THE PERSONAL ART OF DAVID OCTAVIUS HILL

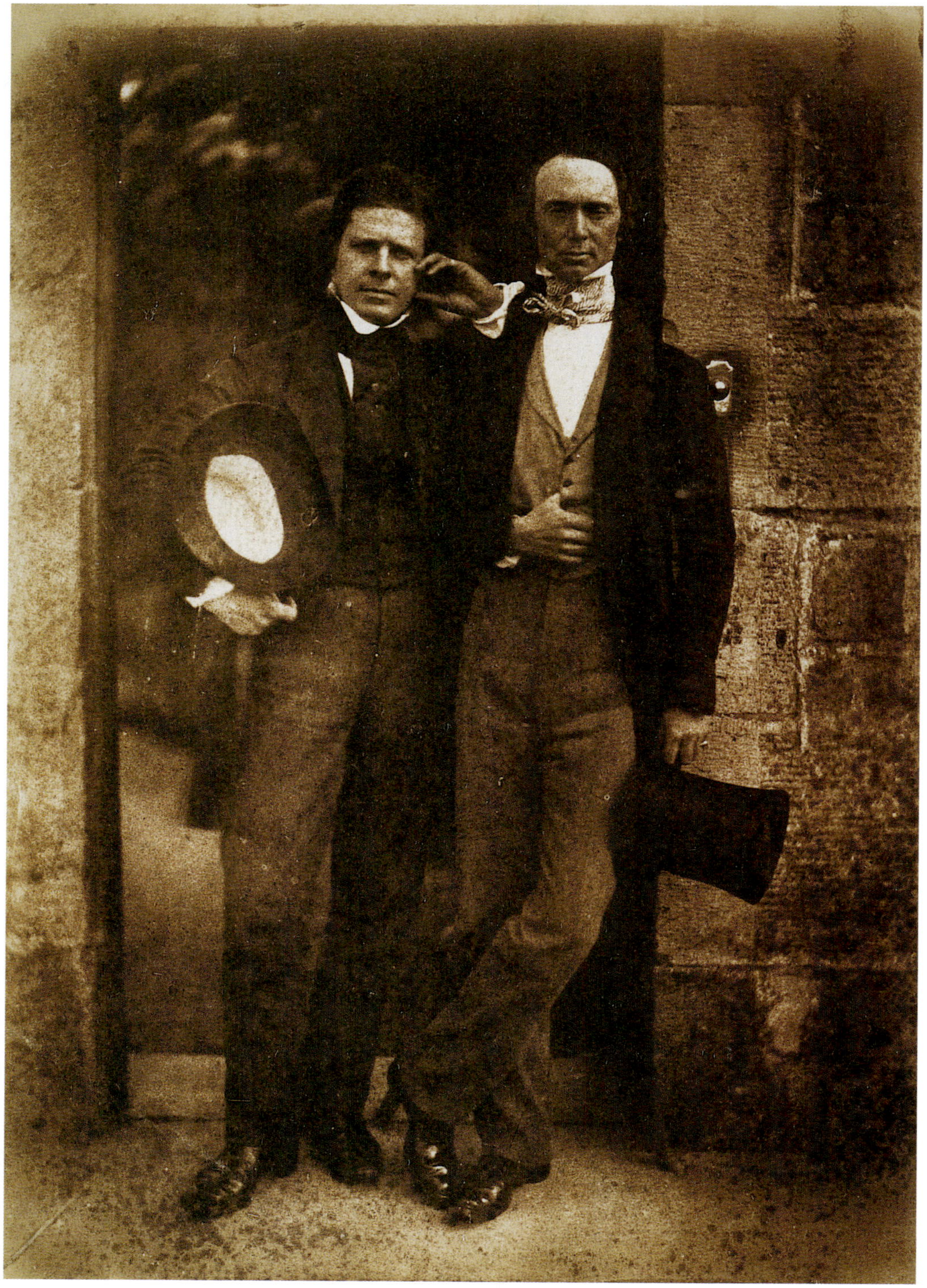

The Personal Art of David Octavius Hill

Sara Stevenson

Published for the Paul Mellon Centre for Studies in British Art by Yale University Press
New Haven & London

Library of Congress Cataloging-in-Publication data

Stevenson, Sara.
The personal art of David Octavius Hill / Sara Stevenson.
p. cm.
Includes bibliographical references and index.
ISBN 0-300-09534-1 (acid-free paper)
1. Hill, David Octavius, 1802–1870. 2. Adamson, Robert, 1821–1848.
2. Photographers—Scotland—Edinburgh—Biography. 4.
Photography—Scotland—Edinburgh—History. 5.
Calotype—Scotland—Edinburgh—History. I. Title.
TR140.H49 S74 2002
770'.92—dc21
2002001247

Typeset in Garamond; typesetting and design by Kate Gallimore

Printed in Italy

Frontispiece: D. O. Hill and Robert Adamson,
D. O. Hill and William Borthwick Johnstone, 1843–7.
Calotype. Scottish National Photography Collection.

For
David Bruce

CONTENTS

ACKNOWLEDGEMENTS

I have worked with Hill and Adamson's calotypes, in my professional capacity as the chief curator of the Scottish National Photography Collection, for around twenty years. In effect, I became a photographic historian because I was asked to produce a catalogue of the five thousand negatives and positives in the Scottish National Portrait Gallery; Hill and Adamson's work was the beginning of my education in the field and they still continue to educate me.

The length of time I have worked with the subject means that I may well have forgotten individuals who have generously helped me with specific questions. The acknowledgements should, therefore, be addressed, in a very broad sense to my friends and colleagues in the world of photography, history and photographic criticism, who have effectively collaborated with me on this project. It is an important argument of this book that creativity may grow from sociability. It has certainly been my experience that much of the excitement and development of my own ideas have come from enlivening conversations rather than formal texts.

My first debt is to David Octavius Hill, whose mind I have attempted to occupy. He is one of the rare historical figures whose company is unfailingly attractive and whose art is a pleasurable extension of that attraction. Secondly, I am indebted to those scholars who preceded me in the field and communicated their enthusiasm to me, particularly David Bruce and Katherine Michaelson. I am more than grateful to the photographers who have illuminated my understanding of the art of photography in relation to Hill and Adamson, especially Thomas Joshua Cooper, Robin Gillanders, Murray Johnston, Patricia Macdonald and David Williams. Amongst the international scholars, I would wish to acknowledge the generous enthusiasm of Keith Bell, Bodo Von Dewitz, Roy Flukinger, Françoise Heilbrun and Will Stapp. Within Britain, I am personally indebted to Janis Adams, James Berry, Alison Boocock, Duncan Forbes, Colin Ford, Barbara Gray, Michael Gray, Mark Haworth-Booth, James Holloway, Julie Lawson, Simon Manfield, Alison Morrison-Low, Richard Ovenden, Allen Simpson, Roddy Simpson, Helen Smailes, Elisabeth Smith, Graham Smith, Christine Thompson and Mike Ware. I am more than grateful to my colleagues at the National Galleries of Scotland for their help and encouragement. I also wish to thank Kate Gallimore for the long-distance editing of this work

NOTE ON SOURCES AND ABBREVIATIONS

This publication aims to examine Hill's world and art in three combined ways. The visual evidence is offered by the Hill/Adamson calotypes and Hill's paintings and engravings – principally the material held in the National Galleries of Scotland and Glasgow University Library, Special Collections, and with reference to the collections of the Royal Scottish Academy, the University of St Andrews, the National Museums of Scotland, the National Library of Scotland, the Gernsheim Collection in the Harry Ransom Humanities Research Center, University of Texas, and the Fox Talbot Museum. This is supported by cross-reference to the work of other photographers and painters, whom we know to have influenced the artist. Because the partnership was established at the beginning of photography, much of the significant comparative photographic material, which may illuminate the subject of photography, comes afterwards. Some comparisons with the future are, therefore, explored to that end.

The second source is the correspondence of Hill and his friends, official and private, which is largely in the collection of the National Library of Scotland, the Royal Scottish Academy and in private hands. The groups of Hill's correspondence which have proved particularly helpful are the letters relating to the affairs of the Scottish Academy; Hill's letters to David Roberts, the Scottish landscape artist living in London; Hill's letters to Joseph Noël Paton; and the letters from the engineer James Nasmyth, to Hill. These are principally in the Royal Scottish Academy Archives, the National Library of Scotland, the Royal Scottish Observatory and private collections.

Thirdly, the book refers to published writing, concentrating on those works written by people Hill knew and admired and, within that category, taking especial account of the people who appear in the portrait calotypes. Since it is clear that the study of Hill's life and work requires a greater spread of contemporary knowledge, the work concentrates more on the documentation and publication of the time than on subsequent criticism.

Abbreviations

ECL	Edinburgh Central Library
FTM	Fox Talbot Museum, Lacock, Wiltshire
GUL	Glasgow University Library, Special Collections
NGS	National Gallery of Scotland, Edinburgh
NLS	National Library of Scotland, Edinburgh
NMS	National Museums of Scotland , Edinburgh
NMPFT	National Museum of Photography, Film and Television, Bradford
RA	Royal Academy, London
RO	Royal Observatory, Edinburgh
RSA	Royal Scottish Academy, Edinburgh
SNPC	Scottish National Photography Collection, Edinburgh
SNPG	Scottish National Portrait Gallery, Edinburgh
SRO	Scottish Record Office, Edinburgh
UOE	University of Edinburgh
UOSA	University of St Andrews

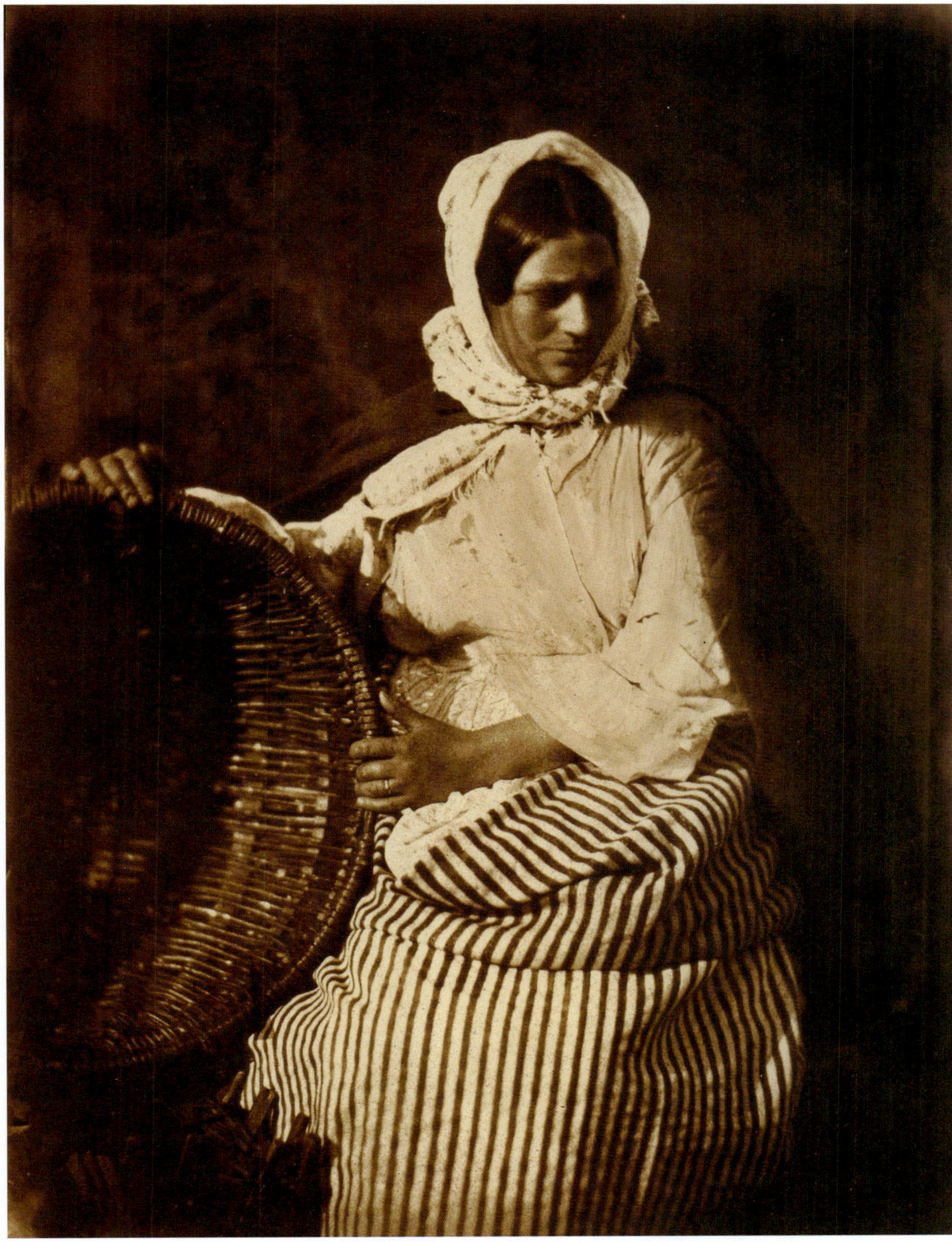

Plate 1
D. O. Hill and Robert Adamson, *Elizabeth Johnstone Hall, Newhaven Fishwife*, sometimes known as *It's no fish ye're buying, it's men's lives*, 1843–7.
Calotype.
Scottish National Photography Collection, Edinburgh.

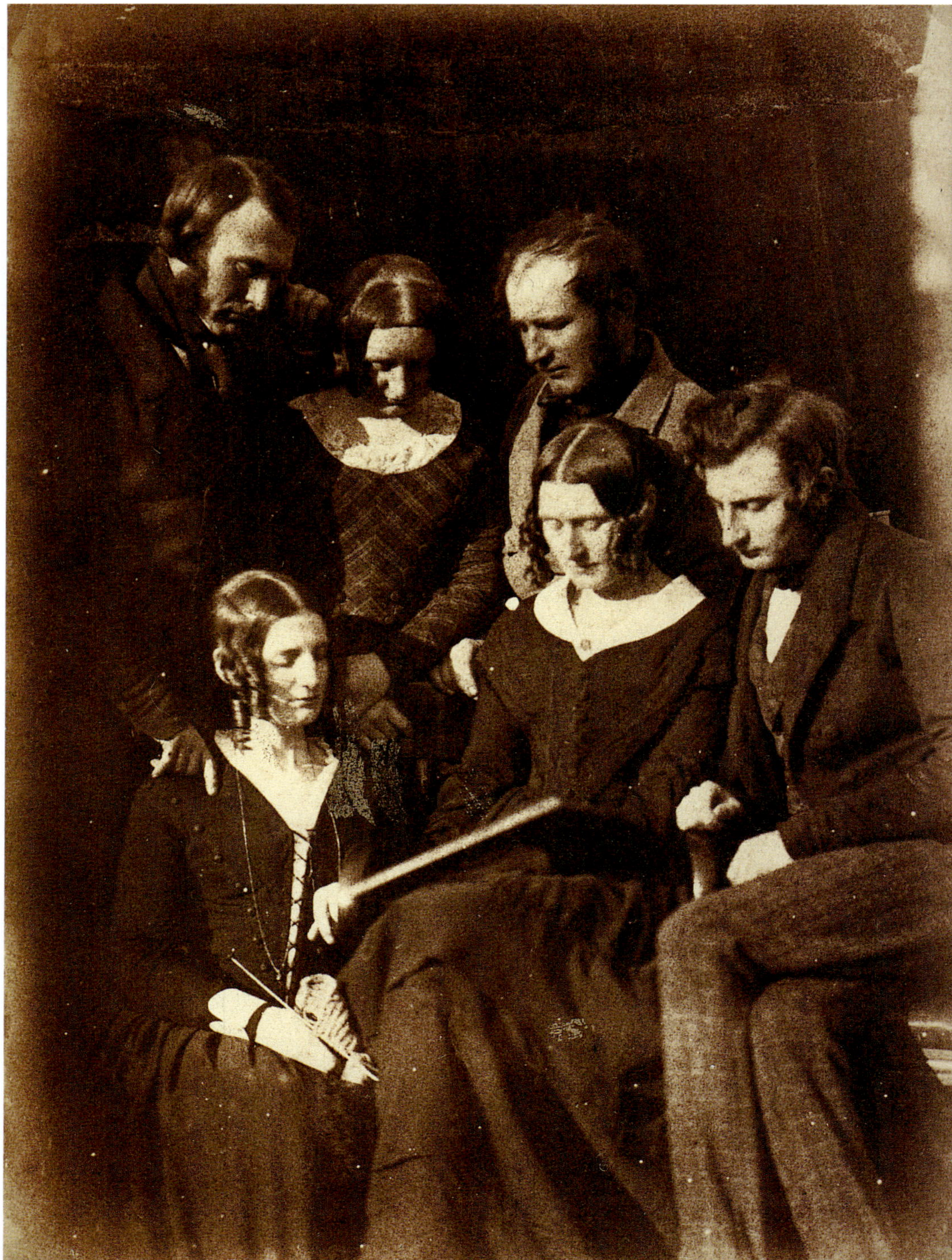

Plate 2
D. O. Hill and Robert Adamson, *The Adamson Family*, with John on the left and Robert on the right, 1843–7. Calotype.
Scottish National Photography Collection, Edinburgh.

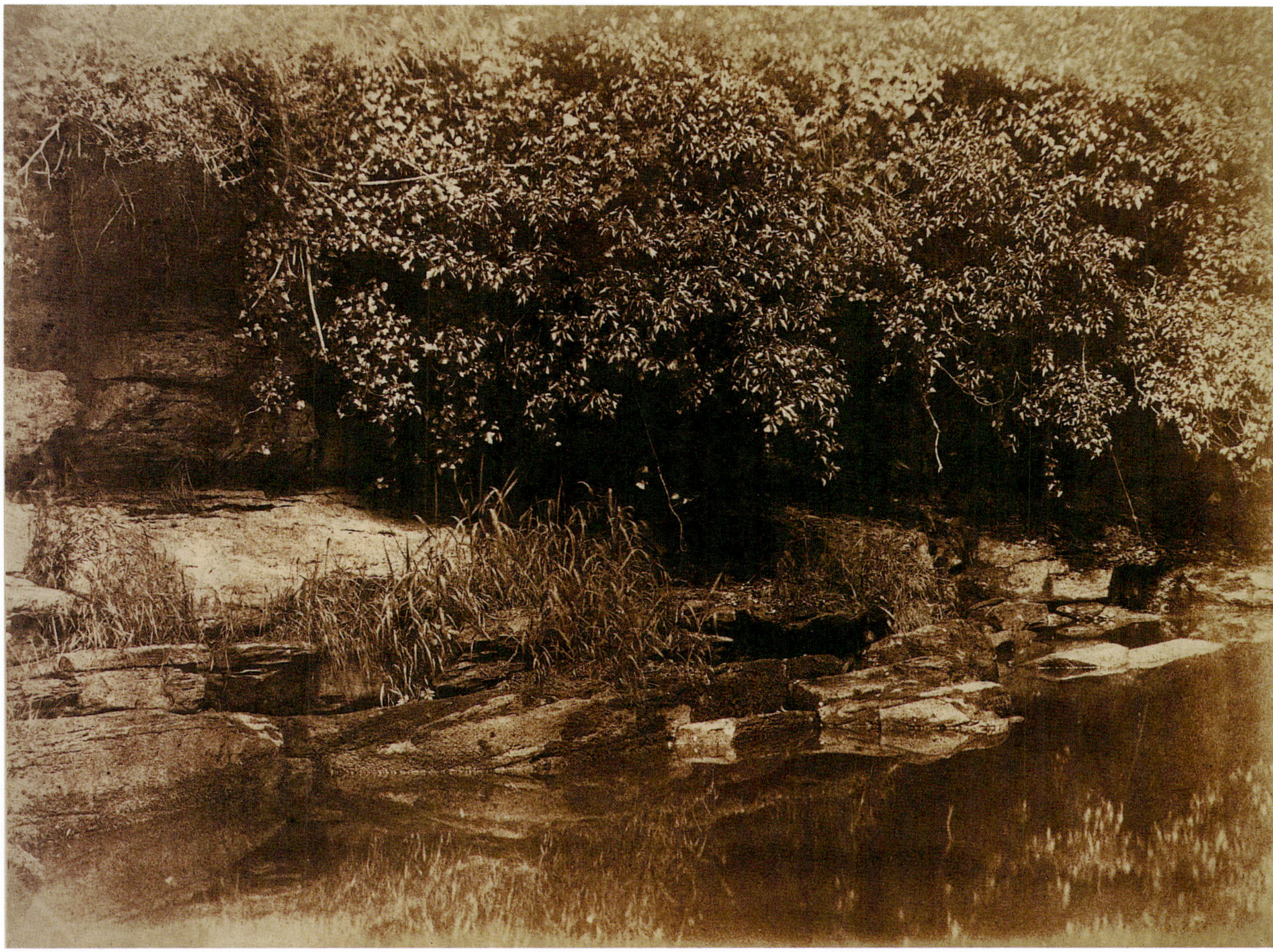

Plate 3
D. O. Hill and Robert Adamson, *Burnside*, 1843–7. Calotype.
Scottish National Photography Collection, Edinburgh.

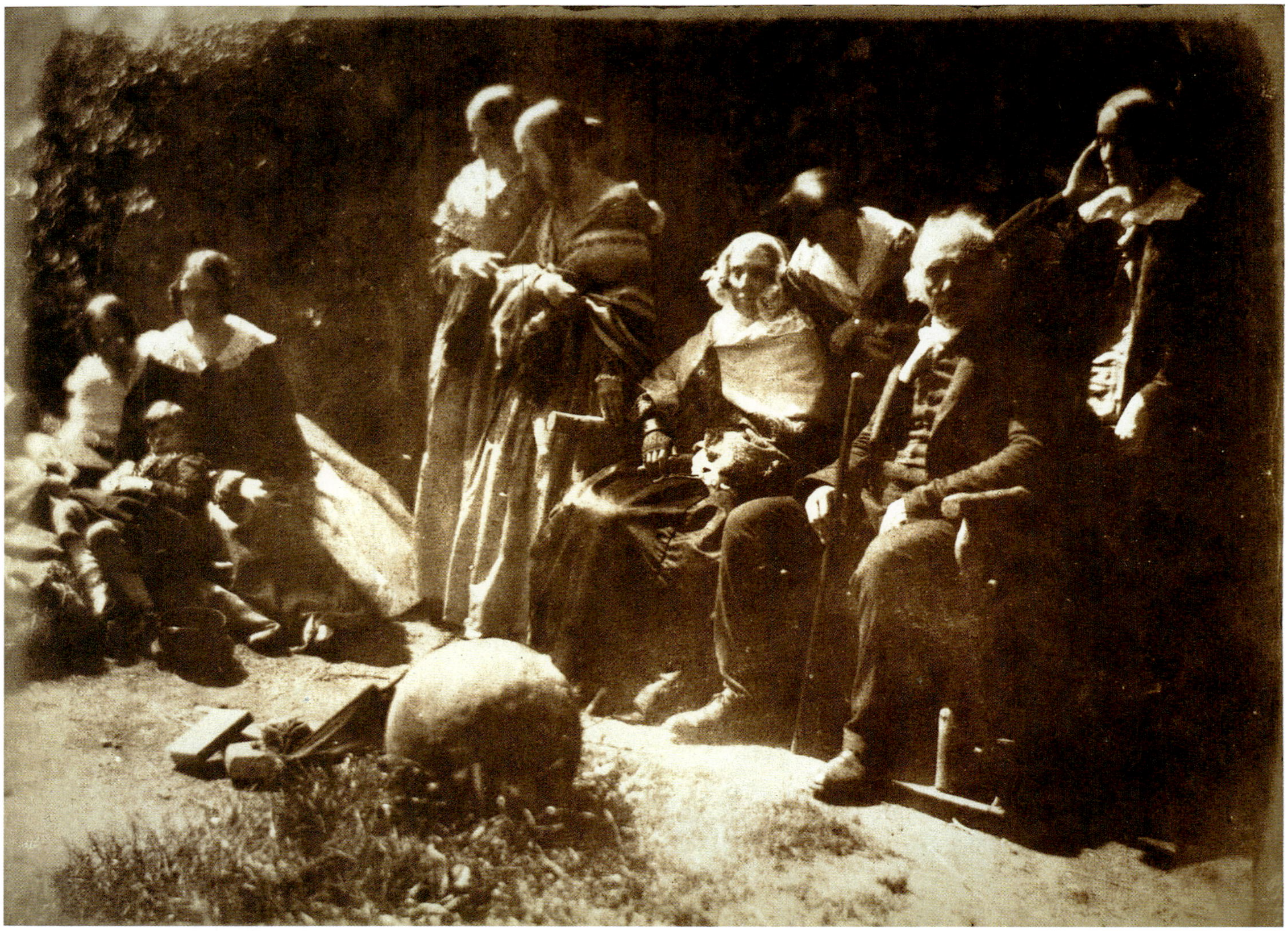

Plate 4
D. O. Hill and Robert Adamson, *Reverend Dr Thomas Chalmers and his Family at Merchiston Castle*, 1844. Calotype.
Scottish National Photography Collection, Edinburgh.

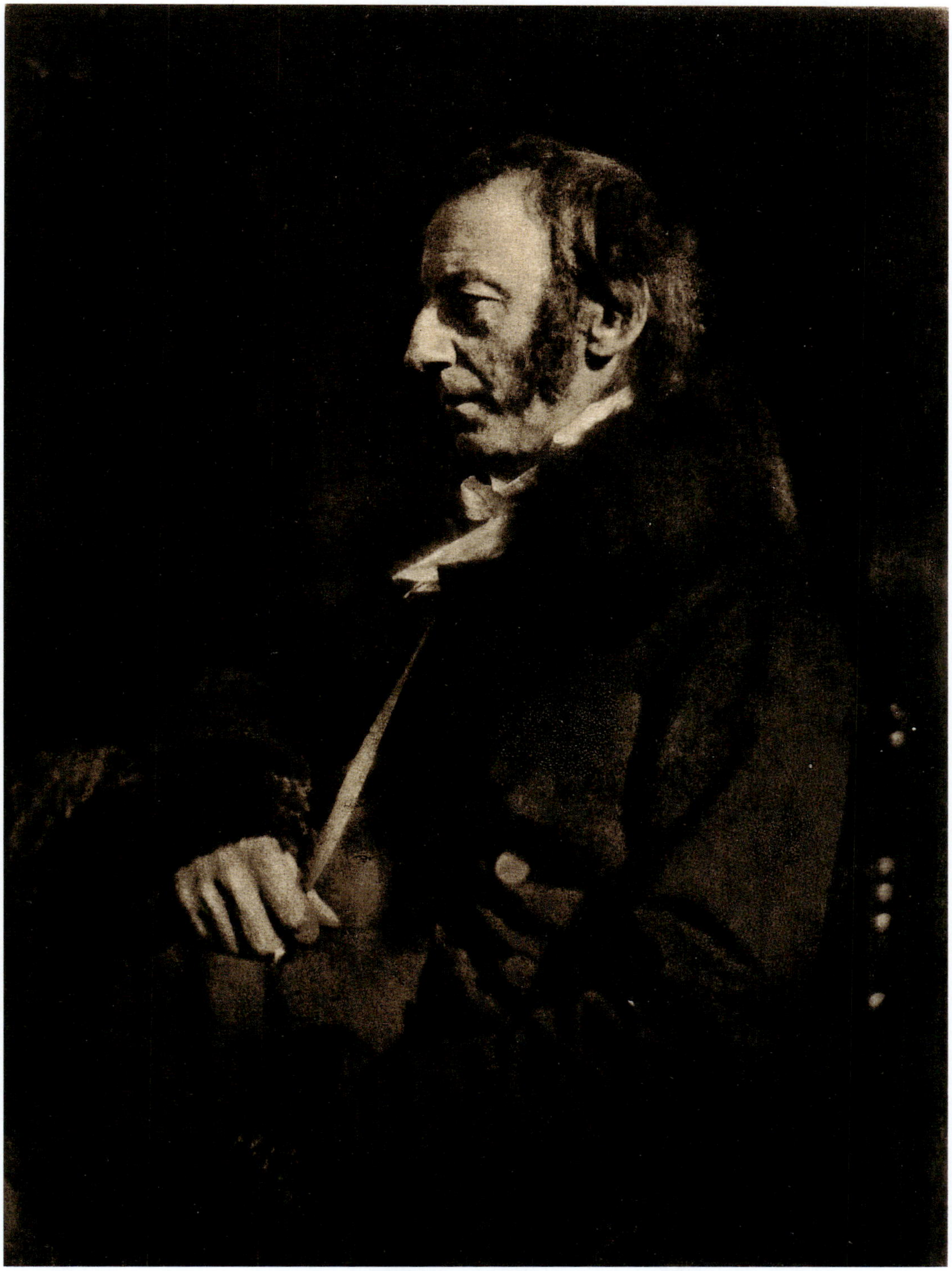

Plate 5
D. O. Hill and Robert Adamson, *The Marquis of Northampton*, October 1844. Photogravure by J. Craig Annan, after the calotype.
Scottish National Photography Collection, Edinburgh.

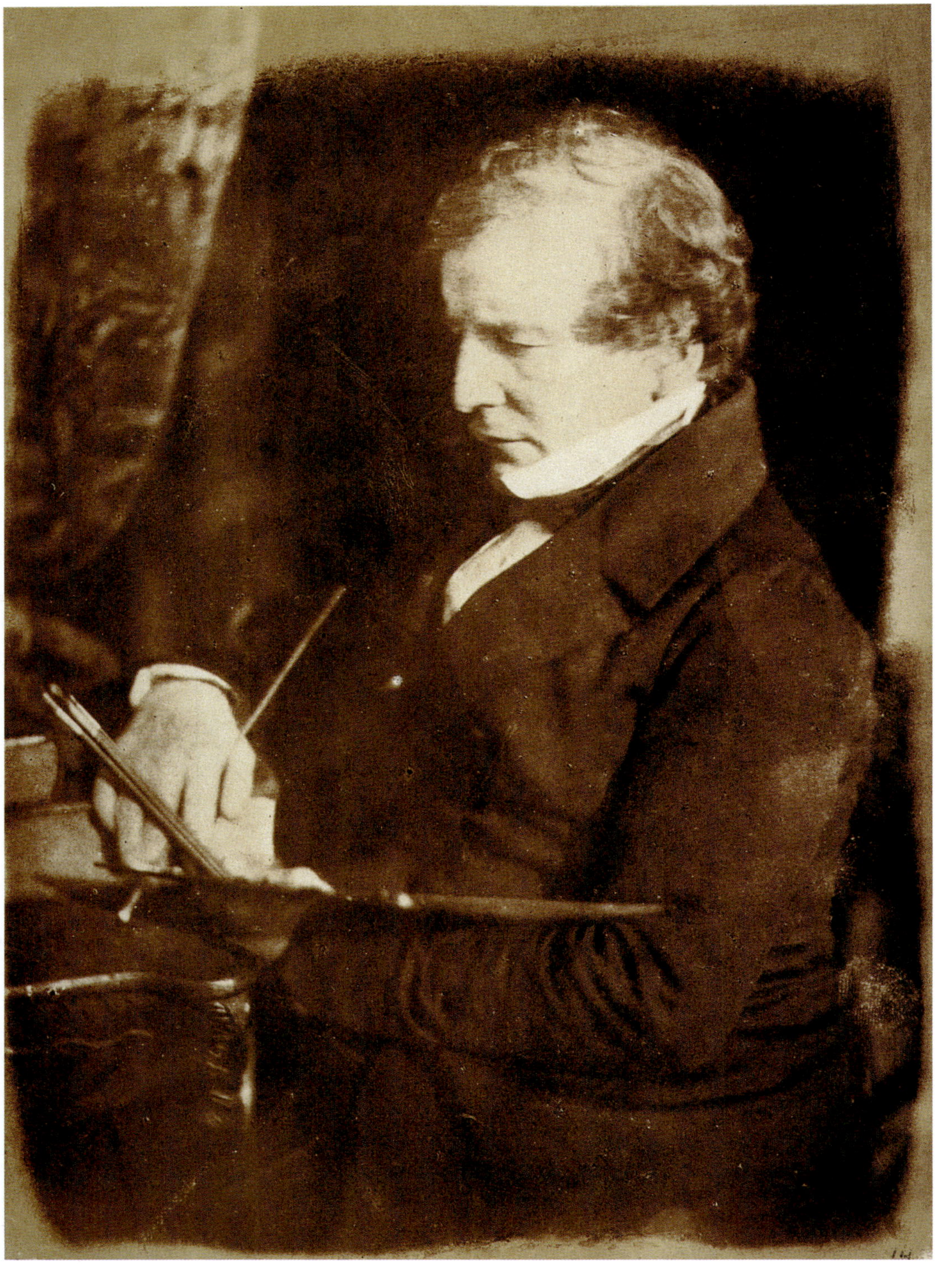

Plate 6
D. O. Hill and Robert Adamson, *William Etty*, October 1844. Calotype.
Scottish National Photography Collection, Edinburgh.

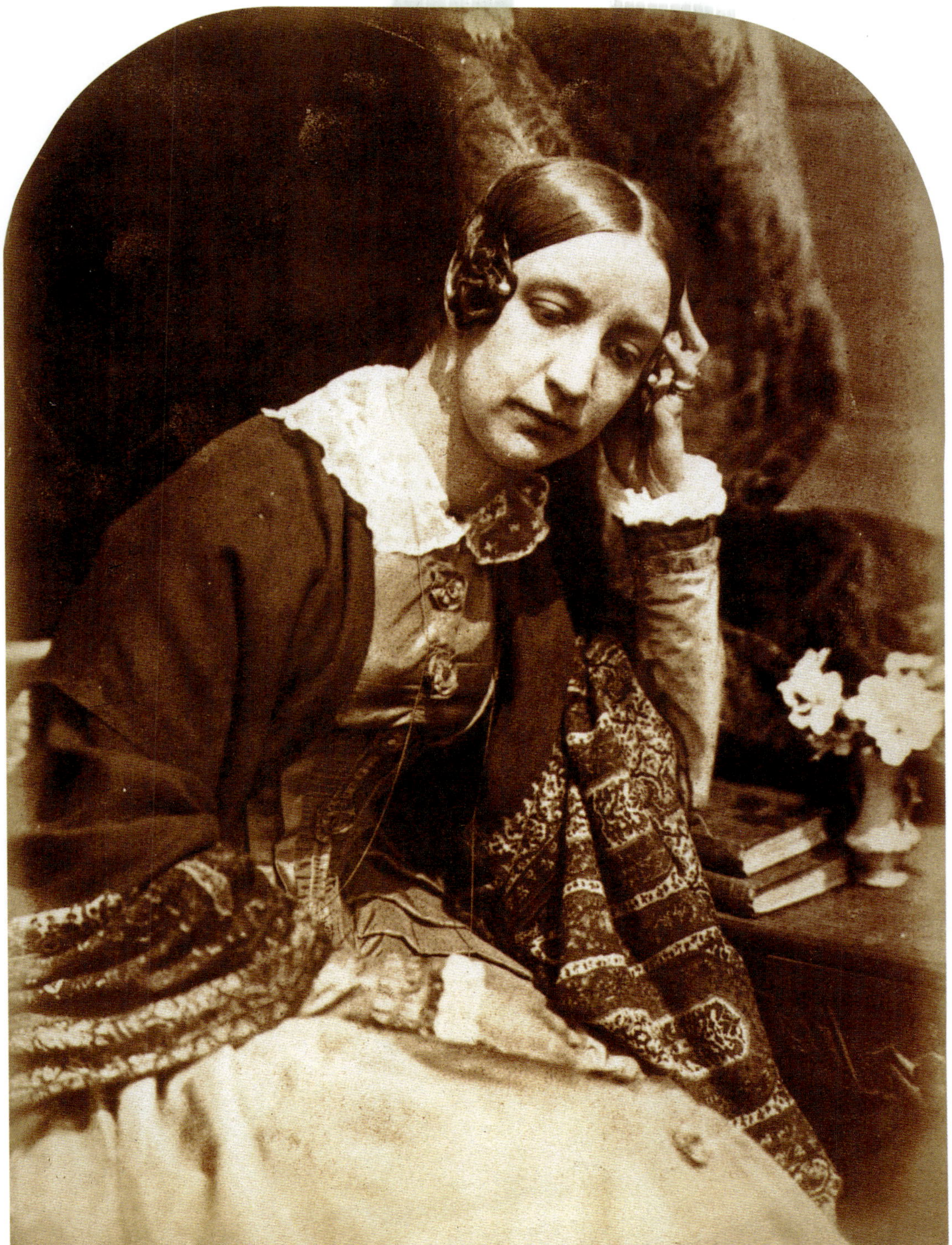

Plate 7
D. O. Hill and Robert Adamson, *Elizabeth Rigby*, 1843–7. Calotype.
Scottish National Photography Collection, Edinburgh.

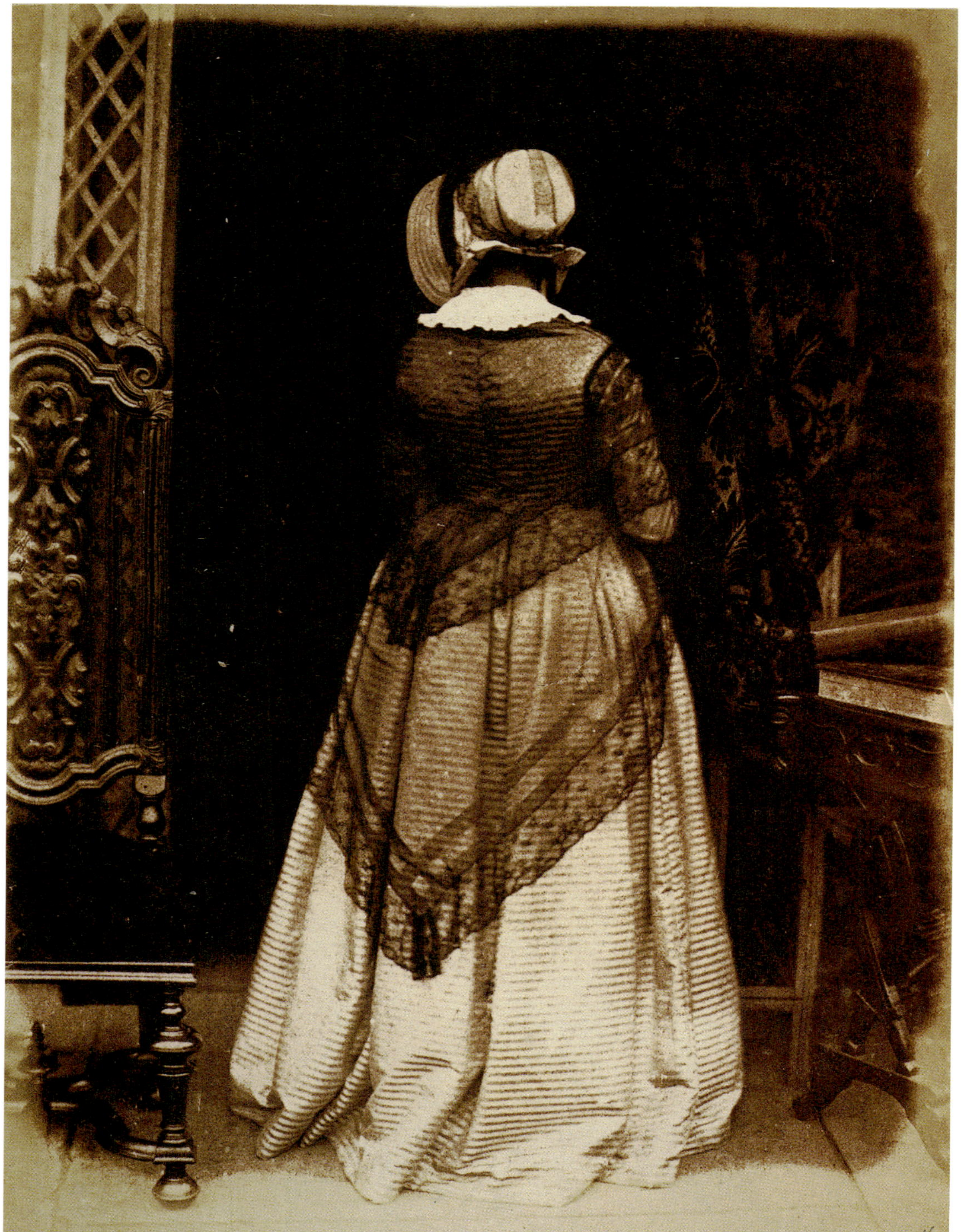

Plate 8
D. O. Hill and Robert Adamson, *Lady Ruthven*, probably 1847. Calotype.
Scottish National Photography Collection, Edinburgh.

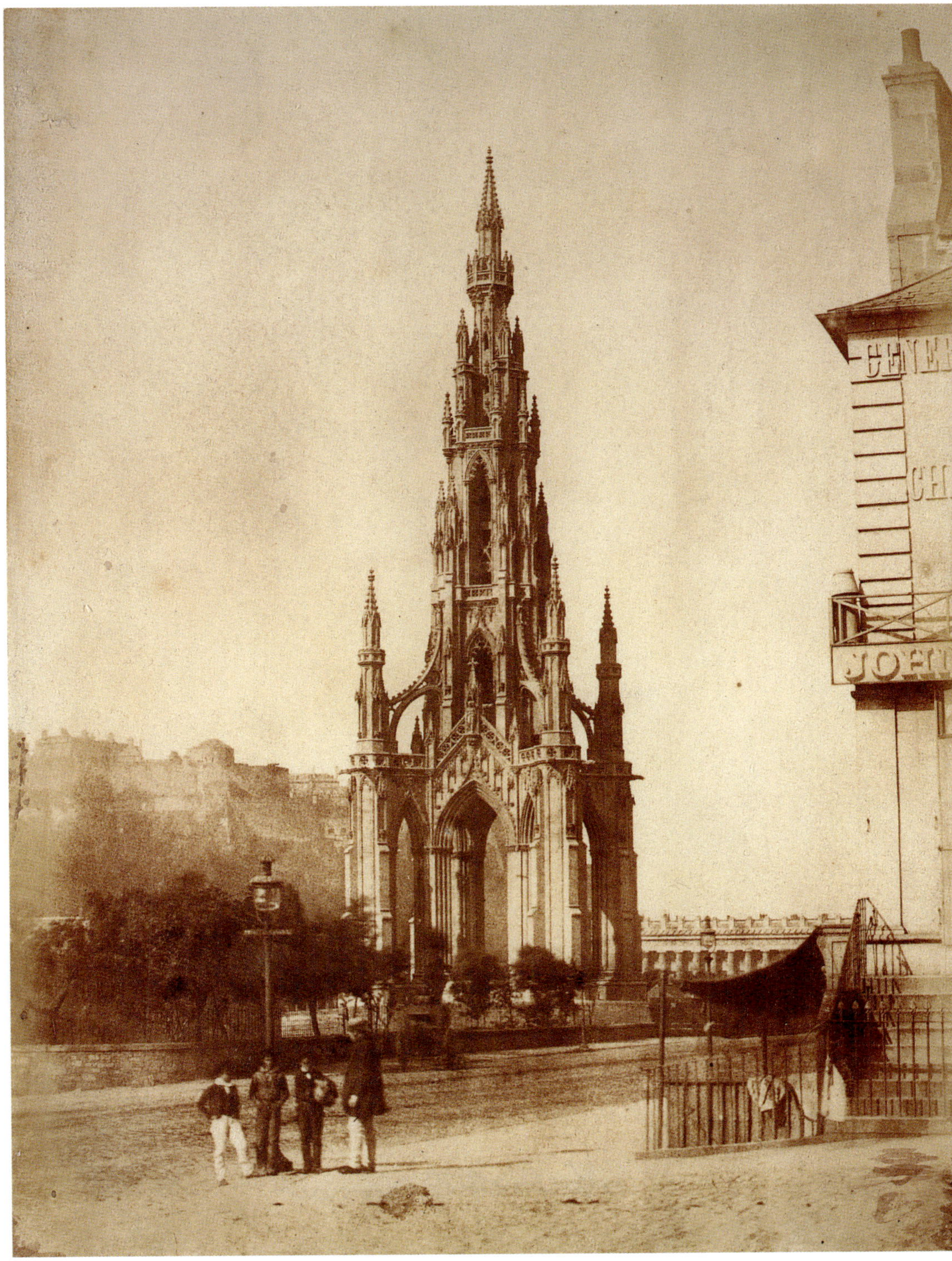

Plate 9
D. O. Hill and Robert Adamson, *The Scott Monument*, 1844. Calotype.
Scottish National Photography Collection, Edinburgh.

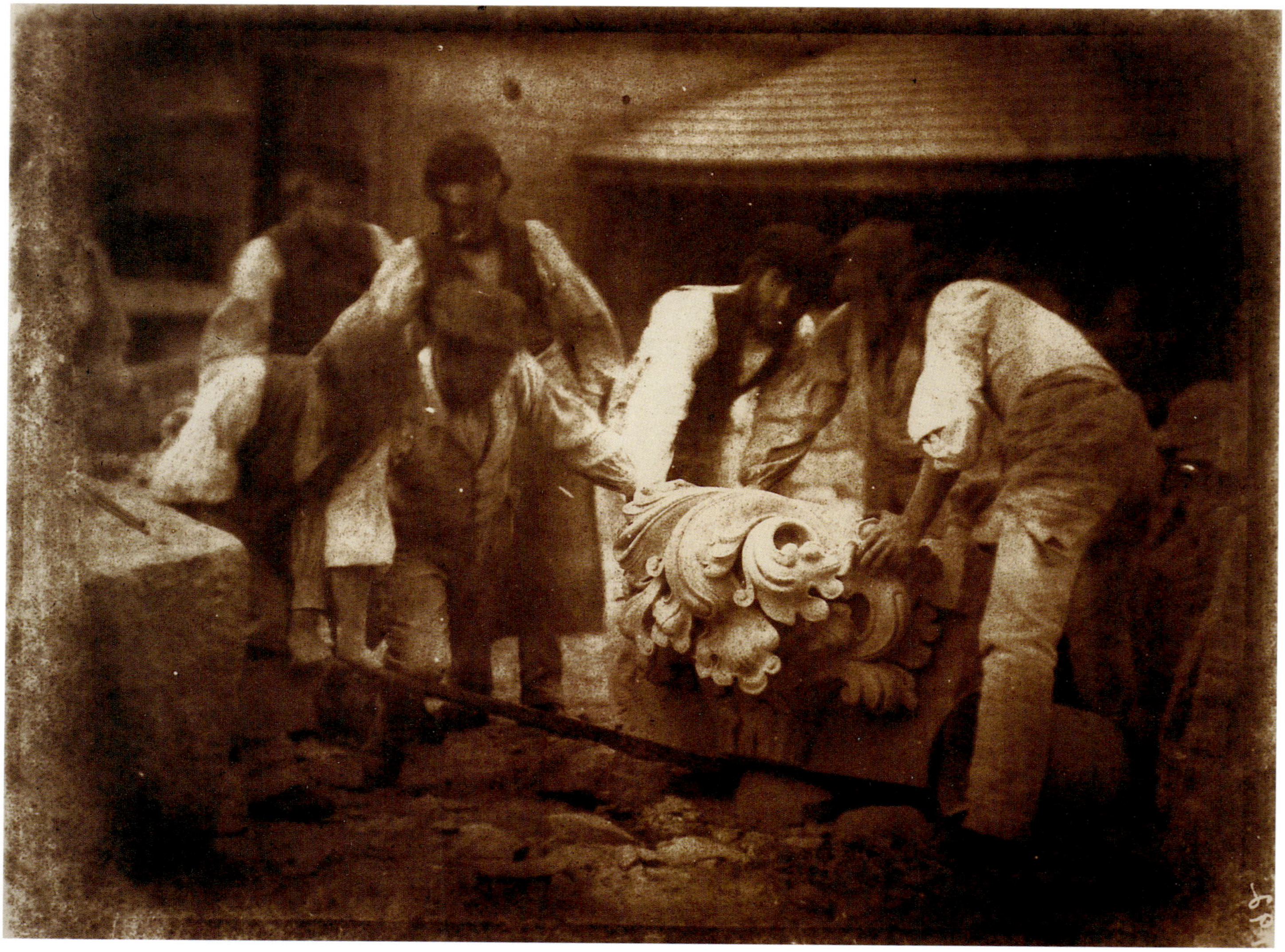

Plate 10
D. O. Hill and Robert Adamson, *Masons Working on the Scott Monument*, 1843 or 1844. Calotype.
Scottish National Photography Collection, Edinburgh.

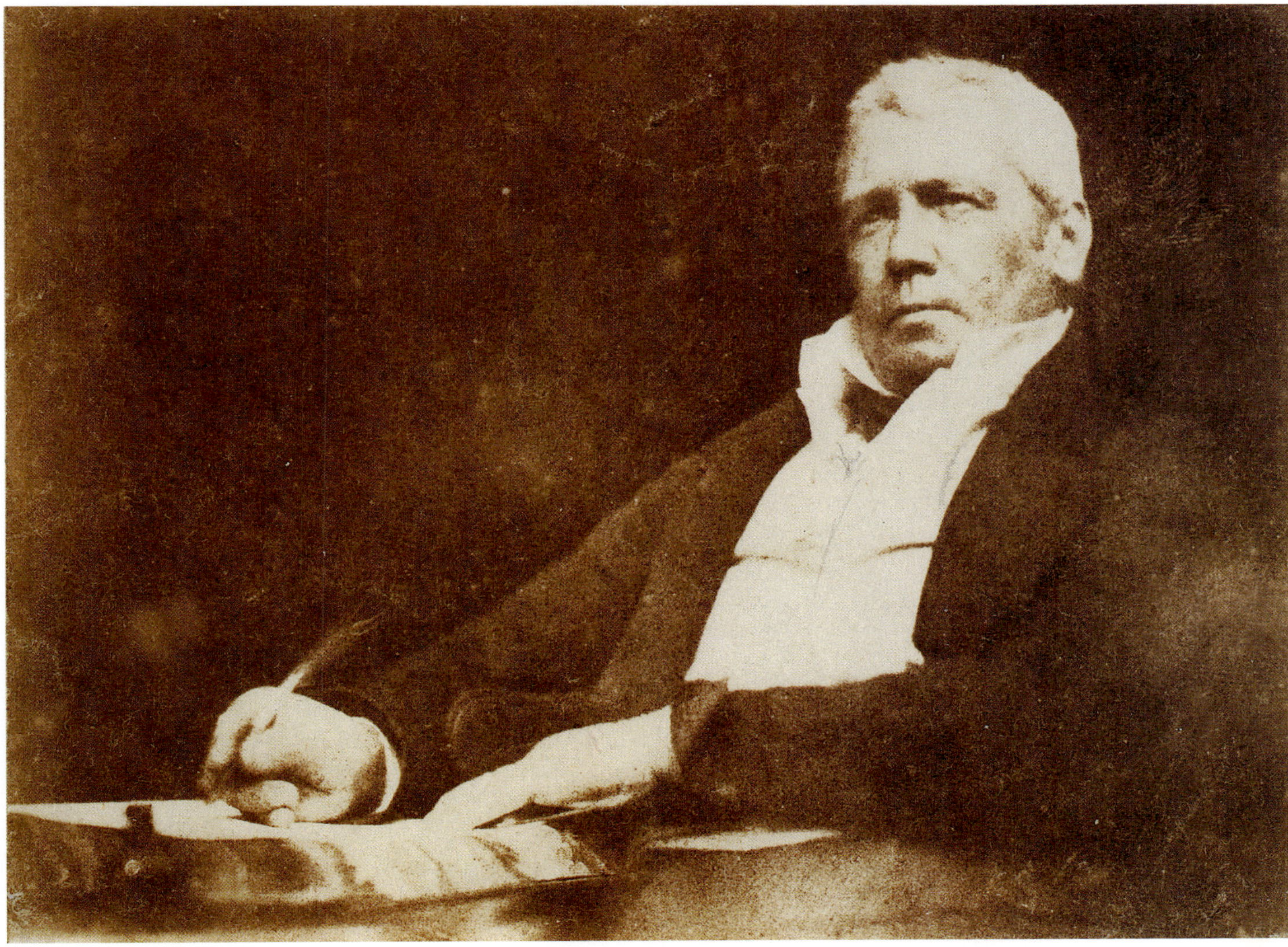

Plate 11
D. O. Hill and Robert Adamson, *Samuel Aitken*, probably 1843. Calotype.
Scottish National Photography Collection, Edinburgh.

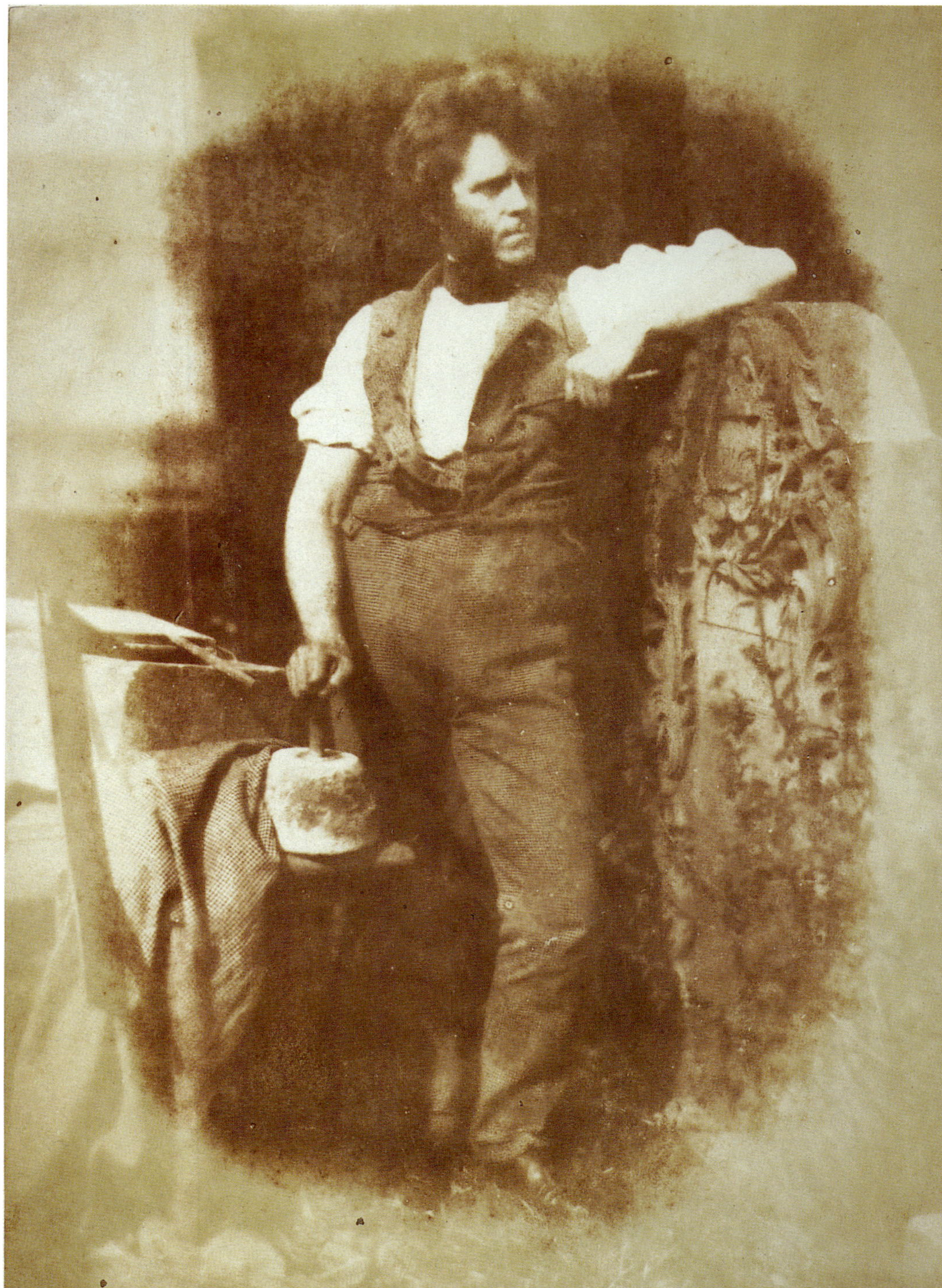

Plate 12
D. O. Hill and Robert Adamson, *Hugh Miller*, 1844. Calotype.
Scottish National Photography Collection, Edinburgh.

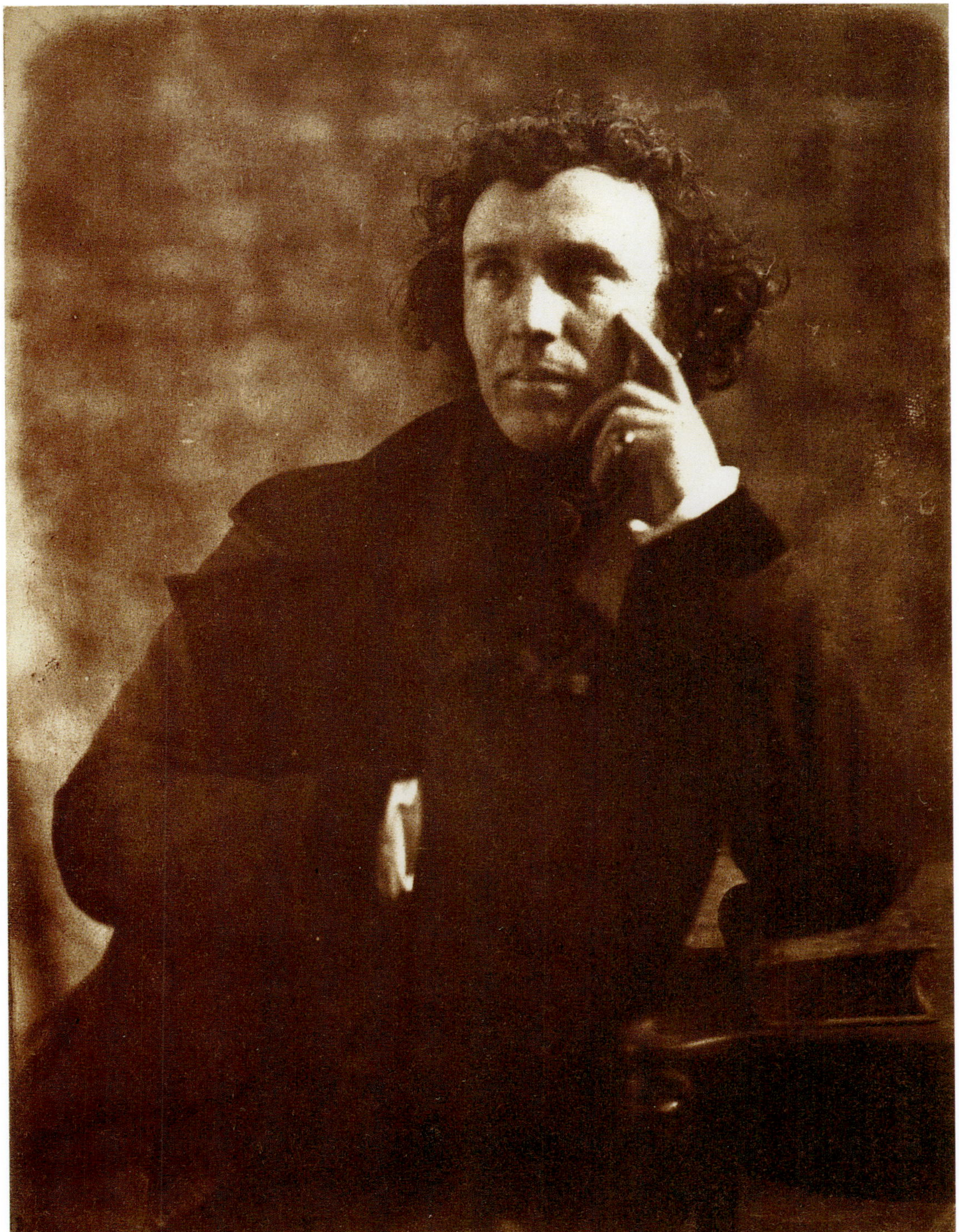

Plate 13
D. O. Hill and Robert Adamson, *Sir John Steell*, 1843–7. Calotype.
Scottish National Photography Collection, Edinburgh.

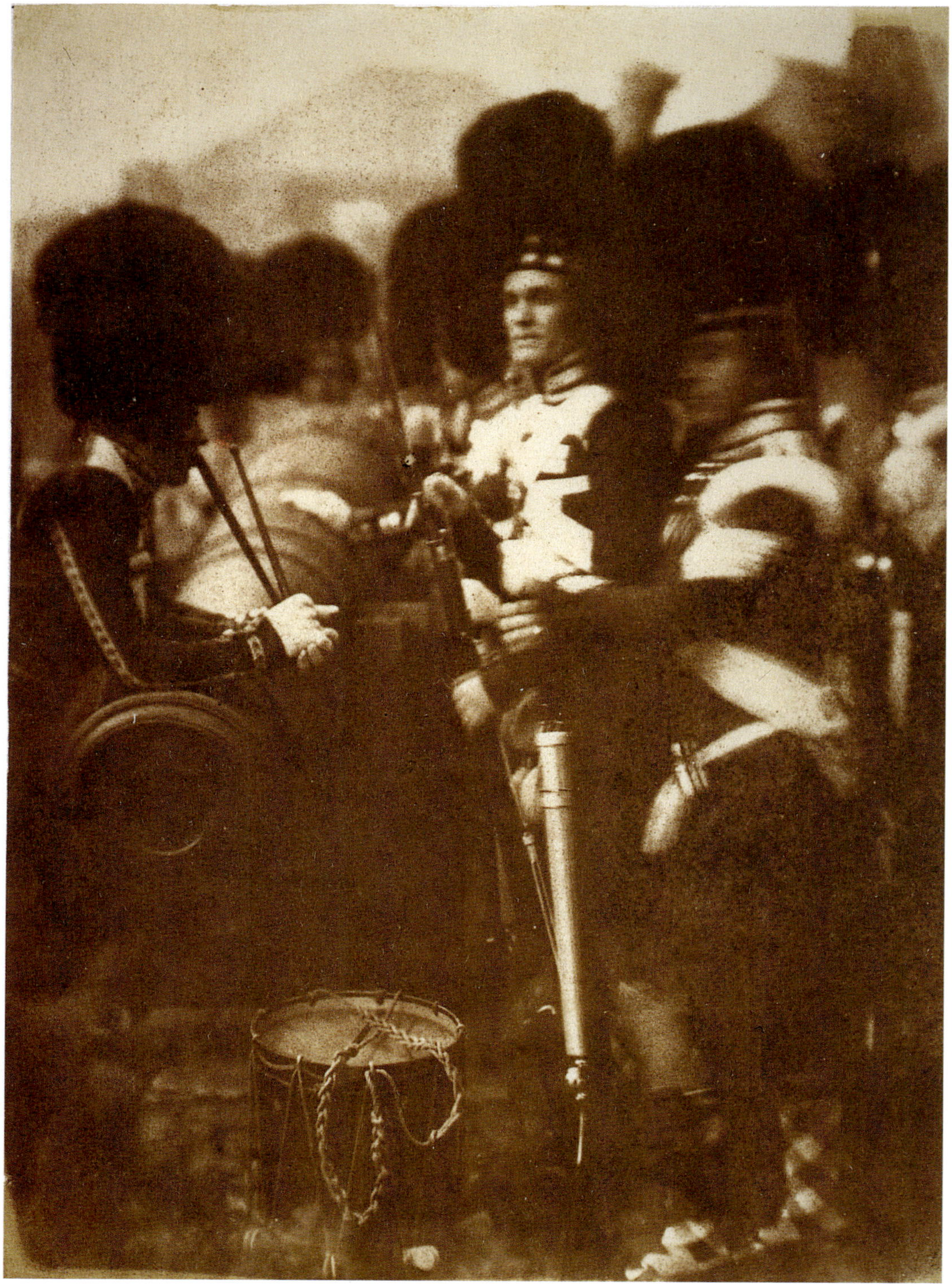

Plate 14
D. O. Hill and Robert Adamson, *92nd Gordon Highlanders at Edinburgh Castle*, 1846. Calotype.
Scottish National Photography Collection, Edinburgh.

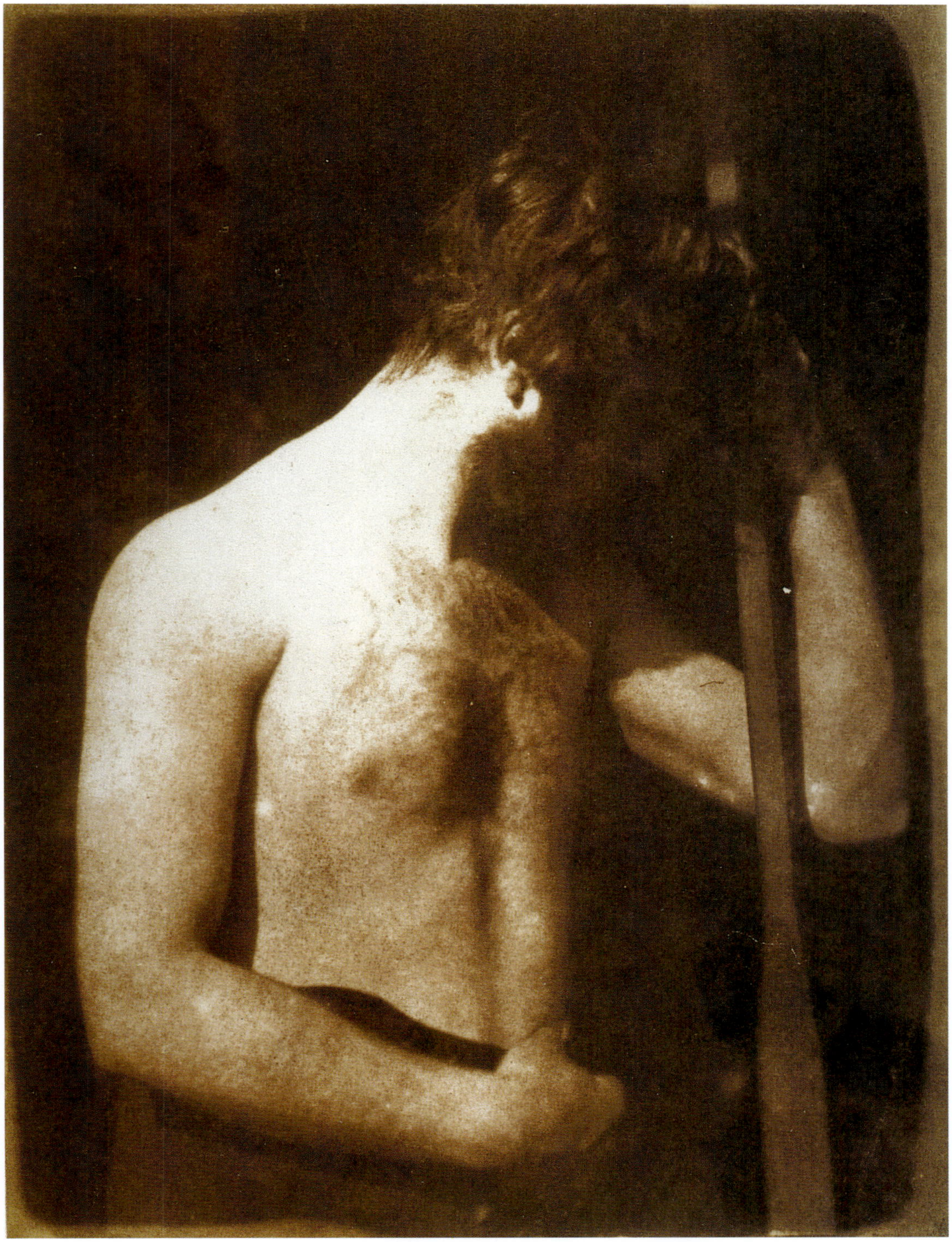

Plate 15
D. O. Hill and Robert Adamson, *Life Study – Dr George Bell*, 1843–7. Calotype.
Scottish National Photography Collection, Edinburgh.

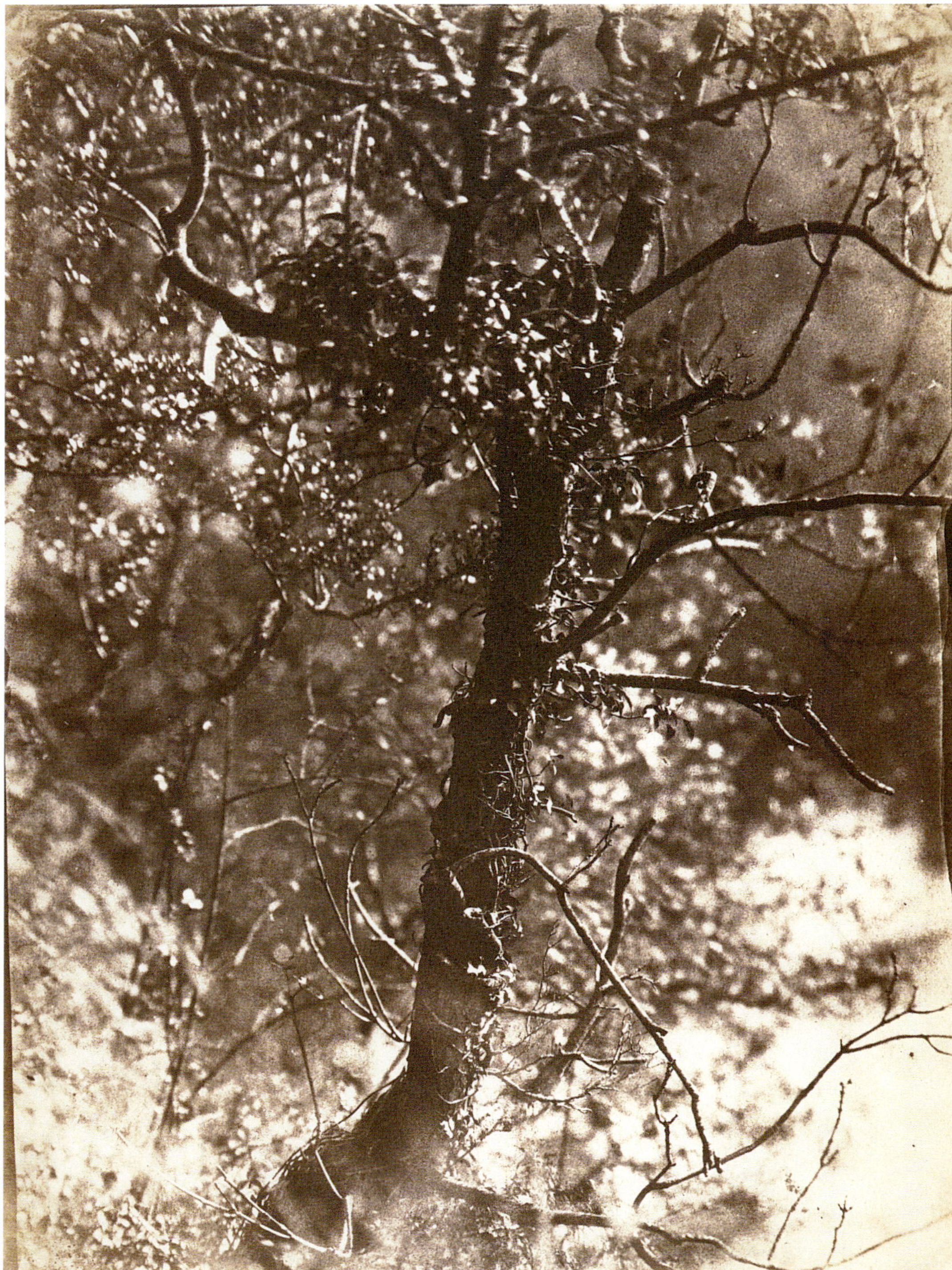

Plate 16
D. O. Hill and Robert Adamson, *The Fairy Tree at Colinton*, 1843–7. Calotype.
Scottish National Photography Collection, Edinburgh.

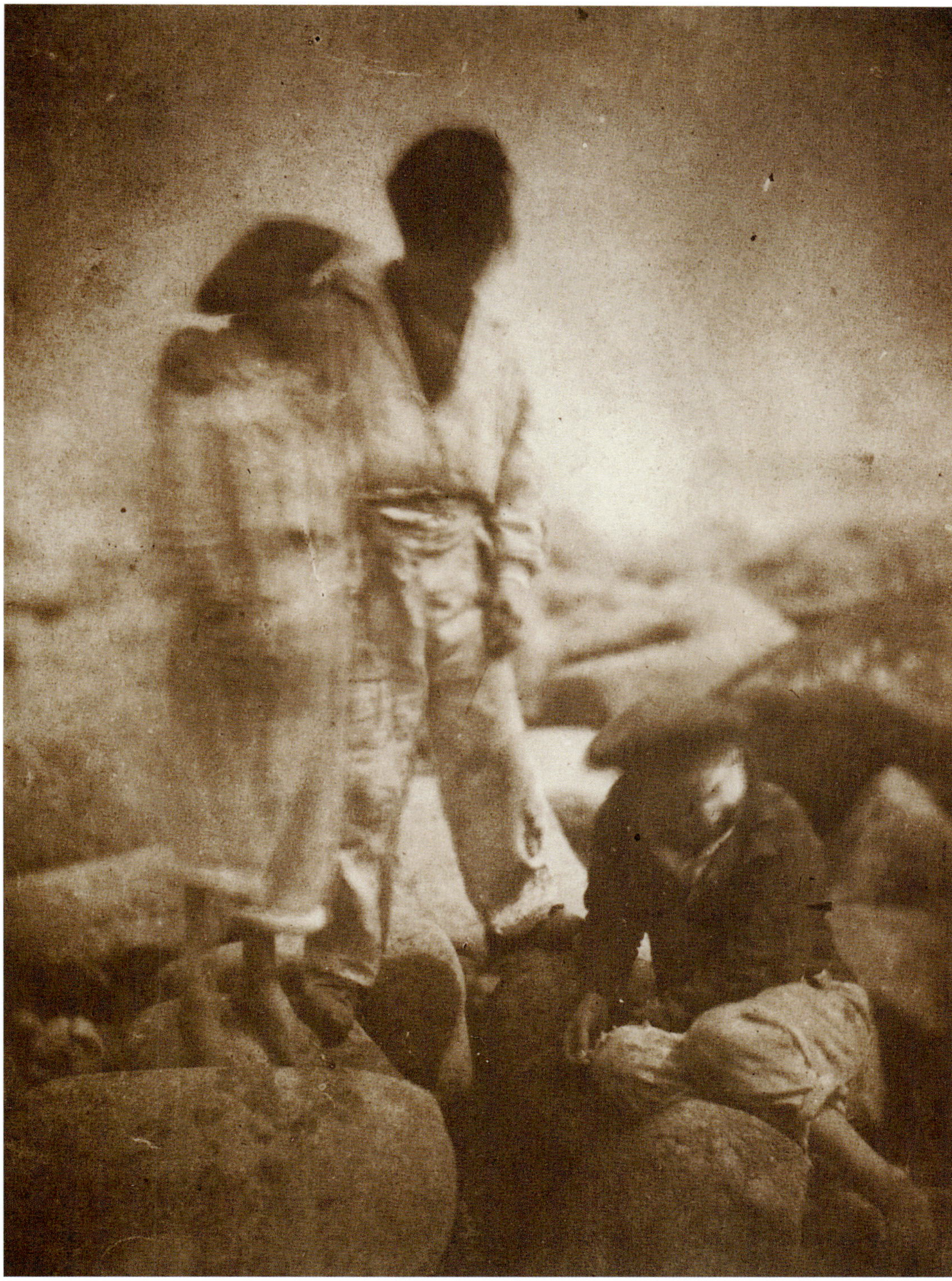

Plate 17
D. O. Hill and Robert Adamson, *Boys Standing on the Rocks at Portobello*, 1843–7.
Modern calotype print, made by Michael and Barbara Gray from the negative in the collection of Glasgow University, Special Collections.

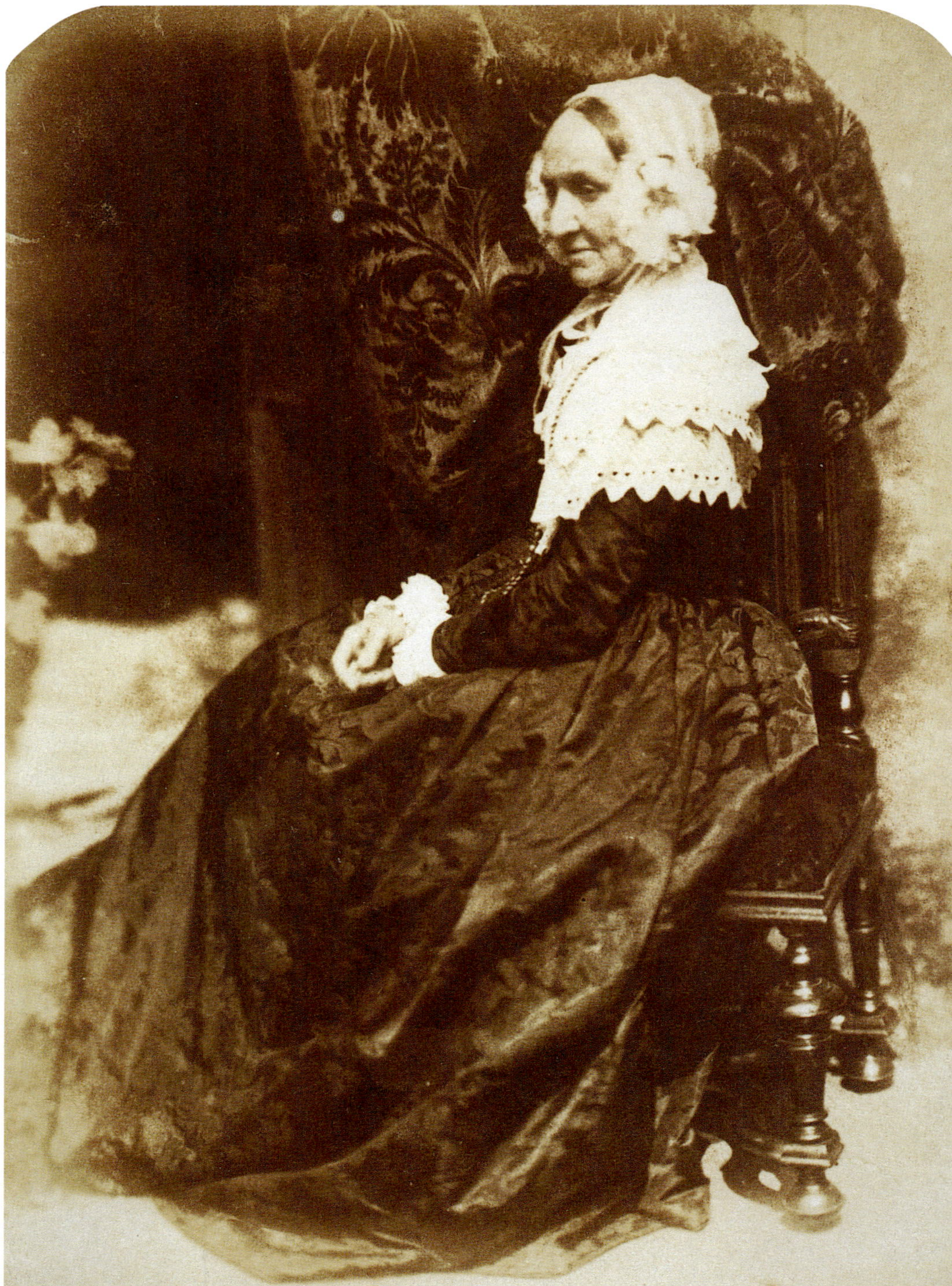

Plate 18
D. O. Hill and Robert Adamson, *Mrs Anne Rigby*, 1843–7. Calotype.
Scottish National Photography Collection, Edinburgh.

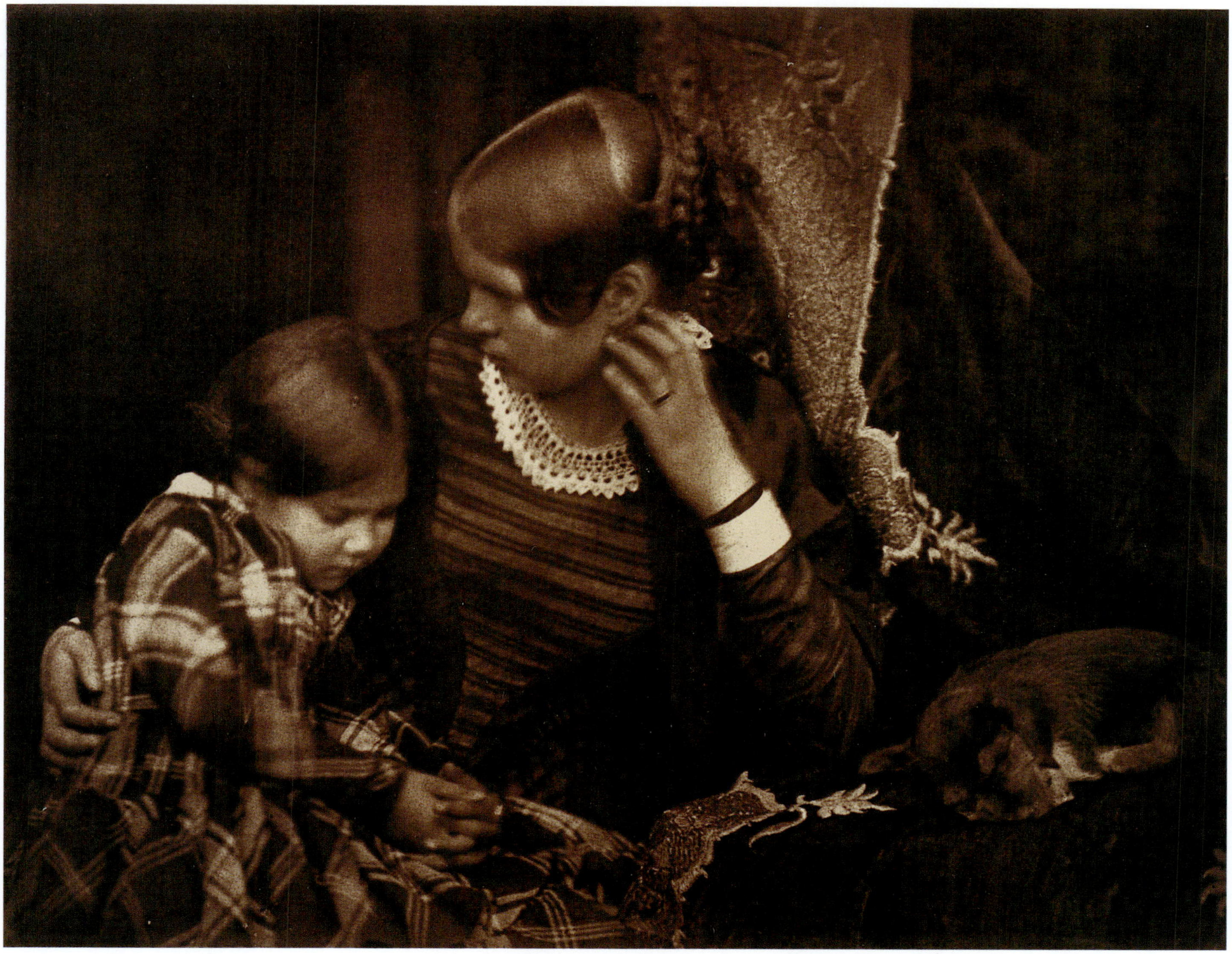

Plate 19
D. O. Hill and Robert Adamson, *Misses Farnie and the Sleeping Puppy, Brownie*, 1843–7. Calotype.
Scottish National Photography Collection, Edinburgh.

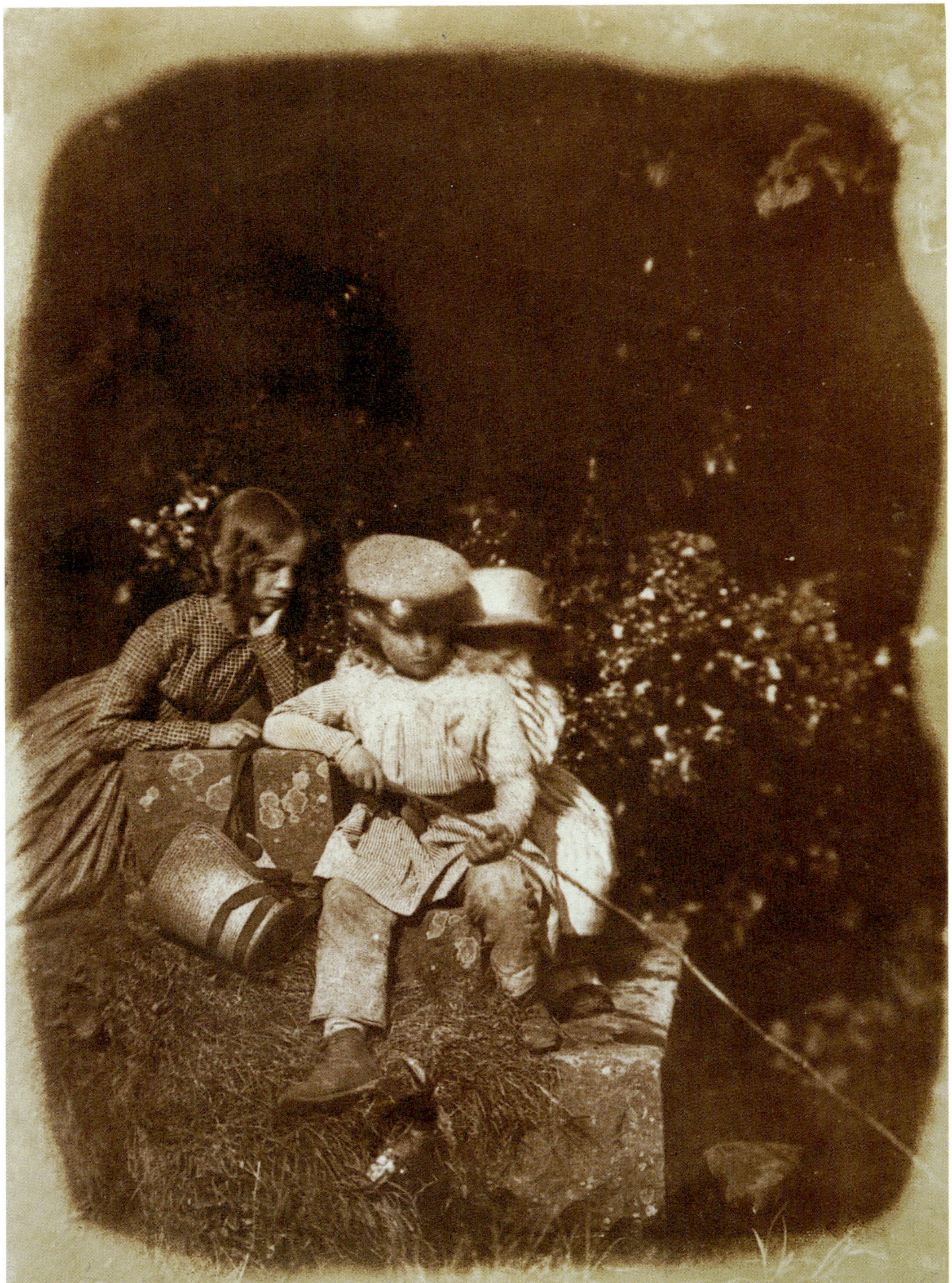

Plate 20
D. O. Hill and Robert Adamson, *At the Minnow Pool* (the Finlay children), 1843–7. Calotype.
Scottish National Photography Collection, Edinburgh.

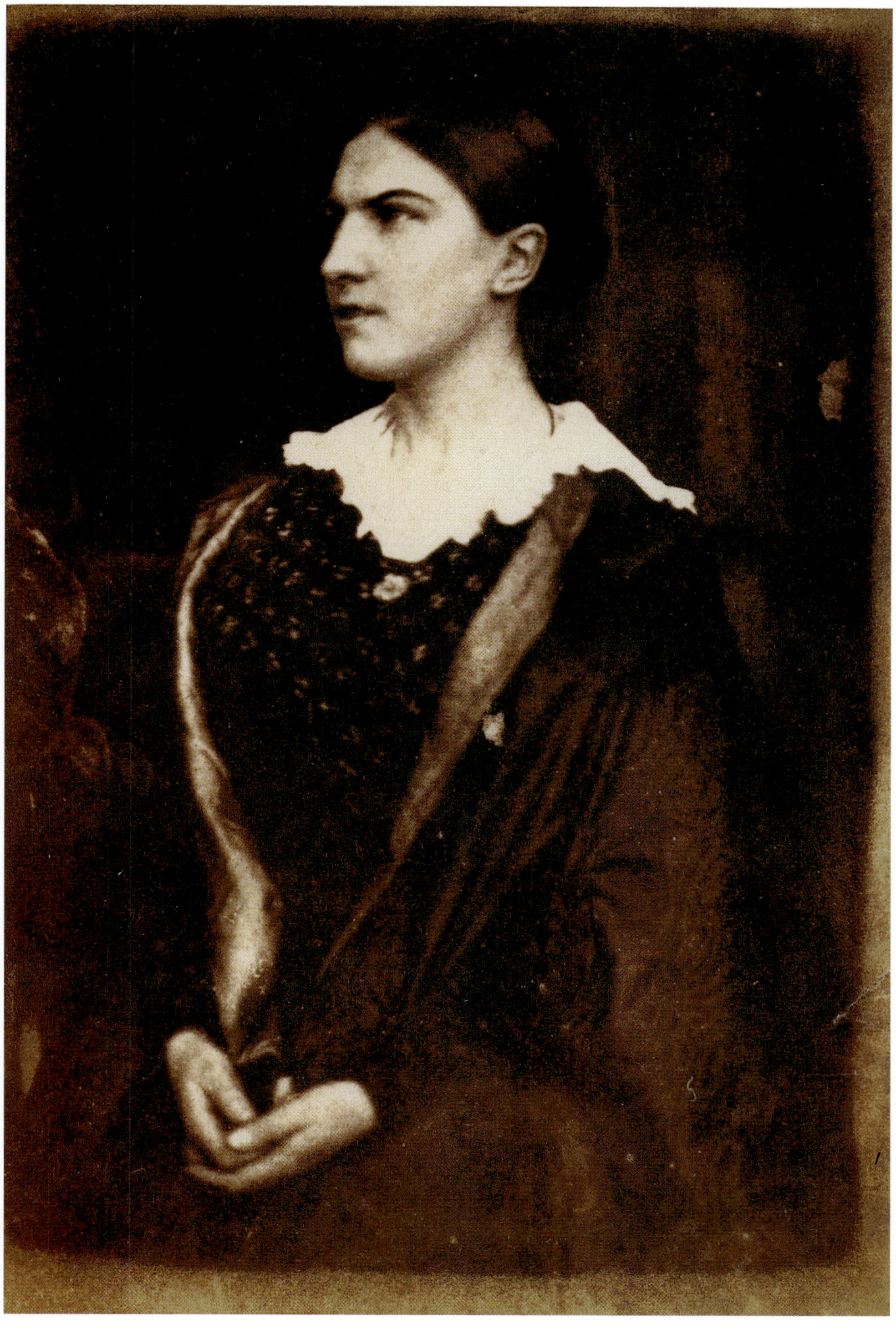

Plate 21
D. O. Hill and Robert Adamson, *Miss Kemp*, 1843–7. Calotype.
Scottish National Photography Collection, Edinburgh.

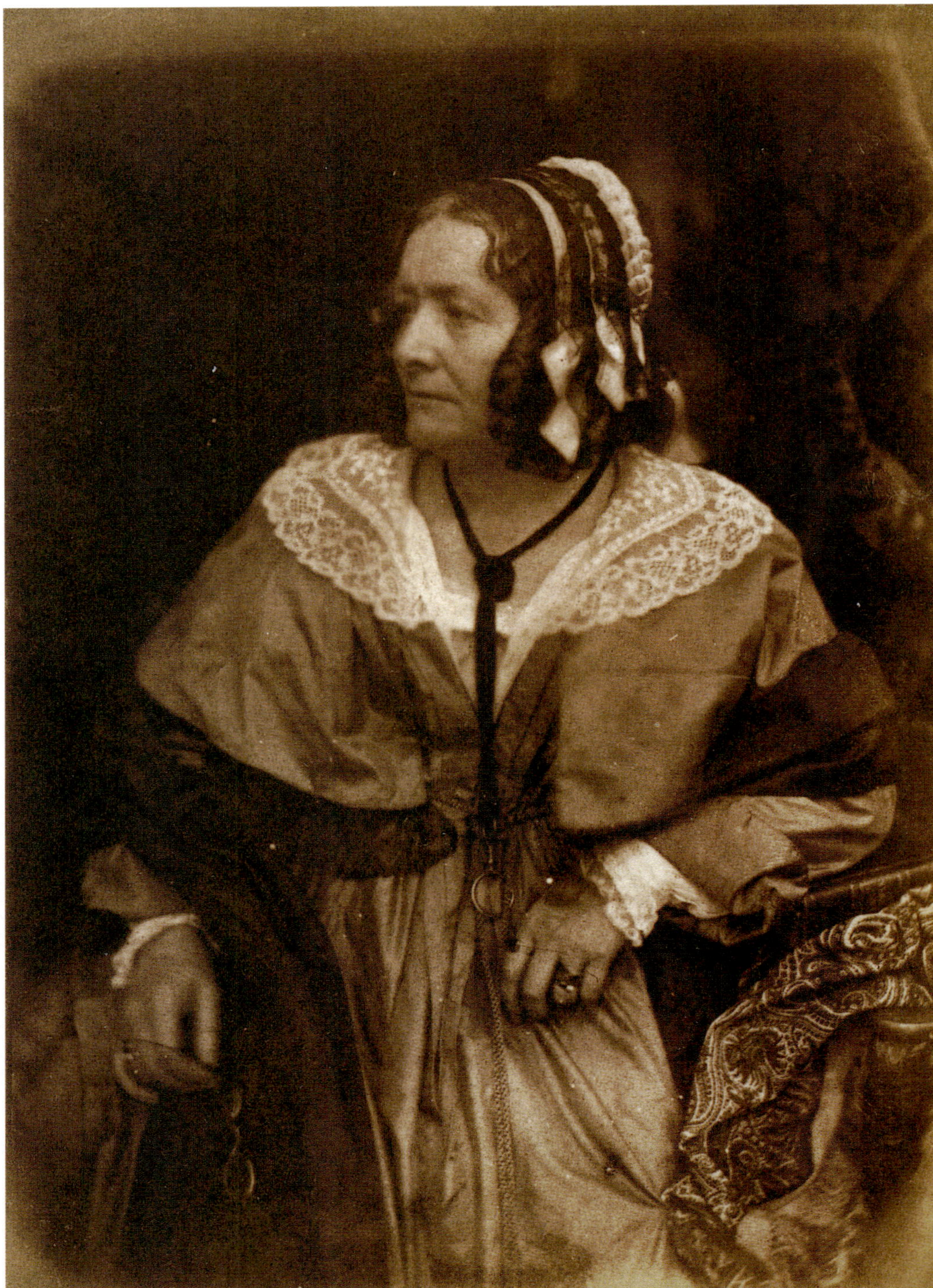

Plate 22
D. O. Hill and Robert Adamson, *Mrs Anna Jameson*, 1843–7. Calotype.
Scottish National Photography Collection, Edinburgh.

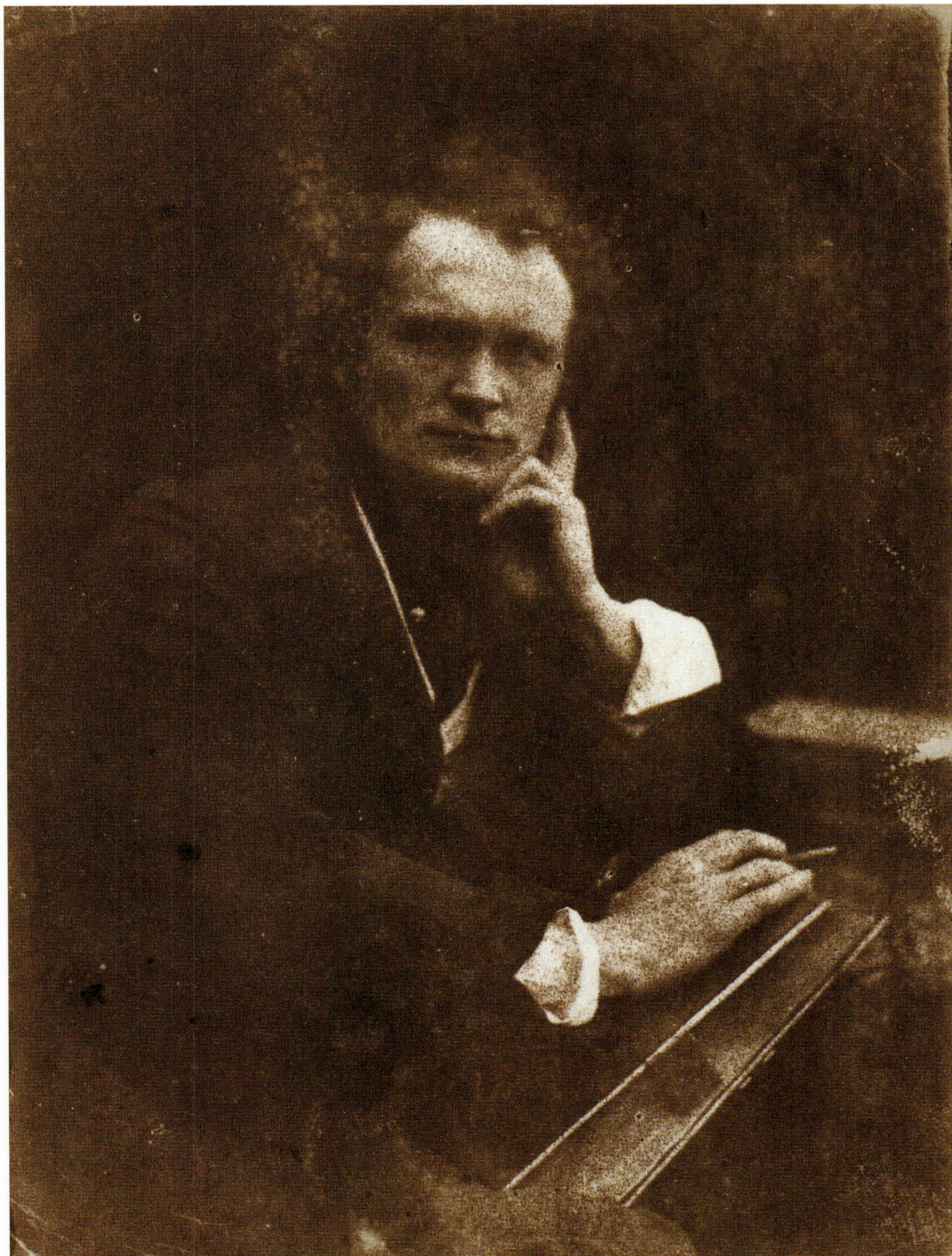

Plate 23
D. O. Hill and Robert Adamson, *Thomas Duncan*, 1843–4. Calotype.
Scottish National Photography Collection, Edinburgh.

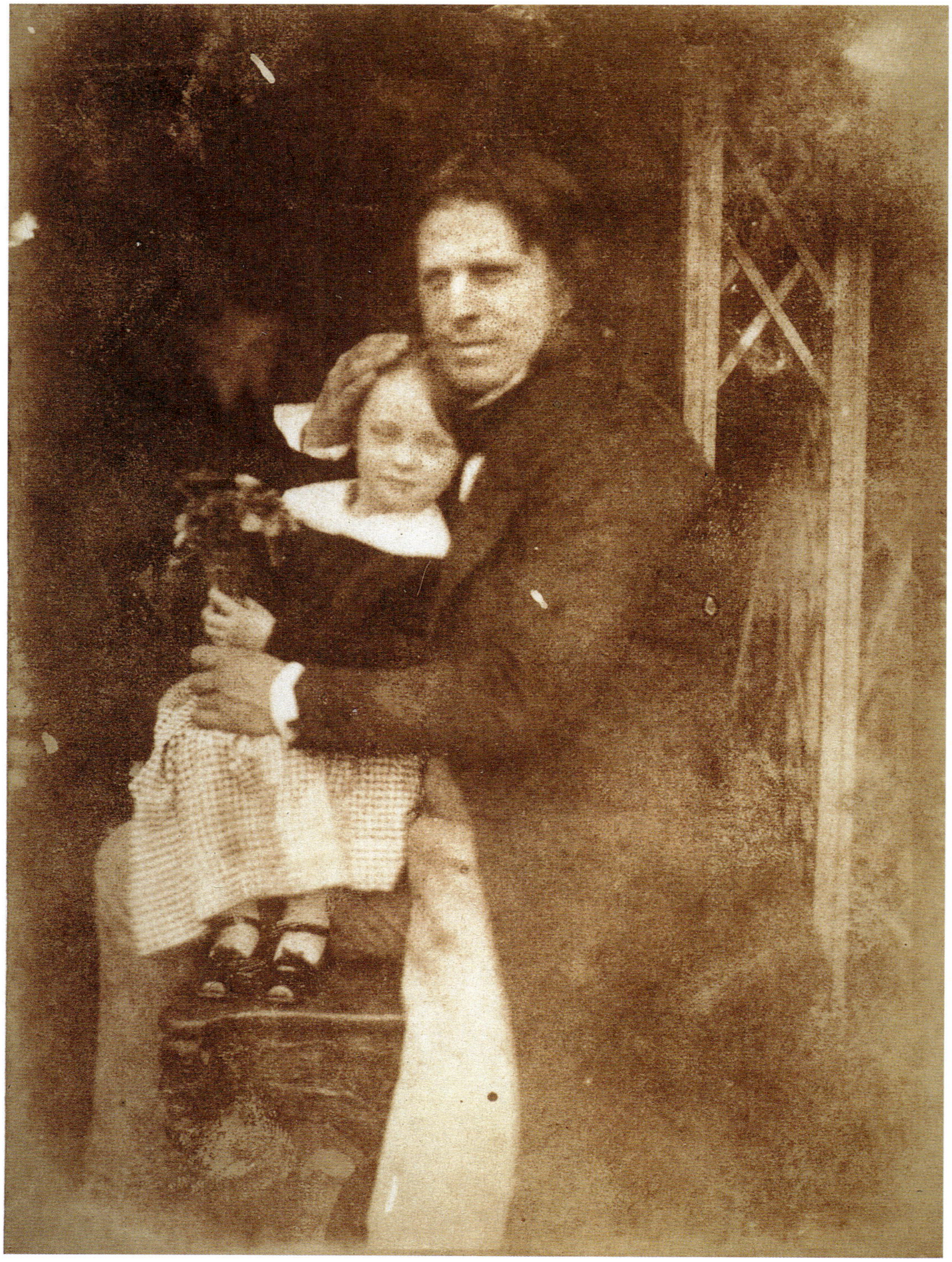

Plate 24
D. O. Hill and Robert Adamson, *D. O. Hill with Charlotte*, probably 1843. Calotype.
Scottish National Photography Collection, Edinburgh.

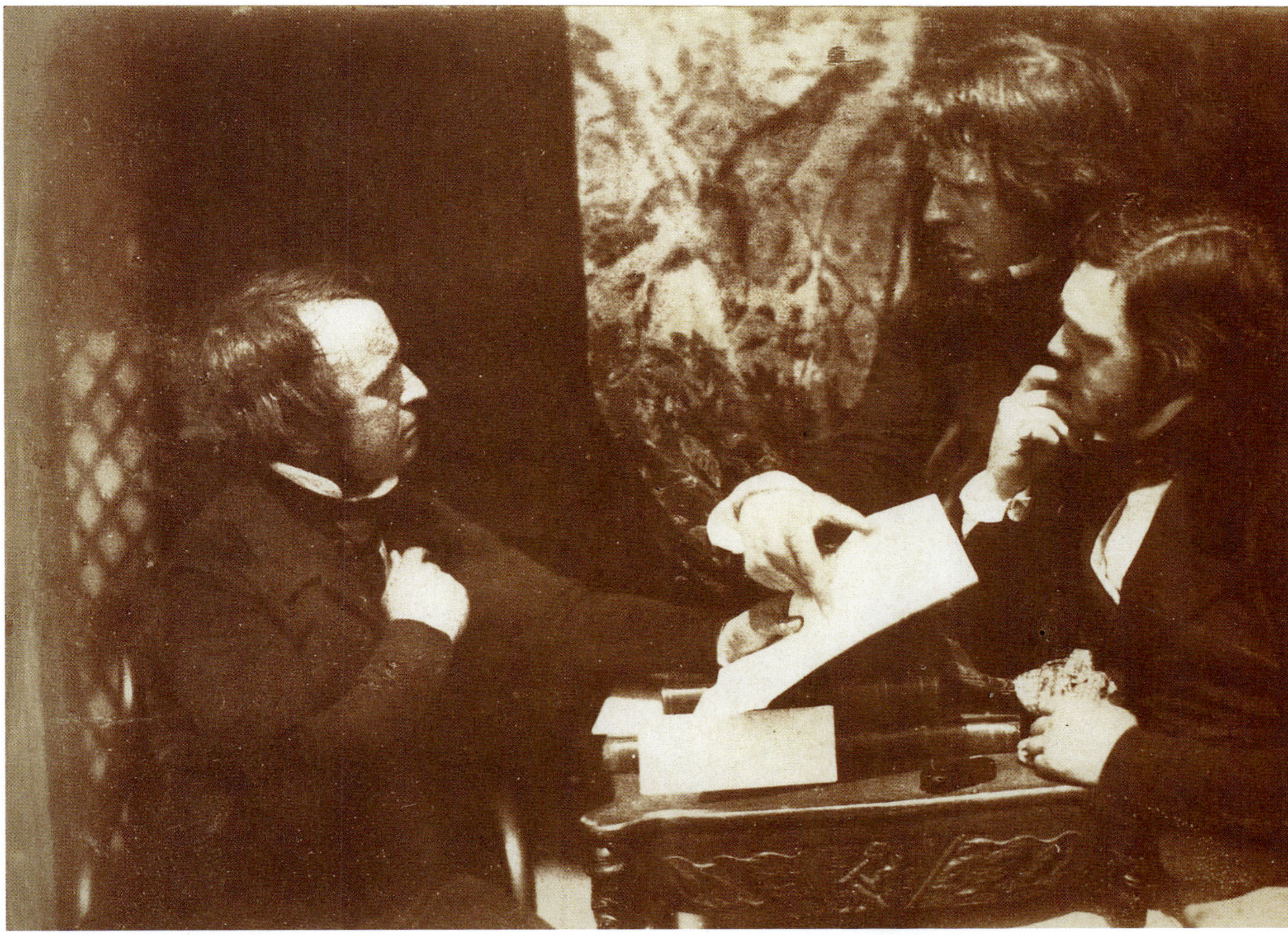

Plate 25
D. O. Hill and Robert Adamson, *James Ballantyne, D. O. Hill and Dr George Bell*, 1843–7. Calotype.
Scottish National Photography Collection, Edinburgh.

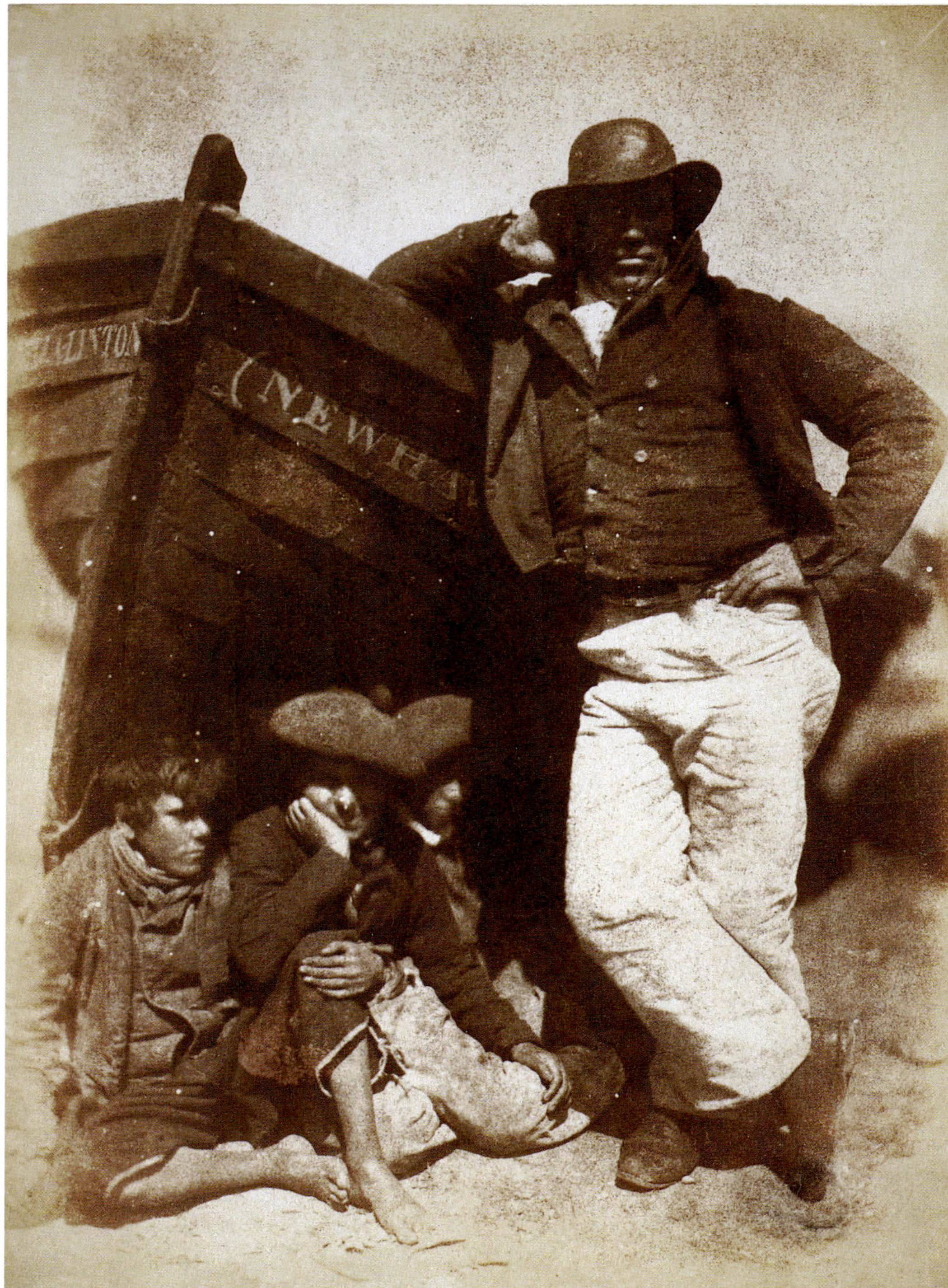

Plate 26
D. O. Hill and Robert Adamson, *James Linton, his Boat and Bairns, Newhaven*, 1843–7. Calotype.
Scottish National Photography Collection, Edinburgh.

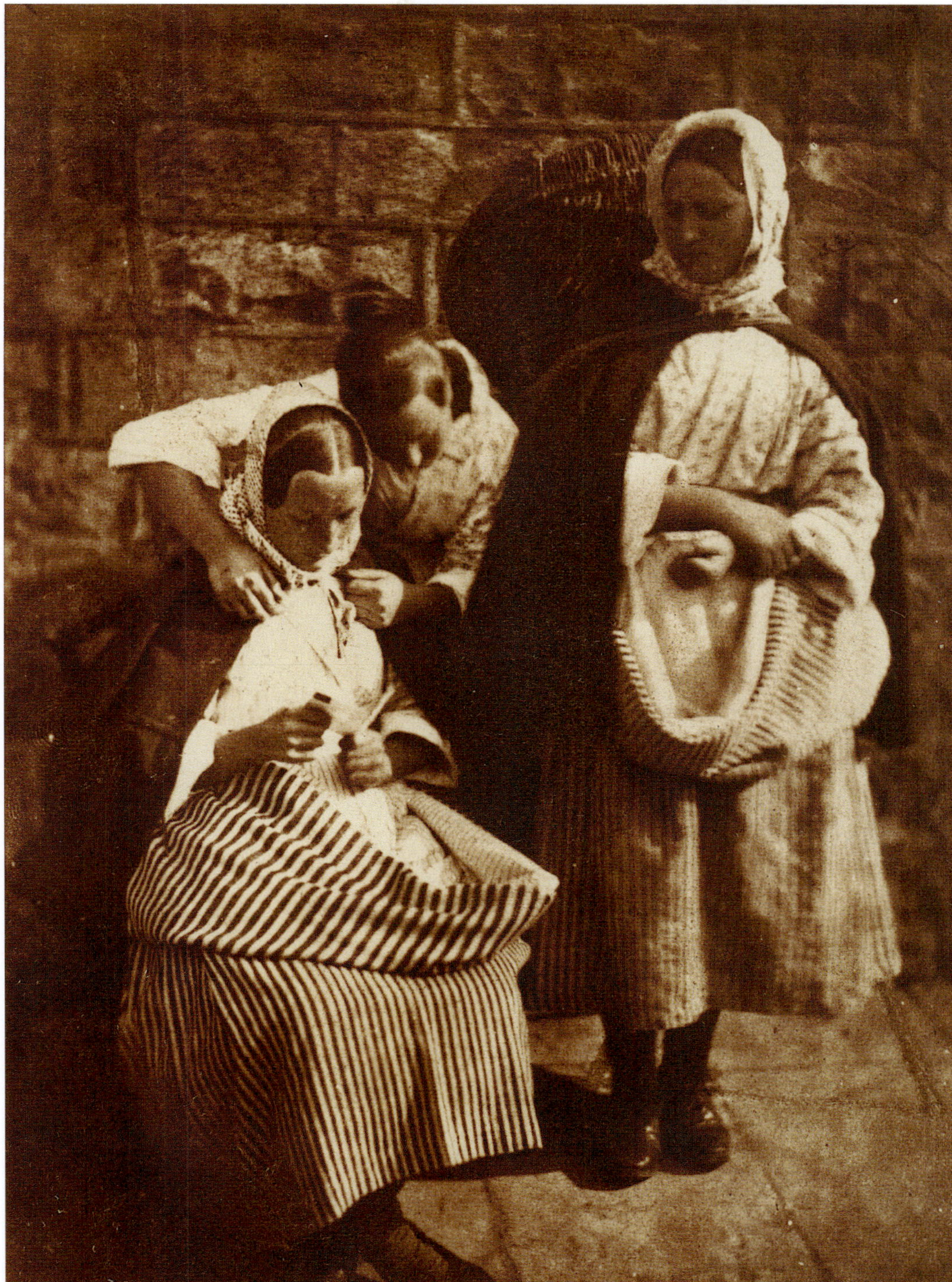

Plate 27
D. O. Hill and Robert Adamson, *Fishwives Reading a Letter, Newhaven*, 1843–7. Calotype.
Scottish National Photography Collection, Edinburgh .

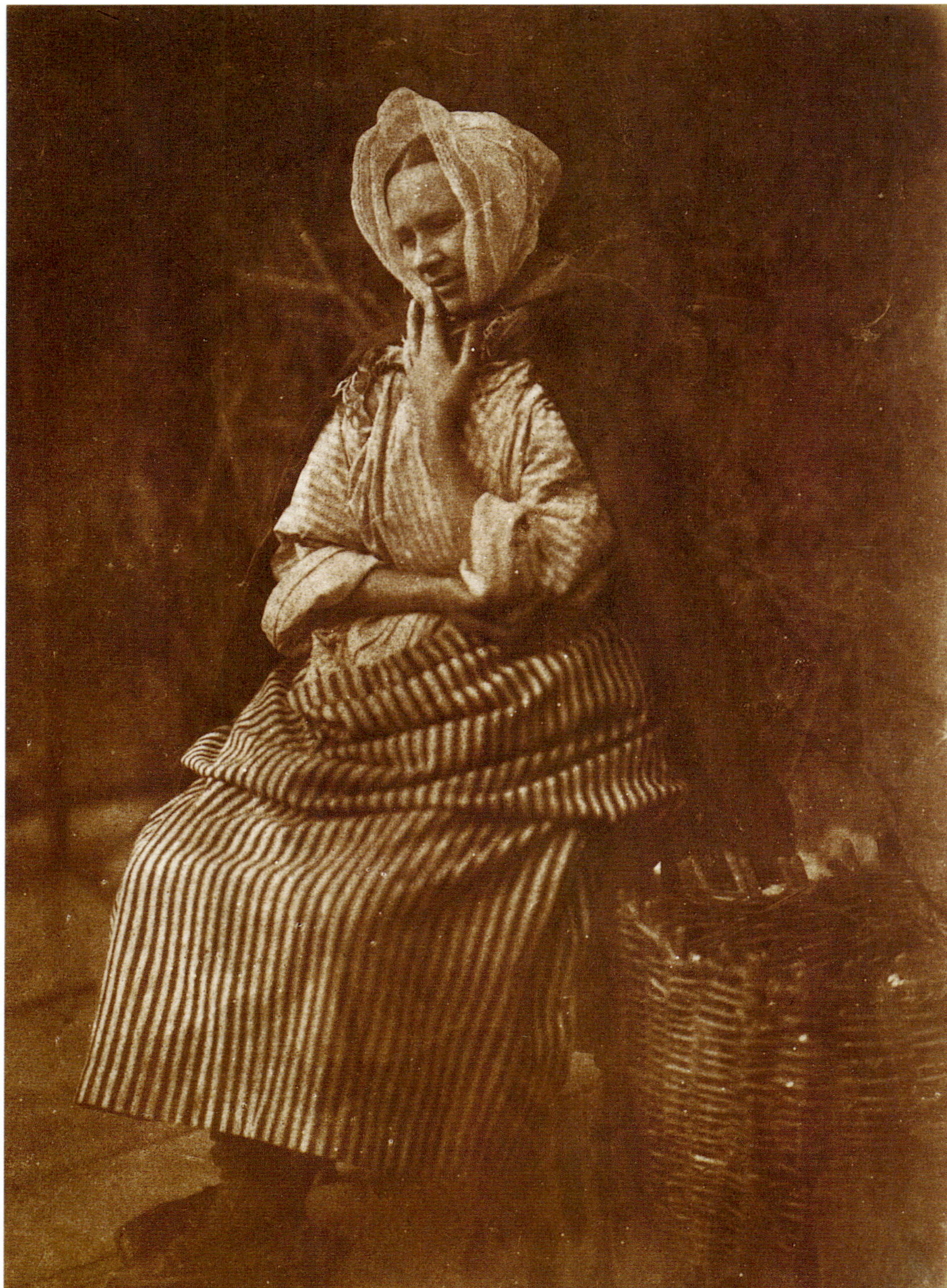

Plate 28
D. O. Hill and Robert Adamson, *Jeanie Wilson, A Love Reverie*, 1843–7. Calotype.
Scottish National Photography Collection, Edinburgh.

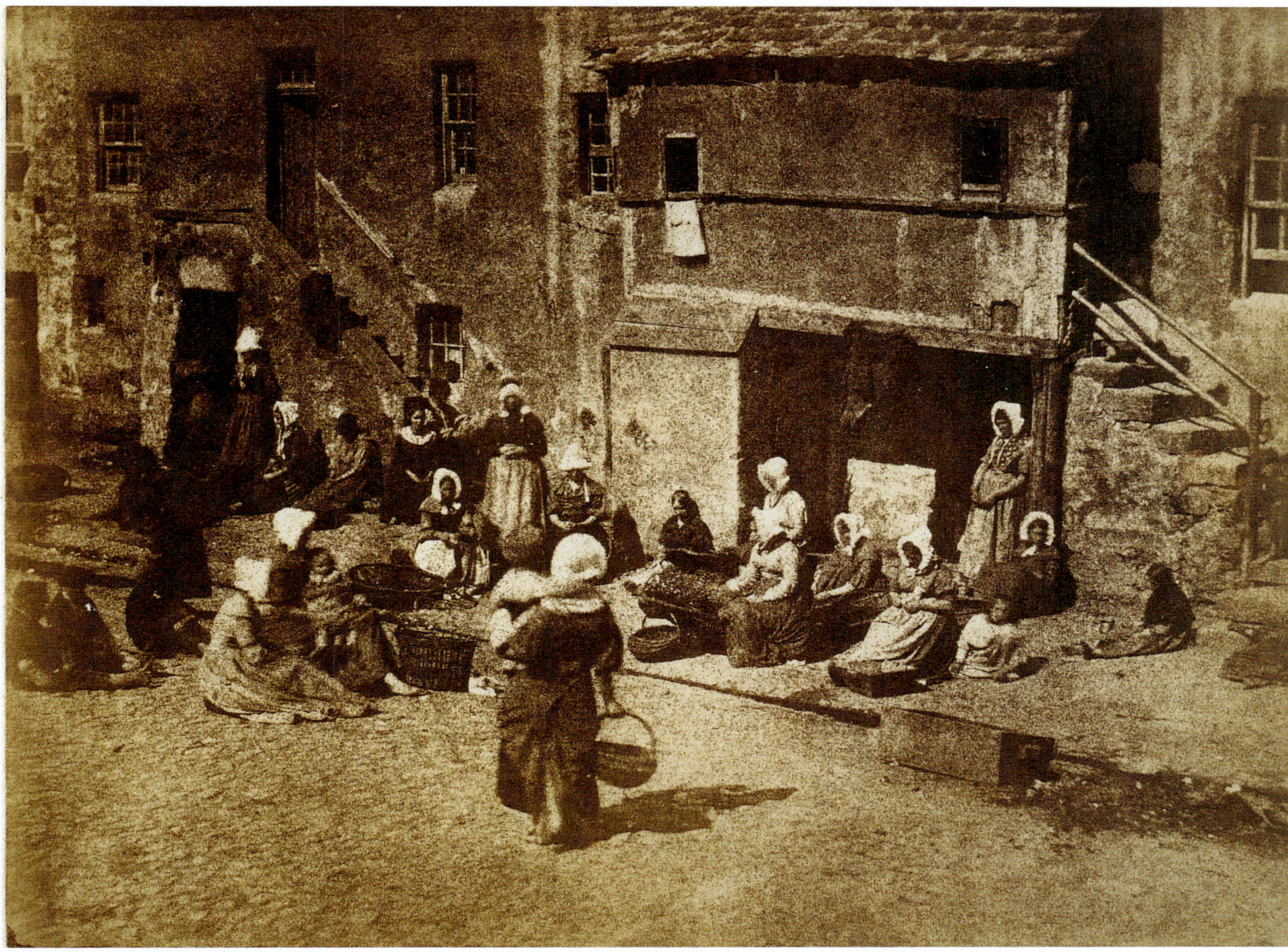

Plate 29
D. O. Hill and Robert Adamson, *Fishergate, North Street, St Andrews*, 1843–7. Calotype.
Scottish National Photography Collection, Edinburgh.

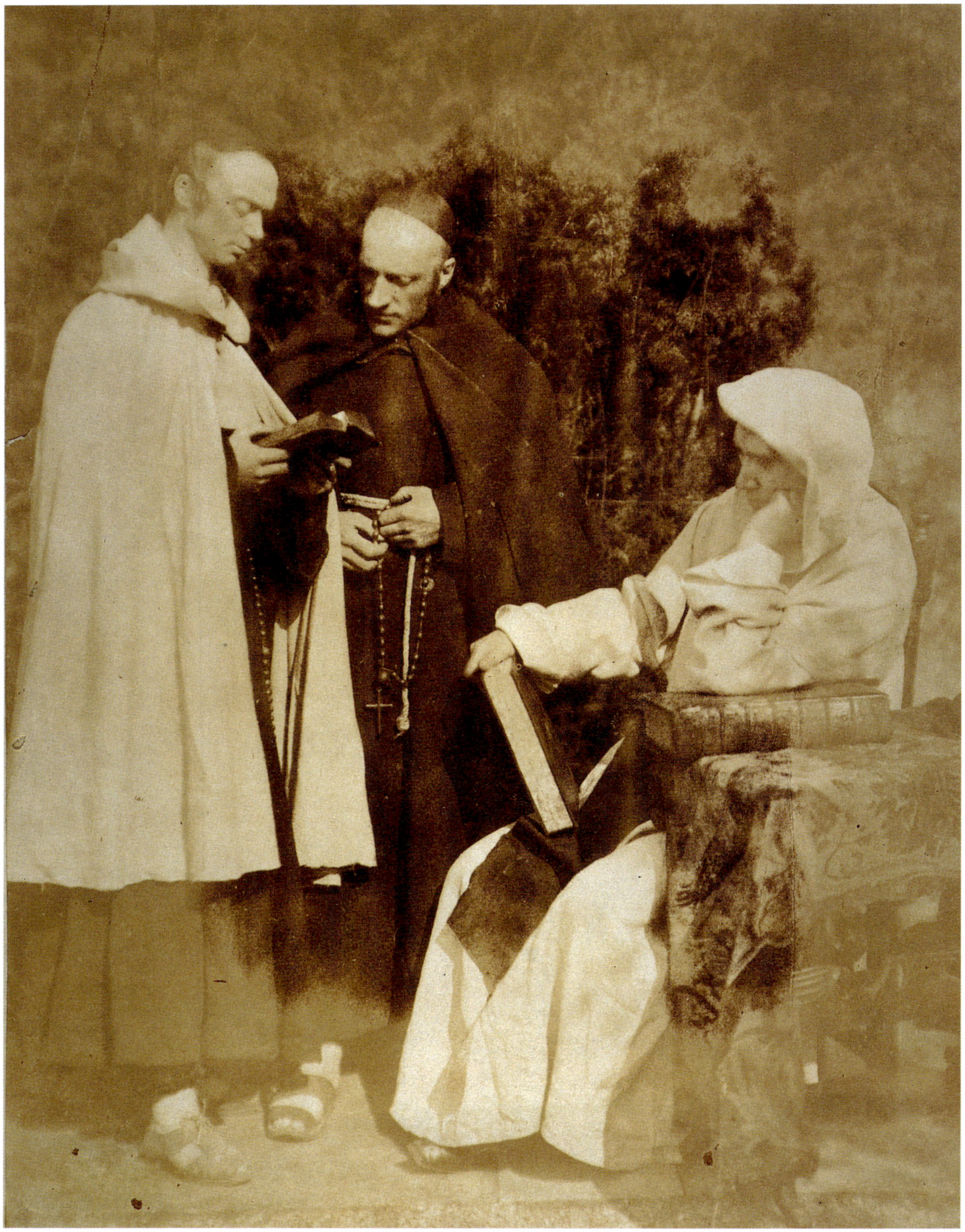

Plate 30
D. O. Hill and Robert Adamson, William Borthwick Johnstone, William Leighton Leitch and David Scott as *The Monks of Kennaquhair*, 1844–6.
Calotype.
Scottish National Photography Collection, Edinburgh.

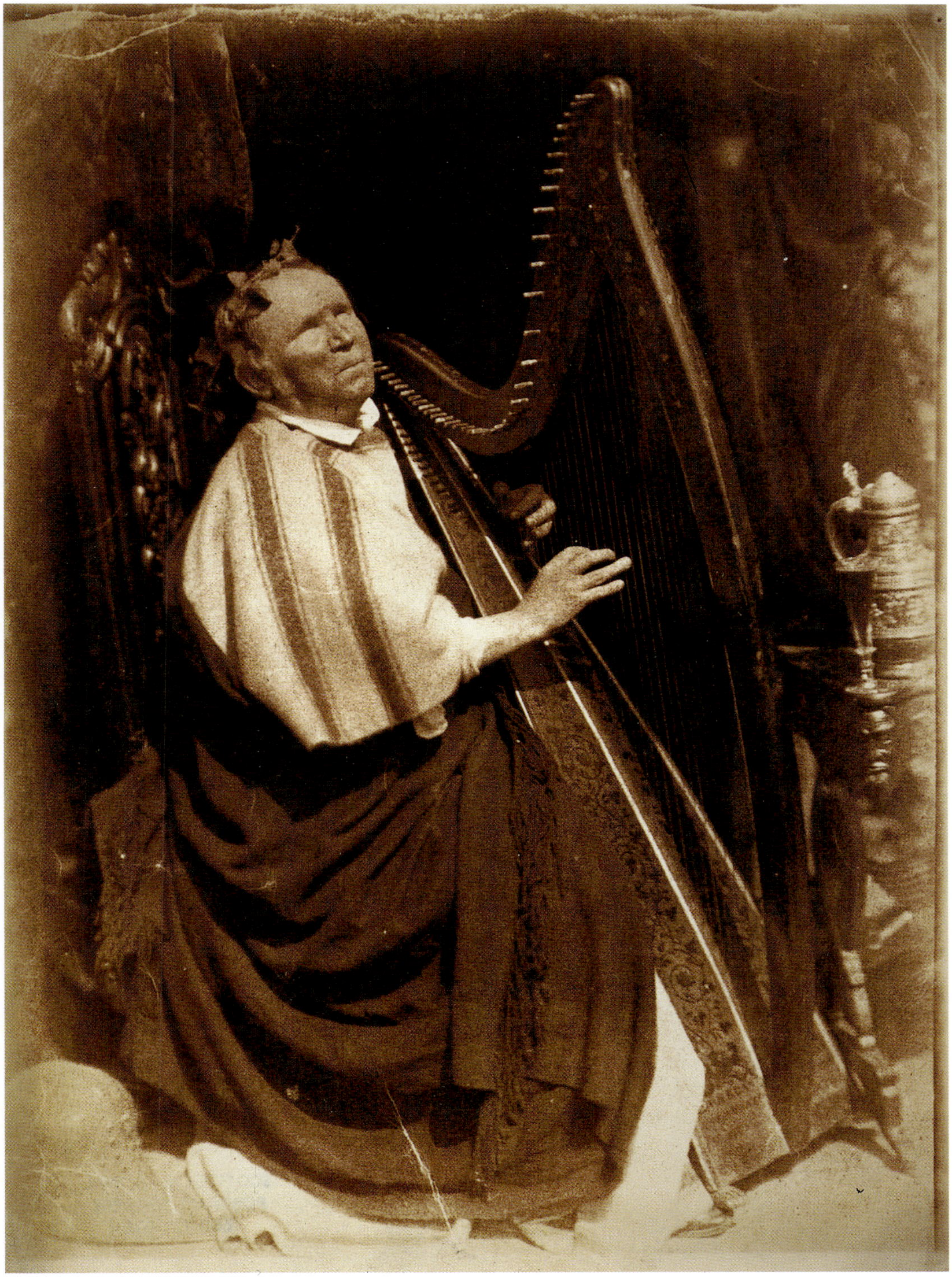

Plate 31
D. O. Hill and Robert Adamson, *Patrick Byrne*, 1845. Calotype.
Scottish National Photography Collection, Edinburgh.

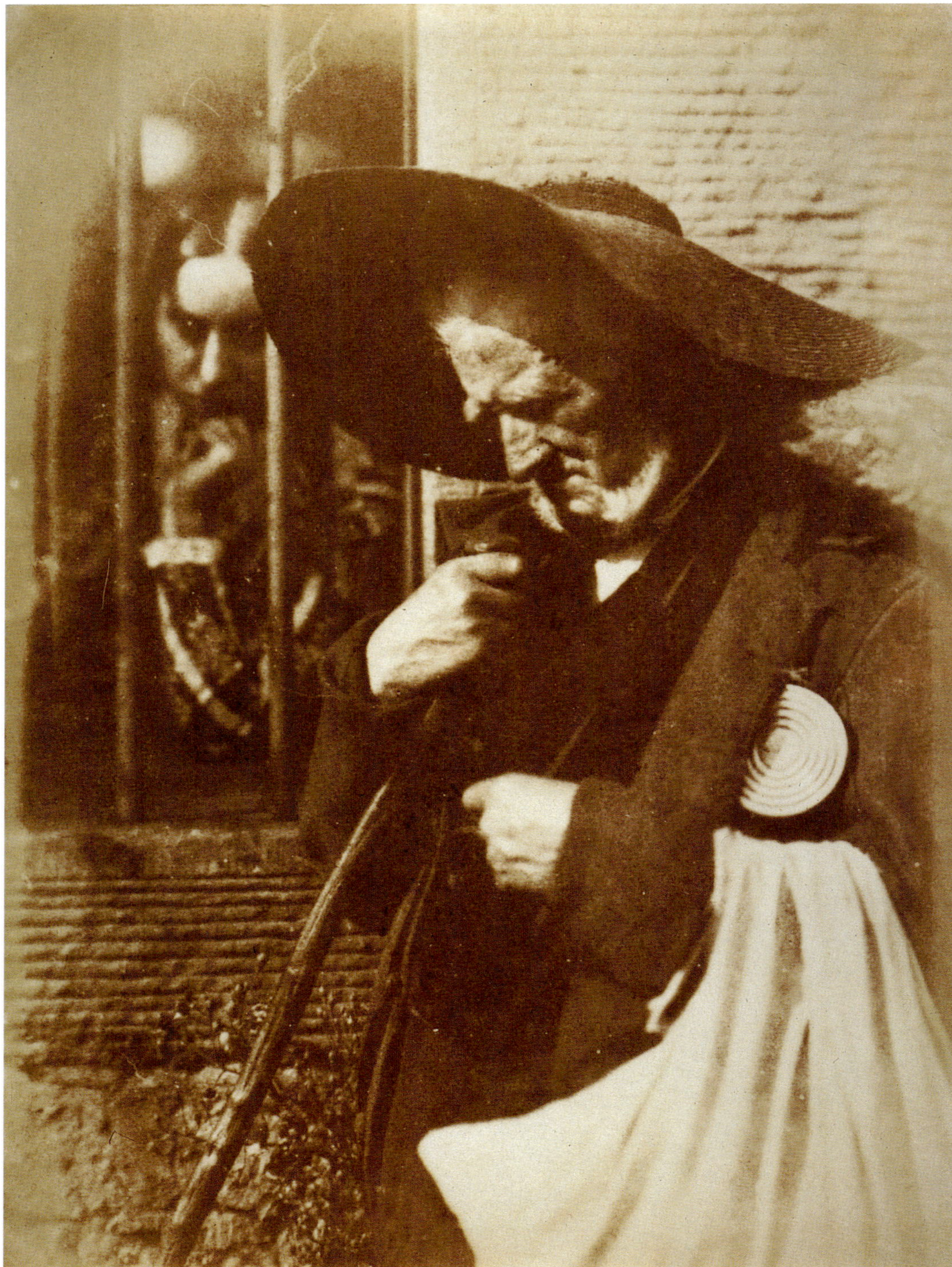

Plate 32
D. O. Hill and Robert Adamson, John Henning and Miss Cockburn as *Edie Ochiltree and Miss Wardour*, 1843–7. Calotype.
Scottish National Photography Collection, Edinburgh.

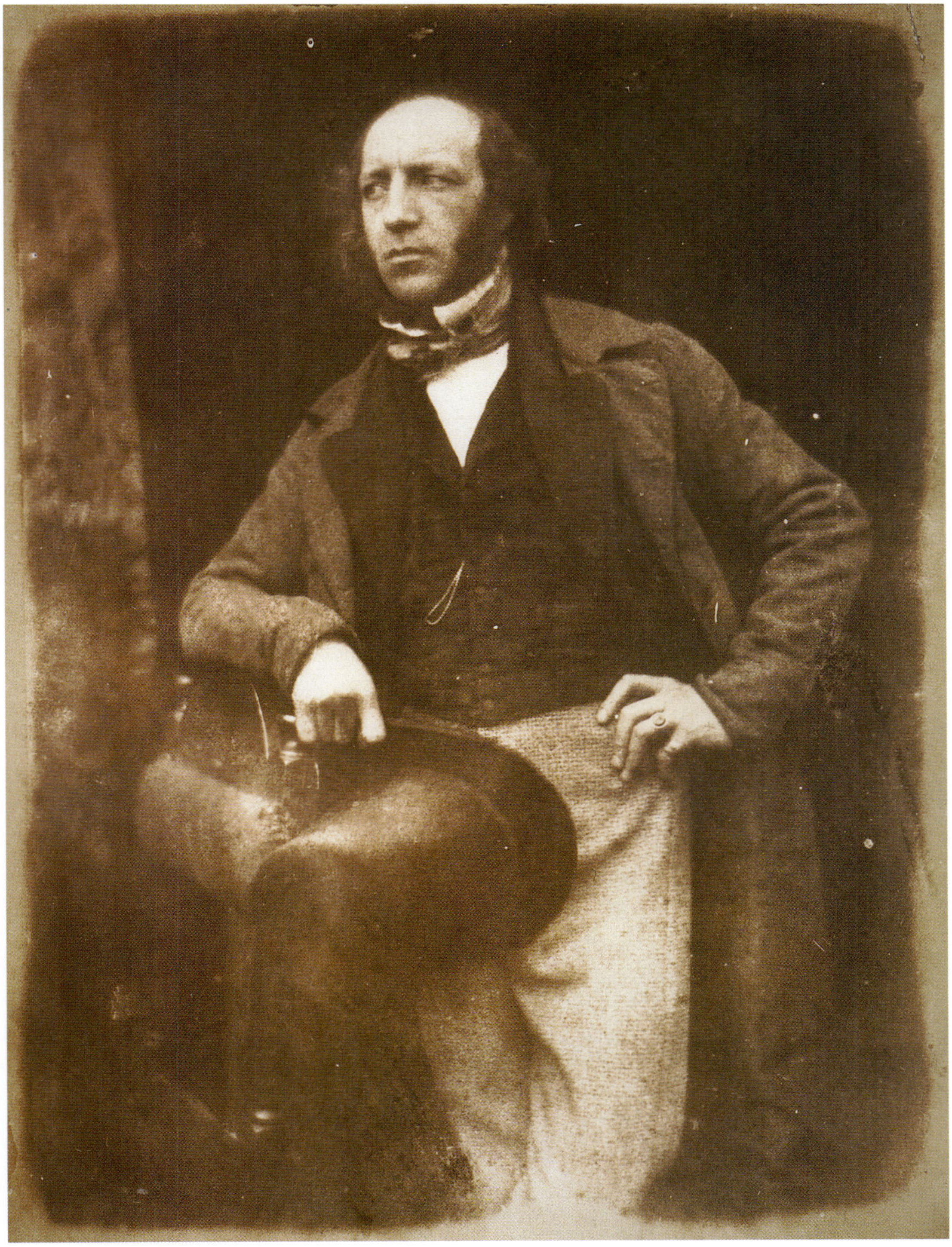

Plate 33
D. O. Hill and Robert Adamson, *Alexander Campbell of Monzie*, 1844–6. Calotype.
Scottish National Photography Collection, Edinburgh.

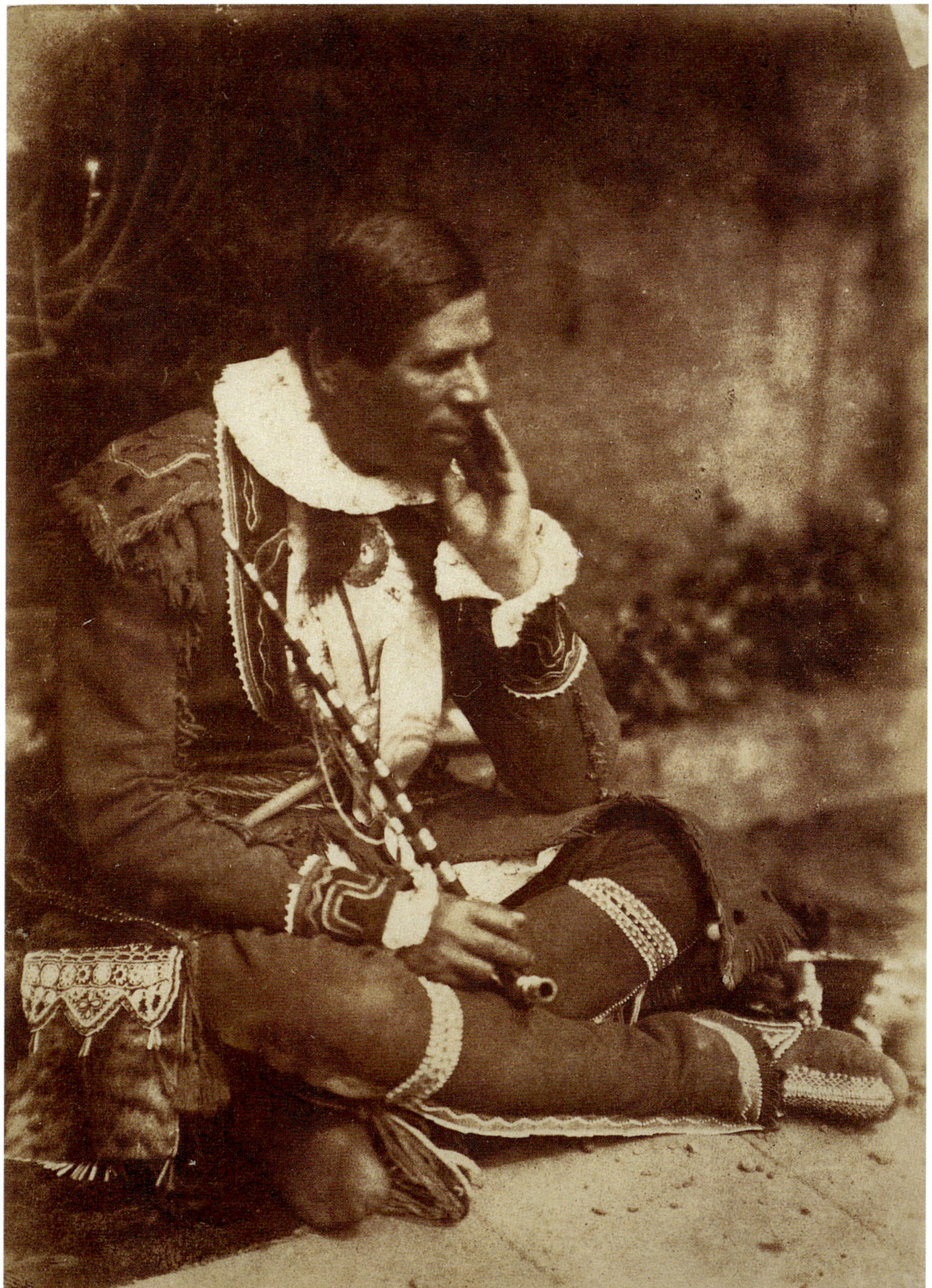

Plate 34
D. O. Hill and Robert Adamson, *Reverend Peter Jones or Khakewaquonaby*, July 1845. Calotype.
Scottish National Photography Collection, Edinburgh.

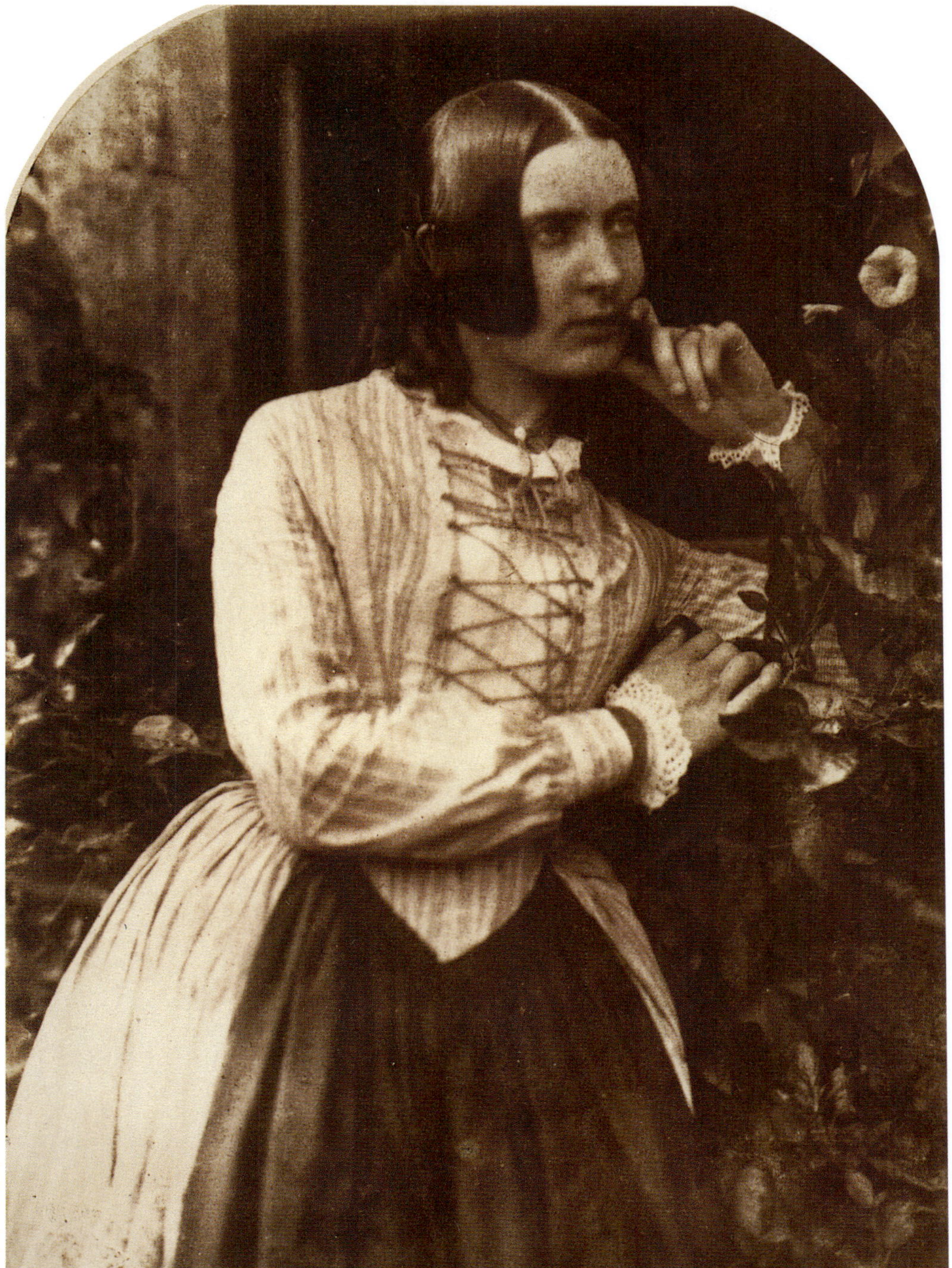

Plate 35
D. O. Hill and Robert Adamson, *Patricia Morris*, 1843–7. Calotype.
Scottish National Photography Collection, Edinburgh.

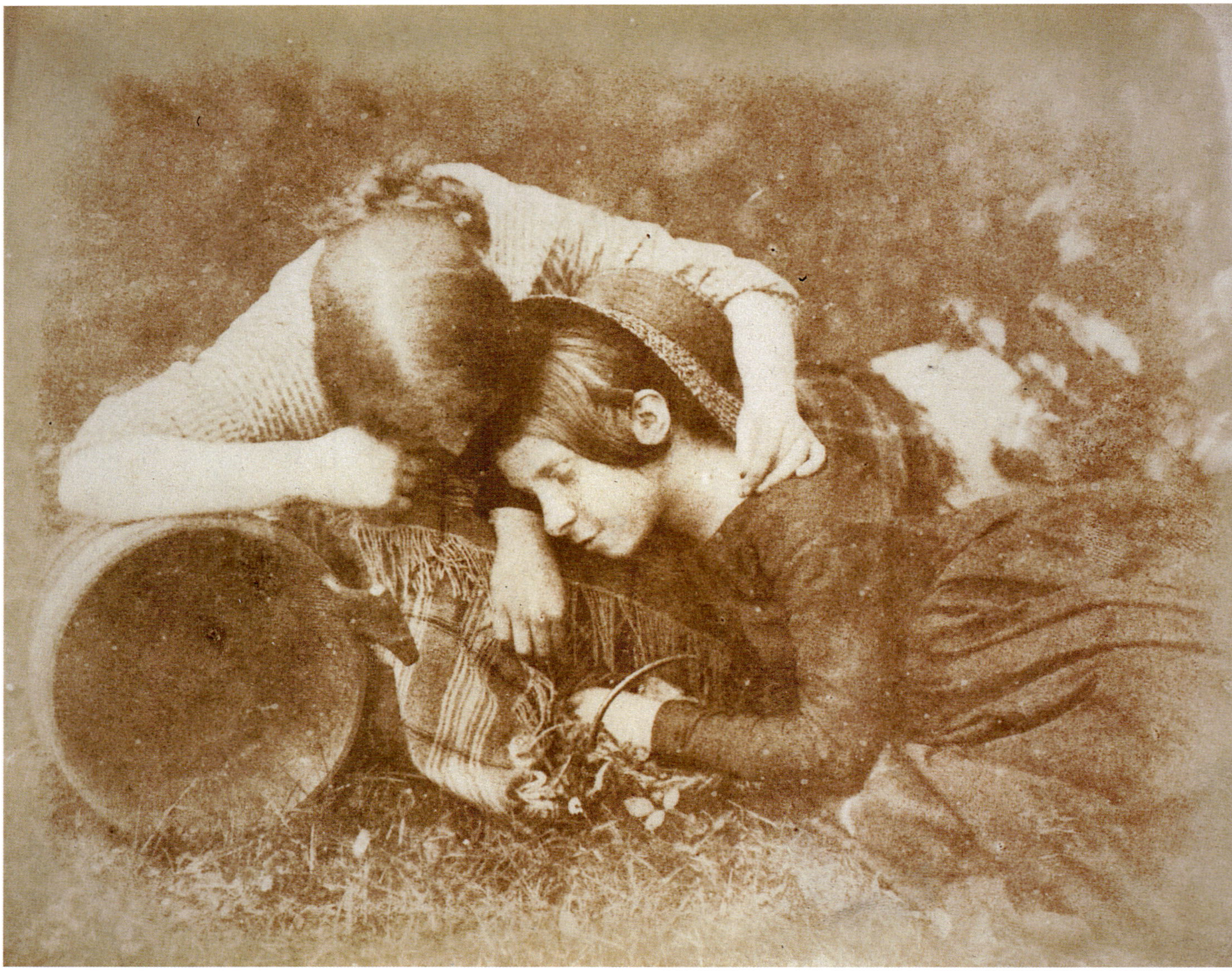

Plate 36
D. O. Hill and Robert Adamson, *Margaret and Mary McCandlish, 'The Gowan'*, 1843–7. Calotype.
Scottish National Photography Collection, Edinburgh.

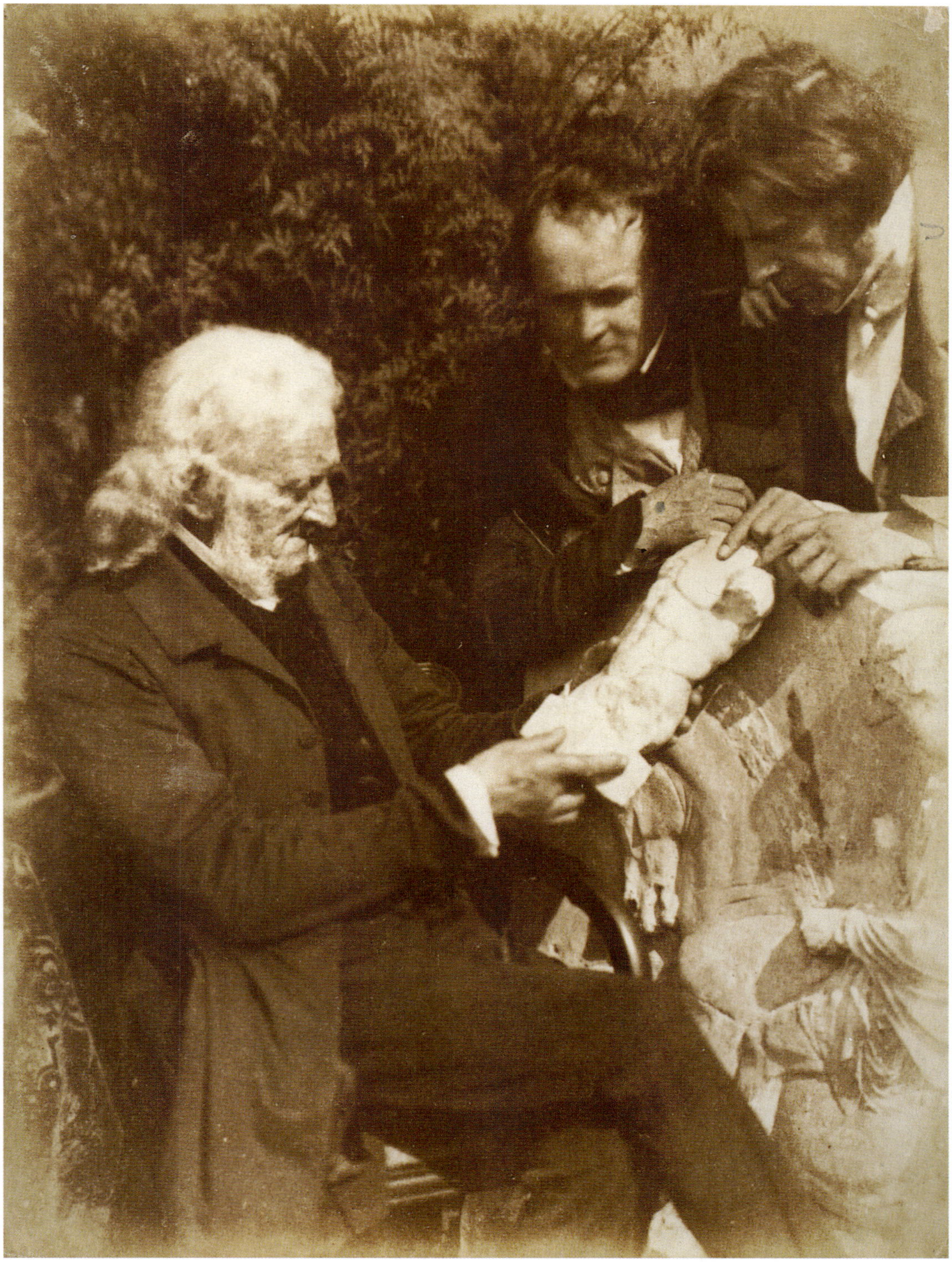

Plate 37
D. O. Hill and Robert Adamson, *Alexander Handyside Ritchie, John Henning and D. O. Hill*, 1843–7. Calotype.
Scottish National Photography Collection, Edinburgh.

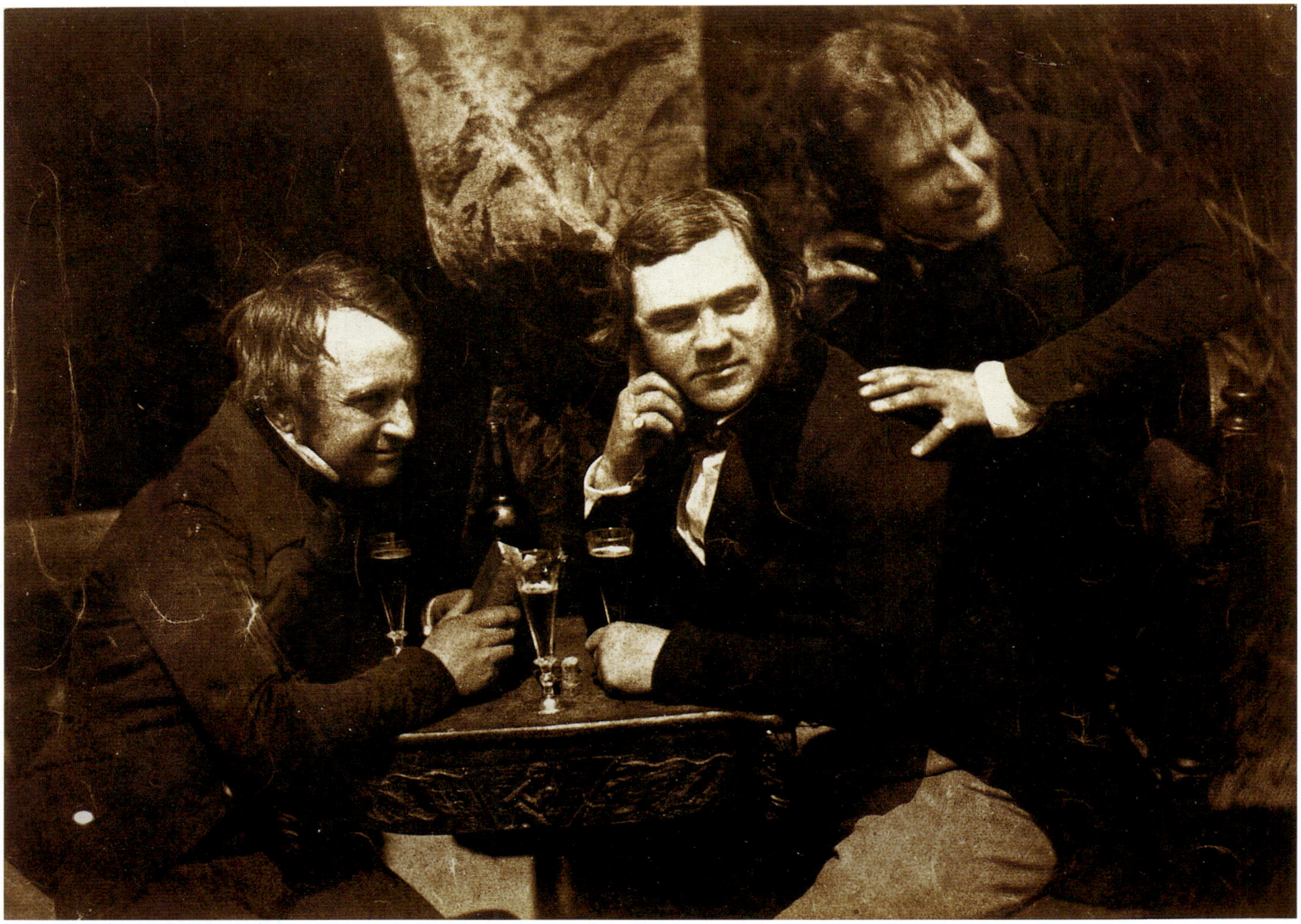

Plate 38
D. O. Hill and Robert Adamson, *Edinburgh Ale*, 1843–7. Calotype.
Scottish National Photography Collection, Edinburgh.

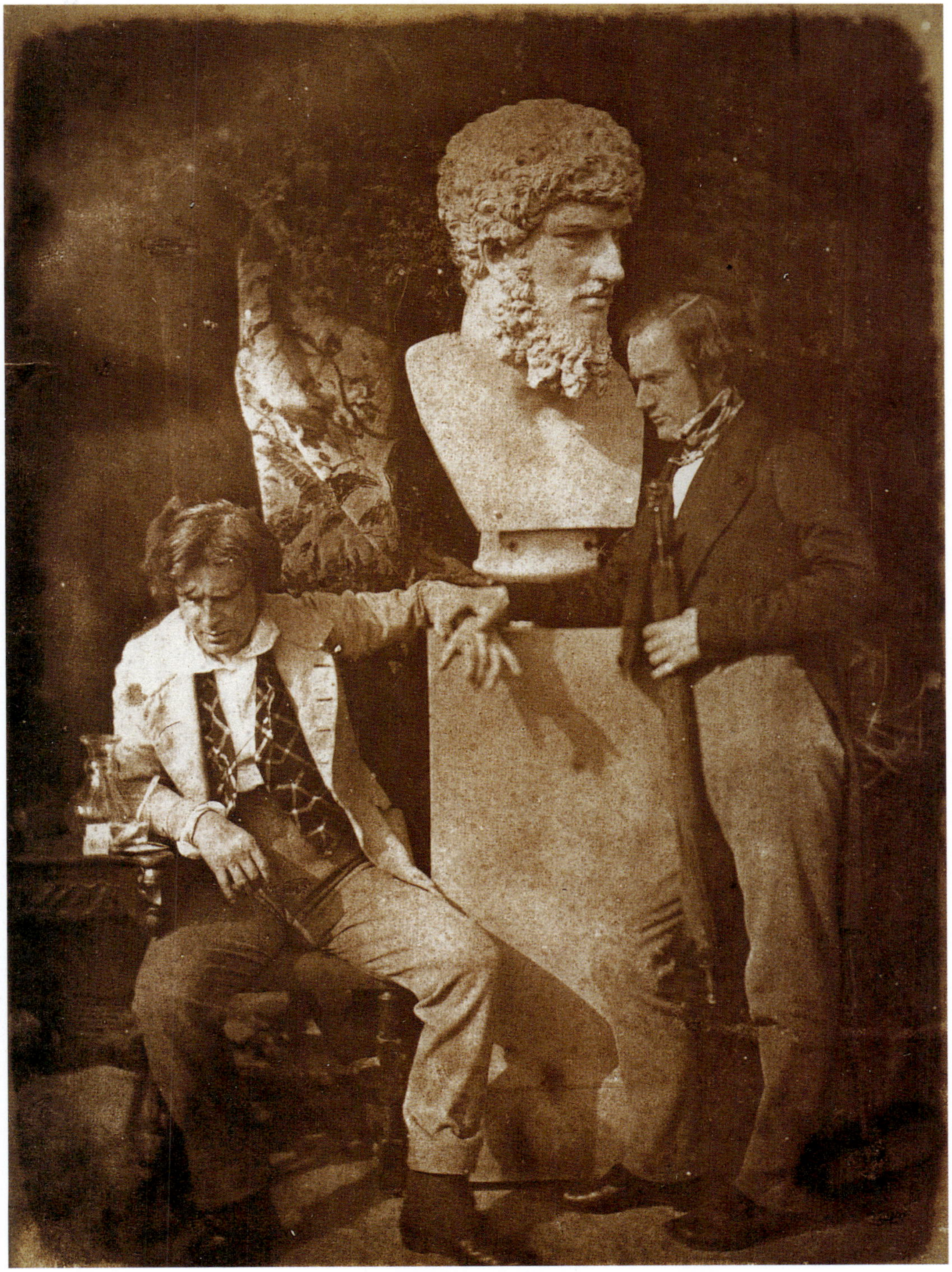

Plate 39
D. O. Hill and Robert Adamson, *The Morning After, 'He, greatly daring, dined"*, 1843. Calotype.
Scottish National Photography Collection, Edinburgh.

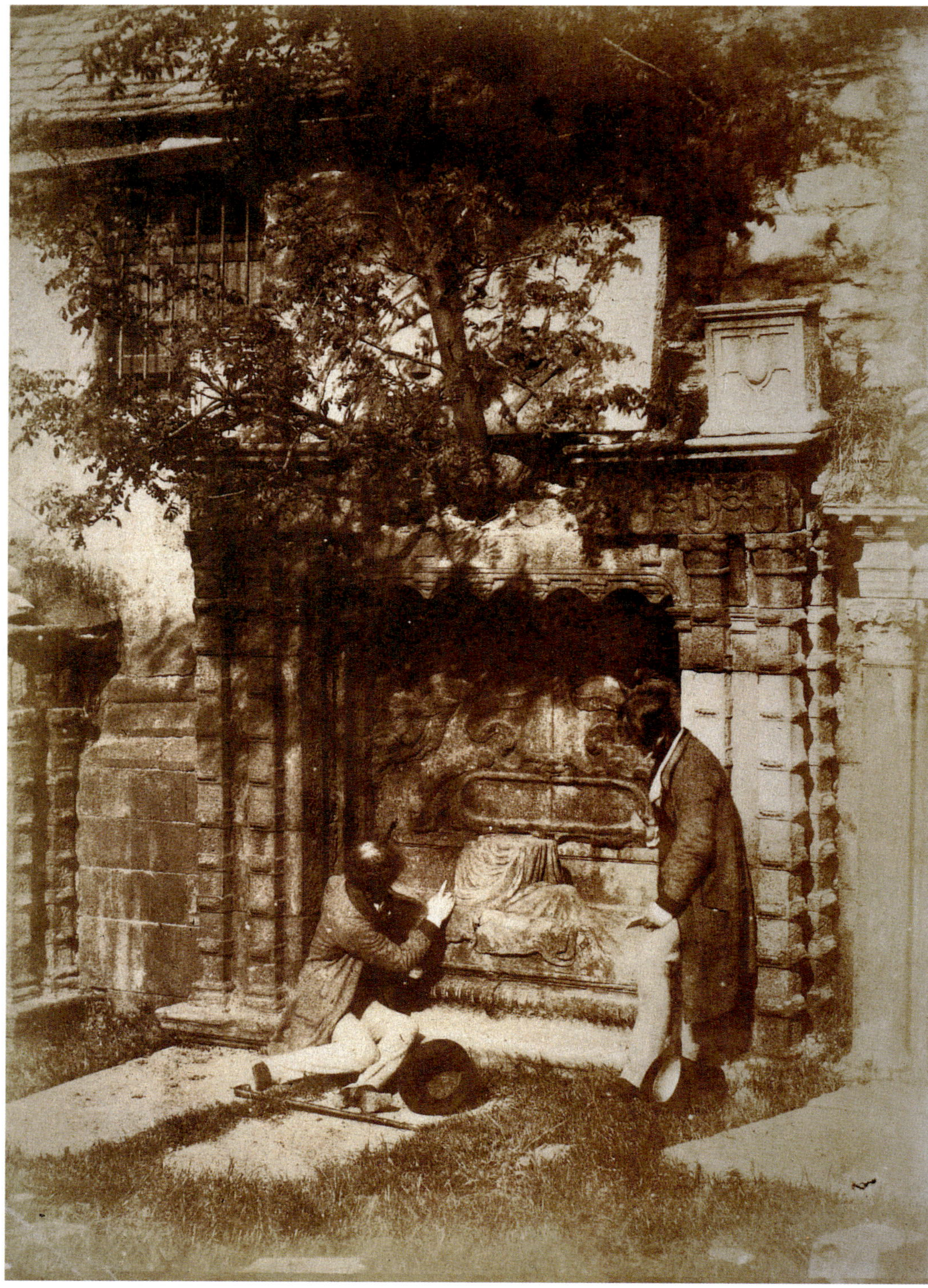

Plate 40
D. O. Hill and Robert Adamson, *D. O. Hill and Thomas Duncan at the Nasmyth Tomb, Greyfriars' Churchyard*, 1843–4. Calotype.
Scottish National Photography Collection, Edinburgh.

INTRODUCTION

David Octavius Hill was born two hundred years ago. He was a landscape and genre painter, and an important actor in the shifting world of the arts in Scotland. His life spanned sixty-eight years from the reign of George III, in 1802, to the first three decades of Queen Victoria's rule (he died in 1870). In our time, however, he is famous for his role in the early history of photo-graphy, his partnership with the young Robert Adamson, which lasted a mere four years between 1843 and Adamson's premature death in January 1848. This has given us a curious and seriously inadequate perspective both on the photographic work and on the way that work should illuminate its own time.

This study is written with several aims in mind. It offers a celebration of the life of a sociable and kind man. It is designed to give a view of his work as an artist beyond photography, and to illuminate his position and influence in the practical workings of the Scottish art world. And, because Hill lived in a highly literary and literate age, to make the connections with the writings of his time (from personal letters to best-selling books), which are a large part of the inspiration behind the photographs. Our focus on Hill centres on the 1840s, so the study is constructed largely to reflect and revolve around that time, with an exploration of history and ideas combined.

Twentieth-century criticism has come up with two broad answers to the problem posed by Hill and Adamson's work, which is: how do we feel the impact and that apparently straightforward sense of familiarity of photographs taken more than 150 years ago? The first response placed the work in a 'golden age' of photography, uncluttered by later mannerism. The second adopted a critical stance in which the viewer achieved a personal or inner understanding on his own terms. These positions should be briefly addressed, because the intention of this book is to open up our knowledge of the history and gain a greater illumination from Hill and his contemporaries. It is here assumed that some of the most enthusiastic twentieth-century responses to Hill and Adamson's work may have assisted in obscuring our full understanding and pleasure, and that Hill's beliefs, enthusiasms and connections in particular justify our attention.

The golden age idea may be illustrated from the twentieth-century writings of the Pictorialist photographer J. Craig Annan and the art historian Heinrich Schwarz. They have attributed Hill and Adamson's success to a kind of photographic innocence, working in a new and open field of exploration. It was Annan who introduced the work of Hill and Adamson to a wider world at the beginning of the twentieth century, through international exhibition and the photogravures, published in the United States in Alfred Stieglitz's critical journal, *Camera Work*. Annan had met Hill briefly as a child but largely inherited his enthusiasm from his father, Thomas Annan, whose own work as a photographer had been encouraged and to some degree directed by Hill. Annan expressed his admiration of Hill and Adamson's photography in such a way, referring specifically to Hill:

> He is indeed a fortunate man who, endowed with talent and courage, finds himself at work in a field where there are no precedents and who must simply follow the guidance of his own instinct . . . Such productions are evolved as unconsciously and as directly from nature as are the trees and flowers, and constitute a pure product . . . To present day pictorial photographers it is extremely interesting and almost humiliating to observe that on the very threshold of the photographic era there was one doing with no apparent effort what they would fain accomplish with eager strivings, and thinking so little of his achievements that when he returned to what he considered his

serious work it was with a sense of having frittered away three solid years in following a most fascinating amusement.[1]

Heinrich Schwarz's immensely influential work on Hill as a 'Master of Photography', first published in Germany in 1932, introduced the photographs to the attention of the next generation:

> Just as Gutenberg's printings have remained the outstanding creations of typography, so are Hill's calotypes examples of photography so brilliant that by the side of them everything which has taken place since pales. As though photography, in the first hours of its existence, had wished to manifest and unfold all its possibilities, as though it had hoped at once to approach all but the farthest reaches of the attainable. Hill's calotypes stand isolated and unequalled at the dawn of a new art . . . From the very insufficiencies of this man's technical equipment grew the subtlest artistic achievements. Alone in a new world of graphic representation, he sensed instinctively all the secrets of a new vision.[2]

The arguments, put by Annan and Schwarz, are appealing because of their wholehearted appreciation. But this is rhetorical prose. It flies a standard well above the common minutiae of explanation, and relies on a concept of general imperative. Both men were practising artists, Annan as a photographer and Schwarz as a lithographer, and both understood the professional skill that lay behind the photographs' success. Annan himself qualified his remarks in the same article:

> One becomes so fascinated by the interest of the persons who sat to Hill and by his magnificent characterization of them that it is only as a secondary consideration that one thinks of the artistic qualities of his pictures. This is really one of the highest compliments that one could pay them if it be true that 'the greatest art is that which conceals art', for there is absolutely no appearance of conscious effort in the arrangement of his compositions, nor is there any feeling of affectation in the striking attitudes in which he frequently portrayed his subjects.[3]

The second stage of the twentieth-century critical assessment relies on the direct internal appreciation of the viewer; the assumption that if a photograph moves me, it can be explained in my terms of reference. The effect is a curious one, of a historical landscape full of me's, or at least people highly compatible with me – either in my emotional condition or in the strict rationality of my brain. This may be illustrated from a passage published by the authoritative critic, Walter Benjamin in 1936, and by a secondary response to his passage, written by Stephen Bann at the end of the century. Benjamin addresses the impact of Hill and Adamson's photograph of a Newhaven fishwife, which he sees as a model of an anonymous, unposed subject (pl. 1):

> In Hill's Newhaven fishwife, her eyes cast down in such indolent, seductive modesty, there remains something that goes beyond testimony to the photographer's art, something that cannot be silenced, that fills you with an unruly desire to know what her name was, the woman who was alive there, who even now is still real and will never consent to be wholly absorbed into art. And I ask: 'how did the beauty of that hair, those eyes, beguile our forebears: how did that mouth kiss, to which desire curls up senseless as smoke without fire' . . . No matter how artful the photographer, no matter how carefully posed his subject, the beholder feels an irresistible urge to search such a picture for the tiny spark of contingency, of the Here and Now, with which reality has so to speak seared the subject, to find the inconspicuous spot where in the immediacy of that long-forgotten moment, the future subsists so eloquently that we, looking back, may rediscover it.[4]

Benjamin's first response to the photograph may be simply defined as the combination of three thoughts: that the photograph presents a beautiful woman; that his emotional feeling for the picture is heightened by the knowledge that she is not fictionalised but alive; and that his reaction is given an edge by the opposite knowledge, she is real but unattainable. Benjamin is able to possess the picture in his own description, because he is describing a sexual impulse – for the twentieth-century, famously an impulse of the subconscious, and an area in which we have established a sense of superior understanding and liberation, with the Victorians as the opposite model of unconscious repression.

The problem created by Benjamin's conclusion is that, while Annan and Schwarz see Hill as controlling the nature of photography, Benjamin makes the assumption that what he, himself, sees and feels go beyond the photographer's 'art'. He is seeking a direct connection or communication with the subject of the picture. He assumes that his response is distinct from Hill's intention. Benjamin's assumption leads to Roland Barthes's idea of 'The Death of the Author', which proposes that the author's intention is inextricably involved in a complex cultural relationship, which allows the reader to take on a significant role in the creation of meaning. The idea was taken yet further by Jacques Derrida, for whom there could be no final authority, and communication was thus rendered problematic between artist and audience.

This removal of the personal was extended by Stephen Bann from the photographer to the subject. Bann criticised Benjamin's passage on the Newhaven fishwife as follows:

> Does she cast down her eyes with 'casual seductive shame'? The idea is a delightful one, but it is almost wholly the result of our own projection. Does the 'something that cannot be silenced' – which we take to be the ontological insistence of the photographic document – really demand the name of the anonymous fish-wife? Does it really require that we supply a civil status for that reticent body? Let us suppose that we found out, through a small miracle of archival research, that she was called Mary Macpherson. Would that in any way palliate the mute challenge of the image?[5]

Bann draws a circle in his argument to say that the thing that speaks is the essential nature of photography. This takes the thinking away from the emotional gut and apparently turns the photograph into a document – but it is a wordless document offering a mute challenge. Without following this line to its conclusions, it reveals a strange method of thinking, which positively ignores available information. The small miracle of archival labour could be achieved by referring to any publication on Hill and Adamson's work from the 1970 exhibition catalogue written by Katherine Michaelson onwards.[6] Moreover, a student of their work looking at the original photographs or albums in public collections would find her name had been written by D. O. Hill under the photograph. She is Elizabeth Johnstone Hall.

Walter Benjamin was concerned with the extremely important relation of photography to reality. It is this relation that has given photography its distinction and much of its emotional power, and that peculiarly quirky, tender or painful character of the unexpected detail. The concept connects with Roland Barthes's idea of the 'punctum', the tiny spark, the almost invisible mark, which nevertheless pricks our understanding or passion. This may seem an ironic observation of a public art, popularly known for its ability to shout from hoardings or replace ten thousand words in a newspaper. Barthes's proposal takes photography back to the personal and the intimate. But it derives from a philosophic idea discussed from the very beginning of photography, when its driving importance was mysterious and moral, connecting the art to humility and mortality. It is, in the end, this sense of mortality that dictates Barthes's choice of the transcendent image – a photograph of his mother, looked at after her death: 'the Photograph was indeed essential, it achieved for me, utopically, *the impossible science of the unique being*'. So focused is his contemplation of the picture that the photograph effectively becomes transparent; the picture's anonymity and aesthetic unimportance is subsumed into verbal possession, and we are not allowed to see it. It is not illustrated: 'It exists only for me. For you, it would be nothing but an indifferent picture, one of the thousand manifestations of the "ordinary".'[7] This is metaphysics rather than photography; the photograph becomes an icon or relic, a focus only for contemplation. In consequence, the shared public language of photography has disappeared, and its potential for democracy has become élitism for the individual.

The pleasures of introspection and the ability of the inner search of the self to illuminate photography – however it is defined – are naturally limited. This may be illustrated again by the same example of Benjamin's analysis of the photograph of the fishwife. His underlying logic is fairly clear. D. O. Hill, a middle-class, academic painter, took photographic portraits of the Edinburgh cultural world, in which we may assume the painter's conventional respect for the person and importance of the sitter. Common sense and the known practice of figure painters suggests that, when he came to picture the 'ordinary' working woman, his interest would not be in her mind or personality, but more simply in her appearance as a potential sketch, a usefully decorative figure. The formal decorative qualities of the photograph's construction would seem to offer support to this argument. The impact of the photograph on posterity may then become something new, something seen with a fresh and discriminating eye, from which the convention and the political and social prejudices of history have fallen away. These ideas lead to Stephen Bann's conclusions:

> It is a curious property of the photograph that its 'naïve' character is not obliterated but actually confirmed by the passage of time. Since it forms (in Barthes's phrase) a 'message without a code', it simply persists, gathering historicity as the distance in time between the moment of photographing and the moment of the spectator's perception grows greater. Walter Benjamin has succinctly pointed out how, while the portrait becomes after a few generations no more than a 'testimony to the art of the person who painted' it, the photograph affords a 'new and strange phenomenon.'[8]

These influential examples of photographic criticism require a confidence in the critic's understanding, which is not supported by evidence – almost by definition it cannot be. They assume that the interest in the fishwife as a person was beyond Hill's intention; that photography is an art in which a significant part of the visible excellence or fascination is the result of accident; that the picture has a separate life, which goes beyond its author. In Barthes's case, we have a picture of his mother in which the communication itself is a monologue, private not public. But these assumptions are peculiarly inappropriate to Hill and Adamson's work.

Benjamin saw in the photograph of Elizabeth Johnstone Hall one of the most remarkable characteristics of Hill and Adamson's photography – an eloquent future. Despite the distance in time, and without any further knowledge, the photographs may indeed communicate a degree of human interest. The impressive nature of their work can be summed up in the fact that they made their art both public and personal – open to strangers as well as friends and, in the proof of history, open to posterity. For whatever reason, we can feel a connection, an interest in the fishwife, before we discover more about her and her life, simply from looking at the picture. The photographs may very reasonably be discussed in the terms of the criticism quoted above. But, I would propose, a working knowledge of the life, the social and professional concerns and enthusiasms particularly of the more prominent figure in the partnership, David Octavius Hill, casts greater light on the photographs and gives us a greater interest in their subjects. The Modernist Paul Strand, one of the great photographers of the twentieth century, identified the personal nature of Hill's work: 'Yet the results of Hill's experimenting have given us a series of amazing portraits which have not until recently been surpassed...They remain the most extraordinary assertion of the possibility of the utterly personal control of a machine, the camera.' Our admiration, our sympathy with and understanding of the photographs come from that personality and that personal control. It is worth our while to know him better.

The disassociation of Hill and Adamson's work from the words of the early nineteenth century is, moreover, particularly ironic. The time was one of great fluency; there was a boom in publishing and the introduction of the penny post encouraged free communication. D. O. Hill was the son of a bookseller and a man of great literary enthusiasm. Many of the people pictured in the photographs, whom Hill admired and knew as friends, were writers of one kind or another. We can know them from the pictures; we can enhance our knowledge and understanding by reading their works. This gives us more than a linear history of the partnership and Hill's own cultural position. It enables us to achieve, from different angles and considerations, both the individuality of his circle and the complicating factors of thought which make a social culture.

1

Mr Hill, Mr Adamson and the Partnership

For David Octavius Hill, the photographic partnership with Robert Adamson was arguably only an episode in his professional life of fifty years. He was forty-one when he first met Adamson, with an established career as a painter and lithographer and the social status of secretary of the new Royal Scottish Academy. He lived a further twenty-two years after Adamson's demise.

A critical focus on the four years of the photographic practice is, therefore, both natural and complete for a study of Robert Adamson, but incomplete and reductive for our understanding of D. O. Hill. It is partly because of this disparity in time and experience that this study, as a whole, will not treat the partnership as part of a chronological sequence in Hill's life. It is hoped rather to achieve a sense of Hill as a man living within a particular social and artistic group and of the kind of thinking and activities of this group. A brief outline of the two men before they met and the story of the partnership is necessary to this aim.

DAVID OCTAVIUS HILL

D. O. Hill was born in the city of Perth in Scotland (fig. 1) in 1802, to Amelia Murray and her husband, Thomas Hill. As his middle name indicates, he was one of a large family of brothers, but with only one surviving sister, Mary. D. O. Hill's deep affection for his mother was expressed after her death. She was, 'most loving, self sacrificing, & pure hearted'.[1] His father had been involved in the re-establishment of Perth Academy at the beginning of the century, and D. O. Hill attended the school as a boy. The academy had an impressive curriculum, which appears in an advertisement for 1811 – subjects included mathematics, physics, (incorporating engineering and optics), chemistry 'with its application to Arts & Manufactures', geography, logic, modern languages, writing, drawing and both portrait and landscape painting.[2] The rector of this school, Adam Anderson, was a most remarkable man. He is described in Kenneth Cameron's biography:

> From a firm belief in Christianity's capacity in the moral sphere, and in the complementary role of science in the material, to transform the quality of life, the theme of reconciliation runs through his diverse activities. He attempted to bridge gulfs between religion and science, amateurism and professionalism, and not least the conflicting aspirations of different groups in society...Fused with a love of humanity in general, and an intense civic pride in his adopted town in particular, this released a veritable stream of creativity.[3]

Adam Anderson's approach to his pupils was kind, in an age when aggression was a common factor in the teaching of boys, and his range of mind and interests was phenomenal. The influence on Hill's character is undoubted and the impact of Anderson's engineering and scientific enthusiasms, as well as his respect for education itself, may be traced in Hill's career as a painter. It is, moreover, a straightforward comment on the virtues of education that three of the contemporary Scottish painters, Hill, Thomas Duncan and John McLaren Barclay, came from this same school. They were taught by David Junor, who was apparently a naïve painter but presumably a good teacher.

In pursuit of further education in art, Hill joined the Trustees Academy in Edinburgh around 1818, where he was taught by the landscape painter, Andrew Wilson, and was able to study the academy's impressive collection of classical casts. He was further advised by the history and genre painter, Sir William Allan (fig. 2), in the 1820s. Hill also

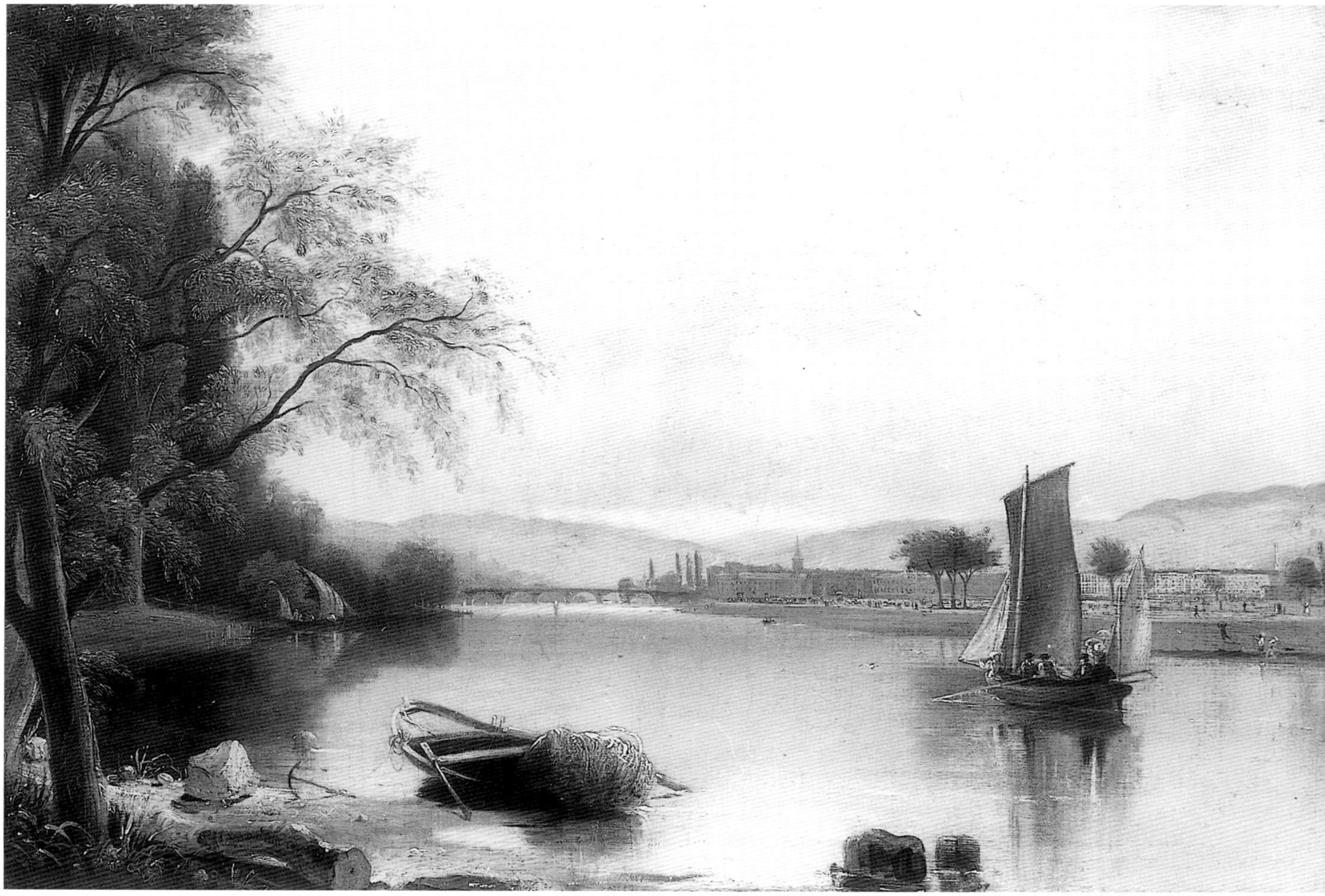

1. D. O. Hill, *View of Perth from the North*, 1826. Oil on canvas. Perth Museum and Art Gallery.

became a teacher. He first appears in the Edinburgh street directories for 1826–7 as a landscape painter and teacher of drawing, and one of the photographs, of Hill sketching with the Misses Morris, suggests that he maintained this role (fig. 3). In 1832, he proposed to establish a drawing academy for figure and landscape with 'a class particularly adapted for the boys of the High School'. This emerges in a letter of support, written by William Allan, in which he adds: 'It gives me great satisfaction in being able to give a Testimony not only of your abilities, but of the power you possess in creating that degree of emulation in the minds of your pupils, which cannot fail to ensure every success.'[4] In October of 1832, Hill was employed to teach drawing, four afternoons a week, by the new 'Edinburgh Institution for Languages, Mathematics, etc' which was set up by Robert Cunningham on a similar model to Perth Academy: 'for those Young Gentlemen, who being destined to employments for the successful prosecution of which a critical knowledge of Greek and Latin is not indispensably requisite, are desirous of devoting a greater portion of their time to studies more immediately connected with their future pursuits.'[5]

Hill's father, Thomas, was a Perth bookseller, who established a branch with Hill's brother Thomas, in Edinburgh in 1825, as 'booksellers, stationers & music sellers'.[6] By the following year, the younger Thomas is listed as living at 27 Elder Street, where D. O. Hill has joined him as a painter and teacher. Another of Hill's brothers, Alexander, who first came to Edinburgh to work with the publishing firm of Blackwood's, joined Thomas in the running of two shops as 'bookseller, stationer, artist & colourman' in 1828–9. While their independence was presumably formally established by their father's death in 1826, they seem to have re-formed as a supportive family group. Alexander's career worked in parallel with D. O. Hill's, as he became increasingly involved in the art world as a publisher and seller of engravings and in the exhibition of paintings in his Princes Street gallery.

Hill first emerged as an artist at the age of eighteen when he published a series of Perthshire landscapes in the new art of lithography (fig. 4). This interest in lithography and the reproduction of fine art also runs as a continuing thread through his subsequent career. As a painter, he was concerned with both landscape and genre, often peopling his landscapes with little figures to bring the two together. In his engaging view of Leith, painted in 1826 (fig. 5), he already exhibits an interest in contrasts of light and shadow and a sense of life and movement in the figures, and in the straining flags, which imply a rapid shift in the cloudscape. The picture also signals an early interest in the fishermen and women, which was to flower in the photographic partnership.

As a young man, Hill was less visible as a public figure than he was in later life. Our earliest glimpse of him is provided by the miniature painter Margaret Saunders, who arrived in Edinburgh around 1830, with a letter of introduction to Hill, who assisted in her career. She attended a dance at William Allan's house and collapsed in inconvenient laughter, when taking part in a mournful tableau. She added: 'I was destined to make a scene that night, for when I was waltzing with D. O. Hill, I felt a little faint and said I would stop, he said "O just one round more", but at the end of the round I fell in a faint; and had to be carried or led into another room and laid on a bed, *quite interesting*.'[7]

2. D. O. Hill and Robert Adamson, *Sir William Allan*, 1843. Calotype. Scottish National Photography Collection, Edinburgh.

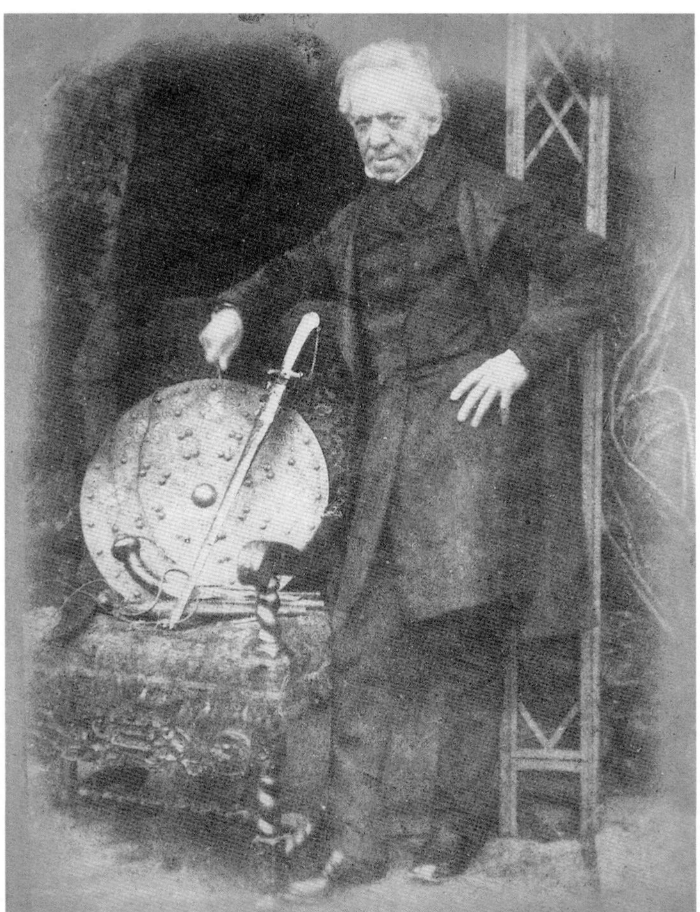

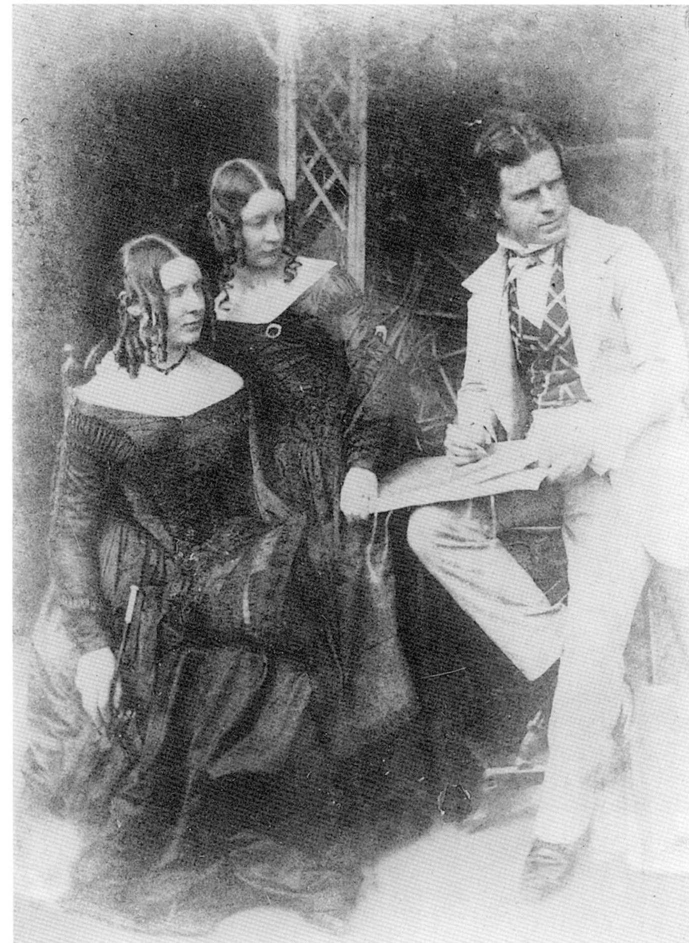

3. D. O. Hill and Robert Adamson, *D. O. Hill with the Misses Morris*, 1843–7. Calotype. Scottish National Photography Collection, Edinburgh.

In 1832, he published one of his most interesting sets of lithographs of the Glasgow and Garnkirk railway line (see chapter ten). This was originally a minor commission from the engineer John Miller, but Hill found the subject so fascinating that he decided to enlarge and publish the images. In 1834, he embarked on his most ambitious publishing venture – a series of sixty-one landscapes related to the life and

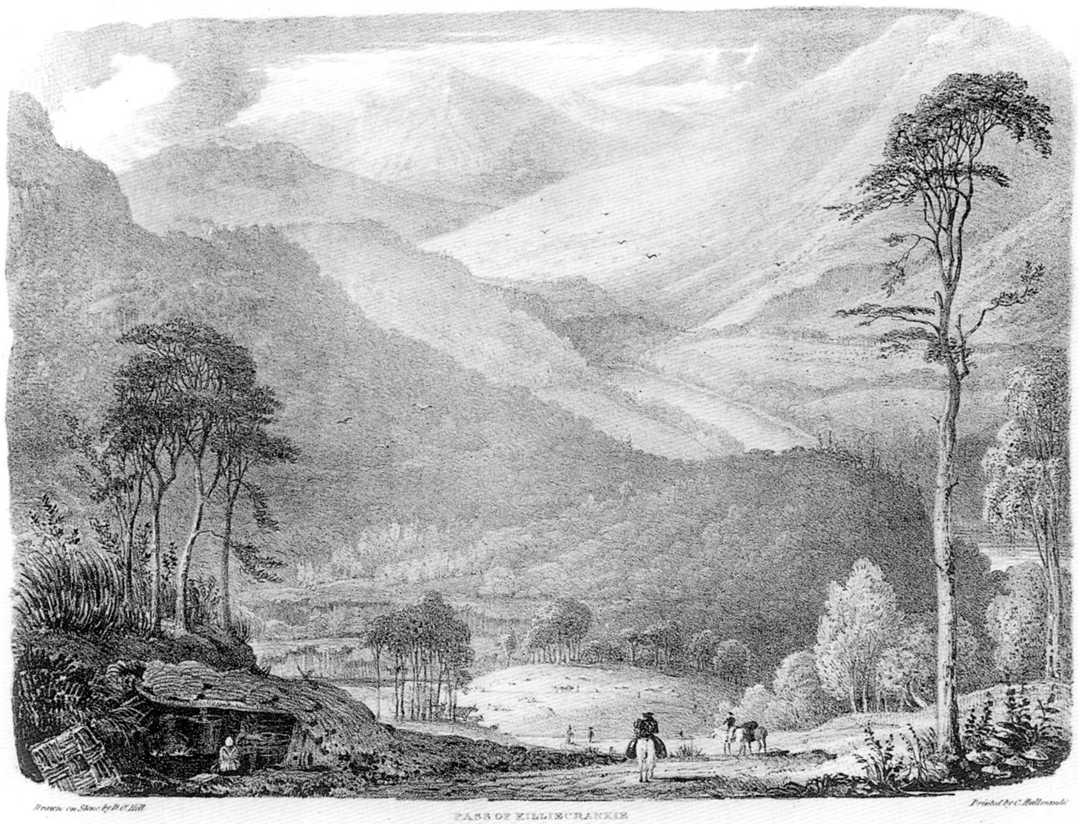

4. D. O. Hill,
The Pass of Killiecrankie, *c.* 1820.
Lithograph. Scottish National Photography Collection, Edinburgh.

writing of Robert Burns. *The Land of Burns* was completed and published by John Blackie in Glasgow in 1840, and was an impressive success. Hill apparently toured through a broad area of Scotland, principally in the west, painting the landscape in all varieties of weather and celebrating as particularly Scottish the shifting extravagance of weather patterns. It is a practical and unsurprising note that a friend wrote to him in 1836: 'Certes, you have not come scatheless from the land of Burns, and I deeply grieve that your accursed rheumatism should so have fettered your good right hand.'[8] This should stand as a comment on Hill as an early *plein-air* painter, not simply because of his ambition to 'paint on the spot', but because it resulted in the chronic condition which hindered and frustrated his manipulative talents.

In the 1820s, the Scottish artists were engaged in a struggle to free themselves from the two government-funded agencies that controlled art education and were responsible for exhibitions. The move for independence was led by a small group of the artists, who established the Scottish Academy. In 1829, the larger group, led by Sir William Allan and including D. O. Hill, considered setting up another independent institution. According to George Harvey, Hill was responsible for the break-up of the meeting in 1829, in which this second group, chaired by William Allan, was supposed to debate the forming of a separate institution. Allan opened the meeting to discussion:

> After a short pause, Mr J. F. Williams rose and addressed the chair in his rather stagey style. 'Mr Chairman', said he, 'in the nature of things there is in society a tendency to progress and where there is progress there must be extension; extension and progress go therefore hand in hand,' – and a little more to the same purpose, when a loud peal of merriment broke forth from the meeting, and Mr Williams sat down, adding, 'Well, the stuff is there, but you may put it in another form and words.' When the mirth had subsided, the secretary asked what he was to minute, on which Mr D. O. Hill, quoting Dogberry, replied, 'To be a well-favoured man is the gift of fortune, but to write and read comes by nature.' [Shakespeare, *Much Ado About Nothing*] At this there was another shout of laughter, when the chairman becoming angry began to scold Mr Hill; and as it was evident from the uproar that

nothing further in the shape of business would be done, they separated – and so ended the only meeting of the twenty-four.[9]

The passage underlines the attractive inexperience of all twenty-four men in the management of committees. In that year, they joined the academy.[10]

In 1830, the portrait painter William Nicholson resigned from the unpaid post of secretary of the academy. Hill accepted the appointment after Nicholson had made it clear that his own work for the academy 'was attended with a very serious sacrifice on my part; and I may mention, in confidence, that I cannot estimate my loss at less than £200 a year.'[11] Hill, therefore, consciously accepted a loss in income, which may have delayed his marriage, and a professional responsibility, which was at odds with his personal ambition. In George Harvey's words, Hill:

> commenced his long period of service to the Academy, so fruitful in much that conduced to its stability and well-

5. D. O. Hill, *On the Quay at Leith*, 1826. Oil on board. National Gallery of Scotland, Edinburgh.

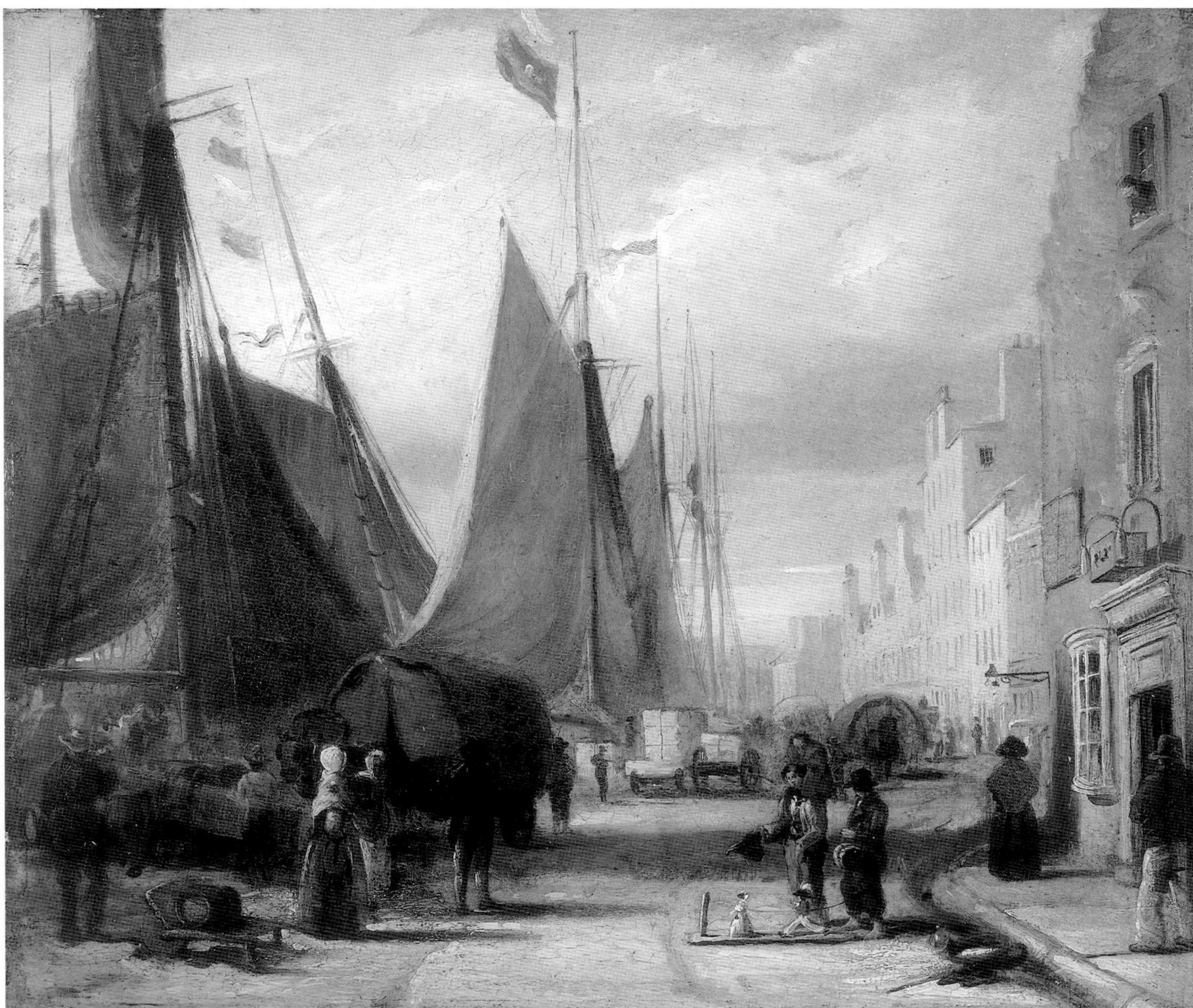

being. Of an impulsive and enthusiastic nature, and at this period but imperfectly acquainted with business, he occasionally required the qualifying regulation of cooler and more practical heads; nevertheless, whatever he did in capacity of Secretary was always done with a singleness of purpose in the direction of what appeared to him the best interests of the Academy.[12]

It is worth noting Harvey's opinion that Hill was not a natural administrator. The heroism involved in tying himself to such work against his natural, ebullient and possibly inefficient character deserves tribute. When he first undertook the secretaryship, he worked for five years unsalaried and was never paid enough to relieve his financial anxiety. In the end, he worked for nearly forty years for the academy, and, in the words of his obituary: 'His zeal amounted to enthusiasm for the cause of the Academy and of Scottish art, and was never wanting.'[13]

Our first indication of Hill's marriage comes in a letter from his friend, the ambitious publisher John Macrone, whose facetiously affectionate and literary manner may present a mirror to Hill's own style. The letter begins: 'My dilatoriness in answering your letter certainly does not give the seeming of extra joy at the receipt, but nevertheless, I do assure you that few events in this world of chequers have given me greater delight than the sight of your well known *illegible* hand.' It ends: 'And now, Bully-boy for thy-self. When is *it* to be? – Now, don't blush and look so confoundedly modest. – Don't pretend ignorance either; – *Corpo di Bacco!* That won't pass! – When is *it* to take place I say! – What, man, dost think I have forgotten the *Fair Maid of Perth*? – not I, by my halidome! – Once more, thou Knave, when is *it* to be?'[14] Hill married Ann Macdonald (1804–41), who was the daughter of a wine merchant in Perth and apparently a fine musician, in 1837.[15] They had two daughters, Charlotte, known as Chatty, was born in January 1839, and a second child died a few hours after her birth in 1840. Ann Hill herself died in 1841, leaving Hill a widower with his only daughter.

DR JOHN ADAMSON, ROBERT ADAMSON AND MISS MANN

The information we have about Robert Adamson, before he met David Octavius Hill, can be fairly simply outlined. He was born in 1821 and brought up in Fife at Burnside, the farm his father leased, on the coast outside the university town of St Andrews (fig. 6). A picture was drawn of his boyhood, at the end of the century:

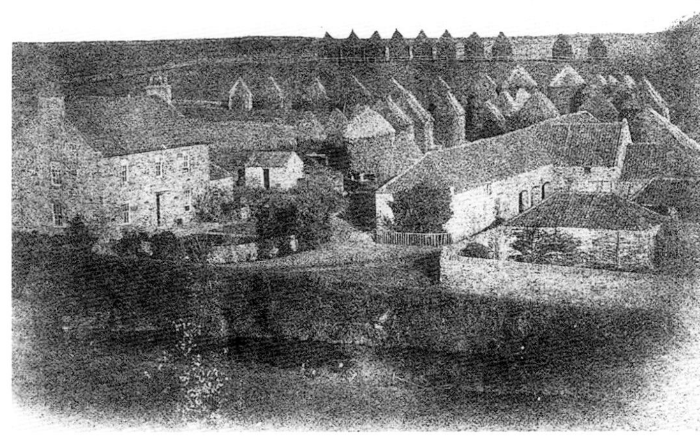

6. John or Robert Adamson, *The Farm at Burnside*, probably 1842. Print from a calotype negative. Glasgow University Library, Special Collections.

> As a boy he was delicate in health and retiring in disposition, with a strong turn for the natural sciences, and an especial aptitude for mechanics; devoting all his spare time to the construction of various models, steam-engines, wheelbarrows and small schooners which he sailed on the burn that ran beside his father's house, and sometimes even building larger rowing-boats, to the no small danger, as we are informed, of those who ventured their persons therein upon the deep. At one time it seemed probable that he would adopt mechanics as a profession; and, indeed, with this in view, he worked for a year or two in a mill-wright and engineer's shop in Cupar, but his frame was hardly muscular enough, his health scarcely sufficiently robust to bear the severe physical strain involved in such a calling.[16]

The possibility that Hill knew this story and relayed it is supported by his reference to the photograph, *Burnside* (pl. 3), after Adamson's death, as a picture that possessed 'to me more than ordinary interest', as 'the youthful haunt of my amiable friend'.[17]

Around the time of Robert Adamson's apprenticeship, St Andrews had become a focal point for the early experiments in photography because of the friendship between the physicist, and resident of the town, Sir David Brewster, and the inventor of the calotype process of photography, William

Henry Fox Talbot.[18] The calotype was the first negative/positive process of photography, based on Talbot's initial invention of the 'photogenic drawing', which he renamed in 1840 on discovering the virtues of gallic acid in greatly increasing the sensitivity of the process.

Talbot and Brewster corresponded on the subject and, in May 1841, Talbot sent a confidential account of the practical details north. For roughly a year, Brewster and his close circle in St Andrews wrestled unsuccessfully with the calotype – a failure they found all the more disconcerting because they had already succeeded in taking pictures by the rival French daguerreotype process. Brewster's principal associates in these experiments were the provost of St Andrews, Major Lyon Playfair, and Dr John Adamson. Dr Adamson (1809–70), the eldest brother of Robert, had been educated at St Andrews and Edinburgh, had qualified as a licentiate of the Royal College of Surgeons in Edinburgh in 1829, and had subsequently studied in the medical schools in Paris. He found employment as a ship's surgeon and travelled as far as the China seas, before returning to St Andrews. But in 1837, he discovered the town had too many doctors and took up the teaching of chemistry for the Madras College School. In 1843, he became closely associated with the lively Literary and Philosophical Society, founded by Sir David Brewster, as its museum curator.

Finally, in spring or early summer 1842, John Adamson succeeded in taking the first successful portrait calotype in Scotland. The careful and calculated experiments behind his success may be judged by the fact that in the subsequent months of the year, he established control over this fickle process, was able to teach his brother, and had sufficient confidence to propose that Robert Adamson set up in business as a photographer by August of 1842 (pl. 2). David Brewster reported to Talbot on 15 August that Robert had been 'well-drilled in the art by his brother'.[19] Brewster had persuaded Talbot, who patented the calotype in England, that it would be unprofitable to extend the patent in Scotland,[20] and wrote to remind him in October:

> You will recollect of promising me your countenance and support to any person whom I could induce to practise the Calotype as a profession in Scotland. When the specimens reach you, you will be able to judge of Mr Adamson's work, and to do what you can to support him. I mean to give him a strong recommendation and I trust you will do the same.[21]

The small album of photographs, sent by John Adamson to Talbot, in November 1842, as evidence of their skill, is principally a technical demonstration, showing a command of portraiture, sculpture and landscape photography. Presumably Talbot offered Robert Adamson formal endorsement or encouragement, and it was at this point that the Adamsons bought the larger camera or cameras, with which he later set up his studio.[22] Photography, which was dependent on good daylight, was a seasonal business. But John and Robert may have been able to practise in the winter months of 1842–3, because St Andrews stands on a peninsula and, on good days, would have been filled with light both from the sky and reflected off the water. This proposal is supported by two calotypes of the town under snow (fig. 7). Although some of the small calotypes are signed in the negative either by John or Robert, they did not sign any of the larger calotypes of St Andrews, so it is not clear from any documentary record which they took between November and the following April, and which may have subsequently involved D. O. Hill. However, John Adamson wrote a list of sites in and around St Andrews with appropriate times of day, at the end of his scrapbook, which may well have been intended as test or control subjects for the new cameras, and which may serve as a clue to this question.[23]

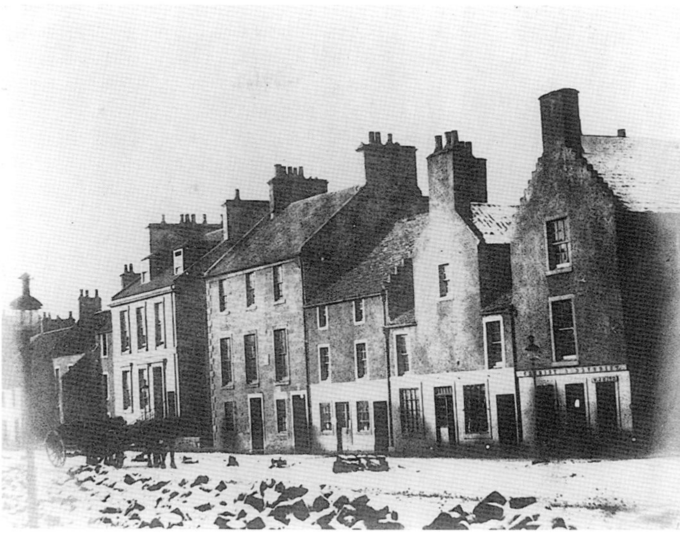

7. John or Robert Adamson, *South Street, St Andrews*, probably taken in the winter of 1842/3. Calotype. Scottish National Photography Collection, Edinburgh.

In May 1843, Brewster reported: 'Mr Adamson…goes tomorrow to Edin to prosecute, as a Profession, the Calotype. He has made brilliant progress, and done some of the very finest things both in Portrait and Landscape.'[24] For a studio, Robert Adamson succeeded in hiring Rock House, the highest private building on Calton Hill in Edinburgh, nearly a

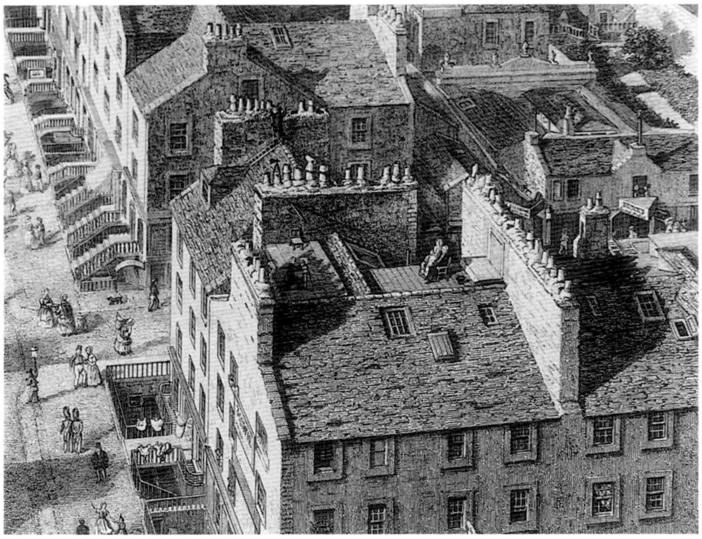

8. James Ebsworth, Detail from a view of Edinburgh from the top of the Scott Monument, showing James Howie taking portraits on the roof of his studio, 1846. Engraving. Edinburgh City Art Centre.

thousand feet above sea level. The activities of the studio mainly took place in the small walled garden at the south front of the house, and this was a clear advantage in printing the calotypes out, which might need as much as two hours bright sunshine. It also gave a natural advantage of both comfort and pleasure over most city portrait studios of the 1840s, which were generally to be found at the top of tall buildings. The contrast between the common practice of the day and Hill and Adamson's work might almost be summed up by this advantage. One of the earliest daguerreotypists in Edinburgh was James Howie (fig. 8), whose own practice was clearly hostile to relaxed portraiture:

> Mr Howie's arrangements were at first of the simplest kind. His sitters had to climb three flights of stairs, and then by a kind of ladder reached a skylight, through which they got access to the roof of the house. The posing chair, with something in the shape of a head-rest fixed to its back, was placed against the gable of the adjoining building [under listing and smoking chimneys], and the operator used to take the sitter and press him down with the observation – 'There! Now sit still as death!' Of course, under such circumstances, with the sun shining brilliantly and the exposure counted by minutes, artistic portraiture was not be expected.[25]

It may have been a few weeks before Adamson met Hill, but in that time, he apparently only took a handful of calotypes on and around the Calton Hill. There is one of the Royal High School, just below Rock House, dated 17 May (fig. 9), which seems likely to be his work alone. The sky of the negative has been painted out to give a smooth blank, rather than the arbitrary mottling generated by the paper of the calotype. This was John Adamson's habit, but the mottling was an effect that Hill approved of (see chapter three).[26] There are two group photographs of Robert and his brother, Alexander, taken at Rock House, which might be an experiment in portraiture for the new studio. However, no advertisement has yet been found to suggest that Robert Adamson had commenced commercial operations. The first public mention of his studio is made in an article published on 24 June, referring to: 'the calotype, – an art introduced into Edinburgh, during the last fortnight, for the first time, by Mr Adamson of St Andrews.'[27]

The problem presented by this minimal account of Robert Adamson's career before he met Hill is that even practical facts about him are missing from the contemporary record. We may, for example, speculate that he was apprenticed to John Annan, a millwright and flax-spinner at Dairsie in Fife, but the census returns for 1841 sank in the ferry on their way across the Forth and no apprenticeship record has been found.[28] Robert Adamson died before it became common to publish obituaries, and he was a young man who had made little public impact, so there is no account of his life or public tribute to him in either newspapers or journals in 1848. His family seems to have been particularly reticent in their grief; he and other members of his family were only added to the

9. Robert Adamson, *The Royal High School*, 17 May 1843. Calotype. Scottish National Photography Collection, Edinburgh.

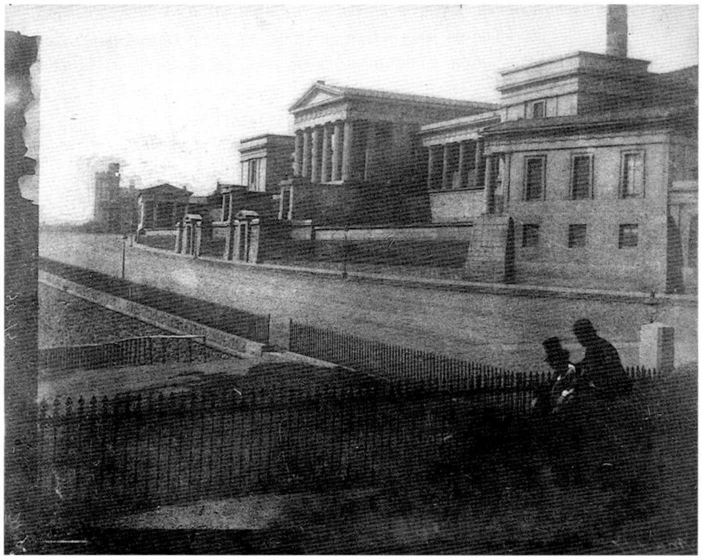

family tombstone in the churchyard of St Andrews Cathedral, *en bloc* in 1900.

The calotype prints are the substantial expression of Robert Adamson's professional work, the product of his entire adult life, cut short by his death in January 1848. This was acknowledged by D. O. Hill in the album he gave to Lord Cockburn in 1850, where he annotated the group of the Adamson family:

> Dr John Adamson of St Andrews was one of the earliest and most skilful improvers of the processes of the Calotype. His brother Robert, during the last five years of his life, devoted himself, with my aid as an artist, in developing the powers of the art. The pictures in this volume are chiefly manipulated by him and are his best monument.[29]

When Hill wrote this, he may indeed have been thinking that the calotypes were effectively Robert Adamson's only monument.

We are, moreover, almost entirely dependent, when looking at the work of the calotype partnership, on the writing of Hill and his friends. No letters by Robert Adamson are known and there are only of two or three by John. It is, therefore, difficult to offer a straightforward view of Robert Adamson as an independent actor.

There is a further complication. In the course of the partnership, the engineer James Nasmyth, wrote to Hill:

> How goes on the divine solar art? and how does that worthy artist Mr Adamson the authentic contriver & manipulator in the art of light and darkness? and thrice worthy Miss Mann that most skillfull and zealous of assistants . . . I have the remembrance of All on Em so clearly calotyped in my minds Eye as last I saw them in full manipulation of the divine art of light.[30]

Miss Mann is a wild card in the discussion of the partnership. Her role as Hill and Adamson's assistant has never been assessed. A very simple argument pointing to the periodic ill health of both partners and the professional preoccupation of Hill with academy affairs could be made to propose the almost invisible woman as a primary actor. The only positive mention we have of her is in James Nasmyth's letters. We know of one occasion, when neither Adamson nor Hill were there, and the King of Saxony and his entourage turned up at Rock House without warning. Two photographs were taken by 'an assistant'.[31] The results were not particularly good (fig. 10). Assuming that the assistant on this occasion was Miss Mann, they might be a measure of her general competence as an independent photographer, but this was a thoroughly disconcerting occasion and therefore not an effective test. Miss Mann apparently also worked for the astronomer Charles Piazzi Smyth, in the observatory on Calton Hill above Rock House.[32] The annotations on the negatives, presumably in Robert Adamson's hand, would appear to be printing instructions and may have been addressed to her; it may be assumed that she was involved largely in the printing of the calotypes. However, the phrase Hill employs in the tribute to Adamson quoted above, 'The pictures in this volume are chiefly manipulated by him', may imply that she was responsible for some part of the critically active manipulation.

The question of Miss Mann's contribution is an interesting problem; we have no further evidence at present, and the case cannot be intelligently argued. Future research may well discover critical information in relation to both Robert Adamson and Miss Mann. However, it is assumed, in the argument of this book, that Hill's prominence was not simply casting a shadow over these two people he worked with in photography, but that his capabilities and ideas both illuminated and led the work.[33] The argument is also based on a concept of growth in partnership – an idea that creativity may expand rather than contract when minds and capabilities are brought together. Without being in a position to propose more for Adamson and Miss Mann than the evidence implies, it will be here taken as read that their skills were similarly inspiring to Hill.

DISRUPTION AND PARTNERSHIP

Robert Adamson arrived in Edinburgh on 10 May 1843, at a time of severe crisis and excitement in the city. A mere eight days later, the formal proceedings of the General Assembly of the Church of Scotland were abruptly stopped by the Moderator, the Reverend Dr David Welsh (fig. 11), who rose, uttered a protest against the Church's proceedings, and left. He was followed then and in the next days, by more than four hundred ministers, who proceeded to set up a new Free Church, independent of the state. The Disruption was the culmination of a long, formal dispute which the Church leaders had pursued through the law courts as far as the House of Lords; it was a protest against the encroachment of the state on the Presbyterian church and particularly against the legal right of landed proprietors to appoint ministers contrary to the will of the church elders. It was a carefully planned event, involving the principal evangelical leaders of the Church, charismatic and influential figures such as the

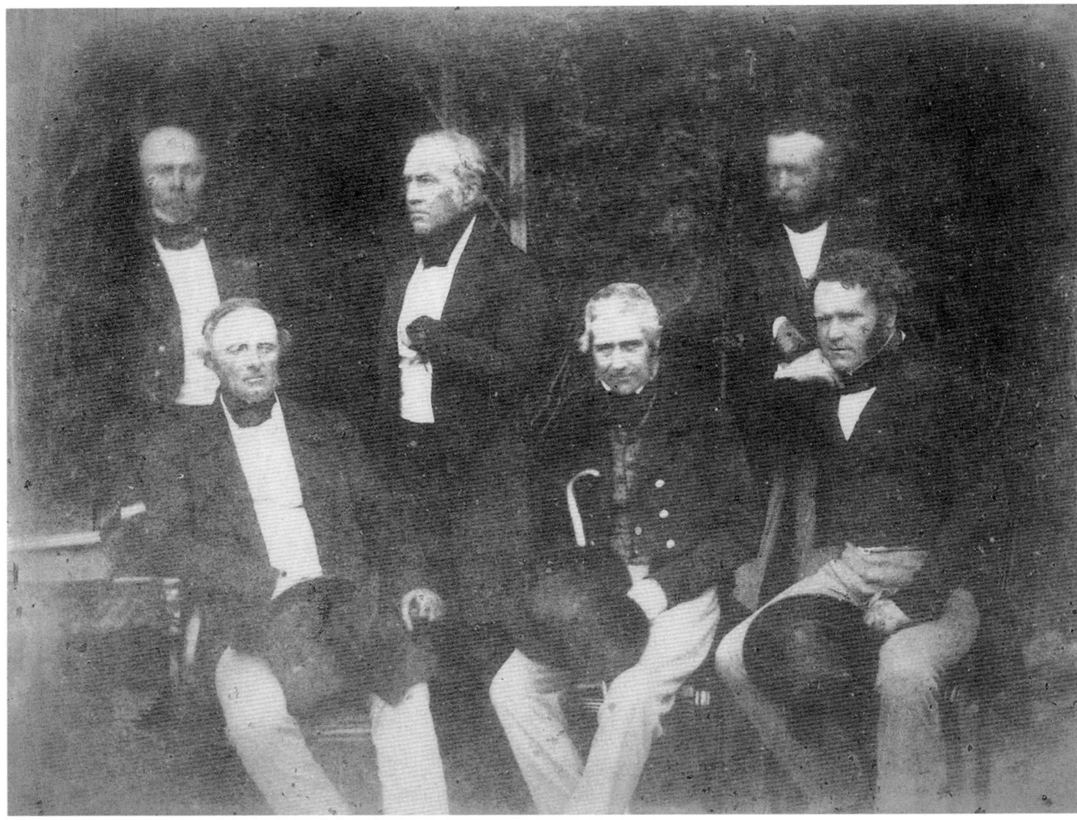

10. Miss Mann (?), *The King of Saxony and his Entourage*, 2 August 1844. Calotype. Scottish National Photography Collection, Edinburgh.

Reverend Dr Thomas Chalmers. But it was also extremely emotional: the ministers abandoned their livings and their manses; they were effectively heading into destitution on principle alone.

The founding of the Free Church was filled with extraordinary excitement, fuelled by principle and generosity. At the time, even observers who were not wholeheartedly behind the movement were deeply affected. Dr John Brown, while expressing a doubt of the principle behind the gesture, still felt 'the wonderfulness, the solemnity, and in a certain just sense, the heroism of the time and act'.[34] It was a source of national excitement and pride. The occasion caused the judge, Lord Jeffrey, to exclaim: '"I am proud of my countrymen!" and Lord Cockburn with like emotion enunciate, when, on the day following, the Painter communicated his intention to paint the event, "There has not been such a subject since the days of Knox – and not then!"'[35] 'The painter' was D. O. Hill, who was one of the many who witnessed the event. His own brother-in-law, the Reverend Robert Macdonald, minister of North Leith, was one of the seceders. Hill was so deeply moved that he decided to paint a grand historical painting to commemorate the act, and gained permission to sketch the meetings of the new church. Six days after the Disruption, he advertised engravings from the painting, which he estimated would take him from two to three years.

One of the leading and influential lay figures in the Free Church was Sir David Brewster, who was present at its first sessions. Brewster observed Hill sketching and saw an opportunity to promote the interests of calotype photography and his protégé, Robert Adamson. He wrote to Talbot to explain, on 3 July:

> A grand historical picture is undertaken by a first rate Artist, to represent the *first General Assembly of the Free Church*. I got hold of the Artist, shewed him the Calotype, & the immense advantage he might derive from it in getting likenesses of all the principal characters before they dispersed to their respective homes. He was at first incredulous, but went to Mr Adamson, and arranged with him the preliminaries for getting all the necessary Portraits. They have succeeded beyond their most sanguine expectations.[36]

By the time Brewster wrote to Talbot, Hill and Adamson's experiments had proved so effective that they were able to hold their first exhibition, both of the painted and drawn sketches for the painting and of the calotypes taken for the painting, in Alexander Hill's gallery, in the week beginning 12 July. Significantly, by this time they were also planning an independent series of calotype portraits of the clergymen and laymen of the Free Church.[37] Brewster's letter to Talbot continued:

> Mr D. O. Hill, the Painter, is on the eve of entering into partnership with Mr Adamson and proposes to apply the Calotype to many other general purposes of a very popular kind, & especially to the execution of large pictures representing difft. bodies & classes of individuals.
>
> I think you will find that we have, in Scotland, found out the value of your invention not before yourself, but before those to whom you have given the privilege of using it.[38]

11. D. O. Hill and Robert Adamson, *The Reverend Dr David Welsh*, 1843. Calotype. Scottish National Photography Collection, Edinburgh.

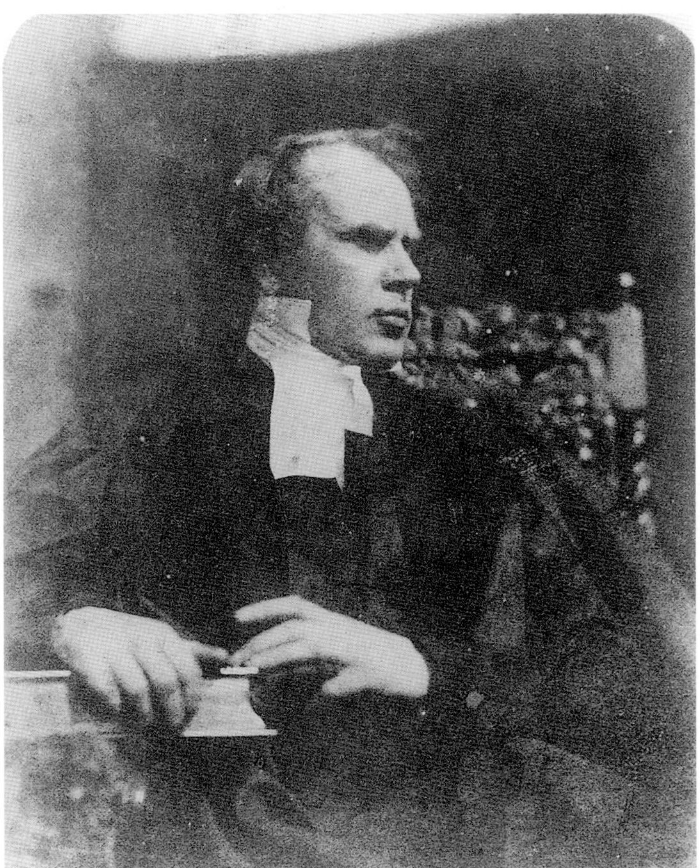

The first critical review of the calotype was published by Hugh Miller, the editor of the Free Church newspaper, the *Witness*, in the same month.

In the first year of the partnership, Hill and Adamson are known to have attended the second assembly of the Free Church, which was held in Glasgow in September, to take further portrait studies for the painting. They took the first of their calotypes in the fishing village of Newhaven. They also worked with at least three other painters: Sir William Allan, Sir George Harvey and John Harden. For Harvey, they took calotypes in the grounds of Greyfriars' church as sketches for a large-scale moral painting, *Children Blowing Bubbles in Greyfriars' Churchyard.* They exhibited their work in the Board of Manufactures exhibition and were awarded a prize of ten pounds, 'for combining in the happiest possible manner artistical freedom of excellence with scientific precision of execution.'[39]

At the beginning of the following year, Hill exhibited seven of the calotypes, including portraits of William Allan and David Brewster, at the Scottish Academy – the first photographs to be shown there. Adamson retreated to St Andrews for the winter months, but in the following May, the partnership was resumed with a new energy. According to Hill's will, he insured his life at this time, perhaps to provide the financial backing for a new contract. Hill moved in to Rock House, and they advertised the publication of a series of six albums of calotypes, 'in a style of great elegance on a paper the size and quality of "[David] Roberts' Views in the Holy Land"'. These were to be *The Fishermen and Women of the Firth of Forth, Highland Character and Costume, The Architectural Structures of Edinburgh, The Architectural Structures of Glasgow, Old Castles, Abbeys &c in Scotland* and *Portraits of Distinguished Scotchmen.*[40] In a letter to David Roberts the following year, Hill substituted *Greyfriars Monuments* for the Glasgow volume.[41] It may be at this point that they acquired a new large camera from Thomas Davidson, the Edinburgh optician who supplied the St Andrews circle with its equipment, and possibly at least one new lens. They took the large camera with them to the town of Linlithgow, west of Edinburgh, on the new railway line. They also carried it out to Merchiston Castle School, to the south of Edinburgh, where they photographed the family of the Reverend Thomas Chalmers (pl. 4), whose brother was the headmaster, and made studies of groups of the schoolboys.

In September, Alexander Christie, one of the directors of the Trustees Academy in Edinburgh, took a collection of the calotypes over to Paris. They were presented by the scientist Dominique-François Arago at a session of the Académie des

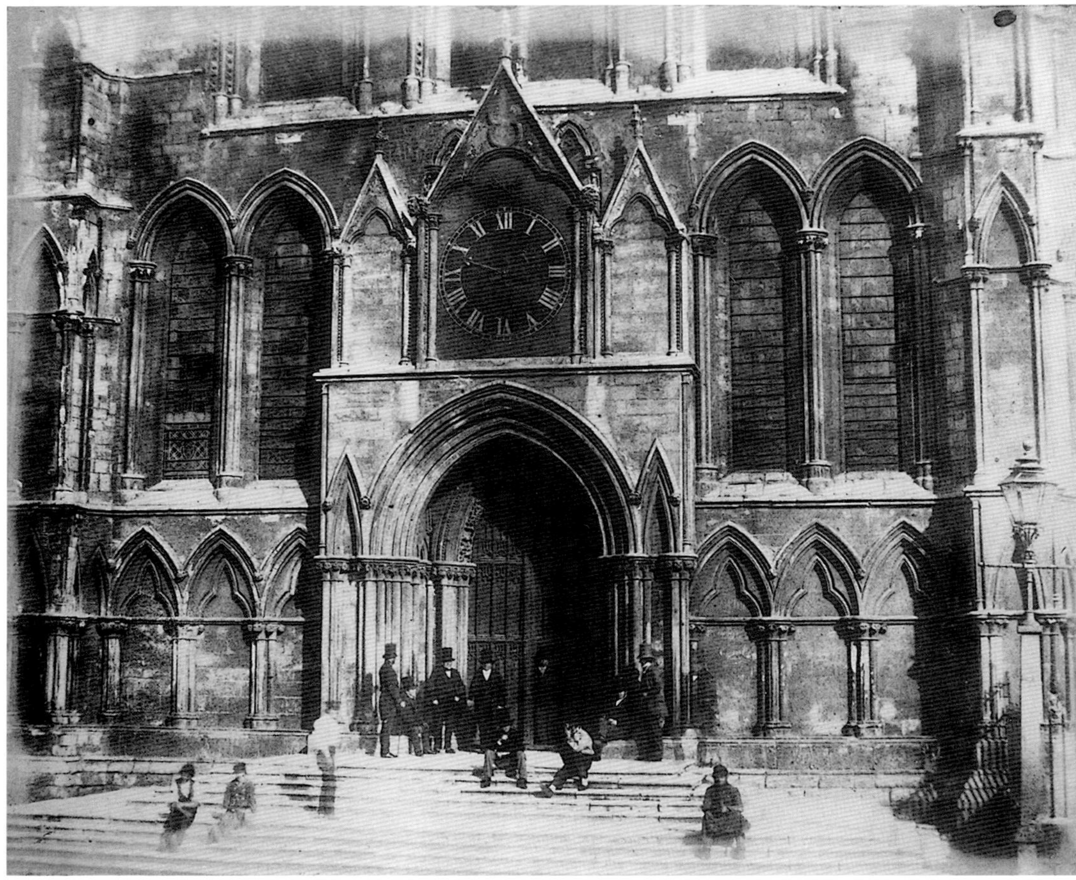

12. D. O. Hill and Robert Adamson, *York Minster*, 1844. Calotype. National Museum of Scotland.

Sciences, apparently at the instigation of the painter, Ary Scheffer. The report, comparing the calotypes, 'une nombreuse collection', with French daguerreotypes, 'très belles', was equivocal, but noted that: 'M. Ary Scheffer les qualifiat de merveilleuses.' David Brewster may have been obliquely involved in this presentation, which properly referred to Talbot as the inventor of the process and credited Brewster in connection with the camera, 'une chambre noire exécutée, sous la direction immédiate de sir David Brewster'.[42]

At the end of September, and more certainly prompted by Brewster's suggestion, Hill and Adamson attended the meeting of the British Association for the Advancement of Science in York. Since they were, on this occasion trespassing over the border into England and therefore entering the territory of the English patent, Hill obtained, a little belatedly, Talbot's permission to take calotypes of the distinguished participants. They also carried with them the big camera and took large-scale calotypes of Durham Cathedral and York Minster (fig 12). The portrait calotypes taken at York included a particularly important one of a notable patron of the arts, the Marquis of Northampton (pl. 5).

In the month of October, they also captured two distinguished visitors to Edinburgh. The first was the English painter William Etty, who had brought his brother up to see the three major works purchased from him by the Scottish Academy. Despite having no change of clothes with him and looking a little travel-worn, he was inveigled by the academy into attending a celebratory dinner in his honour, and Hill took the opportunity to carry him off to Rock House. The portrait of Etty (pl. 6) was one of ten exhibited at the academy during the following winter. The second, more exotic sitter was Mohun Lal, who had travelled from Afghanistan to bring back the papers of Sir Alexander Burnes, killed in the fighting at Kabul, and was given an official tour of the city, 'dressed in a magnificent Hindoo costume' (fig. 13).[43]

At the beginning of 1845, Hill sent a portfolio of the calotypes down to the London printseller and publisher, Dominic Colnaghi and wrote to his London ally, the landscape painter David Roberts, that he should choose any he would like for his own collection. Roberts apparently discovered that Colnaghi had concealed the calotypes from public view, 'by throwing them under the counter instead of on it'.[44] Roberts retrieved the portfolio and proposed to show it at meetings in the house of Lord Northampton and at the influential Graphic Society. Hill's pleased reply unexpectedly ends by expressing doubt about his involvement with photography. He wrote: 'A little more of the Calotype in the Spring months & in all probability I will then leave it to be worked out by less occupied hands.'[45] However, Roberts's report of the response of Northampton and his guests, turned Hill around and injected a new excitement into the partnership. In March, Hill wrote two letters to Roberts. The first reached unprecedented depths of illegibility, because, as Hill explained in the second letter, 'Adamson had subjected it to the process of being copied by putting it through a press – which made such a mess of the original, that my always illegible hand was nearly if not wholly obliterated. I fear in truth it would defy your intelligence to make out.'[46] The letter is, however, readable, and makes a number of important points. Hill expressed his high opinion of the Adamsons' skill and his belief that they had improved the calotype process. He added: 'I believe also from all I have seen that Robert Adamson is the most successful manipulator the art has yet seen, and his steady industry and knowledge of chemistry is such that both from him and his brother much new improvements may yet be expected.'[47] Hill then declared an interest in undertaking an album of English portraits and said that he had asked Talbot's permission to come south to do this:

13. D. O. Hill and Robert Adamson, *Mohun Lal*, October 1845. Print from a calotype negative. Scottish National Photography Collection, Edinburgh.

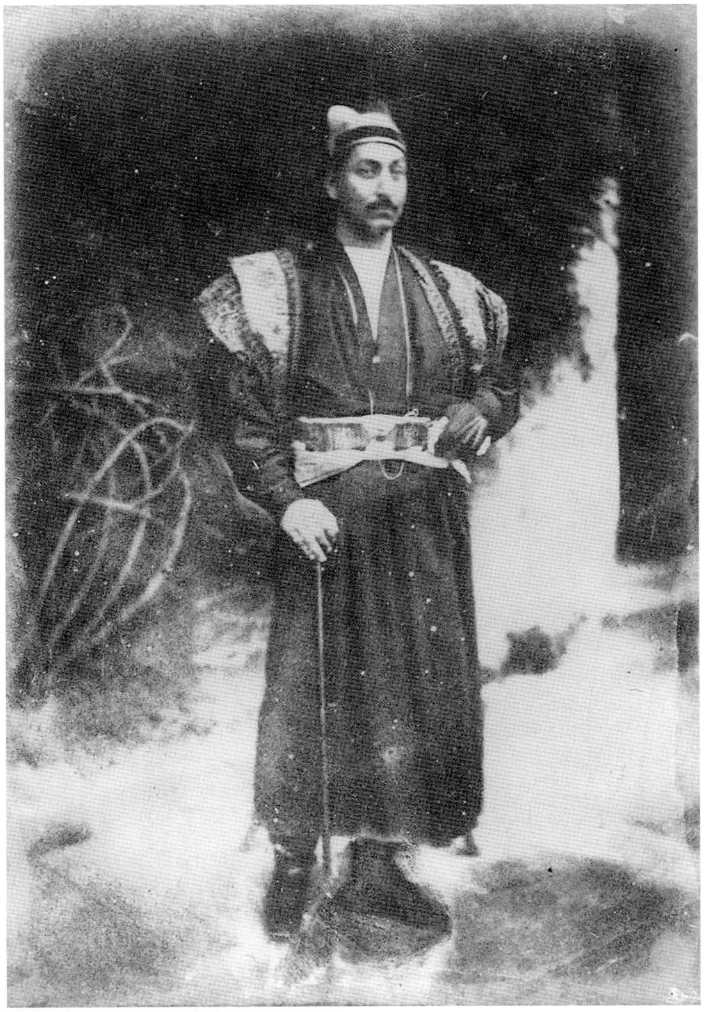

> I am somewhat ambitious in the sort of book I would like to give myself to in bringing out…I say that this first book of English Calotype *pictures*, for really Talbot's examples in his Pencil of Nature are not intended to be such, should be such as to make the French look only second best in their Sun Painting efforts. It should almost be a book worthy of the tables [?] of sovereigns and of the highest cognoscenti. Now there is my naked bosom in the matter, which I hope will not make you rate me as absolute and arragant as Petruccio, making you exclaim, 'Why! This gallant will command the sun.'

Roberts had obviously expressed some anxiety about competition:

> You ask, 'Can it be kept secret?' I can only say that Adamson says the manipulation is very liable to go wrong in the hands of most people – that though several have now and then produced a good specimen – they find it difficult to succeed often – and the arrangement of the picture is as much an effort of the artist as if he was in reality going to paint it . . . I [illegible] therefore that in the common acceptation of the word it cannot be called secret – tho' Adamson thinks he knows some things others do not.
>
> My connection with the art has been purely that of an artist. I know not the process though it is done under my nose continually and I believe I never will. Until I took it up the best things I saw were, though chemically fine, artistically nothing.

Regrettably these plans came to nothing, probably because of the English patent (see chapter two). However, Hill spent some energy in 1845 in promoting the calotypes through his friends and allies. One of Hill's correspondents in London was Charles Heath Wilson, the director of the Schools of Art at Somerset House, who wrote to him in April:

> If I had had the calotypes I could have done a great deal. I have lately had important opportunities under very favourable circumstances. I have one friend especially who will prove an enormous puffer. I can send them to Mr [Samuel] Rogers the Poet & to other people. ½ doz. will answer the purpose perfectly. Mrs Jamieson [Anna Jameson] is going to take them up strong, but you should guide us what to say in case we get upon wrong ground in respect of the English patent.[48]

The partnership must have seemed on the verge of a breakthrough into the English art world. The most enthusiastic of the published reviews was written by Elizabeth Rigby, later Lady Eastlake, who was very closely involved in the calotype work both as a critic and model (pl. 7). Her review, printed in full in chapter three, was published by John Murray in the *Quarterly Review* in 1846 and quoted in an article by Dr John Brown written for the *Witness*. The calotypes were shown that year at the academy, as 'specimens of a volume of Calotypes now preparing for publication'.[49]

The calotype work started early in 1846, a year in which the winter was unexpectedly mild (strawberries ripened in the open ground near Edinburgh in early February), and the partnership was able to take calotypes of the marine painter John Christian Schetky and his daughter on 6 January.

By 1846, the year in which he had expected to complete the painting, Hill's idea of the Disruption picture had been radically altered by the calotypes. During the Free Church assembly in May, he was still advertising for the churchmen to come and sit for their portraits. Hugh Miller commented on this in the *Witness*: 'We understand that a longer period must elapse before its completion, a circumstance which the doubling of the scale of the picture, and the insertion of twice or three times the number of portraits than were at first contemplated, are sufficient to apologise for.'[50] The partnership was involved in another Free Church event in 1846. The Church had bought John Knox's house in the High Street, threatened apparently by new and unsuitable ownership, and were building a monument to him alongside. Hill and Adamson, presumably thinking to offer a photographic record to posterity, deposited seven calotype views of the old building within the foundation stone. Hill, who had exhibited some anxiety that he was 'playing truant' from his landscape painting, was also painting a view of Edinburgh from the castle (see chapter ten). He and Adamson attempted a panoramic series of calotypes of the city (fig. 98), possibly as an independent series, which were used, with other calotypes of people, as studies for his painting.

From the sudden falling off of dated negatives, it may be that the main output of the partnership was completed by June 1846. Hill's view of Edinburgh from the castle was purchased by the engineer John Miller, who commissioned him to paint his railway viaduct at Ballochmyle the following year (fig. 103). There are a substantial number of calotypes taken at Ballochmyle, which from the state of completion of the viaduct may have been taken fairly late in 1847. They are not technically successful calotypes, perhaps because they were prepared beforehand and not on the spot, and may have been taken without Adamson's direction, perhaps by Miss Mann.[51]

Another session, which may be dated to 1847, and might also be Miss Mann's work, produced a group of portrait calotypes, including Lord and Lady Ruthven (pl. 8). Hill sent them with a characteristically deprecating note:

> Lady Haddo's and Miss Baillie's are not what in better circumstances we could hope – and so I may say of your own and Lord Ruthven's portraits – yet yours especially indicates what could be done in this direction with good sitters, good backgrounds and good sunshine: indeed with these appliances a wonderful little family gallery might be made in a few days and to such uses I doubt not that the Calotype will come . . . I am preparing a calotype volume of 100 calotypes which I hope soon to show your ladyship. With its publication, the art and I will probably part company.[52]

In the event, Hill parted company from the art more painfully than he must have hoped. In the autumn of 1847, Adamson fell desperately ill and retreated to St Andrews. There on the 14 January 1848, he died. After Adamson's funeral, D. O. Hill wrote sadly:

> I have today assisted in consigning to the cold earth all that was earthly of my amiable true & affectionate Robert Adamson. He died in the full hope of a blessed resurrection. His truehearted family are mourning sadly especially his brother the Doctor – who has watched [?] him as a child during his long illness. I have seldom seen such a deep & manly sorrow.
>
> Poor Adamson has not left his like in his art of which he was so modest.[53]

Practically speaking, Adamson's death left Hill in a difficult position. A letter from Hill to the editor of the *Art Journal* explains that he hoped to sort out the partnership's obligations with John Adamson in August 1848, and he had returned from painting in the country a hundred miles away to do so.[54] But John, perhaps still distressed by his brother's death, failed to arrive. Hill declared that he was still not sure whether he would become the 'sole proprietor' of the calotypes or give up his interest in them altogether, and he could not deal generously and allow the journal to use the calotypes freely.

Hill's undoubted enthusiasm for the calotypes must have been severely tempered at this point by the knowledge that he had largely shelved his chosen career as a landscape painter, and notably fallen behind his contemporaries as a result, and that his major work, the Disruption picture, was still a long way from completion. The plans for publishing the calotypes had not proved effective, although he had constructed a set of one hundred calotypes for a handsome publication, and was still optimistic that this might find a market. However, he may well have bought out the Adamsons' interest, and it is possible that John Adamson only took back to St Andrews the cameras which Robert brought with him in 1843.

A FAMILY PARTNERSHIP

It is difficult to find an exact parallel to the partnership of Hill and Adamson within the arts. Neither the partnership of Gilbert and Sullivan nor that of Gilbert and George seem wholly effective as a comparison – in one the roles are too clearly defined and in the other too nearly linked. A better comparison exists within the contemporary business world, where it was customary for the older, more knowledgeable or experienced partner to take the lead and adopt a relationship – paternal or fraternal, extending the idea of apprenticeship – towards the younger. Such alliances presumably worked on the generous principle that a responsive working relationship would allow for growth – Adamson was half Hill's age and Hill was a successful teacher. In industry, at this time: 'Partnerships were usually family or extended family concerns having close links through birth, marriage, community or religious affiliation. Mutual trust between partners and knowledge of each other's business affairs and assets was important in the face of unlimited liability.'[55] Their assistant, Miss Mann, came from Perth and may herself have been connected by friendship or blood to the Hill family. This was a more protective and amicable relationship than the idea of business partnership suggests nowadays, but it was an idea operative at the core of the Industrial Revolution: 'Industry in Britain was essentially "family capitalism" in which the aim was to maximise the welfare of the family rather than industrial growth and profitablity.'[56] It may indeed be that Hill was partly caught by this sense of familiar obligation into staying with the partnership longer than he meant. Adamson's ill health may have added to and maintained his concern for the younger man.

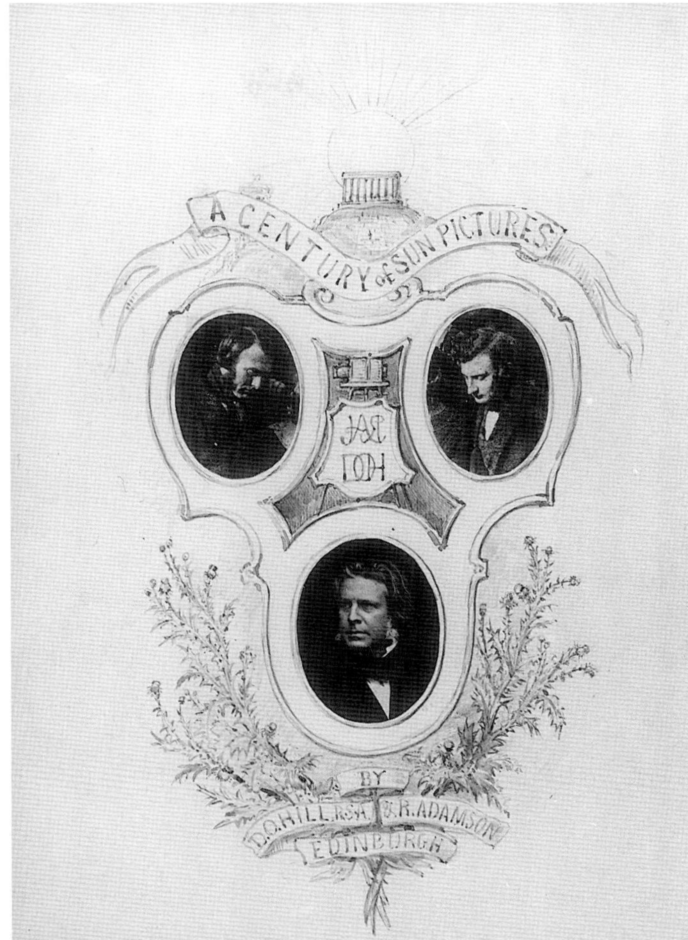

14. D. O. Hill, Album title page, *c.* 1855. Wash drawing and photographs. Museum Ludwig, Agfa Photo-Historama, Cologne.

There is an indication of Hill's continued sense of connection to the Adamsons in a calotype album, which he put together some time in or after the mid-1850s (fig. 14).[57] For this, Hill painted a title page crowned with the sun, shining through the National Monument on Calton Hill. Below are three ovals, with portraits of John and Robert Adamson at the top and Hill below; from the photographs chosen, the two Adamsons appear to look down to Hill. The Adamsons' initials are joined in one monogram, with Hill's underneath, on the same shield. Behind the shield is a camera. The title reads: 'A Century of Sun Pictures/ By D. O. Hill, R. S. A. & R. Adamson/ Edinburgh'. The calotypes in the album are all by Hill and Robert Adamson (with the exception of the portrait of Hill used on the title page, which dates to the 1850s), but Hill is here acknowledging John's role in the development of the calotype. He may also be indicating a personal friendship with John Adamson, who later took photographs of Hill, his daughter and second wife, Amelia Paton, in the 1850s and 1860s (fig. 42).[58]

The idea of relation and connection was clearly a dominant thread in Hill's life and work. His ambition was tempered and directed by this broader moral and social urge. The success of the calotype partnership depended on the warmth of a sociable creativity, which connects both to an amiable view of the workings of society and to theories of association in art, which will be explored in later chapters.

2

The Disconnected Triangle

Brewster, Talbot and Hill and Adamson

SIR DAVID BREWSTER AND THE LAUNCH OF THE CALOTYPE IN SCOTLAND

One of the notable curiosities of early photography is the lack of a convincing or articulated connection between four of the principals: William Henry Fox Talbot, Sir David Brewster and the Hill/Adamson partnership.

Sir David Brewster, the distinguished physicist and principal of the United College of St Leonard and St Salvator at St Andrews University, was the man responsible for bringing the calotype process to Scotland (fig. 15).[1] Brewster had first visited William Henry Fox Talbot, the inventor of the process, at his home, Lacock Abbey in Wiltshire, in 1836, and reported to his wife that the place was 'a paradise'. Talbot's wife, Constance, wrote of the stimulating effect of Brewster's society on this occasion: 'You are perfectly right in supposing Sir David Brewster to pass his time pleasantly here. He wants nothing beyond the pleasure of conversing with Henry, discussing their respective discoveries & various subjects connected with science. I am quite amazed that scarcely a momentary pause occurs in their discourse. Henry seems to possess new life.'[2] Brewster was generally remarkable in his ability to excite interest and enthusiasm in others. His daughter quoted a friend, 'himself the possessor of genial gifts and genius', as saying, 'When I have been with other great men, I go away saying, "What clever fellows they are"; but when I am with Sir David Brewster, I say, "What a clever fellow I am".'[3] She explained his engaging intensity:

> In the walk, at the meal, in society, in solitude, there was a constant observing and experimenting upon some common daily occurrence – the colours and forms of plants, the eye balls of fish and other creatures, the habits of goldfish, the gambols of mice, abounding in his old house, the scratching of snail shells on the window, the jewels and tinted ribbons of his lady visitors, the patterns of wallpapers and carpets, the shadows of carriage blinds.[4]

It was due to Brewster and his relationship with Talbot that the calotype process was pursued through extraordinary difficulties, until Brewster's colleague, Dr John Adamson, finally succeeded with the process in 1842. Brewster's persistence, seen in his correspondence with Talbot, illustrates both the chemical difficulty of the calotype and his own energy. It was, moreover, Brewster who persuaded Talbot not to patent the calotype process in Scotland and to allow Robert Adamson to set up in professional business as a calotype photographer. Robert Adamson moved to Edinburgh in May 1843 and in July, Brewster wrote to Talbot explaining that he had introduced D. O. Hill to Robert Adamson: 'Mr Adamson, who is now established in Edinr. with crowds every day at his studio, will be very grateful for your kindness. He will send you specimens of his progress which I think will surprise and delight you.'

The commentary on the Adamsons' progress, quoted in the previous chapter, comes almost entirely from David Brewster. His own archive of correspondence was destroyed in a fire, so we do not have Talbot's letters in response. Brewster's letter gives us a picture of Hill as reluctant to use photography or more simply ignorant of its possibilities. However, it is most unlikely that Hill did not know about photography. There was in Edinburgh, as in St Andrews, a considerable amount of photographic activity from 1839 onwards.[5] Talbot's own photogenic drawings were exhibited in the Exhibition of Arts, Manufactures and Practical Sciences at the Assembly Rooms in Edinburgh in 1839. Hill might well have known about photography, even before the public announcements of that year, from his personal

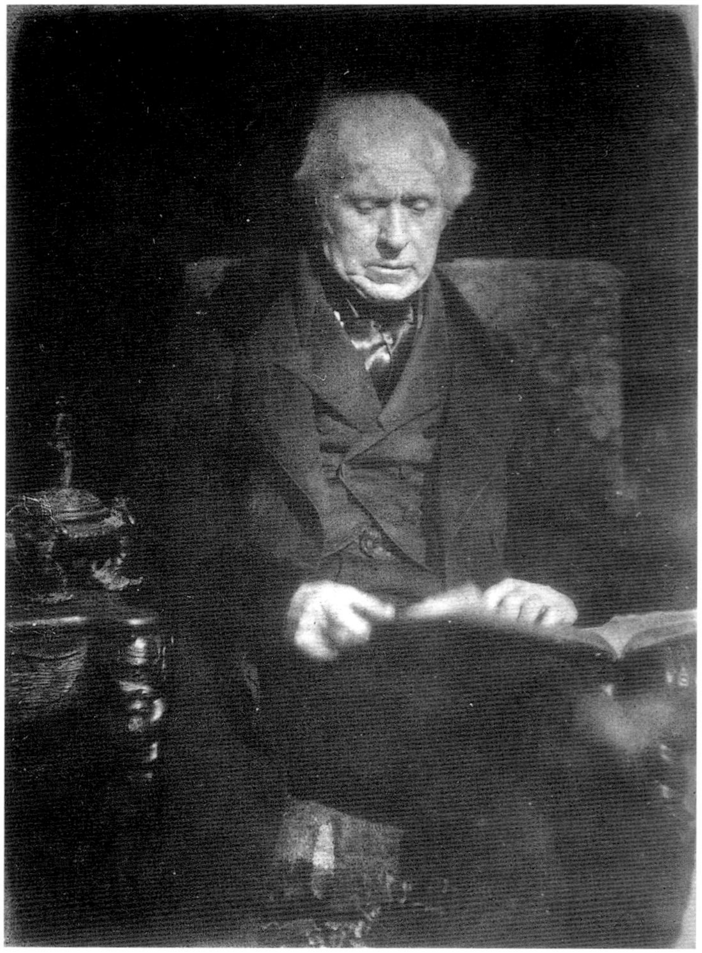

15. D. O. Hill and Robert Adamson, *Sir David Brewster*, 1843 or 1844. Calotype. Scottish National Photography Collection, Edinburgh.

friendship with the engineer James Nasmyth (fig. 16). Nasmyth apparently acquired a photograph by the Parisian instrument maker, Gustave Froment, as early as 1835, and he was friendly with the land agent George Smith Cundell, who published a version of the calotype process in 1844.[6] James Nasmyth, rather than David Brewster, may have been Hill's first conduit to the art.

An article on Hill's plans for the Disruption picture, published by Hugh Miller ten days before Brewster's letter, may qualify Brewster's account:

> Mr Hill has been led by what at first seemed a scarce surmountable obstacle in his way, to have recourse to an expedient which bids fair to exercise no slight influence on his art; and to add greatly to the interest of his picture. Much of the value of a piece such as he contemplates must of course consist in the faithfulness of the portraits. There was an utter lack of time to get these taken in the ordinary way; – and in a very few days, the members of the Free Assembly would have been scattered all over the kingdom . . . in the emergency the artist bethought him of having recourse for his likenesses to the recent invention of drawing by the agency of light. They were first taken by the Daguerreotype in the ordinary way, and with the usual sombre and shadowy effect, and latterly, through the medium of the sister invention, the calotype, – an art introduced into Edinburgh, during the last fortnight, for the first time, by Mr Adamson of St Andrews.[7]

This introduces the interesting possibility that Hill was already working with a daguerreotypist. Brewster might have deliberately deflected Hill from the daguerreotype to the calotype in order to send business in the direction of his own protégé. The circular, lithographed letters sent out by Hill to

16. D. O. Hill and Robert Adamson, *James Nasmyth*, 1843–7. Calotype. Scottish National Photography Collection, Edinburgh.

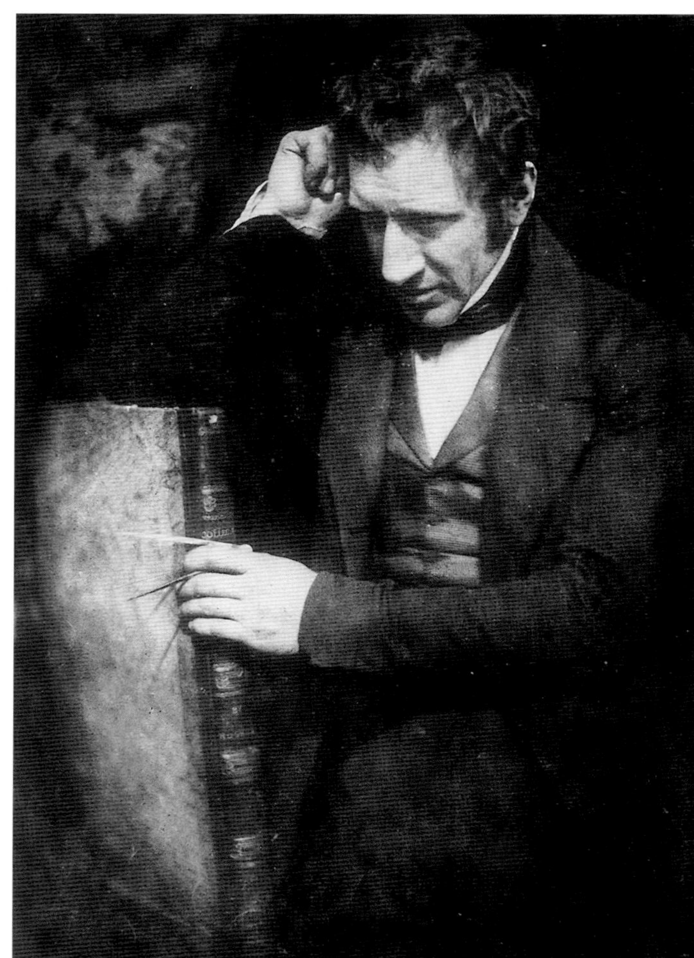

invite people to sit for their portraits confirms that Hill was at this stage considering, if not using, the assistance of a daguerreotypist:

> The preliminary studies of the portraits for this work will in the first instance be made by the use of the Daguerreotype and Calotype – and as Mr Hill has made the necessary arrangements with Mr Adamson a gentleman recommended to him by Sir David Brewster as an adept in the latter process, he requests that Dr Gordon will consent to meet him at Mr Adamson's house – Calton Stairs.[8]

In autumn 1843, Brewster was enthusiastic in his reports of the progress of the partnership. He wrote:

> I wish I could send you some of the fine Calotypes of ancient Church yard Monuments, as well as modern ones taken by Mr Adamson, and also specimens of the fine groups of Picturesque personages which Mr Hill and he have arranged and photographed. Those of the Fishermen & women of Newhaven are singularly excellent. They have been so inundated with work that they have not been able to send me a Collection.[9]

In 1844, Brewster was still actively promoting Adamson's work. He met Carl Gustav Carus, the art critic and physician to the King of Saxony, at Taymouth Castle. It was at his suggestion that the king and his entourage, travelling semi-incognito, subsequently visited Rock House.[10]

It would be reasonable to suppose that Brewster and Talbot would have exerted a strong and guiding influence on the partnership. Talbot may well have expected a return for his generosity, if only in the form of communication. In his letter to Talbot, of 28 November 1843, thanking him for a packet of calotypes, Brewster added: 'I gave your letter and the two calotypes to Dr Adamson who has sent them to his brother in Edinr. who will communicate with you on the subject of his Negatives.'[11] However, on 18 April 1844, he made it plain that Robert Adamson had not responded:

> This delay in writing you, has arisen from his having left Edinr. about the time you wrote me, & from his desire to send you one or two good negatives for your work. Dr Adamson is so annoyed at the circumstance that he has got my camera, for the purpose of getting one or two good negatives for you so that I hope the oversight will be atoned for.[12]

While this could have been simple absence of mind on Robert Adamson's part, it implies a reluctance to proffer his own expert knowledge, even to Talbot. This knowledge was, of course, Adamson's professional advantage; he could not afford the amiable amateur exchange of negatives, but his lack of response was discourteous.

WILLIAM HENRY FOX TALBOT IN CONNECTION WITH HILL AND ADAMSON

The only positively recorded meeting between Hill and Adamson and Talbot took place at the conference of the British Association for the Advancement of Science in York, in autumn 1844.[13] Hill wrote to ask if Talbot would give permission, saying that it had been, 'suggested to Mr. Adamson and myself, to attend the meeting of the British Association at York, for the purpose of making Calotype portraits of some of the eminent men who may be present.'[14] Hill then expressed doubt as to whether they would indeed be able to attend the meeting. The slight awkwardness of the letter and the curious fact that he did not say who had made the suggestion, since it was presumably Brewster, a leading figure of the association, may be evidence of an uncomfortable relationship with both men. However, Hill and Adamson were installed in York by 28 September. Hill seems to have met Talbot before he replied to the letter: 'I have again to return you an expression of the sincere thanks of Mr. Adamson and myself, for your liberality to us in permitting us to Calotype in York. I trust that our efforts here will add some new interest to your beautiful art . . . I hope I may have the pleasure of seeing you again before your train for Scotland.'[15]

Hill and Adamson set up a studio in the grounds of the York Museum and worked until 4 October. Hill reported his dubious reception at York to David Roberts, and added in a later letter:

> Your flattering opinions have been shared by Etty, Allan, [William Leighton] Leitch and many artists and a few [illegible] who know what art is, and these I have used as a warm blanket, to restore me to my natural heat, after a few cold bucketings of ignorant criticism, which my desire to foster and improve this hand maiden of Fine Art, has exposed me to.[16]

The York meeting was particularly unpleasant for Talbot, because several participants were presenting variant forms of photography and attacking his patent rights. Presumably Hill and Adamson were also under critical attack because they were working with Talbot's process. This would have meant that they were trying to calotype cool or even hostile sitters.

It is a sad irony that Thomas Davidson's large camera, with which they photographed York Minster and Durham Cathedral, apparently made no impact on the meeting.

However, Talbot came north with his assistant and printmaker, Nicolaas Henneman, to take the calotypes for his album, *Sun Pictures in Scotland*, immediately after the association meeting. He stayed three nights in Edinburgh, in Rampling's Waterloo Hotel from 10 to 12 October, in Waterloo Place, a few yards away from Rock House, to photograph the nearly completed Scott Monument.[17] It may therefore have been at this point that he had the discussion with Hill, which Hill mentioned to David Roberts six months later: 'Mr Talbot I believe may prevent us publishing in England, but I believe he will be inclined to grant permission on certain terms. Indeed he said so to me.'[18] From the slightly cryptic evidence of Talbot's notebooks, Talbot had seen and approved a number of Hill and Adamson's calotypes, perhaps on the same occasion. In his 1843/4 notebook, one of Talbot's lists includes, '18 Pilots family, 20 do (cast of a figure)/ 4 two fisher men/ 17 Jeanie Wilson??'[19] Talbot sent Hill a copy of part two of *The Pencil of Nature* and contemplated using something of Hill and Adamson's work in part five. A loose notebook page with lists of the calotypes he was proposing to include has: 'frame (with something enclosed)/ 8. Something coloured/ one of Hill's?/ 10 Palais de justice'[20]

In 1845, the favourable reaction from the influential Graphic Society in London and a gathering at Lord Northampton's house excited Hill and Adamson's ambition to produce a grand album of portraits of important Englishmen. Hill's letter is responding partly to Roberts's anxiety that someone else might pre-empt the idea. It contains the following passages:

> Adamson in answer to some of your queries respecting this Photogenic Process. The Art is the invention of Mr Fox Talbot who is the sole patentee: his patent extends in England only. About three years ago this said process was chemically and artistically speaking a very miserable affair. Dr Adamson of St Andrews – brother of my friend R Adamson whose manipulation produced the pictures now with you, took up Mr Talbot's process as an amateur. You are aware how jealous some scientific men are, as to their rights in the paternity of inventions or improvements, therefore I say *entre nous* that I believe Dr Adamson & his brother to be the fathers of many of those parts of the process which make it a valuable and practical art. I believe also from all I have seen that Robert Adamson is the most successful manipulator the art has yet seen, and his steady industry and knowledge of chemistry, is such that both from him and his brother much new improvements may yet be expected. I must tell you that Dr Adamson, up to the time that his brother thought of using the art professionally, was a most liberal communicator to all and every one, of all his improvements – and Mr Talbot had regularly a knowledge of his results. Mr Talbots patent not withstanding Adamsons improvements of his processes you will thus see prevent us from executing, or at least, selling a work in England without his consent. Some days ago I wrote for this from Mr Talbot – a few days will I hope tell me with what success...
>
> P.S. In glancing over this hastily written letter, it has occurred to me that I may be construed as speaking depreciatingly of Mr Talbot – which is not my intention in praising – and justly praising my friends the Adamsons. It may be as well however to avoid a collission [?] with Talbot by asserting what it might be difficult to prove if disputed.[21]

Hill sent a second, more legible letter, which exhibits further embarrassment and an anxiety not to offend Talbot: 'I fear I displayed some bad taste in praising too much the works it adverted to, and perhaps in claiming more for my friends the Adamsons than Mr Talbot or his friends would admit them to be entitled to. The Egotism you must forgive – and the praise of my friends is to *my friend* and to him only.'[22]

Talbot apparently did not reply to the proposal, and Hill's letter or letters are missing. Talbot may have referred Hill's correspondence to Antoine Claudet, who held Talbot's licence for portraiture in London. In 1845, Hill was trying the public approach detailed above. Talbot may well have been seriously offended by Elizabeth Rigby's review, which overflows with enthusiasm for Hill and Adamson's work, and ignores Talbot's publications, *The Pencil of Nature* and *Sun Pictures in Scotland.* She notices Talbot only in a dismissive footnote:

> To Mr Fox Talbot the happy invention is owing, but that artistic application of it, which has brought these drawings to their present picturesque perfection, required the eye of an artist, and for this the public is indebted to Mr. D. O. Hill of Edinburgh, in conjunction with Mr. Adamson, a young chemist of distinguished ability. It is to be hoped that Mr. Talbot, in justice to his own genius, will soon invite these gentlemen to London.[23]

The editor of the *Quarterly Review*, John Murray, responded to a letter from Talbot and presumably a gift of *Sun Pictures in Scotland*, commenting on this and identifying the author of the article:

> I hasten to return you my very best thanks for your valued gift of the Scottish Talbottypes – I am greatly interested in them & in the progress of the invention.
>
> I am also requested by *Miss Rigby* to offer her acknowledgments for the separate specimens wch. will facilitate a comparison between the Art in Edinburgh & in London. I cannot refrain from wishing that it were possible for Mr Hill to act in conjunction with you. There are points in wch. your Calotypes have a decided superiority over his – there are others in wch I think he excels – especially in obtaining artistic effects – a combination of the two would be a step in advance –
>
> I show the specimens English & Scotch to all friends & hope I am making converts.[24]

In November 1843 Brewster had written to Talbot: 'I think your plan of publication excellent. The same idea had occurred to Mr Hill & Mr Adamson, who advertised it some time ago as a plan in contemplation.'[25] He did not amplify this remark. It is likely that Talbot knew of Hill's *Land of Burns* and possible that he may have thought Hill and Adamson's plan to publish would include the obvious step of calotyping the land of Scott. While photographing the landscape associated with Walter Scott was an unexceptional and even obvious idea, and Talbot had an established affection for Scotland, it may be significant that *Sun Pictures in Scotland* was his first publication with a specific subject.[26]

The fourth and last photographically illustrated publication Talbot was involved with may also have entailed some unexpressed rivalry between Hill and Adamson and Talbot's commercial operation with Henneman at the Reading Establishment. Sir William Stirling, later Stirling-Maxwell, who lived at Keir near Stirling, in Scotland, wrote the first scholarly book on Spanish painting in English and by the mid-century owned the most important collection of Spanish art in Britain.[27] For his three-volume work, *Annals of the Artists of Spain* (1848), Stirling commissioned Nicolaas Henneman to make twenty-five sets of calotypes after sixty-six paintings, etchings, engravings, drawings and book illustrations.[28] Amongst the unexplained calotypes in the Hill/Adamson work are a group of prints from five engravings after Velázquez. They calotyped the print of *The Surrender of Breda* three times to give three different negatives, which suggests an intention to publish. These calotypes connect very obviously with William Stirling's project. Hill's interest in the good reproduction of painting (discussed in chapter five) might suggest that the idea originated in Edinburgh, and that Hill and Adamson started work without Talbot's agreement only to find the project taken over by Henneman.

From the evidence of Talbot's notebooks, he was understandably startled by the statement in Brewster's article on photography in 1847: 'The large volumes of Talbotypes published by Messrs Adamson and Hill, at the price of £40 or £50 each, and now in the possession of one or two of the most distinguished artists in London, evince also the perfection of Mr Talbot's process.'[29] Talbot and the Reading Establishment lost money in their photographic ventures and it seems likely that he was unaware that Hill, also, spent more than he recouped – that it was his ambition to sell the albums for such a price, rather than an achievement. Hill seems to have given away the known albums. There were only two ambitious centres of production for Talbot's calotype process in Britain, and the ambitions may have overlapped if not collided.

It is fairly clear that Brewster's role as the intermediary and communicator between the Scottish practice of the calotype and Lacock Abbey ceased to be effective in 1843. Part of this unexpected lack of communication between Brewster, Talbot, and Hill and Adamson may simply relate to personality. Brewster could be not just stimulating and enthusiastic, as he was in the company of the reticent Talbot, but dogmatic and opinionated, which he may have been in his contact with Hill. He expressed his own impatience with the thinking of artists in the following terms:

> Poets and painters have, generally speaking, very imperfect conceptions of the force of mathematical and physical evidence. The predominance of the imagination over the judgement indisposes them for patient and profound thought. The slightest resemblances, the most fortuitous associations, are linked together as cause and effect; and even words unburdened with meaning, and sentences unfreighted with thought, suggest to their fancy ideas and propositions blazing with all the lustre of truth.[30]

In this instance, Brewster is talking of Goethe's theory of colours and Charles Lock Eastlake's translation and commentary upon it. It is a fair comment on Brewster's position that he insists that his own theory of colours is, by scientific law, visually harmonic in the practice of painting. Where Eastlake, a painter, says that scarlet may be balanced by a pearly grey, Brewster maintains that it requires a bright green. Hill, who was described as having 'a rich versatile, rapid, facile mind, crowded with thick coming fancies',[31] would presumably have fallen with fatal ease into Brewster's category of the unthinking artist. This makes it unlikely that Brewster would have respected any opinion or ideas when they ran counter to his own. Hill was friendly rather than confident in Brewster's mould, and lacked the scientific knowledge which might have helped to establish common ground with either Brewster or Talbot.

BREWSTER AND THE PURSUIT OF TRANSPARENCY

Hill and Adamson's aesthetic approach to calotype portraiture (which will be discussed in chapter three), eventually proved antipathetic to Brewster and probably also to Talbot. By 1847, the critical distance between Brewster and the partnership was so great that, when Brewster reviewed the progress of photography, he included a devastating attack on the calotype process as a portrait medium. This was not disguised by his gracious approach:

> In treating of an art so beautiful and enchanting as the Talbotype undoubtedly is, we are unwilling to speak of its defects . . . but when it is employed to take portraits, particularly those of children and females, it invariably presents us with unsatisfactory results . . . The defect is so great, as to deter many persons from sitting for their portraits . . . it is often a hideous likeness, even when female beauty has submitted to its martyrdom. The defect arises, to a certain extent, from the rough grain, so to speak, of the paper, and also from its imperfect transparency – for in the positive picture every imperfection of the paper is copied, and every luminous point re-appears as a black one – so that the positive picture has the appearance of being stippled, as it were, with grains of sand, which give a painful coarseness to the human face.[32]

Brewster was following a line of thought in this paragraph leading to his own suggestion for improving the calotypes, which involved soaking them with varnish or oils to make the image transparent. He apparently believed that making the image clearer would make it not merely more distinct and informative but also more consistent. His affections manifestly belonged to the daguerreotype:

> If we judge of an art by the beauty of its productions, we can scarcely deny that the Daguerreotype, as applied to landscape and inanimate objects, came almost perfect from the hands of its inventor . . . The Talbotype will, we doubt not, make the same start towards perfection; and when a fine grained paper shall be made, and a more sensitive process discovered, we shall have Talbotype portraits the size of life, embodying the intellectual expression as well as the physical form of the human countenance.33

Hill and Adamson must have been appalled by Brewster's sweeping condemnation. Hill tried to redress the situation by using Lord Cockburn's influence to place a further article by John Brown in praise of calotype photography. Cockburn wrote merrily to the editor of the *North British Review*: 'Certain artists here hold that this is the Paradise of Calotype'.[34] The article was not published, and it may have been at this time that Hill gave Brewster a hundred of the calotypes, in the hopes of changing his mind. At the Edinburgh meeting of the British Association for the Advancement of Science, in 1850, when Brewster was president, he exhibited these calotypes. He said:

> This series, and indeed all those taken under Mr. Hill's superintendence, are distinguished by the artistic arrangements and drapery of the figures, a merit quite independent of their excellence as photographs. Hence these Talbotypes have been greatly admired and esteemed by artists, and have been justly regarded as valuable auxiliaries to art.[35]

In the meantime, however, Brewster believed he had found the perfection he sought in the albumen process, in which the chemicals were carried in a transparent film on the surface of a glass negative and on the surface of the paper positive. Hill's pleasure in Brewster's first remarks may well have been destroyed by his second presentation: 'This new process has been brought to such perfection in this city by Messrs. Ross and Thomson, that the Talbotypes taken by them, and lately exhibited by myself to the National Institute of France, and to M. Nièpce, were universally regarded as the finest that had yet been executed.'[36]

Hill was undoubtedly distressed in 1851, when the Great Exhibition jury awarded the prizes in photography, substantially in Brewster's terms. The jury awarded a Council Medal to Samuel Buckle and Ross and Thomson and a Prize Medal to Henneman and Malone.[37] The shortest entry appears for Hill and Adamson, who only received an Honourable Mention for: 'very many Talbotype groups, remarkable for easy and graceful arrangement. They are, in effect, after Rembrandt, being made out in broad and deep-toned masses of light and shade. As a whole, they are very sketchy and spirited. The tints are rich and varied both in depth and colour, and are of a rich sepia.'[38] The detailed commentary afforded to the other photographers reflects the technical lead of the criticism, even in the Fine Arts Section. Photography was also exhibited in the section for 'Philosophical Instruments and Objects Depending on their Use', where Brewster was one of the judges, and the terms of praise are sympathetic to his views in both sections.[39] The awards of the jury were a serious blow. Hill sadly remarked to David Roberts:

> I am glad you have not tired of them. I had some hopes the Chrystal Palace Fine Arts Jury would have awarded me a medal for my artistic application of this process – and I am still of the opinion they should have done so – it would have been some consolation for much time and money spent, I hope not foolishly, in making the art respectable.[40]

THE CALOTYPES
Talbot and Hill and Adamson in Opposition

Unlike Brewster, Talbot was a practical photographer, and both his opinions and his work may be compared with Hill and Adamson's. However, the inadequate communication between Hill and Talbot may have been visual as well as verbal. Beyond the four or five listed in Talbot's notebooks, it is not clear which of Hill and Adamson's calotypes Talbot knew. Hill was not impressed by *The Pencil of Nature* and referred to it disparagingly, when talking of his ambitious plan for an album of English portraits: 'this *first* book of English Calotype *pictures* for really Talbot's examples in his Pencil of Nature are not intended to be such should be such as to make the French look only second best in their Sun Painting efforts.'[41] Passages of Talbot's text were designed as promotional literature, exploring the range of advantages and uses of photography, some of which would have been antipathetic to Hill. In an obvious example, Talbot promoted the ease as well as the factual accuracy of photography. His text for the photograph of the bust of Patroclus reads:

> It has often been said . . . that there is no royal road to learning of any kind. But the proverb is fallacious: for there is, assuredly, a royal road to Drawing . . . Already sundry amateurs have laid down the pencil and armed themselves with chemical solutions and with camerae obscurae. Those amateurs especially, and they are not few, who find the rules of perspective difficult to apply – and who moreover have the misfortune to be lazy – prefer to use a method which dispenses with all that trouble.[42]

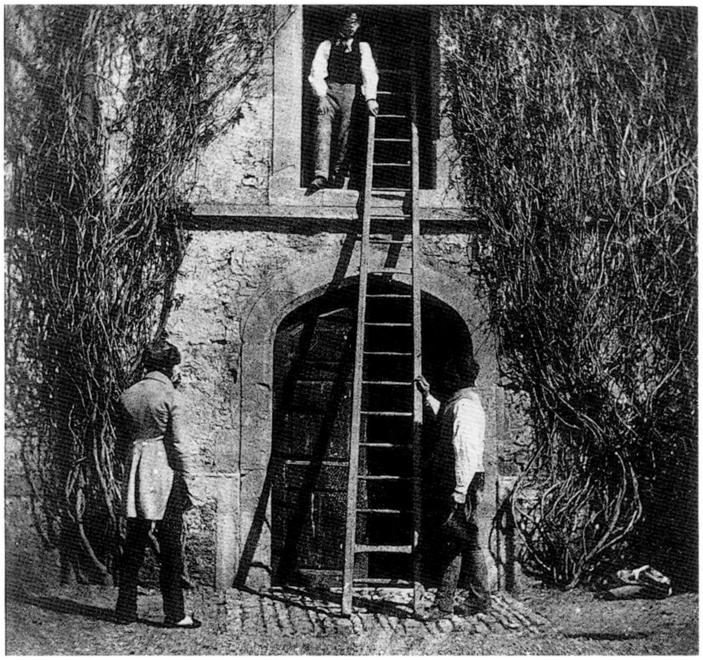

17. William Henry Fox Talbot, *The Ladder*, *c.* 1845. Calotype. Fox Talbot Museum, Lacock, Wiltshire.

Hill had no interest in the idea that photography made art easy. His position was that the making of, or the approach to, fine art, whether in painting or in the calotype process was meant to be difficult.

> I can only say that Adamson says the manipulation is very liable to go wrong in the hands of most people – that tho' several have now and then produced a good specimen – they find it difficult to succeed often – and the arrangement of the picture is as much an effort of the artist as if he was in reality going to paint it.[43]

Certain of the pictures in *The Pencil of Nature* are visibly opposed to Hill's aesthetic sense. Talbot's calotype, *The Ladder* (fig. 17), is presented with a text, which reads:

> Groups of figures take no longer time to obtain than single figures would require since the Camera depicts them all at once, however numerous they may be: but at present we cannot well succeed in this branch of the art without some previous concert and arrangement . . . But when a group of persons has been artistically arranged, and trained by a little practice to maintain an absolute immobility for a few seconds of time, very delightful pictures are easily obtained.[44]

Talbot may have introduced the question of groups to *The Pencil of Nature* because he knew from Brewster of Hill and

Adamson's practice. In theory, a comparison might usefully be made between their calotypes from this example. However, *The Ladder* is the only image in *The Pencil of Nature* with figures, and Talbot may have chosen the image because it had a good negative, which would allow multiple reproduction. Aware of the limitations imposed by this constraint, Talbot had a tendency in *The Pencil of Nature* to write of future ambition rather than what was there in the picture presented. This is a notable example of dislocation between text and picture. It is not an articulated group; the figures are placed like points of reference in a perspective drawing, and there is none of the sociable contact set up in Hill and Adamson's groups. But, while this is an extreme example, Talbot's groups usually maintain a distance between the figures. The distinction between Hill's and Talbot's approach to the group might be expressed broadly as a distinction between the emotional and the cerebral, or perhaps more simply as the resulting difference in practice between physical involvement and the issuing of instructions. Hill could understand the social structure of a group – could demonstrate what he wanted and would physically organise people. We can be reasonably sure that Hill was handling his subjects not just from the evidence of such supports as a pile of books under a leaning elbow but because he occasionally used solidly based metal supports and clamps for inexperienced sitters. Talbot may well have stood back, asked people to move into position and told them to stand immobile.

The contrast between Hill and Adamson's work and Talbot's may also be considered in an impersonal area, in their photographs of the Scott Monument (fig. 18 and pl. 9). In this particular case, Hill and Adamson had the advantage that they lived in Edinburgh and could watch and consider the progress of the monument. They could take advantage of a bright day when one occurred. Talbot was at the mercy of the weather, but he was fortunate, the sun shone at his chosen time of day and his photograph is strong and clear. His experience of lighting, which he practised with the bust of Patroclus at Lacock Abbey, is here demonstrated in the use of a low westerly sun to pick out the carved detail. The principal distinction between his composition and Hill and Adamson's derives from the fact that it is taken from the shelter of an upstairs room in Princes Street.[45] The high viewpoint, which is common in Talbot's work, helped to reduce the problem of vertical perspective, and some of Hill and Adamson's calotypes take the same advantage. However, Talbot's position was fixed too close to the monument and he could not move back from the window. The image of the monument is nearly complete, but the calotype cuts off the top of the spire, squaring off a Gothic monument. All of Hill and Adamson's calotypes, taken at several stages of the building process, show the complete state of the work.

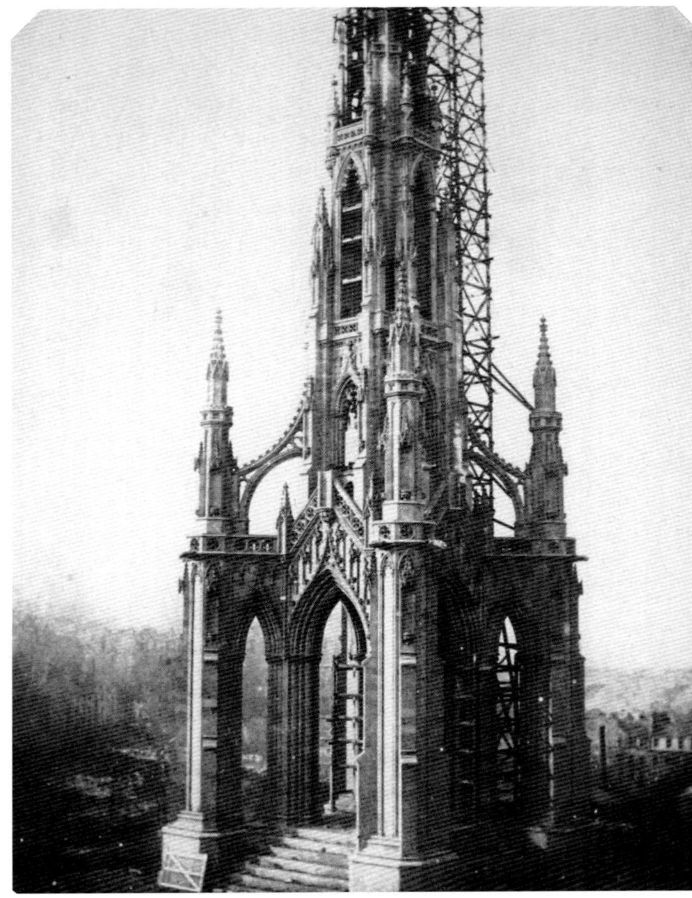

18. William Henry Fox Talbot, *Sir Walter Scott's Monument, Edinburgh, as it Appeared when nearly Finished*, October 1844. Salt paper print from a calotype paper negative. Fox Talbot Museum, Lacock Abbey Collection.

The distinction to be made here is perhaps twofold. Talbot, with his many enthusiasms and pursuits, may simply have been too impatient to look for a different viewpoint – he took five negatives from this one position – or to wait a few days until the monument was complete. He took the entire series of calotypes for *Sun Pictures in Scotland* touring through the country between 10 and 22 October.[46] Talbot travelled with scientific instruments and expected to assess the world as he found it. His impatience as a photographer may derive from his enthusiasm for new paths – the enthusiasm which led him to discover photography. The composition of the photograph might be regarded as an attempt to fill a rectangular frame more fully than a complete Gothic spire may naturally do; it may equally be regarded as a hasty and curiously disrespectful image. His inherent reticence may also have prompted him to retreat indoors to the privacy of a room and a window. Urban photography was too attractive to bystanders and the control of interested crowds was always a problem, which Talbot particularly disliked in photographing views; many of his urban photographs, such as his pictures of the Paris boulevardes and the comparable view of Nelson's column, are taken from indoors.[47] In their calotypes of the Scott Monument taken on the level, Hill and Adamson seem to have dealt with this problem of the intrusive bystanders to achieve the best view.

'NO POETRY IN THE PENCIL OF THE SUN'

In this context, it is not practical to undertake an analysis of Talbot's work as a whole in relation to Hill and Adamson's. It is visually and aesthetically distinct, and from such distinctions as have been noted here we can begin to see such a radical difference in personality and approach that it becomes less surprising that the four men practically concerned with the excellence of the new art failed to connect. The difference was neither public nor overt. However, in the 1850s, Brewster and Hill came to represent positions of public polarity, in which Brewster stood for the scientific and technical character of photography, its representation of reality, while Hill stood for its use as an art form, its capacity for expression.[48]

Hill and Adamson's work was used as a model for the artistic use of photography in an acid debate, in which the authority of professional photographers was challenged. One of the leading professionals in this dispute was James Ross of the partnership of Ross and Thomson, who first appear perched on Calton Hill, above Rock House, in 1847, and whose photographs were promoted by David Brewster: 'Thanks to the praise Sir David Brewster bestowed upon our handiwork (in a lecture given in the Music Hall by that great, good, and influential man), public attention was drawn towards our firm.'[49]

The establishment of the Photographic Society of Scotland in 1856 and the increase in the professional practice of photography between then and the early 1860s widened the division. Brewster was the first president of the society and his introductory speech began:

> Photography is pre-eminently a scientific art; it requires no peculiar genius in its cultivators; the Painter and the Sculptor must bring into the world those high gifts which qualify them for the practice of their divine art, but there is no poetry in the pencil of the Sun . . . The pencil of the artist must be called in, as it has already been, to give perfection and colour to the Photograph.[50]

The artists Brewster refers to here were those who painted on top of the calotypes to give them colour, who included Henry Collen, a miniature painter and the first to take out a licence to practise the calotype process professionally, and the Reverend Calvert Jones, an amateur painter and friend of Talbot. Hill, who respected the calotype's integrity, did not do this. The Photographic Society approached Hill as its potential second speaker, presumably because he would provide an alternative view:

> What is wanted is not so much a *written paper*, as if [illegible] for publication, as a plain & practical explanation of the important points to be kept in view in the selection & arrangement of subjects for the Camera, the management of light & shade, the adaptation of the tone of the print to the nature of the picture &c &c. On all of these matters there is an excessive amount of ignorance among the majority of Photographers, & nothing is more likely to advance the Art, as an *Art*, than a little sound knowledge regarding them.[51]

Hill was unwell at the time but avoided the request to speak at a later date, despite the secretary's warm invitation. However, he exhibited the calotypes in the first and second exhibitions of the new society, with a characteristically modest disclaimer:

> I would not have obtruded these long ago [illegible] works upon the Society had they not, in addition to such pictorial & manipulative merit as may be accorded to them, appeared to you to possess a historical interest, in the early efforts of that wonderful art which has since become so great a fact in the world's history.[52]

The new audience was impressed, and reviews of the exhibitions contained passages that must have been galling to the technologically advanced photographers. One review makes the opposition directly to Ross and Thomson and indirectly to David Brewster, whose pursuit of naturalism had caused him to develop stereoscopic photography:

> First in order of time, they remain first in the order of merit, magnificent beyond comparison in breadth, depth, reality, and pictorial effect, to anything since produced in what are now esteemed the more perfect developments of photographers . . . we prefer the artistic arrangements and

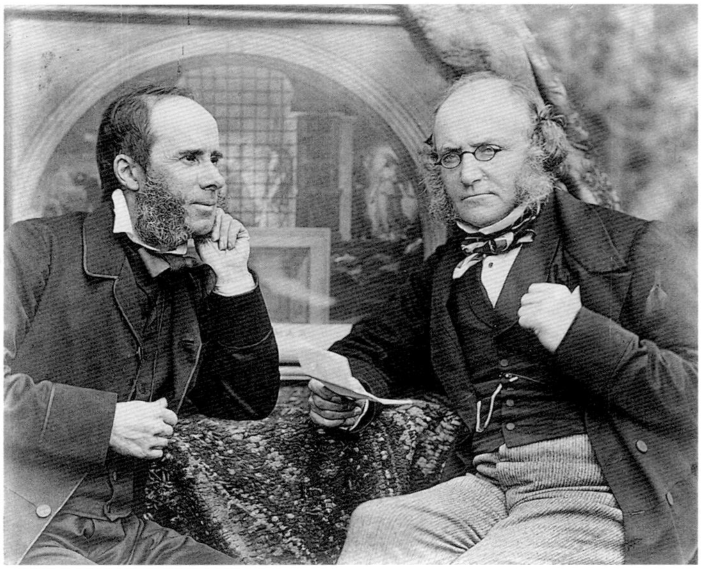

19. D. O. Hill and Alexander MacGlashan, *Horae Subsecivae,* Dr John Brown and John Taylor Brown, *c.* 1860. Albumen print. Scottish National Photography Collection, Edinburgh.

> broad realities of Mr D. O. Hill's portraits and figures to the stereoscopic sugar dolls or the agonising attitudes of recent and more 'perfect' photographers. Next to Mr Hill's examples, we place the 'Lady Reclining', exhibited in the Arts Manufactures Exhibition by Ross and Thomson. The arrangement of the figure is admirable, and the breadth of light and clearness of shadow shows the more perfect state of the art; but the head – that in which Mr Hill's portraits come out – is in this lady dimmed by the superior beauty of the dress.[53]

The dispute within the society was not fought on simple issues. Ironically, James Ross's position echoed the earlier fight between the painters of the academy and the Royal Institution (see chapter five). He objected to the fact that the society's council was composed of gentleman amateurs and painters; professional photographers had no voice in the selection and hang of the exhibitions.

In this context, Hill was promoted as the artist who directed photography. He may well have been actively encouraged by the society to try the brief alliance with Alexander MacGlashon, whose results were exhibited in the society's 1862 exhibition as *Contributions Towards the Further Development of Fine Art in Photography.*[54] The award of a medal to Hill, for the photograph called *Horae Subsecivae*, a group portrait of John Brown and his cousin, John Taylor Brown (fig. 19), drew on Hill lavish praise from Brown himself: 'Did you ever see anything out of Giorgione more subtle and to the life?' and equal invective from the photographer, John Traill Taylor: 'We are at some loss to understand what is meant by a placard attached to some portrait groups photographed by Mr McGlashon . . . to the effect that they are "contributions towards *fine art* in photography by D. O. Hill."'[55] It is no coincidence that the Edinburgh Photographic Society was formed in 1862 by professional photographers disgruntled by the approach of the original society.

The fight within the Photographic Society of Scotland was probably inevitable. The sudden rush of commercial photographers from the mid-1850s made photography a business. The making of money took precedence, and the interested artists were swamped by naïve claims to instant artistry. Within this hostile field, the opposition between Hill and Brewster was set in a public arena and elicited exaggerated feeling and aggression.

However, it may be that one of the critical problems here was not just that Brewster thought Hill was subverting photography but that, in some sense, he was actually subverting photography: Robert Adamson was initially Brewster's protégé; his partnership with Hill closed off that relationship. Hill and Adamson used photography as a means of expression. It could be argued that the seductive expressiveness of their calotypes redirected the art. Without Hill's contribution, it is possible that the technological or transparent character of photography could have been more efficiently established and its eccentricity concealed rather than triumphantly revealed.

3

The Aesthetic Character and Practice of the Calotype

PROCESS

The first two published methods of photography were radically different in character and may be regarded as establishing an immediate debate on the nature of the medium. The daguerreotype was a fragile, jewel-like picture made in grains of silver on a polished surface and encased in a frame or box. Its intimacy was enhanced by its physical character as a hand-held mirror. The difficulty of seeing the picture and the way the viewer and the viewed may be seen alternately in the mirror made it an extraordinarily personal object. The calotype was a multiple: a negative/positive process. The support of both negative and positive was unsurfaced drawing paper, so the photographic chemicals sank into the fibres, blurring the image.

By a nice historical irony, the popular art, with its magical cleverness of detail, was the daguerreotype: the unique, private image. In its first incarnation as the calotype, the repeatable, public image proved the critically demanding work; Hill himself said of his work with the calotype: 'the very excellence of the art exhibited in the Calotype is a bar to its popularity with the unlearned public.'[1]

The distinction between the two processes was exaggerated by the rhetoric of advertisement and admiration. The detail of daguerreotypes invited the magnifying glass. The painter and daguerreotypist Samuel Morse, employed 'a powerful lens, which magnified fifty times' to read a distant street sign.[2] The daguerreotype assumed the authority of machine-made accuracy, while the blur of the calotype was credited with a kind of natural innocence. Partly, this was a result of the daguerreotype achieving a technical perfection before the photogenic drawing, which was improved and patented as the calotype in 1841. The scientist James David Forbes, who was one of the first to examine the two processes in 1839, was sent examples of Talbot's work. Talbot wrote, somewhat nervously, that he only objected to Brewster's showing the specimens he had sent up to St Andrews, because he had sent the only ones available: 'so far from being the ne plus ultra of photogenic drawing they were literally the ne minus ultra.' Forbes then travelled to Paris and was enchanted by the daguerreotype: 'I was pleased beyond my most sanguine expectations; in short it baffles belief:– in promptitude & minuteness one can conceive it even if they cannot believe it upon report, but in beauty, and the perfect representation of nature it must be seen to be understood . . . As to Messrs. Talbot & Co. they had better shut up shop at once.'[3]

The opposition between the processes was set up at the beginning – not least because one was French and the other English. The Napoleonic Wars, which had only ended in 1815, with the Battle of Waterloo, were still a living memory. Hill, despite his initial willingness to consider the daguerreotype, saw the two processes in severe opposition by 1845. He said of his plan to execute an album of English worthies: 'a truly noble work honorable to England . . . would earn more solid applause than the livid pictures of Daguerre.'[4] This opposition meant that the early critical discussions of photography were aware of a contradictory view of nature. Photography was and could be variable.

'A CLEAR IDEA IS . . . A LITTLE IDEA'
Breadth and the Imagination

When Hill differentiated between the calotype and the daguerreotype, he talked of inequality and imperfection: 'The rough surface & unequal texture throughout of the paper is the main cause of the calotype failing in details before the process [or 'precision'] of Daguerrotypy – & this is the very life of it. They look like the imperfect work of a man – and not the much diminished perfect work of god.'[5]

Mary Warner Marien says of this: 'Whereas the calotype process's uneven appearance implicitly negated the complaint that photography was a mechanical art, it also in Hill's phrasing, suggested that photography was an inherently lesser art.'[6] She combines this with Elizabeth Rigby's critique of photography, written from the perspective of 1857: 'if the photograph in its early and imperfect scientific state was more consonant to our feeling for art, it is because . . . it was more true to our experience of nature.' Marien reads this as meaning that Rigby was then constructing an idea of Hill and Adamson's work as naïve.[7] But the two ideas do not mesh. As Marien herself points out, the early practice of photography required so much knowledge that it could not have been naïve.

The torque on the argument comes from a misunderstanding of Hill's vocabulary. He is expressing a form of distinguishing admiration. His comment is sparked off by the innocence of his correspondent, in picking up a magnifying glass to examine the pictures as though they were daguerreotypes, the familiar source of miniature wonders. Hill is trying to convey that his own pleasure in the calotype depends on its breadth and on its rough, apparently lively imperfection. He, like Elizabeth Rigby, distinguished between the surface appearance of nature and the living experience. In so saying, Hill was admiring the calotype as an expressive medium, which belonged within a difficult philosophical and aesthetic interest in obscurity or lack of finish.

The understanding of nature, in the Romantic proposal, comes not from clamorous detail but from a simplification of divine complication: man's rough attempt may come closer to the mark of the ideal because it leaves the imagination free. Hill was rejecting the misleading blandness of the daguerreotype, characteristic of the tailor's fashions, which overlays the structure and the strength of nature. In a broader context, when commenting on an essay on painting, which made a comparison between painters and tailors, Hill recommended that the author substitute a blacksmith, an analogy of strength, for the delicacy of a tailor.[8] Elizabeth Rigby's contemporary admiration of the calotype, which is quoted in full below, was undiluted by her later disillusionment with photography. She planted it in an attack on modern German painting, as a natural model, compared with paintings that displayed the same virtuoso but indiscriminate precision as the daguerreotype and the tailor's work. She refers to the depiction of Tasso in Carl Sohn's *The Two Leonoras:*

> We see the hairs on his beard, the pattern on his vest, the fur of his doublet, the clocks of his stockings, the oranges above his head, the plants at his feet; but we see nothing of Tasso's own expression, or if we do, it is only that of a man who is naturally mortified at finding his clothes running away with all the attention due to himself.[9]

Elizabeth Rigby makes the same opposition, in her later article, in discussing William Newton's views of photography and his preference for the 'whole subject being a little *out of focus*, thereby giving a greater breadth of effect.' She wrote, 'As soon as could an accountant admit the morality of a *false* balance, or a seamstress the neatness of a puckered seam, as your merely scientific photographer admit the possible beauty of "a slight *burr*."'[10]

Hill's view of the calotype follows the religious idea that truth has a certain confusion and that mystery is approached through imperfect understanding. This may be expressed from the Bible, in the Epistle to the Corinthians: 'For now we see through a glass, darkly; but then face to face: now I know in part; but then shall I know even as I am also known.'[11] This relation between naturalism and divine obscurity was made in 1844, when the Scottish Academy exhibited David Wilkie's painting, *Pitlessie Fair*. Hill inserted a long quotation in the catalogue from a review, which praised the picture because it showed: 'No invention, no creation by rule, but the breathing world of Fife seen as through a glass darkly.'[12] It is not a literal obscurity that is admired here, but a view of society, which partakes of a real sense of nature and life; the obscurity is one of time and divine intention.

In addressing the classic distinction between poetry and painting and giving the obscurity of poetry preference over painting, Edmund Burke had expressed the problem of approaching greatness in these terms: 'To see an object distinctly, and to perceive its bounds, is one and the same thing. A clear idea is therefore another name for a little idea.'[13] It was a recurring theme. In the Sublime proposal, confusion itself aimed at the effect of grandeur, through limitation and drama: monochrome and emotional doubt. Horace provided a classical model for this in his praise of the beginning of the *Odyssey*:

> It isn't a flash and then smoke that he plans to give us,
> But light out of the smoke, so that after that
> He may draw from his stores striking and wonderful tales.[14]

This was direct metaphor and one that could be experienced. It was possible to set it in a modern context. Hugh Miller introduced his friend, the hopeful painter William Ross, to a real demonstration of the idea:

> I taught him, too, to light fires after nightfall in the caves, that we might watch the effects of the strong lights and deep shadows in scenes so wild; and I still vividly remember the delight he experienced, when, after kindling up in the day-time a strong blaze at the mouth of the Doocot Cave, which filled the recess within with smoke, we forced our way inwards through the cloud, to mark the appearance of the sea and the opposite land, seen through a medium so dense, and saw, on turning round, the landscape strangely enwrapped 'in the dun hues of earthquake and eclipse.'[15]

There was even an industrial model of such moral illumination, which Hill would have known. His teacher, Adam Anderson, designed the splendid gasworks for the city of Perth. He inscribed on the walls the punning inscription: 'non fumam [*sic*] ex fulgore sed ex fumo dare lucum' (roughly speaking, 'not smoke from flame but light from smoke *or* fumes').[16] From such an unexpected source as this, Hill could have learnt an idea of obscurity as a positive source of enlightenment, which might lead to a readiness to think beyond light and dark as opposites into a sense of one as potentially productive of the other; the thinking necessary to an appreciation of the photographic negative. It was not an easy appreciation; for many people the appearance of the photographic negative was disconcerting. Samuel Morse, for example, had experimented with the idea of photography before the announcement of the daguerreotype, but had abandoned his trials on achieving the negative: 'Finding that light produced dark and dark light, I presumed the production of a true image to be impractical, and gave up the attempt.'[17]

Between the picturesque and the romantic, there are further sites for consideration of the calotype. Both ideas were generalised and used to define whole areas of practice – often contradictory. The lesser ambition of the picturesque, with its occasional dislocation from the ideal, was expressed in reference to such characters as roughness and irregularity. John Brown's appreciation of Hill and Adamson's calotypes was written in these terms:

> True it is, that of imagination and true ideality they can have none, – the sun has none to give; but the painter can by his arrangements make them picturesque. The meaning of which is, that the spectator may, if it is in him, make pictures out of them; and in this sense they are invaluable to the artist as suggestive, and as a fine discipline for the eye. They have all the modesty and all the infinite variety of nature, and, to a man with a shaping spirit, are the very stuff from which to body forth his own thoughts.[18]

Elizabeth Rigby disliked the German painters because they had divorced the Romantic idea from the concept of the wild and fantastic in the chivalric romances of the Middle Ages. Far from leaving the mind free to speculate or dream, they filled it with redundant detail. In her terms, the calotypes, 'broad and true', left the mind able to attempt that dream. James Nasmyth wrote admiringly of the calotypes: 'it is nature reduced to an artistical standard and abounding in the most noble suggestion'.[19] Such verbal echoes underlay and exaggerated the rhetorical opposition of the daguerreotype and the calotype and made the latter particularly attractive to many of the artists of the day.

RESEMBLANCE
Painting and Graphics

In the examination of Hill and Adamson's calotypes, much of the criticism connects with art practice. The importance of breadth in painting had been expressed by Joshua Reynolds in his *Discourses Delivered to the Students of the Royal Academy*, when discussing Titian: 'The excellence of portrait painting, and we may add, even the likeness, the character, and countenance . . . depend more upon the general effect produced by the painter, than on the exact expression of the peculiarities, or minute discrimination of the parts.'[20] Another painter Reynolds admired for his generality was Rembrandt. He wrote: 'Rembrandt's manner is absolute unity.'[21] Whilst not seeing him as an 'elevated' painter, Reynolds approved of his breadth of manner: 'This effect is produced by melting and losing the shadows in a ground still darker than those shadows; whereas that relief [i.e. the illusion of three dimensions] is produced by opposing and separating the ground from the figure, either by light, or shadow, or colour.'[22] The reference to Rembrandt, in the early discussions of photography, occasionally relied on an uncritical and sometimes unsympathetic idea of Rembrandt's work. The logic of the comparison was simply his strong, broadly massed use of light and dark, and those calotypes which employ an exaggerated density of light and shadow would emphasise the reference. Rembrandt was also associated with the kind of direct naturalism which photography might be regarded as inheriting. It was Rembrandt's naturalism which the marine painter Clarkson Stanfield heartily rejected when Hill sent him a series of the Newhaven photographs. He wrote: 'I sat up till nearly three o'clock looking over them. They are indeed most wonderful, and I would rather have a set of them than the finest Rembrandts I ever saw'.[23] Presumably, Stanfield felt that Hill and Adamson's view of the fishermen and women assorted better with an elevated concept of working life than did Rembrandt's.

People were most familiar with Rembrandt's work through his etchings. Hill had tried etching and would have known the blurring of the acid edge, which in Rembrandt's hands was used to such astonishing effect in achieving animation and intimacy. While the movement suggested in line could not be transferred directly to the calotype, the sense of blurring – the equivalent of the burr of etching – was partly inherent and was sometimes deliberately enhanced by Hill.

The relation of the calotype to graphic processes is capable of extensive reference and clearly underlies the satisfaction Hill felt in the results. The experience of printing, in itself, is a practical component in the understanding and appreciation of the negative image. It may reasonably be proposed that Hill's direct experience of the reprographic processes enabled him to visualise the positive in the reversal of the negative, without having to learn a new visual language.[24]

In Heinrich Schwarz's terms: 'The artistic expression of Hill's calotypes is founded entirely on the unique graphic charm inherent in the very being of photography: unbroken continuity from the brightest light to darkest shadow'. Schwarz describes the development of the graphic arts through mezzotint, aquatint and lithography as a search for this quality, which culminated in photography. In a lyrical passage, he compared the calotypes particularly to the richness of the mezzotint:

> The products of Hill's camera are far from being a mirror-image of the visible world uninformed by the spirit. In his work, as in mezzotints, light separates itself reluctantly from shadow. Soft half-tones, emerging from deepest shade, temper the transition to the bright spots of heads and hands. As in the mezzotint, a fluent chiaroscuro plays about the bodies and fuses the figures and the space about them into a harmonious unity. And again, as in the mezzotint, one can actually feel the surface textures in cravats of shimmering satin, waistcoats of dull glowing velvet, collars of thick fur, and shawls made of soft Scottish wool.[25]

Hill's first venture as an artist was his set of lithographs of Perthshire scenery, and he sustained an interest in the process. The new art was potentially a direct creative process like the etching, because the artist could draw freehand on the stone. The print resembled chalk drawing and had something of the same character and arbitrary interference in handling that was later found in the calotype. Hill's taste for this in printmaking was affirmed in 1856, when he defended Robert Macpherson's photolithographs against James Ross's opinion that 'smooth stone would . . . be better adapted for fine subjects.' Hill said: 'There could be no greater roughness than that seen in a fine chalk drawing, which was far from objectionable.'[26] This sense of familiarity may have been emphasised by one of the first descriptions of lithography, which includes a passage, remarkably like an account of the direct printing out of the calotype in sunshine:

> The first state of a drawing is like the dead coloring of a painting. The subsequent touches on the drawing bring it up to life like the second and third paintings of a picture, which improve the lights, strengthen the shadows, and make out local character. Indeed, it is a good plan to imagine that you are at first drawing with so little light that the contours of the masses can only be defined: then suppose a little more light, which exhibits them more in detail; and lastly, that sufficient quantity of light which makes every thing properly obvious.[27]

There is a further point in the making of lithographs, which may have had some significance to the partnership. While etching might be drawn and completed by the artist, the lithograph generally required distinct professional assistance in the printing:

> He [the artist] may supervise, but if he wants the full range of tone in his drawing to be brought out he needs expert aid. This fact distinguishes lithography from etching . . . And fundamentally affects the whole history of the medium. It is perhaps as appropriate to write a history of lithography in terms of the major lithographic printing establishments as in terms of the artists.[28]

This would have given Hill a respect for such complementary expertise, which extended and enhanced his own work, in contrast to the engraved book illustrations from his paintings, which were translations with a separate and often reductive existence. Lithographic practice may therefore have provided Hill with a working model for the calotype partnership.

The resemblance between the calotype, drawing and printmaking is commented on by critics of great and lesser knowledge. Hugh Miller, after his contact with the first work of the partnership, spoke of it in terms of drawing:

The connoisseur unacquainted with the results of the recent discovery, would decide, if shown a set of photographic impressions, that he had before him the carefully finished drawings in sepia of some great master.

The stronger lights, as in sketches done in this colour, present merely the white ground of the paper; a tinge of soft warm brown indicates the lights of lower tone; a deeper and still deeper tinge succeeds, shading by scarce perceptible degrees through all the various gradations, until the darker shades concentrate into an opaque and dingy umber, that almost rivals black in its intensity.[29]

The accomplished amateur watercolourist, John Harden, encountered Hill and Adamson's work in November 1843, and described the calotypes to his daughter as: 'faithfully given & in a sepia like drawing style of the most perfect truth – lovely & veritable . . . the pictures produced are as Rembrandt's but improved so like his style & the oldest & finest masters that doubtless a great progress in Portrait painting & effect must be the consequence.'[30] Harden was used to sketching in monochrome, using the reduced palette of black, brown and white. He acquired and copied two of the Newhaven calotypes in watercolour and his transcription is notably successful – this was neither inevitable nor easy, partly because the apparent monochrome of the calotype is a chemical reaction of some subtlety.[31]

The calotype's generality gave it an affinity with the preparatory sketch for painting, and Hill began by using it for this purpose. In the earliest photographs taken for the Disruption picture, the backgrounds and the furniture are arbitrary and the supports may be visible (fig. 20). The later calotypes are sketches in a different sense. They are both exploratory and finished; they complete the thought which prompted them. The importance of this idea may be illustrated in an analogy with current practice in drawing. The Sketching Society, founded in 1808 in London, was set up to encourage the art. The members attended for two-hour drawing sessions and generally drew on white paper, using sepia ink, burnt sienna, India ink and lamp black. The connection with the calotype is stronger than the physical resemblance. These sketches were consciously designed within a time limit to achieve both immediacy and coherence. J. Hogarth, who published photolithographic reproductions of the society's work in 1858, commented on their 'unity of thought and vigour of execution which is often wanting in the more finished production.'[32] The rapid sketch was admired by John Ruskin, in the same terms, as, 'the invaluable blotted five minute works which record the unity of some single and magnificent impressions.'[33] Such drawings expressed the idea of temporal containment or capture, which became the particular province of photography.

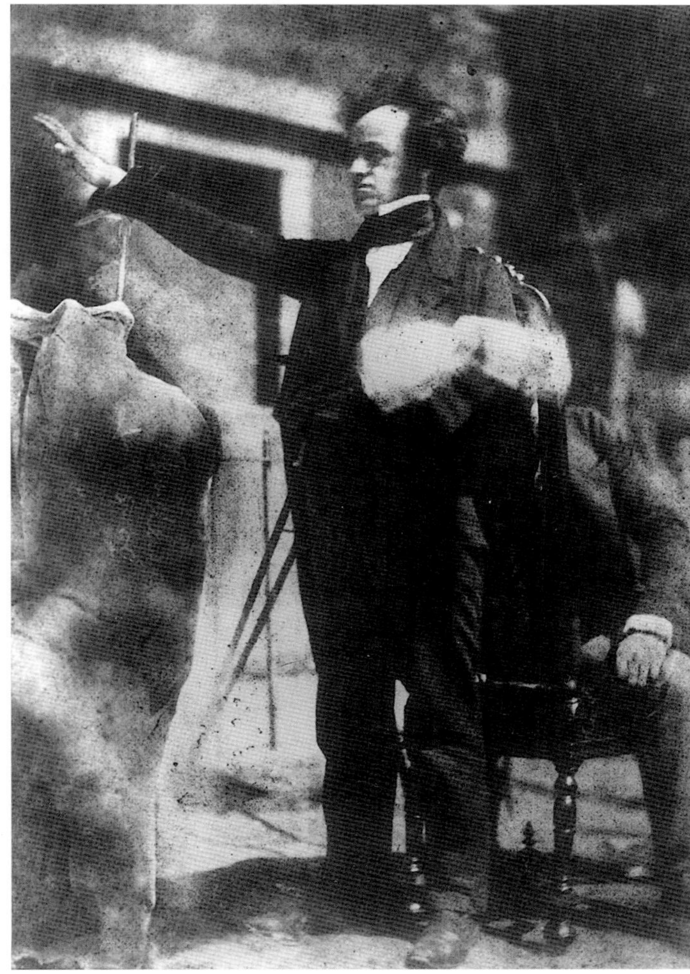

20. D. O. Hill and Robert Adamson, *Reverend Dr Robert Smith Candlish*, 1843. Print from a calotype negative. Scottish National Photography Collection, Edinburgh.

THE CAMERA'S AESTHETIC

It is of notable importance that we have, in D. O. Hill, an artist who lets us see what the camera may have been to aesthetic vision prior to 1839. Whilst retrospective analysis of the previous centuries of portrait and figure painting, from a study of Hill and Adamson's calotypes, is a historical anachronism, the idea deserves a little consideration. The resemblance, for example, between their portraits and the portraits by Henry Raeburn or Reynolds cannot be explained too easily. Hill did not imitate the pose or composition of their paintings, but, nevertheless, a calotype like *Samuel Aitken* (pl. 11) has the look of a Raeburn.

The great excitement of the artists who approved of their calotypes was, understandably, expressed in terms of past painters and sculptors. Hill reported: '[William] *Etty* saw in them revivals of Rembrant [*sic*], Titian and Spagnoletto.'[34] The history painter, Benjamin Robert Haydon wrote, quite wonderfully: 'I am convinced that Calotype is the greatest thing for Art, since the Elgin Marbles.' Haydon's opinion of the Elgin Marbles adds a gloss to this handsome compliment: 'I felt . . . that they would overturn the false beau-ideal, where nature was nothing, and would establish the true beau-ideal, of which nature alone is the basis . . . I knew that they would at last rouse the art of Europe from its slumber in the darkness.'[35]

The extended critical reviews by Hugh Miller in 1843 and Elizabeth Rigby in 1846, both discuss the photographs in relation to painting. They were both calotyped a number of times by Hill and Adamson (pls 7 and 12), and presumably discussed the art with Hill as well as contributing towards it. They comment not simply on the resemblance but declare that the calotypes proved the truth of earlier painters. Elizabeth Rigby used the calotypes to conjure up a roll call of Netherlandish, Spanish and British painters in opposition to the German painters. She wrote:

> One standard, however, there does exist, and one from which there is no appeal, for it rests upon demonstration, and not upon opinion. This is to be found in that wonderful source recently discovered – the only sure test for those artists who, professing to reflect Nature in their works, can by Nature herself only be judged. We mean the beautiful and wonderful Calotype drawings – so precious in every real artist's sight, not only for their own matchless truth of Nature, but as the triumphant proof of all to be most revered as truth in art. Every painter, high or low, to whom Nature has ever revealed herself, here finds his justification. Let Mr Hill apply the Calotype instrument to a simple manly head in a commanding position, it creates a Sir Joshua, – give it an old face wrinkled with age, it returns us a Rembrandt, – summon three or four bare-legged urchins, we see Murillo's beggar boys, – place before it a group of Newhaven fishermen, we have Teniers' Dutch Boors, or Ostade's Village Alehouse, – or against a crumbling brick wall, and Peter Le Hooghe lies mezzotinted before us. Take it to tangled sylvan landscapes, it presents us with a Hobbima, a Gainsborough, or even, what we had not sufficiently prized before, a Constable – give it fretted spires and leafy banks, distant towns and glittering streams, playful shadows and struggling lights, sunny storms and watery beams – and give it lastly, the very motes dancing in the air before them all – and the detractors of Turner lick the dust – the loftiest eulogy of Mr. Ruskin is justified. Every truth that art and genius has yet succeeded in seizing here finds its prototype. Every painter, high or low, to whom Nature has ever revealed herself, here finds his justification.[36]

This idea excited both painters and sophisticated critics. The calotypes apparently endorsed the perceptions of great artists of the past who were true to nature. Hugh Miller wrote:

> one cannot avoid being struck by the silent but impressive eulogium which nature pronounces, through their agency, on the works of the more eminent masters . . . there is an eye of fresh observation required – that ability of continuous attention to surrounding phenomena which only superior men possess; and doubtless to this eye of fresh observation, this ability of continuous attention, the masters owed much of their truth and their power.[37]

Miller was particularly struck with a resemblance between the calotype portraits and mezzotints after Reynolds:

> We have a folio volume of engravings from his pictures before us; and when, placing side by side with the prints the sketches in brown, we remark the striking similarity of style that prevails between them, we feel more strongly than at perhaps any former period, that the friend of Johnson and of Burke must have been a consummate master of his art.[38]

He also commented on a similar resemblance to works by Raeburn:

> There is the same broad freedom of touch; no nice miniature stipplings, as if laid in by the point of a needle – no sharp-edged strokes; all, is solid, massy, broad; more distinct at a distance than when viewed near at hand. The arrangement of the lights and shadows seems rather the result of happy haste, in which half the effect was produced by design, half by accident, than of great labour and care; and yet how exquisitely true the general aspect! Every stroke tells, and serves, as in the portraits of Raeburn, to do more than relieve the features; it serves also to indicate the prevailing mood and predominant power to the mind.[39]

Haydon made a note of painters whose work he admired as models of breadth, in his diary in 1846:

> The artists of the world are divided into Touchers and Polishers. The Touchers – Michaelangelo, Raffaele in his cartoons, Titian, Bartolomeo, Giorgione, Tintoretto, Veronese, Rubens, Velasquez, David Teniers, Rembrandt, Reynolds, Wilson, Wilkie, Gainsborough, Vandyke, – are the great men who had discovered the optical principles of imitating nature to convey thought.[40]

This divides the world of painting into the experts in surface polish and the artists who could express thought through a greater generality of treatment. For Haydon, the immediacy of the 'touch', or rough sketch, connected to optical principles. His practical awareness of the lens derived from his own short-sightedness; he wore three pairs of glasses when painting, achieving four different focal lengths to his vision. He also used a mirror, to check on the progress of a painting for 'faults in balance and drawing.'[41] He was, therefore, aware of the intriguing shifts in focus and appearance that this assistance would give him. Such a practice may well have given him an interest in the camera image.

While it would be unreasonable to suppose that these comments make a direct connection between ideas of breadth and the use of the camera, Etty's slightly odd list of 'Rembrant, Titian and Spagnoletto' may indicate a commonly made connection; in one of the critical works of the previous century, *Essay on Painting*, published in English in 1764, Count Algarotti wrote admiringly of the camera, 'Everyone knows of what service it has been to Spagnoletto of Bologna, some of whose pictures have a grand and most wonderful effect.'[42] The fascinating and contentious subject of the camera's use, before the invention of photography, has been argued at length.[43] The art historical disputes it has generated are evidence of the difficulty of confirming even its straightforward practical application. This derives partly from an anxiety to protect the authority of the artist and the inspirational character of art. But it is presumably also, and far more interestingly, because the response of the painters is not obvious. David Hockney has recently championed the view that the use of optics, both mirrors and lenses, became widespread from the early fifteenth century. His own practical trials with the camera lucida are of particular interest in this context: 'I began to take more care with lighting the subject, noticing how a good light makes a big difference when using optics, just like with photography . . . optics need strong lighting, and strong lighting creates deep shadows.'[44]

Leonardo da Vinci, in his notes on optics, made the connection between the camera and painting. He wrote that the pictures made by light in a dark room, 'will actually seem painted on the paper.'[45] The painters needed to attain a vocabulary of nature, a simplified, intelligible currency. The camera was a tool in the pursuit of this knowledge, which was to grow in usefulness when eighteenth-century improvements in lens making enabled smaller, portable models.

Joshua Reynolds expressed a low opinion of the camera image, in discussing landscapes by Titian and Rubens: 'If we suppose a view of nature represented with all the truth of the *camera obscura,* and the same scene represented by a great artist, how little and mean will the one appear in comparison of the other, where no superiority is supposed from the choice of subject.'[46] It has been assumed from this comment, that Reynolds would not have used a camera obscura as an aid to painting, but he did own one.[47] There is an anecdote, told by the Duchess of Rutland, which suggests that Reynolds was ready to work with a mediated view of his sitters:

> I found a large canvas at one end of the room, and at the other a large looking-glass, and Sir Joshua placed me beside the canvas, so that we were both opposite the glass. I was surprised to see him go up to the glass and attentively look at my face in it. Then, with his back still towards me, he began carefully mixing some paint on his palette; and, after several trials, he turned round, rushed up to the canvas and began to paint at a great rate.[48]

The mirror doubled the distance between Reynolds and his subject, so he was seeing a surprisingly small image. He liked to work 'at the greatest possible distance' from the subject.[49] This, like the camera image, gave him a significantly reduced view. It also agrees with his advice to 'look at the object . . . with your eyelids half closed, which gives breadth to the object, and subdues all the little unimportant parts.'[50] His eyelashes would act as a blurring filter, reducing clarity and colour range, and the muscular contraction would change the length of the eye's focus. Presumably, Reynolds was long-sighted, but this means that he, like Haydon, was happy to see in different ways. Between his half-closed eyes and Haydon's glasses, there is an interest in optical variation, which recognised that individual vision could be assisted and changed. Such exploratory interest would have encompassed the camera image as a matter of course.

Extensive use of the camera, before the invention of photography, may be proposed especially in relation to the later eighteenth- and early nineteenth-century concentration on

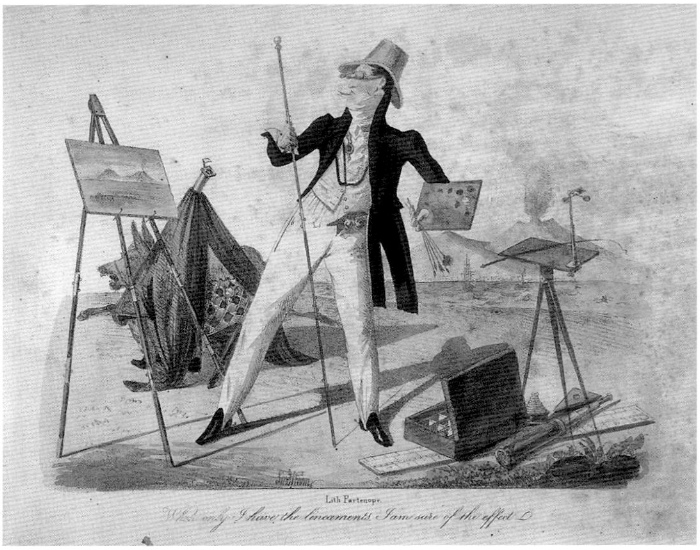

21. Carl Johan Lindstrom, The English (or British) painter – *'When only I have the lineaments, I am sure of the effect'*, *c.* 1830. Lithograph. Private collection.

nature. Presumably, sophisticated painters would have used it for observation rather than for copying. The difficulty of identifying this indirect and thoughtful use of the camera may well militate against the argument. The resistance to the idea is very reasonable, partly because the identification of paintings made with the camera depends on appearance, and even on this ground there are reasonable doubts. The familiar dispute over Canaletto's painting is fuelled by the apparent ease of judging his perspective, which is drawn from a planned city on level islands. However, a painter standing in St Mark's Square in Venice stands in a grand architectural demonstration of perspective; a place where the aid of a camera should be unnecessary. It may indeed be that the British obsession with optical equipment, caricatured by Carl Johan Lindstrom around 1830 (fig. 21), was prompted by the opposite conditions of the eccentric British landscape, exacerbated by local weather conditions.

It is comparatively easy to comprehend the use of the camera as a method of capturing architecture and the formalities of linear perspective. It is more difficult to examine the trickier and more subjective areas of light and atmosphere. This subtler use of the camera in painting may be defined in the terms Martin Kemp uses for his analysis of Vermeer's painting: 'His exquisitely refined grading of simple and compound shadows in response to different kinds of direct and diffuse illumination is obviously the result of many hours of purposeful looking.'[51] The camera image was not static; shadows, like people, move, and while it was practical to draw around a physical outline, the shifting play of light was elusive. In 1569, Daniele Barbaro described his improved camera, as offering the delight of 'clouds, the rippling of water, birds flying'.[52] The camera's glowing, moving image possessed a startling charm; even after viewing a dramatic reality, an audience could be seduced by the camera translation. In 1818 the geologist Charles Lyell described a visit to the Castle of Lauffen, from which visitors had a magnificent view of the Fall of the Rhine, which Lyell noted in one sentence. When they had seen the reality, they were shown a camera version, which he admired in greater detail: 'Afterwards, they darkened the room, and threw a beautiful landscape of the Fall on a white piece of canvas suspended from the ceiling. It was a complete picture, with the addition of motion. The water tumbling over, the clouds of foam, and the agitation of the water in the large basin below appeared beautiful on this flat surface.'[53]

Aids like the camera concentrated the mind: 'in the camera obscura, the visual faculty is brought wholly to bear upon the object before it.'[54] Its use called attention to the virtues and fascination of the incidental, which might correct the gloss of mannerism, imitation and familiar assumption. Peter Galassi has identified a particular movement in oil painting as 'pre-photographic'.[55] The paintings, which are generally small studies, may be defined as a search for nature in terms of controlled accident. One simple way of achieving this lay in the examination of an arbitrarily framed area of sight, the equivalent of a camera's framing but often just a view from a window. Thomas Jones's Italian sketches, taken from rooftops and windows in the 1780s, are a formidable case of the originality this might offer. In one description: 'They are gentle and precise and they illustrate nothing. They simply *are.*'[56] The camera could help to simplify visual experience in a similar manner. Moreover, if the reductive or focussing devices did no more, they would presumably have had the advantage of offering the painters a kind of unified vision – a comprehensible and common reduction or translation, which could be looked at, contemplated and discussed. That Charles Lyell should find a camera image thrown on canvas beautiful is not just a testament to the authority of canvas, it is a comment on a contemporary tool for understanding beauty.

In general, discussions of the relation between nature and art, which may have led to intelligent photography, have concentrated on landscape painting. Examining a person through the pre-photographic camera is not such an obvious idea, presumably because the portable camera contained only a small image – the reduction from reality makes more practical sense

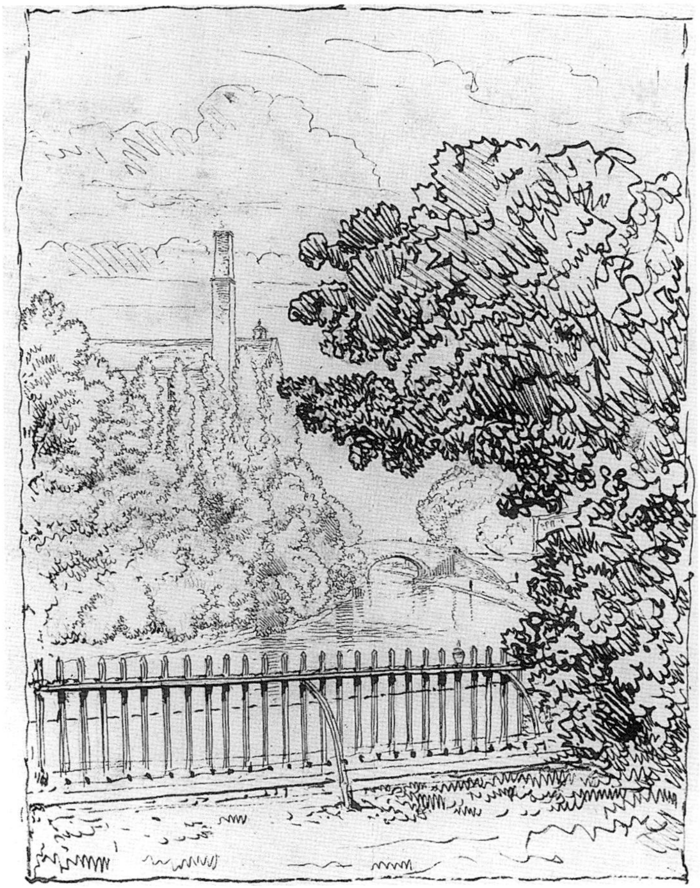

22. James Nasmyth, *View from the drawing room window…*, 13 June 1841. Ink drawing. National Library of Scotland, Edinburgh.

in landscape than in portrait painting, where the face would generally be life size. But Reynolds, who used physical reduction to examine simplification, also owned a camera, and Raeburn's familiarity with the camera image is likely. He was a friend of the landscape painter Alexander Nasmyth, who is known to have used the camera.[57] His son, James Nasmyth, demonstrated his own casual knowledge of the camera in 1841, by making one from 'an old tin box with a spectacle eye as the lens', and sketching the view from his drawing-room window (fig. 22). Raeburn is certainly known to have tried drawing with Francis Chantrey's camera lucida, in 1819.[58] Such familiarity is also suggested in a note made by the landscape painter Joseph Farington, in 1801:

> Some of Mr. Raeburn's portraits have an uncommonly true appearance of Nature and are painted with much firmness, – but there is great inequality in his works. – That which strikes the eye is a kind of Camera Obscura effect, and from those pictures which seem to be his best, I shd. conclude He has looked very much at Nature, reflected in the Camera.[59]

Farington owned and used a camera, so this is an informed comment.

Raeburn's paintings are often notable for their specific use of sunlight, angled from a particular direction and suggesting a particular time of day, even of year (fig. 23). However, in common with the generality of painters, Raeburn had a north-facing studio. His house in York Place in Edinburgh incorporated a tall room with a window so large that it is cut into the ceiling. He increased the light further by angling the

23. Sir Henry Raeburn, *William Forbes of Callander*, 1798. Oil on canvas. Collection of Captain W.F.E. Forbes, on loan to the Scottish National Portrait Gallery, Edinburgh.

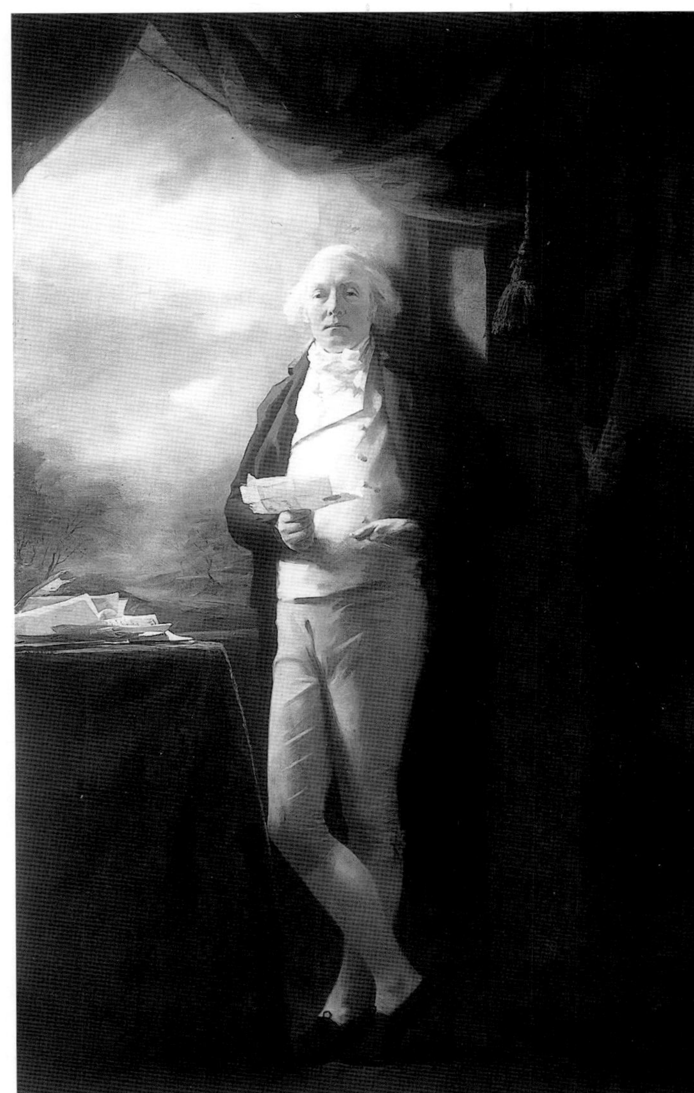

stone surround of the window, and controlled it with a set of shutters, which could block it out and give it a positive direction. By adding what he had observed of sunlight to what he could control of north light, Raeburn achieved the appearance of portraits painted in the rapid shift of the sun. There are no sketches which show Raeburn observing sunlight or its colours, so it may be that he observed without making physical notes: it may also be that he observed such effects through a camera.

The implications of such a study are not simple, but it may be proposed that a way of seeing optically, whether through glasses, mirrors or cameras, was familiar and interesting for many artists, from the Renaissance to the contemporaries of D. O. Hill. Its use may not be easy to identify, because the resemblance was designedly natural and the artists' visual knowledge would have enabled them to correct the camera's obvious distortions. However, the ready acceptance of the aesthetic of Hill and Adamson's calotypes amongst artists and critics, and Hill's almost immediate mastery of the calotype suggests that the camera may well have been a common component of sophisticated thinking and practice in art in his time.

THE HILL AND ADAMSON PARTNERSHIP
Practical Control of the Calotype

In the critical letters written to David Roberts in 1845, Hill established Robert Adamson's authority against hypothetical competition: 'Adamson says the manipulation is very liable to go wrong in the hands of most people – that tho' several have now and then produced a good specimen – they find it difficult to succeed often . . . in the common acceptation of the word it cannot be called secret – tho Adamson thinks he knows some things others do not.'[60] Under these circumstances, Adamson's professional reticence was an advantage, but neither man made it clear just what he was doing, and we can so far only assemble a few ideas of their technical or practical sophistication.

Hill refers to Adamson's steady industry. Robert and John Adamson had cracked the problem of the fickle reaction of the chemicals and paper so that Adamson's success rate was impressively consistent. He understood the difficult chemistry of the process and knew how to control it. This should not be underestimated as an achievement. Robert Hunt published an article in 1855, when Prince Albert had set up a committee to investigate the problem of photographic fading, in which he singled out Adamson's work for praise. In his opinion a properly prepared photograph would not fade. Hunt had exposed photographs:

> to the full influence of sunshine, and under the effects, at one period, of the humid and saline atmosphere of Plymouth and Falmouth, and subsequently to that of the metropolis, a similar set being preserved in portfolios. In some examples the pictures rapidly disappeared, in others they resisted all the influences of light and moisture for years . . . Some of Mr. Talbot's, of Mr. Owen's earliest works, of Hill and Adamson's pictures made in 1844, and a few others, however, now before me, have endured full exposure for many years, without any change in their original degrees of intensity.[61]

One key factor in the chemistry may have been very simple, if laborious. After Adamson's death, John Adamson taught the young Thomas Rodger, who set up as a photographer in St Andrews. In 1855, he and John sent examples of their work to an exhibition connected to a meeting of the British Association for the Advancement of Science in Glasgow. Rodger sent technical notes with his photographs, which include the comment, 'The washing process is for every picture at least 30 hours incessant change of water and in two of those changes the water is made hot'.[62] Rodger's prints from this period have a singular density and beauty of colour.[63] While he and John Adamson had moved on from the straightforward calotype, a similar extravagant and thorough washing out of impurities could explain the stability of Robert Adamson's work.[64] This phenomenal degree of washing would have tested the paper severely, but the paper used for the calotypes was also a concern of controlled and technical interest. Almost without exception, they used Whatman Turkey Mill, the watercolour paper favoured by Turner: a strong, consistent and well-made paper, with a heavy gelatine size for smoothness, combined with a slight nap or tooth, to give the small amount of friction which would facilitate the adhesion of ink, paint and photographic chemicals.[65] It was excellent paper and it had character.

When the Adamsons sent their first successful album of photographs to Talbot, in November 1842, the pictures were all small. They then acquired either one adaptable or two new cameras for Robert Adamson's calotype business in Edinburgh. This enabled them to take larger sizes of picture, roughly 5 × 4 inches and 8 × 6 ½. Between the initial contract of partnership in June 1843 and spring 1844, Hill and Adamson probably acquired a new portrait lens. This, which survives, has been defined as an 'unsymmetrical doublet lens, 17 inch focal length, maximum aperture f/10.'[66] Their equipment probably came from the Edinburgh optical instrument maker, Thomas Davidson.[67] David Brewster had recommended his cameras to Talbot and possibly also to Calvert Jones, who wrote, in May 1842, of a camera by Davidson, 'whose modifications are certainly improvements on Daguerre's system'.[68] Jones mentioned Davidson again in 1845, as supplying: 'capital lenses . . . which arrange themselves for all sizes of paper'.[69] Davidson gave an account of two projects involving his equipment in a letter, headed 'The Solar Camera', to the *Photographic Journal* in 1859:

> It is now more than sixteen years since I assisted Messrs. Adamson & Hill, photographers, Edinburgh, in taking a few copies of magnified representations of minute objects by an achromatic solar microscope, which I had made for Mr. Octavius David Hill, Calton Stairs, Edinburgh . . . The objects I adopted were transverse sections of wood, about 3⁄8″ in diameter. The enlarged copies were, so far as I recollect, about 18″ in diameter. The last time I saw the aforesaid magnified impressions, they were framed & hanging in James Bryson's shop, Princes Street, Edinburgh; & as regards patents, Mr Hill & Mr Adamson had arranged to lodge a *Caveat*, but the premature & lamented death of the latter prevented it.[70]

If Davidson's recollection is correct, this was done at the beginning of the partnership. From his reference to Hill, as the one he made this microscope for, it may be that he is looking at old account books.[71] Taking photographs through a solar microscope was not a new idea; Talbot had done it before he perfected the calotype, and it was demonstrated in Edinburgh by the instrument maker, John Dunn, in March 1839.[72] Davidson's letter was prompted by a discussion in the journal about 'Woodward's Solar Camera', which was able to make enlarged portraits. Davidson comments, 'it is by no means entitled to a patent', presumably because Hill and Adamson were working with a similar idea – precisely what it was is still obscure.

The question of enlargement was also addressed in the second part of Davidson's letter:

> Messrs Adamson and Hill . . . had also a camera, about two feet square, fitted up for taking portraits as large as life; but the imperfections in it, & difficulty of preparing paper so large, were against it. I also made a speculum of 24″ diameter & 30″ focus, for the aforesaid, for taking smaller portraits, or to reflect light on the object; but that was never much used.

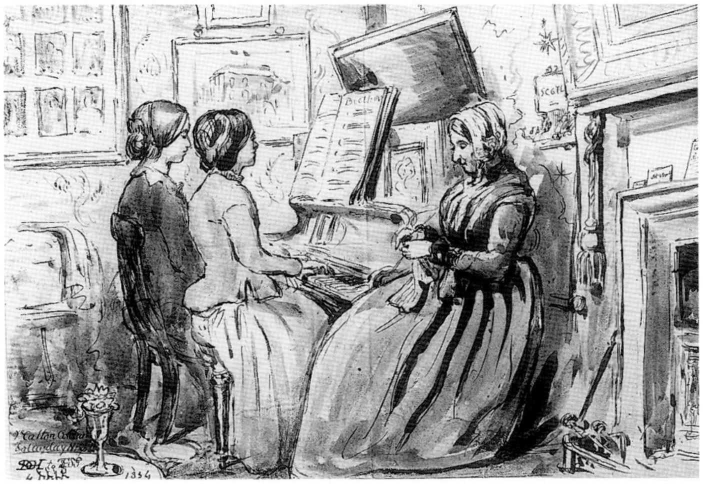

24. D. O. Hill, *The Interior of Rock House*, 1850s. Ink or wash drawing. Present whereabouts unknown, taken from a glass negative in the collection of the Glasgow University Special Collections.

Hill sent pictures, measuring up to 16 × 14 inches, taken with the big camera, to the new Photographic Society of Scotland in 1856. He wrote that they were made: 'when there were no other calotypes in existence a half of the same size. Considering the size – the period & that they were from an Edinburgh made camera – they may also possess an interest to a Scottish photographic society as enabling them to claim for Scotland an honorable priority in certain phases of the art.'[73] With the aid of the big camera, Hill and Adamson were intending to enlarge the scale of the photographs so that they could compete with the grand engravings, currently being published by Alexander Hill. Photographs could then be hung on walls alongside paintings, as they did in Rock House (fig. 24).

The mirror in the camera served two purposes. It had only one, thin silvered surface rather than the two surfaces and thickness of the lens. It was therefore less subject to imperfection and, importantly, would eliminate the potential colour distortion, which might imbalance the tones of the photograph. Moreover, the direct bounce of light should have taken faster exposures. The idea proved practical on a small scale with the Wolcott camera, patented in America, and Thomas Davidson had described a mirror camera of his own, at a meeting of the Royal Scottish Society of Arts on 11 January 1841.[74] There is some doubt whether Davidson's mirror could have been used to take photographs as large as the portraits and groups that Hill and Adamson achieved with this camera, which were approximately 12 × 10 inches, but a later daguerreotype camera, made in 1846 with a ten-inch mirror, is known to have been effective. The photographer who used it wrote: 'The reflector was very quick compared with achromatic lenses (I should say at least three times quicker in exposure), and the portraits so obtained were far more plucky [i.e. strong], had less of the objectionable metallic reflection, and consequently were more pleasing in appearance.'[75]

The potential speed of the mirror presumably indicates a search for more rapid exposure times: the few seconds, which would have justified both the risk of calotyping whole groups of restless children and the attempts at simulated action. Hill and Adamson calotyped groups of schoolboys with the big camera, with varied success (see chapter nine). Hill remarked, laconically, 'The big ones in so far as the figures were concerned did not turn out well – though the architecture was very wonderful.'[76]

How far Hill and Adamson directed and altered the physical nature and appearance of the calotypes by technical means is difficult to assess, partly because the partnership was so brief, being largely confined to the lighter months of the three-year period from mid-1843 to 1846, while their output was numerically large. Rapid development in their thinking may be proposed at the very beginning of the association, because there is a perceptible difference in depth of field and strength, both of detail and impact, between the first groups made for the Disruption picture and later work. A similar distinction may be seen between the first Newhaven photographs, which can be dated to 1843, and subsequent pictures. It is far from clear what they were doing technically, but it may be assumed that Hill as well as Adamson had a meticulous practical concern for the calotypes. This is reflected in his letter to John Scott of Colnaghi, who, he hoped, would assist in promoting the calotype albums. After detailing the binding, mounting, paper, lettering and layout of the album's title page, he apologised: 'Pray excuse all this minuteness on a subject you may consider very unworthy of it – although 'tis one on which I feel somewhat warmly. I would like they should appear in their best attire in taking up their residence with you.'[77]

THE HILL AND ADAMSON PARTNERSHIP
Aesthetic Practice

The calotype was a process severely subject to practical restrictions. This means that Hill and Adamson's practice worked with and against constraints in achieving an aesthetic. Difficulty could be exploited as an advantage. The strength of the portraits was admired by the twentieth-century sculptor, James Pittendrigh MacGillivray:

> [Hill] designed right up to the limit as a sculptor would do in designing and modelling a bas relief. He left no space to let, and he never seems to have relied on cutting or trimming for adjustment. The result, as compared with much in ordinary photography, is an obvious largeness of quality in the picture – such an effect as has caused Mr. Annan to remark that Hill must have possessed in a great measure the power of seeing grandly, and that his compositions are of the noble order.[78]

One of the most impressive portraits, appropriately of the sculptor John Steell (pl. 13), involves a reduction and loss of detail, which leaves his body as a dark, practically undefined shape, almost a silhouette. His right hand is sunk in his coat and only indicated by an edge of white cuff and wrist, which serves to mitigate the potential flatness of the body's shape. His head and other hand are supported on an off-centre and nearly featureless diagonal and the impact is strengthened by the elementary mottling of the background. The hand and one side of the face are strongly illuminated from the right, but the detail is filled in by a bounce of light from the left. This portrait is remarkable for its strength and simplification and could well serve as a model of Romantic practice in photography.

In 1853, when thinking of such a grand effect, the painter E. W. Dallas wrote admiringly of 'those broad masses of arranged and contrasted light and shade which, under proper management, indicate character sufficiently, and leave the imagination to fill up deficiencies'. He worked at the Royal Institution alongside Hill, and later became a professional photographer. He saw what the partnership had done and may have had some knowledge of their practice. But he suggested a technical way of achieving this effect: a lens designed to be defective:

> The perfection of a lens depends in part on the pure and homogenous nature of its material; if this be defective, the definition is affected to a greater or less extent; by using therefore a glass that is partially streaked, some of the sharpness of the image is destroyed, and the more delicate details are lost, but there may still be sufficient left for the purpose intended. It is of course to be understood that the working of the glass must be good, and also that, except the striae in it, the refractive power must be uniform. By taking advantage of this defect, a glass may be produced in which detail shall be obliterated to any extent, even to the entire destruction of the image, if that were required.[79]

The apparent perversity of this is balanced by the qualifying terms: 'the working of the glass must be good.' It seems likely that Hill employed more direct methods of achieving the same end. The comparatively insensitive lenses of the period gave a clear focus only in the centre, and rapidly fell off towards the edge. Most early photographers put the most important element, the sitter's head, at that centre. Hill realised that by moving the important components of the portrait – the head and hands – out towards that edge, he lost the focal point to the advantage of coherence and strength.

In early photography, the photographic focus was out of line with the real focus; the photographer needed to assess the difference and move the focus beyond what he could see through the camera. In the calotypes taken of the soldiers at the castle (pl. 14), Hill seems also to have exploited that eccentric and shallow focal plane, by taking most of a group out of line and out of focus to gain a sense of vigour. This kind of controlled interference may be characteristic of Hill and Adamson's practice. A friend of Hill's second wife, Mrs William Sharp, reported: 'I have been told that when the artist wished to produce a particular blurred effect, he would during the exposure give his camera an almost imperceptible jerk.'[80]

Manipulation of natural light is mentioned in Davidson's description of the concave mirror. Used as a reflector, it could either have been used out of focal range to give a diffused reflection, or in focus as a spotlight, which may have been tried for the nude torso of George Bell, where the focused light on his shoulder has apparently bleached out the detail (pl. 15). Occasionally, light is visibly reflected within the composition where it is appropriate, from primed canvas or open books. Presumably such devices were also used outside the visual frame. Essentially, the calotypes depended on sunlight. By fortunate chance, Scotland was unusually sunny in the 1840s, but that is a comparative assessment. Observation and a remarkable degree of patience must have been essential components of the work. Hill's interest in the accidents of atmosphere on Calton Hill (see chapter ten), may indicate a conscious exploitation and appreciation of the naturally diffused light which fell on Rock House. Robert Louis Stevenson described the view from the hill in 1879: 'on one of those days of sunshine and east wind which are so common in our more than temperate summer. The breeze comes off the sea . . . [bringing] with it a faint floating haze, a cunning decolouriser, although not thick enough to obscure outlines near at hand.'[81] The sunlight falling on the garden from the south was also filtered through the smoke rising from the crowded chimneys of the Old Town, which Hill specifically studied in his painting of *Edinburgh from the Castle* in 1846 (fig. 25). Such pollution would have caused the light to bounce and spread, reducing its hard-edged clarity and harshness. It would necessarily have involved some consideration, since on still days it might have hindered the work. Robert Hunt refers to the undoubtedly greater problems of smoke pollution in London: 'The conditions of the atmosphere most materially influence photographic effects: in the atmosphere of this metropolis it is not at all uncommon for a slight yellow haze to completely obstruct all chemical change.'[82]

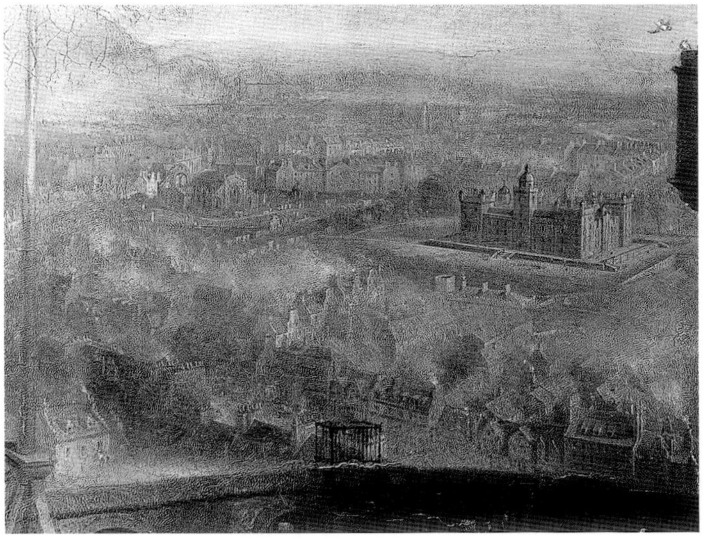

25. D. O. Hill, *Edinburgh from the Castle*, 1846–7 (detail). Oil on wood. National Gallery of Scotland, Edinburgh.

Hill and Adamson had astonishing confidence in their practice. They were prodigal in their experiments and they introduced risks. The calotypes involved not just studied control but patience and adaptability, working from an appreciation of accident. The control of shifts in focus and contrast enabled a subjective response to the character of the subject. They were able and prepared to invent a truthful appearance beyond the mechanical capacity of the medium. This point may be illustrated by examples of landscape photography, which was dominated by two practical problems. Firstly, early photographic chemicals responded differently to different colours; they were slow to react to the green of trees and grass. Secondly, the calotype could not effectively transcribe the delicacy of aerial perspective and atmosphere, without conscious construction (see chapter ten). It is therefore surprising that Elizabeth Rigby praised the calotype for a lively transcription of sunlight. It may well be that Hill was here working from the graphic model, with the same restrictions of monochrome and with the light represented by the paper vehicle, of Turner's *Liber Studiorum* and possibly also David Lucas's mezzotints after Constable.[83] Such a study may even be hinted at in Elizabeth Rigby's new, photographic appreciation of Constable's work: 'Take it to tangled sylvan landscapes, it presents us with a Hobbima, a Gainsborough, or even, what we had not sufficiently prized before, a Constable'. The prints were constructed with a comparatively arbitrary relationship between light and form, which might be used in the calotype to mitigate the strong opposition between the insensitive green of the leaves and the brightness of the light, as well as to explore distortions set up between the two.

One of the engravings for *The Land of Burns* shows Hill exploring the way an oblique or low light may illuminate and shape a landscape unexpectedly, through the obstruction and admission of the sun along paths the eye cannot necessarily see. *Craigieburn Wood* (fig. 26) adopts a low standpoint, where the sun, falling on the house, trees and water, makes a circle of light in the landscape. The glinting path of the water invites us in, and the light leads us up. A similar idea is explored in a large negative, taken in the grounds of Merchiston Castle (fig. 27). The picture is roughly blocked out in opposed light and dark; the downward curve of the wall joins with the upward curve of the tree branch to suggest a circle in the trees above, which is balanced by the circle made within the doorway with the help of the light on the figures and the tail of light running along the path. The composition is unified by blurring and spatial ambiguity. *The Fairy Tree at Colinton* (pl. 16) uses the same idea of constructing a picture with light. The tree, which may just be a dead branch with a few tendrils of ivy, is defined in an almost flat transcript of dark, thinly outlined in light. The background is merely a graded tonality splattered with spots of unreadable light, which could be a bounce from leaves or even from water. These are pictures, which are not merely made with light but which have a central concern for light, largely independent of the tangible reality of the subject.

Presumably, Hill's enthusiasm for the spontaneity and realism of the calotypes meant that he was prepared to lose ideas in technical failure; the negative of Merchiston Castle grounds was not printed. Other unprinted negatives, like the extraordinary image of the boys standing on boulders taken for the *Fishermen and Women* series (pl. 17), illustrate the point; the experiment was not repeated. These pictures were designed to explore accident. Hill seems to have taken an active interest in the idea, and may have deliberately assembled visual information with no certain result but with the aim of achieving natural understanding beyond calculated intention. He had an interest in the calotype for its particular, truthful nature. He was fascinated by 'the very life of it', and was concerned with its independent character. But there is a caveat here. The territory between conscious intention and accident is not clearly mapped out. It may reasonably be supposed that Hill and Adamson, faced with the uncertainties of natural light, movement and chemistry, took a number of experimental photographs, without knowing clearly how they might look, and would have regarded the results as educational: something they could consider and build on. But even the conscious experiments are partially concealed by the method. Where two calotypes are equal in finish, it may not

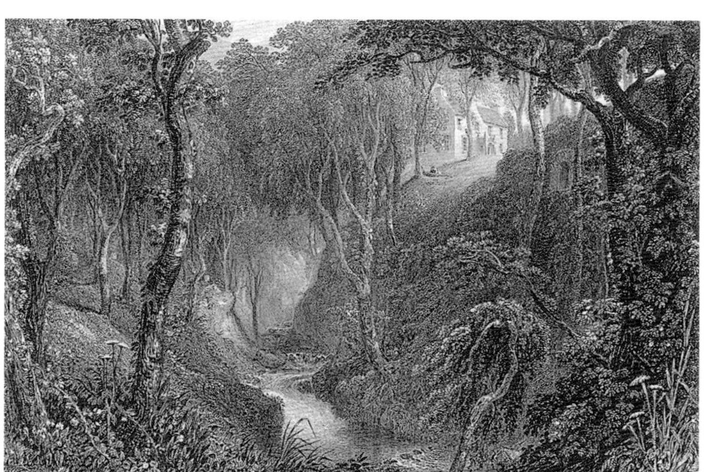

26. William Forrest after D. O. Hill, *Craigieburn Wood*, *c.* 1840. Steel engraving, from *The Land of Burns*, 1840.

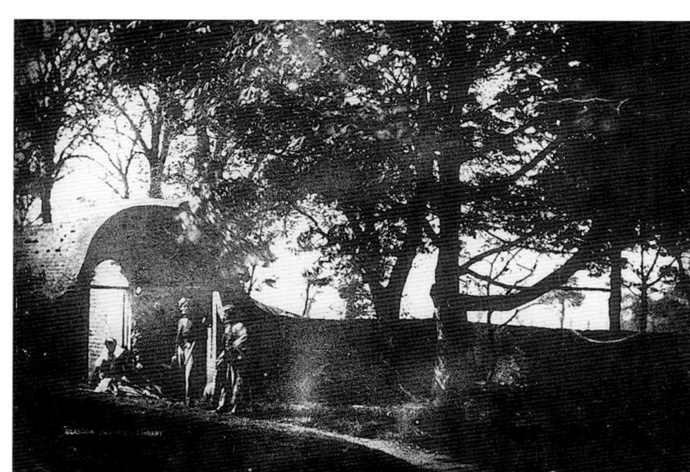

27. D. O. Hill and Robert Adamson, *Grounds of Merchiston Castle School*, 1844. Print from a calotype negative. Glasgow University, Special Collections.

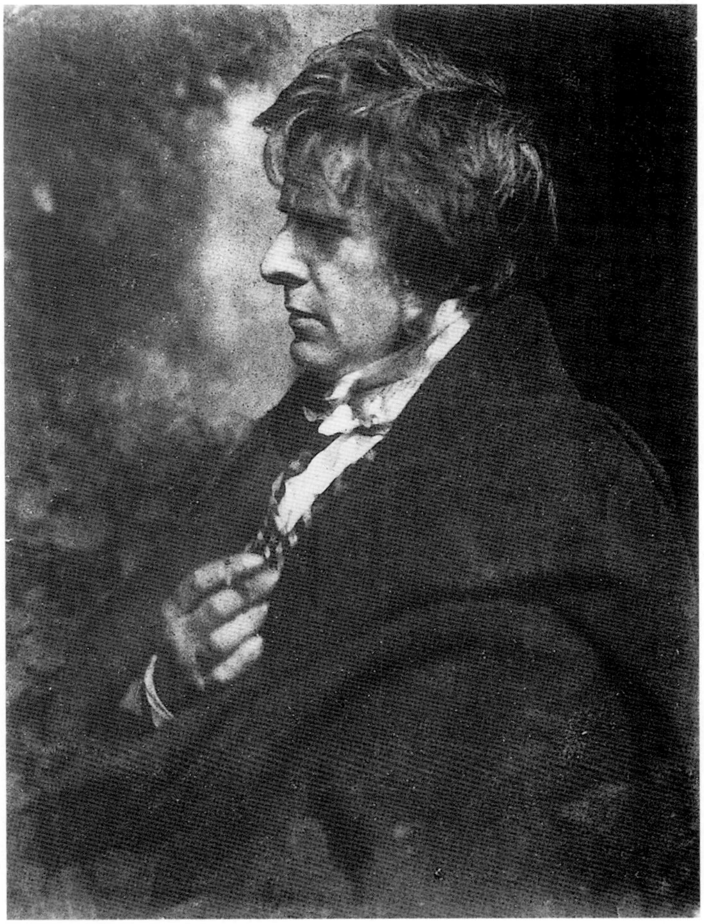

28. D. O. Hill and Robert Adamson, *David Octavius Hill*, 1843–7. Calotype. Scottish National Photography Collection, Edinburgh.

be obvious that one is a trial for the other. Hill appears in many of the calotypes, using himself as a model, to think through an effect or composition. The photograph of Hill draped in a blanket (fig. 28), which is the first plate in Heinrich Schwarz's monograph, is one of two studies for calotypes of the writer and artist in stained glass, James Ballantyne. A calotype of Ballantyne in his own tight jacket and cravat had proved unimpressive (fig. 29), and Hill is looking at the classic design used in the sculpted bust. By examining the pose, the lighting and the background of his self-portraits, he was able to construct a far stronger portrait of Ballantyne (fig. 30).

The intelligent connection between the photographer and the photograph is not severed by the act of photography. Moreover, photography is an inherently multiple art, where a sequence may reflect either in a linear fashion or in a more complex active and re-active group. Hill's use of this elaborate and elaborating idea is evident in the *Fishermen and Women of the Firth of Forth*, which attempts the illumination of a whole society. Calotypes, like *Elizabeth Johnstone Hall* (pl. 1), stand well by themselves but will also gain and give in the company of other pictures. Individual pictures may change character and meaning in the context of other pictures. This extraordinary proposal may be a part of the supposedly casual or unconsidered role of photography – that the medium encourages both additional and speculative picture making and subsequent creative reflection between individual pictures.

The interest of accident may be tied to another and opposite idea: that of difficulty. John Adamson's criticism of the calotype process in 1857 bears an echo of Brewster's earlier complaint, but the emphasis is different:

29. D. O. Hill and Robert Adamson, *James Ballantyne*, 1843–7. Calotype. Scottish National Photography Collection, Edinburgh.

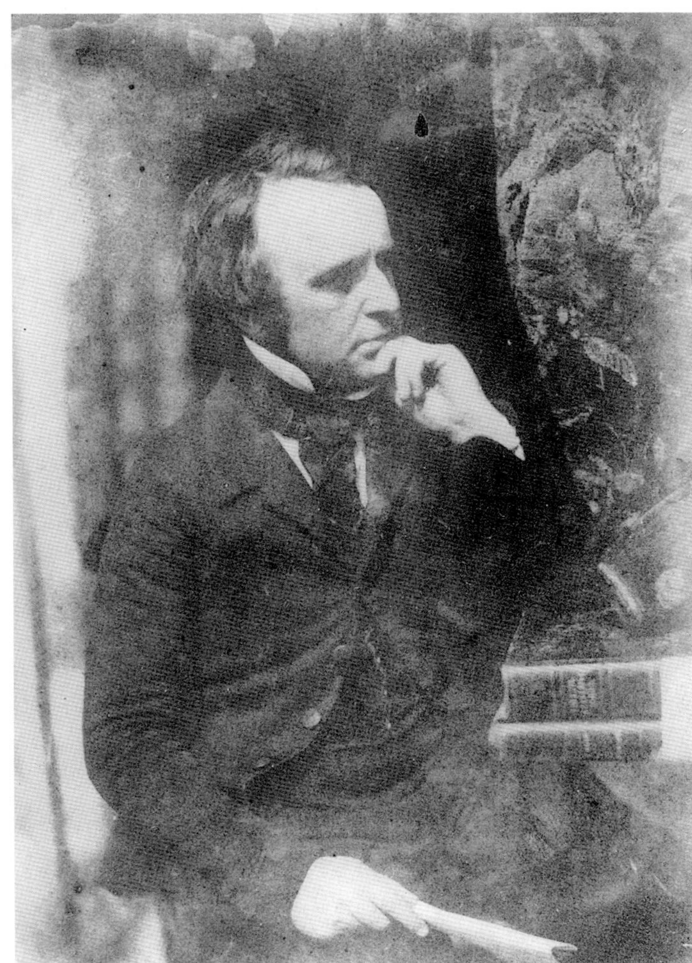

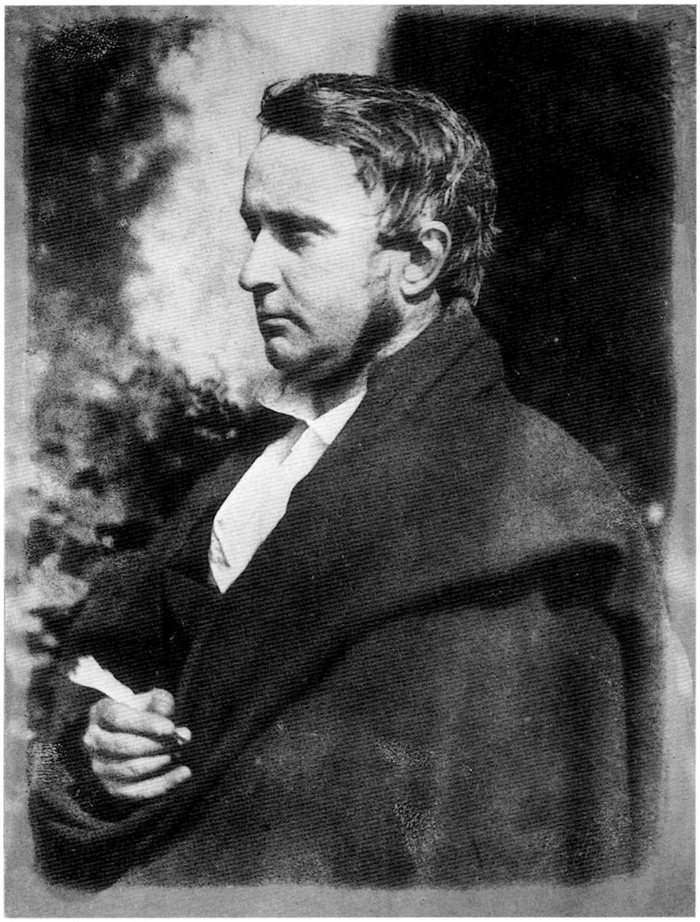

30. D. O. Hill and Robert Adamson, *James Ballantyne*, 1843–7. Calotype. Scottish National Photography Collection, Edinburgh.

> The pictures produced by this process are very artistic and bold in effect, and give fine results for some kinds of landscape and architectural objects; and although excellent results may be obtained in portraiture – as, for example, those produced by the late Mr R. Adamson and Mr D. O. Hill of Edinburgh – yet the amount of light which is necessary to produce the required change is too great to render it very applicable for this purpose.[84]

The concept of difficulty, which Hill briefly mentions in his letter to David Roberts, is important. As will be discussed in chapter five, art could only be achieved through struggle – skill and understanding would be honed against difficulty. Hill did not see photography as an easy performance. He nevertheless used it for large range exercises, such as the *Fishermen and Women* project, which in themselves complicated the work and compounded the risk of failure. Looked at in business terms, the calotype partnership probably was a failure. We can, however, only treat this as a matter of ironical importance in view of the manifest success of the individual calotypes.

Hill made his proposal for the album of a hundred calotypes when he was reading Ruskin's *Modern Painters*. It may be assumed that he was also fired by Ruskin's declaration: 'The teaching of nature is as varied and infinite as it is constant; and the duty of the painter is to watch for every one of her lessons . . . to repeat himself, even in a single instance, is treachery to nature . . . Both [the artist and the preacher] are commentators on infinity.'[85] The calotypes are remarkable for their variation, often dependent on simple shifts in focus and composition. The portraits of James Ballantyne (fig. 30) and Mrs Rigby (pl. 18) are both taken in profile against a counterchange of background light, but they are distinct. The portrait of Ballantyne is solidly composed with a comparatively strong contrast of dark and light in the background. The picture of Mrs Rigby is far subtler, constructed with a kinder light and contrast against a background whose dark is broken up by the pattern of ivy. The two portraits reflect their personal role and public character. Ballantyne was the active, middle aged, creative man and Mrs Rigby, in her daughter's words, is presented as a model of gracious age: 'Think of the moral charm exercised by such a face and figure over the circle where it belongs – the hallowing influence of one who, having performed all her active part in this world, now takes a passive, but a nobler one than any, and shows us how to grow old.'[86]

In a draft of a letter to Lady Ruthven, herself an expert on art, Hill briefly expressed the importance of surrounding and background effects. He was consciously constructing with simple components:

> The group of two young ladies were those you saw here & shows that the art can do something approaching the beautiful; the single portrait (a niece of mine) I send to show what might be done with backgrounds of flowers &c. The Harper, whose costume is made of a blanket and plaid shows how simply one might get up pictures of the old world. I think you will like the sleeping child, which is one of my own greatest favourites.[87]

The sophistication and variation made from that simplicity is impressive. Backgrounds are used for framing, counterchange and relief. Drapery may distract and lead the eye. The careful arrangement even of the fall of material may be seen in the group with the Misses Farnie and the sleeping puppy (pl. 19), which has been set down between the feathered patterns – a care all the more striking in an image that would have invited haste. The practical/sympathetic balance of Hill's organisation may be seen in the puppy itself. The children may be feigning sleep, but the dog cannot be. Presumably, Hill was aware of the opposite patterns of excess energy and profound sleep that are natural to young animals, and very probably he set the children to play with the puppy while he and Adamson waited by the camera. When the dog fell asleep, it seems to have been impervious to movement and apparently allowed itself to be arranged in two poses for different pictures. Patience and care were critical.

Looking at the calotypes taken by D. O. Hill and Robert Adamson, we are faced with a historical dilemma. The work has an excellence, which is highlighted because it stands at the beginning of photography and it is possible that even Hill did not immediately appreciate the skill that he and Adamson deployed in the work. Hill's second letter to Roberts in 1845 about the album continues enthusiastically, but expresses anxiety:

> I have sunk some hundreds of pounds and a huge cantle [part] of my time in these Calotype freaks. I think the art may be nobly applied – much money could be made of it as a means of cheap likeness making – but this my soul loathes; and if I do not succeed in doing something by it worthy of being mentioned by Artists with honor – I will very likely soon have done with it.[88]

It was possibly only in the 1850s and 1860s that Hill could gain a clear idea, by comparison with later photography, of the status of his own work. In the prospectus for the Disruption picture, fourteen years later, he is altogether more buoyant:

> the Portraits made chiefly for the Picture, in 1843 by Mr Hill and his late friend, Mr Robert Adamson of St Andrews, by the then newly-discovered Photographic Process of Mr Fox Talbot, called the Calotype or Talbotype, – until then almost unknown or unapplied as a vehicle of artistic thought and expression, – were mainly the means of first raising the process to the rank of a Fine Art, or rather to that of one of its most magical and potent auxiliaries.[89]

This was written at a period when most painters were denying the connection between their pictures and photography. It is important to realise what Hill was doing here. He has changed the vocabulary from 'art', which was equivalent to our 'craft', to 'Fine Art'. The qualification follows, but this was not a conversation, it was in print. Hill wrote it, and he meant it: the qualification was a mild sop to the many who would disagree with him. It is a most remarkable claim, especially in the context of his large and laborious painting, and suggests that Hill's affections were more tied to the photographs than to the picture.

Hill and Adamson were both reticent about the mechanics of their art, and the technical and practical methods they used to achieve their notable results can still only be suggested rather than clearly defined. However, the reaction of later photographers – their whole-hearted admiration – may be regarded as a reflection of their calculated excellence, and the impact of their work is a matter of considerable significance to the subsequent history of photography.

'ON THE FIRST FLOOR'

Hill's role in photography did not end with the demise of the partnership. The most impressive nineteenth-century photographic work in Scotland, both amateur and professional, had a respect for Hill and Adamson's work, which was reinforced by Hill's continuing enthusiasm. It is by no means clear how many photographers Hill knew and inspired directly, but the probability is that his personal influence was considerable. Hill set up one further public association with a photographer, Alexander MacGlashan, around 1860. This may only have lasted a few days and only involved taking around twenty photographs. Although Hill succeeding in clearing the clutter of MacGlashan's normal studio practice and apparently carried him off to Rock House to work in the garden, the pictures do not achieve the coherence of the earlier work (fig. 19). Hill's largely unexplored relationship with other photographers is more significant.

He remarked, when setting up a photographic library in the Scottish Academy, 'I think I have influence enough with not a few of the Calotypists to get copies of their best', and it is a tribute to Hill's grace that Ross and Thomson were amongst the contributors to that collection.[90]

After Robert Adamson's death, Hill maintained a connection with John Adamson, who photographed both Hill and his daughter, Charlotte, in the mid-1850s and in the 1860s (fig. 31). It seems reasonable to hear Hill's concern in John Adamson's letter to the Photographic Society of Scotland, sent with his photographs for the exhibition:

> I wish very much that the large heads should be exhibited to advantage as I entertain a hope that they may in some small degree help to turn the public taste from the small 'carte de visite' pictures so fashionable at present and in which I think the photographic art has been progressing

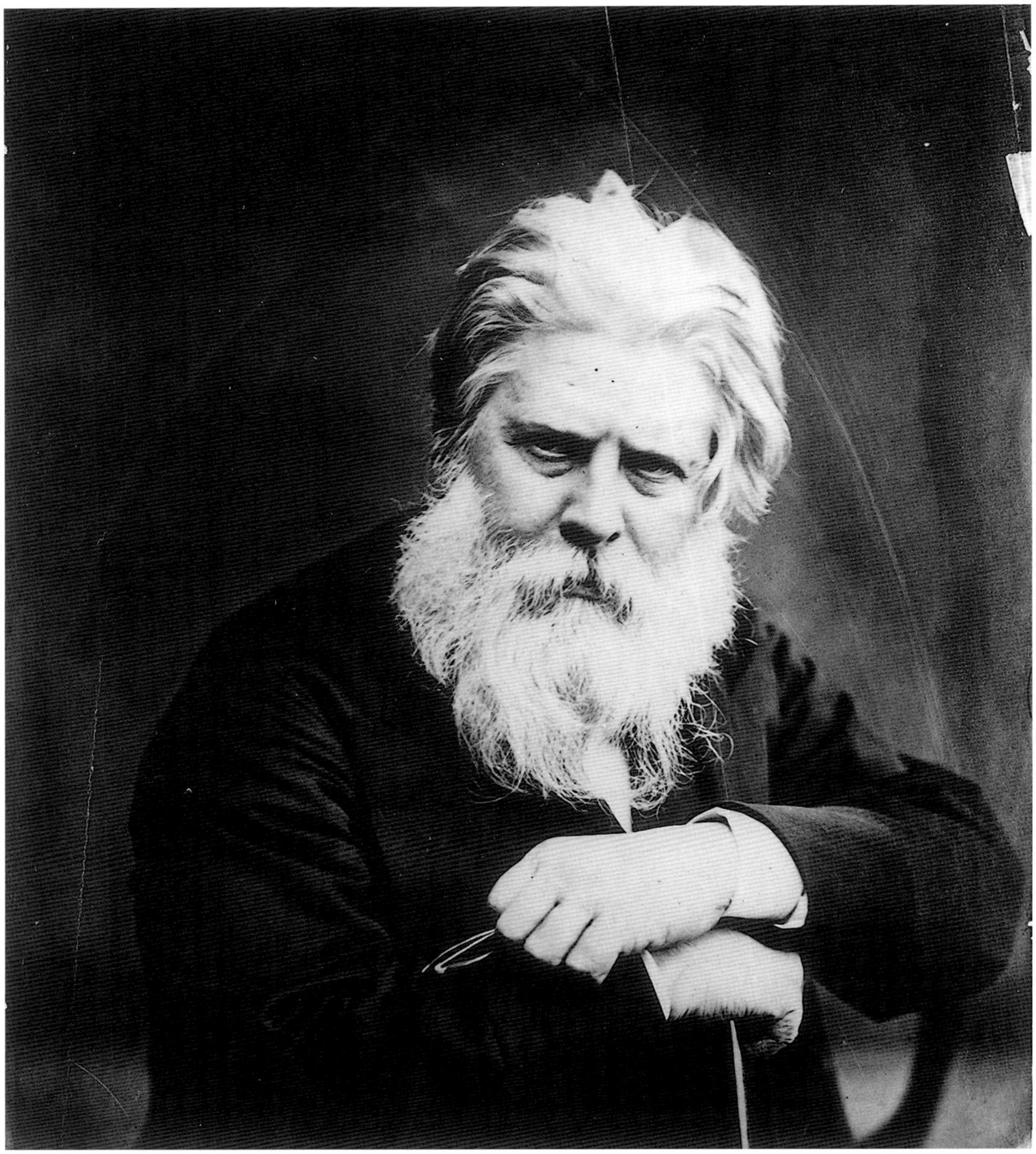

31. John Adamson, *David Octavius Hill*, *c.* 1860. Albumen print. National Museums of Scotland, Edinburgh.

backwards – to portraits of a larger size – and a more ambitious aim in the direction of the painters field of operation.[91]

John Adamson's work developed a power and personality of its own, making him an individual and distinctive portrait photographer. He drew from his sitters a warm response, comparable to Hill and Adamson's portraits, and his strong sense of composition has a similar familiarity.[92]

Whilst Thomas Rodger, encouraged by John Adamson and living in St Andrews, is the natural professional heir of Robert Adamson, the Glasgow photographer, Thomas Annan is a direct inheritor of the Hill/Adamson partnership through Hill (fig. 32). They may have met as early as the 1840s; the Annan family knew Robert Adamson, and were distressed by his death. It is possibly a significant coincidence that Thomas Annan took up a career as a lithographer in 1845, which could have been suggested by an acquaintance with Hill as well as Adamson, and that he became a photographer in 1855 a little ahead of the great popular boom in the art. We know from the record that Hill worked with Thomas Annan to reproduce the Disruption picture in carbon prints

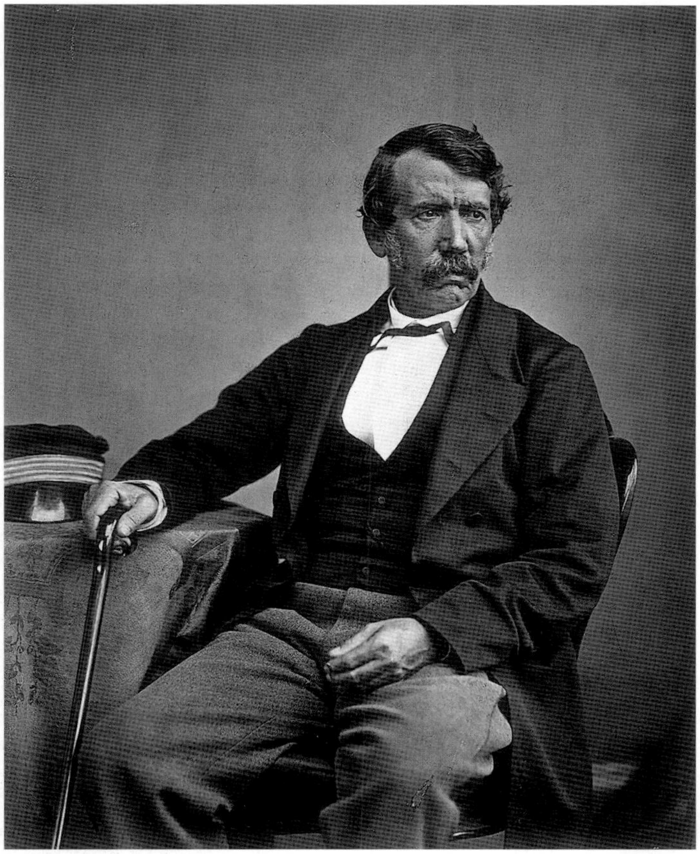

32. Thomas Annan, *David Livingstone*, 1864. Carbon print. Scottish National Photography Collection, Edinburgh.

in the 1860s, and that Annan occupied the Rock House studio for a year in 1869, when Hill retired. His son, J. Craig Annan, recalled that he had 'an intense admiration and appreciation of Hill as a man and as an artist. They were intimate friends'.[93] The younger Annan, who met Hill when he was only six, could remember: 'He gave me a pencil and a sheet of paper and arranged a model while he sat talking to my father'. Later in the century, he and his father printed from the calotype negatives, making new work in the permanent media of carbon and photogravure (pl. 5), which was a translation rather than an imitation of the calotype work.

Through the affectionate agency of the Annans, the enthusiasm for Hill and Adamson's work was transferred to the photographers of their time, especially the international Pictorialist movement, around the turn of the century, which was devoted to promoting photography as an art form. J. Craig Annan's critical writing and his photogravure versions of the calotypes transmitted that excitement to America, particularly through the agency of Alfred Stieglitz and his publication, *Camera Work*, which published twenty-one of their pictures between 1905 and 1912. The calotypes were generously received by the Modernists in turn. In America alone, such influential figures as Stieglitz, Paul Strand and Ansel Adams greeted the work with unequivocal admiration. Alfred Stieglitz wrote for *Camera Work*: 'Hill and Cameron are classics. What they did has not been equaled, in spite of gumming and manipulation and all the modern tricks. They were photographers.'[94] Paul Strand advised Beaumont Newhall, when he was creating his influential exhibition on the history of photography for the Museum of Modern Art, New York, in 1940, on the use of the four floors of the exhibition: 'The first floor should be all David Octavius Hill. The second floor should be Eugene Atget. Give the third floor completely to Alfred Stieglitz. And on the fourth floor you should have Strand.'[95] While not accepting Strand's advice, Beaumont Newhall, wrote of the calotypes' 'astounding modernity of feeling'.[96] Alvin Langdon Coburn, like the Annans, printed in carbon from Hill and Adamson's work and paid conscious tribute to the calotypes in his photographs for Robert Louis

33. Alvin Langdon Coburn, *Under Dark Arches, Edinburgh*, *c.* 1905. Photogravure, from Robert Louis Stevenson's *Edinburgh, Picturesque Notes.*

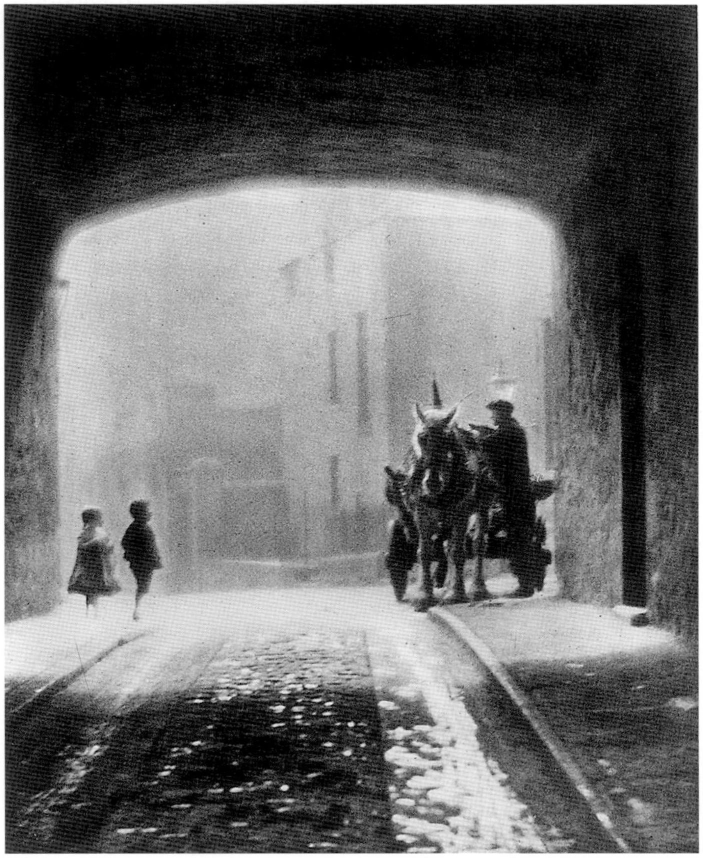

Stevenson's *Edinburgh, Picturesque Notes* (fig. 33). He identified the pleasure in the calotype work: 'Gradually he [Hill] became interested in photography for its own sake, and made a number of landscapes and figure studies for the sheer joy of so doing'.[97] Ansel Adams was even more fluent:

> Were the shade of David Octavius Hill, the great Scottish pioneer of photography, to visit our world and discuss the present aspects of the art and craft of the camera with ghostly objectivity, we could attend the oracle with reasonable devotion . . . a jewel was formed in the matrix of the early nineteenth century, indigenous to its period and sincere in the purity of its presentation. David Octavius Hill succeeded both in making remarkable photographs and in demonstrating one of the basic principles of art: complete expression within the limitations of the medium.[98]

The comments made by these leading authoritative practitioners emphasise the active impact that Hill and Adamson's work had, not just in its own time, but in the twentieth century. Despite the exaggeration of Strand's four-floor history of photography, they have a legitimate claim to have established the ground in the art of photography. In the light-filled months of the years between 1843 and 1847, they generated a 'magical and potent' art.

4

D. O. Hill and Edinburgh Society

I The Sociable City

In the first half of the nineteenth century Edinburgh, by contrast to the far larger city of London, was still a coherently sociable society. Hill's own connections and friendships with a broad range of people, are characteristic of that world. While a man with the status and nature of Sir David Brewster might be regarded as a catalyst of others' action, Hill was, by contrast, a pivot. His central position in the society of Edinburgh, both professionally as the secretary of the Scottish Academy and personally as a man of great amiability, offers the key to the success of the calotype portraits. People constantly referred to him and strangers were directed to him, with the confidence that he would give them a hospitable welcome. This gave Hill access to an extraordinary range of people, and later enabled him to define the practice of the calotype work; the photographs are largely of people of significance to Hill and those who felt positive affection for him.

Around the time Hill arrived in Edinburgh in the 1820s, the eccentricity of the town was described from the London perspective by Benjamin Robert Haydon. He wrote:

> Their hospitality and heartiness were indisputable. Their knowledge and literature were eminent, but their simplicity was the most striking. The greater part of the middle classes believed London was a great, overgrown beast of a city, not to be compared to Edinburgh in point of intelligence, but owing its rank entirely to the accident of its being the seat of government, and not to its enterprise, its skill, its capital or its genius . . . The season in Edinburgh is the severest part of the winter. Princes Street in a clear sunset with the Castle and the Pentland Hills in radiant glory, and the crowd illumined by the setting sun, was a sight perfectly original.
>
> First you would see limping Sir Walter [Scott], talking as he walked with Lord Meadowbank; then tripped [Francis] Jeffrey, keen, restless, and fidgety; you next met [John] Wilson or [John Gibson] Lockhart, or [William] Allan, or [George] Thompson, or [Henry] Raeburn, as if all had agreed to make their appearance at once. It was a striking scene, – foreigners were impressed like myself.[1]

This was a world Hill knew, and the description implies that he was at least familiar with the 'great men' of his day, even as a young man, simply because much of the city's social life took place in public (fig. 34). At this point Edinburgh seems to have had an accessible, outdoor society – common to women as well as men. The mathematician Mary Somerville remarked on the difference between the Edinburgh of her youth and later years: 'Girls had perfect liberty at that time in Edinburgh . . . We walked together in Princes Street, the fashionable promenade, and were joined by our dancing partners. We occasionally gave little supper parties and presented these young men to our parents as they came in.'[2] The judge, Henry, Lord Cockburn, who was associated with Hill in the academy's legal disputes, makes the further surprising point about domesticity in his time that supper was a constantly sociable occasion:

> Almost all my set, which is perhaps the merriest, the most intellectual, and not the most severely abstemious in Edinburgh, are addicted to it. I doubt if from the year 1811, when I married, I have closed above one day in the month, of my town life, at home and alone. It is always some scene of domestic conviviality, either in my own house or in a friend's. And this is the habit of all my best friends.[3]

This general movement involved social meetings in private houses, inns and hotels. One of the focal points was the

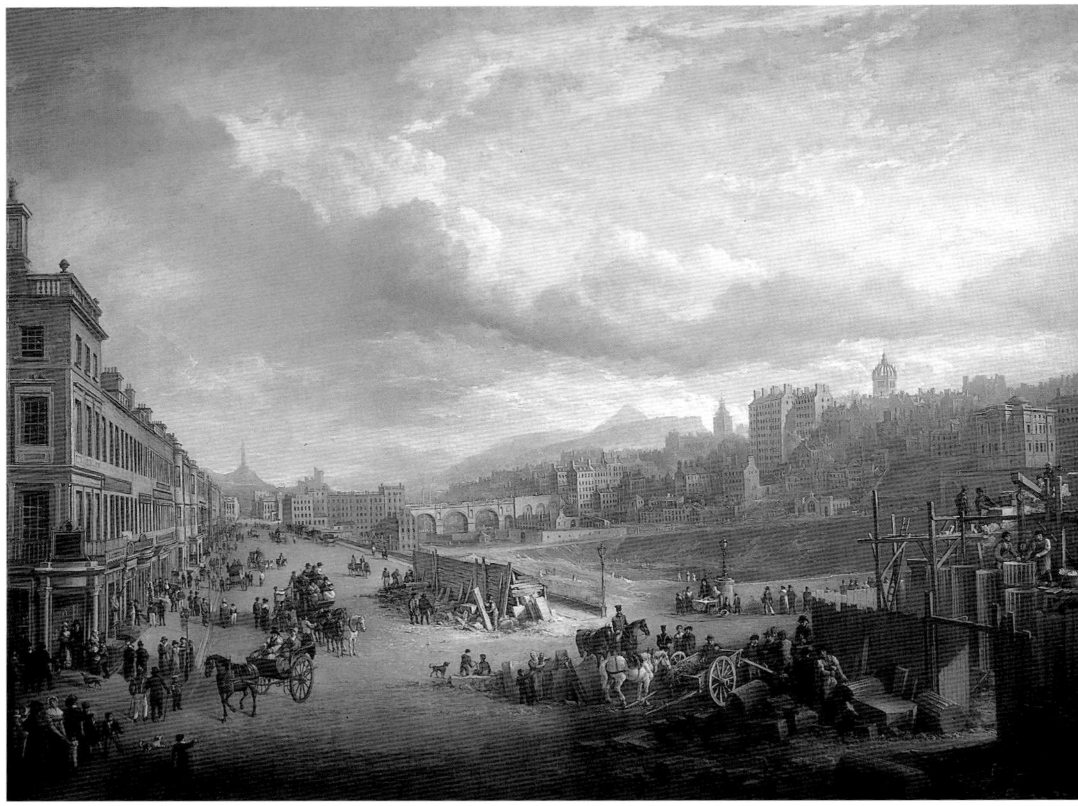

34. Alexander Nasmyth, *Princes Street with the Commencement of the Building of the Royal Institution in 1825*. Oil on canvas. National Gallery of Scotland, Edinburgh.

household of Alexander Nasmyth, in York Place to the north of Princes Street. At the beginning of the century, his house was the gathering place of a wide intellectual group – Mary Somerville was a pupil of his at this time. His son, James Nasmyth, gave an account:

> When the day's work was over, friends looked in to have a fireside crack – sometimes scientific men, sometimes artists, often both . . . There was no formality about their visits . . . Among the most agreeable visitors were Professor [John] Leslie, James Jardine, C.E., and Dr Brewster . . . They brought up the last new thing in science, in discovery, in history, or in campaigning, for the war was then raging through Europe.
>
> The artists were a most welcome addition to the family group. Many a time did they set the table in a roar with their quaint and droll delineations of character. These unostentatious gatherings of friends about our fireside were a delightful social institution . . . I fear they have disappeared in the more showy and costly tastes that have sprung up in the progress of what is called 'modern society'[4]

Hill came into contact with the Nasmyth household in the 1820s (fig. 35). He was a contemporary of the young James, who wrote of him: '"D. O. Hill", as he was generally called, was much attached to my father. He was a very frequent visitor at our Edinburgh fireside, and was ever ready to join in our extemporised walks and jaunts, when he would overflow

35. D. O. Hill, *The Nasmyth Family*, 1829. Ink and wash drawing on paper. Scottish National Portrait Gallery, Edinburgh.

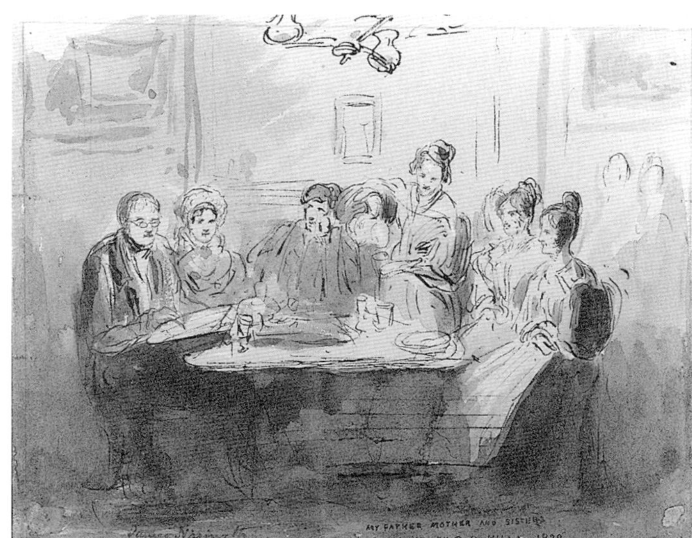

with his kindly sympathy and humour.'[5] Hill's active recollection of the family is reflected in a letter from James Nasmyth in 1845: 'your calotype description of the joys at 47 York Place as of old is beyond all laudation. It made us all live over again many happy joys gone by, in those days. What a pity it is that as time rolls on those who gave character and worth to such times melt away one by one from the picture of living life.'[6]

Between the beginning and the middle of the century, the population of Edinburgh more than doubled, while the population of Glasgow quadrupled.[7] This may in itself have encouraged a shift in behaviour from an open and public world to a more private one. But Hill at least continued this kind of open welcome. In 1836, he entertained the travelling bibliographer, Thomas Dibdin, whom he had met by chance in the west of Scotland while sketching for *The Land of Burns.* Dibdin was well pleased with his reception: 'It was at the breakfast-table of Mr Hill, in London-Street, that I once sat down in the society of very many of the choice artists of Edinburgh. It was a joyous morning and an abundant breakfast.'[8]

In the biographical note on Hill published in the *Art Journal* in 1850, this point is made more broadly: 'His quiet and unassuming residence on the Calton Hill is visited by the best men of the day with pleasure, and left by them with regret.'[9] His obituary added: 'As a friend and companion he will ever be remembered by those who knew him as one possessed of admirable talents for promoting the happiness of the society in which he moved.'[10] This sociability was highly relevant to the success of the calotype partnership in another way. Adamson's professional reticence, coupled with the fact that Hill himself says so little in writing about photography, suggests an isolated and introspective practice. This was far from true. The generally introspective art of photography was, at its inception, a matter of such intelligent fascination that it was surrounded by discussion and experiment; Hill drew at least thirty-four artists to the studio to be calotyped along with an impressive number of critical writers. It is more than probable that they talked, analysed and proposed during the sessions. What Hill and Adamson held in their control was potentially not just a sociable art form but one of communal and active interest. At the heart of this and entwined with it, lay Hill's private life and affections.

CHILDREN AND THE BALANCE OF HUMOUR

In the times he lived through, which were thoroughly exciting in many areas of change and equally distressing in others, Hill maintained his balance most clearly through humour. It was an essential element in his sociability, in generating and maintaining a sympathetic and open response. From his letters, it would appear to be substantially true, as his obituary says, that he combined: 'kindness, wit, and humour, with an innate modesty and propriety which never allowed him to say anything hard or uncharitable of any one.'[11] Even when writing melancholy letters, he managed to make the mood more encouraging by the end. He was not a gossip or a cynic and his writing is less incisive and less entertaining than that of his more acidly critical friends, like Elizabeth Rigby or Lord Cockburn. He was tender-hearted and facetious. James Nasmyth addressed him jocularly, in 1845, as: 'my Dear Friend that rare composition of side shaking jaw wraxing fun and quaint Drollery and sincere and deep feeling for the most serious of subjects.'[12]

Hill had a taste for minor surrealism:

> We have seen, for example, on an occasion when he forgot the day of a party to which he was invited, and appeared in full costume the following evening, a pen-and-ink sketch by him most happily and truthfully representing himself entering the drawing-room and finding the ladies of the family relieving their lassitude by a comfortable nap on the sofas.[13]

This idea of playing with time is engagingly nonsensical and establishes an emotional connection, presumably coincidental, with Charles Lutwidge Dodgson, 'Lewis Carroll'. Hill drew talking animals (fig. 36) for his daughter's amusement and shared with Dodgson a pleasure in entertaining the young and in puns. Hill reported in 1853:

> The 13th being Hope Finlays birthday and that of another little boy . . . we had the 3 eldest young Finlays & 3 other youthies to tea . . . I came out after supper as an Improvisator disdaining to drink any bodys health but in lofty rhyme. I was considered to make some decided hits, especially in proposing the health of Mrs Orr's new Babby under the name of Nuggetina – but dont be afraid – I am not the least spoiled by such flattering encomiums.[14]

The Finlays were Hill's great nephews and nieces, who appear in the engaging calotype, *At the Minnow Pool* (pl. 20). Humour is an important factor in the recognition that

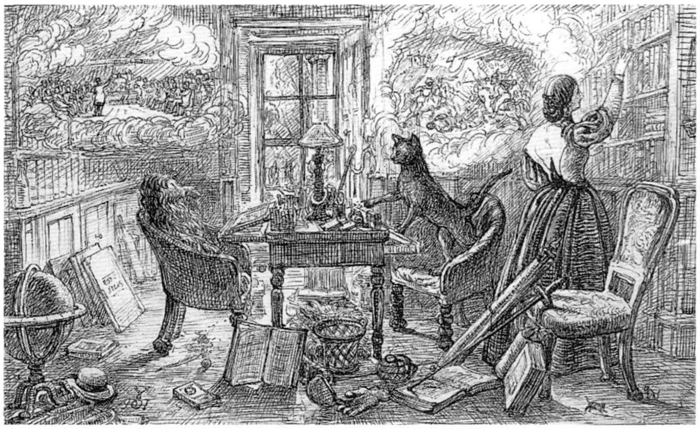

36. D. O. Hill, *A Cat and a Dog Conversing in a Library*, *c.* 1850. Drawing. Whereabouts unknown, taken from a negative in Glasgow University, Special Collections.

people's appearance changes in response to their company – the ability to make a child laugh links to the ability to charm it into posing with an appearance of nature for a photograph. This may be illustrated by a comment on Dodgson's practice, by Alice Liddell (the original for the *Alice* in his books), who wrote:

> We used to go to his rooms . . . [and] sit on the big sofa on each side of him, while he told us stories, illustrating them by pencil or ink drawings as he went along. When we were thoroughly happy and amused at his stories, he used to pose us, and expose the plates before the right mood had passed . . . Being photographed was . . . a joy to us and not a penance as it is to most children.[15]

There is no evidence to propose a direct connection between Hill and Dodgson, but there is a further relationship between photography and nonsense. The understanding that the translation of visual experience into a photograph was an uncertain business may be said to be common ground between the two men. The latter's comic essay on photography, 'A Photographer's Day Out', contains a description of a photographic group, showing:

> The three younger girls, as they would have appeared, if by any possibility a black dose could have been administered to each of them at the same moment, and the three tied together by the hair . . . I kept this view of the subject to myself, and merely said that it 'reminded me of a picture of the three Graces,' but the sentence ended in an involuntary groan, which I had the greatest difficulty in converting into a cough.[16]

This, rather more than the generality of Hill and Adamson's calotype groups, could be regarded as a natural result; it was certainly a common result.

PICTURING WOMEN

Hill and Adamson's pictures of women are, like their portraits of men, remarkable for their individuality and the avoidance of cliché. Roy Strong takes the opposite view. He writes of the women's portraits: 'These are keepsake images calculated to evoke the quintessential ideal of female beauty in the 1840s: fragile and wilting, early Victorian, upper class ladies with huge soulful eyes, upturned noses, dimpled cheeks, and tiny lips, long necks and small waists, forever deployed in poses of contemplative yet seductive resignation.'[17] Strong argues that Hill's model for female portraits came from such watery publications as *Heath's Book of Beauty*. He discusses Canova, Ingres and the delicate engravings after watercolours by Daniel Maclise and Alfred Chalon, and ends with the remark, 'one is struck most by the utter plainness of Hill's lady sitters – early Victorian ladies deprived of any cosmetic help – in spite of their efforts to achieve the contrary'. That is to say, Hill and his sitters were aiming at the keepsake mark, and failed to hit it. This is unlikely. Hill's lack of interest in the elegant distancing proposed here may be demonstrated by the framing of the calotypes. While there are portraits of delicate beauty and restrained elegance amongst the calotypes, even the young girls – the Misses Binney and Monro (fig. 37) – fill the picture: they are not made to look fragile, they are made to look young and close.

The idea that women should be treated differently *en bloc* has been a long-standing fallacy in the profession of portraiture. David Brewster believed that a smoother surface in the calotypes would be more fitting to the prettiness of women. He may have persuaded Thomas Rodger to make this distinction. In 1857, Rodger talked of using two different solutions for development: 'In portraits of gentlemen, No. 1 is also specially applicable . . . as without approaching to hardness, I obtain by it a very pleasing decisiveness of light and shadow. But for ladies, I think too much care cannot be taken to avoid a rapid passage from lights to shadows in photographs.'[18]

It is significant that Hill and Adamson's photographs of women are not all of one type or taken in a particular style. The personality of their sitters is respected – whether they are men, women or children. Hill was clearly a man happy in the company of women and with no nervous impulse to

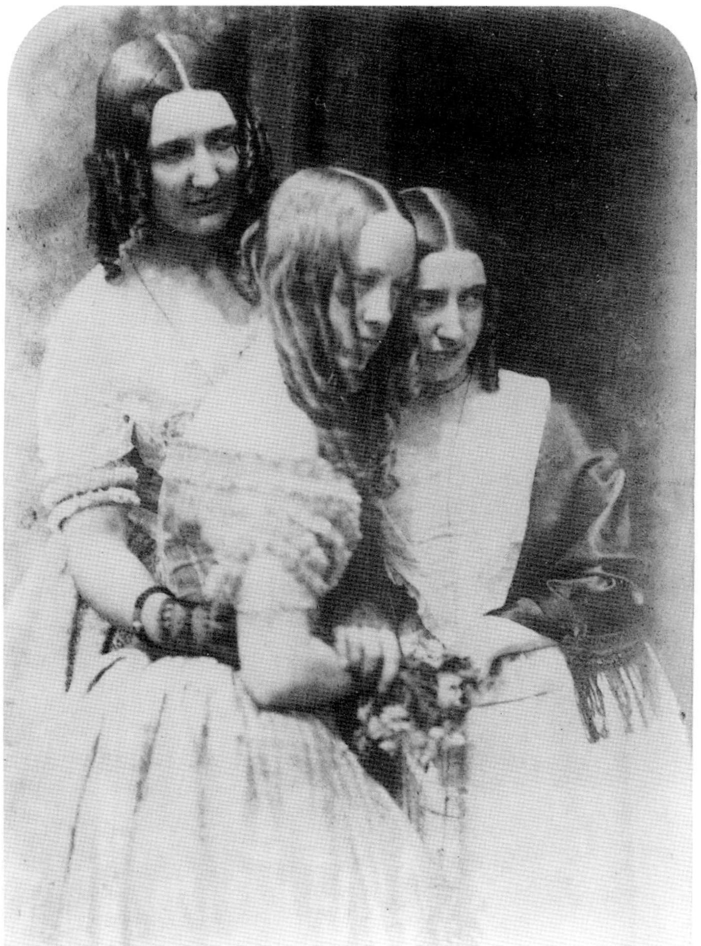

37. D. O. Hill and Robert Adamson, *The Misses Binney and Monro*, 1843–7. Calotype. Scottish National Photography Collection, Edinburgh.

stereotype them.[19] In contrast to the photographs of the Misses Binney, such a photograph as *Miss Kemp* (pl. 21) is so strong in treatment and so lacking in winsome prettiness, as to appear outside its historical context. The women Hill knew and liked were of active intelligence and independence. His daughter and nieces were well educated at the Scottish Institution for the Education of Young Ladies in Moray Place in Edinburgh, where the impressive curriculum included drawing and perspective, taught by an academician, geology and mineralogy, and chemistry taught by Dr George Wilson, FRSE.[20] He talked with affection of a friend of his sister, Mary Watson, who: 'yesterday lost one of her very dearest friends a lady with a somewhat stern face & manner – and one of the most feeling hearts that ever beat – a true Scotchwoman of the old world type – tender & true.'[21] Amongst the women who appear in the calotypes, the art historian Anna Jameson (pl. 22), unnerved Thomas Carlyle, who wrote to his wife in 1833 that she was: 'A little, hard, proud, red-haired, freckled, fierce-eyed, square-mouthed woman, shrewd, harsh, cockneyish – irrational: it was from the first moment apparent that, without mutual loss, we might 'adieu and wave our lily hands.'[22] To Hill she was, 'My friend Mrs Jamesone, the accomplished authoress.'[23] Hill was clearly a popular guest with the amateur painter Lady Ruthven, 'one of those racy and original types of character of which contemporary society seems perhaps less prolific than was that of our great-grandfathers',[24] who was stone deaf in old age and 'could only be communicated with by writing on a slate . . . [she] possessed a monkey, which chattered and seemed able to converse with the deaf lady, who made suitable replies'.[25] He could enjoy the company of women of ribald and acid mind, like 'my old sweetheart, Elizabeth Rigby – the tallest, cleverest & best girl of these parts'.[26] And the direct and strong-minded fishwives of Newhaven seem eminently comfortable in his photographic company.

EMOTIONAL LIFE
Love and Death

In 1851, Hill attempted a little inept matchmaking for his young friend, Joseph Noël Paton, but he was cautious in urging the case:

> you once I thought was a little in earnest in saying that Miss Dodds had made an impression on you. Now I have reason to believe that she has refused more than one – that she is disengaged – and that you by taking the proper means might perhaps carry that prize . . . But dear Noll – let there be no mistake in the matter – if you have not a real leaning that way let what I have written sink into oblivion out of respect to the young lady whose name though I know her not, I have presumed to mention in this strange way. I *am serious* & trust to your honor.[27]

It then became clear that Hill had misunderstood Paton's feelings, and, in a later letter, Hill was thoroughly embarrassed and apologetic. The misunderstanding was based on the natural caution still required in courtship: making a decision was difficult and changing your mind could be destructive, not simply unkind to the woman but potentially damaging to her reputation and status; commitment might require years of constraint before the couple could afford marriage. In a situation where the expression of love and affection for the opposite sex is constricted by these dangers, the same expression could find an outlet in the safer expression of love for the same sex and for children. A tender and even physical friendship could be, socially speaking, expressed between men or women, which could not be expressed with the same freedom for unmarried members of the opposite sex. A man could embrace another man, where he might not risk embracing that man's sister. This may be seen in the photographs, where Hill can, without implication other than friendship, prop men up on each other for physical support and to indicate their intellectual connection. It may be read in the letters, where he can address Noël Paton in emotional terms that he could not use towards his sister, whom Hill subsequently married.

However, Hill was an emotional man. It should perhaps be remembered that he and his contemporaries were only Victorian by adoption. Hill was born during the reign of George III, only two years away from the eighteenth century, and he was thirty-five years old when the young Victoria succeeded to the throne. 'Manliness' did not yet rule out emotional reaction. The stultifying concept of the stiff upper lip, which descended from the earlier traditions of physical courage but stripped that courage of emotion, belongs rather to the other end of Victoria's reign. J. Craig Annan's admiration of the portrait calotypes turns from the interest of the individuals they depicted to this point: 'Breeding is said to be the art of concealing one's feelings, and so highly has our breeding developed nowadays that our faces have almost assumed the uniformity of our clothes. That this was not so in Hill's time is very evident from his photographs.'[28]

The flourishing Scottish evangelist movement was consciously dependent on the exercise of powerful emotion. The lectures of the Free Church minister, the Reverend Dr Thomas Guthrie, were designed to evoke this response. The Reverend Dr James McCosh (fig. 38), who later became the president of the University of Princeton, records his admiration of the first time he heard Guthrie speak at a missionary meeting, when he began by telling a funny story:

> The people began to laugh, and, as he continued, the laughing on the part of the entire audience became so oppressive that an old man of seventy drew himself up, holding his sides, and with some difficulty got out the request, 'Please, Maister Guthrie, *stap*, we can stand this nae langer.' The speaker at once changed his tune, and described a shipwreck which had happened on their coast. The young women began to hide their tears, and at last the whole audience bowed their heads like bulrushes, with the tears flowing from their eyes.[29]

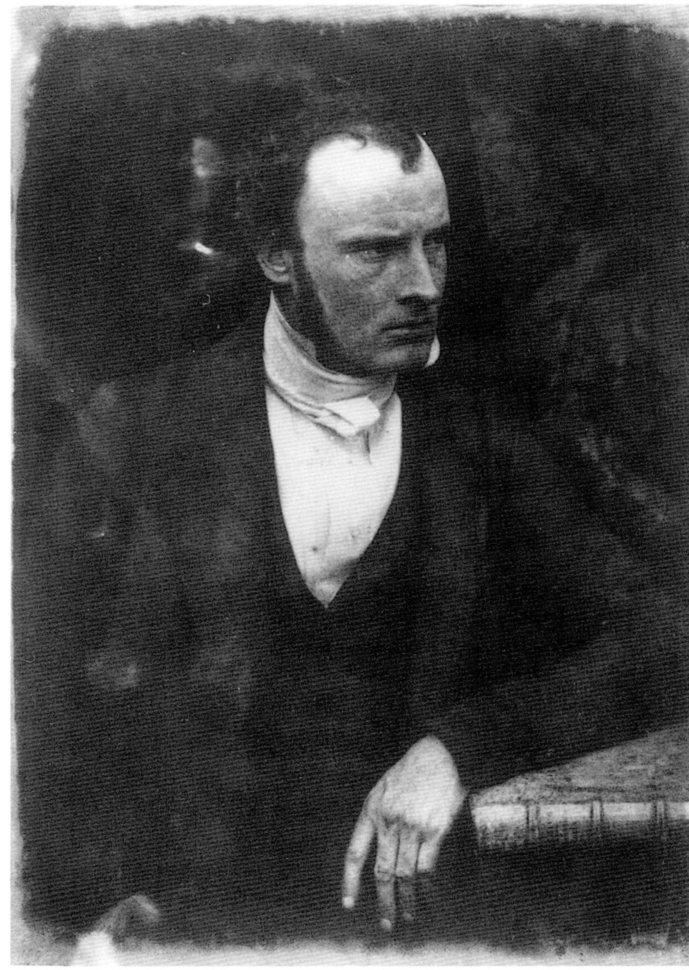

38. D. O. Hill and Robert Adamson, *The Reverend Dr James McCosh*, 1843–7. Calotype. Scottish National Photography Collection, Edinburgh.

The common experience of grief around this time stemmed from an exceptionally high mortality rate, the result of endemic disease and the accidents of childbearing. The very familiarity of the experience, however, should not be taken to imply a hardening to the experience of death.[30] Hill's sadness in the face of infant mortality remained intense to the end of his life. He wrote of his niece and her family in 1869:

> You will have heard of poor Tom & Sarah Gardiner, and how they have had taken from them the two little people. One was to have been D. O. but poor little fellow he has been taken, with his little sister, where they both see the face of Christ. Poor dear people. Sarah's conduct has I believe been admirable. We wait the next letter with anxiety.[31]

The early and mid-nineteenth century coped with grief formally, but allowed and encouraged expression: 'Death evoked the most intense emotions in family life, and Evangelicalism and Romanticism encouraged early and mid-Victorians to give full scope to their expression. They were able to talk and write freely of their sorrow as well as their joy and their love, with a simple sincerity.'[32] However, it is equally true of Hugh Miller, the highly articulate journalist, as it is of the less effectively articulate Hill, that, on the death of a daughter, they retreated into a manual response – Miller picking up his mason's tools to make his child's headstone, Hill to paint two small, commemorative landscapes (see chapter ten).

Witnessing and assisting in the suffering of others and taking responsibility may develop the habit of tenderness. Hill was impressive in his presence, offering practical help to the sick and the bereaved. His correspondence closely follows the fatal illness of his close friend, the history painter Thomas Duncan (pl. 23), and he was there when Duncan died:

> I came direct to our friend's house, from whence I now write, and had the sad privilege of watching by his bedside until all was over, which you will see from the notification sent to you, took place at 5 minutes to 9. All sensation had been gone since Tuesday Evening last, and the immediate cause of dissolution was adupression [?] of the brain. It was a sad sight to see the strong man thus [illegible], his weeping children around his bed – and his excellent wife, half dead from fever, exhaustion and sorrow lifted into the room that she might be present at a scene which could have killed her to have looked on. All was at length over, and bowing to the will of God she allowed herself to be removed to her room, where in the midst of her affliction she has the consolation of reflecting on the spiritual state of mind which her husband had exhibited during his illness – it is now her great support that the Saviour was with him in his dark hour – and that he is in glory. –
>
> Poor Duncan leaves 6 young children for whose maintenance and education it may be difficult to provide in any way approaching to their circumstances when during their fathers life. I have no doubt you will be their friend with the Royal Academy. Will you as a friend privately answer me this question as it has reference to an idea, which as yet I have broached to no one. If any of Mr Duncans friends or countrymen here were to make a fund to assist in educating the children – would the existence of such a fund make the Royal Academy lessen the assistance it would otherwise give the Widow from the Pension Fund? Any information in regard to the assistance Mrs D's friends might expect for her from your fund will be most acceptable. A universal feeling of sorrow prevails here – we know that we have lost one of our best and greatest. My loss is [terribly?] severe but what shall we say of that of the widow and their poor children!!! [33]

Hill's active concern for Duncan's family was followed later by a similar concern for the education of the orphan child of the sculptor Patric Park. This was a Christian interest in good works, visiting the sick and the dying or supporting the widow, but not undertaken in the conscious sense of duty.

THE IMPORTANCE OF RELIGION

It is difficult to estimate the importance of religion in Hill's life, because it depended on a belief and faith, which are not necessarily open to us. Hill's correspondence does not express any particular standpoint in religion. When he speaks in religious terms it is generally in moments of stress or excitement, and his expression is conventional. It is no measure of how intense his belief may have been.

The Disruption of the Church of Scotland in 1843 was clearly a climacteric for Hill, as for many others. He was obviously much impressed by the heroism of the Free Church and admired the Free Church leaders, Reverend Dr Thomas Chalmers and Thomas Guthrie, as well as his own brother-in-law, the Reverend Robert Macdonald. Hugh Miller was clearly convinced of Hill's sincerity in undertaking his great painting of the Disruption, and he wrote an article which opposed a print by David Allan of a General Assembly of the Church in 1783 with the engraving Hill was planning, contrasting the characters of the two artists:

> If Allan, with his quick perception of the ludicrous, his homely truth of character in all cases in which the character was not of an exalted cast, his enjoyment of the low, and his unideal plainness of conception . . . was one of the best fitted in the world for taking the portrait of Moderatism when in its palmiest condition, – Evangelism in the present instance has been not less fortunate in its artist. The one principle required a caricaturist who could confine his love of the ludicrous within the limits of the just and the natural; and such a caricaturist it got. The other demands an artist of nice sensibilities, not unaffected by the moral sublime, and a master of character in its higher departments; and such an artist has it found in Mr Hill, – a gentleman of exquisite taste and fine genius.[34]

Hill presumably attended the Free Church; he was married to Amelia Paton in 1862 by the Reverend Walter Smith of the Free Roxburgh Chapel.[35] However, it is important to remember that in the 1840s, under the leadership of men like Chalmers and Guthrie, the Free Church was founded on broad principles and connected to other dissenting groups. Hill's viewpoint seems to have been, to a degree, non-sectarian and led by the same principles that inform his art. In his relations with the Paton family, he may have been involved in their Quaker and Swedenborgian sympathies.[36]

The religious principle Miller found in Hill's work probably underlies much of his thinking in art. Hill's interest in religious painting, which emerges in his correspondence with Noël Paton, takes him beyond his Presbyterian background and into a wider enthusiasm. He wrote of John Ruskin's lecture in Edinburgh in 1853:

> He is a brave fellow & would be a martyr were it necessary. Was it not a bold thing to [illegible] such on conclusion – that in contrast with the representative Heroes of the Classic & Medieval ages Leonidas and St Louis whose principles of action were duty & religion – Nelson was actuated by duty & no religion. I hope I dont misrepresent what he said. And was it not quite as bold as to bring home to the people he was speaking to and the age to which they belonged – that they seemed to be distinguished by an almost total absence of a recognition of religion – in the creation of great structures or in the embellishment of their private homes.[37]

Hill reacted with similar enthusiasm to the work of a French painter, Louis Janmot, who was hoping to revive the Catholic faith with a series of allegorical paintings on the spiritual and physical progress of the soul.[38] Hill wrote to Paton:

> Look into Hoggs Instructor for the present month – The *letter from Paris* contains an account of a Painter 'Janmot' a new man worth your looking at. I thought it described a man – a good deal like a friend of mine. Janmot is to be here soon, and I am to know him – I think you and he are likely to be good friends. It is curious he has done some subjects such as I have repeatedly spoke to you about as of those you could realize. The regions of Beautiful Spirits.[39]

When Hill wrote this, Janmot had already spent fourteen years on his project, which may have induced a fellow feeling in Hill, still working on the Disruption picture after eleven years. It is nevertheless evidence of a remarkable breadth of sympathy that Hill could consider a Catholic painter's work with such interest and urge his friendship on Paton.[40]

Hill's readiness to understand and indeed adjust to women as to men is expressed in the account of his first marriage:

> I was warned by two or three most loving friends who knew me best, that the lady I married and I were not cut out to make each other happy and the lady herself was somewhat afraid of that and so was I a little – but we both after marriage found in each other qualities we did not look for – as well as those we did look for, and I think we were a very happy couple – and our friends were happy to find themselves wrong.[41]

We know little of Ann Macdonald, except that she is said to have been a fine musician.[42] They were married in 1837 and she probably became an invalid in or before 1840, perhaps as a result of childbearing. Hill speaks of their being confined by his wife's illness. He wrote to Mrs James Hogg, the widow of the poet, inviting her to spend the evening with 'this little friendly circle': 'Mrs Hill's general state of health for some years, has made hermits of us in some degree, and I myself for this reason and others so long delayed calling on you that I grow ashamed to come at last. Should you come to us I will consider that you are inclined to forgive me.'[43] He had a tender concern for his invalid wife. It was a concern echoed in one of her own letters, when she was suffering in pain and pregnancy, and Hill was to be absent in London for a fortnight: 'I shall weary for D. O. but must do the best I can till he returns'.[44]

Ann Hill died in 1841, the eighth child of her generation to die; her mother, who lived until 1850, saw nine of her children die before her. Death was domestic and the women of the household in particular were expected to undertake the responsibilities of nursing. In reviewing an account by 'a delicately nurtured lady' from the Highlands of nursing in the Crimean War, Hugh Miller quotes her as saying, 'I did not feel . . . that we were doing anything better or more praiseworthy than is done in a quiet, unostentatious way at home every day'.[45] Writing in 1853, Hill remembered his sister-in-law (fig. 39), at Ann's deathbed:

> Tomorrow I have to go to Perth to be present at the wedding of my beloved sister in law Jane Macdonald whom I often think of as I used to see her sitting all day and every day by the open coffin which contained the remains of my poor wife. She used to say tranquilly 'I like to be here' and she was – until all was over. I believe Chatty and myself have a very large share of her warm affection and I feel it

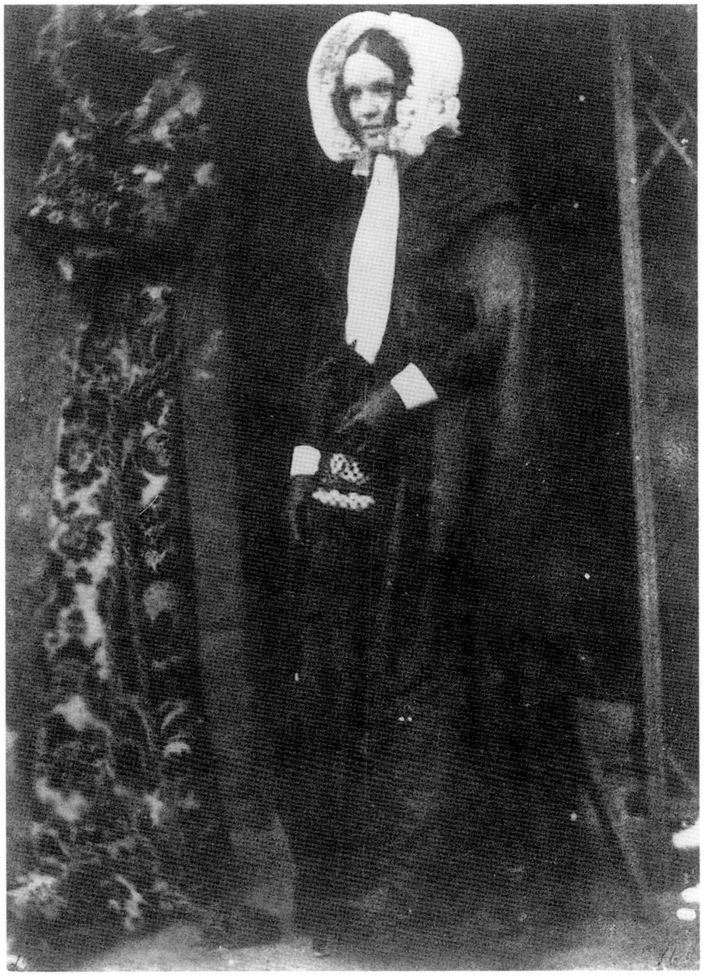

39. D. O. Hill and Robert Adamson, *Jane Macdonald*, probably 1843. Calotype. Scottish National Photography Collection, Edinburgh.

to be a solemn affair to see her united to one she has long known & who will I think make her happy.[46]

The calotype of Jane Macdonald was probably one of the early portraits, taken in 1843. From Hill's account we can see her as a strongly self-contained woman, mourning her sister with her company. What may appear a distanced picture becomes, with this knowledge, a picture about generosity, love and restraint. This is a person Hill saw and admired and loved. Moreover, the connection he makes brings the picture into emotional proximity with another early photograph – the calotype of himself holding his daughter, Charlotte (1839–62).

When Jane Macdonald married in 1853, Hill sent her a letter with a wedding present. The letter reveals the way in which his warmest affection may be expressed, somewhat disconcertingly, through the writing of others and through the facetious pun:

My Dear Love
I will not bother you with the reasons which decided me in selecting a gift in token of my true affection on so auspicious and interesting occasion as your marriage – a thing so very Professional as an Engraving. Had I been richer, my dear Jane, in little engraved Pictures illustrative of 'Ye *Banks* and braes,' it would have been my pride to have sung to you in irresistable notes

'and ye shall walk in silk attire
And siller hae to spare'

The voice being appropriately accompanied by beautiful rustlings of satins and golden chinkachinks. But alas my dearest sister, at this present now, I happen to be as poor as a Poet – though I have very good hopes of being somewhat richer very soon – but being as I said rich in one of the other attributes of the Poet, I here invoke 'myself and all the muses' to 'make oh make' my gift such as it is, to appear in *your* eyes – 'eyes, which do eclipse morn' – estimable – poetical – beautiful seeing that 'a thing of beauty is a joy forever.' Well here it is! – an artist's proof – that is you know – or as an artist's sister you *should* know – one of the earliest impressions – signed by the Painter and Engraver – of Sir Charles Eastlake's [painter and Director of the National Gallery in London] (he, as married my old sweetheart Elizabeth Rigby – the tallest, cleverest & best girl of these parts) chef d [o]euvre – engraved by the best of modern Engravers Samuel Cousins – from whose portfolio I had it with some others, in exchange for some of my Calotypes – those 'wood-*notes*-wild' of mine – which though esteemed by some of the initiated are I confess not so generally popular as the notes of 'Ye Banks &c'

And now my Dear Jane – I know your loving heart too well to think you will not value my gift – because it is not of such value as I wish it to be – may I [illegible] you will love it as you have done me and mine.

May Heaven smile on your union – my true sister, and bless John & you with as much happiness & prosperity as is good for you

Ever your affectionate Brother
D. O. Hill[47]

The letters were written ten years after the calotype was taken and they offer us a view of the pictures from that historical perspective. Hill's love for her may have grown in the meantime, when she helped to fill the void left by Ann Hill's death, but his respect for her command of grief may well have dominated his thoughts when he took the picture. Her very restraint evades the strength and relaxed sympathy of

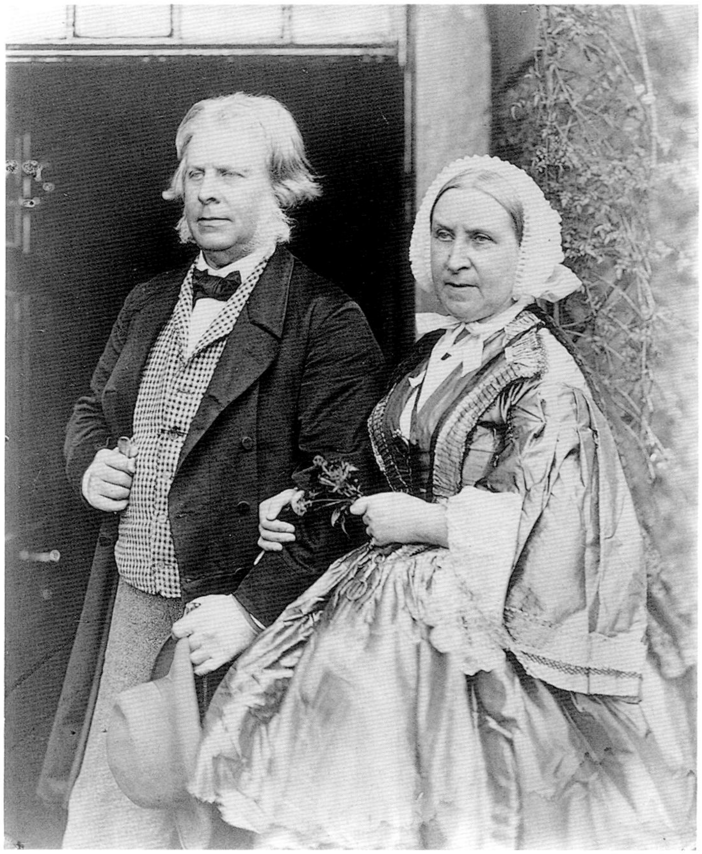

40. D. O. Hill and A. McGlashan, *D. O. Hill and his Sister, Mary Watson*, *c.* 1860. Albumen print. Scottish National Photography Collection, Edinburgh.

Hill's best work – it is a distanced, but nevertheless a touching picture.

After Ann's death, Hill's immediate family was reduced to himself and his daughter. His love for the child is heard in an earlier letter to his wife: 'And now let me ask for Lady-bird, give her as many kisses as she will take from me. I long very much to see the little thing stotting along.'[48] It can also be seen in the early photographs of her – the sense of practical familiarity in the way he holds her is not that of a father who has handed over the responsibility for the child's upbringing (pl. 24). Another picture of her, still as a small child, shows her standing full of merry confidence, her father nearby although he is outside the range of the camera. His active responsibility is confirmed by a letter he wrote to her in 1850: a piece of foolishness to entertain the girl, but including a practical note about galoshes. It is dictated by the family cat, which has injured its paw, to a pigeon called William:

> Along with William & Helen & Vicky & Albert & papa and the rest of the family I was delighted to hear that your cheeks are getting redder than they have been of late and that you were skipping & trundling a hoop at Milfield. I think if I were there I would prefer catching birds – but every one to their taste.
>
> Papa was sorry to leave you in bed on Tuesday morning – but he had made no preparation for staying – he will come and see you soon again – perhaps you would ask him to catch a blackbird or a mavis for me; I am told they are very good eating.
>
> Papa sends your India Rubber shoes as you desire and some other things you may require. Let him know anything else you want and it shall be sent.[49]

Hill was, in our terms, a single parent, but he belonged to a large family. His experience was not unusual and demonstrates how families would reorganise to cope with death. At some stage, he and his widowed sister, Mary Watson, formed an alliance, taking on responsibility for each other's children. They shared Rock House in the 1850s, and the Hill/MacGlashan photograph of about 1860 shows them, arm in arm, looking much like a married couple (fig. 40).[50] In the ribald verse announcing the engagement of his niece Sarah Watson in 1851, it is Hill who acts as her father:

> Who'll give his consent?
> I says Uncle David
> And I'll whistle oer the lave o't
> And I'll give my consent
> This is Uncle David
> Whistling oer the lave o't[51]

He drew himself lolling on the sofa with the lovers and the cat in attitudes of supplication (fig. 41). His character, either as a disengaged Romantic or a Victorian paterfamilias, however, cannot be maintained. His niece's letter to Paton a month later, when he was seriously unwell, is affectionate rather than respectful, offering an unexpected insight into the horrors of his dream life:

> He has very sleepless nights, and is tormented with all sorts of nightmare fancies – last night he was terribly indignant at finding himself a *Cheese* which Mama had packed up and sent in a present to some one – I suppose he was to be 'left till called for' at some Railway Station – He is on the whole very patient. Today he has been much worse as he has had a violent headache – You may be sure this has thrown a gloom over us all, and we are not thinking much of the usual gaities of the season.[52]

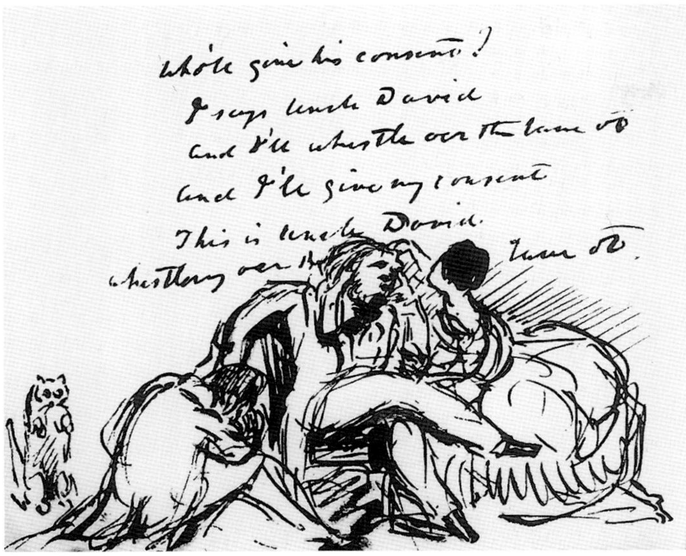

41. D. O. Hill, *Self-portrait with his Niece, Sarah, and her Suitor, Tom Gardiner.* Ink drawing in a letter to Joseph Noël Paton, 19 November 1851. National Library of Scotland, Edinburgh.

A lack of money probably delayed Hill's second marriage as well as his first. His correspondence in the 1850s displays particular financial anxiety. Charlotte's wedding was celebrated in 1861; Hill remarried in 1862, twenty years after the death of his first wife. In a life of sixty-eight years, he was only married for fourteen.

Hill's awareness of the disruptive dangers of a second marriage, that it might cause distress within the family, is expressed in a letter to Noël Paton when the Patons' father proposed to re-marry:

> I am afraid that painful though it be to the children of the departed – it is their true wisdom to submit to the event as one arranged or permitted by providence – remembering that in Honouring our father and our mother there is the promise of reward here and hereafter . . . *It is* ['is' doubly underlined] a trial for you all – but the laws of love and duty and Charity are wise Councillors and dear Noel let them not fail you in this exigency – nor shut you my friend your mind and heart to their teachings.[53]

For himself, Hill had no such confidence in the moral force of duty and, to his credit, he was not a man who would have cared for the submission of his family in preference to spontaneous love. In a letter to his sister-in-law, announcing his second marriage, Hill revealed several important points. It begins by expressing his anxiety, and presumably Amelia Paton's, that their marriage should not disrupt their family affections. He was unable to take a high hand on the issue, almost to the point of absurdity, since it is obvious to him that everyone already knows their intention. He also expressed the same admiration for the tolerance of suffering, as he had in the letter describing Jane Macdonald's fortitude, and it is relevant to Hill's ability to sympathise with others that he actively admired this strength in two women he loved, rather than assuming that it was in some way easier or more appropriate for them. He wrote:

> My Darling Sister Jane
>
> I believe you know all about Amelia Paton and your unworthy brother having agreed some day or other to be man and wife. And since you do know thus all about it, I now venture cautiously to hint to you & uncle John, that such may possibly be the case . . . In my great wisdom I resolved that for a time, it should be a secret – my reasons were I wished to have aunt Watson well & along with me – and Charlotte reconciled & cordial. I dare say both are now the latter – my dear sister I believe is – and dear Charlotte has behaved as I expected she would do, with the most affectionate tenderness, faithfulness and sincerity. All is well so far as those dear ones are concerned and for the first time I today communicate the probable event even to you & Aunt May – asking your sympathy and good wishes & meaning to assure you both, of a faithful & loving & true womanly nature in your new connection. Chatty and Walter know all I could wish to say on this subject. In the religious element I have reason to believe you will be satisfied – and I am indeed mistaken if you do not find that Amelia will do hearts homage to the worth of my dear sisters May & Jane and indeed to worth wherever she meets it – to say nothing of her desire to be beloved by my friends. That we will all like her better when we know her better I doubt it not, for she is a lady in her heart and feelings – and has had much trial and sorrow to bear in silence. All is for the best if we submit ourselves to the discipline of a loving Father, I believe she has done so and that she [illegible] all be blessed of Him. Then she is a good artist & knows artist life – and how to sympathize advise & aid me in my daily work. Her last finished work a bust of Lady Elgin in marble is worthy of any hand it is so good – and she is resolved that the Free [Church?] Picture shall be done! – What a good boy was I – Jack Horner – thou & thy Christmas pie & thy plum on it a discount – when didst thou ever put in thy thumb and pull out a wife with perfections such as I have indicated! But seriously dear sister, do

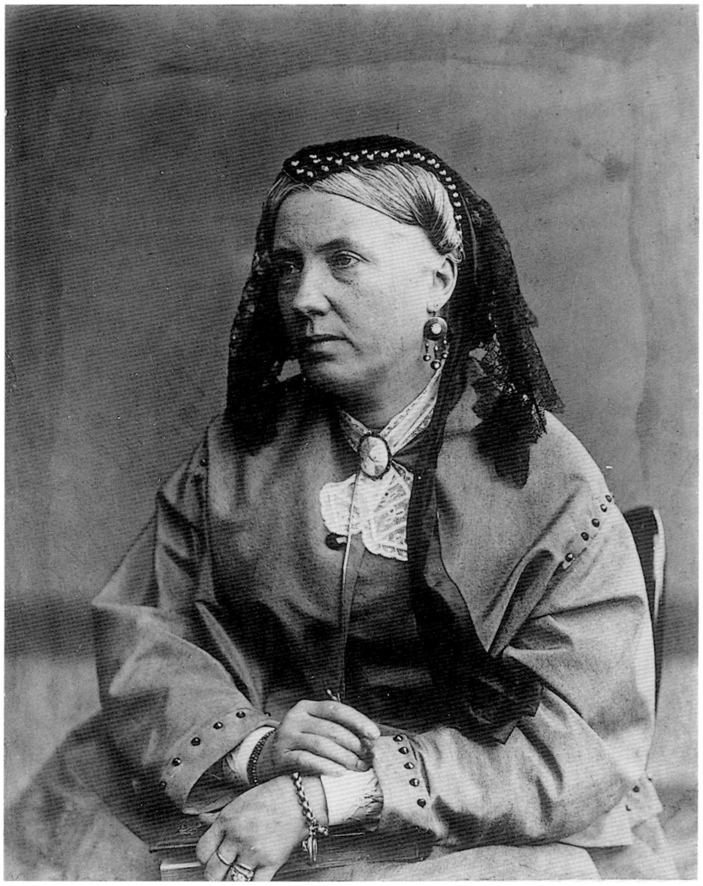

42. John Adamson, *Amelia Paton, c.* 1860. Albumen print. National Museums of Scotland, Edinburgh.

love Amelia – and I know she will love thee dearly.[54]

This letter is arguably conventional in its admiration of Amelia Paton (fig. 42) – she is loving, womanly and religious. However, the compliment to her as an artist, not just able to sympathise and aid Hill but capable of excellent work in her own field, is more remarkable.

A journalist's description of Amelia Paton, written in 1895, tells us of a woman of confidence, character and appropriate generosity: 'She takes a keen interest in the questions of the day, and whether the subject is art or literature, sociology, occultism, or the natural sciences, she is perfectly at home, and talks in a clear fluent manner, interspersed with a little dry humour. Her kindness of heart is apparent even to a stranger.'[55] Her parents were Quakers and the children were brought up 'very much alone, and allowed to roam about as we liked.'[56] This gave her both a sense of independence and a direct enthusiasm for wildlife, which she pursued as an adult in the city, owning not merely the conventional pets: 'Lizards, snakes, and reptiles were wont to give the garden quite a tropical aspect in summer, and a pair of Marmozet monkeys used to sit one each side the dining-room fireplace. Mrs Hill introduced a larger monkey also; but this gentleman, after threatening to break everything in the house, had to be summarily dismissed.'[57]

Amelia Paton's eccentric career as a sculptor was largely of her own direction. She started by painting a miniature at the age of twelve: 'I had had no previous training beyond the fact that all my life I had been accustomed to see my father sketching and my brother Noel too'.[58] According to her friend, Elizabeth Sharp:

> A friend, realising her possibilities, gave her some wax and a modeling tool, and she began to model little portrait heads in relief and in the round. Despite the fact that in those days women who aspired to a profession were frowned upon, this woman-artist persevered and trained herself in the handling of clay, and in due course became known in Scotland as a Portrait-sculptor.[59]

It remains an irony that the passionate letters from Hill to her brother, Noël Paton, in the 1850s, urging and assisting his ambitions in sculpture, largely came to nothing. It proves to be Amelia who received the public sculpture commissions, emerging as a professional sculptor after she married Hill in 1862.[60] That he encouraged his wife's career as an artist, at a time when women sculptors were uncommon in Britain, and when convention would have suggested she live a purely domestic role, is a tribute to Hill's sensitivity.[61] There was a strong group of American women sculptors in Rome in the 1850s and 1860s, but only one of this 'sisterhood' married. Another of the group, Harriet Hosmer, expressed the opinion: 'Even if so inclined, an artist has no business to marry. For a man it may be well enough, but for a woman, on whom matrimonial duties and cares weigh more heavily, it is a moral wrong, I think, for she must either neglect her profession or her family.'[62]

The relation between Hill and Amelia Paton, therefore, gives unusual evidence of a amicable creative relationship. Amelia indeed did help Hill to finish the Disruption picture:

> I well remember Dr Candlish, when he paid us the wedding call, placing his hands on my shoulders and saying, 'Now we look to you to see that your husband's picture of the Disruption is speedily completed', and I promised him that he might rely upon my doing my part in the matter. I used often to work at it in the early morning before D. O. was about . . . putting in the shirt fronts and collars, then I

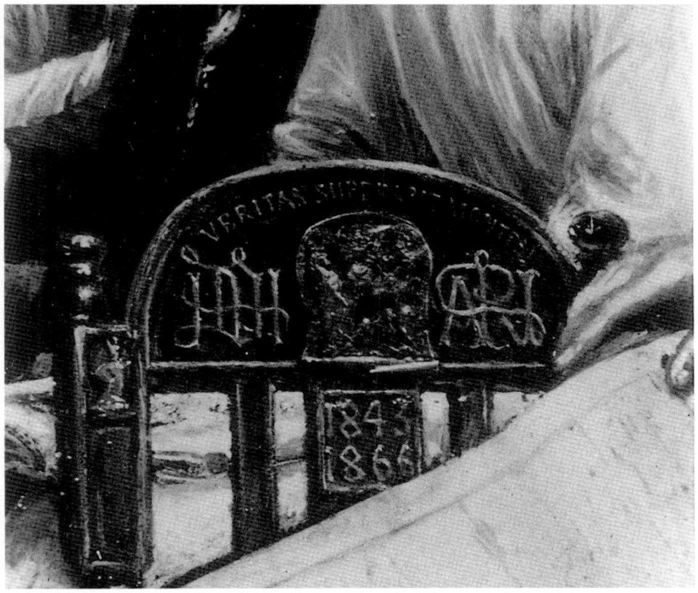

43. D. O. Hill, *The Signing of the Deed of Demission*, 1843–67, detail showing chairback with the monogram of Hill and Amelia Robertson Hill. Oil on canvas. Free Church of Scotland, Edinburgh.

grew more adventurous, and worked at the faces. One day he said to me, 'You need not think that your work has been unobserved by me, but go on.'[63]

Amelia Hill's part in the painting is acknowledged indirectly but prominently (fig. 43). In the foreground of the painting, there is a wooden chair which bears the carved monograms, D. O. H. and A. R. H., over the top is inscribed 'Veritas superabit montes', which appears to be a pun along the lines of 'Truth overcomes [or survives] the Hills'. This was a private acknowledgement placed in full public view – extraordinary as a little personal joke in a major, serious painting. In turn, Hill assisted and applauded his wife in her career as a sculptor. In one of Hill's last letters, he wrote, with pleasure and mock modesty, of the portrait bust she had sculpted of him: 'I whisper in a very low voice that the original was by very many considered the best Bust in the Royal Academy of last year – I mean London. Of course I must not say this but it was said to us by not a few people whose opinions were worth having.'[64]

D. O. Hill seems to have been a rare man: one for whom ambition did not necessitate competition and also a man whose idea of creativity involved his family affections. That her love for him was inextricably tied to art is seen in Amelia Hill's letter after Hill's death in 1870. She wrote to Mrs Blackie on 26 June:

> The sense of loneliness gets stronger every day. You dear have the hope & the certainty of your dear one returning to you from his wanderings – & your heart would be rejoiced to see him so strong looking as he was the day that he had the kindness to come out & see me. I am at a bust but will soon finish it, a commission given me in kindness to try & set me to work once more – I trust I may do it well. The now I have no pleasure in my work. I miss the kind approving word & look. Now it is only a matter of living & that degrades art . . . At times I feel too sad & old to make any chance of rising out of this. Do not think I am impatient. I only feel as if my mission now was done.[65]

II The Old Town and the Village of Newhaven

The Unsociable City and the Problem of the Destitute

The work of the Hill and Adamson partnership would be impressive if it only showed us the religious, intellectual and artistic life in Edinburgh in the 1840s, but it was not circumscribed by these polite confines. In the background of urban society, at the heart of the Old Town of Edinburgh, lay the endemic and appalling problem of the city's slums. By the 1840s the historic centre of the city was trapped in a cycle of fatal disease and destitution, fuelled by the attacks of the potato famine in the Scottish Highlands and in Ireland, and by the regular economic slumps that followed the advance of industrialisation.

The human effects of this are described in a passionate sermon delivered by the Reverend Thomas Guthrie (fig. 00). He began with a description of launching a boat on a calm, summer's day and looking down at the mouldering vestige of a drowned forest below the water, which he then compared with the city slums. Guthrie was rousing his parishioners to undertake a mission to the desperate poor:

> Not a single house, nor a block of houses, but whole streets, once from end to end the homes of decency, and industry, and wealth, and rank, and piety, have been engulfed. A flood of ignorance, and misery, and sin, now breaks and roars above the top of their highest tenements. Nor do the old stumps of a forest, still standing up erect beneath the sea-wave, indicate a greater change, a deeper subsidence, than the relics of ancient grandeur and the

touching memorials of piety which yet linger about these wretched dwellings, like evening twilight on the hills – like some traces of beauty on a corpse.[66]

Lord Cockburn talked of the impact on society of such distress: the genuine sense of helplessness and fear it generated:

> Of all the new features of modern society in Britain, none is so peculiar or frightful as the hordes of strong poor, always liable to be thrown out of employment by stagnation of trade . . . In Edinburgh, besides its fullest complement of ordinary distress, we have a battalion of what are now known by the almost technical term of 'Unemployed Poor' . . . being congregated in numbers and distinguished by a title, they form a separate class, a new state.[67]

These passages are a part of a long debate about poverty. Until 1845, the burden of relieving the poor fell mostly on the parishes, where the inadequate levy was supported by personal charity, and was only expected to protect the disabled. The 'able-bodied poor' were still generally expected to shift for themselves. The system had proved severely inadequate in the face of the steep rise and great movements in the population and the widespread industrial slumps. In 1845, the government passed the Scottish Poor Law Amendment Act, which enabled official interference in the situation. Resistance to the new law was not necessarily cynical. The influential Malthusian theory held that funding the poor undermined self-restraint and would lead to a further rise in population which the country could not feed – that, in fact, extremes of poverty were a painful but natural form of control on a rapidly growing population.[68] The Presbyterian position was that personal responsibility and the need for active charity (both love and giving) were essential in society. Thomas Chalmers, in the preface to his *Christian and Civic Economy of Large Towns*, expresses this difficult idea:

> It is right that justice should be enforced by law, but compassion ought to go free . . . Whatever the calls may be which the poverty of a human being may have on the compassion of his fellows, it has no claim whatever on their justice. The confusion of these two virtues in the ethical system will tend to actual confusion and disorder where introduced into the laws and administration of human society. The proper remedy, or remedy of nature, for the wretchedness of the few is the kindness of the many.[69]

Chalmers saw the personal attention of the rich to the poor as 'nature's own simple mechanism': a moral responsibility, which should not be replaced by a cold political dole.[70] Both his and Malthus's theories were aimed at a future balance of society. They held that an immediate palliative, however generous an impulse, was ultimately destructive. Neither position was wholly misguided; the legal imposition of responsibility enforced by the Poor Law Act was by no means an unmitigated success. Faced by a shift from a self-imposed moral responsibility to a legal responsibility, certain of the Highland landlords pushed forward with the 'Clearances' with a greater vigour; the Act, in effect, increased to unprecedented levels the numbers of emigrants from Scotland.

'DISTRAINING FOR RENT' AND INNOCENT FAILURE
A Model of Distress

In 1846, D. O. Hill and David Roberts solicited the loan of a painting by the Scottish genre and history painter Sir David Wilkie for the Royal Scottish Academy exhibition. This was *Distraining for Rent* (fig. 44), originally painted in the context of the post-war agricultural depression thirty years earlier.[71] It is a picture of human failure in the face of broad economic and social disaster. This was a new idea, and the contemporary reaction to the picture is an expression of the difficulty then inherent in understanding such a subject.

When it was first exhibited, at the Royal Academy in London in 1815, B. R. Haydon wrote:

> Beautiful as the picture was acknowledged to be, the aristocracy evidently thought it an attack on their rights. Sir George [Beaumont, an influential patron and landowner] was very sore on the private day, and said Wilkie should have shown why his landlord had distrained; he might be a dissipated tenant. I defended Wilkie as well as I could, but there was a decided set at the picture.[72]

It is a painting about the effects of war. The chief protagonists are the bankrupt tenant farmer, the man who steers the plough and tends the flocks (notable symbols of peace), the wife and mother, the innocent children and even the miserable working dog. Wilkie presents his subjects as innocent victims and the painting represented tragedy among the lower ranks of society. The painting is set in the present, so the moral was not comfortably swaddled in antiquity. Wilkie was the son of a Scots Presbyterian minister, with the moral leaning this would imply, and it is unlikely that he would exhibit a painting, proposing that the tenant was the victim of abstract economic circumstances.[73] The landlords had a legal right to claim the high rent established in the profitable

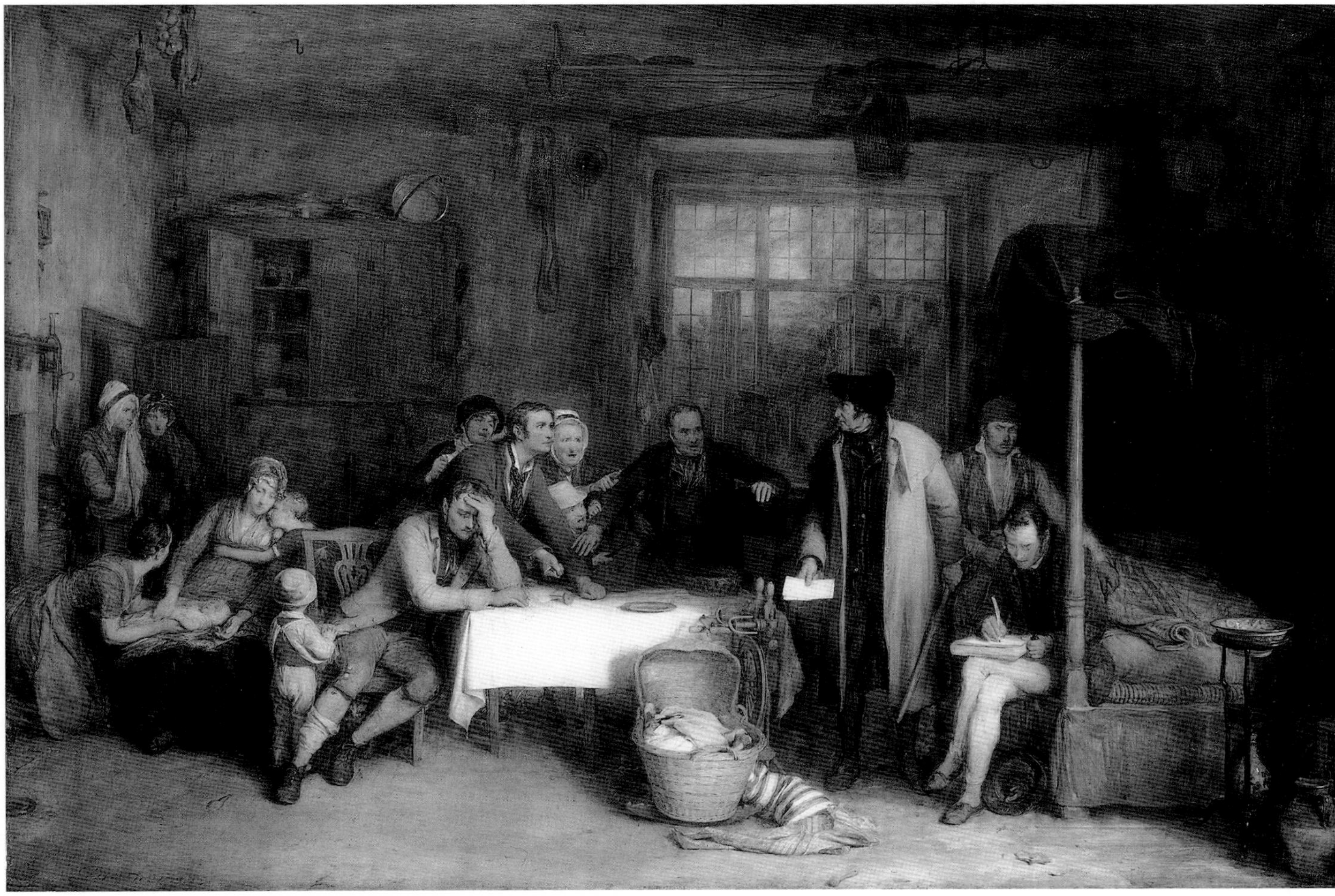

44. David Wilkie, *Distraining for Rent*, 1815. Oil on panel. National Gallery of Scotland, Edinburgh.

war years, but, in Wilkie's view, that right should have been balanced by their moral responsibility towards their tenants. The picture makes the point that the stout officers of the law have come alone to fulfil the letter of that law. The landlord is not in the picture, and did not see or confront the distress in person.

Wilkie's painting was a problem picture – presenting the victims of another man's legal right. It seems likely that Wilkie sought to move the absent landlords to a sense of their responsibility, by facing them with innocent suffering. This was arguably the first of the pictorial attempts to move the social conscience – a conscience that could sleep well because of the divorce between the layers of society.[74] It is a forerunner of the paintings of the mid-century, like Richard Redgrave's *The Sempstress*, designed to draw attention to exploitation and the waste of youth. It heralds the engravings of Henry Mayhew's *London Labour and the London Poor* (issued between 1851 and 1862), and the first use of photography, in such works as John Thomson's *Street Life in London*, published in 1870, as a tool of social reform.

Wilkie had made a difficult picture and it was put out of sight for thirty years. When it was exhibited in Edinburgh in 1846, John Brown's review took a fatalistic view – he saw it as a painting about suffering bravely borne:

> It is to our liking Wilkie's most perfect picture . . . there is more of human nature, more of the human heart, in this than in any of the others. It is full of 'the still, sad music of humanity', – still and sad, but yet musical, by reason of its true ideality, the painter acting his part as reconciler of men to their circumstances. This is one great end of poetry and painting.[75]

However, it is not a painting of resignation (although that was one possible resolution of this moment); it is a picture of people reduced, stunned by despair. Hill recognised the intensity of that despair; that the mother in the painting was stricken out of her very nature and unable to respond to her infant children. He wrote: 'the unutterable woe of the wasted matron reminds me as I write of a still sadder scene.'[76] He was speaking of Mrs Duncan's grief on the death of her husband, Thomas Duncan (quoted above). Characteristically, while John Brown was discoursing on a broad moral proposal, D. O. Hill related it to his own experience of the despair of a woman who had watched her husband sicken and die. As an observer intimately involved – subject to distress himself as Thomas Duncan's friend – Hill saw and felt the experience with her sensibility as well as his own, and judged it aright.

Hill wrote to David Roberts in 1846: 'We all agree with you in your appreciation of the Wilkie – never surely was passion and feeling and sorrow more intensely depicted than this.'[77] It was a model of distress, which he might have considered following in his own work. Despite this, the calotypes do not demonstrate an immediate concern for the dreadful conditions in the centre of Edinburgh; Hill and Adamson did not take a camera into the slums, either to record or draw attention to them. However, it is probable that Hill was not simply well aware of the situation but actively concerned by it.

One of the officials involved in the working of the new Poor Law was Hill's friend, Dr George Bell, 'an estimable, upright, and loving man', who worked with Thomas Guthrie amongst the poor.[78] In 1849, Bell published a pamphlet on the problem. Taking the example of a single room in a slum tenement, he concluded with an impassioned statement:

> It defies the graver of Hogarth, the pencil of David Scott, so familiar with nightmare horrors, the pen of Dickens, and the tongue of Guthrie. How would the artist manage the background and middle distance of the picture, so varied, so full of national history, so pregnant with dark biography? What could an uninstructed gazer make of the little sparks of light upon the black canvass, marking the morning beams of a mortal's day, which became dark as night before his sun had got a footing in the sky? Such lights would seem to him like falling stars – they would not light the gloom.[79]

It takes little imagination to hear this passage as resulting from a serious conversation between Hill and George Bell, and we have two calotypes, taken in 1846, which might be thought to illustrate such a discussion. As a painter, Hill had a passion for the light and physical freedom inherent in the idea of aerial perspective. Bell's sentence beginning, 'How would the artist manage the background', is the voice of a landscape painter, concerned with history. Clearly the confinement and the darkness would have struck Hill with force, as an artist who worked with light and the pleasures of open landscape and sky.

George Bell and Hill figure together again in another calotyped discussion, with the poet and stained glass artist, James Ballantyne (pl. 25). It was a part of the inherent sympathy between the three men that Ballantyne also expressed distress for the slum conditions. The introduction to his book, *The Gaberlunzie's Wallet*, a popular combination of prose, verse and song, describes the misery in the Old Town and offers a sad poem about a little girl crouched in a doorway for shelter:

> An' nae lawfu' bread can the wee thing win,
> Wi' the brand o' shame on her shy wee face:–
> O God! man has justice, but little grace![80]

The picturesque neighbourhood of this poverty was described by James Ballantyne in his account of the High Street: 'this emporium o' character, wi' its lang and tempting array o' penny shows, ballad-singers, speech-criers, baskets o' laces, combs, caps, shoe-ties, an' twopenny mirrors, wi' hurleys fu' o' cherry-cheekit apples an' brown speldings.'[81] A description of this kind might well have appealed to Hill as the idea of a genre painting. However, there are not even street 'types' among the calotypes, of the kind familiar in the work of the Edinburgh engravers, such as Walter Geikie (fig. 45), and in later, commercial photography, which imply surface character and a certain humour in poverty.[82]

It seems likely that Hill would not have thought it right to photograph the destitute. He seems to have followed the moral aesthetic, inherent in Scottish art.[83] As examples of this, it is worth quoting both James Ballantyne and the journalist Robert Stephen Rintoul. Ballantyne wrote, at the beginning of *The Gaberlunzie's Wallet*: 'I am persuaded that it will further the cause we ought all to have in view, namely, the promotion of brotherly kindness, and the elevation of moral sentiment, to draw our illustrations of life from Character, not from Crime, and to exhibit the beauties of Virtue, rather than the deformities of Vice.'[84] Rintoul defined the role of art as follows:

> The contemplation of that which is beautiful and harmonious begets a disposition of mind harmonious and congenially alive to excellency, – a disposition which may be so cultivated as to grow into a habit. By a more positive

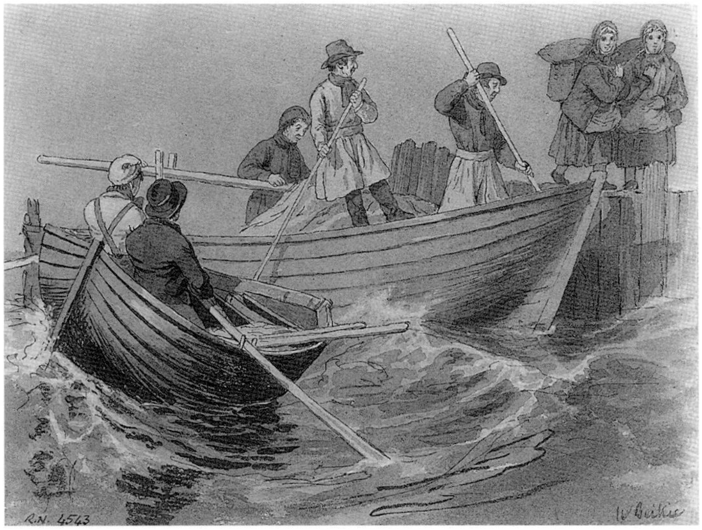

45. Walter Geikie, *Newhaven Boats Coming in to Land.* Watercolour. National Gallery of Scotland, Edinburgh.

re-action, the continued familiarity with the aspect of dignity and grace tends to produce, through outward imitation, similar qualities. And those two processes set a third in motion: the mind, which is familiarized with excellence and harmony, acquires a keener perception of what is discordant and base, and revolts the more from it.[85]

NEWHAVEN
The Working Solution

In 1844, Hill and Adamson advertised the publication of an album of calotypes entitled *The Fishermen and Women of the Firth of Forth.*[86] Standing on top of Calton Hill, above Rock House, Hill would have an extended view of the city. To the south lay the Old Town stretched on a spine of rock between the castle and Holyrood Palace at the base of Arthur's Seat, the focus of the city's desperate poverty. To the west and north lay the neoclassical New Town, the site of the city's new and elegant prosperity. From such an elevated distance, this social disparity might seem a sentimental opposition; in practice it was a savage and immoral contrast. But the height would give Hill a longer view, a mile away northwards to the shores of the estuary of the river Forth, and the small fishing village of Newhaven. Here, it seemed was a true opposition – a natural, working-class, social enclave, a coherent, self-sufficient community, which had kept its feet and was flourishing during the depression, independent of the economic imperatives set up by landowners and mill owners alike.

Here in Newhaven, interestingly, Hill found a solution to the problem of destitution. A large part of the problem within the city slums derived from the influx of desperate people, seeking work or medical help. This distressed and driven population had no active, self-protecting community of the kind that can flourish in difficulty. In 1819, Thomas Chalmers had effected a practical experiment of his social theory of the importance of personal charity and attention in the slums of Glasgow. He took over one of the largest and poorest districts of the city and broke it down into manageable units, each with an elder and a deacon. He deliberately closed his parish from outside poor relief – keeping 'his people' together, paying attention to them and re-building the natural impulse of generosity and neighbourliness. He and his successor in the same parish succeeded in keeping the community together for a surprisingly long time under onslaughts of economic disaster in the 1820s and 1830s. George Bell recommended a similarly contained solution to the problem of Edinburgh's slums in 1849, in the idea of taking over waste land and returning the agricultural workers, who had come into the city and been trapped by poverty, to small coherent communities.

Newhaven had achieved that balance naturally and in the same exclusive way, because the fishermen and women married and made strong friendships within the community – justly arguing that only insiders could be expected to take on such hard and strenuous work. This protected them from what could be thought of as the economic facts of the time, and it kept them successful as a society.

Hill's view of Newhaven was unquestionably admiring and for good reason. The Newhaven pilots had an established reputation for heroism from the Napoleonic Wars and they were known as skilled and effective fishermen, working from open boats both in the inshore fishing with the 'small line', which could carry from 500 to 3,000 hooks to catch haddock, whiting and codling, and in the 'great line' fishing out at sea for several days at a time. To fish the migratory herring, some forty boats from Newhaven would join others travelling north to Wick for six to eight weeks – a minimum of 200 miles, 'no inconsiderable journey as it was often the custom to row the entire distance'.[87] The remarkable professional skill of the Newhaven men was made publicly clear in the context of a disaster in 1848, at Peterhead, when the herring fishery was caught in a summer storm, and a hundred men were drowned, leaving 47 widows and 161 orphans. A Parliamentary enquiry established both the lack of safe harbours and the often poor design of the boats. The Newhaven boat, previously thought to have been one of the best-

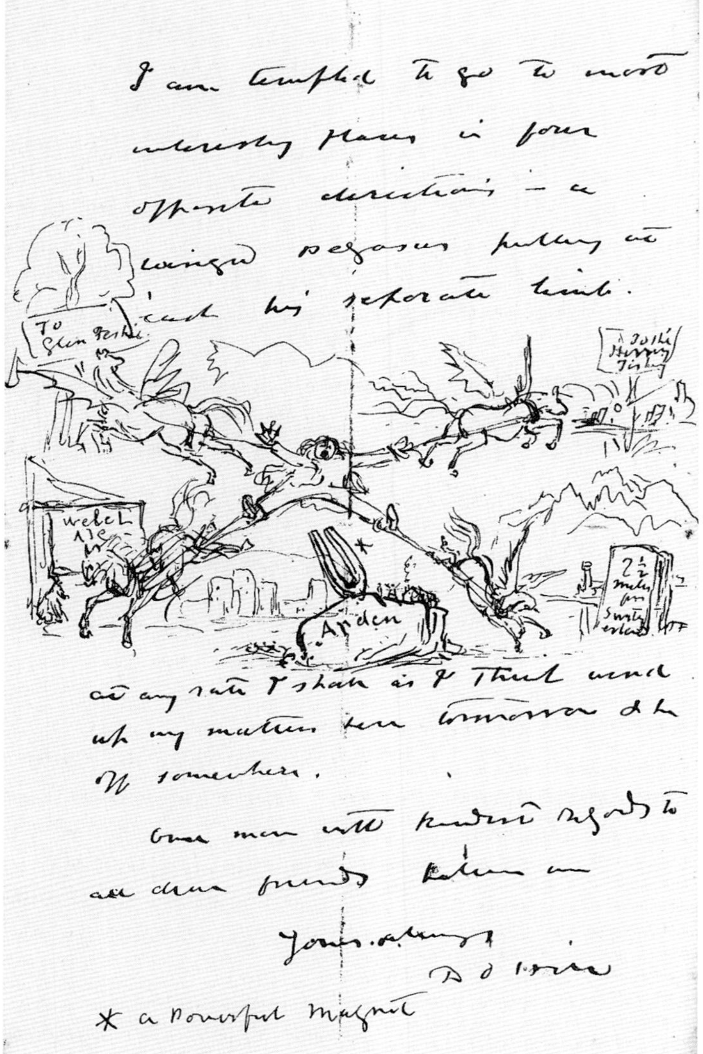

46. D. O. Hill, *Self-portrait Caricature.* Ink drawing in a letter to Joseph Noël Paton, 19 August 1852. National Library of Scotland, Edinburgh.

designed, was finally appreciated as one of the worst – second only in unseaworthiness to the Wick boat, which was condemned as 'the worst shape that could be given to a floating body for the useful purposes of a boat': 'spheroidal' and apt to travel around in circles. The report concluded: 'The character the Firth of Forth boats are said to bear, of being fine sea-going boats, must be attributable more to the skill of the crews than to the form of the boats'.[88] None of the Newhaven men drowned in 1848.

One of the calotypes of the Newhaven fishermen, which shows them lolling idly against a boat after the strenuous work at sea, was entitled by Hill, *Dolce Far Niente.* The landsman's common, cynical view of the fishermen saw them as idlers, leaving the weight of the work to the women. The calotypes are, however, uncritical in the admiration of both men and women, and there is a possibility that Hill had spent time at sea with the fishermen as well as in the village itself. This is hinted in the little caricature he drew in the summer of 1852, when he was uncertain where to go to paint. It shows him torn in five different directions, and one of the arms of the signpost says: 'To the Herring Fishing' (fig. 46). He was certainly aware of the risks and tragedy in their lives.

At Wick, as at Newhaven, the fishwives were more visible to observers than the men, who fished the herring at night, bringing back a phenomenal catch, which averaged 88,500 barrels annually in the twenty years up to 1840 – each barrel containing seven to eight hundred fish. The need to gut and cure so great a catch meant that over two thousand women could be needed and the fishwives might travel with the men to the fishing grounds. A half-appalled, half-fascinated description of the fishwives at work, was given by James Wilson, who had much difficulty in finding the vocabulary to treat the subject:

> Bloody and all-begrimed with slime, [she] stands up with knife in hand, or stoops her horrid head 'with scaly armour bright', and plunging her bare and brawny arms again into the trough as if no bowels of compassion existed any more on this terraqueous globe . . . From what we witnessed of their prowess, we doubt not that if arranged in battle array they would have gained the day at Waterloo, long before Blücher came up.[89]

The load of work the fishwives undertook was unquestionably very great. The actress Fanny Kemble, who was herself an independent woman, befriended a Newhaven fishwife around 1829 and visited her in later years:

> I often went back . . . and more than once saw her and her fellow fish-women haul up the boats on their return after being out at sea. They all stood on the beach clamouring like a flock of sea-gulls, and, as the boat's keel rasped the shingles, rushed forward and seized it; and while the men in their sea clothes all dripping like huge Newfoundland dogs, jumped out in their heavy boots and took their way to their several houses, their stalwart partners, hauling all together at the rope fastened to the boat, drew it up beyond watermark, and seized and sorted its freight of fish, and stalked off each with her own basket full, with which she trudged up to trade and chaffer with the 'gude

wives' of the town, and bring back to the men the value of their work. It always seemed to me that these women had about as equal a share of the labour of life as the most zealous champion of the rights of her sex could desire.[90]

In all probability, this workload was achieved at great cost. As a tourist in Fife discovered at the end of the century: 'They look superbly strong these women; but to be sure, the "weak anes dee", as one of them told me.'[91]

The balance to this situation was the singular independence and confidence of the community, particularly expressed through the women. As James Wilson noted in surprise, at the end of a day of gruelling work, they would wash and dress again in better clothes, and many emerged as 'magnificently fine females'.[92] The Newhaven fishwives especially were noted for their beauty and their picturesque dress, becoming a noted sight for the Edinburgh tourist, both decorating and dominating the scene. Their direct confidence and their outdoor life raised some moral anxieties among other observers, but Hill and Adamson's calotype account of their work is wholehearted in its admiration and aimed to show both the work and the protective social structure of the village – the close relationship between individual fishwives who formed friendships in youth and supported each other, or the protective educational relation of father and sons (pl. 26). The calotypes involved a remarkable number of figures, men, women, children and even babies, in about 120 carefully posed photographs, and clearly required the intelligent co-operation of the community. They go beyond the practical and family view of the village and give us also an idea of its cultural and moral status. The village effectively joined the Free Church and the fishwives are seen reading in a Bible class with the minister, as well as reading letters – a new and notable literacy (pl. 27). There are two photographs where a fishwife and a fisherman are simply shown thinking (pl. 28), and an idea of their known skill as singers is brought out in the captions Hill gave the calotypes. The series is intended as a satisfactory and efficient idea of the community's structure and work and a visible model of a socially successful and heroic community. Regrettably, Hill and Adamson never published this series in a separate volume, so the complete intention of this first 'documentary photo-essay' was not made clear at the time, but it is an extraordinary recognition of the possibilities of photography in social documentary and seems to have no graphic precedent.[93]

The specific enthusiasm for the fishermen and women displayed in the calotypes and the sense of Hill's admiration as both generous and unqualified, may be underlined by John

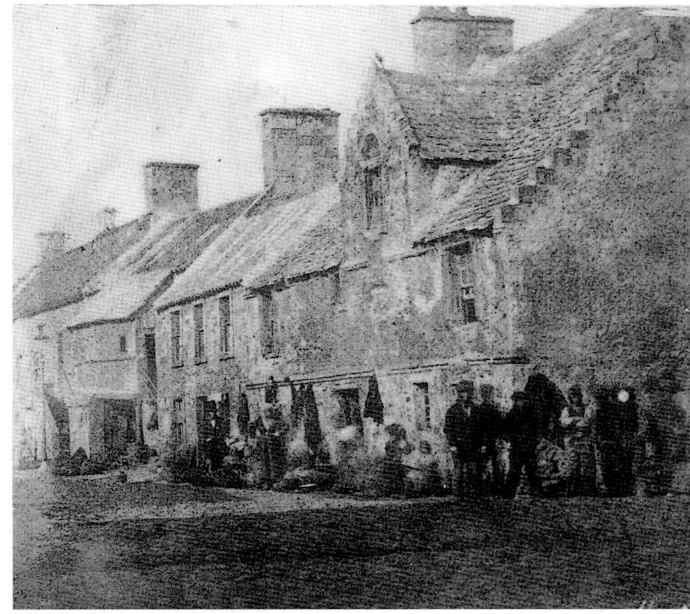

47. Robert Adamson, *Fishergate, North Street, St Andrews*, 1842. Calotype. National Museums of Scotland, Edinburgh.

Adamson's response to the fishermen and women of St Andrews. In 1841, he published a *Report on the Sanitary Condition and General Economy of the Labouring Classes in the City of St Andrews*, in which he roundly condemned the Fishergate, in North Street.[94] He summed it up as a locality of 'filth and dissipation', and recommended both physical and educational improvements. The Fishergate was the subject of one of Robert Adamson's calotypes, taken in 1842 (fig. 47). This provides an extremely interesting comparison with two of the same subject taken with Hill for *The Fishermen and Women* (pl. 29). When Hill and Adamson were working on the series, they moved to St Andrews to take a number of calotypes, two of North Street and several of the harbour, presumably with the idea of exploiting the open space of the Fishergate, as an alternative to the narrow lanes of Newhaven, and of adding calotypes of boats in a harbour – at Newhaven there was only a pier.

The earlier calotype is conspicuously different from the later. The photographic angle is designed to show a line of the buildings, and it may be that Adamson was thinking of the architecture more than the people. However, it might have been intended as a picture of the neighbourhood's depressed condition, illustrating John Adamson's treatise; it could be that, in this one small picture, Robert Adamson invented critical documentary photography, of the kind designed to evoke active concern, in contrast to the later *The Fishermen and Women* series. The people caught in the photograph, perhaps told to stand still by the figure in the top hat to the left, are showing doubt or hostility. The men, whom John Adamson describes as 'lounging at the corner of the street, in full view of the public houses of which there are several for their especial accommodation', are far from relaxed. They are facing the camera in attitudes expressing aggression, one with his arms folded, another with his legs braced apart; in the background, one of the women is standing with her arms akimbo. The contrast is obvious; the later calotype shows people apparently relaxed and unconcerned by the camera – the picture of a reasonable working community. The irony of the same place and people being treated as a matter for civic concern in 1842 and as a picture for admiration around 1845, may be tempered by the knowledge that the provost of the city, Major Lyon Playfair, had undertaken sweeping improvements of the area. The physical condition of the community and, possibly, their moral condition may have radically improved between the two pictures.[95]

It is clear from the concentrated essay of *The Fishermen and Women* that Hill, who admired the prominent figures who came to Rock House, did not adopt a narrow view of importance in society. Hill apparently shared Thomas Guthrie's belief that heroism and virtue came in different guises and that this was an element of social strength:

> Christians have individual peculiarities which, as much as their faces, distinguish them from each other; and this is rather a beauty than a blemish – a charm rather than a fault . . . It is a power, an element of the highest utility in the Church. Hence the mistake of those who would have all Christians modelled on their own pattern, as, for example, of some modest, retiring, gentle spirits, who cannot appreciate the worth and usefulness of those whom God has cast in a rough mould and made of stern stuff.[96]

This was not a common view. Elizabeth Rigby said of Guthrie's preaching:

> He is a regular O'Connell in the pulpit – cringing to the people, and telling them that they were able to judge, for it was the people with whom Christ was popular, and the elders and higher classes who persecuted. I wonder who it was that crucified Him! . . . This is a lesson to all parties: a perfect agitator and an excellent specimen of how the pulpit is made use of to quicken the worst species of pride in the Scotch mob. No wonder they are so turbulent and sanguinary when excited – they are utterly democratic in religion.[97]

Words like 'democracy' and 'enthusiasm' had for many people a sinister relation to mob rule and, in the context of the social and economic distress in the 1840s, the idea of revolution was near and troubling. Britain might well have been swept into the European political revolutions of 1848. D. O. Hill took a more generous and optimistic view of his world.

Elizabeth Rigby's approach to the Newhaven fishwife was distinguished from Hill and Adamson's. She wrote an admiring passage in her journal in 1843, which nevertheless shows an element of patronage – the lady distributing advice:

> Went down to look at Jinny [Jeanie] Wilson – a tremendously hot day, and she with as heavy a load of petticoats as of fish: a lovely blooming creature, with a complexion of that transparent kind of which our aristocracy are most proud; her eye laughing, her hair, without any figure of speech, golden – such a colour as an indoor life never permits. She was laden with clothes, petticoat over petticoat, striped and whole colour, all of the thickest woollen material, and one of a kind of dreadnought frieze; also a tremendous serge coat with long sleeves, that hung flat upon her back, over it a striped butcher's apron 'To wipe ma haunds' – and she made a graceful gesture over her shoulder with a fine pair, full in the palm and slender in the fingers – perfect pictures. Altogether, guessing roughly, I should say she was carrying to the amount of five ordinary box-coats, or fifteen conventional flannel petticoats. She wore, she told us 'sax on common days, four at hame, and twa of a Sunday, and nae cheap, thirteen shillings the pair', and she had 'sax pair' . . . She told me that this quantity of apparel was necessary to prevent the creel from hurting her back, and I suggested a pad for the necessary part, and a little less weight of material, and expenditure of shillings upon the rest; but Jinny had an unanswerable: 'It was verra true - a piece upon the bock might be better, but ye ken it's juist the fashion o' the place.'[98]

This text offers some illumination on the calotype of Jeanie Wilson (pl. 28). If it is a casual record of the voice of a working woman, it is an astonishing coincidence. Elizabeth Rigby clearly did recognise not just the beauty but the confident authority of the other woman. She records the dismissive riposte, and her own interest in fashion is calmly reflected back by Jeanie Wilson's remark. A sympathy or perhaps tolerance seems to have been established between the two, who shared the fact that they were both independent and earning their own livings.

The idea of a 'common heroism' implicit within *The Fishermen and Women* was picked up at the end of the decade and made explicit by the novelist Charles Reade. He wrote a popular novel called *Christie Johnstone*, set in Newhaven, which was published in 1851.[99] Reade may not have met Hill, but it seems reasonable from coincidences in the plot of the book that he at least knew the photographs and understood Hill's admiration of the people.[100] Reade was interested in pictures and press cuttings and kept a series of scrapbooks, which he used as inspiration for his novels and plays. Reade, like Hill, believed in an idea of ordinary heroism and admired the lively culture of the village, which he also saw as an influential model or standard. The book's hero, an effete viscount, is sent up from England by his doctor to live among the fishermen and run their physical risks – in the course of this, his elegant idleness turns to activity and intelligent judgement.

Photographing a working community as a model, rather than a desperate society as a problem, is also an answer to the twentieth-century concern about the potentially voyeuristic attitude of the wealthier classes to pictures of poverty. In *The Fishermen and Women* series, neither patronising concern nor dubious relish is invited, only admiration. This extended series of photographs has to be considered as a large-scale, serious work. It is not a set of distanced sketches by a purely aesthetic or anthropological observer; it is a close and loving study of a community that Hill greatly admired; here was an ideal and possibly here, if attention was paid, was a solution to a grievous problem.

5

Personal and Professional Ambition

PREDESTINATION AND PHRENOLOGY

D. O. Hill belonged to a society that emphasised the personal responsibility of the individual and regarded both hard work and struggle as a necessary background to success. Samuel Smiles's publications in the *Self-Help* series, regarded nowadays as characteristic of Victorian values, emanated from such work as Hugh Miller's *My Schools and Schoolmasters* and included the lives of others of Hill and Adamson's subjects, Robert and William Chambers and James Nasmyth.[1] All are built on the assumption that formal education was only partly of benefit to a future career. Smiles, whilst declaring in his autobiography that, 'A good education is equivalent to a good fortune', adds, 'I fear I was fonder of frolic than of learning' and concludes, 'On the whole, provided there was perseverance, those young men succeeded the best from whom little was expected.'[2]

The question of personal responsibility for success was complicated by the Presbyterian idea of predestination, which meant that worldly failure, as well as success, was part of God's intention.[3] Like life itself, ambition was in God's hands and subject to the same condition of perilous and obscured hope. Hill expressed this after his niece, Patricia Orr, underwent an operation in 1853: 'let us hope she may be spared and that God has some good work for her to do which this dreadful shadow may point the way to.'[4]

The supposed science of phrenology, which had a particular stronghold in Edinburgh from the 1820s, partly aimed to simplify or alleviate the stress of religious predestination by proposing that inherent capabilities could be judged by an examination of the surface structure of the head.[5] The leading phrenologist, George Combe (fig. 48), explained his enthusiasm for the subject as a revolt from the arid formalities of his Calvinist upbringing: 'There was neither within nor around me any atmosphere of consistency, goodness, and truth; but a constant conflict of emotions and ideas one with the other; *and the world was a chaos.*'[6] In the words of another phrenologist: 'The world will give it [phrenology] a long trial, were it only that it deals with the substances of character, and seems to create a solid play-ground, away from the abstractions of the old metaphysics. Colour and life, substance and form, are dear to mankind, as homes against the wind of cold speculation.'[7] In an age when self-determination was beset with new fears and problems, from the erratic nature of industrial progress to an unstable population, such certainty was particularly attractive. For young men wanting to know what trade to adopt, for masters wanting confidence in new servants, for people looking for marriage or business partners, phrenology purported to give practical answers. George Combe made phrenology both popular and subsequently respectable by attaching it to a moral and educational system. His book, *The Constitution of Man*, published in 1828, sold 17, 000 copies in one year, and became fourth of the best-selling books of its time.[8] The well-established commercial practice of phrenology in Edinburgh in the 1840s may be seen in the diary of the publisher James Gall, who joined himself to the Newhaven calotype of the minister taking a Bible class with the fishwives, in his role as a Church elder (fig. 49). Gall took his whole household to a consultation with a Mrs Hamilton in 1842, and copied out her chart of 'Phrenological Developments' in forty-one different categories. Mrs Hamilton's measurements showed that the largest and most impressive bumps in the household belonged to the housemaid. She managed to explain this away and to present Gall with an analysis of his own nature, which was as splendid as it was implausible.[9]

In 1843, Hugh Miller introduced his article on the calotype with a sardonic comparison between the impact of

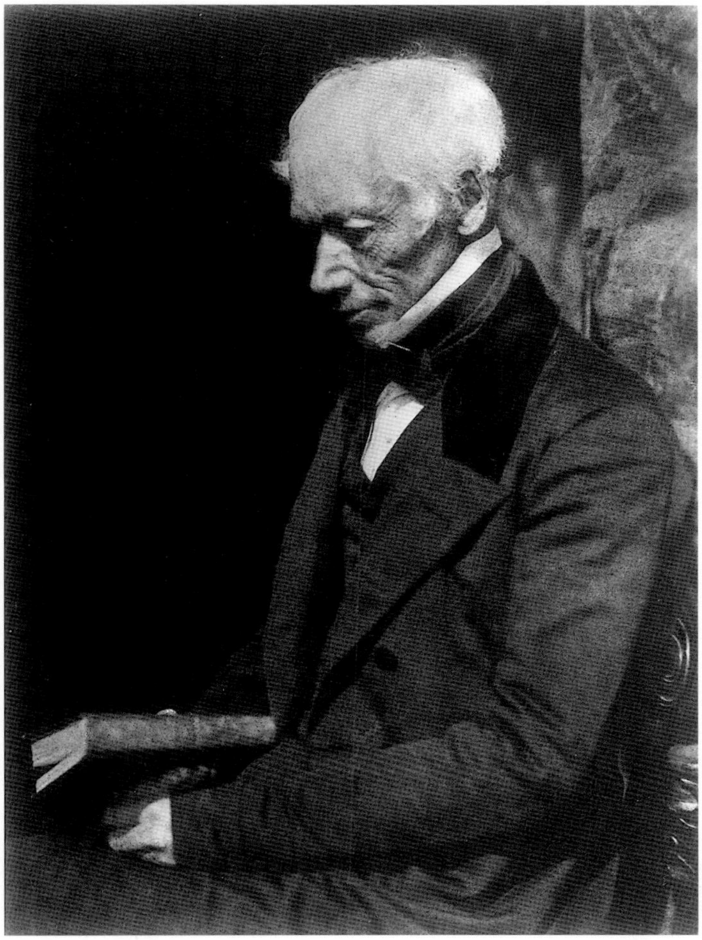

48. D. O. Hill and Robert Adamson, *George Combe*, 1843–7. Calotype. Scottish National Photography Collection, Edinburgh.

photography and a blatantly fraudulent version of phrenology:

> Phrenomesmerism and the calotype have been introduced to the Edinburgh public about much the same time; but how very differently have they fared hitherto! A real invention, which bids fair to produce some of the greatest revolutions in the fine arts of which they have ever been the subject, has as yet attracted comparatively little notice; an invention which serves but to demonstrate that the present age, with all its boasted enlightenment, may yet not be very unfitted for the reception of superstitions, the most irrational and gross, is largely occupying the attention of the community, and filling column after column in our public prints.[10]

Phrenomesmerism was a public performance, in which the expert first (apparently) hypnotised the subject and then pressed the relevant bumps to generate the behaviour of loving children, miserliness and so forth. The subject then capered about the platform displaying these characteristics, to considerable admiration. One of the travelling performers, a Mr Mair from Dundee, walked, by a nice irony, into the arms of Dr John Adamson in the same month Hugh Miller published his article, and the story may have prompted Miller's remark. Mair began his performance in St Andrews by first putting a boy into a 'cataleptic state':

> He then invited any gentlemen present to examine the boy. Dr Adamson, who happened to be present, having procured a weight of about 14lbs, attached a cord to it, and put it over the boy's arm, and suddenly cut the cord, when the arm started up, plainly shewing that the weight had been supported by an ordinary voluntary exertion of the boy. The performers were a little abashed.[11]

Since the medical profession was currently in desperate pursuit of anaesthetics to alleviate the pain of surgery and one of the proposed solutions was hypnotism, Adamson's interest and suspicion here may have related rather to the mesmerism than the phrenology.

However, the more serious impact of phrenologists' opinions on the Scottish art world, which will be further examined for its influence on art practice in chapter nine, may be judged by two instances. In 1826, John James Audubon, a relatively obscure naturalist, came to Edinburgh, where he secured agreement to publish his great work on the *Birds of America* with the engraver and phrenologist, William Home Lizars, because phrenological analysis of Audubon's skull confirmed him as a painter and 'compositor', and earned him a place next to Titian and Rubens as a colourist.[12] The artist and his partner and, indeed, all convinced phrenologists now had an investment of belief in Audubon's success.[13]

Part of the virtuous intention behind phrenology was educational – to match the young to appropriate careers. The Swedenborgian minister and phrenologist, D. G. Goyder, was filled with enthusiasm for the fourteen-year-old Joseph Noël Paton:

> Of the different heads brought under my notice I do not remember one more strikingly characteristic and harmonious with phrenology . . . His head was very large, measuring at that early period upwards of 23 inches in circumference, and every part was fully and freely developed. The organs of Constructiveness, Form, Size, Coloring, Ideality, Imitation, Wit, and Language, were very large indeed . . . I recommended the father of this

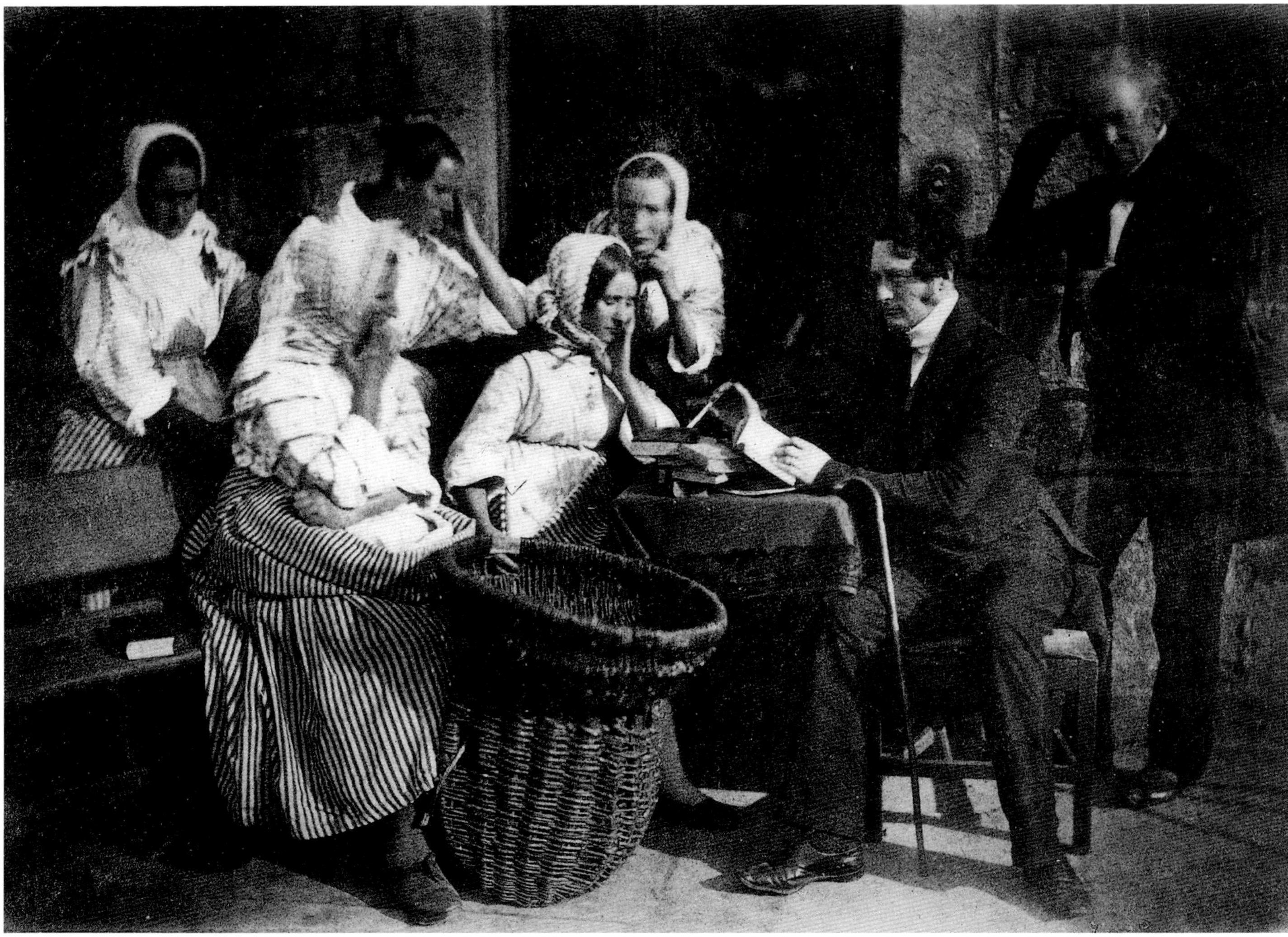

49. D. O. Hill and Robert Adamson, *Newhaven Fishwives with the Reverend James Fairbairn and James Gall*, 16 July 1845. Calotype. Scottish National Photography Collection, Edinburgh.

youth to allow him to cultivate the arts, affirming that I was yet young enough to see him at the head of his profession as an artist.[14]

Regardless of the actual influence of Goyder's words on Paton's career, such a positive opinion can only have been cheering and added to Paton's youthful confidence. It would also have been attractive to his close friend, D. O. Hill. But the same respect for phrenology could be undermining. Hill's career as an artist was settled and begun before phrenology became respectable. What if his head was the wrong shape for the Fine Arts?

In a series of letters on phrenology and art in the 1840s, George Combe wrote:

There are numerous instances in which the individual has possessed the temperament of genius, and even a combination of cerebral organs adapted to art, but in which the size of the organs has been so deficient, that it was not adequate to give vigour and impressiveness. Such artists are haunted by a demon of genius: their fine and active temperaments give them some inspirations; they appreciate art, and are able to a certain extent, to body forth, in their own minds, original conceptions of beautiful figures and groups; but owing to the smallness of their brains, there is a feebleness in the execution which mars their best efforts.[15]

There is an uncomfortable echo here in anxieties expressed by Hill's friends and particularly in John Brown's criticism of his painting, written in 1846: 'There is sometimes a provoking carelessness, and even feebleness in execution, and harshness of contrast. These show that his power of performance, – of sustained effort, – is not equal, or at least not by his will made equal to his conceptions.'[16]

Brown's intention, to persuade Hill to work harder on his landscape painting, involved a doubt of his capacity. Whether or not Hill believed in phrenology, a nervous suspicion that his brain was wrongly developed might well have been as discouraging as the opinion of Paton's head was encouraging.

AMBITION AND FINE ART

The high ambition of an artist's work was seen, by observers, as necessarily surrounded by the failure of those lacking in talent and drive. Bathos was omnipresent in the art world of the time; the grander the project, the more foolish the intensity may be made to look. Hill helped the history painter David Scott, when he was on his deathbed, to dispose of his unsold heroic picture of *Vasco da Gama Passing the Cape of Good Hope*. Hill was attempting to alleviate Scott's distress, but he may also have been attempting to lessen the tragic irony, inherent in the theoretical necessity of failure.[17]

The ambitions of genius in art were tempting and could be fatal. Benjamin Robert Haydon's suicide in despair in 1846 is a desperate case of the stress between ambition, talent and success.[18] It was presented in the *Sun* newspaper as the consequence of appalling official meanness, in the face of 'the anguish of destitute genius'; a failure of public patronage, which led to 'starvation, and the lunacy, and the sudden and sometimes violent deaths, which impart such a melancholy but significant gloom to the memorials of some of the most gifted beings in the land'.[19] Hill, like many others, must have been strongly affected. Haydon had written to him in April, admiring the calotypes and adding: 'I never paint now without one of your heads on my easel'.[20] He shot himself in front of the easel and there is a macabre possibility that his life blood blotted out a calotype.

There was even an appropriate literary model of such failure in Walter Scott's satire on the idea of the native genius, Dick Tinto. In a letter to Paton, describing John Ruskin's Edinburgh lecture in 1853, Hill wrote:

> There was great amusement occasioned by a magnified drawing of one of the sixty four Lions of the Royal Institution – as contrasted with a drawing by Millais of a Tiger from the Life. Dick Tinto's Horse standing a-la Tripod on its hind Legs & Tail, I doubt not produced exactly such emotions in the minds of the Guests of the Wallace Head of Gandercleugh.[21]

Hill is referring to the first chapter of Scott's *The Bride of Lammermoor*, in which Tinto introduces the tragic plot of the main story, and, in particular, to Tinto's inept painting for the Wallace Head Inn, which compensated drinkers for the poor quality of the beer: 'one glance at his sign was sure to put them in a good humour.'[22] Tinto, an innocent and untutored painter, emulated the natural art of David Wilkie, 'amid hunger and toil'. He pursued his career in Edinburgh and London, was briefly patronised, but died bankrupt, earning the brisk epitaph: 'So ended Dick Tinto! a lamentable proof of the great truth, that in the fine arts mediocrity is not permitted, and that he who cannot ascend to the very top of the ladder, will do well not to put his foot upon it at all.'[23]

Tinto's ruin was completed by the caprice of patrons, who briefly supported him as a fashionable novelty. The idea has its precedent in the eighteenth-century sentimental proposal – specifically related to poetry – that genius springs from nature and that irresponsible patronage might spoil the man of genius, by introducing him to the corruption of sophisticated society. Ill-considered patronage might not merely encourage the ineffectual but offer the accomplished artist too easy an advance. This anxiety is expressed in Henry Mackenzie's praise of Robert Burns in *The Lounger* in December 1786, which is introduced by a nervous paragraph: 'We have had repeated instances of painters and of poets, who have been drawn from obscure situations, and held forth to public notice and applause by the extravagant encomiums of their introductors, yet in a short time have sunk again to their former obscurity.'[24]

James Nasmyth, a successful engineer and *laissez-faire* industrialist, wrote to Hill, in 1835, expressing doubt about the unnatural encouragement offered by academies of art:

> there is such a native elasticity in true genius that it will by its own efforts leap over the stumbling blocks and by making nature and not art its model for the most part. I do think we should then have more real originality – in as much as none but the true genius could fight his way through. for I am a bit of a tory in these as well as some other matters. which makes me think that every facility should *not* be given for young men joining the profession as it is one in which the supply has so fearfull a tendency to exceed the demand and these academys do tend I think to cultivate potatoes under hot beds.[25]

Nasmyth was being disingenuous. His career as an engineer was based on his parents' own knowledge and wide circle and their even more remarkable readiness to allow their teenage son to turn his bedroom grate into a foundry. But this idea, of the importance of stumbling blocks, was common. It reappears in the article on the history of painting written by James Skene, who was both an amateur painter and a patron, for David Brewster's *Edinburgh Encyclopaedia.* Skene devoted a large section of this to a moral lecture on the founding of the Scottish Academy. Skene required not just difficulty but suffering in the pursuit of art:

> It is not an unusual error in institutions of this description, to defeat their purpose by overshooting the mark, and endeavouring to do too much, – to present the means of encouragement uninvited, and to urge its acceptance, before the privation it is meant to supply is keenly felt, and a consciousness of its value awakened in the minds of those for whose behoof it is intended.[26]

Hugh Miller wrote an account of his friend, William Ross, who wished to become a painter, which lays out an example of the problem of the natural ideal based on individual, unsupported struggle:

> His boyhood had been that of the poet: he had loved to indulge his day-dreams in the solitude of a deep wood beside his grandmother's cottage; and he had learnt to write verses and draw landscapes in a rural locality where no one had ever written verses or drawn landscapes before. And finally, as, in the North of Scotland, in those primitive times, the nearest approach to an artist was a house-painter, William was despatched to Cromarty, when he had grown tall enough for the work, to cultivate his natural taste for the fine arts, in papering rooms and lobbies, and in painting railings and wheel-barrows. There are, I believe, a few instances on record of house-painters rising to be artists . . . but the fact that the cases are not more numerous serves, I fear, to show how much oftener a turn for drawing is a merely imitative, than an original, self-derived faculty.[27]

Miller's direction in this passage is unexpected. He starts with the idea of the young poet in natural solitude, follows with a sardonic account of his apprenticeship and concludes that Ross was unsuccessful because he lacked the 'original faculty'; for Miller, as for Nasmyth, genius would have fought its way through. This now seems an uncompromising and unkind idea. Miller's fatalism was presumably a part of a search for the explanation of his friend's failure and early death and he did not allow that Ross might have flourished with encouragement.

EDUCATION AND UNITY
The Alleviation of Individual Responsibility

Hugh Miller was resigned to his friend's failure as natural. For a modern audience, untrammelled by assumptions of predestination and divine purpose, it is arguable that William Ross's talent was wasted by a lack of professional education. But Miller had only a partial interest in formal education. The title of his autobiographical work, *My Schools and Schoolmasters*, was sardonic; he presents himself as largely self-educated and much of that education as coming direct from nature.

Hill would have sympathised with a more generous view. His own formal education had been both good and encouraging, and he was experienced and open as a teacher. Hill taught in association with the Edinburgh Institution from 1832 to 1835. He set up his classes, which were also advertised separately and directed at the High School pupils, both in the rooms of the Institution and in the large classroom below the Scottish Academy's exhibition rooms in Waterloo Place. In his advertisement, he wrote:

> To endeavour to render the study general and to induce Pupils to continue their attendance for an adequate period, it is intended to open these Classes with a rate of fees reduced to an equality with the ordinary branches of education.
>
> The plan of study to be pursued will embrace Perspective – The Elements of Landscape – Historical Picturesque Composition in Landscape – Sketching from Nature, Drawing the Human Figure, etc. [28]

He was expressing a conscious intention to broaden the range and base of a sophisticated training in art. The school was also remarkable as only the second in Edinburgh to be based on co-operative lines. The teachers themselves took responsibility without a controlling or proprietary board – a fact significant in the context of the reform of politics, just achieved with the Reform Bill of 1832.

Hill was also fortunate to be a member of the close circle around the landscape painter, Alexander Nasmyth. This offered an unstructured and unofficial forum for advanced education, which the Edinburgh painters seem to have maintained. Moreover, Hill's association with the Nasmyth family would have encouraged the interest in an interchange between art and technology. Alexander Nasmyth was a ready inventor, devising ingenious methods to enable people to run down hill at speed or improving lawnmowers (fig. 50). His son, James, Hill's close friend, was an engineer, not a painter, but he could model and draw and took a knowledgeable interest in the arts.

It would appear that the artists and their friends discussed their work with each other and offered practical assistance. Hill was given much advice by his friends, presumably mostly verbally but sometimes in their letters. As an example, the advocate and poet, Sheriff Henry Glassford Bell, wrote to him: 'O! man! paint your lights & shadows in large masses – use less green & yellow & more black & red, & then you may defy the foul fiend, who always is Yours very truly.'[29] The artists' anxiety for excellence involved an unselfish concern that art should succeed generally rather than just individually – a properly social impulse. Hill's tribute to William Allan, written in 1849, is of this order, combining a note on his enthusiasm as master of the Trustees Academy with a comment on his 'genial, hospitable and liberal private character'.[30] Thomas Dibdin was impressed by the artists he met when entertained by Hill in 1836: 'The fact is . . . there exists at Edinburgh a warm and generous feeling about the FINE ARTS. There is a sort of heart's worship in the cause; and, I will honestly add, a very general disposition among artists to render ample justice to the merits of each other.'[31] It is unquestionably significant that the generosity Dibdin admired was found in Hill's enlivening company.

Scotland seems also to have taken an energetic role in publishing art criticism in the 1840s and 1850s, with the idea of educating the artist as well as the audience. Dr John Brown partly justified taking up employment as art critic for the *Witness* in 1846 in Hill's interest: 'I was anxious to do it very much on account of David Hill. I want to tell the truth about him to himself and the public'.[32] At a later date, Hill urged Noël Paton to exhibit in Edinburgh as well as London, on the grounds that:

> Our press here would do you more justice than your great Picture can receive from any Metropolitan Journal, called upon to discuss the whole of the Royal Academy Exhibition – and little as the Metropolitan Press would confess to being moved by the provincial it is not the less certain that an Edinburgh reputation has not unfrequently preceded, at least, if not led to one that was world wide.[33]

This opinion is confirmed by a letter from the Pre-Raphaelite painter, John Everett Millais in 1852, when his picture

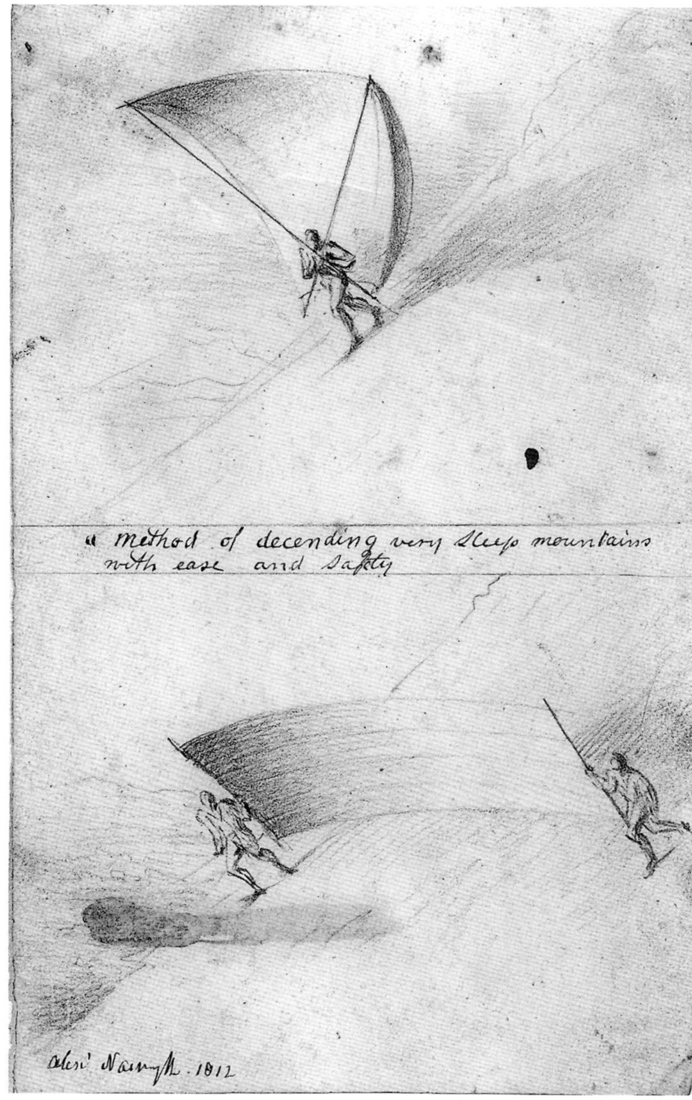

50. Alexander Nasmyth, *A Method of Descending Steep Hills.* Drawing. National Gallery of Scotland, Edinburgh.

Marianne, was in the Scottish Academy: 'I am continually receiving Scotch papers with frightfully long criticisms, a vast quantity of praise and, of course, advice.'[34] This critical distinction helps to explain John Ruskin's remark in 1853:

> I have many friends and admirers in Edinburgh, and am in some respects far better understood there than in London. The Edinburgh artists – Harvey, D. O. Hill, Noel Paton, etc., are all eager to meet me, while the London ones are all too happy to get out of my way, and the only letter you have yet got, showing true appreciation of my book, except George Richmond's, is from the Edinburgh Dr. Brown.[35]

It is presumably not a coincidence that John Ruskin, who became the most influential critic of the time, was born of Scottish parents and imbued with a deep religious training, which emphasised the need for moral criticism throughout life.[36] When he met Hill in 1853, he noted that Hill was, 'a landscape painter, amiable and unobtrusive; must be attended to'.[37] Hill wrote to him in 1867, hoping that he would write a criticism but received the melancholy reply:

> I have kept your kind letter by me very sorrowfully it is one of the painfullest results of the state of health I am in at present that I must seem so unkind to my friends —but I have been obliged – by sweeping and irrefrageable rule – to give up all critical work. It is very laborious to me, & very killing and I believe *utterly* useless. Popular will must direct art at present – no single voice can be heard in the hubbub. But if it could – I have no voice to raise – I never look at any pictures now.[38]

THE SCOTTISH ACADEMY AND THE REJECTION OF OFFICIAL PATRONAGE

James Skene and James Nasmyth were thoroughly dubious of academies. Lord Cockburn was more sympathetic. He was involved as a mediator in the early stages of the Scottish Academy and wrote of its history: 'There is an advanced state of art at which probably all artificial associations of artists are useless, if not hurtful. But in an infant stage, during which the public taste requires to be excited and educated, and artists need importance and protection by formal brotherhood, such unions are nearly indispensable.'[39]

The academy was joined by the large group of artists, including Hill, who had stood back in the first instance, in 1830.[40] The preface to the exhibition catalogue of that year is telling in its vocabulary, challenging and echoing the authority of the official patronage of the Board of Manufactures and the Institution for the Promotion of the Fine Arts:

> The Council rejoices to state, that with a view to their own freedom and independence, a Union has been formed between the Original Members of the Academy and the Associates of the Royal Institution, and other Artists . . . The Scottish Academy aims at promoting the advancement of Scottish Art, and the dignity and independence of Scottish Artists; and they fondly anticipate that these objects will be attained by cordial co-operation, and by the absence of contracted and selfish views.[41]

Hill became the secretary of the Scottish Academy, and was later one of the principal actors in freeing it from the amateur toils of the Board of Trustees for Manufactures in Scotland (established in 1727) and the associated Institution for the Encouragement of the Fine Arts (founded in 1819).[42] The membership of the Board and the Institution was composed of noblemen and men of wealth, patrons rather than professional artists. Essentially, the painters had set up the academy and withdrawn their associate membership of the Institution because, as interested artists, they were not allowed a voice in its actions.

This curious relationship lasted until 1844, when the essential flaws within it cracked open. After the opening of the academy exhibition, Hill received a letter from the secretary to the board of trustees, Sir Thomas Dick Lauder. Lauder wrote to complain that the academy's hanging committee had re-hung a painting by his son in a poor position in the exhibition. This was a contentious issue. The difficult decisions involved in hanging such crowded exhibitions, and the naturally jealous concern of the artists that their own work should be hung on the line, rather than raised to the ceiling, meant that the committee worked in well-guarded secrecy. The unpleasant character of Lauder's letter may be summed up in one of his comprehensive sentences:

> It is evident that no public confidence can be placed in future in a Council which can allow, not only the judgement of its Hanging Committee, but its own determinations corrobative thereof, and these so long confirmed, to be swayed and overturned by every unworthy intrigue that may be originated by selfish individuals in the body which it ought to govern.[43]

The fight that ensued had the distressing character of a domestic dispute – these were all men who knew each other well, occupying the same building and all, theoretically, concerned with the same public work. Thomas Dick Lauder's role on the board was formally that of a disinterested patron. By voicing precisely the kind of private jealousy attributed to artists, which had justified depriving them of control over their own affairs, he generated the anger which made this impossible situation public, and gave the academy the ammunition they had needed to break free.

The fight occupied more than a decade, and the extraordinary stress and indignation it generated can be heard in Hill's letters. It was he who acted as the official focus of the complaints, from Lord Meadowbank and James Skene amongst others, constantly responsible for 'another shell which we are just in the act of throwing into the citadel of the Royal

Institution.'[44] James Nasmyth's doubtful attitude towards academies was shattered by this dispute and he responded to one of Hill's letters:

> The attack they made on the Scottish Academy is outrageous and insolent beyond all sufferance and I only hope it will put the finishing toutch [*sic*] to a final and most complete emancipation of Scottish art and artists from the driveling but abortive attempts to degrade the artists of Scotland to be the creeping things that they would apparently wish to see them become. Patrons of the Fine arts. Meadowbank and Skeens their very names stink i' th' nostril of every thing that is small and spirit cramping.[45]

The results were a substantial measure of independence for the academy and the establishing of a separate building to house the academy and its schools with the new National Gallery of Scotland. It was a compromise position, which Hill notes in 1855:

> We go to it with the debt of many thousands on our shoulders – the Board look to us for the art knowledge necessary for conducting their schools & exhibitions – they have a noble gallery of antiques which may be ours in effect – and in short with frank & manly sincerity our position, the Government being along with us, may be made better than we ourselves could have made it. There are many considerations to make us rest more than satisfied with our new position. These I doubt not would have occurred to your mind – they frequently did to mine – even when I was striving to convince others & myself that nothing could do for us but sole possession. If we had got it I think one of my first acts would have been resignation of office – for woe betide the [fearless?] secretary who had three Exhibitions a year instead of one to attend to.[46]

Hill along with George Harvey was then appointed one of the members of the Board of Trustees, finally placing artists alongside the 'disinterested' patrons.

INDEPENDENCE OF PATRONAGE AND THE ASSOCIATION FOR THE PROMOTION OF THE FINE ARTS

The success of the academy involved a union of people and ideas: challenging the Scottish painters; educating and interesting the public; and widening the audience. This, in itself, is a clue to the way Hill thought and worked. His enthusiasm was not narrowly directed but expressed broad ambition. The strange situation in which the academy flourished until 1844 may well have been made possible by this attitude of mind, in which ambition was approached through the opening influence of generosity.

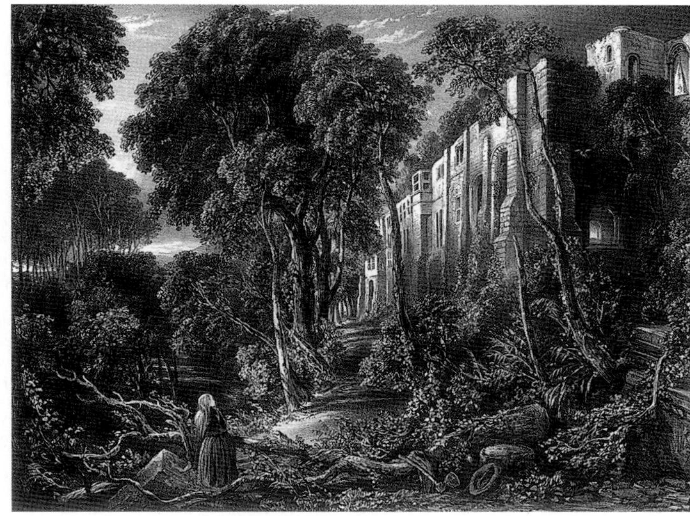

51. W. Gauci after D. O. Hill, *Dunfermline Palace*. Lithograph, published 1853. National Library of Scotland, Edinburgh.

It was obvious that fine art was encouraged almost entirely by the wealthy. The rejection of patronage – in the ownership and control of politics, religion, education and the arts – is critical to Hill's career, which was particularly driven by the search for independence for the artist, and the urge to disseminate art to a greater public. Despite the elevated theory that a small class of educated, discriminating men would encourage and monitor the productions of art, it was obvious that patronage could lack stability, generosity and even sense. Hill's own experience with Mr Hunt of Pittencrieff, whose senile forgetfulness caused him to reject the painting he had ordered, underlined the problem that the artist was not commonly arguing from a position of strength. Hill had painted a picture of Dunfermline Palace, which Mr Hunt admired and commissioned a variant. The original was painted in moonlight with the contemplative foreground figure of the woodcutter's daughter (fig. 51). For Mr Hunt, Hill repainted the subject in sunlight, substituted the fashionable figure of Hunt's daughter strolling through the wood with a little dog, and painted his house in the background – alterations which would have made the picture difficult to sell elsewhere. In letters to Joseph Noël Paton in 1853 and 1854, and thinking of the palace wall, Hill referred to him as 'Hunty Dunty' and wrote with uncharacteristic anger: 'Indignation is not the thing and ridicule is not the thing for such an animal.'[47] At the time, Hill was painfully short of money. Eventually, the situation was resolved by Mr Hunt and his family accepting responsibility for a piece of senile forgetfulness. This was for Hill an experience of the distorted world of old age, where the authority of the adult is mixed with the irresponsibility of the child; where the words, the denial and insistence that it is the other who is wrong, spread confusion and increase the injury. The accidental connection between Hill's and Lewis Carroll's Humpty Dumpty (as opposed to the familiar nursery rhyme) is this use of words as flat statement, against good sense or morality: '"When *I* use a word," Humpty Dumpty said in a rather scornful tone, "it means just what I choose it to mean, – neither more nor less."'[48]

Hugh Miller expressed a sense of the danger of dependence, inherent in such a close and potentially demeaning relationship: 'no man *is,* or no man ought to think himself, above the high dignity of being independent . . . Some of the greatest wrecks we have seen in life have been those of waiters on patronage.'[49] Cockburn, after reading Allan Cunningham's *Life of David Wilkie* in 1843, commented: 'His life does not impress me with a favourable idea of the position even of a successful artist in this country. In Wilkie's case, it produced little money and constant anxiety about patronage.'[50]

In the new cycles of economic depression, the most impressive artists might fail. David Roberts's friend, the Glasgow merchant John G. Kinnear, himself affected by the slump in 1848, wrote slyly but accurately to him: 'I suppose the times will affect your *sect* also – a falling off in the demand for works of Art – Exhibitions glutted – Landscape looking down – great fall in the Historical line – Eh?'[51] In that year, George Harvey wrote in despair, 'It is now three years since I *sold a picture of any kind* and *seven* since I sold one in Edinburgh.'[52] This explains the enthusiasm with which the exhibition receipts were counted, which may be seen in Hill's letters to Roberts: 'The Exhibition continues to draw hugely – that is even more so than any previous one. and the Treasurer gets more particular and *generally* confidential in announcing the sum total.'[53] It also justifies Hill's pride in the financial position of the academy and of the painters, which he summed up as his achievement, when he retired in 1869:

> I entered upon the duties when our income from visitors was 5 or 600£ a year – now they are £3000 from that source. Our sales were contemptible – now for the last three years they average more than £6000. And this great result has in a great measure flowed from beginnings by myself, which have stirred up the artistic [or 'intense'] love of art of England and its colonies – so that a few years ago – the income of the associations founded on ours – which was my devising – was 60,000£ a year in Great Britain. Then the activity it has made with private purchasers is amazing – But this is perhaps nothing to the implanting of notions of art throughout the whole empire – and to a great extent the love of nature [?] which it has opened up. I have also the satisfaction of having introduced the evening Exhibitions which show their success by producing some £500 or 600 a year to our funds at smaller prices of admission.[54]

This was not simply Hill's view. From the mid-1830s, the academy had apparently achieved a situation, in which:

> All expenses connected with the general management, also what was expended in the purchase of works of art for the National Gallery, the Library, and the support of its schools, were defrayed solely from the proceeds of the annual Exhibitions, the income from which continued to show a steady increase, the result of the Academy's efforts to make these annual displays increasingly attractive to the public, not only from the contributions of the members, but by acquiring for the time the loan of works distinguished for their merit and value.[55]

The success was partly the responsibility of the Association for the Promotion of the Fine Arts in Scotland, an idea whose very name declares its encroachment on the responsibilities of the Institution for the Encouragement of the Fine Arts.[56] This was a system invented by Hill, with Henry Glassford Bell and John Steell – the first of the art unions – set up in 1834 to enlarge the narrow base of patronage. Hill was prompted into action by the drop in sales in the academy's exhibitions from nearly £500 in 1831 to £338 in 1833.[57] The Association was a kind of lottery in which, for a pound a year, each of the subscribers received a print and the opportunity to win oil paintings at the academy's exhibitions. *The New Statistical Account of Scotland* in 1845 noted that, in 1840, the Association collected £6,396; in 1842, £6,590. The text comments: 'Those who recollect the time, when instead of £6,000 being collected in one year for the encouragement of the fine arts, there were not £1,000 distributed among our native artists in six years, will best appreciate the importance of the change which has taken place.'[58]

There were several advantages to the lottery. It stimulated the art of engraving and, both through the prints and the distribution of the paintings, reached and educated a new audience. However, despite these manifest advantages, the lottery attracted moral opposition, on the original grounds that art should be achieved through struggle. Disconcertingly, one of the fiercest opponents of the idea was Hill's friend, John Brown. In his review of Ruskin's *Modern Painters* he added a passage irrelevant to the text of his argument, contrasting the public benefit of Robert Cadell's illustrated edition of Scott with the harm generated by the art unions, and it is probable that the argument was aimed specifically at Hill:

> The heavy and certain evils to the public as well as to art, which all such unnatural and self-sufficient associations must, in our opinion, produce . . . by tending to make void the natural law of reward and production – depreciating what is truly valuable, and encumbering it by their help, and as a natural consequence of their encouragement, producing and over-rating and over-rewarding an inferior – often false – art, which would other wise have either not existed, or been left to be dealt with according to its desert.[59]

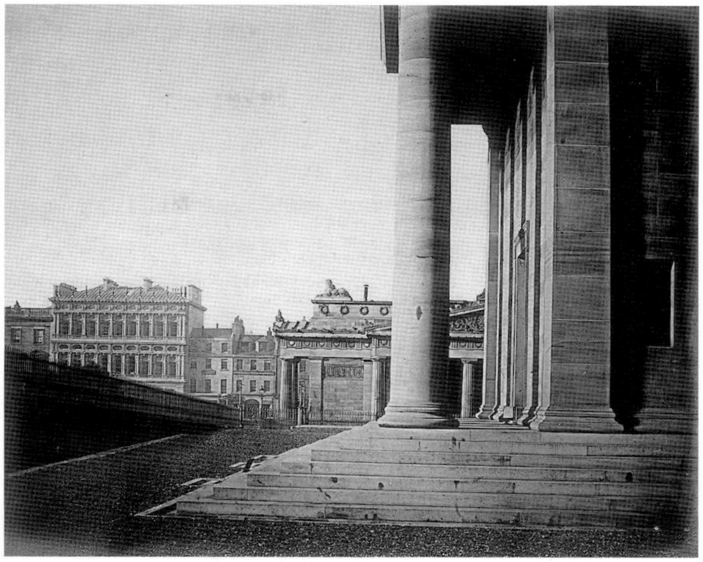

52. William Donaldson Clark, *The National Gallery and the Royal Institution*, *c.* 1859. Albumen print. Scottish National Photography Collection, Edinburgh.

EXHIBITION AND EXAMPLE
The Education of the Artists and their Public

From the evidence of Hill's letters, we can see his energy in setting up the annual exhibitions, bringing in challenging and important pictures from outside Scotland to help raise standards and widen the horizon of the artists and their audience. This was undertaken at a period when most important paintings were privately owned and only to be seen as a personal favour. Hill's pursuit of paintings from private collections began in 1830, with a flurry of letters requesting the loan of work from artists including Raeburn, C. R. Leslie, Edwin Landseer, John Constable, Turner and Wilkie. It may be seen later, particularly in the letters to David Roberts in the 1840s. In 1845, paintings by Clarkson Stanfield, Turner and Roberts himself were among those lent, and Hill responded: 'Many many thanks to you for your great exertions – I trust they will lead to the growth of a cosmopolitan spirit in regard to Art as well as the increase of a National emulation in the race of genius.'[60] A similar impulse lay behind Hill's personal gifts of hundreds of the calotypes to the English and Hibernian Academies as well as the Scottish Academy, where he started a photographic library in 1851:

> A nucleus has already been formed by 500 of the best specimens executed by him and the late Mr Adamson. He stated that there were many other Calotypists, both professional and amateur, who would be found equally ready to contribute the best of their works, were they assured that they would be considered fitting additions to a National Art Library, and would be valued and preserved accordingly. [61]

Much of this activity was designed for the benefit of the painters, but Hill was also concerned with the education of the public at large. From the late 1840s, he was involved in soliciting and acquiring paintings for the proposed National Gallery of Scotland. He was also concerned that it should encourage and generate new art and he urged Noël Paton's designs for sculpture for the building on the committee of the academy and the architect. His correspondence with Paton on the subject is lengthy and impassioned:

> I have high hopes that a public subscription will *do them all.* I think our President will come down handsomely. I shall with plêasure give my first year of my advanced salary – the advance is £25 – the great matter is to delight people with *the designs* and that speedily . . . I promise you I shall not easily be beaten off the execution of them all. If a personal solicitation & representation will raise the needful. So never say die.[62]

The gallery opened in 1858 in the handsome new building designed by William Henry Playfair, on the Mound behind the Royal Institution – without Paton's sculpture (fig. 52). However, Hill's enthusiasm had continued to overflow in ideas of this kind. In 1854, he proposed a national collection of art at Holyrood: 'It might be made one of the most delightful & extraordinary collections in the world – the History Poetry Romance – superstitions sylvan sports & Landscapes of Scotland and by Scottish artists – and all this in Holyrood – depend upon it there is life in it.'[63]

Hill's interest in spreading the base of art education emerges in the free and the cheap evening openings the academy organised. The intention was laid out in the leaflet printed, in 1846, to re-publish John Brown's critical piece on *Distraining for Rent* for the benefit of the visitors, which is signed by Hill as secretary. It was designed to promote an understanding and love of art among the people:

> It is not more to the honour and fame of Scotland, that she produced a Burns from the bosom of the people, than that they – the masses – know intimately, understand thoroughly, and feel and love intensely, the writings of their own poet. We would also have them know, feel, and love in equal degree, the immortal works of one who may be truly said to be *their own Painter* . . . In order to assist in the study of this and other works, those of our readers who might be liable to fall into the mistake that pictures are meant to gratify the eye without interesting the mind or the affections, we extract from a contemporary . . . a lengthened essay on the work above alluded to, as we think we recognize in it a style of criticism of the highest class, likely when read, to exercise a most wholesome and genial influence on the Art, and the feeling for Art throughout Scotland. [64]

This leaflet was economically reprinted from a copy of the *Witness* text in the *North British Advertiser*, which allowed the academy the free use of its set-up type. The first print run was 3,000, and Hill was authorised by the academy to print as many more as he needed. These were circulated to 'individuals having workmen in their employment, with a printed letter stating the intention', thus serving as an advertisement and promotion for the cheap evening openings as well as an advance preparation for the experience.[65]

Hill obviously had executive control of the academy catalogues, as in so much that applied to the exhibitions. He shared an interest with other painters, like Turner, in supplying his own paintings with printed texts. His admiration for Ruskin's writing on Turner turns to this point: 'When reading his glowing pages I was so fascinated by the truth and beauty of his remarks, that I more than once thought of communicating to the Author my entire sympathy and admiration of his labours . . . it might serve the cause of the criticism if public attention were called to it while Turners Picture was with us.'[66]

In previous decades, the political attack on the Royal Institution was partly based on the complaint that its exclusive evening opening of exhibitions deprived the generality of art education.[67] Having seen the idea of cheap evening openings work well in Edinburgh, Hill urged the idea on David Roberts for the London Royal Academy, and, knowing how even admirable plans will founder on detail, provided the answers to the most practical questions. It is a good example of Hill's pursuit of excellence through technology that he recommends the Royal Academy to find or make its own supply of gas for the purpose: 'I am told your London gas is not of the purest – but if you found it worth your while you would find ways & means to come by a supply of a purer sort – many private gentlemen in Scotland have their country houses supplied with beautiful gas – made at their own place by their Gardener or other domestic.'[68]

THE MULTIPLE IMAGE

It was important to Hill and his colleagues that the academy should provide an example of excellence in all fields to encourage and educate the Scottish painters and their public. For many artists the understanding of both historical and modern painting was a particular difficulty and dependent on reproductions. The desire to acquire equivalents or copies appears in several instances in Hill's correspondence in the 1850s:

> I may mention to you (in strict confidence) that Mr J. F. Lewis [John Frederick Lewis] the painter of 'The Hhareem' was reported to have made drawings from Massaccio & Ghirlandajo & on my writing to him . . . he mentioned incidentally that he had about sixty drawings in water colours from the great Spanish Italian Flemish & other masters some of them very elaborate others slighter. This led to a desire of possessing these. Lewis is a cracksman in his way . . . Lewis writes me that his drawings are 62 – and pricing them moderately such as he thinks they would sell at Christie & Mansons they come to about £540 or thereabouts – but he seems a man of generous spirit and says if the Academy wish them he would part with them at some loss for their purpose.[69]

> We have bought 200 casts in imitation Ivory – from Medieval Ivory Carvings extending over seven centuries – and I believe giving a capital view at a glance of the sculpture of those ages. They are early casts & sharp.[70]

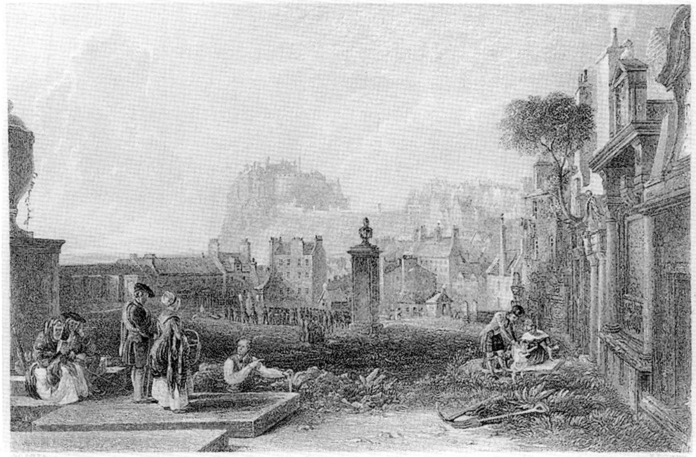

53. W. Richardson after D. O. Hill, *Edinburgh Castle from Greyfriars Churchyard.* Engraving from *The Land of Burns*, 1840.

This urge for understanding through a comparable, equivalent work explains Ruskin's enthusiastic letter to Hill in 1853, responding to the academy's initiative in proposing to send accomplished students abroad to copy pictures of significance. He wrote:

> Art has been entirely debased all over Europe by the habit of copying great works in the modes supposed most likely to render them attractive, when engraved, to the public eye: a system which has necessarily destroyed the veracity of the copyist, as well as the sincerity of admiration for the true virtues of great works of art. To teach the student to copy at once faithfully & spiritedly; and to put the public in possession of the series of copies so obtained, will be the easiest & the most effective means of reviving the perception of the nation both to the powers of its own artists, & to those of the dead.[71]

Nineteenth-century painters took a particular interest in reproducing their work. The idea of making art public within people's private lives, was of immense importance to Hill, and the idea was a continual thread in his career. His first public artwork was the set of lithographs, *Sketches of Scenery in Perthshire Drawn from Nature and on Stone.*[72] Hill was connected with the boom in the publishing trade, in the production of illustrated books, newly enabled by the use of the hard steel plate for engraving. He was involved in illustrating Walter Scott's Waverley novels for Robert Cadell in 1831–2, which meant that he worked closely with sophisticated engravers – some of them the same men who worked with Turner.[73] In 1837 to 1838, he was the principal illustrator of the *Tales and Sketches* and *Poetical Works* of James Hogg. His major literary publication was the series of engravings from sixty-six landscapes painted as *The Land of Burns*, which he embarked on in 1834 (fig. 53), the same year Cadell published Turner's landscape illustrations for Scott's *Poetical Works. The Land of Burns*, published by John Blackie in 1840, was ambitious. An article on Hill in the *Art Journal*, in 1850, says: 'This beautiful book originated entirely with himself, and was one of the most spirited and expensive speculations in Art-Literature which had been attempted by a Scottish publisher.'[74] Hill's pride in it is seen in the early 1850s, when he wrote to Paton:

> I am working away washing & putting new faces on the Land of Burns pictures – all of them. The week I was in Glasgow I did this to 7 or 8 of them, so as to prove to their proprietors that I could improve them beyond their conception of what was meant by putting them in order – but that if I did it at all I must do it thoroughly, and there was a work of time & labour – with a little brains to make them work sweetly. They were so satisfied with the experiment, that they have made it worth my while to do the whole set well – & I am well pleased that these members of a somewhat ragged regiment will now take the field with their pockets full of pollashs [?]. I trust to fill the world with new admiration. But seriously I am very well pleased to have this opportunity of blowing the noses of these bubbly boys – of putting clean shirts on them, and of otherwise giving them the necessary brushing up to enable them to pass in society – and as Ailie Dinmont [ref. Walter Scott, *Guy Mannering*] said of her bairns to behave themselves *distinctly*.[75]

The following year, he exhibited the pictures as 'The Burns Gallery' in his brother's premises in Edinburgh.[76] He thought of taking out a two-page advertisement in the academy's exhibition catalogue: 'for my Burns Gallery & my Calotypes – with the opinions of artists thereon, it would be well for me that the first should not be a gone coon – and that the latter should a little more be made a dropping green [might be 'goose' or 'dripping goose', perhaps a variant on 'dripping roast'].'[77] According to Hill's obituary, he had proposed to house the paintings permanently in a special gallery on the banks of the River Doon, where Burns had lived: 'but for want of funds the proposal fell through, and one half of the series has since been destroyed by fire, the remainder being dispersed by public auction in Edinburgh.'[78]

The surviving paintings for the *Land of Burns* are all in oil. By 1842, it was clear to Hill that the terms for book illustration were not always adequate for the effort concerned in making drawings. He wrote two consecutive letters to Thomas Constable about illustrations of Queen Victoria's visit to the Highlands, between which his concern about this problem is clarified:

> As to the price of these drawings for the steel plates, I would propose 12 Guineas each for the landscape ones – and perhaps more for the Dunkeld reception should it prove ultra elaborate which indeed it must be – say 20 Gs if the drawing turns out good and very elaborate – if but medium as to quality and labour say 16 Gs. As to the woodcuts I am more in the dark about them. Mr Duncan tells me he charges Mr Caddell from 5 Gs the very small to 15 Gs the large he had done for Old Mortality of the Abbotsford edition . . . If you think this is a fair standard to go by I will do the best I can with the subjects proposed.
>
> I will endeavour to get the drawing for Cousins ready by the time you mention but hardly think it possible. These drawings take me a much longer period than matters of greater apparent importance.
>
> In looking forward to what I must do this month I find it will be absolutely impossible for me to undertake the woodcuts – that is with the expectation of doing them in a way satisfactory to myself & otherwise I will not.[79]

By this time, Hill was probably more interested in Alexander Hill's promulgation of fine art prints as independent objects rather than book illustrations, both because they were bigger and would make more impact, and because they would represent a better proportion of effort to financial result. His obituarist wrote:

> Mr Hill, who was all his life of a speculative turn, and was animated at the same time by a warm desire for the improvement of the public taste, took an active share in various enterprises connected with the diffusion of artistic productions. It is understood to have been through his influence that his brother, the late Alexander Hill, was induced to enter upon the print publishing business, through which so many fine and costly engravings have been placed at the disposal of the public.[80]

Alexander Hill ran a gallery in Princes Street for the exhibition of paintings, the loan and sale of prints and watercolours, and artists' supplies. He became the official print publisher to the academy and bequeathed proofs of his engravings to the academy on his death.[81] Thomas Dibdin recounted a visit to his premises, in 1836, when he saw the evidence of Hill's 'first decided success':[82]

> You look before you, and a white pennant streams down, as from the top mast of a first rate [ship], upon which are inscribed the names of the subscribers to the plate of Sir David Wilkie's 'preaching of John Knox'. The publisher rubs his hands in a sort of modified ecstacy. 'A thousand pounds, Sir, are upon yon scroll.' – 'With all my heart, good Mr Hill, and may it be doubled before the day of publication. How did you manage to raise such an army of subscribers?' – 'Wrote to every Scotch peer and to every Scotch gentleman in the Kingdom; and behold the fruits.'[83]

It was principally through his brother that Hill published his own large-scale engravings, which included the *Views of the Glasgow and Garnkirk Railway* in 1832, the posthumous portrait of the Reverend Thomas Chalmers and his grandson, *Edinburgh from the Castle* and *Windsor Castle.*

Hugh Miller's introductory article on the calotype, in 1843, offers evidence that Hill was thinking of photography as a substitute for drawing in book illustration:

> For a large class of works the labours of the artist bid fair to be restricted to the composition of *tableaux vivants*, which it will be the part of the photographer to fix, and then transfer to the engraver . . . Compared with the mediocre prints of nine-tenths of the illustrated works now issuing from the press, these productions serve admirably to show how immense the distance between nature and her less skilful imitators.[84]

The calotypes, which illustrate Walter Scott's novels, were presumably intended as an experiment in photographic publication. The seriousness of the intention may be seen in the fact that for the group of *The Monks of Kennaquhair*, one of the models, the painter, William Leighton Leitch, has shaved his head (pl. 30).

It is probable that Hill's established interest in publication is responsible for the scope and scale of the calotype partnership's work. When he moved in to Rock House, Hill and Adamson immediately announced six volumes of calotypes in preparation. None of those advertised was issued, though they did publish *A Series of Calotype Views in St Andrews* in 1846.[85] In the end, their principal publication proved to be the album sets of a hundred calotypes. W. H. F. Talbot granted licences to professional men like Henry Collen and Antoine Claudet, who both worked subtantially in response to their subjects – people came to them and asked for their portraits. Hill showed little or no interest in what was, in effect, small-scale patronage – 'cheap likeness making'. This

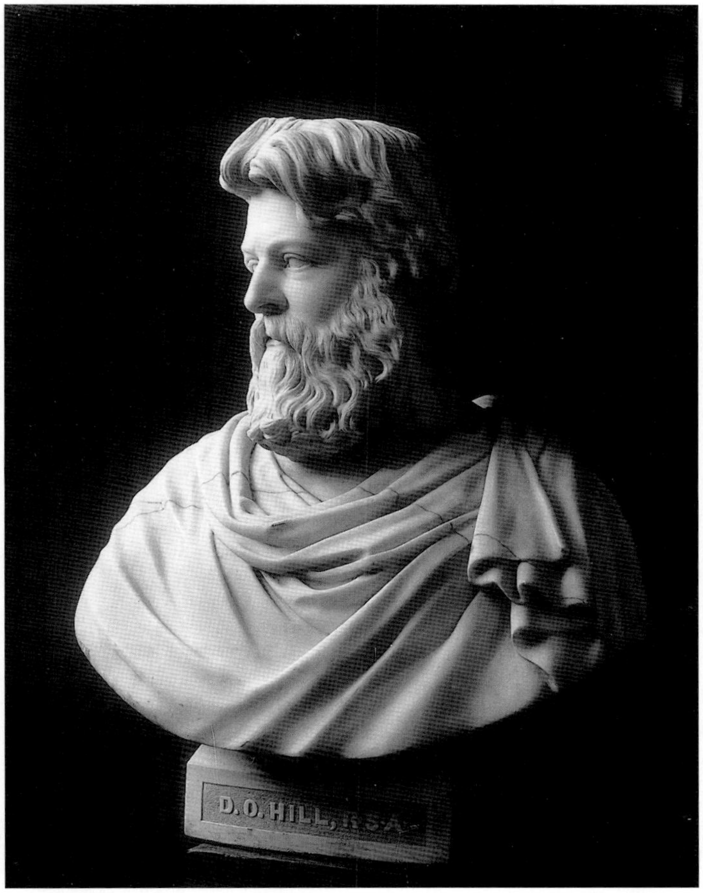

54. Amelia Robertson Hill, *D. O. Hill*, 1869. Marble. Scottish National Portrait Gallery, Edinburgh.

point is obscured by the predominance of portraits in Hill and Adamson's work, but they were mostly pictures taken for public consumption, as the impressive number of surviving prints may demonstrate.

There are indications in the calotype work that Hill was already considering substituting photographs for engravings in art reproduction. Here the concern would be for the potential accuracy of such copies – a direct, or at least closer transcription than the translations of many engravers. Ruskin's original enthusiasm for photography stemmed from this idea: 'It is such a happy thing to be able to depend on *every*thing – to be sure not only that the painter is perfectly honest, but that he can't make a mistake.'[86] There are copies of several engravings and paintings amongst the calotypes, including the work of Henry Raeburn, William Allan and William Etty. Hill later urged the need for expert photographic reproduction on Thomas Annan, probably directing his career substantially into this field, so that Annan: 'was never so happy as when endeavouring to faithfully translate some masterpiece into monochrome through the medium of his camera'.[87] One of Annan's most important commissions came from Hill. While Hill's first advertisements for the Disruption picture, in 1843 offered subscribers an engraving of the painting, in the 1860s, he turned to photography. Annan held the patent rights for Joseph Swan's 'permanent' carbon process. Hill persuaded him to purchase 'a large Photographic Camera of the latest and most perfect construction' from Dallmeyer, and to print photographs in three sizes – the largest, half the size of the painting and put together from three negatives.[88] It was not his intention just to produce one grand picture, which might disappear into a private collection, but to publish it in an enduring edition of thousands.

Hill's maintained enthusiasm for reproduction was expressed in one of his last letters, where he spoke with great satisfaction of ordering a multiple edition of Amelia Paton's marble bust of him (fig. 54): 'The day before your welcome package arrived – we had just issued orders to Leopoldo Aeroghi [?] – our honest & admirable & handsome [illegible] maker – to get a few copies of Mrs Hill's Bust of myself ready – with which we intend to try the temper of our friends by asking their acceptance of a copy – as New Years gifts.'[89]

The obvious financial advantage of producing more than one copy of an artwork was balanced by the more important argument behind publication. The educational advance, offered in literature through book publication, could be extended to aesthetic education: 'implanting notions of art throughout the whole empire'.

PERSONAL AMBITION

The Signing of the Deed of Demission

It is clear from the foregoing that Hill's ambitions as an individual were strongly affected and often re-directed by his concern for broader ambitions in the arts. He had, however, the responsibility for his own individual creativity and, although interrupted, he continued to follow the dictates of high ambition and struggle expected in the concept of genius. His most laborious work was *The Signing of the Deed of Demission* (fig. 55), which may usefully be analysed here for its conscious complication and its arguable failure. The original intention to paint a memorial of this great historical event was straightforwardly ambitious and unquestionably difficult. Hill expected it to take three years of his professional life; it took twenty-three. As late as August 1860, he could write: 'I have brought out my big figure Picture here

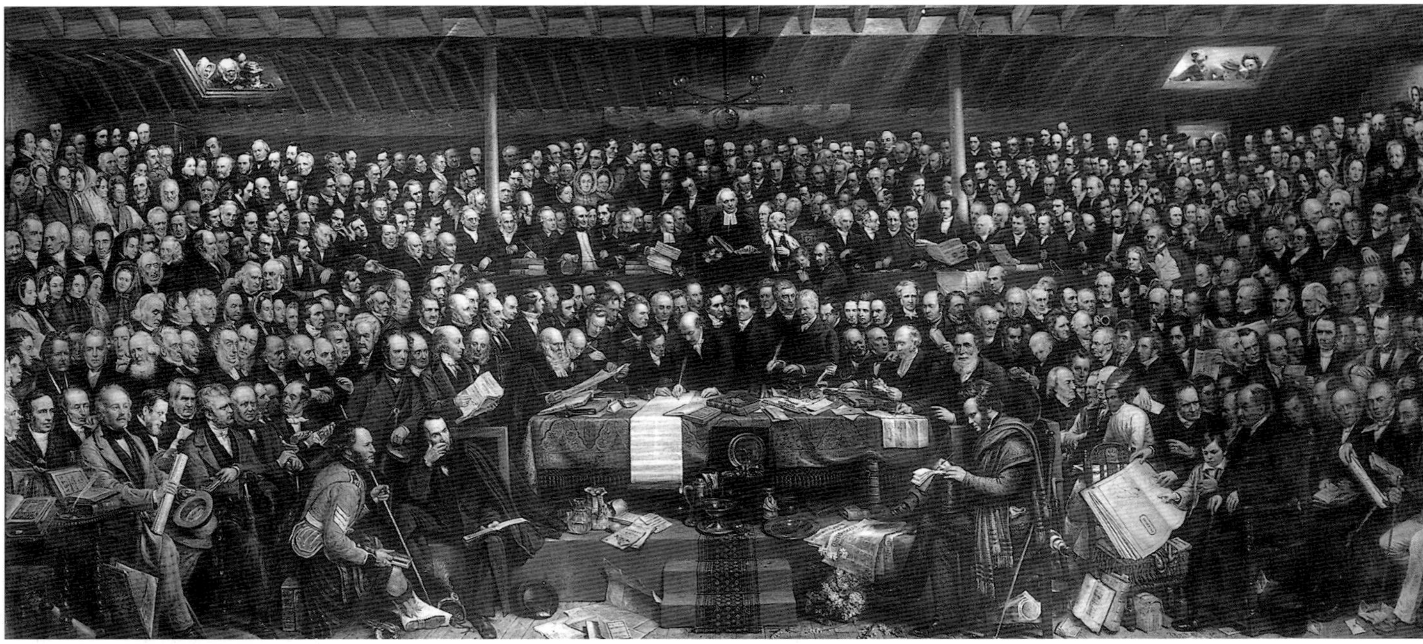

55. D. O. Hill, *The Signing of the Deed of Demission*, 1843–67. Oil on canvas. Free Church of Scotland, Edinburgh.

[Grange House, south of Edinburgh], desiring to dedicate the summer in pushing it on towards completion rather than in sketching. There is a great deal of gin-horse work to be gone through before the end is in sight.'[90] And as has been seen, he was only able to finish it six years later, with the assistance of Amelia Hill. This was no idleness on Hill's part. George Harvey wrote of the finished picture:

> I consider it a noble work, and can conceive no more precious bequest to future generations of the Free Church by the present than such a record of the men – painted at the time – who so valiantly fought the battle of its independence. The painting, moreover, is unique of its kind: I know of nothing like it existing; and strongly feel that but for Mr Hill's enthusiasm, it could never have been produced, requiring, as it did, such an amount of heroic self-denial and continuous labour of a kind which few could give, and which no one unacquainted with the production of figure-pictures of a much more subordinate character could possibly imagine.[91]

However it was done, it would be an image involving large numbers of ministers in the ordinary, dull clothes of their profession – by definition, a painting difficult to infuse with any decorative aesthetic or colour. Hill and others continue to refer to it as the Disruption picture, a title promising drama, but the painting he finished in 1866 was far different. He could have used the model of David Wilkie's *John Knox Preaching to the Lords of the Congregation* (fig. 56), which had been such a success for his brother's print publishing business, and he was apparently first considering such a subject. Either the reading of the protest by the Reverend David

56. David Wilkie, *John Knox Preaching to the Lords of the Congregation, 10 June 1559*. Oil on wood. National Gallery of Scotland, Edinburgh.

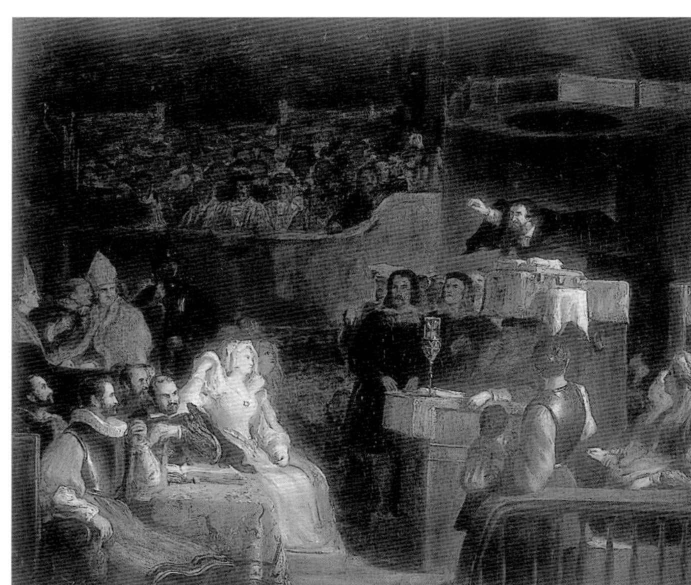

Welsh or the first sermon preached by the charismatic Thomas Chalmers would have given him a psychologically dramatic composition; instead he focused the painting on the figure of a minister quietly signing his name to the Deed of Demission – signing away his living as an act of sacrifice – and Hill gave the painting that title. The actual Disruption took place in the neoclassical church of St Andrew and St George (fig. 57), a fine building with an elegant and visually interesting circular interior. The first sessions of the Free Church took place in Tanfield Hall, an old oil and gas works. Hill chose the latter site. With all this, it should come as no surprise that ultimately his use of photography, intended as an aid to simplify his painting, only compounded the problem, by giving him more than 450 recognisable portraits to include in one composition. Hill clearly followed inspiration and the advice of people equally moved by the event. Friends who were not emotionally involved were taken aback, and some expressed doubt, even in the early stages. Charles Heath Wilson wrote to him in 1845:

> Your large picture made a great impression on me, I thought you a little crazy when I heard of it, but you have proved what heart of sentiment can do, you think that it is a great event which you are commemorating, you enter with fervour into the feelings of the men you paint, you admire them (I dont) if you succeed as you have begun the production of that picture will be an event & a very remarkable one in the history of Scottish arts, a remarkable phase in the history of the artist mind. I often think about it & hope earnestly that you may succeed. *Forgive* my frankness & eschew plastering *alla scozzese.*[92]

Elizabeth Rigby, when reviewing the calotypes, published her dislike of Hill's concentration in an acid footnote, which must have caused him to blench, referring to 'the fat martyrs of the Free Kirk, as yet seemingly their favourite subjects'.[93]

Hill, through his own excitement and enthusiasm, made it nearly impossible to complete the picture. The early sketches had a coherence, which might well have led to a better picture and certainly one easier to achieve (fig. 58). Hill eventually recognised this. He admired Paul Delaroche's grand painting, the *Hémicycle des Beaux Arts*, when it was on exhibition in his brother's gallery in 1853, in just these terms: 'It is really a beautiful thing . . . I wish I had seen the original ten years ago – my Free Kirk picture would in that case long ago been done'.[94] Delaroche's painting was based on Raphael's *School of Athens* and is huge, designed to curve half-way round the École des Beaux-Arts in Paris, but it is a comparatively sparse composition of around seventy figures.[95] The simple implication of Hill's remark is that he had realised that his project had got out of hand; he could see the advantage of a less crowded composition, perhaps both a smaller and a more symbolic group.

Hill's general despondency in the 1850s (partly brought on by ill health), was obviously loaded by his sense of failure

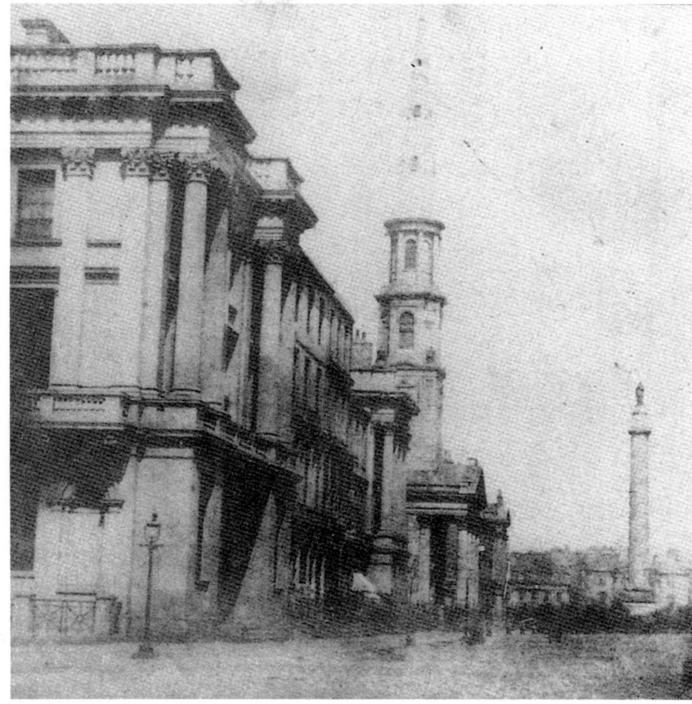

57. D. O. Hill and Robert Adamson, *George Street, Edinburgh, with the Church of St Andrew and St George*, 1843. Calotype. The Janos Scholtz Collection of Nineteenth-Century European Photography. The Snite Art Museum, Notre Dame.

58. D. O. Hill, Sketch for *The Signing of the Deed of Demission*, c. 1843. Oil on board. Free Church of Scotland, Edinburgh.

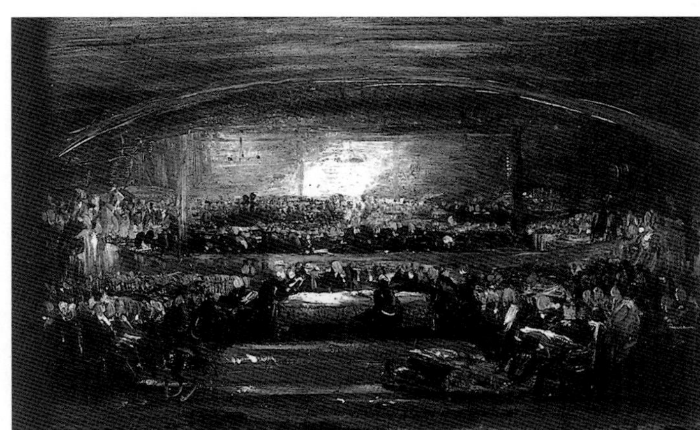

at not completing the task. Moreover, by the time the picture was complete, the public excitement had died down and he was addressing a new generation, which had no direct knowledge of the warmth and passion behind the Disruption. The response to the finished picture was generally not good. The painter Sam Bough, 'compared the grouping of the numerous heads to "Potatoes all in a row", and satirized the various weak points of the picture in a very comical manner'.[96] The editor of the *Art Journal*, Samuel Carter Hall, saw it as 'the weary Disruptive Portraiture, which must have lain like an incubus on his genius'.[97]

We feel the failure of the painting, partly because the photographs are so much better. Our view of it suffers from the historical intervention of the composite group photograph, with its inescapable aura of scissors and paste, or of modern digital manipulation. For photographic historians, it is the impulse behind the partnership and little more than a foil for the photographs. Heinrich Schwarz referred to it disparagingly: 'he squandered his marvellous and inspired portrait photographs on a frigid setting and a huge and clumsy background.'[98] Helmut Gernsheim said of it: 'we can only consider it as a misspent labour of love, for the subject was clearly beyond Hill's capability – if not beyond the capacity of most artists.'[99] More recently, Colin Ford has written: 'the inescapable fact is that the Disruption painting . . . is a monumental flop'.[100]

It was not, for many of Hill's peers, a great painting; it is not a great painting for us. But it would be fair to examine the picture, not so much for its success as for its intention, as a radical experiment and a most impressive ambition. In its directly personal or democratic character, the painting offered a series of histories. Hill set up a kind of democracy of perspective, by moving the dominant figure of Thomas Chalmers to an elevated position at the back. He is a small figure in the flat plane of the painting; we can understand his dominance from the height of his position and by the shaft of sunlight shining down on him, which picks him out among the crowd. It nevertheless requires historical understanding to see him fully as the leader of the Disruption. He is offered as a focus rather than a figurehead; the other figures in the painting have equivalent status. The heroism of each one within the picture could be told, detailed, as the face was, in its contribution to the greater whole. It was designed as an educational work, on a par with Delaroche's *Hémicycle*; although Hill did not have Delaroche's certainty of the painting's location, it was equally designed as a didactic and elevating picture, a model for posterity.[101] It offered not just the communal heroism, but an understanding of the Church's drive and success in the hands of determined individuals and groups. It rejected the dramatic, destructive character of the Disruption, in favour of the constructive, successful and quieter Evangelical future of the Free Church. This is partly brought out by Hill's prospectus for the picture, which takes the narrative line, but the individual members of its audience could develop the theme from their own local and personal knowledge.[102] It is a demonstration of Presbyterian principle and morality.

Harvey's response makes the point that the painting itself involved a comparable heroic effort, which was justified by the importance of the subject. The calotype practice was motivated by the painting, and we owe the unchallenged success of individual portraits to the same driving idea. They are not separate; they are not squandered or misspent. They are a successful realisation of a religious, historical and democratic idea, which the painting itself did not wholly achieve (these ideas will be developed in later chapters). They illustrate a similar, conscious search for the challenge of difficulty and the parallel idea of sacrifice.

'TILL THE WORLD BRINGS OUT ITS HISTORY'

> I must tell you that the meeting of the Academy on the 25th November, in approving of my salary being paid for life – passed two pages of resolutions of great interest and value to me & to my relations. I will at another time send you a copy of them, and an account of the queer way in which I was deprived of thus being presented in the Report. Douglas is a new secretary [?] therefore I do not blame him but strange to say our President has manifested a strange [strong?] and seemingly jealous dislike to [illegible] being said of me – so the paragraph at the end instead of being in the words of the Report, which it would have been had I been writing it [illegible] – is reduced to a simple pecuniary affair. I understand that the members instead of ['resenting' or 'rewriting'] this in a minute [?] – consider the Institution itself would suffer – and so we must bide our time till the world brings [it?] out its history.[103]

Hill left the academy in ill health in 1869, and the above is part of a letter expressing some sadness about the ungenerous treatment of his pension. Its illegibility is a part of that expression. Hill was distressed that the work he had done had not been formally recognised.

In the Christian ethic Hill followed and admired, personal responsibility for advancement was balanced by the contrary idea of sacrifice; this, rather than obvious, individual success, may have proved to be God's intention. In the words of his obituary: 'Mr Hill fought the battles of the Academy with a singleness of purpose and a devotion of time and talent which in effect impaired his efforts towards attaining the first-rate place in art otherwise in reach of his fertile and felicitous genius.'[104]

The text on Hill's gravestone, which may have been written by Amelia Hill, reads: 'He was a man of upright, noble and unselfish character, who sacrificed much to the advancement of the fine arts of his country'.[105] The idea of sacrifice runs consciously through Hill's career. He chose the moment of sacrifice, the minister signing away his right to the richest living in Scotland, as the central focus of his Disruption painting. George Harvey talked of the painting as an act of sacrifice in itself. More importantly, in adopting a responsibility for the community of art, and devoting himself to its broad advancement, he lost the individual, or selfish concentration that might have made him a celebrated painter.

6

Writing Fact and Living Fiction

THE LATENT SPIRITS

In the first half of the nineteenth century, western art was heavily influenced by literature. It dominated D. O. Hill's own professional work, both as a painter and as a photographer. His father and brother were booksellers, which gave him a natural link and presumably the opportunity to read more books than he could afford to buy. But it is nevertheless remarkable that the bibliographer and librarian, John Taylor Brown, said that Hill's 'knowledge of Shakespeare and Scott was greater than of any man I ever knew'.[1] A thorough familiarity with these two authors alone would imply both a wide range of poetic and historic inspiration and a potential knowledge of humanity.

As has been seen, throughout his career, Hill worked with the idea of publication uppermost. He was a friend and associate of publishers, like John Macrone, Robert Cadell, John Blackie and John Murray, and a friend of and collaborator with the prominent authors and speakers of his time: poets, novelists, the writers of sermons and memoirs, essayists, biographers, journalists and critics; James Hogg, Professor John Wilson, Robert Chambers, Hugh Miller, Elizabeth Rigby, Lord Cockburn, Dr John Brown, Anna Brownell Jameson. The calotypes serve as a literary roll-call for the Edinburgh of the 1840s and illustrates its connection to a wider world. This familiarity goes beyond a social connection into an intelligent connection – these are people whose thinking and enthusiasm informed Hill's work; he, in turn, affected them with his own enthusiasm and pleasure in life. Dr John Brown wrote of Hill that he had, 'a rich, versatile, rapid, facile mind, crowded with thick-coming fancies'.[2] A better understanding of this complication may be achieved by looking at the literary field and the way it interlocked both with Hill's art, and with his social behaviour and understanding.

Hill was present as a young man during an extraordinary revolution in publishing and authorship. A sense of the excitement of this may be gathered from Lord Cockburn's account (coloured by his politics) of the release of Scottish society and culture at the end of the Napoleonic Wars. Amongst the most impressive changes was the great literary revolution begun by Archibald Constable, the publisher of the *Edinburgh Review* and the works of Walter Scott, who:

> rushed out and took possession of the open field, as if he had been aware from the first of the existence of the latent spirits, which a skilful conjurer might call from the depths of the population to the service of literature. Abandoning the old timid and grudging system, he stood out as the general patron and payer of all promising publications, and confounded not merely his rivals in trade, but his very authors, by his unheard-of prices . . . [which] drew authors from dens where they would otherwise have starved, and made Edinburgh a literary mart, famous with strangers, and the pride of its own citizens.[3]

The literary emphasis of the portraits in the calotypes is based on this cultural revolution – the sudden, wide spread of independent and combative literature and criticism, in books, journals, newspapers and encyclopaedias. It became increasingly possible to acquire an informal education in the form of biographies, scientific explanation or literary criticism, which were entertaining and pleasurable. The massive increase in output and consumption had, moreover, a marked effect on the authorship and character of the writing. Many more writers were published and the manner of writing became biased towards the personal and physically or emotionally descriptive: looking less to a classical or philosophical model and more to one that was widely intelligible.

The writers and public speakers Hill particularly admired had the ability to make what they were saying visible in the mind's eye. Notable examples amongst the popular writers were Walter Scott and Hugh Miller; there are radical differences of principle and approach between the two authors, but they shared this character. Scott died in 1833, and there is no evidence that Hill met him, but he would have known him, if not directly certainly by reputation, through Sir William Allan, whose work Scott admired and promoted. Hugh Miller was a friend and exact contemporary of Hill.

The pictorial character of Scott's writing was admired as early as 1810 in a review of *The Lady of the Lake*:

> He sees everything with a painter's eye. Whatever he represents has a character of individuality and is drawn with an accuracy and minuteness of discrimination, which we are not accustomed to expect from verbal description . . . The rocks, the ravines, and the torrents, which he exhibits, are not the imperfect sketches of a hurried traveller, but the finished studies of a resident artist, deliberately drawn from different points of view.[4]

A recent critic has emphasised the character of this vision, as an aesthetic based on reality, the equivalent of landscape painting rather than topography: 'Whatever fictional gloss may be applied, when he is writing of Scotland, and especially of his own Border region, Scott is recording not inventing; his vision grows out of an objective world, a place of time and the senses. Before Scott . . . landscape rarely appeared as an organic element in prose.'[5] Hugh Miller's writing was praised in the same manner by Thomas Carlyle, in 1852: 'You have, as you undertook to do, painted many things to us; scenes of life, scenes of Nature, which rarely come upon the canvas; and I will add, such Draughtsmen too are extremely uncommon in that and other walks of painting.'[6] The following is part of a passage of geological enquiry, written by Miller, which is offered as an example of such physical and local description. It is quoted at length to emphasise its loving and seductive detail, and the drive of intense curiosity that lies behind Miller's thinking. It begins by taking us deep into the Doocot Cave on the Cromarty Firth:

> We strike a light. The roof and sides are crusted with white stalactites, that depend from the one like icicles from the eaves of a roof in a severe frost, and stand out from the other in pure, semi-transparent ridges, that resemble the folds of a piece of white drapery dropped from the roof; while the floor below has its rough pavement of stalagmite, that stands up, wherever the drops descend, in rounded prominences, like the bases of columns. Here, however, is a puzzle to exercise our ingenuity. Some of the minuter stalactites of the roof, after descending perpendicularly, or at least nearly so, for a few inches, turn up again and form a hook, to which one may suspend one's watch by the ring; while there are others that form a loop, attached to the roof at both ends. Pray, how could the descending drop have returned upwards to form the hook, or what attractive power could have drawn the two drops together, to compose the elliptical curve of the loop? The problem is not quite a simple one. It is sufficiently hard at least, as it has to deal with only half-ounces of rock, to inculcate caution on the theorists who profess to deal with whole continents of similar material.
>
> Let us examine somewhat narrowly. Dark as the recess is, and though vegetation fails fully fifty feet nearer the entrance than where we now stand, the place is not without its inhabitants. We see among the dewy damps of the roof the glistening threads of some minute spider, stretching in lines or descending in loops. And just look here. Along this loop there runs a single drop. Observe how it descends, with but a slight inclination, for about two inches or so, and then turns round for about three quarters of an inch more; observe further, that along this other loop there trickle two drops, one on each side; that, as a consequence of the balance which they form the one against the other, their descent has a much greater sweep; and that, uniting in the centre, they fall together. We have found the solution of our riddle, and received one proof more of the superiority of the simple art of seeing over the ingenious art of theorizing.[7]

Miller has brought us in to this grand setting, carrying the flaring torch; he then offers a small problem, which is solved by visual observation. It is a precise piece of prose, which is hung engagingly round the idea of a pocket watch on a spider's thread. While it is manifestly not scientific in any rigorous sense, it would be a mistake to think of Miller simply as a populist. Despite the immense popularity of his work, he was more certainly an educationalist, opening people's minds to the visible world. The message is essentially that human thinking is faulty, liable to make grand assumptions based on too great a respect for the printed word, and that solutions may be found by going into the landscape and looking intelligently.

Scott had examined the detail of nature with equal concentration. He was observed with amazement 'noting down even the peculiar little wild flowers and herbs':

> [I] could not help saying, that as he was not to be upon oath in his work, daisies, violets, and primroses would be as poetical as any of the humble plants he was examining . . . he replied that in nature herself no two scenes were exactly alike, and that whoever copied truly what was before his eyes, would possess the same variety in his descriptions, and exhibit apparently an imagination as boundless as the range of nature in the scenes he recorded.[8]

Miller treated fact in a broad, poetic manner, bringing narrative and fiction into his province. Walter Scott, by contrast, looked at surrounding reality with respect and brought *that* into the province of fiction. The distinction between the two approaches became most interestingly blurred. Scott, like Miller, had an eccentric education. It had been divided because of ill health in his youth, between a direct experience of nature and the vernacular tradition of history and poetry, learnt from the company of country people, and formal university education. This meant that, while his thinking was tempered by irony and classical learning, he was ready to accept the value of pragmatic experience or real life. [9] He stood out against the concepts of the uniformity of human society generally accepted in the Enlightenment.

Scott and Miller both approached truth through reality and the examination of present nature: in a half ounce of rock and a small flower. Their underlying motives were distinct but the effect was similar – they were both fascinated by their findings. Scott employed the idea of assembling unimportant fragments to generate an imaginative world. Hugh Miller's aim was largely moral and consciously depended on humility. Casting the eyes down, away from the fearful sublime to a local comprehension, had the attractions of familiarity. It offered an understanding of facts within reach of the hand and comprehensible through a knowledge of their context. Through the creative use of such familiar or rediscoverable facts, writers as diverse as Scott and Miller transferred a sense of direct experience to their readers and merged the pleasures of fact and fiction.

'DISSOLVING VIEWS' AND THE USE OF ANALOGY

The particular Scottish affection for fact surfaced in the collected information of the *Statistical Accounts*, published in 1792.[10] The accounts were put together by the clergy and were as much idiosyncratic as systematic. The often unexpected and intriguing information published in the accounts opened up creative possibilities. This is directly seen in the novel *Annals of the Parish* by John Galt, who was both a novelist and a statistician. Galt was particularly skilful in the use of small facts – details of furniture, dress or garden plants – which proved to be a natural way, both of generating historical realism and of satirising his characters. The taste for such literalness was the cause of a sardonic comment from a friend of David Roberts in 1844: 'It has been often said that we are not an Artistic people, and I fear it is not altogether untrue – Not because Genius cannot ripen in the Northern climates, as the Abbate Winckelman asserts, but because our minds are so occupied with "great facts", and little facts, that we have no capacity for the Ideal.'[11]

Hill, himself, was not looking for raw fact so much as for nature. He disliked the 'livid' accuracy of the daguerreotype and its indiscriminate focus, which would coldly delineate surface and outline. Authors imitating Scott sought to achieve his effects by inserting facts in such cold slabs, and it is interesting that a Scottish review of Charles Dickens's work in 1845, attacked him in terms of the daguerreotype: 'Ludicrous minuteness in the trivial descriptive details induces us to compare Mr. Dickens' style of delineation to a photographic landscape. There everything within the field of view is copied with unfailing but mechanical fidelity.'[12]

One of the notable characteristics of the writing and preaching that Hill knew lies in the extension of this interest in the actual, the use of natural analogy – the direct poetic and moral reference to reality. A London critic heard Thomas Guthrie (fig. 59) preach in 1856, and wrote with some cynicism:

> Guthrie's faith seems to be a lurid Calvinism, refined by that poetic fervour and love of nature which is so intense among the Scotch . . . Guthrie's preaching was a finished performance – tones, gesture, diction highly spirited and sometimes highly effective – but I could hardly trace an idea. He passed from one topic to another, as if he were exhibiting dissolving views of the perdition of man.[13]

Dissolving views were devised in the early part of the century, before the invention of photography.[14] Essentially they were images superimposed from two or more magic lanterns, to demonstrate changing effects and scenes – one picture could melt into another as the lighted wicks were turned up and down. In the 1840s, the Polytechnic Institution in London had a particularly impressive version of this using mammoth painted slides. It was brought up to Edinburgh in October

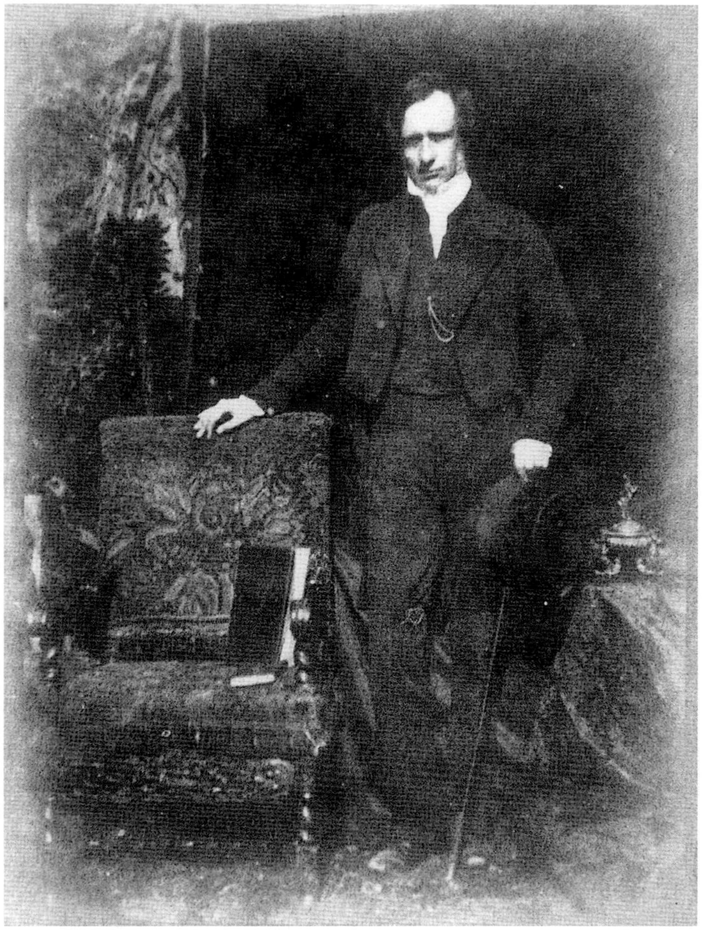

59. D. O. Hill and Robert Adamson, *Reverend Dr Thomas Guthrie*, 1843–7. Calotype. Scottish National Photography Collection, Edinburgh.

1843 and shown in the Calton Convening Rooms, with 'an efficient number of Performers, both Vocal and Instrumental, to assist with their combined efforts in rendering the illusion of each picture effective and complete'.[15] As a public entertainment, it was popular for forty years.

Guthrie's friends were conscious that his habit of analogy needed defence:

> His mind moved not in the logical, but the analogical plane, and swept forward, not in the rigid iron line of the railway excavation, but with the curves of a river that follows the solicitation of the ground. And so, too, his sermons were constructed. They had not exhaustive divisions enclosing subjects, as hedges do fields, but outlines, such as clouds have, that grow up by electricity and air; or such as the breadths of fern, and heather, and woodland had on the hill-side opposite his door, where colour melted into colour, with here a tall crag pointing sky-ward, and there an indignant torrent leaping headlong to come glittering out again among flowers and sunshine. Some tell us that analogy is a dangerous guide, and that metaphors prove nothing; but where they rest on the unity between God's world and man's nature they are arguments as well as illustrations.[16]

The curiosity of this lies in the newly factual interest which underlay it. It is a historical way of thinking, based on the seeing of parallels and of relating things through types: the three-part view of the cultured world in which the New Testament had its natural precursors in the Old Testament and the classical age, or the association of animal, vegetable and mineral forms through their surface resemblance, which dates back to Aristotle. It is not wholly impractical; much of our knowledge of the world is based on the recognition of resemblance – the understanding that similar things and situations are likely to present us with similar problems and benefits. This was not, in an eighteenth-century sense, rational – it rejects sophisticated education – but it did connect common sense with faith.

Analogy was carried into the area of mystery by the Christian assumption that God had built the metaphorical message into nature. Because man was God's central creation, nature would be filled with moral intimation. Thomas Guthrie naturally related this idea to the biblical parables:

> With this end I used the simplest, plainest terms . . . I turned to the gospels, and found that He who knew what was in a man, what could best illuminate a subject, win the attention, and move the heart, used parables or illustrations, stories, comparisons, drawn from the scenes of nature and familiar life, to a large extent in His teaching; in regard to which a woman – type of the masses – said, 'The parts of the Bible I like best are the *likes*.'[17]

Guthrie's preaching was admired in 1846, in terms that relate his arguments to the new authority of science: 'He derives a wonderful power from the use of analogy . . . brought fresh from the streets in the everyday publicities of life . . . He deems the affections more assailable for good than the judgment, and we think him right . . . It is like a beautiful experiment in chemistry.'[18]

Guthrie felt the need to know and communicate with other people. He also appreciated the beauty of nature and made his preaching consciously visual. He went so far as to advise one artist – possibly George Harvey:

> on whose easel lay an unfinished historical picture. He suggested some change, and ventured somewhat freely to

criticize some object or attitude on the canvas, when the artist, with just a little warmth, interposed – 'Dr Guthrie, remember you are a preacher and not a painter.' 'Beg your pardon, my good friend – I *am* a painter; only I paint in words, while you use brush and colours.'[19]

Guthrie has here taken the classical idea, that the two arts of writing and painting are so closely interlinked that they involve the same underlying vocabulary, and applied it to the Romantic study of nature as the source of inspiration for poet, preacher and painter.[20] Hill's admiration for him was expressed in the gift of a painting in 1847. Guthrie responded appreciatively: 'I came last night to find my drawing room adorned by your kindness, talent & taste – It is an exquisite Picture – a Masterpiece – I pity the Poet who has to follow the Painter – If this world with its [illegible] Palaces is so beautiful what must Heaven be. May we inherit a house "Eternal in the heavens".'[21]

Thomas Guthrie retreated to the Highlands for respite from the terrible work in Edinburgh's city slums when he fell ill in 1849. He wrote from Lochlee, comparing the countryside with Edinburgh's Canongate:

> If I could make a satisfactory picture I would hang these two scenes up side by side before the world. Such a contrast! God made the one, man and Satan the other. I can roam here by loch and streamlet, with my eyes now up on the blue heavens, now on the majestic hoary crags, now on the calm blue waters, now on the leaping, rejoicing falls and see neither sight nor hear sound of sin, – of the groans wherewith the whole creation groaneth. If Jesus Christ did not say – pointing to yon outer world where the battle is a-fighting – 'Arise, let us go hence'; if duty to Him and our fellow-men did not come in and say with Martha to her sister, 'the Master is come and calleth for thee', I would be content to spend the remainder of my days in this sweet quiet solitude.[22]

It is particularly appropriate that George Harvey, who used the analogical idea to paint scenes of Scottish religious significance that would offer a parallel to the Bible, painted a picture of Guthrie preaching on the shores of the loch and a sketch of him fishing on Lochlee (fig. 60).[23] The latter is a picture of his pleasure in the outdoor world and in nature; it also offers an unstrained parallel with the Lake of Galilee. 'This loch,' Guthrie wrote in a letter, 'like the Lake of Galilee and all such mountain-girdled waters, rises on a sudden like a hot angry man.'[24] By natural comparison he could be seen as an apostle, an evangelist, 'a fisher of men'. This meant that, by picturing the reality, the painters and, by inheritance, the photographic partnership were able to offer an analogical reading, offering the same reflective possibilities to their contemporary audience.

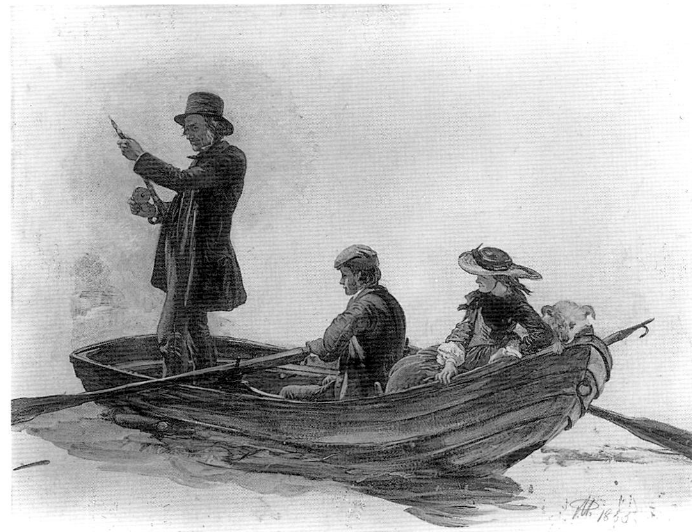

60. George Harvey, *Thomas Guthrie and his Children Fishing on Lochlee*, 1855. Oil sketch on millboard. Scottish National Portrait Gallery, Edinburgh.

'LIKE MEN ACTING A PART'

Through authors like Walter Scott, fact and life had flowed into fiction. The expressiveness and visual excitements of fiction had flowed into fact, and that fiction itself influenced the actual life of the people pictured in the calotypes. Henry Reeve wrote of Thomas Guthrie's sermons, as:

> *Noctes Ambrosianae* in the pulpit; there is the exuberance of [Professor John] Wilson over a punchbowl, and sometimes the pathos of the Shepherd [James Hogg]. The Scotch have almost repudiated the theatre, but they are more theatrical than the English. Jeffrey, Cockburn, and Rutherford [all three men were judges] always talked and behaved like men acting a part.[25]

This opinion would not have surprised Guthrie. His biography quotes an old woman as saying, 'Eh, Mr Guthrie, if it hadna been for the grace of God, ye would have made a grand play-actor.'[26] It was so far a serious question that Thomas Chalmers, himself an impressive preacher, warned of its dangers: 'as much delight may emanate from the pulpit on an arrested audience beneath it, as ever emanated from the boards of a theatre; and with as total disjunction of mind too in the one case as in the other from the essence or the habit of religion.'[27] Cockburn confirmed the idea of the theatricality of the Scottish courts in an account of a civil court in Liverpool, where he found the proceedings remarkable for quiet and brevity: 'I heard no voice strained and did not see a drop of sweat at the Bar in these eight days. Our high-pressure Dean [John Hope] screams and gesticulates and perspires more in any forenoon than the whole Bar of England in a reign.'[28]

This suggests that Edinburgh was literally self-conscious. Whether in continuing, regenerating or even fabricating a simple-hearted heroic tradition, they were keeping a Romantic emotionalism alive. One example of this lies in the particular admiration for old ladies of character, which Hill clearly shared. It is a recurrent theme in the writing of the time – expressed by Walter Scott, most notably, but also by Lord Cockburn:

> There was a singular race of excellent Scotch old ladies. They were a delightful set; strong headed, warm hearted and high spirited; the fire of their tempers not always latent; merry even in solitude; very resolute; indifferent about the modes and habits of the modern world; and adhering to their own ways, so as to stand out, like primitive rocks, above ordinary society. Their prominent qualities of sense, humour, affection, and spirit, were embodied in curious outsides; for they all dressed, and spoke, and did, exactly as they chose; their language, like their habits, entirely Scotch, but without any other vulgarity, than what perfect naturalness is sometimes taken for.[29]

This admiration of 'ancient' character enabled one of the period's more eccentric fictions – the impersonations by Clementina Stirling Graham, who would turn up in the houses of her friends, disguised as a perverse old party. She invented and acted the litigious 'Lady of Pitlyall', who amongst other implausibilities, had inherited a flea from the very person of the Young Pretender:

> I have a flech that loupit aff him upon my aunty, the Lady Brax, when she was helping him on wi' his short gown; my aunty rowed it up in a sheet of white paper, and she keepit it in the tea canister, and she ca'd it aye the King's Flech, and the Laird, honest man, when he wanted a cup of gude tea, sought aye a cup of *Prince's mixture* . . . It is now set on the pivot of my watch, and a' the warks gae round the *flech* in place of turning on a diamond.[30]

People were fascinated by her performance and believed her, because they wanted to believe that such a woman existed. Hill, who knew Clementina Stirling Graham and photographed her in her sixties, referred to her as 'a dear little woman'.[31]

This, inherently Romantic view of a world maintained in an older character, was supported by a broad generosity. The autobiographies and biographies I quote in this book, written by people Hill knew and admired, are written in a manner of heightened enthusiasm and are entertaining to read. This was a true reflection of the subject, in relation to the writer and the expectations of the time. Dr John Brown, who wrote a number of biographical essays, including the one telling the story of Clementina Stirling Graham's performances, was an especially receptive man. His friend, John Stuart Blackie, said of him censoriously: 'In point of emotional character he was the most womanly man that I ever met with. His judgment was often at fault when his affections were engaged, and I do not think I ever heard him say "No" with decision during the whole time of my long intercourse with him.'[32] Brown himself was aware that his own kindness was perhaps a critical failing:

> You are quite right about my tendency to excess in praise. This arises from two causes: 1st, from my constitutional vice (for it amounts to one) of wishing *to please* at all hazards: this is one of my greatest weaknesses. 2nd, From a real exaggerative tendency, arising from my passionate nature; this really interferes very much with my trustworthiness as a critic.[33]

This, a self-conscious sensitivity, should not be taken too straightforwardly. Brown knew that his encouraging criticism was to a degree optimistic, but it is part of the purpose of criticism to influence the future. Moreover, such a recognition should only undermine our sense of his veracity if we have no doubts of the truth of other less self-critical authors and know their purpose. What is interesting in this potential confusion is that Brown and his friends were well aware of the doubt. They acknowledged authorship rather than claiming objectivity. It is a similar warmth or passion that Hill was seeking in his portraiture: closeness rather than perspective or a false appearance of objectivity. We meet his sitters on friendly terms.

Hill himself did not think of human virtues as necessarily absolute or flawless. He did not excuse, he defended the faults of his heroes. For *The Land of Burns*, he drew an elaborate vignette of Burns sleeping on the grass by Lincluden Abbey, surrounded by fairies debating what dream they

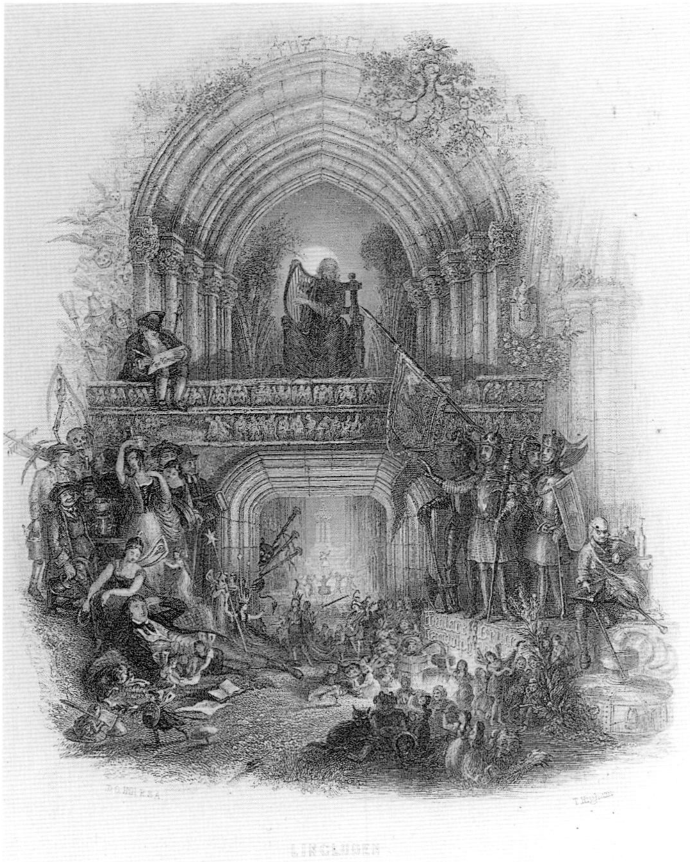

61. David Octavius Hill, *The Poet's Dream at Lincluden*. Engraving from *The Land of Burns*, 1840.

should give him. In the foreground, is a little Highland fairy in a kilt attacking a pen-wielding toad (fig. 61), which:

> personates one of those critics or biographers, whose blackened pages, throwing their shadows before, sometimes while the poet lived, clouded his serenity. In the present instance, a friendly fairy shields him from the venom of the reptile, and annoys it in turn by the application of a sprig of Scotch thistle; the moral of which is, that the countrymen of the bard will not permit even his frailties to be further drawn from their dread abode without administering the merited castigation.[34]

Such a view of character is not Hill's idea alone but is common to much of his circle. The reason we are so clear of his faults or failings lies in the habit the writers of the time had of dealing with these together with the virtues of their friends – whether this was moral criticism or an expression of character, the two are presented side by side. One surprising example is the biography of Sir David Brewster written by his daughter, who was at times consciously disrespectful. She wrote, in explanation: 'That would be an unsuccessful picture which was all light and no shadow . . . that would be a poor biography which told only the better part and threw a veil over the rest.'[35]

Two examples of accounts of Hill by his friends may help to make this, admittedly obvious, point. The first is written by John Stuart Blackie, professor of classics at the University of Edinburgh. Blackie lived into the third generation of Victoria's reign and is looking back from that, perhaps less expansive, perspective:

> Next to [George] Harvey, my great friend amongst the artists was David Octavius Hill. Hill was an extremely agreeable and a remarkably handsome fellow. In art, his conceptions were poetical, and his execution ready: at the social board he was always jovial, and sang a good song. He made a great mistake in middle life by undertaking an historical picture of the Free Church Disruption, which he removed altogether out of the province of art by making it a gallery of portraits instead of a single effective group. The labour devoted to this work took away several of the best years of his life, and when it was finished it remained a mere historical curiosity, for which he received neither fame as an artist nor money as a merchant. What may have been the faults which prevented him from attaining the first rank as a painter, I never took pains to enquire. I loved him so much as a man, that his merits or defects as a painter seldom came within my view. What I used to object to in his landscapes, when I first began to look at Scottish pictures, was a certain flimsiness about his trees, which seemed to indicate either hasty work or a deficient eye for nature; perhaps a want of laborious persistency and ambitious determination to attain first-rate excellence in some one department may have been the weak point in his character. But I systematically avoided making curious criticisms on the productions of artists, that I might not attempt to combine the incompatible functions of a warm friend and a just critic; because I was profoundly conscious that a man who criticises paintings, not being himself a painter, is certainly liable to run into blunders from which even rare modesty and caution can with difficulty save him.[36]

A criticism of this kind may be intelligently filleted by the understanding of its author, which it helpfully contains – Blackie makes the aesthetic criticism he claims to avoid. He has indeed offered an unconscious criticism of his own understanding in the matter by pointing out in a previous sentence, that the work of the Calvinist-inclined George Harvey fails to resemble the painting of Rubens.

Another friend of Hill, James Nasmyth, presented him in similar terms, but with more understanding and sympathy:

> His name calls up many recollections of happy hours spent in his company. He was, in all respects, the incarnation of geniality. His lively sense of humour combined with a romantic and poetic constitution of mind, and his fine sense of the beautiful in Nature and art, together with his kindly and genial feeling, made him, all in all, a most agreeable friend and companion. 'D. O. Hill', as he was generally called, was much attached to my father. He was a very frequent visitor at our Edinburgh fireside, and was ever ready to join in our extemporised walks and jaunts, when he would overflow with his kindly sympathy and humour. He was a skilful draughtsman, and possessed a truly poetic feeling for art. His designs for pictures were always attractive, from the fine feeling exhibited in their composition and arrangement. But somehow, when he came to handle the brush, the result was not always satisfactory – a defect not uncommon with artists. Altogether, he was a delightful companion and a staunch friend, and his death made a sad blank in the artistic society of Edinburgh.[37]

'AND BE ANOTHER'

Hill would appear to have shared the ability of the great literary figures he admired, not simply to understand but to be, sympathetically, someone else. In John Brown's words:

> Though little known as a delineator of human character, he has many of the mental qualities proper to this department: he can throw himself out of himself, and be another; he has humour, which implies, we have always thought, not merely character in its owner, but a power of seeing into the character of others; and he has that thorough human-heartedness and love of his kind, that makes him lay out his affections on them wherever he sees them.[38]

This ability involves an understanding of how life looks from inside someone else's head. Stanley Cursiter, the painter and curator of the National Gallery of Scotland, identified and admired this understanding in a review of the calotype work in 1928: 'In single figures the pose is always simple and natural, and invariably personal in that we feel it to be true to the sitter rather than a preconceived attitude determined by the photographer'.[39] Such empathy, which sees both virtues and faults with an eye of generosity, is one of the most sophisticated, albeit often confusing, human traits.

In the early nineteenth century, empathy was a notable character of literature in Scotland. The idea of occupying another personality relied on the convention of writing anonymously, particularly for journals like *Blackwood's Magazine* and *The Edinburgh Review*. Sarah Green's *Scotch Novel Reading; or, Modern Quackery: A Novel Really Founded on Facts*, published in London in 1824, offered the engaging possibility that such anonymity was a Scottish commercial plot to monopolise the novel-writing market.[40] However, it proved useful to women authors, who were taken more seriously if they were anonymous or pseudonymously male. Elizabeth Rigby, for example, wrote anonymously for the *North British Review*, and implied in her text that she was a man; the anonymity may have allowed her to be more acid in her criticism. It enabled protected critical writing, but it also had the positive creative purpose of writing in other personae. Scott, who played with its possibilities as 'The Great Unknown', wrote, when his anonymity was broken:

> As it is the privilege of a masque or incognito to speak in a feigned voice and assumed character, the author attempted, when in disguise, some liberties of the same sort . . . the present acknowledgment must serve as an apology for a species of 'hoity toity, whisky frisky' pertness of manner, which in his avowed character, the author should have considered as a departure from the rules of civility and good taste.[41]

The assumption of another's name, most evident in the form of parody, extended the idea further. Hill's taste for this is shown in a letter of encouragement to Noël Paton, where he rewrites one of the parodies of James and Horace Smith:

> Joseph Muggins stir your stumps
> Why are you in such doleful dumps
> A dancer & affraid o pumps
> What are they fear'd on, eh! ad raten
> Here's the last sketch of J. N. Paton.[42]

The Smiths' *Rejected Addresses* was one of the first significant works of parody, based on the unlikely award of a prize for a speech to reopen the Drury Lane theatre after a fire. It became a popular and critical success when eighteen pages of *The Edinburgh Review* were devoted to admiration of the work. The proposals of character and parody, when regarded as an alternative to caricature and satire, offered the nineteenth century a kinder and closer view of their subjects. The

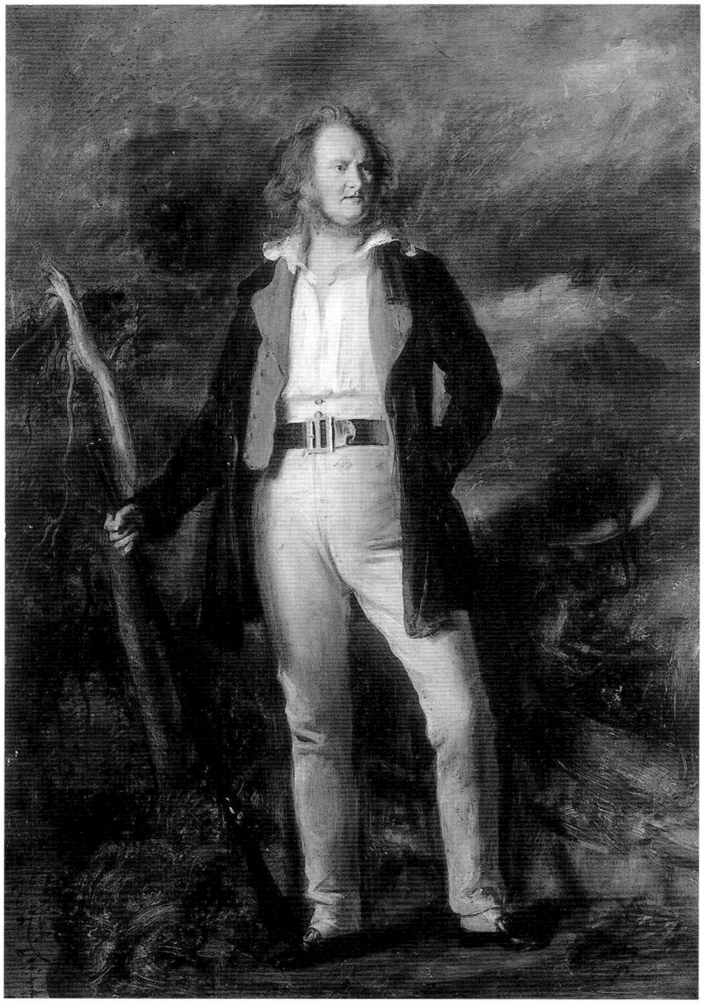

62. Thomas Duncan, *Christopher in his Sporting Jacket*, 1844. Oil on millboard. Scottish National Portrait Gallery, Edinburgh.

wider education of the time, based on the publishing revolution, which made their assumed authors so familiar, meant that the earlier, more aggressive theatricality of approach became subtler and could offer both humour and understanding of the subject. In Dwight Macdonald's terms parody is 'an intuitive kind of literary criticism, shorthand for what "serious" critics must write out at length. It is Method acting, since a successful parodist must live himself, imaginatively, into his parodee . . . Most parodies are written out of admiration rather than contempt.'[43] The parody accepted the idea of individuality and was a humorous celebration of 'marked and peculiar style', adding to the pleasure and public currency of the original. The anonymous writing had, moreover, the interesting consequence that parody would not necessarily be distinguished from true authority.

The most extraordinary literary example of this confusion of personality known to Hill was the *Noctes Ambrosianae*, largely written by John Wilson for *Blackwood's Magazine* between 1822 and 1835. This series was presented as conversations between real people, lightly disguised under pseudonyms: John Wilson was 'Christopher North', James Hogg was 'The Shepherd', Thomas De Quincy was 'The Opium Eater', and so forth. It was an extended bravura performance of multiple personality – poetic, ribald and critical – which Wilson maintained for thirteen years, until James Hogg's death. Wilson's son-in-law, who edited the *Noctes* for re-publication, made the astonishing claim:

> The Ettrick Shepherd of the Noctes Ambrosianane is one of the finest and most finished creations which dramatic genius ever called into existence . . . In wisdom the Shepherd equals the Socrates of Plato; in humour he surpasses the Falstaff of Shakespeare. Clear and prompt, he might have stood up against Dr Johnston in close and peremptory argument; fertile and copious, he might have rivalled Burke in amplitude of declamation; while his opulent imagination and powers of comical description invest all that he utters either with a picturesque vividness, or a graphic quaintness peculiarly his own . . . He is intensely individual and also essentially national. Hence he is real – hence he is universal.[44]

In writing as 'Christopher North', Wilson also presented himself as fictional. Thomas Duncan painted a small full-length portrait of him, known as *Christopher in his Sporting Jacket* (fig. 62), after one of Wilson's essays, in which Wilson is portrayed in a physical, outdoor pose, hair windswept and shirt open, holding a gun. [45] He was a large man and proud of his strength. In youth he wrestled with fairground champions; at the age when Hill knew and photographed him, he is known to have attacked and defeated a carter for maltreating his horse. The kind of invention involved here is basically truthful; he was assuming an alternative view of his own personality. So it is curious that the painting was later attacked for its ambiguity. It was said, in 1879:

> Except in Edinburgh, where Professor Wilson could be, do, or say anything, the idea was little cherished. The man and the picture are out of keeping. At the desk or in the field he was masculine beyond his fellows, but here, dressed in character, he becomes trifling and effeminated. The head is veritably that of Professor Wilson, while the accessories are more fitted for T. P. Cooke.[46]

Cooke was an actor, and it is hard to see what is meant here by 'the accessories'. It may be the pose, with its suggestion of an eighteenth-century idea of elegance, which strikes the writer as compromising.

The critic of Thomas Duncan's painting was troubled by a possibility of 'trifling effeminacy'. A concern for status lies behind a hostility roused by David Wilkie's picture of Scott's family as a country farmer and his household (fig. 73, see chapter seven) in 1818. When shown in London, it was attacked as 'a most conceited design . . . a picture which creates pity for the painter and disgust at the objects, while it violates decency and good taste'.[47] A similar concern emerges nearly two hundred years later in modern criticism of the calotypes of Hugh Miller. Miller was a man who had led an extraordinary career, beginning life as a stone mason in Cromarty, becoming a knowledgeable collector of and best-selling writer on geology, writing poetry and prose, acting as a banker and finally working as a combative journalist. At the time Hill and Adamson photographed him, Miller was the editor of the Free Church newspaper, the *Witness*. But it was not a role he was happy with – 'the editor writes in sand when the tide is coming in', he said.[48]

At the same time as the partners were taking the sketches for the Disruption picture, in May or June 1843, they took two small photographs of Miller as a stonemason, leaning on a grave in the Calton cemetery (fig. 63). The importance of these calotypes is emphasised by the fact that they restaged and improved the picture with the large camera in 1844 (pl. 12). Here, the background trees are masked off to remove the distraction; Miller's bonnet is off, allowing the characteristic springing bush of his hair to be seen, his shirt sleeves are rolled up and his waistcoat is open to the waist to allow a more muscular pose. The effect is a far more successful rendering of a working sculptor and a clearer idea of Miller's own pride in his size and strength.

Miller wrote of the stonemason as 'the hermit' and philosopher of the graveyard:

> I have risen from my employment to mark the shadow of tombstone and burial-mound creeping over the sward at my feet, and have been rendered serious by the reflection, that as those gnomons of the dead marked out no line of hours, though the hours passed as the shadows moved, so, in that eternity in which the dead exist, there is a nameless tide of continuity, but no division of time.[49]

The calotype of him as a sculptural mason therefore shows him as the independent man of strength and skill, and a modern philosopher. Moreover, in Miller's opinion: 'he is but

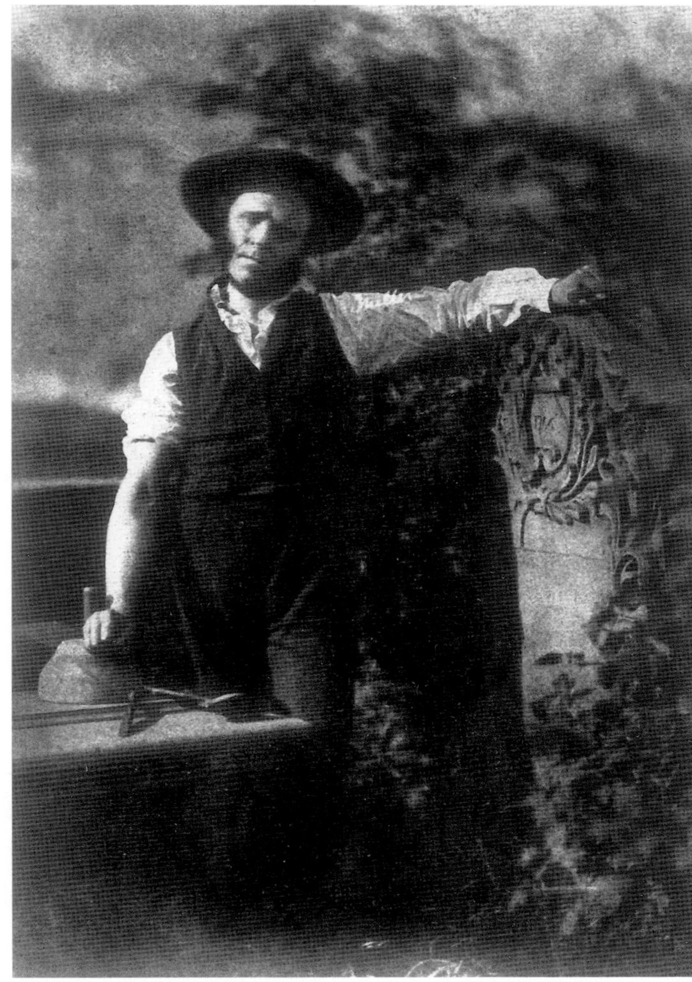

63. D. O. Hill and Robert Adamson, *Hugh Miller*, 1843. Calotype. Scottish National Photography Collection, Edinburgh.

a sorry, weak fellow who measures himself by the conventional status of the labour by which he lives.'[50] These calotypes express a pride in, and respect for, physical work, which allowed that it could be united with intelligence and philosophy – that it was not necessary for the man to 'rise' in society and sit at a desk. This idea is combined with a more difficult character, of deep importance to Miller as a Presbyterian. There is a story that he kept a photograph, probably one of these, on his desk; a lady asked him why he kept it there, and he replied that it kept him humble. This disconcerting combination of pride and humility gave both the force and the moral stress to Miller's personality.

It seems likely that the hostile response to these three pictures stems from their cultural dislocation, transplanted from their time or place. The critics' anxiety is focused on their own ideas of dignity, the importance of appropriate dress and the display of worldly status, and probably implies a dislike of the exploration of duality in the character of the three men.[51] The balanced historical opposition of the public and the private man, the serious and the relaxed, the mental and the physical, seems to have still been a common idea in Edinburgh in Hill's time – at least within his circle. Lord Cockburn, in inviting a friend out to the country wrote of himself:

> His Majesty's Solicitor General is a decorous person – arranged in solemn black – with a demure visage – an official ear – and evasive voice – suspicious palate – ascetic blood – and flinty heart. There is a fellow very like him, who traverses the Pentlands in a dirty grey jacket, white hat, with a long pole. That's not the Sol. Gen. That's Cocky – a frivolous dog.[52]

Thomas Carlyle was a leading voice in advancing the contrary idea of a monolithic, severe character for great men, which supplanted this variable idea, and bred a world nervous of duality: 'man's spiritual nature, the vital Force which dwells in him, is essentially one and indivisible ... All that a man does is physiognomical of him. You may see how a man would fight by the way in which he sings.'[53]

THE FACT IN FANTASY

Hill may have enjoyed fancy dress occasions – like the curious forerunners of the work of Gilbert and Sullivan that he helped his friend, the editor of the *Glasgow Herald*, George Outram, to compose and perform – partly because they allowed him to try being someone else. He referred to one of these performances, which was a satirical musical based on an attempt of the clergy to raise their stipends:

> I heard last week the whole of the Plea for Augmentation – it is almost a tragic performance and at the same time irresistiby comic. The greed, sensuality and worldiness of the clerical Elegant [?], is almost too dreadful to laugh at were it not for the ludicrous way in which the legal phraseology of the tiend court is interwoven with the ministers appeal.[54]

This occasion was ribald and satirical, but there was an additional seriousness behind the idea of such role-playing, which is exemplified by the immense solemnity of an earlier event. The Eglinton Tournament was staged in August 1839, by the Earl of Eglinton and a group of aristocratic friends.[55] The event was first prompted by the disappointing lack of historic

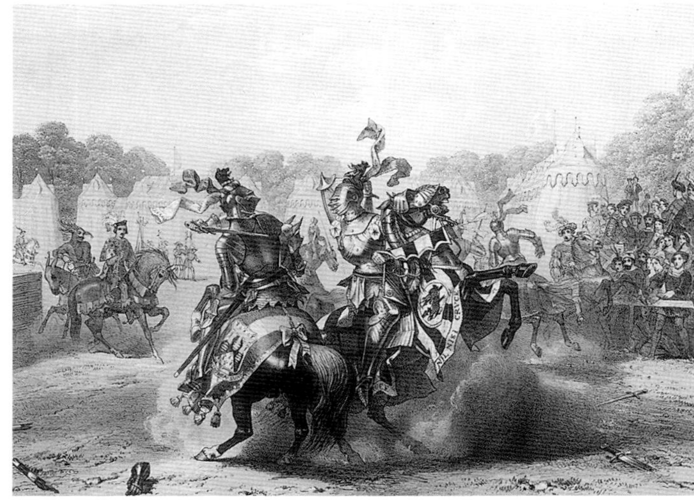

64. After Edward Corbould, '*The Melée*', *Eglinton Tournament*, 1839. Lithograph. National Library of Scotland, Edinburgh.

ceremony at Victoria's coronation – and in particular the omission of the queen's champion entering on horseback, to throw down a mailed glove in challenge to her enemies. The planning of the tournament was elaborate, and the cost of the exercise was extraordinary, involving the making and adapting of armour and historic costume, an enormous silver trophy and a splendid series of engravings detailing the action and events in highly imaginative precision (fig. 64). It took place in the wettest valley in Scotland and was, unsurprisingly, rained off. A reduced version of its original plan took place a few days later and the 'knights' performed respectably – it was not the complete fiasco experienced in earlier attempts to rekindle chivalry, in that the knights were capably athletic: they succeeded in hitting each other with the lances. One hundred thousand people are estimated to have been in the audience. D. O. Hill was one of the artists present on the occasion and one of the fancy dress calotypes may well be a reminiscence of the event, since it was inscribed at a later date as 'D. O. Hill in Tournament Dress' (fig. 65). This shows him as a minstrel playing the lute, an appropriate role, given his fondness for singing.

Amongst Hill's friends, an affection for the Middle Ages can been read in letters from James Nasmyth and Kenneth MacLeay, who is also seen in mediaeval dress in the calotypes. In 1835, Nasmyth wrote to Hill:

> I trust we shall i'the end save a few 'pieces of eight' and at a fitting season take my departure to some high and lonely tower where to converse on a dais of old, with one D.O. of happy memory. when to keep out the winter and colde

weather I shall have a mug of nut Brown Ale and a crabb laid i'the fire (a sea cole one as old song hath it) Ah these be the daies to look forward to, then shall we imagine the sound of pipe and tabour in the hall, while we sit and gossip olde daies. while said crab bobs gainst nose in gossips bowl.[56]

Hill's antiquarian taste is seen in the calotypes, where his fifteenth-century helmet is placed beside the harpist, Patrick Byrne (pl. 31), and Jimmy Miller, *The Young Savage*. This helmet is a south German sallet for the tournament and an important piece.[57] He also possessed and calotyped 'an ancient oak door', carved with the figure of a man fighting a lion, which he showed to the Society of Antiquaries in 1848, and was himself one of the group who revived the moribund society at the time.[58]

Behind the wistful affection for the decorative idea of the Middle Ages, lay a reasonable concern for generous morality, lost in the Industrial Revolution and the faltering principles of Free Trade. Thomas Chalmers, for example, recommended a hierarchical system of class, on the grounds that: 'There is a soul in chivalry, which though nursed in the bosom of affluence, does not cloister there, but passes abroad from mind to mind, and lights up a certain glow of inspiration throughout the mass of the community . . . where there are nobles, the common people are not so ignoble.'[59] It was not a wholly distanced admiration. The unexpected impact of the tournament may be judged by a letter written by Hugh Miller in the 1840s, which reads:

> Could you lend me a glance of your volume on the Eglinton Tournament? Lord Glenlyon who acted so conspicuous and gallant a part then has been dealing by the Church with a degree of meanness and rancour not yet reached by any of the other aristocracy. It would be perhaps well to give him a gentle cutting up, and begin by a detail of his past [?] exploits. The knightly and brave should be generous and merciful.[60]

The belief that someone enacting a role might be regarded as having its virtue or true character is a significant part of the interest in fancy dress and amateur theatrical performance. It is a serious and optimistic belief that the successful expression of emotion or virtue must be based on true experience. The idea had been transferred to painting through the Renaissance classical tradition that held 'the painter himself, like Horace's tragic actor, if he is to move the beholder of his picture must first feel these emotions himself. Si vis me flere, dolendum est primum ipsi tibi, is Horace's famous maxim.'[61]

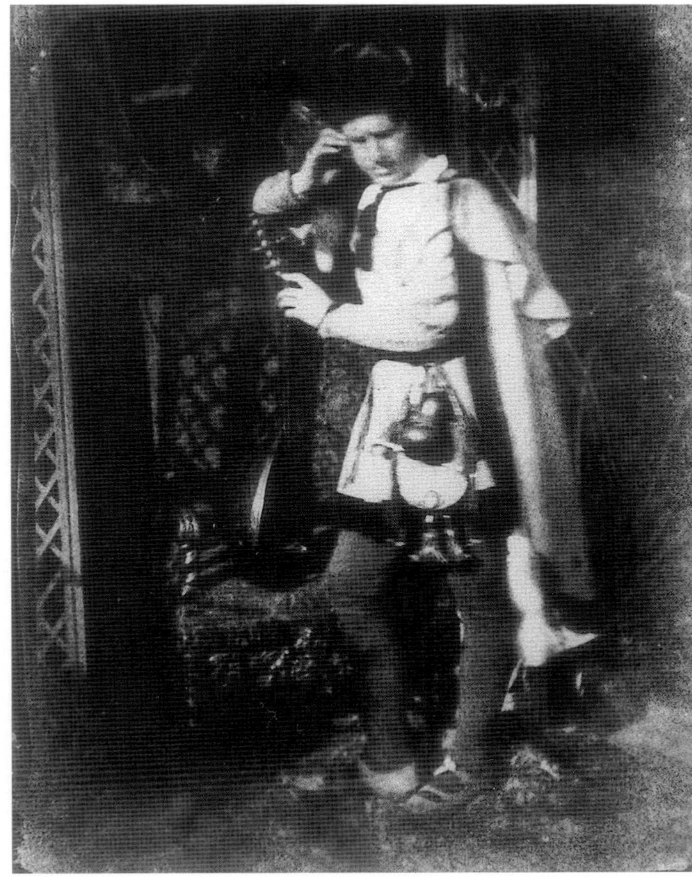

65. D. O. Hill and Robert Adamson, *D. O. Hill in Tournament Dress*, 1843–7. Calotype. Scottish National Photography Collection, Edinburgh.

LORD COCKBURN AND *THE ANTIQUARY*

Within the calotypes, the session at Lord Cockburn's home, Bonaly Tower, mostly clearly demonstrates the confusion of historical and modern ideas, blended by the influence of literature. Here again, the prominent writer was Walter Scott. He invented characters who were recognisably human, allowing his readers to sympathise and imagine themselves in the same circumstances. Moreover, in his words, Scott invited the painters, obliquely and overtly, to consider passages for illustration. He emphasised and directed their role by imagining scenes in their terms and offering them subjects to paint. The effect of this was as disconcertingly widespread as the popularity of his work. Scott inspired painters worldwide and offered the prospect of a great, new range of familiar stories and scenes for interpretation.

At Bonaly, Hill and Adamson took photographs connected with Scott's *The Antiquary*, which include the fancy picture of the sculptor John Henning and Miss Cockburn

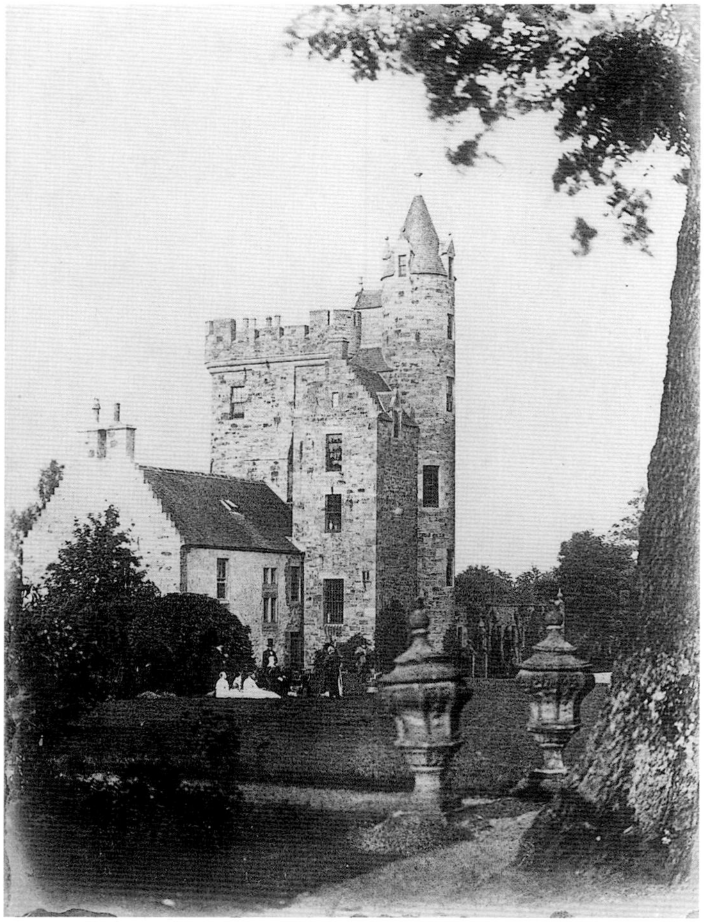

66. D. O. Hill and Robert Adamson, *Bonaly Tower*, 1843–7. Calotype. Scottish National Photography Collection, Edinburgh.

(pl. 32). The particular text that was used as inspiration comes from the account of the meeting between the characters Edie Ochiltree and Miss Wardour:

> Edie Ochiltree, old man and beggar as he was, had apparently some internal consciousness of the favourable impressions connected with his tall form, commanding features, and long white beard and hair . . . At present, as he lay half-reclined, with his wrinkled yet ruddy cheek, and keen grey eye, turned up towards the sky, his staff and bag laid beside him, and a cast of homely wisdom and sarcastic irony in the expression of his countenance, while he gazed for a moment around the courtyard, and then resumed his former look upward, he might have been taken by an artist as the model of an old philospher of the Cynic school . . . The young lady, as she presented her tall and elegant figure at the open window, but divided from the courtyard by a grating, with which, according to the fashion of ancient times, the lower windows of the castle were secured, gave an interest of a different kind, and might be supposed, by a romantic imagination, an imprisoned damsel communicating a tale of her durance to a palmer, in order that he might call upon the gallantry of every knight whom he should meet in his wanderings, to rescue her from oppressive thraldom.[62]

John Henning was usefully picturesque in appearance but was also similar to Ochiltree in cast of mind – a self-educated man with his own high-flown and confusing philosophy. He was described by the painter William Bell Scott:

> About 1841, he was aged with a noble presence; he had lost no hair, but it was pure white, and long, falling down upon his shoulders. His favourite subject was Biblical criticism, for which he had cultivated Hebrew and Greek to some extent, and he was fond of reading papers to a club of enthusiasts. These papers he would bring and re-read to me night succeeding night, especially one about the bottomless pit, which seemed appropriately endless.[63]

Cockburn himself was an enthusiastic antiquary and built himself Bonaly Tower, a Scottish sixteenth-century-style tower house, in 1836 (fig. 66). A self-determining hermit crab. he represented himself in Scott's terms; consciously, if ironically, placing himself in his own national history.[64] His daughter was unmarried and possibly being courted at the time of the pictures, like Miss Wardour in the book.[65] All three, Henning, Cockburn and Miss Cockburn fitted convincingly into the imaginative invention of Scott's fictional characters.

There is another echo of significance here, which may have prompted the idea. An undated letter from Cockburn to Hill says:

> I shall be very glad to see Mr Adamson & the Apparatus on Thursday . . . Be so good as to step down from Pie Mont & put a note into the post office, as soon after receiving this as you can, saying whether you be all acquainted with Mr Ballantyne – the Gaberlunzie. If he be not a stranger to the party, I should like to have him out here.[66]

James Ballantyne, who wrote *The Gaberlunzie's Wallet*, was one of the group calotyped on this occasion. His book was an extension of Scott's idea, in which the wandering beggar moved about the landscape to different houses, where stories were told, poems recited and songs sung.

It seems probable that Hill, with his knowledge of Scott, started, not with the idea of illustrating *The Antiquary*, but the other way about – recognising in the people a resemblance to the fiction. Such fancy photographs have an innately real character, which stays comfortably within a concern for the truthfulness of photography.

Within this one photographic session, there is a remarkable nest of associations. Scott himself is involved. He was an antiquary and there is an element of self-satire in the portrait of *The Antiquary.* In building his mansion, Abbotsford, Scott launched an enthusiasm for the baronial in Scottish architecture, which overtook Cockburn.[67] Moreover, Scott's story presents a narrative before and after the passage quoted, giving it dramatic life – the contemporary audience looking at the calotype would know that the beggar had saved the lives of the antiquary and his daughter during a dramatic storm the night before, and that she was about to offer him a substantial reward, which he would reject. The text offered a further layer of implication in the romance of a resemblance to earlier figures. The photographs would have thereby adopted an apt typological character, with three layers: the present actuality, the factually based fiction of the recent past and the Romantic distant past.

Hill had a long-standing professional and affectionate relationship with Lord Cockburn, especially in the academy's affairs. It may be expressed by Cockburn's letter to him, in 1847, thanking him for a set of calotypes:

> But are you not too munificent? – when I look on that splendid 'Land of Burns' , which adorns my shelves – & recollect sundry precious prints – & read your present intimation of still further generosity – I am abashed by the contrast of the little I have given with the greatness of what I have received.
>
> However, the true value of the donations, in my sight, consists in the kindness that sends them, & in the reciprocity of this feeling, I am conscious that I am not unworthy of your favour – for I have a very strong & sincere esteem for you – extending far beyond the artistic matters with which so much of our intercourse has been connected . . .
>
> Weather & Adamsons health have been adverse to the completion of the Bonaly Book, but Hope, which fortunately for mortals never dies – hints about 1848 . . . I don't believe that either Eastlakes or Stanfields appreciation of the coming volumes is a whit too high. My chief interest in it is, my Interest in the artist.[68]

The Bonaly Book was part of the entertainment offered by Cockburn at one of his country picnics. Hill sent Cockburn's daughter an album of the Bonaly photographs as a wedding gift in 1849, as:

> containing a few memorials of a very pleasant day at Bonaly . . . [which] I intended to have sent to you on your marriage day – with an expression of my devout wishes for your happiness. I waited however to get impressions of the calotypes my London friend made at Bonaly last autumn – but I waited too long and the volume could not be got ready for the day.[69]

There is an interesting mystery here. Apparently neither Cockburn nor Hill regarded the photographs we know as complete; they had other ideas, which were delayed and finally dissolved by Adamson's fatal illness. Hill apparently took a 'London friend' to Bonaly as a substitute for Adamson in 1848. Neither the friend nor the work has been identified, so we are left with a question and a sense of incomplete work.

But in these various ways, the Bonaly photographs have an extended and fascinating range of reference and the memory of pleasurable company, made poignant by this incompletion. They contained the personal and public, the literary, historical and actual. They are an expression of Hill's circle and knowledge – his admiration both for Scott and Cockburn. It is not a coincidence that the affectionate account of Hill given by James Nasmyth, which is quoted above, comes at the end of his lengthy and appreciative account of a Bonaly picnic in 1853.

7

Nationality and the Vernacular

The study of Scottish nationalism in the eighteenth and nineteenth centuries has a similar dependence on the literature discussed in chapter six. In the early and mid-nineteenth century, the history of the previous century was understood more from a reading of Walter Scott's novels than from books of history:

> The Romantic revolution in historical writing was born of Walter Scott and Scotland. The man and the place combined a blend of past and present, uncertainties and assumptions, physical realities and philosophical ideals which met the growing yearning of Europeans and Americans to receive (in the words of Heinrich Heine) 'history from the hand of the poet not from the hand of the historian . . . dissolved back into the original poetry whence [it] came.' Scott's historical legacy was both personally unique and yet representative of the experience of his country, compounded as it was of the tensions and contradictions of a traditional Scotland merging into a changing British nation, part of a great world empire.[1]

The three political crises in Scottish nationalism in the eighteenth century can be seen as the Union of 1707, which drew Scotland closer to England, principally by withdrawing Scotland's independent parliament and by shifting the seat of power to London; and the Jacobite wars in 1715 and 1745. These two rebellions in Scotland, in favour of Prince James Francis Stuart and his son, Prince Charles Edward Stuart, were, practically speaking, civil wars. The line of division, Jacobite against the Hanoverian government forces, was far from clear-cut in any terms, historic, religious, political, geographic or family, and clans who supported the Stuarts in 1715, stood back in 1745.[2] The wars left an acid sense of divided and confused loyalty and lost nationhood.

However, the effective defeat of the Jacobite cause at the battle of Culloden in 1746, eventually withdrew the threat of violence. After the death of Prince Charles Edward, his brother, Cardinal Henry Benedict the last of the Stuart line, made the Hanoverian line his heirs. The Jacobite movement became sentimentally attractive; within a generation of the war of 1745, a Romantic idea of the Scottish Highlands was advanced which helped to give a new coherence to the broader Scottish idea. One of the striking cultural phenomena of the late eighteenth and early nineteenth centuries in Scotland was the development of this Highland idea into a leading national theme. This was itself largely achieved through literature.

In the 1760s, James Macpherson published his 'translations' of the ancient Gaelic poet, Ossian, which promoted the Highlanders as a grand primitive society, and offered an opposition, not so much between Highland and Lowland Scots or Scots and English, as between a Romantic vision of the past and the present.[3]

Walter Scott's first novel, *Waverley*, published in 1814, was designed to consider the contradictions of the Jacobite/Hanoverian conflicts from an individual rather than political viewpoint.[4] Scott was, from childhood inclination, a Jacobite – he knew men who had fought in the war and some of his relatives had been executed by the Duke of Cumberland, son of King George II – but his adult judgement 'inclined for the public weal to the present succession'.[5] The idea of the Jacobites, which he proposed in the book, was attractive for its heroism, but he balanced the narrative by introducing the human factor. Waverley was an Englishman, caught up in the Highland fighting, who could see his old commander and fellow soldiers on the English side as equally heroic. When King George IV visited Scotland in 1822, Walter Scott orchestrated the event and filled Edinburgh with a Highland host. The king himself theatrically symbolised the reconciliation by wearing the Highland dress, which had been proscribed by royal decree after the battle of Culloden.[6]

D. O. Hill believed that opposing forces could be reconciled and united in sympathy for heroism. This is expressed in his support in the 1850s for Joseph Noël Paton's grand plan for a national memorial in Princes Street in Edinburgh. This, disconcertingly, featured a plaque commemorating the trial in London of the thirteenth-century Scottish patriot, William Wallace, which related it to the mocking of Christ. Hill defended the memorial with great passion against the doubt of David Roberts, who was resident in London:

> England then as now recognized in Wallace a noble martyr for Liberty, done to death by a powerful and sagacious but unscrupulous and tyrannical Norman King. Englishmen should and do revere the memory of Wallace . . . I believe they will aid the monument, if this aid is wanted. And as to Bruce – the opinion of the late Dr Arnold of Rugby is one that Englishmen will listen to, and he has said that, 'Englishmen should keep the anniversary of Bannockburn as the day which conferred on England her right arm.' Consider the sort of Union we would have had, had Scotland been a downtrodden & conquered people: – contrast such a Union with that whose blessings we now enjoy.[7]

Hill and Roberts were at odds here, but Hill's enthusiasm was deeply rooted in a concept of union based on sympathy.[8] Hill's idea of nationality is culturally respectful or assimilated. He had no difficulty associating Burns and Shakespeare, as he did in his captions to the *Fishermen and Women* series.

The great advantage offered by the influence of the eighteenth-century Scottish Enlightenment – led by such figures as the philosopher, David Hume, or the economist, Adam Smith, but more emphatically by the wider, literary influence of such authors as James Macpherson, Robert Burns and Walter Scott – was precisely that Scottish nationalism could be approached from a position of international strength. Isolation from England was not necessary to generate distinction; such distinction had flowered within the Union – and primitive heroism could be brought together with modern sophistication. Hugh Miller, who was doubtful of Scott's temporising humanity, wrote approvingly of his influence in the balance of the Union, at the inauguration of the Scott Monument in 1844:

> He has interested Europe in the national character and in some corresponding degree in the national welfare; and this of itself is a very important matter indeed . . . the European celebrity of the fictions of Sir Walter must have had the inevitable effect of raising the character of his country – its character as a country of men of large growth, morally and intellectually.[9]

'HIGHLAND CHARACTER AND COSTUME'

One of the six albums of photographs Hill and Adamson announced in 1844 was *Highland Character and Costume*. This was presumably meant to involve the Highland ministers as well as the more obvious Highland figures, and Hill probably intended to include the large calotype of the Highland laird and Free Churchman, Alexander Campbell of Monzie (pl. 33). He was described with such enthusiasm by John Stuart Blackie that he sounds fictional:

> He received me with great frankness of old Highland hospitality, gave me a splendid dinner of venison-tripe and full-bosomed grouse, with a magnum of most excellent claret, capped with a tumbler of brandy-and-water . . . we had all sorts of laughing and talking and explosive outbursts. He took me through all his various and strange museums, introduced me to his magnificent deerhounds, and mingled deer-stalking and good fellowship with pious scraps of Gospel and Revival hymns in a manner quite original and refreshing . . . he is full of natural vigour and nobleness, but like a wild horse has never been accustomed to the rein, and is not quite understood by the quiet jogging people of whom the respectability of this world is mainly made up. He and I got on like gunpowder, and came down the glen in the dark, singing song for song.[10]

The volume would certainly have contained the piper John Ban Mackenzie (fig. 67), the miniature painter Kenneth MacLeay, the celebrated deerstalker Finlay, and the 'Sobieski Stuart' brothers, who all appear in the calotypes in Highland dress.

Charles Edward Stuart was calotyped in full Highland dress, in a suitably melancholic pose, lying on a rocky ledge (fig. 68). He and his brother John, who were known by the names of Hay Allen and Sobieski Stuart, lived as a Romantic fiction, claiming to be the legitimate heirs of the Stuart line. They told their own story in print in 1847. It is a mysterious and wonderfully unconvincing tale, told through the doctor summoned in secret to the childbed of Princess Clementina Sobieska, wife of Prince Charles Edward. She bore a child

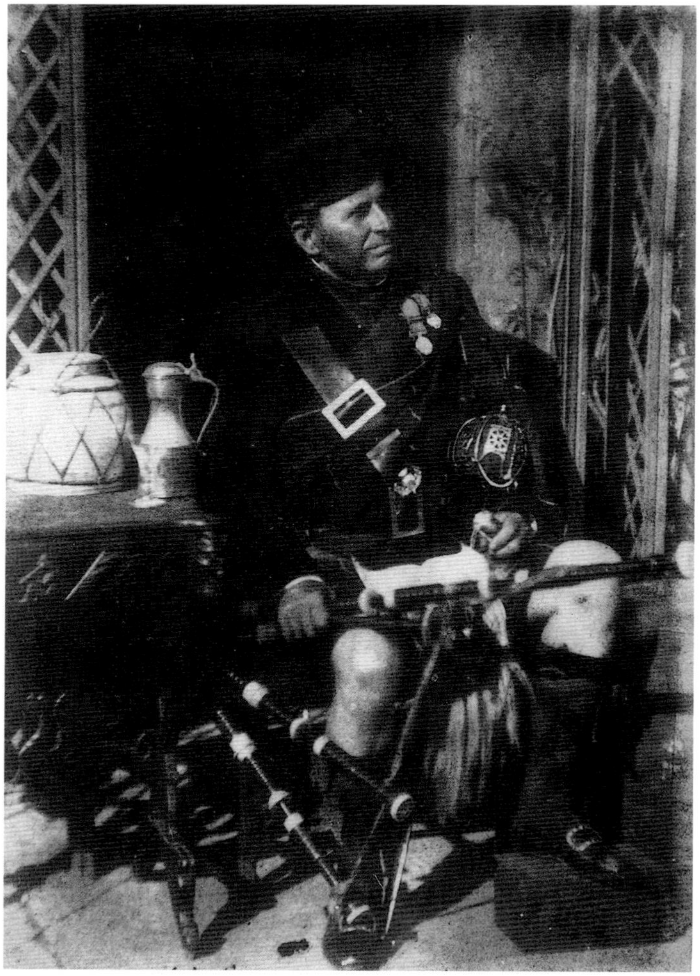

67. D. O. Hill and Robert Adamson, *John Ban Mackenzie*, 1843–7. Calotype. Scottish National Photography Collection, Edinburgh.

who was smuggled away, unacknowledged, to save his life. This child, the Sobieski Stuarts said, was their father. They made no rash attempt to lay claim to the throne, but presented themselves as the melancholy survival of a great historic past. They established themselves on an island in the middle of the River Beauly, in a neo-gothic house decorated with Highland shields, swords, coats of arms and stags' antlers.[11] In 1848, they published a verse account of their life on the banks of the Findhorn River, as *Lays of the Deer Forest.* A romantically minded sympathiser described their life there: 'Here the two brothers entirely realised the old border ideas of gallant young huntsmen, – superb figures, attired in the ancient dress of the century, and full of chivalric feeling, – who, giving up the common pursuits of the world, spent most of their days in following the deer through the pathless wild.'[12] To the cynical eye of Elizabeth Rigby, they were immediately transparent. She met one of them in 1843 and remarked: 'the man was dressed in all the extravagance of which the Highland costume is capable – every kind of tag and rag, false orders, and tinsel ornaments which could be heaped on an ill-made clumsy person; the whole surmounted by a face very like the portraits of Charles II, but nothing like the descriptions of the Pretender.'[13]

By creating themselves a setting which belonged to the distant past, the Stuart brothers managed to live a life that symbolised a primitive Highland ideal in the middle of the industrial age. It was arguably only one step further than the taste for baronial gothic architecture, which overtook Lord Cockburn, and belonged within the same framework as the Eglinton Tournament. Walter Scott, presumably conscious that they were to an extent his own invention, remarked cautiously: 'I have understood that the Messrs. Hay Allan are young men of talent, great accomplishments, and an exaggerating imagination, which possibly deceives even themselves.'[14] From the calotype of Charles Edward, which Hill exhibited in the academy in 1844, it may be presumed that Hill was prepared to accept the brothers as genuine. The obvious invention in their lives and work fitted so pleasingly into the taste for the Highland romance of life that people wished it to be true, although the sustained examination of their printed arguments made that truth more doubtful. Their two principal works were the *Vestiarum Scoticum*, which purported to be an ancient manuscript, published in 1842, and *The Costume of the Clans*, which appeared in 1845. It is not impossible that the publication of *The Costume of the Clans* was prompted by Hill and Adamson's own proposal. The calotype volume would have been one of a number of such grand publications, which included Ronald Robert McIan's *The Clans of the Scottish Highlands*, issued in parts from 1843 and Kenneth MacLeay's *Highlanders of Scotland*, published in 1868 at the instigation of Queen Victoria.[15]

Macleay was recommended to the queen's attention by Noël Paton, as, a 'Highlander of Highlanders', but his work was monitored with some suspicion by the Dowager Duchess of Atholl, the queen's adviser, who wrote: 'Having lived for many years in a town, he has rather adopted stage effects, and exaggerated views, altho' fortunately these do not appear in his drawings.'[16] MacLeay himself, who appears in the calotypes in a theatrical Highland dress, was proud of his own Jacobite ancestry, and claimed descent from King Robert I. He and his wife, who were known to Hill as 'the King and Queen', responded to an academy invitation in 1847, in appropriately regal and mediaeval style: 'Be it known unto our trusty & well beloved Cousin & Secretary of the Mount

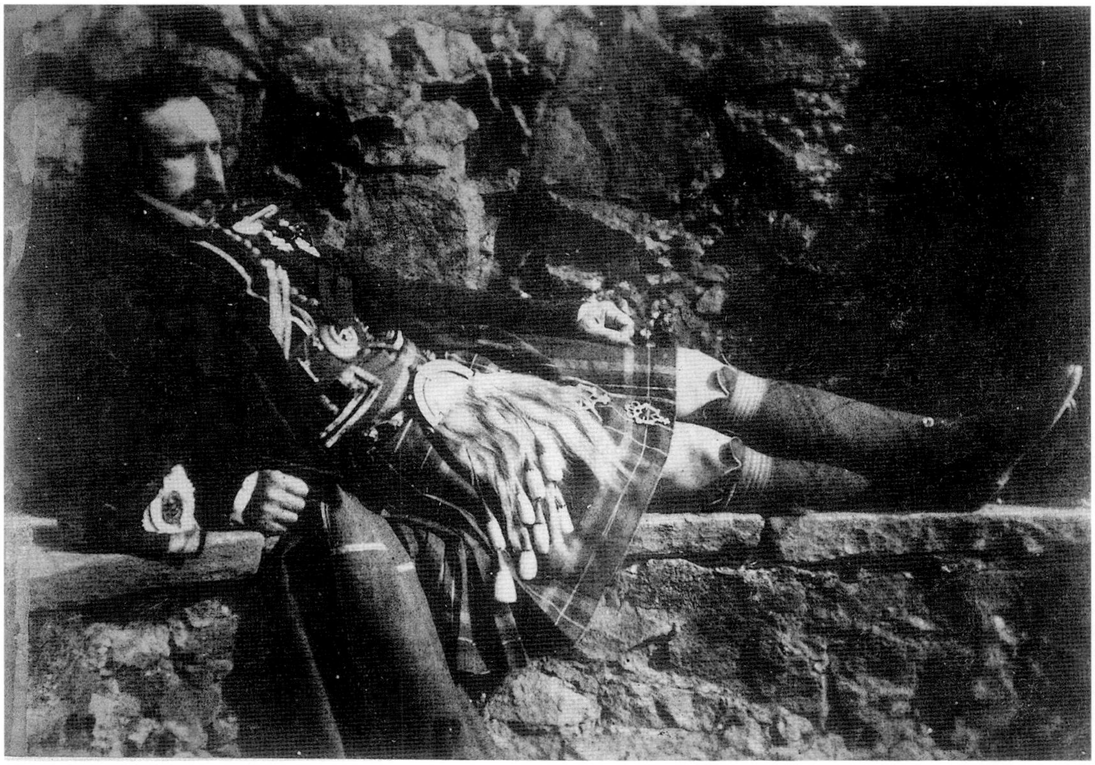

68. D. O. Hill and Robert Adamson, *Charles Edward Stuart*, 1843. Calotype. Scottish National Photography Collection, Edinburgh.

that it is her Majesty Queen Louisa's intention along with ourself this night to Grace your Banquet & that in time to remark upon the pane of our Juvenile Subjects.'[17]

THE DISRUPTION PICTURE AND NATIONALISM

The exaggerated and theatrical element in the behaviour of the Sobieski Stuarts and Kenneth MacLeay lies within the context of a wider admiration for the combined historic and picturesque idea of the Highlander. It was promoted pictorially by the grand Highland portraits of Henry Raeburn, painted in the late eighteenth and early nineteenth century (fig. 69). It gave warmth and strength to the figures Hill admired: the Gordon Highlanders, heroes of the Napoleonic Wars (pl. 14) and, more extraordinarily, the Free Churchmen.

In the foreground of the Disruption picture, the composition is anchored by the only two wholly unobstructed figures: Hugh Miller and Sergeant Mackenzie of the 42nd Highlanders (figs 70 and 71), 'Pipe-major of the regiment at Waterloo, where he behaved with great gallantry', who acted as 'one of the Officers of the Assembly'.[18] Mackenzie is wearing Highland dress and is sitting, leaning forward in an attitude of attentive contemplation; there is no military stiffness in his attitude (fig. 70).

The pose is reminiscent of the figure of the native American in Benjamin West's *The Death of General Wolfe.*[19] West's painting was immensely popular; he painted at least five replicas, and the engraving by William Woollett was 'one of the most commercially successful prints ever published'.[20] It was much debated in its time for breaking the convention of showing heroes in classical dress, in favour of contemporary uniforms, giving the picture that core sense of specific time and respect for nationality, which is critical also to the Disruption picture. John Galt later quoted West's justification: 'The same truth which guides the pen of the historian should govern the pencil of the artist. I consider myself as undertaking to tell this great event to the eye of the world; but if instead of the facts of the transaction I represent classical fictions, how shall I be understood by posterity?'[21] West's painting may not have been factual in a literal sense. The American is unnamed and was presumably meant as a representative national and historical figure, posed as the melancholic observer. Sergeant Mackenzie, who was an identified individual, serves a similar purpose in the Disruption picture, locating the event in its national context and offering the respect of a military warrior to fighters in another arena.

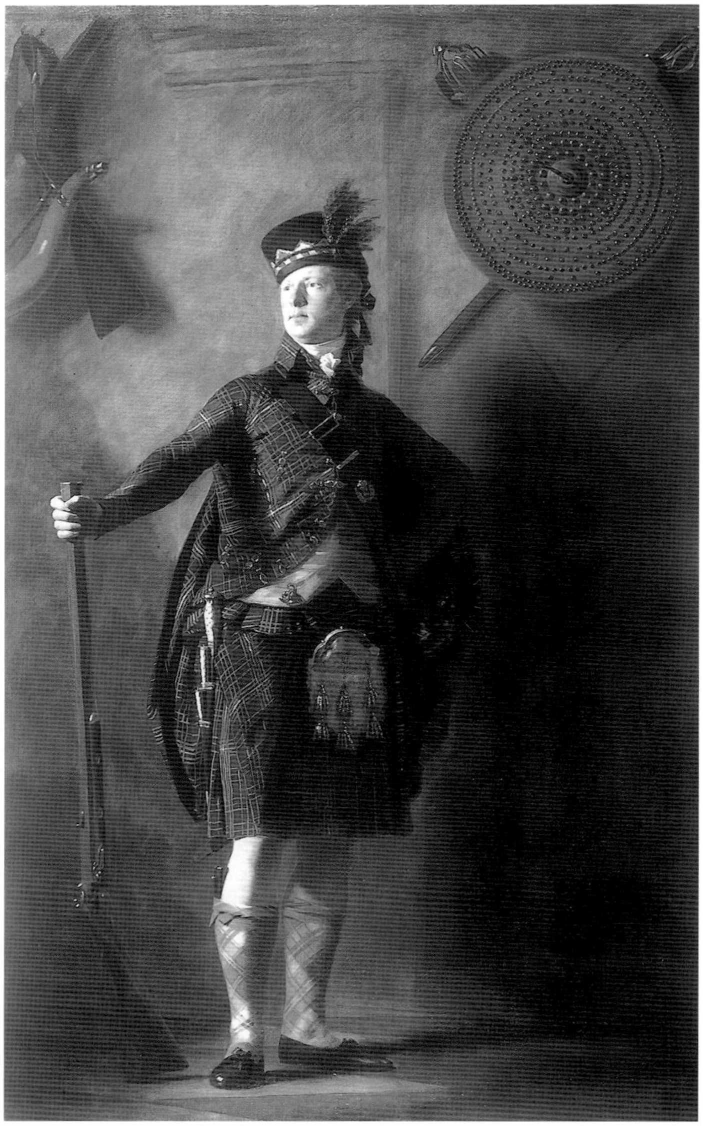

69. Henry Raeburn, *Colonel Alastair Ranaldson Macdonell of Glengarry*, c. 1811. Oil on canvas. National Gallery of Scotland, Edinburgh.

This comparison may be underscored by a group of photographs Hill and Adamson took in 1845. In August of that year, Hill and Adamson were able to take the earliest photographs of an American chieftain. Their subject was the Reverend Peter Jones or Khakewaquonaby (pl. 34), an Ojibeway from north-west Canada, the son of a Welsh methodist and an Ojibeway woman.[22] Jones was touring Britain both to defend his own culture and to raise money for schools to promote western civilisation and Christianity among his people. He preached in the churches of the Reverend Thomas Guthrie and the Reverend Dr Robert Smith Candlish in Edinburgh, and addressed a public meeting.

Jones was not, in some eyes, a sufficiently Romantic figure. John Stuart Blackie's response to him is in striking contrast to his lyrical description of Campbell of Monzie: 'He is a tall, dark-haired, dark-eyed, rather poor looking fellow, but with a big bulging mouth.'[23] Very probably, both for Guthrie and Hill, he was a model of assimilation. Hill, it should be emphasised in this context, did not look for beautiful models to symbolise his ideal but looked to the admirable reality.

Peter Jones appears in two groups of photographs, one in tribal dress and the other in western clothes. The calotypes thus show him in two roles: the historic, American figure both standing, wearing the war bonnet and holding an axe, and sitting on the ground, contemplative, with the pipe of peace; and the western man of religion with the Holy Bible. The pictures offer the optimistic potential of assimilation – the proposal that the history and simpler virtues of the older culture may combine with the new.

It seems probable from the calotypes that Hill could see an analogy between Khakewaquonaby and the Highlanders – the plumed headdress and the skirted tunic of the native American were visually in tune with the Highland chieftain's eagle feather and kilt. Thomas Guthrie used the parallel of the native American to admire Hugh Miller's fighting spirit in 1843:

> On the eve of what was to prove a desperate conflict, I have seen him in such a high and happy state of eagerness and excitement, that he seemed to me like some Indian *brave*, painted, plumed, leaping into the arena with a shout of defiance, flashing a tomahawk in his hand, and wearing at his girdle a very fringe of scalps, plucked from the heads of enemies that had fallen beneath his stroke.[24]

The calotypes of Miller, like the calotypes of Jones, offered alternate readings (see chapter six), as the journalist and the stonemason. In the Disruption picture, Hill painted him as the editor of the *Witness*, noting the proceedings (fig. 71), taking the pose largely from the group with another journalist, John Robertson, but isolating the figure. Miller is wearing a Lowland plaid, an untailored drape of material, which may imply the simpler and stronger virtues of the past. It echoes Hill's remark to Lady Ruthven, about a picture of the blind harper, Patrick Byrne (pl. 31): 'The Harper, whose costume is made of a blanket and plaid shows how simply one might get up pictures of the old world.'[25] However, the painted figure is also Miller the intellectual, which is emphasised by the profile, adopted from another calotype, showing him with his hair combed back to give the height of the temple – the visible sign of intelligence. In effect, both Guthrie and Hill were

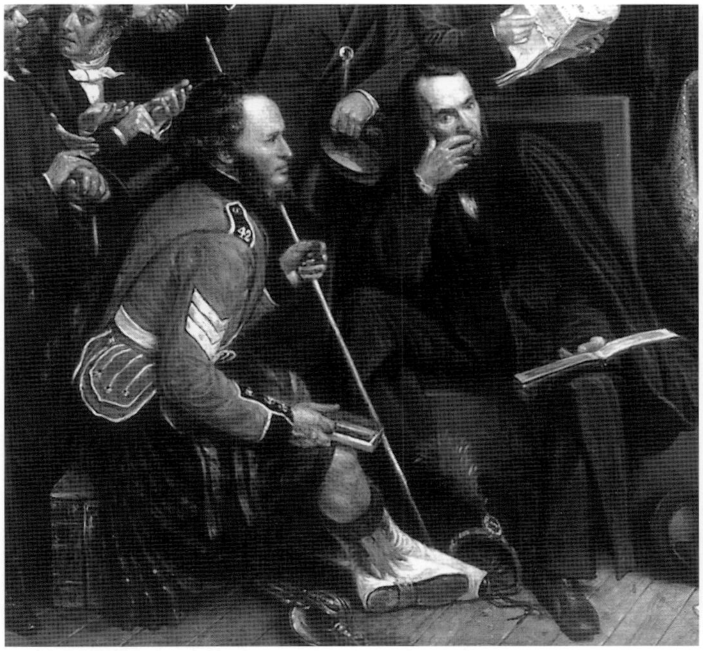

70. D. O. Hill, *The Signing of the Deed of Demission*, detail showing Sergeant Mackenzie and Mr Hately. Oil on canvas. Free Church of Scotland, Edinburgh.

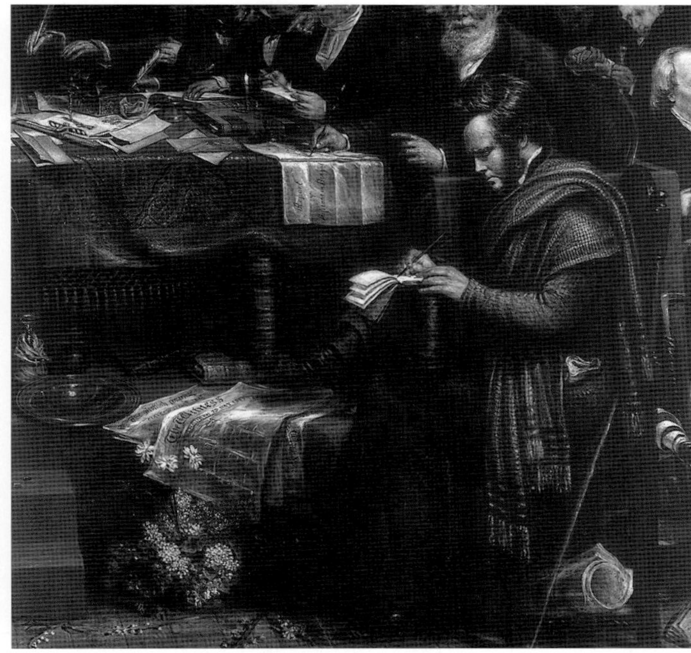

71. D. O. Hill, *The Signing of the Deed of Demission*, detail showing Hugh Miller. Oil on canvas. Free Church of Scotland, Edinburgh.

presenting an idea of assimilation that was far from bland; it allows for a combination of the passion and courage of the primitive and the intelligence and fluency of modern man. It may additionally be significant that the figure of the Highland sergeant is more inclined to passive melancholy, and that the upright, active figure of Miller is aligned with the column supporting the upper level of the hall, which bears so many of the leading figures of the Disruption.

The composition of the painting changed radically within the twenty years Hill worked on it. I do not know when Hill placed Miller in this position but the idea was not a part of the original designs. It may be that the prominence of the portrait is a personal tribute. Given the friendship between Hill and Miller, there can be no doubt that he was deeply shaken when Miller shot himself, overwhelmed by the pain of a brain disease, in 1856. Hill's text for the painting says:

> The plaided form . . . employed in taking notes near the Clerks' table, is the editor of the *Witness* newspaper . . . a name very dear to Scotland, and admired wherever the English language is read – whose figure does not bulk more prominently in the picture than did his remarkable writings in the controversy evolving the Disruption, of which it may be said emphatically he was one of the greatest leaders.[26]

The idea that this is a memorial tribute is supported by the explanatory leaflet, which refers to the portrait of Robert Adamson, placed much higher in the composition, immediately before this passage. On the ledge beside Miller lie copies of the *Witness*. On the ground, scattered at his feet are flowers, the natural tribute of affection to mortality.

The position and choice of these two key figures underline the historic and national character of the Disruption picture, but it was a nationalist painting in a broad sense. The Free Church was a focus of international attention. Hugh Miller wrote of Hill's projected painting in June 1843:

> His picture bids fair to possess an interest, not limited to one age or one country. One of the most pregnant events in modern history is the disruption of the Scottish Establishment; and it is an event for which Evangelism all over the world feels a deep concern. The Christian is the only true cosmopolite; his sympathies are co-extensive with the human family; and those feelings of love and admiration which a narrow patriotism confines within its limited ranges of hills, or its bounded lines of coast, he extends to wherever, for the sake of Christ, there are great dangers encountered or great sacrifices made.[27]

This explains Hill's apparent optimism in promoting the finished picture: 'The Painter entertains the hope . . . that the

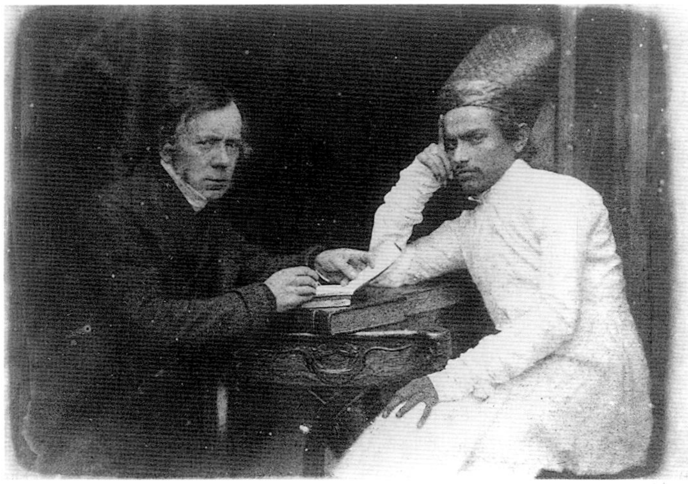

72. D. O. Hill and Robert Adamson, *Reverend John Jaffray and Dhanjiobai Nauroji*, 1843–7. Calotype. Scottish National Photography Collection, Edinburgh.

representation of an event so evidently designed to fill a large place in history, and to exert a far-reaching influence, will find ready admission into the houses and Art Collections of men of all denominations of religious opinions.'[28] It was not an optimism founded on local enthusiasm alone. The painting includes such significant international figures as Dr Jean Henri Merle D'Aubigné, a leader of ecumenical Protestantism from Geneva; the American Presbyterian and father of Harriet Beecher Stowe, Lyman Beecher; Dhanjiobai Nauroji from Bombay, who was ordained as a Free Church minister in 1846 (fig. 72); and Karl Heinrich Sach, professor of theology at Bonn, who made a special study of the Free Church and wrote *Die Kirche in Schottland*, which was published in 1844. In 1862, Thomas Guthrie spoke of a discussion with the Chevalier Bunsen, expatiating with rapture on the Free Church and Scotland:

> The idea that had seized his mind, and on which he dwelt so eloquently, was this – that God had, in His providence, raised us up in this country, and placed us in circumstances favourable for its solution, to try the problem, whether a Church, without aid or countenance from the State, could by the resources of its own members and nothing else, fulfil the two grand objects of every living being – sustain and extend itself.[29]

The act of secession from the Church of Scotland was based on the Presbyterian need to separate the political government from religious morality. In 1917, Harold Laski's *Studies in the Problems of Sovereignty* talked of the Free Churchmen in these terms: 'They were fighting a State which had taken over bodily the principles and ideals of the medieval theocracy. They urged the essential federalism of society, the impossibility of confining sovereignty to any one of its constituent parts.'[30] Laski identified a surprising fact about the Disruption, viewed from the early twentieth-century perspective, in the context of political nationalism: that Scottish historians had not written an adequate history of 'the central event of nineteenth-century Scottish history'.[31] Ironically, the painted history of the event, offered so expansively by Hill, did not take on any of the authority of the missing writing. In the last twenty years, it has proved necessary and interesting to Scottish historians to explain the importance of the Disruption: 'It was an age of revolution in Scotland, more far-reaching in its impact than that surrounding the Union of 1707, and the Disruption crystallised and symbolised the transformations being unleashed on the nation.'[32]

The evangelical movement may indeed have been responsible for undermining or, more strictly, replacing the political radicalism of the Chartist movement in Scotland. Both the Chartists and the evangelists were aware of this conflict, and sometimes met head on.[33] The Disruption effected an equivalent to the political revolutions in the other countries of Europe, although the arguments of the Free Church leaders were firmly set in a non-revolutionary structure. While it is doubtless a coincidence that Karl Marx wrote, 'religion is the opium of the people', in 1843, it is an extremely interesting coincidence. The evangelists provided the excitements and pleasures of combat and righteousness, which absorbed political anger and redirected it. They specifically upheld the current social stratification, regarding its failure as a breakdown, which could be restored by ameliorating the conditions and raising the moral status of the poor at the base of the pyramid. The principal aim was elevating the minds, or rather the souls, of the people, not their comparative circumstances. The advantage of the Free Church idea, which helped to distinguish it from a state or political concern, was the concentration on the individual's responsibility, to think and act with direct moral consciousness – an individual responsibility and an individual freedom.

MUSIC AND HISTORIC TRADITION

In 1830, when Hill first took on the responsibility, as secretary of the Scottish Academy, for pursuing important paintings for the annual exhibitions, he wrote an especially enthusiastic letter to David Wilkie, which makes the connection between painting and music in his own mind. He is writing about Wilkie's painting, *The Highlander's Return*:

> It is with profound respect I venture to transcribe my own more than half suppressed emotions on studying the picture of calm contentment, of domestic endearments, of manliness, modesty, innocence, and grateful attachment. The feelings it awakens are not less intense, nor less delightful in their intensity than those called forth by the most touching of our melodies or the most perfect Lyrics of our heart strung bards, while the exquisite art by means of which the conception is embodied, furnishes a pleasure unknown to the mere lovers of song. The chord you have touched so delicately & yet so masterly, will find a responsive echo in many a Scottish bosom and will, if possible, enshrine the artist still deeper in the hearts of his admiring Countrymen.[34]

Beside Sergeant Mackenzie in the Disruption picture is another thoughtful figure, Mr Hately, the precentor who led the singing during the Free Church sessions (fig. 70). His presence was designed by Hill to:

> remind the spectator of that opening song of praise, given forth by Dr Chalmers as the Church's first act of Devotion after the Disruption – 'O send Thy light forth and Thy truth' – and joined in by the nearly four thousand voices with a joy and fervour of devotion seldom experienced; while the immense hall, till then but dimly seen from the dark and clouded nature of the day, was now filled with beaming light, from the bursting forth of the sun dispelling darkness, a change in the face of the heavens in wonderful harmony with the words of the psalm and the feelings of the worshippers.[35]

This was the emotional, mysterious focus of the day and the creative rather than combative aspect of nationalism. When painting the picture and thinking of the event, Hill heard the hymn, and in the picture the sun streams in through a skylight to celebrate that moment. The song is in the sunlight.

The prospectus ended with a discussion of 'the objects of still life in the Picture', including the flowers (fig. 71), which:

> were a feature in the first Assembly, being the everyday gifts of the ladies of the Church . . . Scotch in their associations, they also mark the month of May, and call up many beautiful thoughts and sayings dear to the heart of Scotland, and applicable to the situation, from that of the greatest of her poets – 'The hyacinth's for constancy, wi' its unchanging blue'–to that of HIM who spoke to the multitudes on the Mount, and now, here to the hundreds of homeless men who had that day given their all for Him . . . 'Consider the lilies of the field; they toil not, neither do they spin: yet I say unto you, that Solomon, in all his glory was not arrayed like one of these.'[36]

The first quotation comes from Robert Burns's love song, 'The Posie'.[37] Hill is making a reference to the month of May, when the Disruption took place – the singer picks different flowers in succession and the refrain is: 'And a' to be a posie to my ain dear May'. The justification for quoting the work of a reprobate in the context of a religious painting is Hill's generous belief in analogy within the arts and within nature. For him, 'The Posie' could be an equivalent of 'The Song of Solomon', a love song and, on another plane, a song offering a reflection of divine love. The celebration within the song of the beauty, simplicity and sweetness of a girl would not have struck Hill as incongruous as an expression of the crowd of Presbyterian ministers. It is not a direct analogy, but it is reflected in the true impulse of the ladies in 'their everyday gifts', to add physical beauty and sweetness to the moral beauty of the occasion.

Hill's talent for singing helped to make him popular at social gatherings and he even figures in a song, written by George Outram, to celebrate a housewarming, in which the warmth of the house is measured against the general state of inebriation.

> When Bell begins to falter in his boisterous career,
> And Mackenzie's merry voice begins to sound a
> little queer,
> And Hill's becoming tuneless – we may the question
> pit,
> In whispers to each other – Is the house warm yet?[38]

Hill joined Outram in Glasgow, in 1844, at a 'Scotch Denner':

> a purely national meal, to which each guest was to come in the costume of some favourite Scottish worthy, and which was to be a gathering ironically renewing the once popular lamentations over the Union with England, as destructive of the independence and ancient position of Scotland. The 'denner', to which only a small and select party was invited, each of whom appeared in a historical character and dress, came off on 22d July 1844, being the 138th anniversary of the Treaty of Union . . . With the toasts, on the occasion of the 'denner', were intermingled many of the Chairman's most delightful songs – some of them

being composed for the occasion – together with other songs, hardly less delightful, by a favourite Scottish landscape-painter, now, alas! no more [i.e. Hill]; and with the irresistible stories of another Scottish artist [Daniel Macnee], who, happily, still survives to charm his countrymen alike with his word and colour painting.[39]

This was a consciously historical occasion, a mock revolutionary gesture, with Scottish food of both the finest and the least pretentious kind and a menu written in verse quotations. The food included a serious dish called 'crappit head', described as a variant on haggis, 'stuffed into the heads or skulls of large haddocks, and . . . roasted in a Dutch-oven'.[40] It is of some interest that the two aspects of the vernacular tradition, original song and storytelling, were represented by two artists.

The connection between song and nationality was longstanding, and was even used in the political context of the Union of 1707. Andrew Fletcher of Saltoun, 'the archetypical Scottish patriot of modern history', wrote at that time a dialogue on the regulation of governments for the common good, which contained the celebrated passage: 'I knew a very wise man . . . [who] believed if a man were permitted to make all the ballads, he need not care who should make the laws of a nation.'[41] The concern for the decline of song as a critical part of Scotland's social culture was expressed by James Hogg as part of a wider concern for farm workers, whose material conditions had improved but who were, in his opinion, less devout and less happy:

> On looking back, the first great falling off is in Song . . . the young men attended at the ewe-bucht or the cows' milking, and listened and joined the girls in their melting lays . . . I never heard any music that thrilled my heart half so much as when these nymphs joined their voices, all in one key, and sung a slow Scottish melody . . . Where are those melting strains now? Gone and for ever![42]

The Scottish publishing revolution had helped to spread new songs but also made available the collected editions of old ballads, gathered by poets like Allan Ramsay in his *Tea Table Miscellany* in 1724 or Walter Scott in his *Minstrelsy of the Scottish Border* of 1802–3. The idea that the vernacular should be a spring of sophisticated creativity was well established; ironically sophisticated writing became vernacular and authorship was often concealed to make a song historical.[43] Jacobite songs were invented by such as Baroness Nairne, who also wrote 'Caller Herrin' – one of the fishwives' songs.[44]

One of the reasons why the old songs had a considerable impact, both within Scottish culture and abroad, lay in the Scottish poets' continuing concern, not simply to collect what in some instances were fragments but to rewrite and improve them. At the end of the eighteenth century, an English enthusiast for historic song identified as peculiarly Scottish and peculiarly irritating the habit of rewriting historical texts: 'Why the Scotish [*sic*] literati should be more particularly addicted to literary imposition than those of any other country, might be a curious subject of investigation for their new Royal Society . . . The history of Scotish poetry exhibits a series of fraud, forgery and imposture, practised with impunity and success.'[45] The Scots had established a thoroughly ambiguous but lively idea of rewriting, which falls comfortably within established convention in the creative arts but is antipathetic to antiquarianism. The problem, and the justification of the complaint, lay in the extraordinary Scottish tendency to deny authorship.

Robert Burns was the principal figure in this combination of historical discovery and invention.[46] He subsumed his own energies in the rewriting of old songs, both respecting and joining his work to the creativity of the ancient bards, who, he wrote: 'described the exploits of Heroes, the pangs of disappointment & the meltings of Love, with such fine strokes of Nature . . . O ye illustrious names unknown! The last, the meanest . . . one who though far inferior to your flights, yet eyes your path . . . pays this sympathetic pang to your memory.'[47] Burns's songs have a seductive force, appealing to the emotions through a combination of the sophisticated and the simple. He melded the old and the new, rewriting old songs and inventing new songs in a traditional manner. There is a remarkable range of emotional impact in his songs, not just from satire to sincerity, but from love to patriotism, from carousing to despair, from tragedy to tiresomeness, from the extraordinary to the ordinary. The range of emotional experience offered in singing such songs must have been not just uplifting and cathartic but part of the whole proposal of being another and of exploring human nature.

As a singer and inventor of songs, Hill would have been well aware of the concentrated skill involved in writing and singing songs of such apparent simplicity. The act of singing is ephemeral and we cannot hear Hill's voice. For John Brown it was an equivalent or illumination of Hill's painting. Brown wrote in his 1846 review: 'His works always exhibit something of the highest beauty, – often a sort of tenderness as unexpected and as plaintive as the 'owercome' of an old border ditty *sung by himself*.'[48] Brown's comment suggests that Hill could cope with musical sophistication. It is reasonable to assume that he knew how a song was constructed and could achieve subtle effects.

From the outsiders' point of view, the Scots had a notable affection for music. The readiness of Scottish society to burst into song and dance was commented on by Benjamin Robert Haydon in the 1820s:

> I never had a complete conception of Scotch hospitality till I dined at [Andrew] Geddes' with Sir H. Raeburn and [George] Thompson (who set Burns' songs to music), and a party of thirty at least.
>
> Thompson sang some of the songs of Burns with great relish and taste, and at the chorus of one, to my utter astonishment, the whole company took hands, jumped up and danced to the tune all round till they came to their seats again, leaving me sitting in wonder.[49]

Elizabeth Rigby described an Edinburgh dance in 1843, as a wild, national and historical impulse:

> Nobody would believe in England what an immense expenditure of animal spirits goes on, on these occasions. Young men and children, old men and maidens, all jumping and whirling, and toiling alike. You can hardly believe your eyes till you see the oldest and gravest in the land cutting capers, snapping fingers, tossing their heads, twisting round, brandishing their arms, shaking their legs, clapping hands, whooping, yelling and screaming, till you expect them to sink down with sheer exhaustion, like the dervishes.[50]

The poet Leigh Hunt expressed a similar feeling about Scotland in the 1850s, in writing to John Hunter of Craigcrook, who held the solemn position of a solicitor and official witness to the Free Church Deed of Demission:

> It has always appeared to me, that Scotland, by some unaccountable freak of latitude, – or was it a consequence of an infusion of the blood of France? – was a more southern region than England. – I mean as to its songs and dances, and other evidences of animal spirits, not omitting certain escapades of the wise over their bottles, called High Jinks.[51]

Such an enthusiasm for music and dance was not just a historical survival, it was consciously fostered, and it offered relief from the constricting politeness of modern life.

THE ANTIQUARY, NEWHAVEN AND SONG

Sir Walter Scott's preface to his novel *The Antiquary*, says:

> I have . . . sought my principal personages in the class of society who are the last to feel the influence of that general polish which assimilates to each other the manners of different nations. Among the same class I have placed some of the scenes, in which I have endeavoured to illustrate the operation of the higher and more violent passions, both because the lower orders are less restrained by the habit of suppressing their feelings, and because I agree with my friend Wordsworth, that they seldom fail to express them in the strongest and most powerful language. This is, I think, peculiarly the case with the peasantry of my own country, – a class with whom I have long been familiar.[52]

In 1817, David Wilkie made a little oil sketch of Scott and his family as a farmer and his household (fig. 73). Wilkie wrote to his sister, mentioning the painting, from Abbotsford in October 1817: 'the Misses Scott are dressed as country girls, with pails as if they had come from milking: Mr Scott as if telling a story.'[53] This obviously links with Scott's idea that the national character and culture of Scotland were preserved among the country people. Scott was not yet publicly known to be the author of the Waverley novels, but his authorship was only thinly disguised; the painting may therefore involve an element of wry humour, taking his anonymity at face value and presenting him and his family, not simply

73. David Wilkie, *The Abbotsford Family*, 1817. Oil sketch on wood. Scottish National Portrait Gallery, Edinburgh.

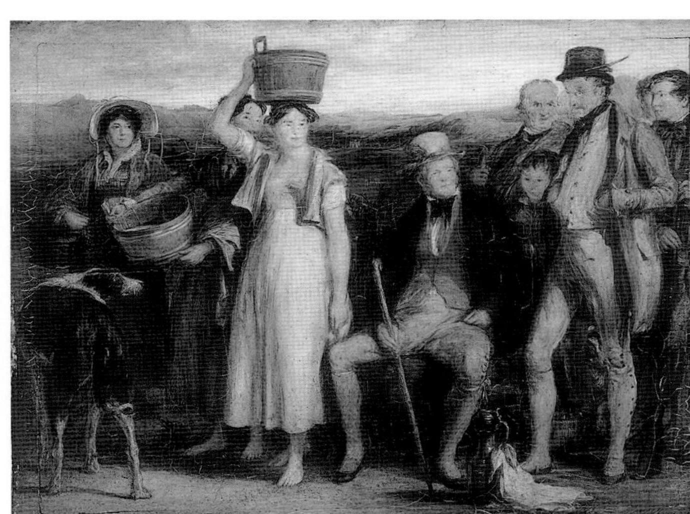

with a rustic bloom but with a manifest appearance of rustic innocence.

While Walter Scott had addressed the Highlands of Scotland in *Waverley*, *The Antiquary* was set in the Lowlands, in Fife. The book is narrated on two levels. Ostensibly it is a social comedy, centred on the antiquary's gullible enthusiasm for historic remains and on the courtship of his daughter. This part of the plot revolves around unlikelihood and melodrama. The climax is the grand tragic setting of the storm and raging tide which threaten to trap the antiquary and Miss Wardour. They are safely rescued by the beggar and the young lover in the scene just previous to the one pictured in the Bonaly calotypes (pl. 32, see chapter six).

The apparent subplot concerns the people Scott refers to as his 'principal personages', which means that, despite the title of the book, the real plot centres on the fishing village of Auchmithie. Here, the central action is the wholly undramatic disaster when the active young man of the Mucklebackit family dies in a swamped boat. It is the factual relation in the book. Scott looked for the passion and language of Scotland in the poorer classes of society. He could express history and nationality in the terms of a fishing village. This, clearly, relates to Hill and Adamson's series, *The Fishermen and Women of the Firth of Forth*. This publication was advertised with others, including *Highland Character and Costume*, and the two may well have been intended to represent the historic nation of Scotland. They express a series of distinctions: north and south, warlike and civil, clan and family, and male and female, on the double grounds that the historic, picturesque dress of the Highland clansman might be balanced by the equally picturesque dress of the Lowland fisherwoman and that the fisherwomen ruled their society. In a note to *The Antiquary*, Scott wrote: 'In the fishing villages on the Firths of Forth and Tay, as well as elsewhere in Scotland, the government is gynecocracy'.[54]

In *The Fishermen and Women*, Hill was extending Scott's idea that they, rather than the higher ranking or more educated members of society, represent the distinctive national history and vernacular culture. Hill emphasised the connection with Scott's poetry and naturalism in the calotype album he gave to James Wilson.[55] In this, two of the pictures of fishwives are supported by quotes from the matriarch Maggie Mucklebackit. The calotype of James Linton and his boys is captioned 'Saunders Mucklebackit of Musselcraig', offering the idea of the close affectionate and working relationship between father and son, which the father utters in his grief on Steenie's death. Two of the songs Hill quotes also appear in Scott's chapters on the fishing village. One is sung by the old woman of the Mucklebackit family, and Scott describes her as:

> chanting forth an old ballad in a wild and doleful recitative.
> The herring loves the merry moonlicht,
> The mackerel loves the wind;
> But the oyster loves the dredging sang
> For it comes of the gentle kind.[56]

Song was of particular importance in the cultural strength of Newhaven. The beauty of the fishwives' singing was often remarked on, and was celebrated in a lyrical passage by John Wilson:

> Saw ye them ever marchin hamewards at nicht, in a baun of some fifty or three-score, down Leith Walk, wi' the grand gas lamps illuminating their scaly creels, all shining like silver? And heard ye them ever singing their strange sea-sangs – first half-a-dizzen o' the bit young anes, wi' as saft vices and sweet as you could hear in St George's Kirk on Sabbath, half singin and half shoutin a leadin verse, and then a' the mithers and granmithers, and ablins great granmithers, some o' them wi' vices like verra men, gran tenors and awfu' basses, joining in the chorus, that gaed echoing roun' Arthur's Seat, and awa ower the tap o' the Martello Tower, out at sea ayont the end o' Leith Pier? Wad ye believe me, that the music micht be ca'd a hymn – at times sae wild and sae mournfu' – and then takin a sudden turn into a sort o' queer and outlandish glee? It gars me think o' the saut sea-faem – and white mew-wings wavering in the blast – and boaties dancin up and down the billow vales, wi' oar or sail, and waes me – waes me – o' the puir fishing smack, gaun down head foremost into the deep, and the sighin and the sabbin o' widows, and the wailin o' fatherless weans![57]

The importance of song and storytelling, related specifically to Newhaven, is further brought out in Charles Reade's novel, *Christie Johnstone* (see chapter four). One of the principal scenes in the book sets two picnics, side by side, on the island of Inchcolm in the river Forth. The aristocratic and wealthy party prove unable to entertain themselves. For the party of fishermen and wives, two hundred yards away, 'a merry dance, succeeding a merry song, had ended, and they were in the midst of an interesting story.'[58] The distance was that between a fatuous reliance of the over-civilised and moneyed on others' formal instruction and the active vernacular tradition. The heroine, Christie Johnstone, is both physically heroic and a creative storyteller and singer, and the irony of her story is that it was a retelling of *The Merchant of Venice* in the vernacular. She herself sums up this distance, inverting the common meaning of vulgarity: 'Voolgar folk sit on a chair, ane twa, whiles three hours, eatin an' abune a' drinkin, as still as hoegs, or gruntin puir every day clashes, goessip, rubbich . . . they canna gie ye a sang, they canna tell ye a story, they canna think ye a thoucht, to save their useless lives.'[59]

From John Brown's account, Hill sang the old ballads. According to his obituary, he also wrote them: 'not unfrequently entertaining his companions with ballads of his own composition'.[60] His relationship with the village of Newhaven may have involved a readiness to join in with the singing. In James Wilson's album, Hill subscribed the Newhaven group of the women carrying the washing, 'The Dredging Sang, Newhaven', and added the touching song from *The Antiquary*. The dredging song, sung impromptu by the fishermen, was described, prosaically, by Charles Reade:

> Dredging is practically very stiff rowing for ten hours. I have heard the song and seen the work done to it; and incline to think it helps the oar, not only by keeping the time true, and the spirit alive, but also by its favourable action on the lungs . . . The song, in itself, does not contain above seventy stock verses, but these perennial lines are a nucleus, round which the men improvise the topics of the day, giving, I know not for what reason, the preference to such as verge upon indelicacy.[61]

A news report emphasised the combined pleasure of watching and listening to the fishermen: 'On Friday . . . a little after sunrise we counted fifty boats in the offing, all hands busy at the dredge, and making the water musical with the oyster song. Nothing can be finer than the movements of the tiny squadron.'[62] Logically, Hill and Adamson could not calotype the oyster dredging, because the photographic process was not sufficiently sensitive to catch movement. It is a measure of their sense of its importance as a picture that they staged the group with the boat on shore, with its sail pushed out by a pole stuck in the beach (fig. 74). Part of that importance lay in the song Hill heard. We know, moreover, from Hill's letters to Paton in the 1850s, that he himself invented songs on topical issues. He wrote jocularly of himself, 'He was such a Poetical genius that frequently on beginning a note in plain prose – a spirit of song would burst upon his path.'[63]

The analogy with the calotypes is unforced. Hill referred to them as 'wood-notes wild'.[64] The phrase, written in admiration of Shakespeare, was first coined by John Milton in his *L'Allegro*: 'sweetest Shakespeare, Fancy's child,/ warble his native wood-notes wild'.[65] It was adopted by Robert Burns as

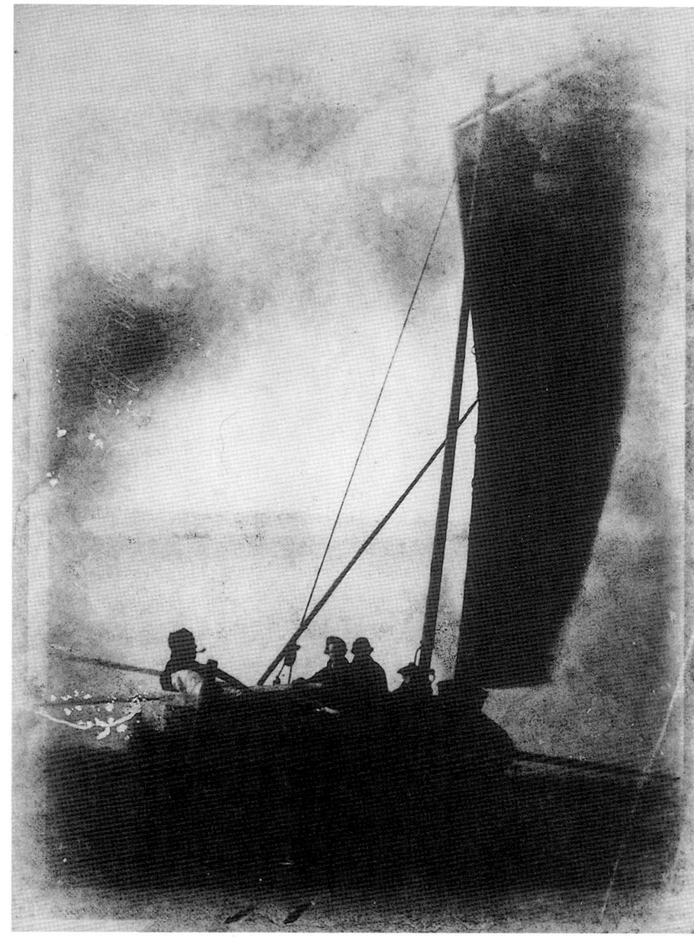

74. D. O. Hill and Robert Adamson, *Oyster Boat*, probably 1844–6. Modern calotype by Michael and Barbara Gray, from the negative in the Scottish National Photography Collection, Edinburgh.

a motto and he also used it to describe his wife's singing: 'she has (Oh, the partial lover! you will cry) the finest "wood-note wild" I ever heard.'[66] Such a musical connection was also made by James Nasmyth in relation to the landscape calotypes:

> that Durham and York minster! Its sure they are noble very *pitch* forks of art to set me a [illegible] on the right key at once. It is nature reduced to an artistical standard and abounding in the most noble suggestion. Bloody Mackenzie's Tomb [in the Greyfriars' Churchyard] what a perfect Romance. Oh had I the power of music what a theme I could make that suggest in the grand solemn style.[67]

In the culturally sophisticated view of the balance and interchange between the vernacular and the polite, involving

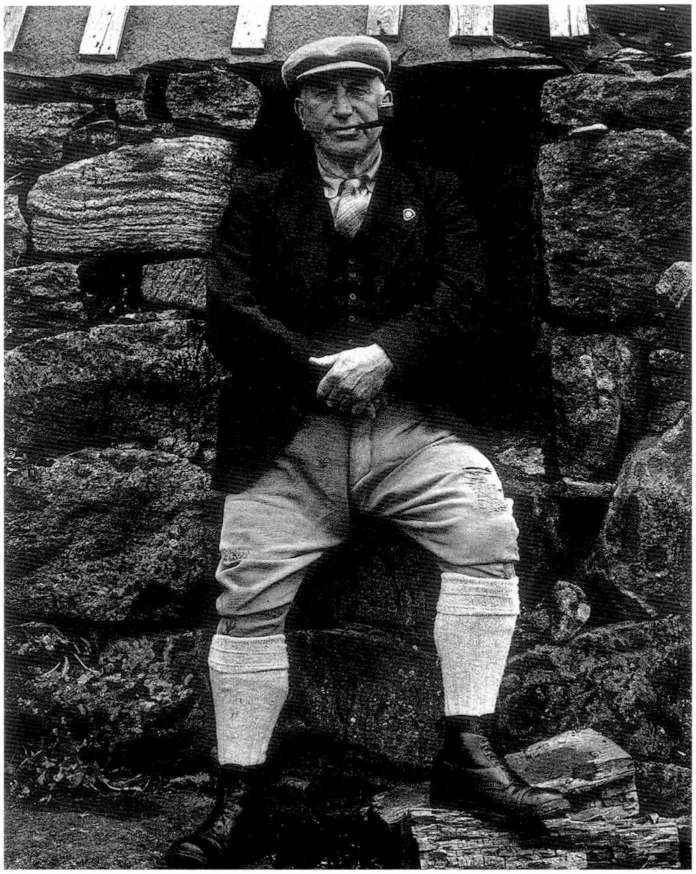

75. Paul Strand, *Portrait of a Man, South Uist*, 1954. Photogravure. Stills Gallery Collection.

nature with artifice, simplicity with complication and history with the present, Hill found a model for the calotype itself. Its natural life and vigour escaped precise control and generously offered a variable beauty in return.

Hill sent James Wilson the calotype album as a farewell gift, because he was going to India. Wilson had been concerned in an examination of the Scottish fishing industry in the 1840s, and therefore knew the people. Hill would have expected him, looking at the pictures and reading the captions from songs like, 'The boatie rows', to see the representative people of Scotland and to experience the emotional force of the music. Through the familiar musical revivals and reconstructions, the eye and the responsive ear could connect the calotypes with the vernacular tradition of song, and recollect the sound of the people added to the sight of the photographs.

The importance of vernacular culture is expressed in the calotypes and mirrored photographically in the work taken a hundred years later by Paul Strand in the Hebrides (fig. 75), which involves a visual tribute to the heroic, beautiful and popular strength of the Newhaven calotypes. The text for this, written to Strand's photographs by Basil Davidson, says:

> The telling of stories still keeps alive the ancient and honoured tradition of the bards . . . Within these last few years it was still possible to meet old men and women who could remember many of the ancient stories – strange and magical, often immensely long . . . But these Uist bards had also the gift . . . of composing poems and stories from contemporary events. . . I have heard Mrs Archie's mother sing two or three of her oldest songs; and the effect is strange. Here in a living mouth are the hint and music, faint as a rustling amid dry leaves, of a time when the Romans were comfortably settled in Britain . . . when those who would make and chant the Song of Beowulf, oldest of surviving English songs, had several hundred years to wait for birth.[68]

The romanticism inherent in this account should not obscure the understanding that both for Strand and for Hill such romance was sounding in their ears and was a leading part of the motive and the character of the work. In both cases this is, in some active sense, photography that sings of history and the present time together.

8

Time and Mortality

PRACTICAL TIME

The only account we have of Robert Adamson at work was given by the photographer James Good Tunny:

> Time after time have I gone and stood on the projecting rock below Playfair's monument on the Calton Hill, and drawn inspiration from viewing Mr Adamson placing a large square box upon a stand, covering his head with a focussing-cloth, introducing the slide, counting the seconds by his watch, putting the cap on the lens, and retiring to what we now know to be the dark room. Oh! if only I could have got an introduction to these men, it would have been the consummation of my happiness![1]

This wistful note tells us little beyond the obvious point that Adamson used a watch to measure the length of the exposure and thereafter to regulate the printing time for the negatives. Photography has this straightforward relation to time.

It was not a coincidence that the uniform appreciation of time became both public and personal in the early to mid-nineteenth century. It was, through the advanced mass production of clock parts, increasingly possible for people to own a time piece; by about 1850, even poorer families might have their own clock, and the watch became a common possession. The development of the Post Office, the telegraph companies and the railways had brought the need for consistency and the drive for it coincided with the great railway boom of the 1840s. At the beginning of the decade, Captain Basil Hall wrote to Rowland Hill, who introduced the penny post, proposing:

> to regulate all post-office clocks in the Kingdom, by means of the time brought from London by the mail-coach chronometers; and he had no doubt that, ere long, all the town clocks, and, eventually, all the clocks and watches of private persons, would fall into the same course of regulation; so that only one expression of time would prevail over the country, and every clock and watch indicate by its hands the same hour and minute at the same moment of absolute time.[2]

Basil Hall was particularly conscious of the need for consistent time because he was a sailor and navigation depended on the relation of the stars, the landfall and calculations of time. Uniform Greenwich time was established throughout the country through the readiness of individual towns on railway routes to accept it over the natural time established by the rising of the sun. Glasgow and Edinburgh were only persuaded to adopt Greenwich time by the chairman of the Edinburgh and Glasgow Railway in January 1848. By 1852, Britain was still divided between towns that kept, publicly, to Greenwich time and those which held to local time. Time, what it was or should be, was a general concern, if only in such banal terms as catching a train or the post.[3]

FRAMING TIME

The image of Robert Adamson standing with his watch in his hand, counting seconds, seems a specifically photographic idea. The photograph is tied to the time of its exposure; in that time, the camera has to stand in front of its subject to take the image. Photography, therefore, apparently allows us the privilege of the photographer's place and time. It is an illusion, but it is an important illusion, and it maintains, through our belief in it, a sense of historical immediacy.

Painting is supposedly free from such elementary limitations. But the painter's interest in time could be as precise;

the study of nature, as the base of painting, required that same attention to the passage and the effects of time. A practical textbook owned by Hill included the following:

> As the best practical hints are derived from accidental combinations in nature, whose sudden changes prevent the possibility of sketching, the mind ought to be trained to the most regular and even mechanical mode of arranging the ideas; that in an instant we may be able to determine whether the effects, which we perceive, depend upon a particular form, upon particular arrangement of the light and shade, or upon the manner in which the hot and cold colours are brought in contact.[4]

The ability to catch the character and appearance of transient effects and action involved a kind of mental snapshot. It is clearly true that celebrated painters had that ability – Rembrandt, for example, could catch the moment of an elderly woman wrestling with a furious child, the child escaping from her grip and its slipper flying.[5] The purpose of this study was to secure the psychological or active components of a visibly unified sense of time within a picture (something, which, on a surface level, could be seen as through a window). Such history and genre pictures as David Wilkie's *Distraining for Rent* (fig. 44) were constructed to present a meaningful point in time. It was a virtuoso contrivance, an ideal, but apparently particular, frozen moment: 'A painter … can select the best possible moment of action, the striking event upon which the whole tenor depends . . . Well may it be called the mirror of the mind, which it is the painter's peculiar province to hold up to view.'[6] The playwright, Douglas Jerrold, wrote a play based on *Distraining for Rent* and on another of Wilkie's paintings, *Rent Day*, which was performed at the Drury Lane Theatre, London, in 1832 and staged in Edinburgh's Theatre Royal the following year.[7] After viewing the play, Wilkie wrote to Clarkson Stanfield asking him to pass on a compliment to the author:

> whose inventive fancy has created out of the dumb show of the picture all the living characters and progressive events of real life and while paying an unprecedented honour from the Dramatic to the Painter's art, has with the help of life, movement, space and time shewn us in comparison how stationary and confined, is that *one instant* to which our elaborate art is limited.[8]

Wilkie's response was courteous and belittles his own achievement. The painting is remarkable precisely because it is not confined; it contains the implications of a number of potential stories. It occupied the minds of its viewers in considering how the protagonists had come to that point and what would happen next, what they were thinking and what they would do; unlike the play, the picture leaves us without certainty and it achieved its poignancy from the surrounding doubt. George Bell, in his work on the destitution in the Edinburgh slums (see chapter four), expressed the difficulty of understanding such desperate conditions in a way that suggests he may have been thinking of *Distraining for Rent*: 'The describing of such a scene involves very much more than the telling of what one has beheld. It involves a reference to the past and future of the people as well as to the present. It involves the transfer of our perception of their moral condition, which is the spirit, or rather the demon of the scene.'[9]

Hill was concerned to contain known history within his paintings. His landscapes were often exhibited with historical narratives to give his audience the associations to draw their minds into the picture and towards historical contemplation. His Disruption painting is, at first sight, picturing the moment of the signing of the Deed of Demission by the Reverend Dr Patrick MacFarlane on 23 May 1843, and this gives the painting its title. His concern for the subject was far wider. Even when he began work on the picture, Hill was thinking of a broad expression of the activities of the Church around 1843 rather than a precise time and act. The first advertisement for the proposed engraving after the picture, published on 24 May, only six days after the Disruption, says that it will contain not just the Free Church ministers but their sympathisers from other groups of dissenters and, 'other personages who have taken or may yet take part in the eventful proceedings of the Assembly.'[10] The picture finally contained groups representing the later activities of the Church: home and foreign missions, the new church buildings and schools. People who were not present at the Disruption, like the vice-chancellor of the University of Bombay, Reverend Dr John Wilson, who was entering Jerusalem on the day of the Disruption and was calotyped in arab dress, were added to give a complete idea of the Church's membership and actions. One review of the finished painting expressed it thus: 'The picture is not chronological. It does not present events in succession as they occur in time, but simultaneously as they occur in a dream. Several incidents are thus indicated which were yet undreamt of in 1843, but without which the story of the Church would be so far incomplete . . . He has given us a twenty years' history.'[11]

One of the curiosities of the picture is the way in which the age of the people in the portraits has spread over the twenty-year period in which the work was underway. Hill's own face is probably drawn from a photograph taken in the mid-1850s, ten years away from the calotype image of Adamson (fig. 76). The portrait of George Bell, standing behind Hill, has been aged from the calotype by the addition of grey hair and whiskers. Thomas Annan, the photographer commissioned to make the carbon photographs for sale in 1866, was added to the doorway at the back of the painting just before it was photographed.[12] Hill felt the need to connect the picture to a living future, as much as to a particular past.

The painting was also designed to offer echoes of history. The four-square composition, with the central table parallel to the frame and the grouping of the foreground figures and objects, is reminiscent of David Wilkie's unfinished painting of *John Knox Dispensing the Sacrament at Calder House* (fig. 77), which itself is based on Leonardo's *Last Supper.*[13] The signing of the deed, at the heart of the picture, connects it with the signing of the National Covenant in 1638, a connection that was made deliberately by the Free Church leaders, who used the vocabulary and the ideals of the seventeenth-century action. Thomas Guthrie was himself described in these anachronistic terms: 'athletic, castle-built, and towering, bearing on his front the signet of a rude independence – you see before you the outward representative of the sturdy Covenanter . . . an anomaly in the nineteenth century.'[14] The still-life element of the picture included 'a piece of the handwriting of Knox, a copy of the "Solemn League and Covenant" and "The Cloud of Witnesses" borrowed from the antiquarian, David Laing.'[15] The Free Church was making the point that it was returning to the principle and propriety of the Presbyterian Church, that it was the Church of Scotland itself that had strayed. Even the frame of the Disruption picture has a consciously historical inscription written round it, echoing an inscription in the entrance hall at Abbotsford: 'These are the effigies and memorials of the men quha keipit the marches of the Scottish Kirke in the days of the Ten Years' Conflict; they were gude men in their time, and in their defence God he them defendit.'[16] Hill is promoting the view of the Free Churchmen that they were reclaiming a kind of moral time with its ancient and simpler religious standards.

CONTAINING TIME

In painting the Disruption Picture, Hill became conscious of the problem of time in an elementary sense, because it took him twenty-three years to finish. The picture developed a visual disjunction as his subjects died or grew older. He was

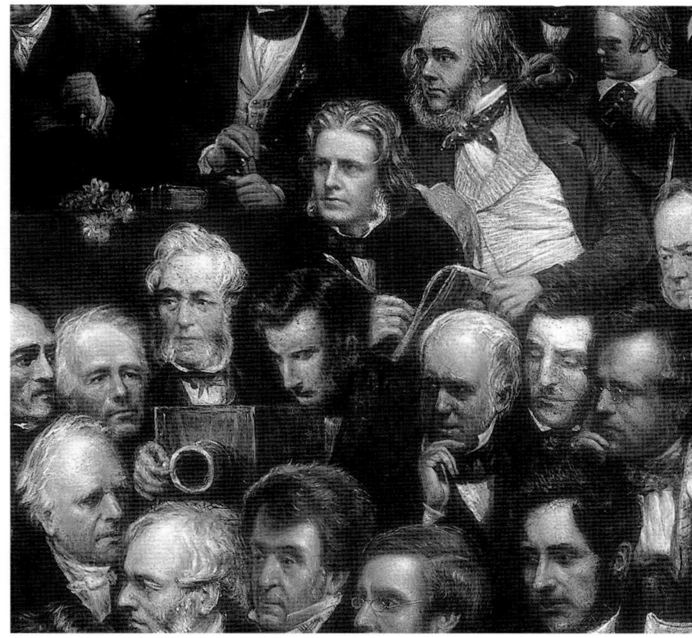

76. D. O. Hill, *The Signing of the Deed of Demission*, detail showing Robert Adamson, D. O. Hill and Dr George Bell. Oil on canvas. Free Church of Scotland, Edinburgh.

able to build on an established, religious idea of presence in absence: of a broad Church existing in the past, present and future, which was composed of the dead as well as the living: the 'Church invisible'. But here it was transposed to a corporeal reality, rather than separated, through such conventional symbols as people perched on clouds or wearing wings.

In working with photographs and by aiming to make natural groupings within a real setting, Hill made the painting

77. David Wilkie, *John Knox Dispensing the Sacrament at Calder House*, 1840. Unfinished oil painting on wood. National Gallery of Scotland, Edinburgh.

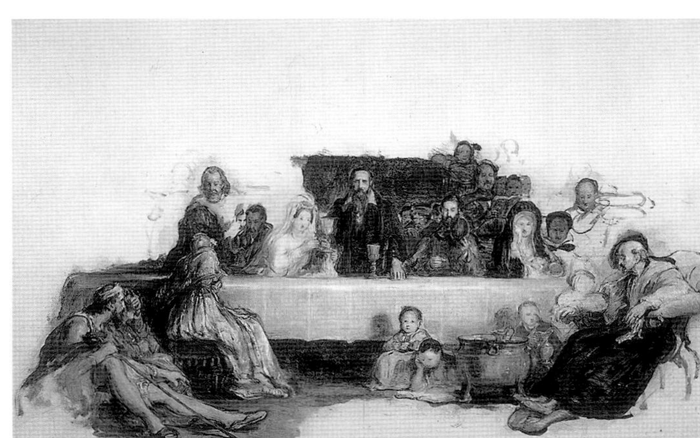

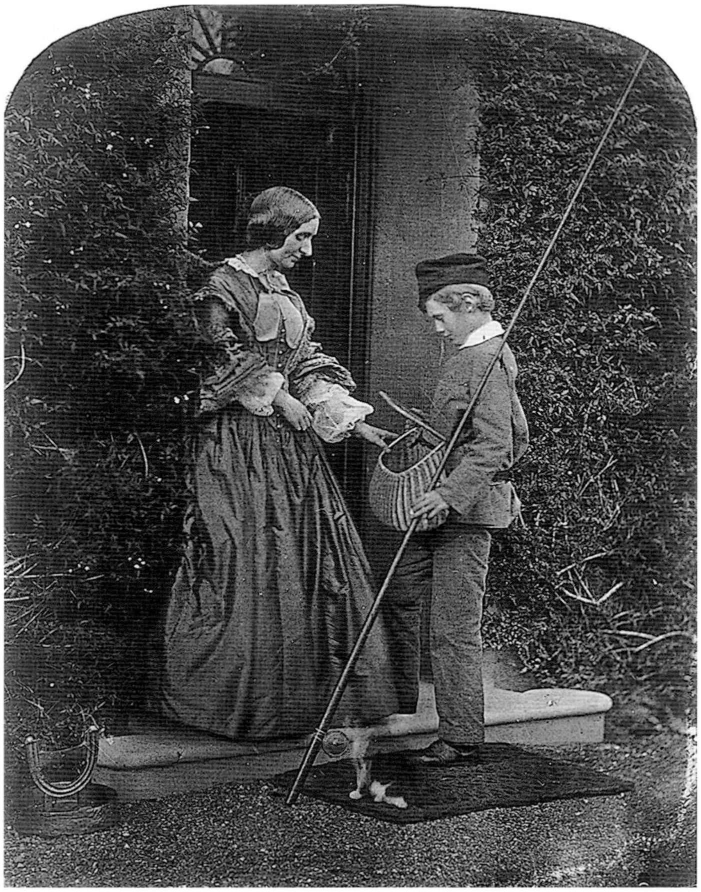

78. John Adamson, *Home from the Burn*, *c.* 1860. Albumen print. University of St Andrews Library, Special Collections.

oddly surreal in its sense of time. It looks strange to us, because we are comparing it with the photographs; we shift our glance from one to the other and the subjects age ten or twenty years. Reality obscures the symbolic character of the picture and gives it the arbitrary reflection of a dream. When the finished picture was exhibited, it was probably less startling to his contemporaries, because they were both remembering the dead and turning from the living people, whom they knew in old age, to look at the painting. However, the effective, emotional impact of this may be judged by the way Hill and George Bell have grown older, while Robert Adamson was halted in his youth by death.

In combining the photographic idea of the instant or specific time of the photograph's taking with the conscious construction and reworking of the painter's idea, Hill may have meant to combine the characters of mortal immediacy and immortal future – adding the poignancy of the one to the depth of the other. This is possibly a case where the failings of photography inspired a philosophical idea. One of the notable facts of the long exposures of early landscape photography is that people could walk through a picture, leaving only a blur to mark their presence. Hill would have been familiar with this in the calotype photographs taken in the city, which appear unpopulated but in which human or wheeled traffic has simply passed by. The camera has collected a generalised rather than a specific image, something that would not have been seen intelligently by the photographer. Such partial appearance was far from evident in the blurring of the calotype, but became clearer in the later paper processes. A good example of such absence/presence was taken by John Adamson around 1860, in the albumen print, *Home from the Burn* (fig. 78)[17]. In the picture, Adamson's nephew is showing the contents of his fishing basket to his aunt. On the step beside him is the family cat. But the cat is transparent; it has presumably moved away after discovering that there is no fish in the basket.

As a matter of study, rather than a practical difficulty, the part-time cat is an interesting idea.[18] In the photograph, it registers as 'not really there'. But the cat was there in precisely the same way as the humans. It occupied space, formed part of the group and influenced the way the other two were thinking. Moreover, it continued to have that influence after its departure. It is possible to assume the thoughts of the two people – concerned to enact an engaging subject, distracted by the wandering cat but consciously staying still for the photographer. Presumably, they and John Adamson found the result entertaining, as such mild anarchy is liable to be.[19]

Hill may well have involved this photographic knowledge with his practical use of photography in the Disruption picture. His scene presents a Free Church, nominally placed in Edinburgh in May 1843, but actually spanning twenty years of life and death. The dead are part of the church and still affect its living representatives.

Hill's developed interest in this idea can be connected to a landscape painting he made in memory of his daughter, when she died in 1862 (fig. 100, see chapter nine). She is not there as a visible figure, but she had been there. She had touched and altered that landscape – run up the hill, cast a shadow, planted a flower. The intensity of Hill's photographic experience may have provided a natural metaphor, which he could transform into the comforting thought that Chatty was – like Robert Adamson and even like the cat – still there within the frame.

Generally speaking, the urge to catch has a troubling edge – it is a metaphor of hunting and prey. In theory, speed obviates the need for human contact, and reduces the social element of photographing people to a fragment of time. The photographer, again in theory, is hidden by that speed. In practice, modern experience has shown that subjects can react with similar speed to the presence of a camera. Human life is sufficiently brief; to sum it up in a fractured second is liable to pile authority on action, beyond its capacity to bear meaning.

Hill was not working with a process that would freeze life in a pin-point measurement. He liked his portraits breathing and he was looking for an emotional or sociable moment; a time in which personality might be expressed. This time was not encompassed within the calculation of the photograph's taking. It was likely to have been built up beforehand by conversation, generating a warmth of response, which left a trace of the exchange of ideas and pleasure in the face and stance of the subject.

Part of what we are looking at in the calotype portraits is a straightforward extension of the portrait painter's search for the broad, timeless expression of personality. Here, the Reverend Thomas Chalmers's family group is critically important (pl. 4). The calotype is an impressive expression of Chalmers's role in history and within his own family. The idea of a religious leader as a source of light is expressed through the diffused light of the picture – the way the sun seems to radiate through the man and illuminates the stone ball, the little World, at his feet with the books of the Word. Through his family, his daughters and grandson, we have not just the idea of the patriarch but of his legacy to the future; his human and mortal role is offered in parallel to his religious authority.

John Brown wrote a posthumous essay on Thomas Chalmers, which may serve as a text for the calotypes. It began with a lyrical account of the sinking sun, and continued: 'It is no small loss to the world, when one of its master spirits – one of its great lights – a king among the nations – leaves it. A sun is extinguished; a great attractive, regulating power is withdrawn.' He then wrote of the portraits:

> Mr. Hill's Calotypes we like better than all the rest; because what in them is true, is absolutely so, and they have some delicate renderings which are all but beyond the power of any human artist; for though man's art is mighty, nature's is mightier. The one of the Doctor sitting with his grandson '*Tommy*', is to us the best; we have the true grandeur of his form – his bulk . . . The Daguerreotype is, in its own way, excellent; it gives the externality of the man to perfection, but it is Dr Chalmers at a stand-still – his mind and feelings 'pulled-up' for the second that it was taken.[20]

Brown's article has a close relation to the photographs. The breadth, the sense of the spread of time and the bulk of the man are common to both. There are other lines of connection. Brown talks of Chalmers's enthusiasm and the simplicity of his heart and life as childlike – the child in the photograph is his grandson, but may also represent himself as a child. He is clearly restless and will stand for the innocent energy of the young in Chalmers's own words: 'When a child is filled with any strong emotion by a surprising event or intelligence, it *runs* to discharge it on others, impatient of their sympathy.'[21] The presence of the boy also expresses Chalmers's pleasure in children, modelled on that of Christ. Brown tells how:

> being out one Saturday at a friend's house near the Pentlands, he collected all the children and small people . . . and took the lead to the nearest hill-top – how he made each take the biggest and roundest stone he could find, and carry – how he panted up the hill himself with one of enormous size . . . [At the top he set the stone rolling down the hill] how he watched him setting out on his race, slowly, stupidly, vaguely at first, almost as if he might die before he began to live, then suddenly giving a spring and off like a shot – bounding, tearing . . . how the great and good man was *totus in illo*; how he spoke to, upbraided him, cheered him, gloried in him, all but prayed for him, how he joked philosophy to his wondering and ecstatic crew, when he (the stone) disappeared among some brackens – telling them they had the evidence of their senses that he was in, they might even know that he was there by his effects, by the moving brackens, himself unseen; how plain it became that he had gone in, when he actually came out! – how he ran up the opposite side a bit, and then fell back, and lazily expired at the bottom . . . [he then rolled all the stones down the hill one at a time] till he came to the Benjamin of the flock, a *wee wee* man, who had brought up a stone bigger than his own head; then how wonderfully IT ran! what miraculous leaps: what escapes from impossible places: and how it ran up the other side farther than any, and by some felicity remained there.[22]

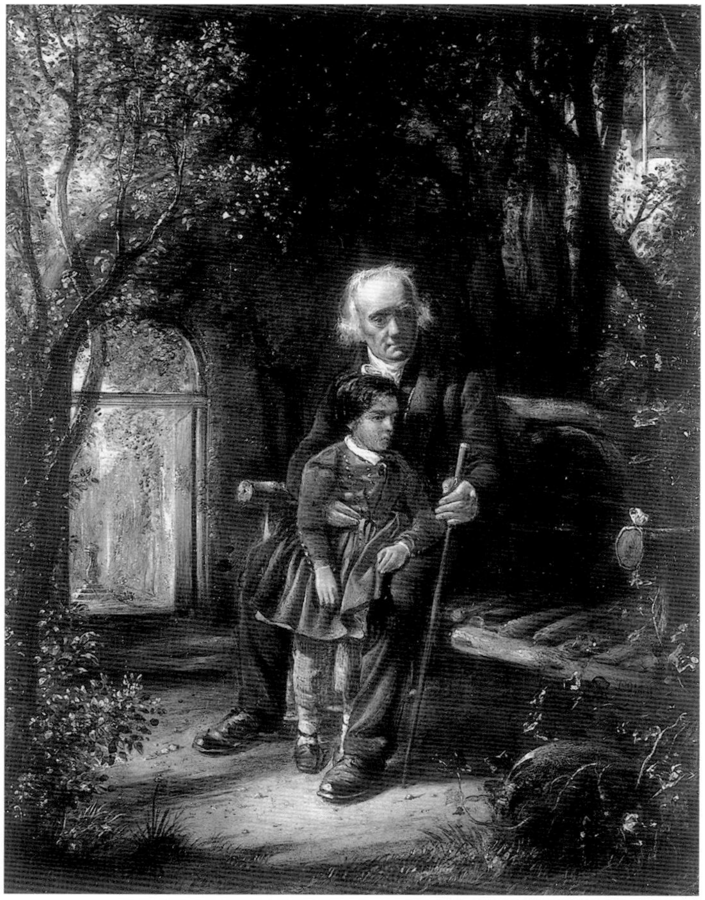

79. D. O. Hill, *Dr Thomas Chalmers and his Grandson, Thomas Chalmers Hanna*, 1847. Oil on millboard. Scottish National Portrait Gallery, Edinburgh.

The stones that rolled in the story and the stone at Chalmers's feet in the calotype make a natural point about Chalmers, based on his own impulse to teach through nature. Presumably, Hill found the ball there in the garden, fallen from a gatepost, though he may well have rolled such a pleasing and meaningful shape into the best position for the photograph. It is an analogically layered object that will mean more to people the more they know of the man. That it should represent the world in little and mortal concerns is a proposal reinforced in the painting Hill made from the photograph of Chalmers and his grandson as his own posthumous tribute in 1848 (fig. 79): there he perched a butterfly on the arm of the bench, the fragile symbol of passing time, and, through the gateway into another part of the garden, the sun is falling on a sundial with a scythe propped against it. The stone further adds the human, touching memory of Brown's story. The photograph, through elementary gestures of this kind, could open up the imaginative mind to philosophical speculation and a sense of time that ranges through Chalmers's life and the following generations. It offers an approach to his immortality through a knowledge of his mortality.

It is of some interest that John Ruskin's response to Brown's essay on Thomas Chalmers makes the three points: how pleased he was by the memoir, how he found the actual extracts from Chalmers's writings disappointing and how valuable he thought a calotype would be:

> I do not recollect anything that has given me greater pleasure than the account of the Doctor's Sisyphian labours and ratiocinations on the Pentlands . . . The worst of it was, that after all that we hear of your noble old friend's Thunder and Lightning, one is – at least I was – a little disappointed by the quietness and sobriety of the extracts from the Scripture readings. Is it at all possible to get a Calotype of him? I suppose it must be now. There is certainly nothing like them for rendering of Intellect, nor to my taste for everything else except beauty.[23]

Chalmers was more effective as a preacher than as a writer; but it does remain an extraordinary proposal that Ruskin hoped to understand Chalmers's mind from a calotype rather than from his written work.

NEW LIGHTS

Hill wrote of the calotypes, 'you will find they will always be giving out new lights.'[24] In the photographs of Thomas Chalmers, the great man advanced in age and reputation, it may be that Hill intended the full implications of the work; that he had heard the story of the stones rolling downhill. In another case, the portrait of his young niece, Patricia Morris, the picture probably meant more to him years later (pl. 35).

In 1853, Hill wrote an account of an operation undergone by Patricia Morris, when she is Mrs Orr. On first reading the letter, we do not know her fate. This is, in historical terms, a rare position to be in, because our knowledge usually works from the end of the story. We are placed, as Hill was, in suspense. The letter reads:

> The news of Mrs Orr, I rejoice to say are wonderfully encouraging. You know that [Professor John] Syme who saw her on Saturday week last was to go back on Tuesday to operate – Her sufferings meanwhile – on Sunday and Monday were something awful to hear of – & to witness

as [her sister] Mrs Finlay did – never to be forgotten. She could not have lived a week under them. But she was ready & eager for the Doctors. On the Tuesday she ordered in the table on which she was to be disposed – when under the knife – and when the awful hour of twelve came – she the only composed person in the house asked for her watch which the Nurse had kindly removed from the bed curtain where it generally hung, and the good soul returned it having put it back 1/4. Patricia said it is twelve – I know by the shadow on the floor – the Doctors will soon be here – she was told they had arrived. She said she was ready – and resigning her husband's hand which she had a long time held – she told him to go away – Syme had with him Dr Duncan from Edinburgh & Dr Macfarlane of Glasgow with two of his principal assistants. The Cloroform did its work completely and Syme as was said by the other Doctors men of great eminence [?] & experience – said with blanched faces – had that day done a wonderful work. Syme thinks it is removed – so does Macfarlane. Duncan still doubts it may be in the system. But Syme speaks cheerfully giving much hope. Meantime Patricia has had rest peace & absence from pain – she has now been 8 days in one position which you may well believe is of itself hawful [*sic*] while the natural course of the discharging of such a wound must entail much suffering, though as compared to the first of a modified nature. Syme saw a letter today from Isabella telling these symptoms, and he says the pain of the wound, its discharge & the other symptoms are life – another abscess now would be fatal, and so you see wonders are not yet ceased. Let us hope she may be spared.[25]

Mrs Orr benefited from James Young Simpson's recent discovery of the anaesthetic properties of chloroform: her operation was the more likely to be successful, but the need for antisepsis was only demonstrated efficiently by Joseph Lister in the 1860s. Hill's next reference to her is, in clinical terms, not surprising: 'I fear poor Mrs Orr is in a very bad way. She has retrograded for 8 or 10 days – and the hopes of her doctors, her husband and relations are very low indeed.'[26]

Hill's account alters our view of the calotype, but was not in his thinking when he made it. The photograph is only a pre-vision of her fate in the broad sense of the vulnerability of young women when they married and bore children. However, Hill's interest in the photographs as 'giving out new lights' would mean that he saw them as revealing truths after time. In this case, it is not simply the young woman but the flowering plant in the picture, which could be read, after the fact, for its natural meaning. The flower is a common symbol of mortality, as for example, 'The grass withereth, the flower fadeth: but the word of our God shall stand for ever.'[27] It is possible that Hill saw more – a natural, revealed message – in the plant after Patricia Morris's death than he may have seen or meant in the first instance.

Hill had given a literary meaning to the calotype group of the McCandlish girls, in which Margaret figures as a milkmaid with a wooden bucket and Mary has a small basket of flowers, by titling it *The Gowan*, or daisy (pl. 36). The calotype shows the young Mary asleep, and Margaret leaning over and tickling her neck with the flower. The photograph echoes Robert Burns's poem, 'To a Mountain Daisy, On turning one down with the Plough, in April – 1786.' This is a moral verse, which compares the little flower growing unprotected in the field, vulnerable to the cold blasts and the plough's casual ruin, to the fate of a simple country maid and the country poet:

> Such is the fate of artless maid,
> Sweet flow'ret of the rural shade!
> By love's simplicity betray'd,
> And guileless trust,
> Till she, like thee, all soil'd is laid
> Low i'the dust.[28]

The specific date of the title and the idea of Burns halting the plough to consider the flower, unites the photographic idea of precise time with anxiety for the future. Hill complicated his own picture by adding the line, 'As if a fly had tickled slumber', linking it to the Roman Britain of Shakespeare's *Cymbeline*. The phrase is spoken of Imogen who, being heavily drugged, appears to be dead and is assumed to have died of melancholy whilst 'smiling, as some fly had tickled slumber,/Not as death's dart being laughed at.'[29] *Cymbeline* has a complicated plot but there are connections beyond the simple coincidence of the idea of tickling a sleeper. The play opposes the corruption of the court to the simplicity and honesty of the country, and the language of the men exiled to the country is more natural. The son of Cymbeline, who has brought out the 'corpse', proposes to put wild flowers on the grave:

> thou shalt not lack
> The flower that's like thy face, pale primrose, nor
> The azur'd hare-bell, like thy veins, no, nor
> The leaf of eglantine, whom not to slander,
> Out-sweetened not thy breath.[30]

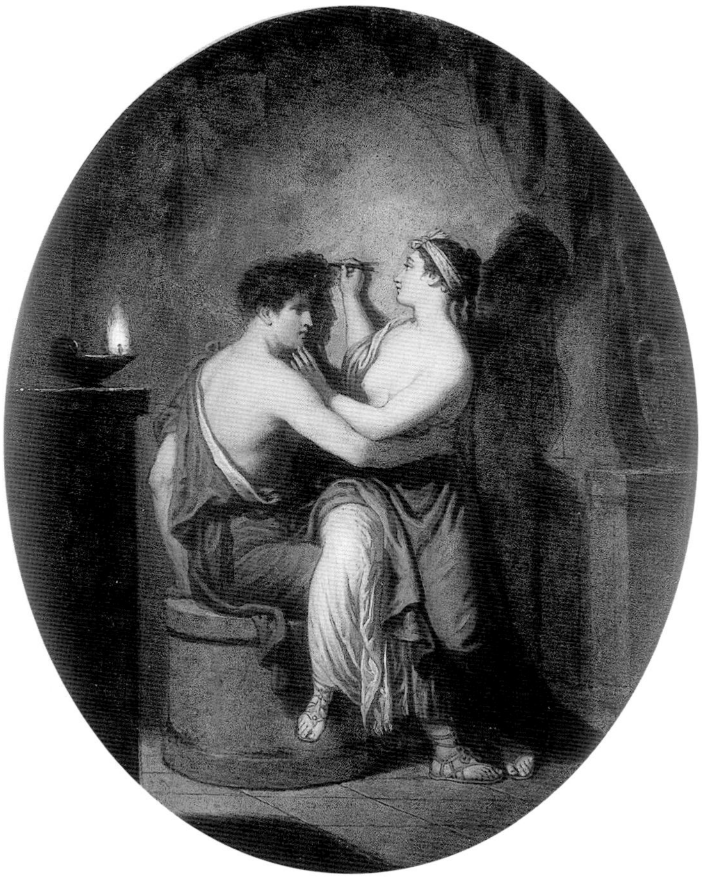

80. David Allan, *The Origin of Painting*, 1775. Oil on wood. National Gallery of Scotland, Edinburgh.

The ideas of change and mortality in these connections to *The Gowan* suggest a comparable meaning for the flower in Patricia Morris's portrait. It is a convolvulus or bindweed and, judging by the heart-shaped leaves, is the cultivated version, the Morning Glory. Miss Morris is not just standing beside it, she has her arm partly through it. The convolvulus is a twining plant, an obvious symbol of love and affection; it flowers in a day, its beauty is lost rapidly in fruition and it dies in bearing its seed. Hill may have seen the picture with a new eye, as having an in-built message that the divine proposal was for her, as for the flower, that she had fulfilled her purpose – a consolation for his wasted hope that: 'she may be spared and that God has some good work for her to do'. This idea would include the extraordinary proposal that a natural photograph, constructed with the idea of truth uppermost, could convey the kind of divine truth that a sensible examination of nature would achieve.

'ONLY A SHADOW'

The fragility of photographs on paper and the tendency of ill-fixed photographs to fade naturally proposed an analogy between photography and human mortality. This moral and emotional idea connected photography to the humblest end of the art market, the making of silhouettes. This, in turn, had inherited the respectability of classical tradition, from the story told by Pliny of the Corinthian maid who traced her lover's shadow on the wall, which he described as the origin of painting. The subject was treated by two Scottish painters, David Allan and Alexander Runciman, in 1773 and 1775 respectively (fig. 80), and by Joseph Wright of Derby for Josiah Wedgwood in the 1780s.[31] Oscar Rejlander staged a photograph of it in the 1850s, entitled *The First Negative*.[32]

An anonymous, hyperbolic article, published in 1856, made the link to photography:

> The production to be sure was only a shadow on the wall: but it was the first likeness on which complacent love could dwell, and the original prototype of the portrait, dear to the heart even when so faint and imperfect . . . And here the simple effect rested for centuries, unless the black, unmeaning silhouette stirred up a disagreeable memory of it . . . Photography . . . is of splendid descent. Its fountain is the glorious luminary of life and day; its medium is the wonderful hyparxis of Plato, light (the *what it is!*); and its production is the realization of the third and last element of this sublime philosophy, the work of ineffable agencies applied to material purposes by human ingenuity and skill.[33]

Victor Burgin has discussed *The Origin of Painting*, in the same terms, as the motivation for photography: 'the origin of the graphic image is in the portrait, and . . . the origin of the portrait is in the desire for protection against the loss of the object'.[34] The human need behind the portrait makes it far from surprising that photography, invented generally as a method of public reproduction, became popular as a method of private portraiture. The mortal relation of the photograph to its subject is often underlined by the reflex terminology of the snapshot: 'old, faded, torn'. It has seen life, like the person it represents, and touchingly shares his mortality. The Reverend Edward Bradley provided an example of this analogy in 1855:

> The widower holds before him the likeness of her who was his wife. It is a Calotype, and was but the work of an amateur; and yet, how he values it! upon the wall hangs

> another portrait of her; it was painted by a skilful artist, but it has the artist's conventional face, his conventional attitude, his conventional background. How it sinks in interest before that little Calotype! In it the husband sees the living likeness of his wife . . . She lives before him again; she is snatched once more from the tomb, and he is permitted to gaze on her for a time. Amid the blinding tears of recollected love, he presses the portrait to his lips, and speaks to it with child-like affection. And yet it is but a Calotype![35]

John Brown's general critical comment on photography, written as a preamble to a review of Hill's second essay in the art in 1861, made the same association between photography and death:

> When death comes . . . you take out these, it may be, wasted, shadowy, almost vanishing images – how you treasure them for ever, beyond all trim and graceful miniatures by man's hand. That is the very turn of the head, the shape of the bald head, the child's look you so well knew, the restrained smile, the waistcoat, the shawl – the *reality* you can never more forget or see – all are brought back to you, and in that *camera lucida* of your own brain, in that chamber of imagery, from out this poor, imperfect sun-sketch there blooms into life, untouched by time or change, your idea of that face.[36]

This respect for photography, independent of the province of art, is a focus for meditation. The fading photograph echoes the Bible: 'All our righteousnesses are as filthy rags; and we do fade as a leaf.'[37] It is significant that Sir John Robison's report on the daguerreotype to the Edinburgh Society of Arts in 1839, focused on such symbols of mortality: 'on examining them by microscopic power, details are discovered which are not perceivable to the naked eye in the original objects; a crack in the plaster, a withered leaf lying on a projecting cornice, or an accumulation of dust in a hollow moulding of a distant building, are faithfully copied in these wonderful pictures.'[38] The photograph could be held in the hand or, like a miniature, be framed and worn close to the heart. It could become a personal relic, alongside the lock of hair, as an object of transferred devotion or melancholic contemplation. In this sense, its very unimportance and lack of artistry was supposed to increase its personal and private impact; practical ineptitude on the part of the photographer (or better still, anonymity) made the photograph more real or more poignant, because it suppressed or eliminated the intermediary. In the later discussions of spirit photography, the ignorance of the human medium, attempts to fake results and manipulative incompetence were all turned around and used as evidence for belief: the medium was not just the photographic chemistry, it was also the bland transparency of the manipulator.

Hill observed the phenomenon that the calotypes might change in their meaning with time, but he does not seem to have concluded that the growing distance in time removed them from the province of art. Indeed his reaction was apparently the opposite; while he referred to the calotypes with qualified diffidence in the 1840s, by the 1860s he was convinced of their aesthetic importance. He was impressed by the magical or shifting properties of the photograph, while realising the need for artistry in making them appear.

PAPER AND STONE

Brown's passage on the memory evoked by the worst of photographs leads, by contrast, into his praise of Hill's work: 'You get a shock of surprise and pleasure when, in the midst of others, you come on them, powerful, gentle, full of space, full of the play of light and shadow, of the play of human life and feeling, of that same element that makes Sir Joshua, Velasquez, or our own Raeburn and Duncan and their subjects immortal.'[39] One of the necessary attractions of photography, approached from the weighty traditions of formal portraiture, is its close relation to humanity. It was, apparently, in opposition to the ideal looked for in the public portraits of great men. But even in conditions of pomp, that idealising formality might be informed by a concern with time and its effects; mortality was a key moral concern – it was not the opposite of immortality so much as its precursor. Certain of Titian's grand portraits, for example, his group portrait of Pope Paul III with his nephews, express that evanescence – the connection with a time that will, inevitably, pass. Henry Raeburn's portraits may appear oddly photographic in their effect perhaps for this same reason. The age of his sitters is noted in the bloom of the young and the flatness of tired eyes, and his breadth of treatment suggests, like the calotypes, the blurring of breathing life.[40]

Hill and Adamson's work may, however, be regarded, in the context of formal painting, as temporal. Here is the human and touchingly factual contact. The humanity of the calotypes (and such humanity is not a necessary factor of photography) may be seen in comparison with other images. The photographs of John Wilson (fig. 81) may be compared with John Steell's monumental sculpture of him, which was

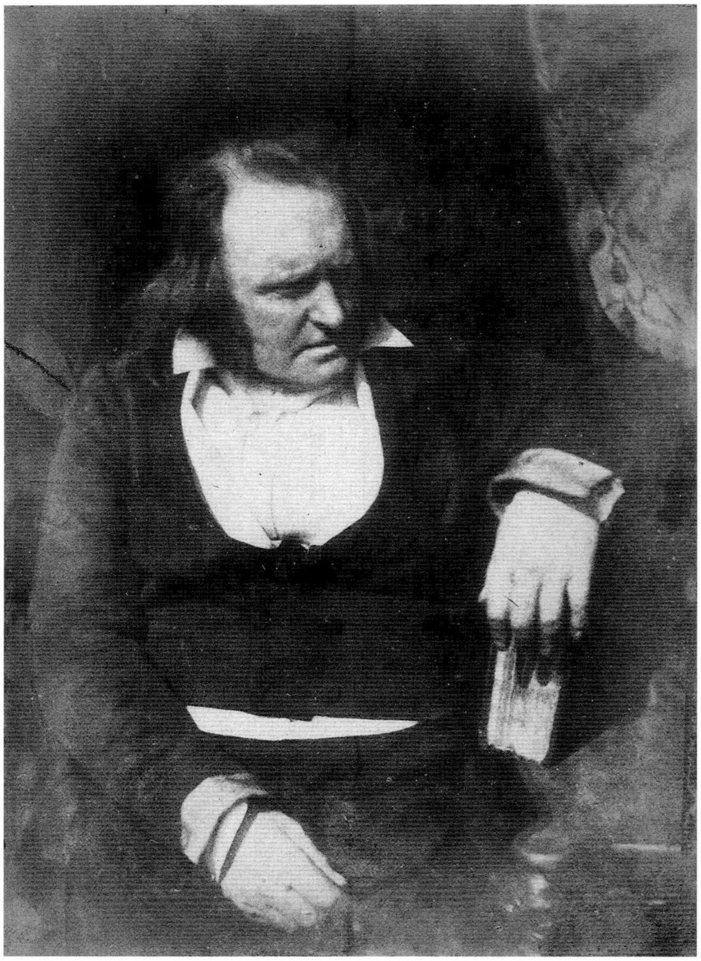

81. D. O. Hill and Robert Adamson, *Professor John Wilson*, 1843–7. Calotype. Scottish National Photography Collection, Edinburgh.

erected in Princes Street beside the Royal Scottish Academy. The immediate difference between the works lies in the size and elevation of the sculpture and the important fact that the paper image may be held in the hand. But the difference in approach and medium may be better understood by a comment made by Elizabeth Rigby in her journal:

> Met D. O. Hill . . . and went with him to his brother's rooms to see a bust of Professor Wilson. Such a grand Jupiter, very fine and very like, but wanting his exquisite colours to lighten and refine – the tender, child-like bloom which seems, like his mind, to have survived all the wear of time and care of this world. The substance of the hair can't be imitated: it is a mere halo round the head, of which heavy marble locks give no idea; still the bust is a majestic thing.[41]

In a longer passage, John Wilson's daughter talked of him with reference to the calotype photograph:

> despite increasing infirmity, his step was free, and he looked leonine in strength and bearing. So did he when he sat for his photograph to Mr. D. O. Hill . . . In this product of that wonderful art, then in its infancy, comes out the character of the man; the block, as it were from nature, not softened down or refined away by that delicacy which so often makes portrait-painting insensate, but great in its original strength; with a something, perhaps more of the man, and a little less of the poet in his look, than painting would have given, yet unmistakable to the very character of the hands, broad and beautiful in form. The hair, not so fine, is rather lost in the hazy shadows of the photograph, but all else is good and true. Why, some one may ask, are those '*weepers*' on his sleeves? This was a mark of respect he paid to the memory of his wife, and which he continued to wear as long as he lived, renewing these simple outward memorials with tender regularity. The solicitude he showed about his weepers was very touching. Many a time have I sewed them on while he stood by till the work was finished, never satisfied unless he saw it done himself.[42]

In Joshua Reynolds's words: 'Sculpture is formal, regular and austere; disdains all familiar objects, as incompatible with its dignity.'[43] It is petrifaction, designed to endure after the death of the fragile, mutable flesh. It involves formal discrimination – Wilson justifies elevation to a pedestal on the principal street of the grand New Town of Edinburgh. He stands by a truncated palm tree, which is presumably a classical reference to his fame and to his own poetic work, *The Isle of Palms*, but it is not a tree native to Scotland. Photography, and especially paper photography, had from its inception a connection with life and people of 'lesser importance'. It was straightforwardly less heavy, less serious, more fragile – emotionally rather than intellectually affecting. While Hill took no interest in the daguerreotype's accurate depiction of costume, his family affections suggest that he would have shared the view of John Wilson's daughter that the weepers – his sustained affectionate tribute to his wife – were important: part of the truth of the man. However, the distinction between the sculpture and the calotype was not as great as might be expected. Mrs Gordon is applauding the calotype for its strength in sculptural terms. Hill's photographic practice was designedly public rather than private, although informed by personal knowledge.

BETWEEN HILL AND ADAMSON AND JULIA MARGARET CAMERON
Humanity and Immortality

Hill was concerned with the calotype as an expression of life. His interest was temporal, relating to what he knew of present life but giving that knowledge of present life to immortality. This may be better understood in comparison with the approach of Julia Margaret Cameron.

Hill and Cameron had certain interests and characteristics in common. They were both sociable, both generous and both highly ambitious. They shared an interest in the imperfect and the broad effects of photography. It is easy to oversimplify the distinction between the two bodies of work. It is a distinction that is exaggerated by Cameron's personality and her fluent enthusiasm. She was working twenty years later, in the next generation, in England rather than Scotland and with a radically different attitude to religion and the depiction of the religious ideal – the distance between the Anglo-Catholic Oxford Movement and the Free Church of Scotland.[44]

It is regrettable that we have neither Hill's opinion of Cameron nor Cameron's of Hill and Adamson. It seems plausible that Hill would have largely concurred with Cameron's comments on Sir David Brewster's 'eloquent speech' on photography, in December 1864:

> I could not help wishing . . . that you had spoken of Photography in that spirit which will elevate it and induce an ignorant public to believe in other than mere conventional topographic Photography – map making & skeleton rendering of feature & form without that roundness & fulness of force & feature that modelling of flesh & limb which the focus I use only can give tho' called & condemned as '*out of focus*'. What is focus – & who has a right to say what focus is the legitimate focus – My aspirations are to ennoble Photography and to secure for it the character and uses of High Art by combining the real & Ideal & sacrificing nothing of Truth by all possible devotion to Poetry & *beauty*.[45]

However, while there is an expressive sympathy between Hill and Adamson and Cameron, the difference in practice and aim was radical. Hill was looking more for a result of social interaction. Cameron was looking for the effects of introspection: the inward turning, even facial blankness, generated by the self-hypnotic effect of posing for long minutes at a time in bright light. Cameron's sitters stare beyond us; they do not connect. She deliberately extended the exposure times to achieve this, and the ribald accounts of such mild torture illuminate what she was doing, both physically and psychologically. The botanical painter, Marianne North, who submitted to twelve attempts to photograph her in Sri Lanka in 1877, recalled: 'She . . . dressed me up in flowing draperies of cashmere wool, let down my hair, and made me stand with spiky cocoa-nut branches running into my head, the noonday sun's rays dodging my eyes between the leaves as the slight breeze moved them, and told me to look perfectly natural (with a thermometer standing at 96°)!'[46]

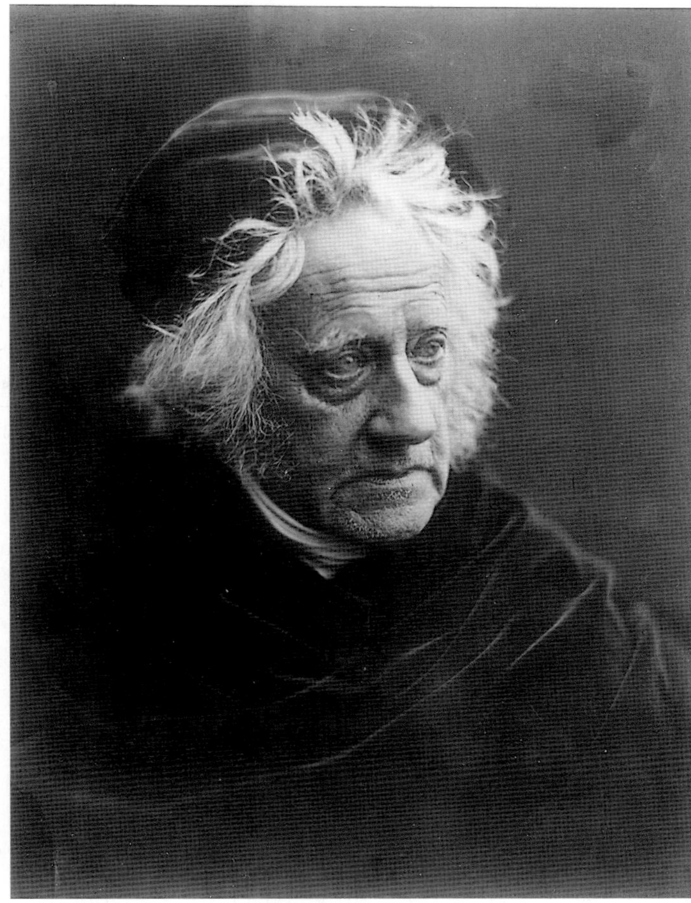

82. Julia Margaret Cameron, *Sir John Herschel*, 1867. Albumen print. National Portrait Gallery, London.

The difference between Hill and Cameron, both of whom admired their subjects uncynically, lay in this. Hill wanted the human warmth of a conversation and contact. His portrait of Thomas Chalmers sits in a family group; his picture of John Wilson shows him with the weepers on his sleeves to mourn his dead wife. Cameron wanted the sitter to express an individual ideal of genius or beauty, as an abstract of her enthusiasm as much as a reaction to their personal nature. Hill's photography is more responsive and more understanding. He had more humour; it is hard to imagine Hill instructing his sitters to look natural. They were both generous, but Cameron's generosity was aggressive, she sometimes pursued rather than courted her sitters. There is an element of unkindness in her photographs of Sir John Herschel at the age of seventy-five (fig. 82), one of which has been described as 'one of the most moving images of a great intellect caught in the process of physical dissolution.'[47] In seeking sociable and temporal dislocation, she has here achieved an abstraction of despair – tragedy rather than nature. Cameron wanted to fit her sitters into a mould of immortality; Hill was offering a framing of mortality – it was a kinder vision.

9

The Figure and Expression

FIGURE STUDY
The Classical Cast, Anatomy and Phrenology

The two earliest of Hill's surviving letters were written to the Board of Trustees for Arts and Manufactures in Edinburgh. The first was written when he was eighteen years old, and formally requests readmission to the Trustees Academy. It says: 'his principal reason for residing in Edinburgh is that he may have the benefit of attending this institution, as he has no other opportunity of drawing from the Figure.'[1] The second is dated seven years later, when Hill was a practising artist:

> having of late given part of my attention to the painting of Figures, (of which class of subjects my first picture viz 'A Scottish Bridal' is now in the Royal Institution) I am deeply impressed with the importance of obtaining a better knowledge of *drawing* the figure, to which end I have the strongest desire of being allowed to attend the Academy in the evenings . . . I have . . . with the advice of Mr Allan of the Academy who has kindly expressed his desire that I should continue my studies under him, taken the liberty of addressing you to request you would, if it meets your approval, further my desire of being admitted to draw in the Academy in the evening during the pleasure of the Honorable Board.[2]

Hill is known principally as a landscape painter, so this repetition of an interest in drawing the figure is a little surprising. In fact, his ambitions lay also in the practice of genre, and his decision to paint his great *Signing of the Deed of Demission* was based on an efficient knowledge of the human figure and face. He did not need photography to aid him, and had started work on the studies for the picture before Brewster introduced him to Robert Adamson. There is a group of small oil sketches of individual ministers, which Hill apparently decided not to use in the Disruption picture and gave to an aspiring painter to study, which make it clear that he was a competent portrait painter (fig. 83).[3] Certain figures in the painting, like the foreground figures of Sergeant Mackenzie and Mr Hately seem to have been painted from life, without the aid of photography. This proven competence in the field makes it less surprising that the practice of the calotype partnership was substantially the expression of an informed interest in photographing people rather than city and landscape.

The two contemporary painters Hill most admired were Turner and David Wilkie. It is in relation to Wilkie's painting that David Brewster's letter to Talbot, announcing the partnership, should be read. The letter first expresses the initial success of their experiments and Brewster's own excitement at the results they were achieving. It then continues:

> They have succeeded beyond their most sanguine expectations. They have taken, on a small scale, Groups of *25* persons in the same picture all placed in attitudes which the Painter desired, and very large pictures besides have been taken of each individual to assist the Painter in the completion of his picture. Mr D. O. Hill the Painter is on the eve of entering into Partnership with Mr Adamson, and proposes to apply the Calotype to many other general purposes of a very popular kind, & especially to the execution of large pictures representing difft. bodies & classes of individuals . . . I have seen one of the groups of *25* persons with our distinguished Moderator Dr Chalmers sitting in the heart of them, and I have never seen anything finer.[4]

Having been persuaded to consider the calotype as an aid to the one large painting, which he expected to occupy him full time for three years, Hill was already, after just a few weeks,

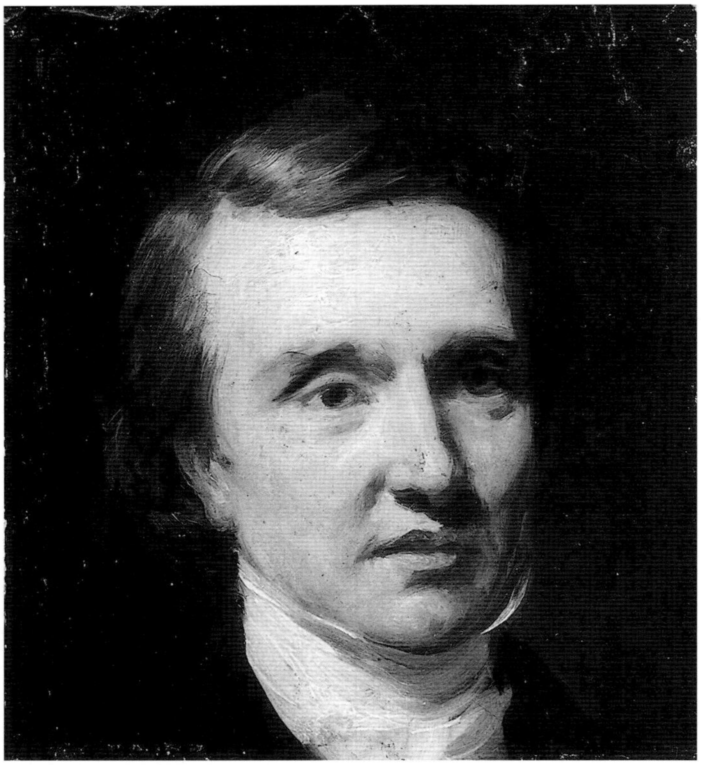

83. David Octavius Hill, Probably *Reverend William Bevan*, *c.* 1844. Oil on millboard. Scottish National Portrait Gallery, Edinburgh.

struck with the exciting possibility of extending his interest to 'purposes of a very popular kind, & especially to the execution of large pictures representing difft. bodies & classes of individuals'. This brief and confusing phrase has not signalled clearly that this – figure study – was the focus of the partnership.[5]

For the Edinburgh painters, the principal aid to the study of the human figure was the impressive collection of classical casts owned by the Trustees Academy – housed in the same building where Hill worked as secretary for the Scottish Academy.[6] It is this collection Hill referred to when he requested permission to study from the figure. Thomas Dibdin commented in 1836:

> The rooms upstairs devoted to the *casts* in plaister of Paris, are admirably arranged: for instead of the sepulchral, lateral light of Somerset House, you have the light immediately descending from above. If the Chantreys, Westmacotts and Baileys, that are to be – in Scotland – do not feel the Phidias-flame rising in their bosoms, it will not be from the want of classical stimulants, in casts of the most approved marble-forms of antiquity.[7]

Hill himself referred to the collection as: 'the finest gallery of casts perhaps in the world.'[8] A young painter who studied there from 1853, described the advantage:

> In Edinburgh we had a long gallery with windows on the roof at intervals . . . I shall never forget the exquisite beauty of the middle tint or overshadowing which the statues had that were placed between the windows; those which were immediately underneath them were of course in a blaze of light, and we had all gradations of light, middle tint, and shadow.[9]

It is worth consideration that Hill had followed here, as a draughtsman, the study proposed by Talbot and others for the camera, of statuary seen and defined in different angles and strengths of light.[10]

Alongside the study of the cast, stood the more difficult study of anatomy. From the Renaissance to the later nineteenth century, the anatomical study of the human form was a theological and aesthetic consideration as much as a professional concern of surgeons.[11] The idea of man, both in Protagoras' phrase, 'as the measure of all things', and as the focus of Christian creation meant that the study was sanctified and elevated by religious and philosophical principle. It was a study of the highest order, and anatomical lectures and dissection took place in public theatres. Such painters as Leonardo and Michelangelo exemplify the idea of the artist-anatomist, who contributed to the knowledge of the human body in the Renaissance and offered a model to later painters. It was understood that physical examination of the body would illuminate greater truths.

The Edinburgh of Hill's time was a centre for surgical teaching and practice. He may well have studied within the extensive collections, housed in the 'magnificent galleried museum', of the Royal College of Surgeons.[12] The continuing, essential interlink between art and surgical anatomy may be expressed by the two museum casts noted in the college, which were of the Greek Discobolus and an *écorché* (cutaway) anatomical figure by Jean-Antoine Houdon.[13] The first curator of this museum was Dr Robert Knox, who was himself an anatomist. Knox maintained in his practice the idea of a grand 'theatrical' tradition:

> Knox was a famous and brilliant teacher and attracted large audiences, sometimes as many as 500. Unprepossessing in appearance – small pox had left his face severely marked and unattractive – he compensated with a flamboyance of dress, a superb histrionic ability, and the complete assurance that men small in stature often display. His lectures –

sometimes repeated several times a day – were regarded as the greatest intellectual treat in 'Modern Athens.'[14]

There are three calotypes which show men in the act of lecturing or preaching, with the right arm outstretched in the dramatic gesture, seizing the attention; two are of the ministers, Thomas Chalmers and Robert Candlish (fig. 20), and the third is of Robert Knox (fig. 84). This grouping may be coincidental, but it may contain an echo of the tradition linking theological and anatomical exposition.

However, there was an inherent difficulty to this honourable study: 'The secular and religious laws that reluctantly sanctioned dissection of human cadavers from the late Middle Ages to the nineteenth century, generally reserved the violation of dissection for those condemned to die at the hands of an executioner.'[15] The bodies of executed criminals were the only certain supply for anatomists. William Hogarth's moral series, *The Four Stages of Cruelty* (1750–1), ends with *The Reward of Cruelty* and the hanged man on the dissecting table. In Edinburgh in the early nineteenth century, surgeons were supplied by the sinister 'resurrection trade', the theft of newly buried bodies. The problematic morality, which lay behind this criminal collusion, was brought to light in a drastic fashion in 1827, when it was discovered that the criminals Burke and Hare had been supplying corpses to the anatomy schools not just by stealing the bodies of the dead from the cemeteries but by murdering people. Dr Robert Knox was the surgeon involved in this case and, while many people were persuaded of his innocence, the scandal effectively finished his career in Edinburgh. The natural revulsion the murders caused may have made practical anatomical study as difficult for the painters as for the surgeons.

Another consideration may have come into play. Anatomy depended on death. The often mannered results of the study were criticised in a letter from James Nasmyth to Hill:

> The disgusting pedantry of showing forth the mean knowledge of the position of a few muscles and by mistaking the means for the end and giving us skinned men placed in attitudes to show off the artists knowledge of anatomy in place of telling the story of the picture is a species of affectation . . . I am your mere goth who can see no beauty but in a noble and yet true representation of nature in her best moods either quiet or excited. Give me your Rembrandt [illegible] and they may walk off with all the skinned men as have such muscles as shine through the dress be it never so thick. I am really not up to that mark of the sublime yet.[16]

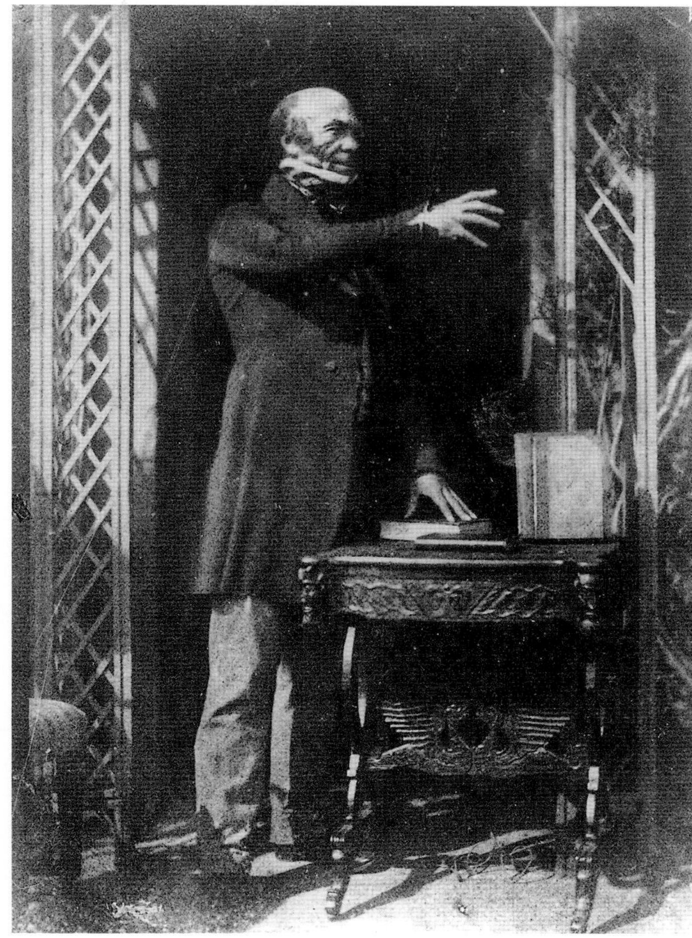

84. D. O. Hill and Robert Adamson, *Dr Robert Knox,* probably 1843. Calotype. Scottish National Photography Collection, Edinburgh.

The Royal Institution opened the first official life class in Edinburgh in 1829. In 1838, Dr David Monro offered a course of lectures on anatomy to the Trustees Academy, using the collection of classical casts and drawings. In 1839, he was assisted by a life model, Private Davis of the Third Dragoon Guards.[17] This turn to life may also have made the study of phrenology or physiognomy more attractive.[18] Historically, it was the purpose of the portrait to reveal something of the greatness or the soul within the subject; theoretically, phrenology, as the analytical study of the surface structure of the head, might help to shift the onus from the artist as ideal image-maker to the artist as respectful observer. However, this does not necessarily imply a simplistic belief in phrenology. A little wit and knowledge of humanity would introduce doubt. George Harvey expressed a bias in favour of phrenology in a letter to George Combe in 1844, responding to his work, *On Phrenology and the Fine Arts*:

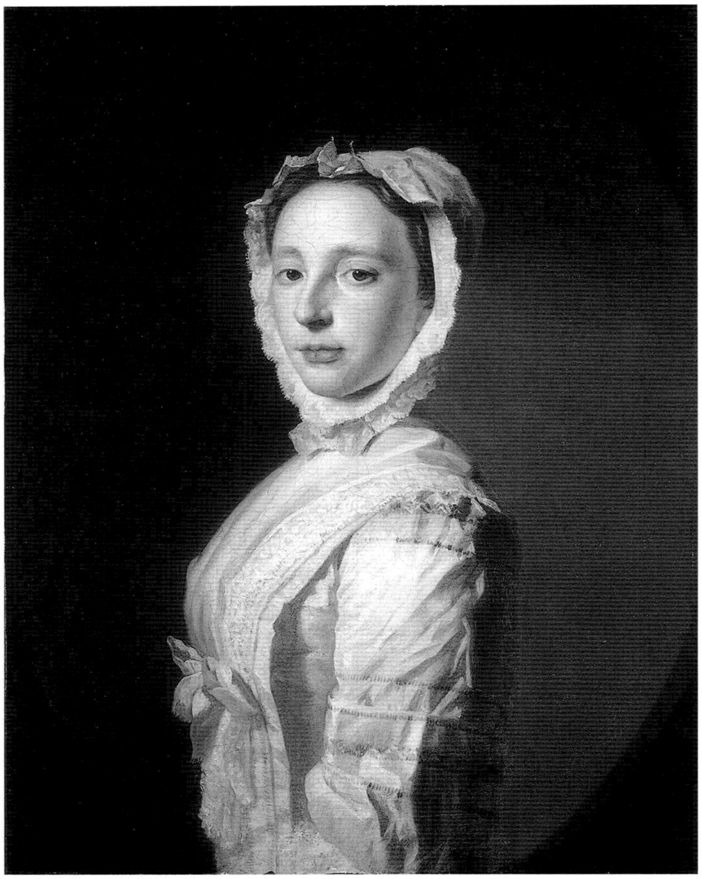

85. Allan Ramsay, *Anne Ramsay*, 1739–43. Oil on canvas. Scottish National Portrait Gallery, Edinburgh.

> I have read the letters with deep interest and cordially concur in the views which you have adopted as to the superiority of that class of Art, in whatever department which embodies most of the qualities of mind, as opposed to that which rests its claims for the supremacy on the merely beautiful in form. This opinion I have long entertained, but have found little sympathy in regard to it among my professional brethren, particularly those who may have been for a time resident in Italy.[19]

For Harvey, the depiction of character or mind through a drawing of the real face was not so much an opposition to the perfection of the ideal, as a proposal contrasting a Protestant truthfulness with a Roman Catholic untruth. The Dutch painters were Protestant and acted upon the principle of personal responsibility and individuality, which Protestantism presupposes. This interest helps to explain the attraction of the Dutch model to the Scottish genre painters, led by David Wilkie. Moreover, the Protestant idea released both Harvey and Hill into a method of religious expression, based on national character and history. It lay behind Hill's interest in the calotype and added strength to his motive in making such an inherently truthful picture of the Free Church.

BEAUTY AND EXPRESSION

In 1755, the Scottish portrait painter, Allan Ramsay, published his *Dialogue on Taste*, which proposed that beauty was a matter of personal affection, and that the classic ideal was a reduction: 'in the antique, we find a sort of common measure, but which falls mightily in its value when we consider that it is only of a negative kind, from which no striking grace can be expected.'[20] This is in contradistinction to Johann Winckelmann's aesthetic theory that the ideal beauty of the classical artists, whilst built on nature, was constructed to achieve a harmony, free from emotion, and 'had no existence but in their elevated conceptions.'[21] Ramsay's belief in the beauty of individual humanity (fig. 85) was reinforced by later authorities in Scotland: the philosopher David Hume's proposal, 'Everything in nature is individual', and Archibald Alison's *Essays on the Nature and Principles of Taste*: 'If in the human countenance and form there were only certain colours or forms or proportions, that were essentially beautiful, how imperious a check would have been given, not only to human happiness, but to the most important affections and sensibilities of our nature!'[22]

These arguments opened the field of aesthetics to subjectivity and variability. They imply, moreover, that need for a sociable relationship between the artist and subject, which was the key to Hill's work. Artist and subject connect and reflect. This attractive proposal was to be found in the work of the surgeon Charles Bell, *The Anatomy and Philosophy of Expression as Connected with the Fine Arts.*[23] Bell believed that emotion made beauty:

> A countenance which, in ordinary conditions, has nothing remarkable, may become beautiful in expression . . . When we look forward to the meeting with those we love, it is the illuminated face we hurry to meet; and none who have lost a friend but must acknowledge that it is the evanescent expression, more than the permanent form, which is painfully dear to them . . .Those who have professedly written on the antique say, that, to arrive at the perfection of the ancient statue, the artist must avoid what is human, and aim at the divine. But we speak of what stands materially before us, to be seen, touched, and measured. With

what *divine* essence is the comparison to be made? . . . the idea of representing divinity is palpably absurd; we know nothing of form but from the contemplation of *man*.[24]

Bell, like Ramsay, was challenging the dominant idea of the classical or platonic ideal – the proposal of the superiority of a universal design. It was Plato's belief that the individual was a mere imitation of a divine pattern and that the further imitation, by art, of nature was destructive of that ideal. In the Renaissance, Neoplatonism answered this problem by moving the artist into a higher sphere, endowing him with divine inspiration and the ability to perceive and seize the eternal pattern. The great respect of the artists, who lived in and after the Renaissance, for classical statuary meant that they learnt their idea of this abstract harmony from the physical, classical model.[25] The establishment of the classical cast collection in Edinburgh was in itself a continuation of this uneasy proposal – offering standards of inspiration and models from a supposedly invented divine ideal. The calotype of Hill with the sculptors John Henning and Alexander Handyside Ritchie, and Henning's casts of the Parthenon frieze, implies the kind of serious admiration and discussion, which must have been a commonplace among the Scottish artists of the time (pl. 37).

It was not, however, necessary to reject the classical ideal in order to pursue nature; the classical model could be reassessed in terms of nature. Benjamin Robert Haydon's opinion of the Elgin marbles as 'the true beau-ideal, of which nature alone is the basis', helped to unravel the confusing obligation to classicism. Haydon sent his note admiring the calotypes in comparison with the Elgin marbles to Hill in April 1846 (see p. 36), the same month that Dr John Brown was composing his review of Hill's work for *The Witness*. Hill presumably showed Brown this handsome compliment, which re-emerges in Brown's text, when he is discussing the Newhaven calotypes:

> These clean, sonsy, caller, comely, substantial fishwives, – what a refreshing sight! As easy, as unconfined, as deep-bosomed and ample, as any Grecian matron. Indeed, we have often been struck, when seeing them sitting together round their oyster creels, with their likeness to those awful and majestic women, the Fates of the Elgin Marbles, the casts of which are in the Gallery of the Royal Institution.[26]

Hill's interest in the calotype process, like Bell's argument, offered an alternative to the uncritical imitation of a classical ideal, in examining the natural and the individual, and, more importantly, in ideas of human variability and change. Bell and Hill were both considering the appealing idea of the 'illuminated face': 'Peace, comfort, society, and agreeable studies, preserve the features mobile, and ready to conform, as an index of the mind, to the sentiments we love'.[27] Bell had a sophisticated understanding of love and the working of society – that when communicating with each other, people are relaxed into an openness, a readiness to reveal their own nature; when studied coldly for an abstraction, their faces will close communication. Individual beauty may disappear under a cold touch. It is a portrait painter's understanding, exemplified in the story told of Leonardo, that while he was painting the Mona Lisa, 'he engaged people to play and sing, and jesters to keep her merry, and remove that melancholy which painting usually gives to portraits'.[28] Bell's argument derived from the dominant tradition of portraiture in Scotland, with its necessary relation both to nature and courtesy, expressed by Allan Ramsay and Henry Raeburn. David Wilkie, who was a pupil of Charles Bell, was seeking the same principle in genre painting. His work was appreciated for this grace by G. F. Waagen, the director of the Berlin Museum: 'I find in Wilkie a close affinity with his celebrated countryman Sir Walter Scott. Both have in common that genuine, refined delineation of character which extends to the minutest particulars. In the soul of both there is more love than contempt for man.'[29]

This approach shifted the balance of elevated representation from the imagination to sympathetic observation and contact. It made art a sociable business – the artist had a responsibility to draw out socially, rather than to create, what he wished to see. Hill's talent for generating affection is important – the openness of the calotype portraits depends on this. He wrote to Roberts of his plan for a work on British statesmen, that he needed to be assured that potential sitters liked the work and to know the scheme to be: 'well backed . . . coldness on the part of those to be calotyped unmans me quite.'[30] The responsive warmth of the sitters underlies the relaxed appearance of nature, revealing rather than concealing character. The emotional strength of the calotype portraits lies in a restrained interaction with his sitters, where the mind is kept attentive. Hill knew his sitters.

There is a practical distinction between the social skill discussed in chapter four, of communicating with and accommodating people, and the unnatural construction of the same appearance for art. The difficulty of achieving this apparently natural relationship may be illustrated by comparing Hill's practice with that of the successful commercial photographer, Antoine Claudet, who instructed his sitters: 'If ladies, however, *must* study for a bit of effect, we will give them a recipe

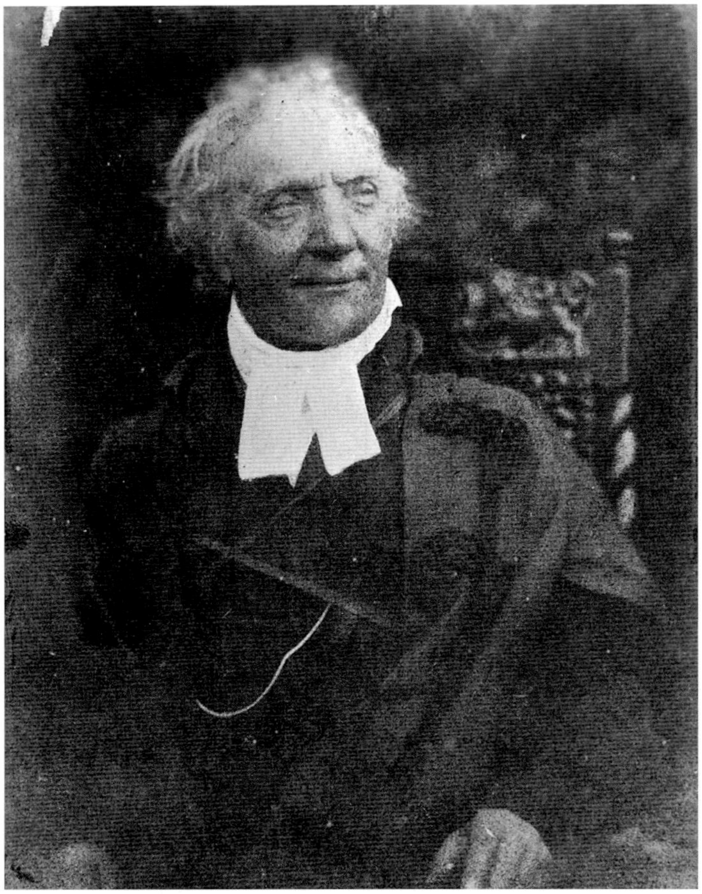

86. D. O. Hill and Robert Adamson, *Reverend Dr Thomas Chalmers*, probably 1843. Calotype. Scottish National Photography Collection, Edinburgh.

for a pretty expression of mouth – let them place it as if they were going to say *prunes.*'[31] However skilful Claudet was as a photographer, this is extreme social ineptitude. It justifies John Brown's hostile criticism of Claudet's work, which he contrasted with Hill's in 1862:

> Take Claudet's best – everything is there that the perfection of skill, manipulation, materials, light, and infinite practice can achieve, and what have you? A clever, leaden, flat miniature, with a background as hard and as *blae* as a slate – no spaciousness, no substance, no ease or grace, power, or life, or play – nothing but surface, and a poverty of invention, of posture, of meaning, of total result quite odd and lamentable.[32]

Among the early calotype studies for the Disruption picture, the series of Thomas Chalmers attempts a number of different angles to the face and includes one of him smiling (fig. 86). Here, Hill was presumably intending to give himself a number of possibilities in composing the painting around the critical figure of Chalmers. Hill's interest is generally distinguished from the later, scientific explorations of expression, conducted by G.-B. Duchenne de Boulogne or Charles Darwin. Duchenne de Boulogne applied electrical impulses to different muscles in the face to create expressions for the camera, with the intention of building a thesaurus of human expressions.[33] Charles Darwin, who used one of Duchenne de Boulogne's most troubling images – the man showing horror – also employed Oscar Gustav Reijlander's photographs of himself acting emotion: 'Indignation', 'Disgust', 'Helplessness'.

Hill did not attempt either the comprehensive or analytical approach to expression. He used neither models nor actors in his photographic work, presumably to avoid professional mannerism in a field of nature – this is all the more remarkable because William Allan, who taught him figure study, manifestly did use actors for his knowledge of physical expression.[34] Hill and Adamson did photograph the Shakespearean actress, Isabella Glynn, but she is shown turned away from the camera. The only life study made from a nude figure is not a professional model but Dr George Bell (pl. 15).

RESEMBLANCE AND THE PHOTOGENIC

Sir David Brewster signalled an unease with the calotype process early on when he found that portraits were not consistent in their resemblance. He wrote to Talbot:

> I have been very much struck with the *different calotypes* of the *same person.* In many of them, where the sitter was steady, – the family likeness is scarcely preserved [note below 'Compare the enclosed one of myself with those taken by you.'] Does this arise from the camera? I have seen among Mr Adamson's calotypes pictures of men & women in one of which the sitter was decidedly *good looking* and in the other *hideous.* There is something yet to be done in reference to this point.[35]

Brewster saw this photographic variation as a technological failing, and pursued its solution to the end of his career. By 1852, he had discovered that the clarity of the albumen process did not resolve the problem, and he turned his attention to the camera lens. He proposed to a meeting of the British Association that 'all the photographic portraits taken with large object glasses or mirrors must necessarily be distorted', because the pupil of the eye was only 2/10 inch diameter.[36] His last correspondence with Antoine Claudet, in 1867, showed him still in pursuit of 'the greater perfection of photo-portraiture by means of small lenses made of materials of different dispersive powers.'[37] Hill can be found mutely expressing the same problem in a story told of his attempt to photograph Thomas Duncan's wife, Mary: 'I can remember my grandmother telling us that D. O. Hill had been set on making a really good photograph of her: so she duly posed for him, and he disappeared to develop it. When next they saw him, he just came and sat down in a chair, and buried his face in his hands, and that was the last of it!'[38]

From the evidence of Hugh Miller's article on the calotype, Hill apparently accepted the variability of human appearance as part of the interest of calotype portraiture. Hill probably discussed with Miller the resemblance between the calotypes and mezzotints after Joshua Reynolds, and showed or lent him an album of the prints for comparison:

> There is one particular kind of resemblance between the two, which strikes as remarkable, because of a kind which could scarce be anticipated. In the volume of prints there are several likenesses of the artist himself, all very admirable as pieces of art, and all, no doubt, sufficiently like, but yet all dissimilar in some points from each other. All this dissimilarity in the degree which it obtains, one might naturally deem a defect – the result of some slight inaccuracy in the drawing. Should not portraits of the same individual, if all perfect likenesses of him, be all perfectly like one another? No; not at all. A man at one moment of time, and seen from one particular point of view, may be very unlike himself when seen at another moment of time, and from another point of view. We have at present before us the photographic likenesses of four several individuals – three likenesses of each – and no two in any of the four sets are quite alike. They differ in expression, according to the mood which prevailed in the mind of the original at the moment in which they were imprinted upon the paper. In some respects the physiognomy seems different; and the features appear more or less massy in the degree in which the lights and shadows were more or less strong, or in which the particular angle they were taken in brought them out in higher or lower relief.[39]

The problem revealed here has a number of strands, both in human perception and in technological mutation. The portrait presents us with something abstracted from experience, because it does not move; our knowledge of people is based on a constantly shifting reality, which builds up a generalised idea.[40] This is the critical problem of portraiture; how to make a face recognisable within one static image without eliminating much of the sitter's character or, even more simply, different facets of appearance. Ernst Gombrich has addressed this problem and concludes that the viewer must be invited to take an active part: 'The portraitist who wants to compensate for the absence of movement must first of all mobilise our projection. He must so exploit the ambiguities of the arrested face that the multiplicities of possible readings result in the semblance of life. The immobile face must appear as a nodal point of several possible expressive movements.'[41] The sophistication of response, which Gombrich requires, had been expressed in different terms by John Ruskin in the 1840s. He qualified the recognition of portraits as dependent on the intelligence of the artist and the intelligence of the viewer: 'Recognition is no proof of real and intrinsic resemblance . . . A man is known to his dog by the smell, to his tailor by the coat, to his friend by the smile: each of these knows him, but how little or how much, depends on the dignity of the intelligence. That which is truly and indeed characteristic of the man, is known only to God.'[42]

Brewster's complaint against photography, which Miller neatly identified with painting, is critically connected with physiognomy and its representation. The photogenic character, defined as the unexpectedly eccentric ability to maintain a consistent image, is one of the most interesting questions raised by photography. Previously such inconsistencies could be blamed on the painter; the supposed objectivity of the camera made it plain that humanity could be divided into the photogenic and non-photogenic. It is now almost a precondition of public life, to be reliably photogenic – important not just to film stars or television presenters but to politicians.[43]

It is difficult to quantify the photogenic character, partly because the rejection of an image by the sitter is usually attributed to vanity and not taken seriously. Moreover, the bystanding audience often urge the resemblance in a curiously conciliatory manner – as though to bring the picture and the person together. However, a significant example of the non-photogenic may be found in the face of Robert Louis Stevenson. He was continually critical of his portraits and, indeed, did not 'take' well either in painting or photography. He wrote to his cousin: 'Dew-Smith has taken a photograph of me which is like you, drunk; very odd, it has your nose instead of mine.'[44] Strange though the idea is, Stevenson's nose proved to be a photographic difficulty:

> *A-propos* of the odd controversy about Shelley's nose: I have before me four photographs of myself, done by

Shelley's son: my nose is hooked, not like the eagle indeed, but like the accipitrine family in man: well, out of these four, only one marks the bend, one makes it straight, and one suggests a turn up. This throws a flood of light on calumnious man – and the scandalmongering sun. For personally, I cling to my curve.[45]

The objection that the mouth is wrong is an understandable and frequent complaint levelled at portraitists. That such an inexpressive feature as the nose could be transcribed wrongly is extraordinary.

This natural difficulty in portraiture further illuminates the skill of the calotype partnership. We can recognise people from a very generalised image, which might be regarded as an inherent advantage in the blurring of the calotype. But the generalisation of the calotype was arbitrary. It was an awkward medium, offering less control and more accident in this key question of recognition. It may be said, therefore, that Hill and Adamson's portraits were remarkable both for being good pictures and, for that apparent photographic tautology, being like the sitter. This is a proposal that is still difficult to understand. It depends heavily on the interpretative sympathy of the photographers, who inherited the responsibility of the portrait painters whilst working with different materials.

THE GROUP AND TABLEAUX

In painting, figure groups were usually constructed from sketches of isolated individuals. Physical and emotional interaction between figures would have to be recalled or invented. The frustration this caused explains the impulse behind the performance art of the painting world in the nineteenth century, the *tableau vivant.*[46] It is no coincidence that David Wilkie was a passionate enthusiast for *tableaux* and that Hill had followed his interest. The *tableau* was a frozen performance or a 'real' representation of a painting. The first Wilkie encountered, in Dresden in 1826, was an imitation of Teniers. He regarded it as, 'the most beautiful reality I ever saw . . . but so evanescent is the group, that the curtain drops in twenty seconds, the people being unable to remain for any longer period in one precise position'.[47] The time was brief, but it enabled a sustained contemplation of a situation which, in reality, would have passed by in a fraction of a second. Where it was the imitation of a known painting, it offered a different experience of the idea and potentially a measure of understanding of the painter's vision. Hill spoke of organising *tableaux* in a letter to Noël Paton in 1852: 'We rehearse at Miss Murrays tomorrow night some tableaux – [James] Archer assists me . . . Now do you think you could lend me your armour and perhaps the Highland Shield – any dresses [?] any, everything that would be useful I think I would like to get up your eve of St Agnes. Come and suggest some [affecting?] subjects.'[48] It is a measure of the seriousness of this idea of real translation and the need for such experience that Hill expected Paton to be interested in a staging of his own painting.

From Hill's point of view, photography immediately opened up the possibility of real groups for study and publication. Hugh Miller saw the early pictures of himself as a stonemason and the studies of ministers in these terms. He wrote, in his article, after the description of his own portrait as a stonemason:

> The other drawing presents a *tableau vivant* on a larger scale, and of a much deeper interest. It forms one of the groups taken under the eye of Mr Hill, as materials for the composition of his historic picture. In the centre Dr Chalmers sits on the Moderator's chair, and there are grouped around him, as on the platform, some eighteen or twenty of the better known members of the Church, clerical and lay. Nothing can be more admirable than the truthfulness and ease of the figures. Wilkie, in his representations of a crowd, excelled introducing heads, and hands, and faces, and parts of faces into the interstices behind, – one of the greatest difficulties with which the artist can grapple. Here, however, is the difficulty surmounted – surmounted, too, as if to bear testimony to the genius of the departed – in the style of Wilkie.[49]

Practice in designing and taking part in *tableaux* was naturally useful to Hill in approaching his calotype groups. It was useful not simply in the costume groups, where the relationship is obvious (pl. 30), but in the practical confidence to be found in most of these compositions. The most natural are apt to be those of the people used to posing in *tableaux* – especially the calotypes in which Hill is expressively relaxed or involved in conversation with others. The painters in particular had an interest in picture-making, which meant that they could think beyond the experience of being pictured, to the purpose of the exercise; they were involved in the work and had not just an idea of what was intended, but how it could be achieved. They were conscious rather than self-conscious. This helps to answer the question posed by Stanley Cursiter, in admiring the skill and organisation behind the portraits and groups: 'One wonders how he managed to instil into his sitters the dramatic sense which allows them to become groups, rather than merely conglomerations of individual figures, a distinction which is due to the presence of some unifying thought or concentration on a single idea on the part of the sitters.'[50] The thinking behind such groups may be examined in two photographs where the idea is offered in a title: *Edinburgh Ale* and *The Morning After, 'He, greatly daring, dined'* (pls 38 and 39). The two pictures are not formally designed as a pair, but they have the obvious moral and narrative relation: the pleasures of alcohol followed by the hangover. We know from the letters, that Hill was not averse to drink. His explanation of *The Poet's Dream at Lincluden* (fig. 61) accepts cheerfully the idea that Robert Burns's inspiration comes to him in drunken sleep. The innocent sociability of *Edinburgh Ale* depends on our idea of the title. James Nasmyth's reminiscent letter to Hill recalling the family gatherings at 47 York Place, sheds light on the convivial aspect of the picture: 'ah sirrah! them was the days for right pleasant songs, when old 47 was in its glory and Finnan Haddies, Ale of potency and most worshipfull toddy sent each its radiating aroma around and erected cracks worthy of being put in print.'[51]

Robert Chambers spoke of Younger's Edinburgh ale, in the context of alcoholism in the late eighteenth and early nineteenth century, as 'a potent fluid, which almost glued the lips of the drinker together', and required careful decanting.[52] He recorded the pleasurable and interesting social mixture achieved in consequence of this insobriety in his descriptions of the fashionable resort to oyster cellars:

> One of the chief features of an oyster-cellar entertainment was, that full scope was given to the conversational powers of the company. Both ladies and gentlemen indulged without restraint, in sallies the merriest and wittiest; and a thousand remarks and jokes, which elsewhere would have been suppressed as improper, were here sanctified by the oddity of the scene, and appreciated by the most refined and dignified.[53]

This was the social background of much of the literary life and inspiration of the time, which can be seen particularly in the work of Robert Burns, James Hogg and John Wilson. It may indicate an appropriate literary reference for the calotype, in Burns's 'O Willie Brew'd a Peck o' Maut':

> Here are we met, three merry boys,
> Three merry boys, I trow, are we;
> And mony a night we've merry been,
> And mony mae we hope to be![54]

It became a commonplace of the descriptions of this sociability that the wit and intelligence improved with the quantity of drink and the lateness of the hour. A conscious model for this idea appears in John Gibson Lockhart's account of the Burns festival, at which John Wilson was one of the principal speakers and praised James Hogg. Lockhart drew Hogg, hilarious on praise and champagne, and the drawing accompanied his text.[55] William Allan, who was clearly charmed both by the description and the drawing, constructed a painting around Lockhart's sketch, which illustrated this culturally profitable hilarity with a party including Hogg, John Wilson, Walter Scott and Alexander Nasmyth (fig. 87). Allan's readiness to use the work of an amateur caricaturist is, in itself, notable evidence of the difficulty in capturing natural expression. Hill would have known the painting, and it is reasonable to suppose that a similar idea of catching that particular sociability lay behind *Edinburgh Ale*.

Looking back from the mid-nineteenth century, Chambers commented:

> It seems difficult to reconcile all these things with the staid and somewhat square-toed character which our country has obtained amongst her neighbours. The fact seems to be, that a kind of Laodicean principle is observable in Scotland, and we oscillate between a rigour of manners on the one hand, and a laxity on the other . . . In Edinburgh, seventy years ago, intemperance was the rule to such a degree that exception could hardly be said to exist.[56]

There is no visible suggestion of the dark side of alcohol in *Edinburgh Ale*, and it may be that *The Morning After* was constructed to offer a balance. It shows Hill hung over, his wrist held by the surgeon and anatomist, Professor James Miller. The lax shadow of Hill's hand is cast by an appropriately low light onto the plinth of the heroic classical bust, known as *The Last of the Romans*.[57] The slumped and dishevelled figure Hill is personating is in a condition he has experienced. He made a jocular reference to a hangover after a dinner at Sir John Watson Gordon's house: 'I delivered myself of a speech drinking Craigs health and soon after went off . . . with a splitting headache, having taken a roasted potato at dinner – the effects of which were not obliterated by seven or eight glasses of capital champain – because my dear friend of a vegetable diet. Take a warning by me.'[58]

The bust of the emperor, whose profile is turned pointedly away, offers a wry comment on the difference between the ideal of man and wayward humanity. In contrast, Hill, the real man, could be the Goth, the democrat and student of nature.[59] He is making a comparison between himself, the

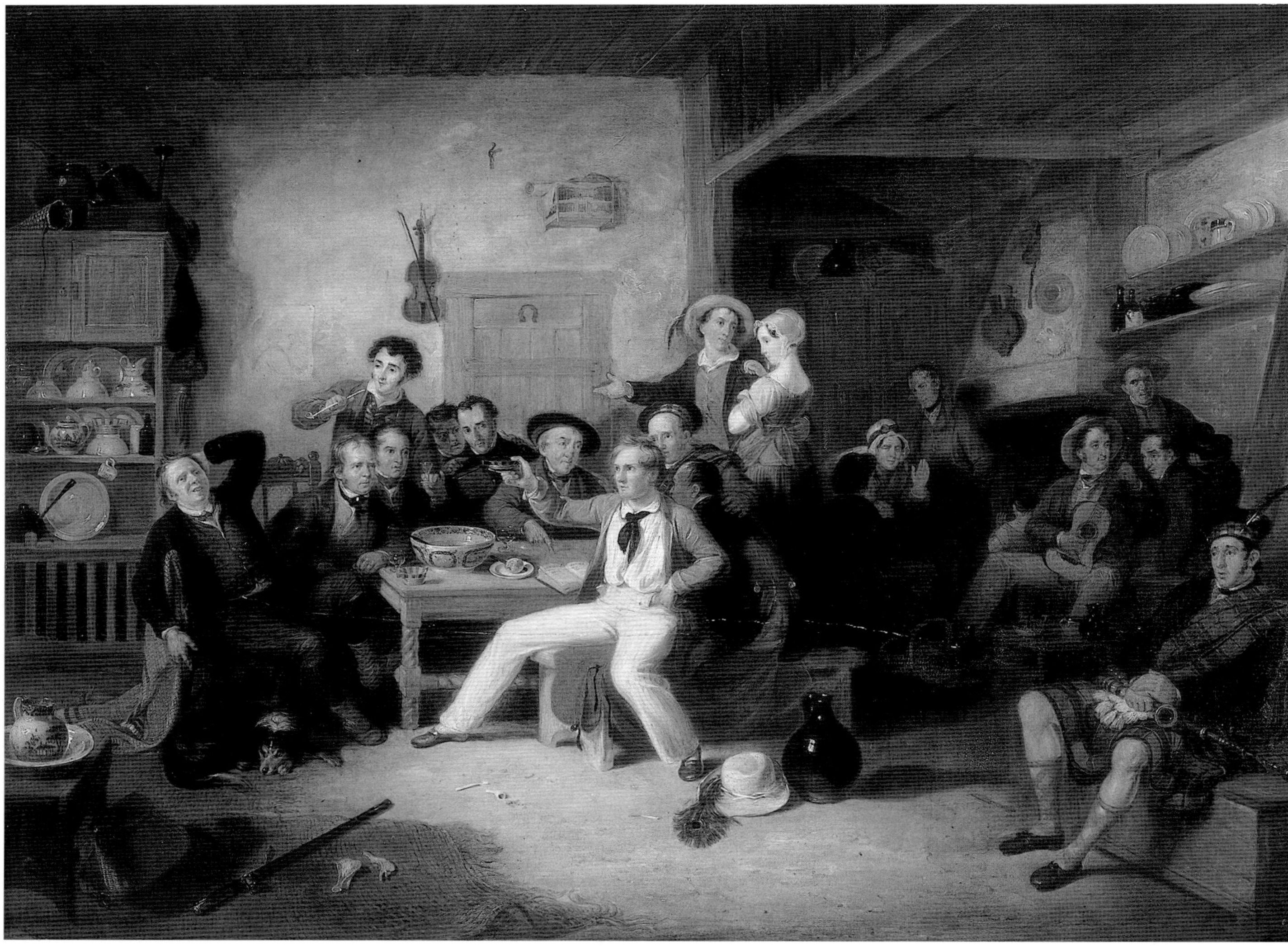

87. Sir William Allan, *The Ettrick Shepherd's Birthday*, *c.* 1820. Oil on canvas. Scottish National Photography Collection, Edinburgh.

sculpted Roman and the upright doctor, carefully and properly dressed, holding his furled umbrella like a defensive sword to his breast – a figure of Christian and medical rectitude. Miller was a temperance reformer. As a doctor he had seen too much of the appalling effects of drunkenness to take it entirely lightly, so the joke has a serious meaning as well. Hill, it may be supposed, was torn between admiration of the sociability and its pleasurable and productive character and the contemporary realisation of the destructive force of alcoholism. He wrote to his wife from Ireland in 1840, in admiration of 'the great apostle of Teetotalism', Father Matthew:

> who has already got more than 500,000 disciples to take his pledge of total abstinence. I asked the waiter at the Inn where I now am if the people ever broke it . . . he replied there were 500 in that town and he did not know of any who had broken it – they will break an oath but not the pledge. He says I was never a drunkard sir but was fond of porter and all that, and rather than not have my fun out of a night, I would think nothing of a pound for my frolic – and now sir, the family gets it, and it does them good. Many's the poor family, sir, that have got both meat and quiet by it, and I think it is the gift of God Almighty himself – So much for Father Mathew. I think I could almost take the said pledge myself, if a poor friend of ours would join me in it.[60]

The calotype's title added a play on words. The phrase, 'he, greatly daring, dined' comes from the epitaph of Phaeton – 'he, greatly daring, died', in Ovid's *Metamorphoses*.[61]

Phaeton, discovering he was the child of the sun god, asked to drive the sun's chariot for a day. He proved too weak to control the four wild, winged horses, caused dramatic destruction on earth, and was felled by a thunderbolt from Jupiter. This implies that the joke is also an offering – an apology to the sun for the arrogant attempt to harness its power to photography – and a propitiation for the inevitable, sunstruck headache. It echoes Hill's awareness of his high ambitions for the calotype when he wrote of his plans to Roberts and added: 'which I hope will not make you rate me as absolute and arrogant as Petruccio making you exclaim. "Why! This gallant will command the sun."'[62]

Hill's interest in Ovid's story surfaces again in the comic drawing of himself being dragged four ways by the sun's winged horses (fig. 46). The light of the sun was, of course, the critical factor in Hill's atmospheric landscape painting. The drawing illustrates his difficulty of decision – he is not heading into the country solely for recreation, despite the sign that reads 'Welch Ale', but to paint.

There is yet another potential layer of meaning. The punning version of the original, 'he greatly daring dined', comes from Alexander Pope's *The Dunciad*: 'Judicious drank, and greatly daring din'd.'[63] Hill may be making another moral point about heroism and its dissipation.

There is, for both calotypes, the precedent of a Netherlandish, genre painting tradition, both the drinking scene and the theme of the doctor's visit.[64] Both kinds of picture were notable as illustrating emotion and tension. Both pictures involve expression, and both, it is reasonable to assume, may be related to Charles Bell's ideas. James Miller was the professor of surgery in the University of Edinburgh and professor of pictorial anatomy to the Board of Manufactures' School of Design. The presence of the medical men in the two pictures, *Edinburgh Ale* and *The Morning After*, makes a further connection with the historic conjunction of surgeon and artist in the study of the human body.

THE UNSUPPORTED GROUP

The two groups are also remarkable because only James Miller was provided with artificial support. *Edinburgh Ale* is the more relaxed picture. Hill has arranged his friends through the camera and then entered the composition, apparently laughing. *The Morning After* is carefully posed and calculated, with Hill fixed in position by Miller's hand on his wrist – it may even be that this picture is a conscious expression of Hill's interest in the classical idea of construction, and that by contrast *Edinburgh Ale* is consciously about unfettered nature. I would not assume that the less structured picture necessarily predated the other. *Edinburgh Ale* has its own ambition.

An idea of the support required by an inexperienced subject may be gathered from the image of Robert Candlish, shown preaching (fig. 20), which was presumably one of the early trials for the Disruption picture. There is an upright support to his outstretched arm, a diagonal support disappearing behind his back and someone is sitting on a chair behind him so that the chairback will steady him in position. Despite this, his other hand, holding the book, has moved and blurred the image. This is a single figure. The group took time to organise and involved establishing a relationship between the figures, which they could maintain for the minutes of organisation as well as the actual time of photography. Hill did not abandon the use of supports, and certain of the pictures, such as those of Alexander Campbell Fraser and his class, would have been impossible without them (fig. 88). Within his closer circle of artists, family and friends, he preferred to risk the natural support that other people and furniture could offer. This would ensure the muscular balance required by the idea of physical expression. Bell had pointed out the problem in using academy models:

> When the academy figure first strips himself, there is a symmetry and accordance in all the limbs; but when screwed up into a posture, they indicate constraint and want of balance. It cannot be supposed that when a man has the support of ropes to preserve him in a position of exertion, the same action of muscles can be displayed as if the limbs were supported by their own efforts; hence in all academy drawings we may perceive something wrong from the ropes not being represented along with the figure. In natural action there is a consent and symmetry in every part . . . The painter, therefore, cannot trust to the man throwing himself into a natural posture; he must direct him, and be himself able to catch, as it were intuitively, what is natural and reject what is constrained. Besides those soldiers and mechanics who are employed as academy figures are often awkward and unwieldy; hard labour, or the stiff habits of military training, have impaired the natural and easy motion of their joints.[65]

Hill attempted the unsupported pose in calotypes where the risks were great – the radical Chalmers family group is a prime example (pl. 4). Because this was an important photograph, he risked not using supports and, because he persuaded Chalmers and his family of that importance, they

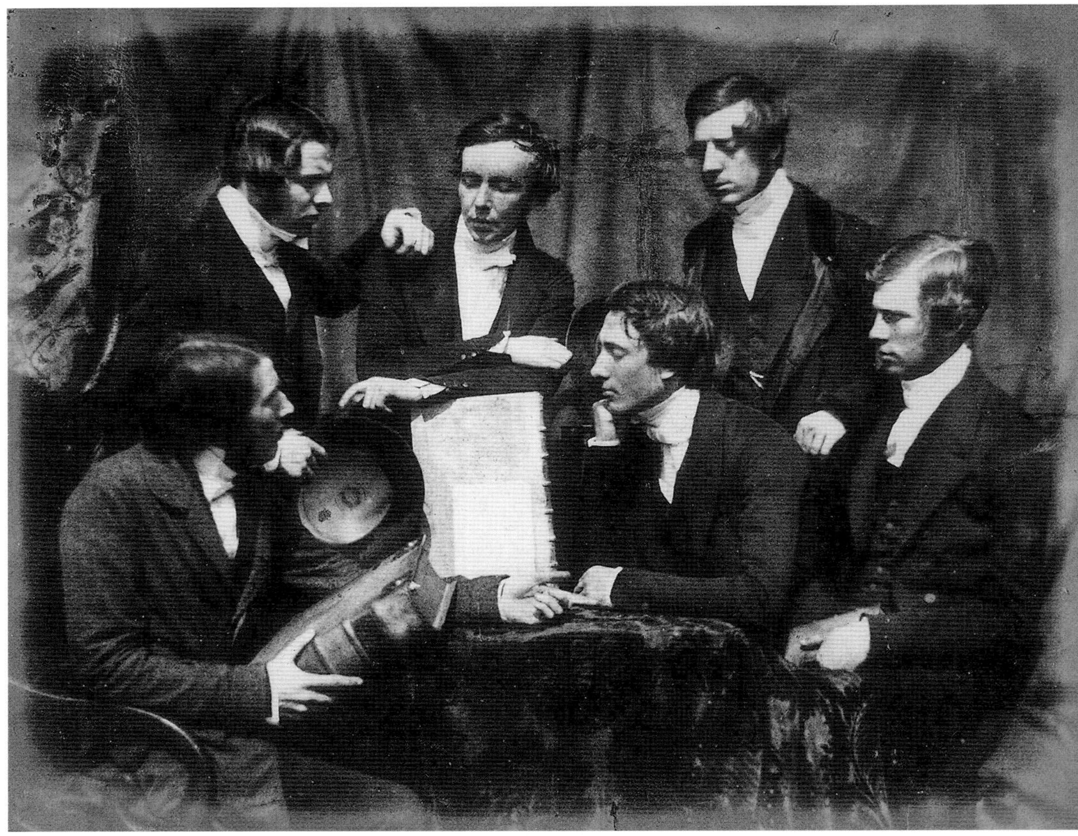

88. D. O. Hill and Robert Adamson, *Professor Alexander Campbell Fraser and his Class*, 1844–6. Calotype. Scottish National Photography Collection, Edinburgh.

were prepared to pose in a difficult and potentially tedious manner. There are several photographs in this group, which were taken in the grounds of Merchiston Castle School, where Thomas Chalmers's brother, Charles, was headmaster. The photographs of adolescent schoolboys, presumably taken on the same occasion, demonstrate a remarkable capacity for human organisation (fig. 89) – one of the successfully realised groups contains around fifty, unregimented people, including a boy up a tree.[66]

The Gordon Highlanders, stationed at Edinburgh Castle in 1846, figure in some of the finest of Hill and Adamson's groups. The regiment was notable for its heroism at the Battle of Waterloo. The photographs vary in character, but include one of the most remarkable of the calotypes, which is an extraordinary compositional blur (pl. 14). It is not even clear how many men are involved in the group. This is all the more striking, because it pictures men who were trained to stand immobile and were employed in life classes for this discipline. But a static pose fails to express the energy of the military. While the man on the left is supported by the cannon and is comparatively still and calm in effect, he is imbalanced by the apparent movement in the men on the right and the sense of suppressed activity. The picture is crowded, especially at the top, by the blurring fur of the busbies, which are used as a compositional mass to fill the space and break the pale line of the architecture. It expresses the strength and energy of the regiment and may be intended to offer an idea, as opposed to a narrative, of unexpressed Highland history, through the ambiguity of the blur. This is the distance between anatomy and animation.

DIRECTION AND NATURE

In his passage on the academy model, Charles Bell described something similar to a film director's talent – the ability to direct people in being natural. The role of construction and direction in still photography may need restating, because it sounds contrary to nature. The problem in capturing nature is that the photographer is there, and the subjects will respond to his presence. Even later photographers with concealed detective cameras or faster film were obviously there and affected the reactions of their subjects.[67] If the photograph was designed to show what someone was normally

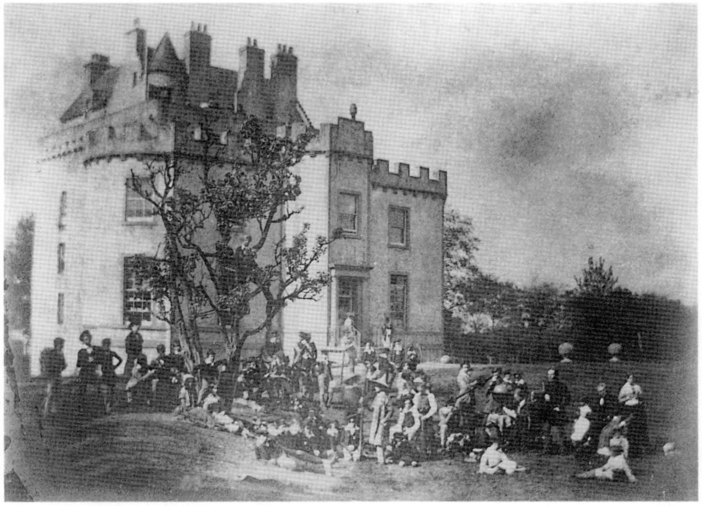

89. D. O. Hill and Robert Adamson, *Boys at Merchiston Castle School*, 1844–6. Calotype. Scottish National Photography Collection, Edinburgh.

doing or how they usually were, the presence of both the camera and the photographer was an interruption, an abnormality increasing the self-consciousness of the subject.

The projected series, *The Fishermen and Women of the Firth of Forth*, was an important demonstration of Charles Bell's advice to watch people in action in their natural setting: 'At the gaming house, on the exchange, in the streets, this study affords amusement of the highest interest and gratification.'[68] Hill was concerned to photograph the fishermen and fishwives within the village and on the shore, rather than inviting them up to the photographic studio. The candid appearance of the Newhaven photographs is based on thoughtful observation of how people behaved in their own territory. Hill had painted in the village in earlier years and his sense of the importance of the location of the figures is seen in the titles of his pictures. In 1835 he exhibited in the Academy three paintings: *The Peacock Inn – Sketch at Newhaven, Evening: Scene on the Beach at Newhaven – Painted on the Spot, Sketch of an Oyster Boat Painted on Newhaven Beach.* The fishermen and women were both willing and, presumably both through discussion and the experience of posing, capable of the same kind of relaxed or interested participation as Hill and his friends.[69] Within the series, two of the most impressive examples, in terms of the risk and the control established under difficulties, are the two pictures taken in the Fishergate in St Andrews (pl. 29). The site and the high camera angle, enabled by a convenient ledge at the top of a flight of steps, were calculated to offer an elevated view of the scene. In practical terms alone, Hill should be admired as a prototype film director; where people, especially children, and animals are concerned, an outside location is an open stage. The Fishergate was a thoroughfare and the photography must have blocked North Street. The photographs demonstrate an impressive capacity for management even beyond the frame – the number of children, who must have been induced to take the work seriously, rather than as a free entertainment, is in itself remarkable. The Cuthbert Bede drawing, from the 1850s, of a man photographing a landscape on a long exposure, with the assistance of a small knot of keenly interested children (fig. 90), is a fine illustration of the problem of photographing in public: 'giving an opportunity to children of a speculative turn of mind, to solve their doubts as to what your camera really contains'.[70] In the actual construction of the calotypes, the co-operation of around thirty women and children would have been secured beforehand. They have been arranged, looking through the camera, in a structured and balanced composition centring on the female figure who appears to stride across the street, carrying a child on one arm and a basket

90. 'Cuthbert Bede', *How to procure a photographic negative.* Illustration to *Photographic Pleasures*, 1859 .

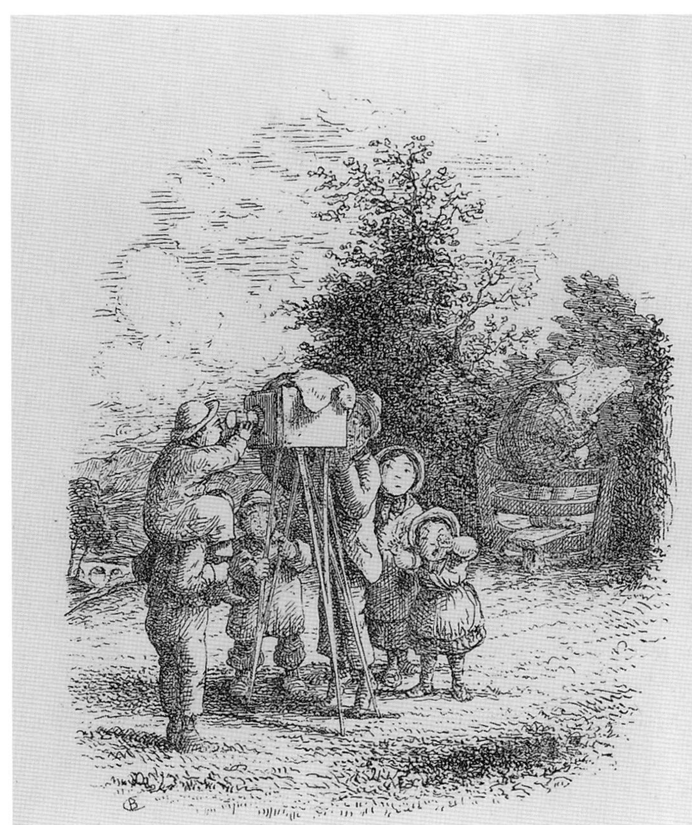

in the opposite hand. The triangle of white in the split of her dark skirt gives the sense of forward movement and the whole thinly grouped composition around her is constructed in the balance of light and shade, dark and light. The picture is dependent on a lack of wind (in a coastal town), and on the appearance of the sun to lay the critical shadow of the woman on the ground. The calculation and organisation behind the photograph is phenomenal – it resembles and anticipates a film still; it is also a happily contrived expression of nature, and the result is convincingly easy.

Photography has a close relation to film making; construction is as important to the still as it is to the moving picture. *The Fishermen and Women* series is the earliest example of a documentary sequence in photography, and it shows extraordinary control and organisation in achieving natural effect, balanced by an equally extraordinary tolerance, which we cannot see in the pictures. This is outdoor photography, wholly dependent on natural light and the generous co-operation of a complete age range of people from an infant in arms to elderly fishwives. The calotypes are not merely a tribute to Bell's idea of physical expressiveness, they are a most effective demonstration of the virtues of the idea.

10

D. O. Hill's Landscape

THE TRADITION OF LANDSCAPE

After Hill's death in 1870, Amelia Hill sold part of his collection of paintings, engravings and books. Amongst the works included were 'brilliant impressions' of Richard Earlom's engravings of Claude's *Liber Veritatis* published in 1774.[1] The *Liber Veritatis* was one of the essential models for the British landscape artists of the day, and it is reasonable to see Hill as influenced by Claude, the leading exponent of the classically poetic in landscape; the painter of calm and beautiful rural idylls, made lyrical by a unifying golden light and the introduction of figures from Virgil, Ovid and the Bible.

Murdo Macdonald has traced a connection between Hill's work and the landscapes of Claude, through the Scottish painters Jacob More, Alexander Nasmyth and John Thomson of Duddingston. It is his contention that Hill was 'the final representative of the mainstream Claudian tradition in Scottish landscape painting.'[2] It is possible to construct a sequence, which traces such a classical connection, in the frontispiece of the second volume of *The Land of Burns* (fig. 91).[3] The painting was exhibited at the Scottish Academy in 1834, as *Scottish Merry-Making: View of Nithsdale from the Dalswinton Hills, with Friarscarse, Burns' Farm of Ellisland, Criffel, Solway Firth & Part of the Cumberland Mountains.* The design resembles an engraving after Alexander Runciman of a landscape treating Milton's *L'Allegro*, which was itself based on Virgil's *Georgics* (fig. 92). Runciman's landscape was removed from its Italian setting and placed in Scotland with a distant view of Hill's native town of Perth.[4] Hill took the idea a stage further. He presents a real landscape with the country people of the area, and his poetic inspiration is Scottish – although the picture is still arguably linked to classical reference, by the thought of Robert Burns as the farmer poet and a natural heir of Virgil.

As Murdo Macdonald suggests, Hill's connection with Claude may be largely indirect. The essential link between Hill and the classical tradition is his reputation as a poetic painter. The critical relation between poetry and painting was initially designed to give the weight of classical authority to painting.[5] The attempts to unify the two, made from the Renaissance to the eighteenth century, caused practical difficulties, but the subject matter of one was regarded as appropriate for the other. Joshua Reynolds's *Discourses*, delivered to the Royal Academy in 1778, spoke of this need for a landscape painter to improve on the imperfections of reality by associating his work with the ideal of classical literature:

> Like Nicolas Poussin, he transports us to the environs of ancient Rome, with all the objects which a literary education makes so precious . . . or, like Claude Lorrain, he conducts us to the tranquillity of Arcadian scenes and fairy land.
>
> Like the history-painter, a painter of landscapes in this style and with this conduct, sends the imagination back into antiquity; and like the poet, he makes the elements sympathise with his subject.[6]

When John Brown was persuaded to take up art criticism for the *Witness* in 1846, his article on Hill included the following passage: 'Mr Hill has, in one word, as many faults, but more beauties, – greater reach of imagination, – more of the true poetical temperament, – more power of rendering his own, and bringing out the emotions of others, – in a word, more *genius,* than any other of our native landscape painters.'[7] Brown's meaning is far different from Reynolds's. Essentially, Hill's poetry was personal and local. His work, *The Land of Burns*, took advantage of this character in Robert Burns's writing. But his idea of poetic association and of beauty was based on familiar admiration and experience.

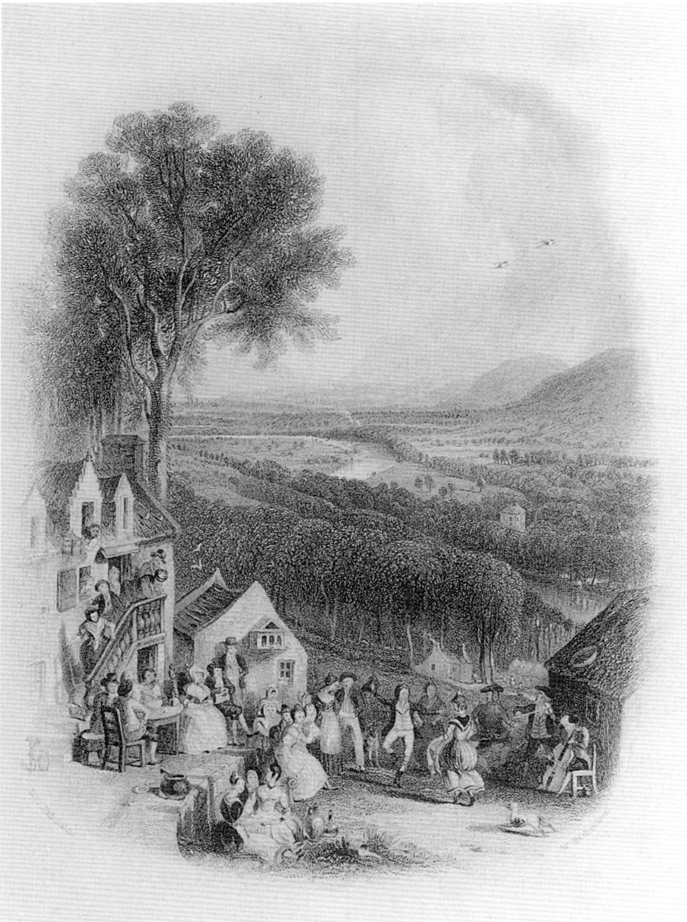

91. D. O. Hill, *Scottish Merry-making: View of Nithsdale*, frontispiece to *The Land of Burns,* volume 2, 1840 .

POETRY AND THE NATIONAL LANDSCAPE

Through the intervention of the British poets, the country had become an object of educated admiration. Following in their wake, respectful tourists headed into the country to experience the same emotions, carrying with them not just the guidebooks and guides to the Picturesque but the poems and novels set in that real landscape.[8] Lord Cockburn was moved by Allan Ramsay's poem, 'The Gentle Shepherd', to hold regular picnics in its setting, Habbie's Howe in the Pentland Hills. He satirised this respectful idea in a letter to his daughter in August 1833, which recounted the gathering of twenty-three friends and the riotous preparations:

> I sat on a stone retired, and reasoned high of Patie and of Ramsay. My soul was with the Gentle Shepherd. But I trust that I kept my temper sufficiently not to let them see how I despised their low tastes. Their food (Oh! to think of food in such a place) consisted of rolls, butter, honey, marmalade, jelly, eggs, cold veal pie, tongue (no want of that) broiled salmon hot (Oh! Oh! hot salmon under the ray of an August morning sun in a pastoral, classical valley) tea, coffee, chocolate – closed on the part of the male, and a few of the female, brutes by a dram – an absolute dram – God bless me – of Whisky!![9]

But it was a serious occasion. He had established the picnic on Allan Ramsay's ground and regularly gathered his friends together there to experience its beauty and associations. Hill was, in Cockburn's terms, 'one of the faithful', and there is a calotype of one such picnic on the hillslope (fig. 93). These parties had their formal graces. In 1852, Hill noted with pleasure the carefully presented flowers:

> A pleasant day of Idlesse at Bonaly yesterday . . . Sally [Hill's niece, Sarah Watson] was with me at Lord Cockburns . . . & enjoyed him much, he was full of mirth & good stories . . . the delicate daughter was with us at breakfast & lunch, and as usual decorated the dinner table to each guest an exquisite bouquet – a peculiar and most beautiful feature of the Bonaly banquets.[10]

James Nasmyth devoted three pages of his autobiography to another meeting at Bonaly, when all the guests were artists: David Roberts, Clarkson Stanfield, Louis and Carl Haag, George Harvey, James Ballantyne and Hill. He described this

92. Alexander Runciman, *Landscape illustrating Milton's 'L'Allegro'.* Engraving. National Gallery of Scotland, Edinburgh.

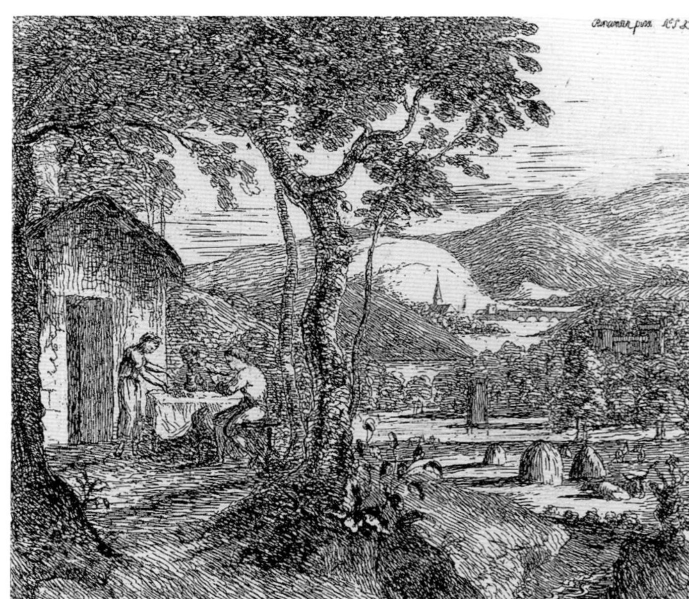

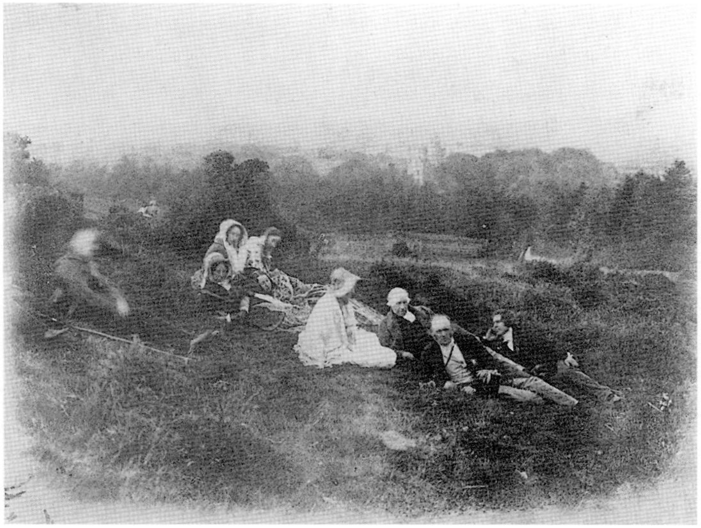

93. D. O. Hill and Robert Adamson, *Picnic at Bonaly*, 1846 or 1847. Calotype. Scottish National Photography Collection , Edinburgh.

favourite spot as 'a semicircular hollow in the hillside, scooped out by the sheep for shelter. It was carpeted and cushioned with a bed of wild thyme, redolent of the very essence of rural fragrance'.[11]

John Gibson Lockhart's account of the beginning and end of Walter Scott's career is specifically written to make the physical connection between the man and the country. He tells of Scott lying on the turf as a crippled child and first hearing the history and poetry of Scotland: 'He says that the consciousness of his existence dated from Sandy-Knowe; and how deep and indelible was the impression, which its romantic localities had left on his imagination, I need not remind the readers of Marmion and the Eve of St John.'[12] Lockhart rounded off the story of Scott's life with an echo of his adult admiration of the Eildon Hills from the viewpoint, still known as Scott's View, where his funeral cortège was delayed: 'on the summit of the hill at Bemersyde – exactly where a prospect of remarkable richness opens, and where Sir Walter had always been accustomed to rein up his horse.'[13]

The idea of the Scottish landscape acting as the poet's muse appears in Robert Chambers's account of Lincluden Abbey, written for *The Land of Burns*:

> To stroll in the evening along the bank of the Nith, to lounge amongst the ruins of Lincluden, to linger there till the moon rose upon the scene, formed a favourite recreation of Burns. His eldest son . . . pointed out to the present writer a little knoll to the south of the church, from which a view is obtained of the landscape beyond the Cluden, set as it were in a pair of picture-frames formed of two ruined windows. On this spot Burns used to fix himself, and gaze on the scene for many minutes at a time. Dr Currie [editor of Burns] states that the muse was favourable to him during these delightful walks.[14]

Hill's own interest in this idea of a fictionally possessed landscape is expressed from the same place in *The Poet's Dream at Lincluden* (fig. 61). Burns lies asleep on the turf before the abbey, surrounded by the figures of a dream – a 'phantasma' of historical characters and fairies, helpfully catalogued by Hill: 'elves, spunkies, brownies, kelpies, mermaids . . . witches, warlocks and worricows'.[15] His concept consciously derives from Shakespeare's *Midsummer Night's Dream*:

> As on another 'mid summer night' a difference of opinion arises between the royal pair, in regard to the nature of the vision to be presented. The voice of the king is still for war, and he wishes to inspire the poet to sing of high and noble deeds. The queen gives her voice for gentler and humbler themes; and the poet accordingly profits by the dispute, for instead of one class of subjects, his soul is gladdened with a varied series of spectral tableaux, which go to fit him for excelling in all the walks of his art.[16]

John Wilson commented on this picture: 'It is but justice to Mr Hill to add, that much of the expression, and particularly the *national* expression, of his sketch, has vanished in the process of its transference to steel, notwithstanding the best skill of an excellent engraver.'[17] This is a somewhat obscure remark but it leads to an important point. This frontispiece is a counterpart to the frontispiece of the second volume, discussed above, which addresses the reality of Burns's setting – the natural or visible inspiration of his work. *The Poet's Dream* offers Burns's historical and fictional inspiration, but the figures in the dream are equally British. Spunkies and worricows have replaced nymphs and dryads.

Here again, Hill was following Walter Scott's lead. His *Minstrelsy of the Scottish Border* (1801–2) published a number of ballads with fairy themes and included an essay on 'The Fairies of Popular Superstition', which related the fairies to lesser classical gods. He wrote of the land around a Roman altar erected near Roxburgh Castle: 'a vicinity more delightfully appropriate to the abode of the silvan deities can hardly be found . . . altogether a kingdom for Oberon and Titania to reign in.'[18] Scott distinguished fairies as the invention of the Celts, and claimed they displayed 'that superiority of taste and fancy which, with the love of music and poetry, has been generally ascribed to their race'.[19] This seductive idea of the fairies he added to the historic idea of them holding a kind of medieval court: 'At their processions they paraded more beautiful steeds than those of mere earthly parentage – the hawks and hounds which they employed in their chase were of the first race. At their daily banquets, the board was set forth with a splendour which the proudest kings of the earth dared not aspire to.'[20] Scott was offering a visual and poetic idea in which remarkable beauty was tied to a historic and cultural nationalism. This helps to explain the particularly Scottish obsession with fairies in the nineteenth and early twentieth century. Scott's fairies were an ancient part of the country's culture, to be preserved and respected in the same manner as a ruined abbey. They became earthly personifications left over from a sophisticated Celtic culture: historical spirits of the land.

The affection for fairies, which has been addressed recently as a Victorian idea, comes from the poetic convention, starting obviously with Edmund Spenser's *Fairy Queen* and Shakespeare.[21] It seems possible that the impulse at the end of the eighteenth century is more a part of the Romantic movement than has been allowed: both William Blake and Fuseli painted Oberon and Titania. With the celebrations of Ossian and the increase in Christian spirituality, Romanticism followed imagination and a line of faith rather than rationality. It is ironic that the rationality of the eighteenth and early nineteenth century took the fairies out of the nursery – declaring such imagination damaging to the infant mind – and they were only allowed to return there in force in the 1840s.[22] The sense that they were an adult concern was perhaps exaggerated by the dream convention and the related consumption of alcohol or narcotics, which might lead to such fantasies. The fairies in Hill's *Poet's Dream* are an adult set if only because they have their own whisky still: '[The scene] is lighted up from the fire of a fairy distillery, which [shows] the very nature of that spell of power which has conjured up the vision; namely the very potent "but very natural necromancy of the punch-bowl".'[23]

The past, both historical and imaginative could occupy the landscape invisibly and intangibly – the fairies could ride through cornfields and in the morning 'the fient of a hoof mark was there nor a blade broken.'[24] Hill's paintings naturally contained that sense of allusion and absent/present opposition. Here the idea of 'dissolving views' or the pantomime transformation scene, whilst childish, provide an easy analogy to the more profound attempt to express spirituality in the spirit or association of place. For Hill this could be human, modern, fairy, religious, historical, literary or mythological.[25]

The complete distinction between this exaggerated imaginative work and the photograph, *The Fairy Tree at Colinton* (pl. 16), is a template of the opposition between Hill's earlier illustration and his work with the calotype. In the photograph, nature is offered unaltered by the construction of artificial whimsy. We are shown the kind of inspiration – suggestion rather than definition – which the real landscape would offer, dancing light, the shifting flicker on the edge of vision, but no more. The one is a literal expression of his imagination; the other is a constructed sketch of the experience that rouses the imagination. It is an opposition that cuts to the heart of the calotypes' success.

HILL AND TURNER

One ostensible connection between Hill's painting and the model of Claude is simply his interest in sunset light, which emerges strongly in the 1850s. In 1851, for example, four of his paintings in the academy exhibition had the word 'sunset' in the title. Here the connection may well have been made or at least reinforced by Hill's overt admiration for J. M. W. Turner.

When Hill moved in to Rock House in 1844, it could be assumed that his reason was practical – to work more closely with Adamson on the development of the calotype and to share the rent. He unquestionably had a second motive. Rock House was the highest private building on Calton Hill, with a magnificent view of the city. It is no coincidence that the first 360 degree panorama was devised by Robert Barker in the 1780s from Calton Hill.[26] J. G. Lockhart wrote, from this standpoint:

> Here there must always be present the idea of the comparative littleness of all human works. Here the proudest of palaces must be content to catch the shadows of mountains; and the grandest of fortresses to appear like the dwellings of pygmies, perched on the very bulwarks of creation. Everywhere – all around – you have rocks frowning over rocks in imperial elevation, and descending, among the smoke and dust of a city, into dark depths, such as nature alone can excavate. The builders of the old city, too, appear as if they had made nature the model of her architecture. Seen through the lowering mist which almost perpetually envelopes them, the huge masses of these erections, so high, so rugged in their outlines, so heaped together, and conglomerated and wedged into each other, are not easily to be distinguished from the yet larger and

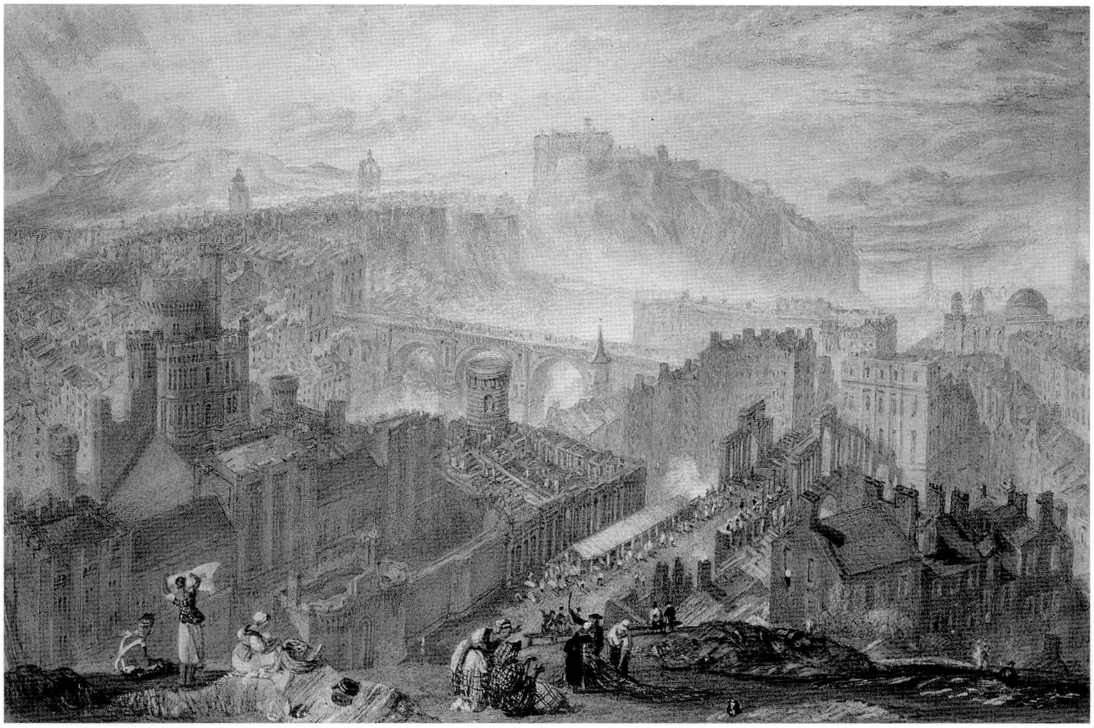

94. J.M.W. Turner, *Edinburgh from the Calton Hill*, *c.* 1819. Watercolour. National Gallery of Scotland, Edinburgh.

bolder forms of cliff and ravine, among which their foundations have been pitched. There is a certain gloomy indistinctness in the formation of these fantastic piles, which leaves the eye, that would scrutinize and penetrate them, unsatisfied and dim with gazing.[27]

Turner's watercolour, taken from just above Rock House for Walter Scott's *Provincial Antiquities and Picturesque Scenery of Scotland* (1819–26), has the same kind of sublime exaggeration inherent in Lockhart's description (fig. 94); he sketched a panorama of nearly 180 degrees and contracted it to within half the real proportion.[28] In the watercolour, Rock House, an ordinary brown building, occupies a prominent position as a foreground anchor to the golden view of the city. Scott wrote in the text: 'The point which Mr Turner has selected for the view is precisely that upon which every passenger, however much accustomed to the wonderful scene, is inclined to pause, and with eyes unsatisfied with seeing, to gaze on the mingled and almost tumultuous scene which lies before and beneath him.'[29] This means that, by the time Hill moved in to Rock House, the site of Calton Hill had become a notable Romantic platform, endorsed by the poetic presence of Scott and Turner. That Hill looked at and discussed the view in these terms is suggested by an entry in Elizabeth Rigby's journal, in December 1844: 'The view from Mr Hill's garden of the city with its wreaths of smoke reminds you of Turner more than Turner does you of it, because he has seen Nature more truly than most that look on her.'[30]

Hill's enthusiasm for Turner is first revealed in a letter requesting the loan of a painting for the academy's 1831 exhibition, asking: 'if it is in your power, favour the Exhibition with one of those splendid achievements in Landscape which have raised your name so high in that most delightful department of art.'[31] In the 1840s and early 1850s, Hill also managed to secure, with Roberts's help, important examples of his work to show in the academy's exhibitions.[32] In 1845, the year Turner's *Palestrina* was sent up to Edinburgh, Hill retired to bed with a cold and the first volume of Ruskin's *Modern Painters*:

As I felt on Saturday Evening that *something* was coming on, from a most presaging & uncomfortable shiver all over, I before going home purchased the Oxford Graduates Modern Painters, which I have devoured with intense interest and gratification. I rejoiced to find that my early admiration of Turner which has increased upon me, is and has been raised on no sandy foundation, but that what the world has called his caprice is in reality to be considered as almost divine revealings. I envy you coming in contact with the head which could conceive – and the hand which

> could execute such a work as your kindness has procured to gladden and revive us here – and no less the mind which could so analyse and the pen so describe the creations of that mortal mind.[33]

After Turner's death, Hill described him as: 'A most glorious artist.'[34]

In the earlier part of the century, Turner was a familiar figure in the Scottish landscape.[35] There is, indeed, a possibility that his appreciation of the idea of painting in atmospheric terms was first learnt in Scotland, in 1801: 'Finberg points out the novel freedom and rapidity of many of the drawings in the Scottish sketchbooks, suggesting that they mark the final disconnection from the topographical discipline of Turner's youth. It seems likely that the atmosphere of Scotland, especially of its mountains, contributed largely to his sense of emancipation.'[36]

The idea of Turner's reception in Scotland has been coloured by Walter Scott's apparent preference for the landscape work of the Reverend John Thomson.[37] Lockhart's opinion of the state of landscape art in Scotland in 1819 offers a different and more complimentary view:

> For the first time is Scotland now possessed of admirable landscape painters, as well as historical painters. With regard to landscape painting, it is very true that she has not yet equalled the present glories of the sister kingdom; but then the world has only one TURNER, and Scotland comes far nearer to the country which has had the honour of producing that great genius than any other country in Europe.[38]

This was published when Hill was only seventeen years old, but he was by then already studying in the Trustees Academy in Edinburgh. Some five years later, James Skene, who worked alongside Turner, wrote:

> One of the greatest landscape painters of the present age, Mr. Turner, seems to have grappled so vigorously with this important desideratum in the art, that much may be expected from his system of study and acute observation. So far as he has gone, eminent success has attended his footsteps; and, aided by the discoveries daily making in the mysteries of light, his scrutinizing genius seems to tremble on the verge of some new discovery in colour, which may prove of the first importance to art.[39]

Despite his admiration, the only written indication Hill gave that he might be emulating Turner comes unexpectedly when he is discussing his intention of publishing a hundred calotypes as a 'sort of Liber Studiorum in its way'.[40] In his calotype of the publisher John Blackie, a volume of *The Land of Burns* (with Hill's name written on the spine in the negative) leans against Turner's *Liber Studiorum*.

The influence of Turner's work may be seen in the general sense that Hill may have been spurred by its ambition to offer an exploration of the different characters and conditions of the Scottish landscape. In 1850, Hill responded to the loan to the academy of Turner's *Wreck of a Transport Ship*: 'Nothing I am sure could better show to this portion of the island, the greatness of the mind and the giant power of the poet-painter of the ocean, than this most noble work; indeed I feel that its presence among us would give new aspirations, – and higher resolves to our whole school.'[41] This admiration suggests a possible connection between one of Hill's sea pictures for *The Land of Burns*, *Turnberry Castle* (fig. 95), and a picture in the *Liber Studiorum*, Turner's *The Lost Sailor*. In Turner's picture, the storm is at its height and the sailor is: 'yet living, dashed in the night against a granite coast, – his body and outstretched hands just seen in the trough of a mountain wave, between it and the overhanging wall of rock.'[42] In Hill's picture, the storm is retreating out to sea with a last flash of lightning in a black sky, leaving the rolling sea, which has wrecked a ship and cast up a sailor on the shore. Hill may have been paying tribute to Turner, acknowledging his transcendent power in the field, by offering the next scene in the drama. Robert Chambers points out in the text that Burns did not write about Turnberry Castle, so the design and inspiration are certainly Hill's in this case.

While they lack the bravura of Turner's interpretation, *The Land of Burns* landscapes are defined in terms of Turner's poetic idea of immediate experience of light and weather, where landscape is a shifting proposal made by and seen through the atmosphere. When the paintings were exhibited at the academy, they were given titles of this kind: in 1835, *The Field of Bannockburn: Effect of Moonrise and Sunset*; in 1837, *Roslin Castle and Glen: Summer after Heavy Rain – Painted on the Spot*; in 1840, *Abbey and Bridge of Kelso: Summer Night: Effect of Aurora Borealis.*

Hill's interest in atmospheric effects was remarked on in John Brown's first review of Hill's work, where he made a deliberate distinction which elevated and defined Hill's poetry: 'I mean, if allowed to go on, to set D. O. Hill above Horatio [MacCulloch] as a Poet or maker.'[43] He made this distinction by comparing the sky in Hill's *Durham* with the sky in MacCulloch's painting: 'the one is a medium and an element; the other looks like a curtain of clouds, hanging straight down'.[44] Brown's subsequent review of the first two

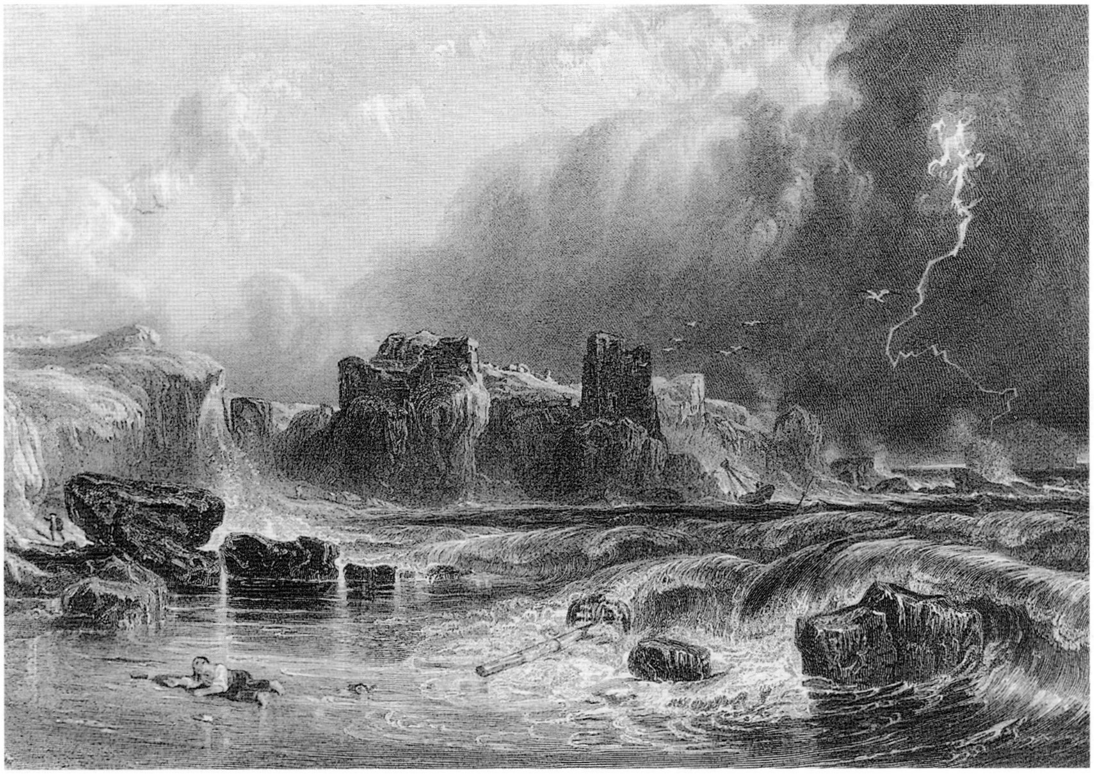

95. D. O. Hill, *Turnberry Castle*. Steel engraving for *The Land of Burns*, 1840.

volumes of *Modern Painters* ends with an analysis of three pictures in Ruskin's terms: one of Turner's sketches for the *Liber Studiorum*, George Harvey's *Glen of the Enterkin* and a sketch by Hill done from his window in Inverleith Row, which was:

> done in a fine frenzy of an hour; it has exquisite colour, and is as sweet and deep in its tones as his own voice; but what is it? Look and you will see, wait and you will feel. There is nothing of earth to be seen but the tops of some great trees, among them an old fir with its cones of last year. Lying across them and giving them power, and getting for itself distance and freedom, is a long line of evening sky: under it and above it clouds of unimaginable colours. The broad sun is sinking, all but sunk down 'in his tranquillity' and in that line of light, added by the painter (for though the sea was not visible to his eye, he wanted it to be there) you see the sea! and on it is the gentleness of the upper heavens. There we have a scene in itself imaginative to all minds of ordinary sensibility, made more so by a mind of higher sensibility, which works under an exalted condition of its whole nature. And fixes for ever upon that mere sketch, the strong and delicate but evanescent feeling as well as sensations of that hour.[45]

A later opinion of Hill's work, by Elizabeth Sharp, also refers to the idea of Hill as a painter who worked best with an accidental immediacy. Her opinion is presumably based on discussions with Amelia Hill and examination of the works she owned after Hill's death:

> A greater individuality, however, is seen in his slight sketches, impressions rapidly noted down in a few seconds on paper, with chalk, pencil or watercolors, or when none of these implements was at hand, with the point of a finger dipped into ink. There are stronger contrasts, greater boldness, in these sketches than in his finished work. A careful observation of the play of light characterises his painting and his photography; in his paintings it is of that peculiar quality of light that belongs to a moist climate. He was very sensitive to that wonderful 'swimming' effect of the sea's surface on the sky, an effect often seen in hilly islands, or when the sea's inlets are long and tortuous. With water-colors, in his youth a comparatively new medium, his effort was to keep his colors pure and simple. He learned from William Leech [William Leighton Leitch] . . . how to draw with three colors only, red, blue and yellow.[46]

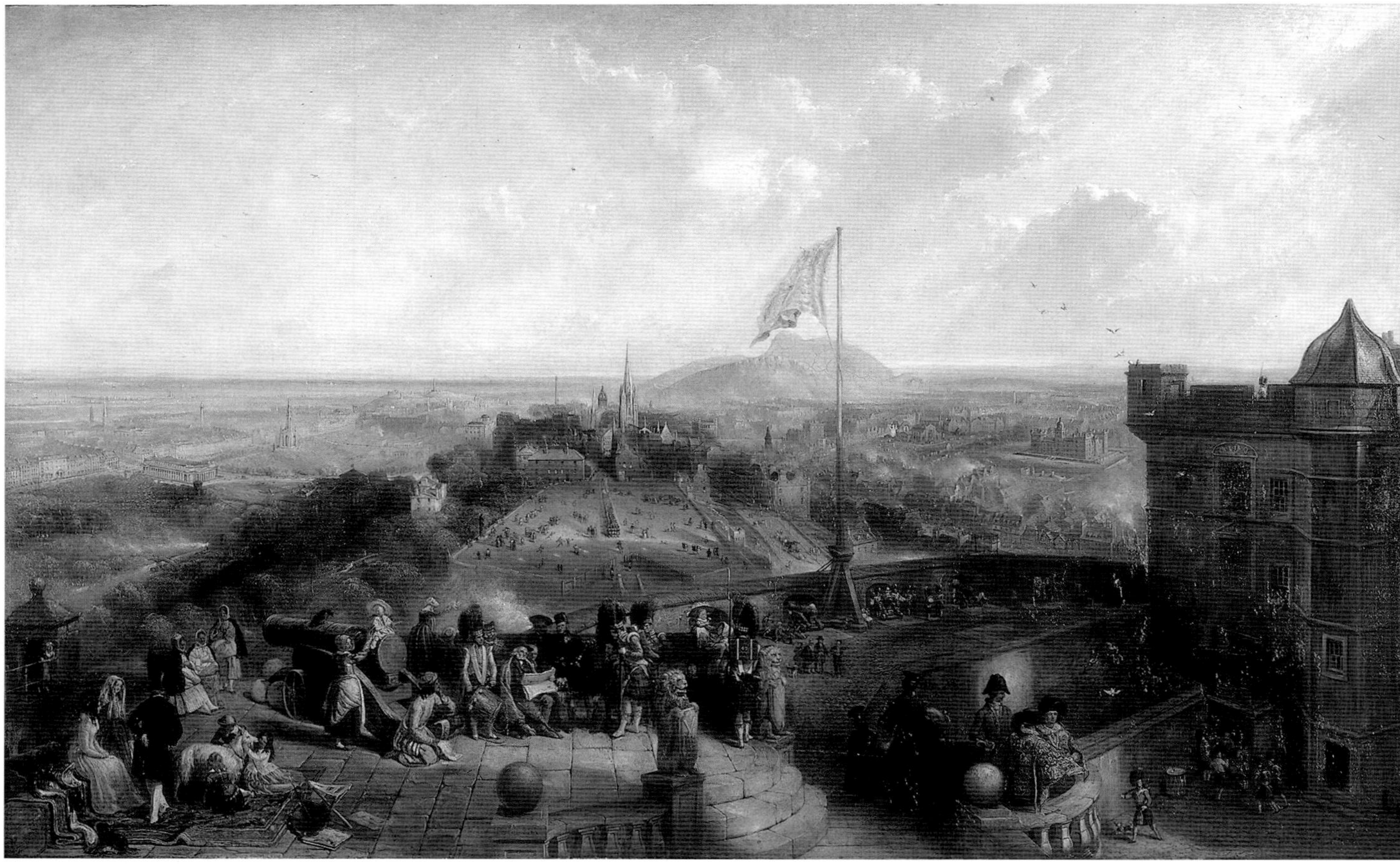

96. D. O. Hill, *Edinburgh from the Castle,* 1846–7. Oil on canvas. National Gallery of Scotland, Edinburgh.

Ruskin's *Modern Painters* was both stimulating and embarrassing to Hill: 'The exalted views there [illegible] of Landscape Painting made me as well they might blush for the truant part I had played from a noble profession.'[47] We might assume from this, that the sketch Brown admired was an attempt by Hill to paint in response to Ruskin's criticism. However, Brown gave the picture a specific domestic location to stress its immediacy. Hill lived in Inverleith Row from 1839 to 1844, when he moved to Rock House. The drawing was therefore at least two years old, when Hill read *Modern Painters*. It may be that Hill responded to Ruskin in exploring another familiar reality, *Edinburgh from the Castle*.

EDINBURGH FROM THE CASTLE

By a useful coincidence, Hill and David Roberts painted this same subject in 1846–7, and the comparison is telling (figs 96 and 97). Hill was such an amiable man that he rarely expressed dislike, and his aesthetic taste could well have been biased by his friendships. He admired Roberts and relied on his help in bringing in important works for the Academy exhibitions. But an opinion of Roberts's painting emerges inadvertently in a letter Hill wrote to him, in which he said of *Modern Painters*: 'when reading his glowing pages I was so fascinated with the truth and beauty of his remarks, that I more than once thought of communicating to the Author my entire sympathy and admiration of his labours.'[48] This 'entire sympathy' fails to consider the passage Ruskin wrote shortly before the praise of Turner, which criticised David Roberts's painting of Roslin Chapel for a lack of interest in natural light. It may be that Hill was tacitly in agreement with Ruskin, who added:

> The general feebleness of the effect is increased by the insertion of the figures as violent pieces of local colour unaffected by the light and unblended with the hues around them, and bearing evidence of having been painted from models or draperies in the dead light of a room instead of sunshine . . . it is bitterly to be regretted

that the accuracy and elegance of his work should not be aided by the genuineness of hue and effect which can only be given by the uncompromising effort to paint, not a fine picture but an impressive and known *verity*.[49]

Roberts's painting of Edinburgh is a grand architectural compilation, based on controlled perspective – a splendid, uncluttered stage. His foreground figures are mostly designed to direct the eye to the view, and the soldiers (taken from a calotype group) act as a decorative indication of his standpoint on a corner of the castle.[50] Hill's picture is both less structured and more animated; there are a remarkable number of people in the castle, on the esplanade below and in the windows of the various buildings. The people are the living embodiment of the city's history. They are identifiable individuals, not stock figures – some of them are visitors to the capital, like John Ban Mackenzie the piper, and Finlay the deerstalker, or the Indian man. Others, like the fishwives, are its normal inhabitants. They range in age from the infant in arms to the old man; and in historical and social reference from the fashionable group on the left to the heralds on the right, from the wealthy to the working man. The very buildings of the scene make a reference to the famous individuals of the past, from the newly built Scott Monument on Princes Street to the sunlit house, left of the esplanade, where the poet, Allan Ramsay, had lived.

The painting was exhibited in London in 1852 with the particular title, *Edinburgh on the Queen's Birthday, Viewed from the Mons Meg Battery, Castle – News from India*. The picture has the immediacy of natural light and movement, with a stiff breeze ruffling the standard and shifting the clouds and their shadows, and a puff of smoke from a fired cannon to celebrate the royal birthday. This is a landscape animated by the present time, filled out by the human histories. The distance is confused by the foliage of trees and the smoke of the Old Town.[51] Hill and Adamson took two sets of panoramic calotypes from the castle, with the standard and large camera,

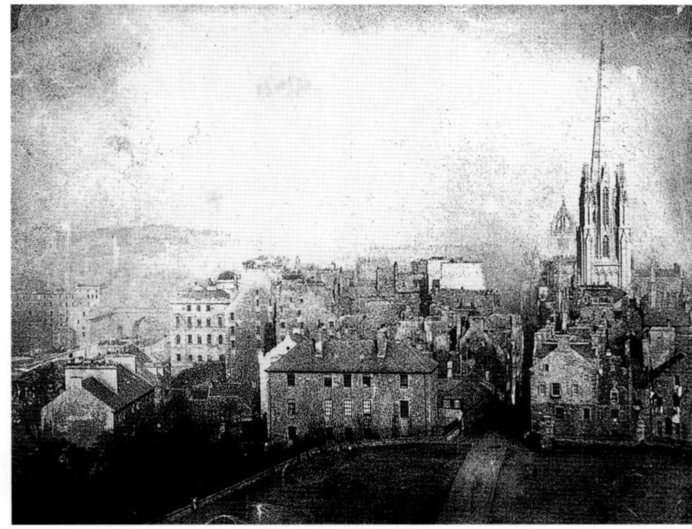

98. D. O. Hill and Robert Adamson, *High Street from the Castle, part of a panorama*, 1846. Calotype. Glasgow University, Special Collections.

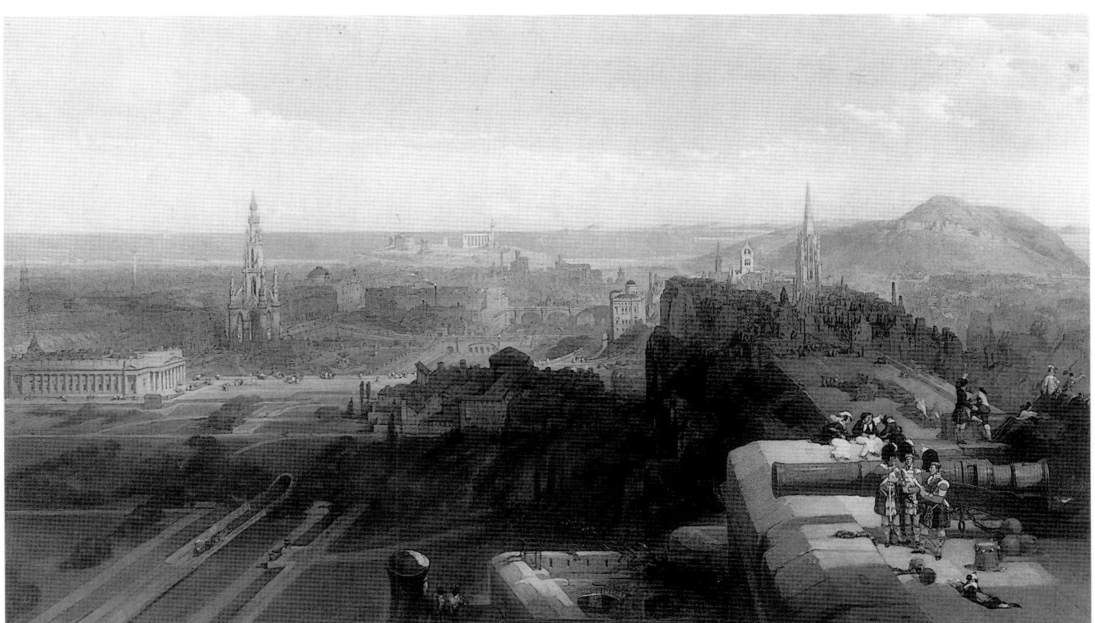

97. David Roberts, *Edinburgh from the Castle,* 1847. Oil on canvas. Yale Center for British Art, Paul Mellon Collection, New Haven, Connecticut.

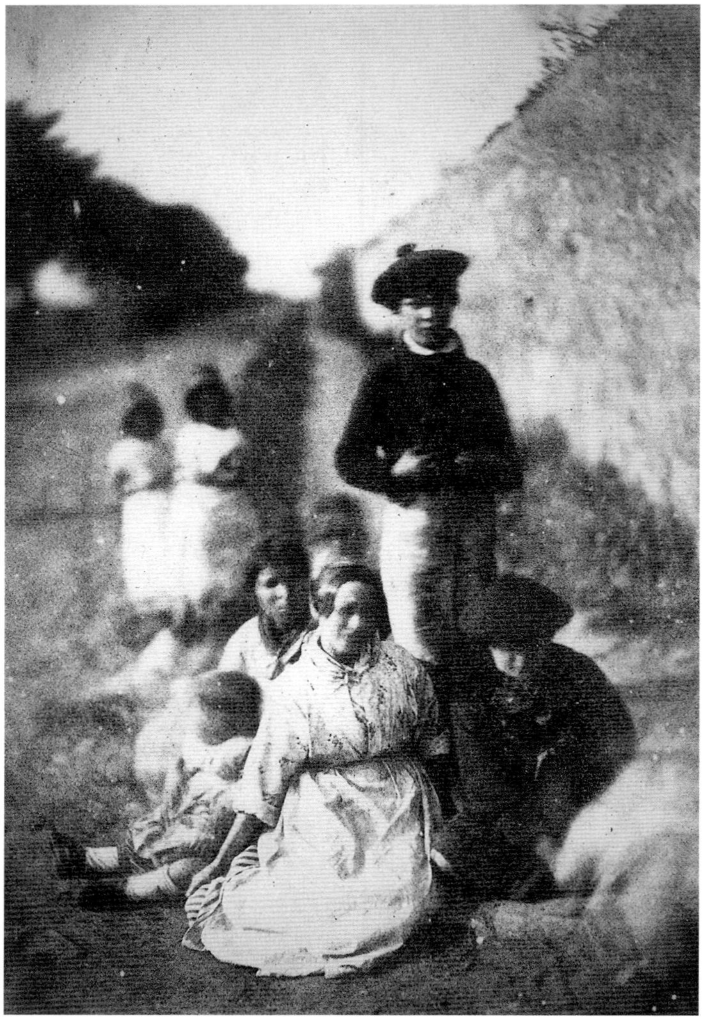

99. D. O. Hill and Robert Adamson, *Unknown Group in the Landscape*, 1843–7. Carbon print from the calotype negative. Scottish National Photography Collection, Edinburgh.

for this painting (fig. 98). In translating them into paint, Hill exercised particular care with the calotype looking south, where the view is veiled by smoke from the chimneys below. This photograph he apparently first turned into a monochrome oil sketch, to feel his way from the one medium to the other before adding the colour: a reverse of the engraver's habit in working from the painting to the engraving.

The picture is an extension of Hill's first interest in the calotype process: the proposal to apply the calotype to: 'the execution of large pictures representing difft. bodies & classes of individuals'.[52] In taking the panoramic series of calotypes, Hill was presumably attempting the naturalism of true perspective. This was one of the great obsessions of art, from the invention of linear perspective by Filippo Brunelleschi in the fifteenth century: the problem of making a convincing view of the three-dimensional world on a flat surface.[53] The difficulty of achieving both accurate and convincing perspective had been evident in the limitations of the treatises on the subject, whose geometry was most appropriate to the distinct lines of classical architecture.[54] In Hugh Miller's essay on the calotype, there is a passage about perspective, relating to a picture of the neoclassical George Street in Edinburgh (fig. 57):

> In this little brown drawing . . . the truth is truth according to the rules of lineal perspective, unerringly deduced . . . Here for the first time, on this square of paper, have we the data on which perspective may be rendered a certain science. We have but to apply our compasses and rules in order to discover the proportions in which, according to their distances, objects diminish . . . in the architectural drawings of the calotype the perspective is that of nature itself; and to arrive at just conclusions, we have but to measure and compare, and ascertain proportions.[55]

However, Hill presumably found that the advantage of the calotype lay more in the appearance of a landscape than in the geometric measurement of its buildings. He was attempting to express not just the architecture but its necessary relation to the volcanic site of the Royal Mile, which appears to roll and shift as it did in geological history. It might be supposed, from the reduction of distance and flattening of light in the calotypes, that Hill could not seek information on aerial perspective in their construction. There is, however, one engaging example in the calotype work, which is almost a textbook illustration of both linear and aerial perspective (fig. 99). The wall, the path, the lines of grass and trees all recede conformably to a vanishing point. The pyramidal foreground group is arranged with a visual balance of weight to the right, depending on the two boys in dark jackets and bonnets. Behind the group to the left, some feet away, are two girls wearing straw bonnets, whose position is defined in a lighter range of tone and a lesser focus, expressing the aerial perspective.

The known problem, in using optical devices to measure perspective, was that they offered a one-eyed view from a fixed point. In taking a series of calotypes covering roughly 180 degrees, Hill presented himself with the immediate difficulty that he had a swivelled, rather than fixed, position for his factual images. He solved the problem in two ways. Firstly, he stepped back and up, so that his swing of vision was hypothetically reduced; secondly, he had the more interesting idea of building a warp into the foreground – not just flattening the actual curve of the half-moon battery but making a sprawling visual curve of stone and shadow. He constructed an S-shape between the sunlit stone ball on the right, round the castle wall, back up to the left, downwards into the valley, coming back up again to the right through the dark shadow over the old city. This exaggerated the sense of life and movement in the picture and encouraged sympathetic movement in the viewer.[56] The use of light and shadow enabled him to suggest the poetic and moral truth in such details as the light stone of the new Free Church buildings, which pierce the real and moral shadow over the Old Town. A lesser detail, like the illuminated stone ball, echoes the ball in the calotype of Thomas Chalmers and his family (pl. 4), and might serve as an indication of a little world, expressing the function of the foreground groups.

An examination of the landscape calotypes in relation to the *Edinburgh* painting shows that Hill had considerable respect for their truth. Even minor detail, like the drawn blinds in the windows of the building at the end of the esplanade on the left and the awnings on the shops in Princes Street, was transcribed, albeit selectively, to indicate the human activity indoors. This engaged the idea of trivial and unimportant truth, captured naturally by the camera, as a poetic idea of transience and humanity. The manifest difference between Hill's view and Roberts's is simply that in Hill's picture the buildings are proportionately smaller.[57] Roberts enlarged and squared the buildings to his frame, built arbitrary parallels and flattened the land to achieve greater dignity for the New Town – his city is a stage for drama. Interestingly, there was a doubt expressed of the truth of Roberts's painting when it was published as a lithograph in 1847, and the test was photography. According to James Ross's commentary on his old ledger:

> September 20, 1847 – Received from Mr Crighton, printseller, £1 14s for a view from the Castle. This gentleman had just received for sale Roberts's lithograph of Calton Hill. While every one praised and admired the beauty of this picture, there were those who denied its truth of outline. This calotype was taken for the purpose of settling the matter.[58]

Hill's city is organic, it is built and lived in by real people and grows from a real landscape.[59]

Like his interest in the figure, Hill's approach to landscape was less concerned with ideal construction than with the visual experience, which might be tied to a knowledge of its structure but was not dictated by it. The indication, in *Edinburgh from the Castle*, of an interest in the underlying geology of the city connects the painting with an attempt, probably initiated by Hill, to improve the understanding of landscape. A proposal was put to the academy in 1851:

> The Council considering the widely spread study of Physical Science and particularly of Geology and that a knowledge of the phenomena is now as necessary to the Landscape Painter as Anatomy is to the Historical Painter resolved to recommend to the General Meeting the propriety of adding a Professor of Geology to the Academy's list of its other Honorary professors – and . . . to recommend to them to elect to this office Mr Hugh Miller as a gentleman whose knowledge and genius would do much honour to the Academy and probably much advantage to its members and students.[60]

The idea was eventually dismissed, on the grounds that: 'this application and elucidation can only be made by one who is both a geologist and a painter – because he ought to be competent to instruct the student how to apply that science to his art'.[61] The proposer on record is John Syme, a portrait painter. Hill, as secretary, did not have a voice in the proposals or voting of the Council, but he was the man who prepared the agenda (ensuring that the question was raised at four meetings), and he spoke positively of the proposal to Noël Paton.[62] It seems reasonable to suppose that it was Hill's idea.

Geological discoveries and speculation were amongst the most dramatic and disconcerting explorations of the time, unsettling the established concepts of human history.[63] Hill's advocacy was presumably based on the assumption that a knowledge of the structure of the landscape would lead to an understanding of something more than the composition of stone and the character of the vegetation it supported. The apparent practicality of this study was still designed to explore areas of poetic inspiration. Miller, himself, saw no division between such reality and its potential meaning or ultimate import. He wrote:

> It is said that modern science is adverse to the exercise and development of the imaginative faculty. But is it really so? Are visions such as those in which we have been indulging less richly charged with that poetic pabulum on which fancy feeds and grows strong, than those ancient tales of enchantment and *faery* which beguiled of old, in solitary homesteads, the long winter nights. Because science flourishes, must poesy decline? The complaint serves but to betray the weakness of the class who urge it.[64]

THE HISTORIC AND MORAL LANDSCAPE
Greyfriars Churchyard

In common with Miller and Turner, Hill wanted to explore the real landscape. The end purpose was the Romantic proposal, suggesting 'a deeper and otherwise unknowable reality behind what can be perceived'.[65] His landscapes were full of history and often a melancholy sense of the past. There is only one picture of Edinburgh in *The Land of Burns*, and that was *Edinburgh Castle from the Gray Friars Churchyard* (fig. 53).[66] The castle is seen behind and above the tombs, in a haze of distance. The churchyard offers a frame and a support to the castle as the religious and mortal base to the secular power, reflected in the painting's exhibition title, *In the Greyfriars Churchyard, Edinburgh: Cameronians Visiting Martyrs' Graves*. Robert Chambers's text for this engraving makes no particular connection with Burns, but he does add a verse written in defence of the Covenanters:

> The solemn league and covenant
> Cost Scotland blood – cost Scotland tears;
> But it seal'd freedom's sacred cause –
> If thou'rt a slave, indulge thy sneers. [67]

Greyfriars was historically important as the place where the Presbyterian Covenant was signed. When Thomas Guthrie was appointed as minister to the parish, a friend wrote:

> within its walls the first signatures were appended to the Covenant; and I doubt not many on that day felt that the Lord was there. The ground that encircles it is sacred, and the man must be dead to all feeling whose soul is not stirred within him, when everything that meets his view reminds him that he is 'compassed about with a great cloud of witnesses', and brings him into contact with 'the noble army of martyrs'.[68]

Several hundred of the Covenanters were imprisoned here after the Battle of Bothwell Bridge in 1679. It was therefore a place of religious pilgrimage. The Cameronians were both the regiment formed originally of Presbyterians, who rallied to the cause of William III, and the seventeenth-century sect who later became the Reformed Presbyterian Church of Scotland. In the choice of setting and the identification of the figures, Hill had made a picture admiring the purer form of Presbyterian worship, in advance of the Disruption.

Hill debated issuing an album of calotypes of Greyfriars alone. The churchyard is remarkable for its seventeenth-century tombs, vigorously carved from designs equally appropriate for bookplates, and one of the Greyfriars calotypes appears as a frontispiece for the album of a hundred calotypes. This resemblance underlines the purpose of graveyards as a kind of textbook, where the inscriptions on the tombs were intended to be read for their moral and historical content.[69] Hugh Miller's passage, quoted in chapter seven, endorses the natural authority of the gravedigger and the stonemason, as the interpreters of the place. In one of the calotypes, *The Artist and the Gravedigger*, Hill posed with two of his nieces, listening to the gravedigger at the Dennistoun tomb. In the painting, a gravedigger directs the attention of two elderly people, and there is also a soldier, with his wife and child, who is reaching out to the tomb.

To the left of the soldier's family in the Greyfriars painting is the Nasmyth monument. There are at least six calotypes of this. Probably the most significant shows Thomas Duncan, sitting pointing to an inscription while Hill listens, sketchbook in hand (pl. 40).[70] The tomb commemorated the ancestors of Alexander Nasmyth, who was the friend and teacher of both Duncan and Hill and who had died in 1840. The two painters are, therefore, offering respect to his memory. The stone apparently bore several inscriptions.[71] An early eighteenth-century account offered a translation from the Latin inscription, which read:

> Here lyes a Flower, that with the too much haste,
> Of fates cut down, did in her blossom waste;
> What graver Eye, contemplating thy dust
> O happy Nasmyth, after thee, will trust
> The smiles of Nature? Or presume to say,
> This well set morn foresigns a hopeful day?
> O may thy grave untainted like thy years,
> Grow ever green, bedewed with Sister-tears.[72]

The monument originally showed a shrouded figure, rising up from the dead, but the figure has broken. A sapling has lodged in the stone and split it, turning the grave to green. The tree is a powerful symbol in Christianity – it is the 'tree of knowledge of good and evil', the origin of death in the Book of Genesis; it is its counterpart, the Tree of Life, the cross that Christ dies on and the source of human redemption.[73] The actual tree breaking the grave is an ash, the natural tree of graveyards. It takes no particular taste for punning to see the living ash springing from the ultimate sign of death – dust and ashes – and with it, such complementary poetic reference as:

> Ev'n from the tomb the voice of Nature cries,
> Ev'n in our ashes live their wonted fires.[74]

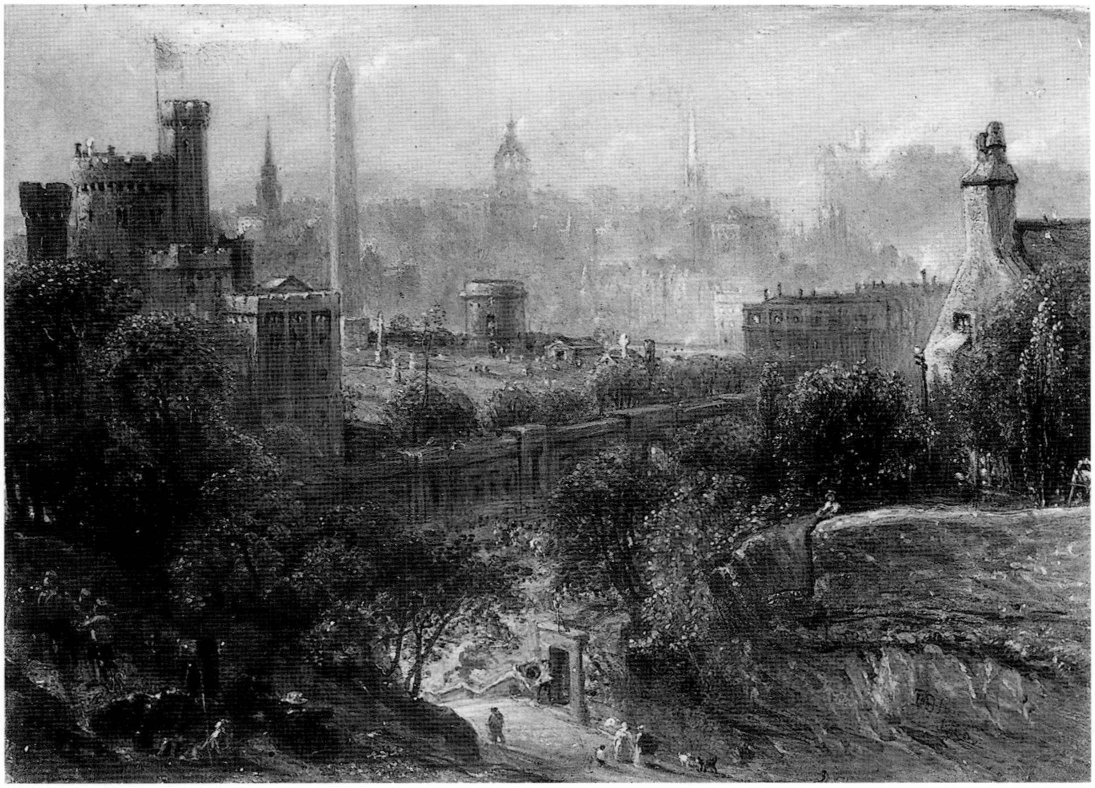

100. D. O. Hill, *In Memoriam: the Calton*, 1862. Oil on canvas. Edinburgh City Art Centre, Edinburgh.

And it may be that Hill also thought of the Norse Yggdrasil, the universal tree, described by Thomas Carlyle:

> Igdrasil, the Ash-tree of Existence, has its roots deep-down in the kingdoms of Hela or Death; its trunk reaches up heaven-high, spreads its boughs over the whole Universe . . . At the foot . . . sit Three Nornas, Fates, – the Past, Present, Future; watering its roots from the Sacred Well . . . Its boughs are histories of Nations. The rustle of it is the noise of Human Existence . . . the breath of Human Passion rustling through it . . . It is the past, the present and the future . . . I find no similitude so true as this of a Tree. Beautiful; altogether beautiful and great.[75]

The tree may have had a further personal meaning for Hill and Duncan. James Nasmyth talked of his father's enthusiasm for old trees when assisting landowners with landscape design. He made little models for his painting, and one of these was known as 'The Family Tree', each of the family making a twig or small branch.[76] Such a historical, natural and literary focus for contemplation was a phenomenal argument for the potential revelation of truth in nature and, by extension, in photography.[77]

IN MEMORIAM

Hill's most poignant pictures were the two he painted for his son-in-law after his daughter's death in 1862.[78] These were the scenes of her childhood at Rock House (fig. 100) and her adult life in Newington.[79] The historical precedent for painting a landscape as a memorial comes from John Constable's tribute to Joshua Reynolds, which was exhibited in 1836, and from Turner's *Peace – Burial at Sea*, in memory of David Wilkie, exhibited in 1842.[80] Constable's picture uses the landscape to encompass the carved stone memorial to the artist. The patron, Sir George Beaumont, built the monument in his grounds, and planted an avenue of arching trees as a natural Gothic aisle. Wordsworth wrote a tribute in verse. Constable added imaginary busts of Michelangelo and Raphael to the scene and introduced nature itself in the presence of the deer and the robin. It is a landscape weighted with authority: constructed by the patron, the sculptor, the gardener, the poet and the painter. Turner's picture, by contrast, is a Romantic and atmospheric expression of grief, using the sea, the sky and the stark blackness of the ship in that expression. In both cases, the subject was one of public and professional admiration.

Hill's paintings dealt with the death of his only child. *In Memoriam: The Calton* is a metaphor, which carries consolation. It is not just about her death but about her life and her hope of redemption. In the foreground is Rock House, with the slope of the hill where Robert Adamson's camera is perched. A larger camera or canvas is being carried out of the gate and the family dogs are playing on the steps. A woman is laying out a rug to air on the wall and Hill has a painting on an easel in the garden. This is the 1840s and the world of life, facing south into the sun. The Calton Cemetery sits in the centre of the picture representing death, with the obelisk of the Political Martyrs' Monument springing up towards the skyline. There, the Royal Mile, with its church spires and the crown of St Giles's Cathedral, is seen through the light, misted and obscured by smoke from thousands of chimneys. It presents an idea of the mysterious, invisible city of immortal life in an extraordinarily unstrained analogy – the poetry of a reality. It was a landscape that Hill had examined at length. The scene was real but it was true in the deeper, spiritual sense and was designed as an act of mourning and a focus of sorrowful contemplation – a familiar place where Charlotte's absence was an acute part of the grief. When the two paintings were exhibited they were described as: 'gems of the opal kind with the colour and the fire, as it were, not laid upon the surface but all coming out from within . . . Both pictures are gems into which . . . we gaze, and could gaze for hours without wearying.'[81] The Romantic gaze of Lockhart and Scott from the standpoint of Calton Hill is here offered as a Christian idea, and the visual hunger they express has become the hunger of mourning. In these pictures, Hill had taken the poetic concept of association from its grand classical origins to the truly personal.

THE CHANGING LANDSCAPE
Right and Responsibility

The emotional connection with the land was based on physical knowledge. The principle of common right in the land was declared in the 1840s in a test case against the Duke of Leeds for denying access to Glen Tilt, ostensibly to protect the deer. Lord Cockburn described the situation:

> His grandfather, the last sane duke, who died about twelve or fifteen years ago, made a private drive several miles up the glen, and although he was by far the greatest deer-killer in Scotland, he not only permitted but encouraged strangers to use it freely . . . ever since, it has required a ducal ukase to see this portion of God's creation . . . I wrote a note with respectful compliments, etc., and re-duking and re-gracing him, and humbly begging that such a worm might be permitted to set its base wheels on this once free drive.[82]

The idea of liberty in the land was important to Hill as a landscape painter, and he took a practical interest in it. He wrote to David Roberts about the committee set up in Edinburgh in 1845 to protect public rights, 'in and through interesting portions of the scenery around Edinburgh, which have been wrested from the public by proprietors'.[83] At the first meeting, Hill was principally concerned to raise the question of the railways coming into the city but he later became one of the directors of the committee.

The issue became a religious concern for the Free Church, because landowners could block its progress by refusing to sell land to build new churches. One of the Free Church celebrities was Janet Fraser, a stocking-weaver:

> This woman, Jenny Fraser, occupied a few yards of ground in one of the Duke of Buccleuch's parishes which, it was discovered, were not his but hers, being the only spot in that inconvenient condition. She was offered an extraordinary price for it. Though but a poor crofter she had the spirit to say – 'Na! It cam' frae the Lord, an' the Lord wants't again, an' he shall hae't' And now there is a Free Church erecting upon it.[84]

Some landowners had refused the congregations the right to meet at all on their territory. Hugh Miller wrote a series of articles for *The Witness*, subsequently published as *The Cruise of the Betsey*, concerning one displaced minister, the Reverend Mr Elder, who lived substantially on a small yacht sailing between the Hebridean islands.[85] Hill provided the illustration for a fund-raising prospectus for a floating church for the western congregations, capable of holding 1,500 people. Hill was further involved in this particular battle in the production of a series of lithographs issued with the ironic title, *Illustrations of the Principles of Toleration in Scotland*, which had a polemic intention on a par with Miller's articles. The preface expressed the unexaggerated veracity of the drawings, 'taken on the spot', and explained the action of the artists:

> The existing state of things has been patiently suffered for three years, during which every effort has been made to conciliate them, but in vain; and it has occurred to some friends of Religious Liberty, to adopt the present mode of making known to the Public the nature and extent of an abuse which, short of ocular proof, could scarcely be

believed to exist in Great Britain in the nineteenth century, in the hope that such publicity may aid them in their efforts to obtain from the Legislature what they have been unable to obtain from the toleration, humanity, or justice of individual Proprietors.[86]

The lithographs showed services held on arbitrary patches of common land, a road, a gravel pit or the sea shore, to evade the legal rights of the landed proprietors. Hill drew the first two of the lithographs (fig. 101), and led the attack in depicting the parishes of Canobie and Wanlockhead on the Duke of Buccleuch's estates. Wanlockhead was an isolated lead-mining village, where all the inhabitants were employed by the duke, and it was a telling fact that three-quarters of the village had seceded to the Free Church. They were obliged to worship outside the village in a ravine 1,500 feet above sea level. Hill's drawing illustrates the villagers struggling uphill against the wind in a shower of sleet, the kind of weather they must have experienced for much of the year, mostly standing and for hours at a time.

Wanlockhead was the most dramatic image. The drawings are deliberately factual rather than impassioned, designed, like later documentary photographs, as an 'ocular truth' for public judgement. The prints were on sale in five major cities, Edinburgh, Glasgow, London, Manchester and Liverpool, and were intended to make a national impact, to shame the landlords.

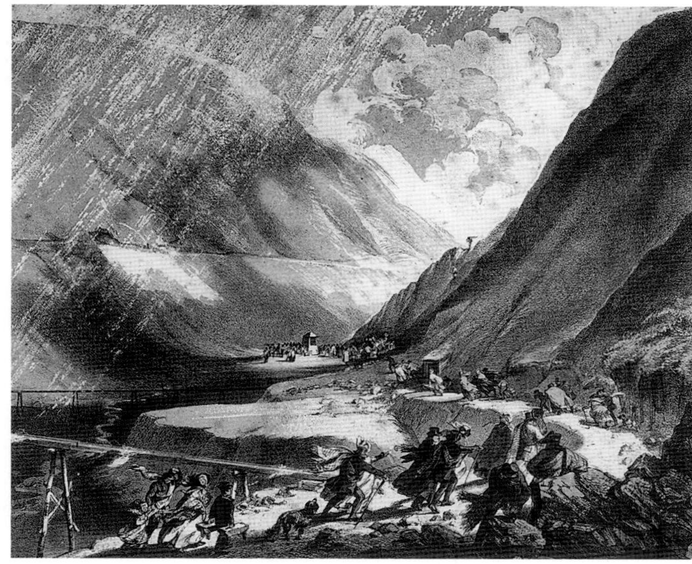

101. D. O. Hill, *Wanlockhead, c.* 1846. Lithograph from the series *Illustrations of the Principles of Toleration in Scotland.* National Library of Scotland, Edinburgh.

IMPROVING THE LAND

The sense of right in the land implied responsibility for its development. Hill saw landscape as open to improvement, rather than hallowed ground to be preserved in its historical state. His mentor, Alexander Nasmyth, was a practical planner who was so far involved in the building of the New Town of Edinburgh that, although he had no official position, he was regularly consulted. We know, from an account sent by Hill to the Royal Institution in 1826 for '3 large drawings in Pencil of Views in Edinburgh shewing the different proposed situations for placing his Majesty's Statue', that he was involved in landscape planning from an early stage.[87] His particular contribution to the development of landscape, in terms of admiration, criticism and such drawing for development, may relate to the great railway boom of the 1830s and 1840s. Hill's first commission of this kind, in 1831, came from the railway engineer John Miller, who continued a friend and patron. Characteristically, Hill improved the commission and enhanced its ambition (fig. 102). His preface to *Views of the Opening of the Glasgow and Garnkirk Railway* explained the situation:

The author of these Views, while on a sketching excursion in the West of Scotland last autumn, was requested by a friend connected with the Glasgow and Garnkirk Railway to supply one or two drawings of objects on the line, which were intended to be engraved on a small scale, and a limited number printed, for the gratification of a few of

102. D. O. Hill, *View near Proven Mill Bridge, looking West,* 1831. Lithograph, from *Views of the Opening of the Glasgow and Garnkirk Railway.* National Library of Scotland, Edinburgh.

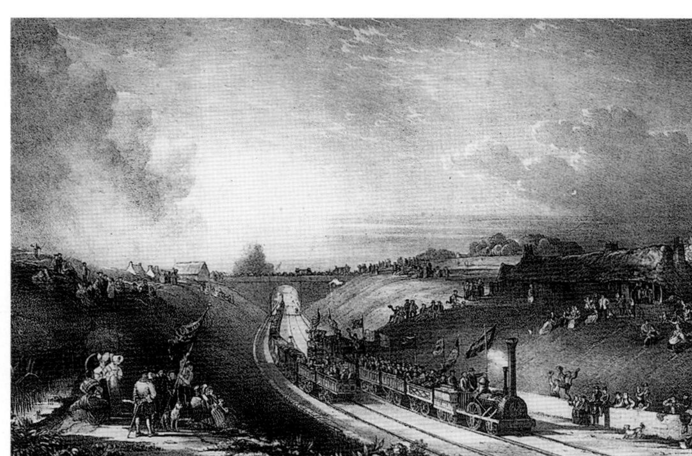

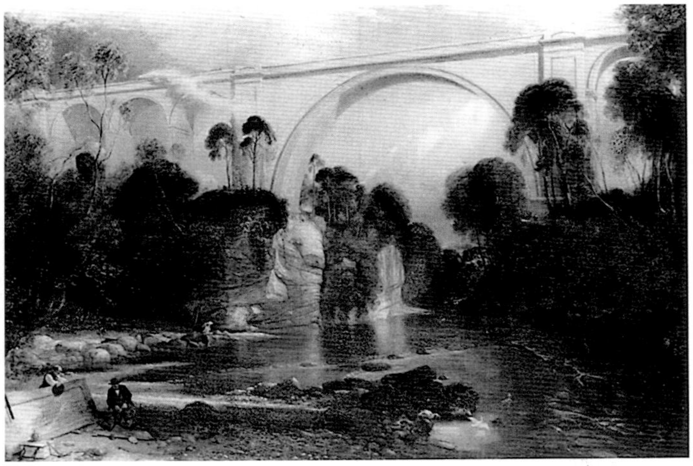

103. D. O. Hill, *The Ballochmyle Viaduct*, 1849. Oil on canvas. Glasgow Museums and Galleries.

> the Directors and Shareholders. These drawings, when executed, suggested the more extended plan of the present series which, without any pretensions as works of art, are respectfully submitted to the Public as professing to give, not only a tolerably correct picture of the localities of the Railway in question, but a characteristic and unexaggerated view of the generally important subject of Railway travelling.[88]

According to the railway historian, Jack Simmons, Hill alone of the early illustrators of the railways displayed an understanding of the way trains worked in his drawing, 'attesting careful observation; he could draw railway machines very well'.[89]

In 1840, Hill wrote to his wife of his satisfaction in sketching Sir Samuel Brown's suspension bridge over the Kenmare Strait, in County Kerry, Ireland: [90] 'it would have proved an interesting subject under any circumstances – doubly so you may be sure, when my hopes were not very high as to its picturesque capabilities.'[91] He developed this enthusiasm for engineering projects in his later work on the railways, painting John Miller's great railway viaducts at Falkirk, Linlithgow and the Almond Valley on the Glasgow–Edinburgh line, which were exhibited in 1843. He apparently intended a series of engravings of this line, in parallel with his Glasgow–Garnkirk lithographs.[92] The large calotypes of Edinburgh and Linlithgow may have been designed for the same purpose, or as further designs for the engraved views on the Glasgow–Edinburgh railway line. If so, then the calotypes of Linlithgow, which are significantly the first photographs known of a railway scene, could have been a part of that project.

Like Turner, Hill was one of the first painters to treat the railways as a serious and large-scale subject. But Turner's *Rain, Steam, and Speed*, exhibited in 1844, was a virtuoso impressionistic performance, 'not a view of the Great Western Railway but an allegory of the forces of nature'.[93] Turner was interested in the feel and the sense of trains and the effect of speed. His painting expresses the dominance of the black train on the dark viaduct arching over the still, golden landscape.

Later in the 1840s, Hill painted the Ballochmyle Viaduct spanning the beautiful 'Braes of Ballochmyle' (fig. 103). Simmons again admires Hill's two paintings of the viaduct as 'a proper tribute to a magnificent work of engineering. Here the main arch, accurately depicted as high and wide beyond any other railway bridge, leaps across an Ayrshire river, portrayed with no less truth to nature as romantic.'[94] Hill's text for the academy's catalogue unites the grandeur of the engineering with the beautiful landscape:

> This celebrated portion of Coil's 'banks and braes, her dens and dells',– a favourite haunt of the poet Burns, and otherwise hallowed by many national associations, – extends for several miles along the right bank of the River Ayr, and forms part of the pleasure grounds of Ballochmyle House. The ravine has lately been spanned by a viaduct of stately proportions, designed by John Miller, Esq., Engineer, which forms part of the Glasgow, Dumfries, and Carlisle Railway. The great central arch, one of the abutments of which is founded on the rock where Peden had his hiding place, is 180 feet in span, and there are six smaller arches, each of 50 feet. The Bridge stands 178 feet above the level of the river.[95]

This description cheerfully associates the romantic haunt of the poet and the refuge of the Covenanting minister, Alexander Peden, with a specification of the new bridge. Another, uncommissioned large-scale picture, *The Valley of the Nith from the Uplands of Dalswinton*, was exhibited in 1850. The catalogue entry described a landscape, which includes Burns's farm of Ellisland, and follows with a quotation from James Nasmyth, which connects Burns himself with engineering. For Nasmyth it was classic ground:

> in the year 1788, the first vessel that ever moved through water by *the agency of steam*, did on the 14th November of that year skim over the surface of said loch; – a great day was that for mankind: an event of the first magnitude, big with the good fate of nations, as after times have proved. The parties present in the boat on that

memorable occasion, were 'Miller' (proprietor of the mansion), 'Taylor' (the engineer), 'Robert Burns' (the poet and farmer of Ellisland), 'Henry Brougham', (the future Chancellor), 'and Alexander Nasmyth', (the father of landscape painting in Scotland), 'a fit and worthy crew to celebrate so great an event'.[96]

Hill's view of industrial development within the landscape is in opposition to earlier models like P. J. de Loutherbourg's *Coalbrookdale by Night*, which is a Sublime concept and a hellish image.[97] The Ballochmyle painting is a celebration of the great viaduct but the beauty of the landscape it strides across remains redolent of the rustic, poetic and historical. *The Valley of the Nith* contains a new component, in the Romantic past of technology. The letter Hill wrote to the Museum of the Commissioners of Patents in 1858, when James Nasmyth suggested the picture might find a home there, is revealing both of Hill's ineptitude in dealing and of his anxious approach to the painting's lack of success:

> I shall be happy if it meets your approbation as a work of art, as much as the subject is one not unlikely to excite your sympathy from its interesting associations. It is one of the most elaborated of my pictures, as I have painted all over it again and again since it was exhibited. It would indeed be an event as agreeable as unlooked for that it should have its home in the same hall with the paddle wheels which moved the craft on the little lake of Dalswinton – the [livening?] germ of the Titanic family of sea-going steamers, of which family I observed with satisfaction that the Leviathan, one of the youngest of the brood, had sent a miniature of herself for the delectation [of] the good old grandmother of the Dalswinton lake.[98]

In the event, the Commissioners did not buy the picture because it was too wide a landscape and did not concentrate on this one point. *Edinburgh from the Castle* was purchased by John Miller and may, from Hill's concern with the planning of the railway lines and station, have been painted partly with that in mind. Below the castle in the valley a little train steams past – a comparatively unobtrusive presence. In all three pictures discussed here, Hill is presenting the fusion of old and new rather than a battle between them; he is expressing a positive affection for good engineering. Hill's energy in promoting good design for the structures of the railways, driving into the heart of the city, is in contrast to Lord Cockburn's hostility. Cockburn regarded the railway boom as insane: 'Britain is at present an island of lunatics, all railway mad.'[99] Hill urged David Roberts, in several letters, to make his voice felt; Hill himself talked to the engineers, and redirected the town meeting designed to consider rights of way in the country:

> I took the liberty of directing their attention to the trouble you have taken in conjunction with Sir William Allan and myself & afterwards in the matter of getting the three Railways Cos whose termini are to be in the Nor Lock near the North Bridge, so far to unite their measures in the designing and erection of these termini, as to get one architect of genius and skill to design and superintend the erection of the whole. I told them . . . of my having been asked by Mr Miller the Engineer of the Edinburgh & Glasgow Line about two years ago, to give a design shewing the effect of the works – that the first thing I recommended was the employment of an architect – either Playfair or Hamilton, to design the Buildings . . . I gave them what I believed to be your views generally in regard to the mighty [or 'weighty'] importance to the beauty and form of Edinburgh – of having these buildings well designed – and I tried to represent to them the effect of the entry into our city by the railway dashing round the [illegible] of Arthurs Seat – skirting the palace grounds beautiful as this [or 'they'] will be – curving in by the cliff rock of the Calton where the norman castle of the prison and Governors house are situated – and then emerging into an area surrounded with tasteful structures composing the various buildings connected with the terminus. – then the gardens laid out round the Scott Monument – and the deformity of the mound removed, to give place to our contemplated collonades [the National Gallery of Scotland] and the New College.[100]

This is characteristically difficult to read but Hill seems to be regarding the railway as a dramatic idea, appropriate to good architecture. John Miller had asked Hill to draw the effect. It may well be that some of the photographs taken by Hill and Adamson of the Mound and from the castle, around this time, were designed with a similar town-planning intention – for the benefit of the grand plans for building on the Mound behind the Royal Institution as well as the railways and to achieve a coherent and beautiful design for the area between the Old and New Towns.

Hill was also involved in the development of the railways in taking photographs of the eighteenth-century Lady Glenorchy's Chapel and the medieval Trinity College Church (fig. 104), which were demolished in 1845 and 1848 to make way for a railway-goods yard.[101] These pictures fit into the

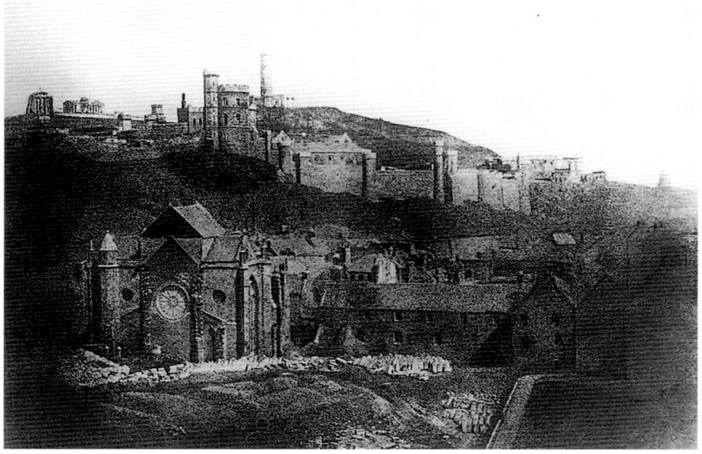

104. D. O. Hill and Robert Adamson, *Trinity College Church and Lady Glenorchy's Hospital*, 1845. From the calotype negative. Scottish National Photography Collection, Edinburgh.

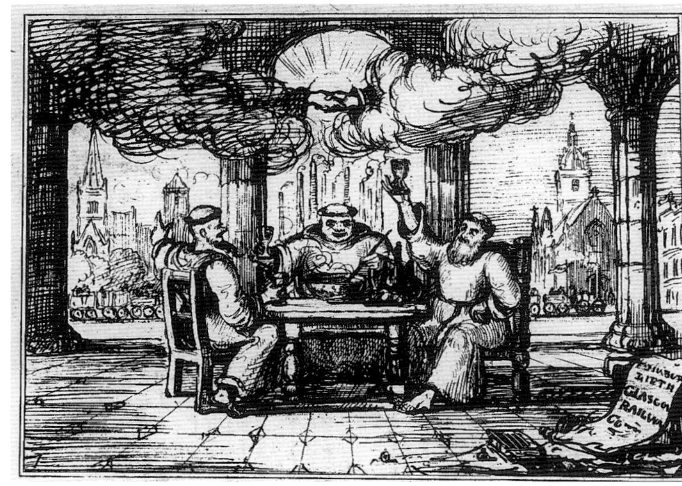

105. D. O. Hill, *St Mungo, St Rollox and St Giles*. Lithograph. Tailpiece to *Views of the Opening of the Glasgow and Garnkirk Railway*, 1831. National Library of Scotland, Edinburgh.

custom of recording old buildings before demolition, which became a common photographic practice later in the century.[102] But there is a twist to the story of Trinity Church. As a result of the protest led by the antiquarians and the Lord Provost, the railway company agreed to rebuild the church elsewhere. Disputes about the site delayed the demolition until 1848, when the city accepted payment from the company to take on the responsibility. The masonry was removed to the slopes of Calton Hill. The disputes on re-siting continued, involving ecclesiastic with aesthetic and antiquarian arguments, and the academy itself joined in the discussion. Hill wrote to Lord Cockburn, with their opinion: 'that the site in the Woodyard would bury the Church, defeat a chief object of its conservation & lower the character for taste of the City. That while the Garden site is immeasurably superior neither the Academy nor the public [?] were in a position to pronounce that it was absolutely the best.'[103] Hill does not mention that another potential site was Calton Hill. The Lord Provost had already purchased the ground he favoured there, in 1851: ironically, this turned out to be the site occupied by Rock House.[104] He was proposing to rebuild the church in place of the house where D. O. Hill lived.[105]

Curiously enough, this inverted involvement of the Gothic and the railways was prefigured in Hill's *Glasgow and Garnkirk Railway* by a small lithograph at the end of the text, which concluded with the ambition of extending the railway line to Edinburgh (fig. 105). Hill drew the three figures of St Mungo, St Rollox (patron of the engineering works) and St Giles as monks, celebrating with a bowl of whisky toddy, while a train, seen through gothic arches, steamed through to connect the three places in the modern world. It was an optimistic vision: the vision of a man who saw the world as complicated and fascinating and who could accommodate a whole range of history and change within his taste and affections.

CONCLUSION

David Octavius Hill was a peaceful revolutionary. In him and in his society we may find the apparent opposite concerns for individuality and union, for originality and combination, for ambition and self-sacrifice. He may be regarded as one of the leading figures and as one of the hardest workers in forwarding the interests of Scottish art with the Scottish public, at a time of recession and depression. His pursuit and support of a creative and personal freedom can be seen in his work for the Scottish Academy, in his circumvention of the toils of patronage in art, and in his enthusiasm for the promulgation and education of the public and artist alike. His curiosity and openness is seen in areas as diverse as lithography, the railways and photography. His generous responsiveness may be seen in his wholehearted promotion of artists as diverse as Turner and Joseph Noël Paton.

All these considerations in Hill's life and actions, as a private man, as an administrator and promoter of the arts and as an ambitious artist, had an impact on his approach to the calotype partnership with Robert Adamson – for us, the focal point of Hill's life work. These impulses and this knowledge lay behind his direct confidence and enthusiasm, and help to explain both the control and the excitement of the photographic work that they achieved between them. That much of this feeling and understanding were particular to Hill may be better understood by examining the Scottish calotypes in the light of the opinions of Sir David Brewster and William Henry Fox Talbot and Talbot's own work. The authority, which these two men, the natural patrons of the Hill and Adamson partnership, should have held, was abrogated by Hill's enthusiasm and the way he redirected not just the partnership but this form of photography. Principally, the distinction lay in Brewster's preference for an idea of photography as a measured and comparatively unmediated method of record and his need for accuracy, both of which he held to some degree in common with Talbot.

One of the arguments put forward to establish the superior judgement of the patrons over the artists was that of critical distance – their very lack of practical experience could be seen as an advantage; that is to say that they would not be misled by admiration of the practical difficulties involved in a work into believing that it was good because it was clever or laborious. The very confusions natural to the art of photography – that it was the direct transcript of the sun with no manual interpretation – inverted the critical difficulty. Here the problem was rather to appreciate the grasp of nature through artifice; the 'art that conceals art' admired by J. Craig Annan. The effect and the concealed skill behind it has proved most evident to photographers looking back to the work from the perspective of their own knowledge and experience. In the words of a painter, Joshua Reynolds: 'Simplicity, being only a negative virtue, cannot be described or defined.'[1] The aesthetic of Hill and Adamson's calotypes was based on a number of critical decisions and preferences, which may be related to the practice of painters and their use of camera technology in the later eighteenth and earlier nineteenth centuries. The actual practice of the Hill and Adamson partnership was demonstrably sophisticated in its use of technology and in its understanding of constraints and advantages. Their approach respected nature, and its effectiveness may be judged by the lack of mannerism, the relaxed response of the sitters, which allows us to see and think of their subjects as individuals familiar to us, more than 150 years later. Hill had taken the art of association into the personal world of his own circle, and then made that emotional, personal art public.

In the biographical note on Hill published in the *Art Journal* in 1850, apology is made for a life lacking in incident.

He was resident for most of his life in the city of Edinburgh and was an important participant and a focal point within its society. In his private life we may examine and understand both his emotional sensitivity and the kinds of encouragement and constraint, which helped to direct his art. His humour as well as his moral concerns helped to balance and stabilise his life at a time of considerable social and economic distress. His affections and his social conscience were important to his understanding of his own family and circle and to his sympathetic admiration of the Scottish fishermen and women, which inspired what may be his most original and significant work. This was the planned *Fishermen and Women of the Firth of Forth*, which saw the effective invention of the photographic documentary essay, and was a project remarkable for its origins in a formal consideration of working society, which had no obvious precedent in the visual arts.

The society Hill lived in emphasised the personal responsibility of the individual within a framework of religious and phrenological determinism. The particular responsibility of artists to succeed was thought to be generated by a natural background of struggle and failure. Hill's own career and interests worked both from within these assumptions and contrary to them, to alleviate, by social and educational means, the stress of individual effort and isolation. Hill actively promoted the advance of art education and the organised support of the arts, through the Scottish Academy and the Institution for the Promotion of the Fine Arts. His professional career is remarkable for its extension of his sociable and co-operative private life, and for what may well be regarded as his sacrifice of personal advance to a higher ambition. The first is exemplified in his work for the academy. The second may be seen in the laborious attempt of the Disruption picture to make a great religious and historical work, advancing the concept of responsibility and the heroism of the individual within a large and democratic social grouping, driven by moral and religious enthusiasm.

Scotland in the later eighteenth century and through to the mid-nineteenth century was a centre of literature and literary production. As the son of a bookseller, Hill was surrounded by books, and his understanding and inclinations were strongly literary. The character of much of the writing he knew and admired, from the work of Walter Scott to the work of Hugh Miller, combines the factual with the poetic and relies on nature and familiar experience as a source of creative inspiration. The emotional and analogical impulse combined with anonymity in writing to introduce a strong vein of ambiguity, and the readiness to accept such confusion is also a part of Hill's exploratory aesthetic, which admired and endorsed natural variation and duality. It does indeed seem reasonable to encompass Hill's own thinking and enthusiasm for literature and ideas in John Brown's words of praise, as a man with, 'a rich versatile, rapid, facile mind, crowded with thick coming fancies', and he was doubtless encompassed in Brewster's general terms of censure for artists:

> The predominance of the imagination over the judgement indisposes them for patient and profound thought. The slightest resemblances, the most fortuitous associations, are linked together as cause and effect; and even words unburdened with meaning, and sentences unfreighted with thought, suggest to their fancy ideas and propositions blazing with all the lustre of truth.[2]

The impact of Scottish literature, and especially the writing of Walter Scott, had taken Scottish history into the realm of fiction and made it powerfully affecting. Through the influence of James MacPherson, Robert Burns and Scott, international knowledge of Scotland had developed from the intellectual impact of the Enlightenment to Romantic sympathy. The idea of Scotland as a place of heightened reality, which was built on ideas of Highland and Jacobite character and romance, was widely attractive. That idea was extended by the enthusiasm of the Evangelists in their struggle to free the Church of Scotland from the political interests of the state. Hill's Disruption picture may therefore be presented as a celebration of heroism and moral conviction which expected a world audience. The painting contains significant elements of the Romantic history of Scotland in the Highland figures of Hugh Miller and Sergeant Mackenzie who support the composition, and in the indication of the third figure, Mr Hately, the precentor concerned with the music. Hill, who was himself an accomplished singer, was aware of the significance of song to Scottish culture, and addressed that concern both in his painting and in his photography.

One of the critical debates within the historic discussions of art, which was examined both for its interest in distinguishing and in connecting the arts of poetry and painting, was the concern of time. The painters' search for emotional focus in historic and figure painting may be exemplified in Scottish practice by David Wilkie's *Distraining for Rent*, where the actors in the drama have reached an emotional pivot of human tragedy. Hill's interest in the idea of layering and complimentary time, which may keep the narrative argument or discussion alive in the criticism of painting, can again be seen in the model of his Disruption painting and relates to examples of his photography, such as Thomas Chalmers's family group. The interest in the natural authority of the photograph as a direct transcript of reality was broadly adopted for its particular emotional poignancy by critics of photography. However, Hill was not looking at the calotypes for their poignancy as objects of humility or little worth, where the absence of artifice might be supposed to reveal simply the persons pictured in them; his concern was for the human liveliness – human mortality and its revelation, through art, of immortality.

Within the particular social and human emphasis of Hill's life, it has not been clear that his initial concern with the calotype process was the study of the figure. He was both a genre and a landscape painter, often combining the two. The traditional methods of study – the cast, anatomy and the infrequent life class – suppressed physical and facial liveliness and the sense of nature, which had been a concern in Scottish painting from the time of Allan Ramsay. Hill's interest followed the model of David Wilkie, a pupil of the surgeon Sir Charles Bell, for whom it was the act of emotion which made beauty. Bell's advice to study life as it was, in social interaction and in the streets, was crucial to Hill's use of the calotype. His knowledgeable study enabled him to effect the calculated social direction, which may be defined as persuading the sitters to reveal their true nature.

Hill's figures occupied the landscape of Scotland. He was a poetic painter, in a sense inherited from the classical tradition; his landscape was enlivened by the people of history and fiction. But his poets were British – principally Robert Burns and Scott – and he inherited their direct inspiration from the land. Hill was poetic in the interpretive sense and he followed Turner's lead in attempting landscape defined by atmosphere and light. Hill's Romantic, moral impulse is evident in the connections he makes through his figures and the choice of location. His particular emphasis on Greyfriars Churchyard, which he used to express both his admiration of the seventeenth-century Covenanters and the nineteenth-century Evangelists, is revealed in his work on Burns and James Hogg as well as in the calotypes. His idea of the humanity of landscape is most poignantly shown in the memorial landscapes painted after his daughter's death, which are a truly personal expression of grief in absence.

Hill's sense of responsibility for the land, as for his fellow men, was also expressed in a practical manner in defence both of the right of access to the land and the freedom to worship on the land. He understood the importance of planning for the future. Hill was clearly sentimental and an antiquarian, but he also appreciated the advantages of his own times. He admired civil engineering and was ready to promote and celebrate its importance in the landscape.

Hill was a man for whom the land and the people, in the heightened reality of poetry, painting and calotype photography, were themselves poetic. In looking at Scotland and the Scots he saw history and Romance. But he saw truly – his lithographic railway trains would run; the calotype photographs he took with Robert Adamson give us the personality and a kind of intimate nobility or heroism in the individuals he knew and admired. It is a generous and connected view of the world. For the modern audience, it is Hill's collaboration with Robert Adamson, which has given us the grand commencement to the art of photography. But that art is closely involved in Hill's own character and connections. It resonates from his life and his broader relations to society and the arts.

NOTES

INTRODUCTION

1. J. Craig Annan, 'David Octavius Hill, R.S.A. 1802–1870', *Camera Work*, no. 11 (July 1905), p. 17.
2. Heinrich Schwarz, *David Octavius Hill, Master of Photography*, trans. Helene Fraenkel, London 1932, p. 18.
3. J. Craig Annan, 'David Octavius Hill, R.S.A. 1802–1870', *Camera Work*, no. 11 (July 1905), p. 19. The idea was important to Annan. His bookplate, etched by D. Y. Cameron, bore the motto, 'Ars est celare artem', illustrated in William Buchanan, *The Art of the Photographer: J. Craig Annan 1864–1946*, exhibition catalogue, National Galleries of Scotland, Edinburgh 1992, p. 19.
4. Walter Benjamin, 'A small history of photography', *One-Way Street and Other Writings*, trans. Edmund Jephcott and Kingsley Shorter, London 1979, pp. 242–3.
5. Stephen Bann, 'Erased Physiognomy: Theodore Géricault, Paul Strand and Garry Winogrand', *The Portrait in Photography*, London 1992, pp. 39–40.
6. The name of the fishwife was published in Katherine Michaelson, *A Centenary Exhibition of the Work of David Octavius Hill 1802–1870 and Robert Adamson 1821–1848*, exhibition catalogue, Scottish Arts Council, Edinburgh 1970; David Bruce, *Sun Pictures: The Hill–Adamson Calotypes*, London 1973; Colin Ford and Roy Strong, *An Early Victorian Album. The Photographic Masterpieces (1843–1847) of David Octavius Hill and Robert Adamson*, New York 1976; John Ward and Sara Stevenson, *Printed Light. The Scientific Art of William Henry Fox Talbot and David Octavius Hill with Robert Adamson*, Edinburgh 1986; Sara Stevenson, *Hill and Adamson's 'Fishermen and Women of the Firth of Forth'*, Edinburgh 1992.
7. Roland Barthes, *Camera Lucida, Reflections on Photography*, trans. Richard Howard, London 1993, pp. 71 and 73.
8. Stephen Bann, 'Erased Physiognomy: Theodore Géricault, Paul Strand and Garry Winogrand', *The Portrait in Photography*, London 1992, pp. 39–40.

CHAPTER ONE

1. Hill to Paton, 11 July 1853, NLS Acc 11315.
2. Advertisement quoted in Edward Smart, *History of Perth Academy*, Perth 1932, pp. 100–1.
3. Kenneth J. Cameron, *The Schoolmaster Engineer*, Dundee 1988.
4. Allan to Hill, 14 September 1832, RSA.
5. T. R. S. Young (ed.), *The Edinburgh Institution*, Edinburgh 1933, p. 180.
6. 'Thomas Hill & Sons, booksellers, stationers & music sellers, 53 South Bridge.' *The Post Office Annual Directory for 1825–6*, Edinburgh 1825. The following year, Thomas Hill and Alexander Hill, 'of T. Hill and Sons', appear, Thomas living at 27 Elder Street, where D. O. Hill is listed as 'landscape painter & teacher of drawing', and Alexander at 17 Montague Street. Thomas Hill & Sons is listed in the directory until 1827–8, and in 1828–9 Alexander and Thomas junior are both listed, one at 50 Princes Street, and the other at 53 South Bridge.
7. Undated manuscript memoir of Margaret Saunders of Dundee, miniature painter, in the collection of Dr Patrick Mullin, 1991.
8. John Macrone to Hill, 10 January 1836, NLS Acc 11608.
9. George Harvey, *Notes of the Early History of the Royal Scottish Academy*, Edinburgh 1873, p. 19, footnote. Harvey was a very serious man and, I suspect, continued to think of Hill as a possibly frivolous juvenile throughout his career.
10. For the history of the Scottish Academy, see Esmé Gordon, *The Royal Scottish Academy of Painting Sculpture and Architecture 1826–1976*, Edinburgh 1976.
11. Quoted in Harvey, *Notes of the Early History of the Royal Scottish Academy*, pp. 68–9.
12. Harvey, *Notes of the Early History of the Royal Scottish Academy*, pp. 69–70.
13. *Edinburgh Evening Courant* (18 May 1870).
14. Macrone to Hill, 10 January 1836, NLS Acc 11608
15. Katherine Michaelson, *A Centenary Exhibition of the Work of David Octavius Hill 1802–1870 and Robert Adamson 1821–1848*, exhibition catalogue, Scottish Arts Council, Edinburgh 1970, p. 11.
16. John M. Gray, 'Robert Adamson' in *Calotypes by D. O. Hill and R. Adamson Illustrating an Early Stage in the Development of Photography Selected from his Collection by Andrew Elliot*, Edinburgh 1928, p. 11. John Miller Gray was born two years after Adamson's death, and his information probably came from Dr John Brown who, as a friend of Hill, could have heard it from him rather than from the Adamson family. Gray wrote Brown's obituary, in which he said that Brown was, at the time of his death, 'writing a Preface to a series of calotype portraits to be shortly published – a task for which he was specially qualified by his interest in art and his comprehensive knowledge of the Scottish society of the last generation.' *John Miller Gray. Memoir and Remains*, Edinburgh 1895, vol. 1, p. 149.
17. Hill to Henry Bicknell, 17 January 1849, George Eastman House Collection MS AC H645 acc 830.
18. This account of the progress of John and Robert's work is substantially based on A. D. Morrison-Low, 'Brewster, Talbot and the Adamsons: The Arrival of Photography in St Andrews', *History of Photography*, vol. 25, no. 2, 2001, pp. 130–41.

19. Brewster to Talbot, 15 August 1842, NMPFT 1937-4905.
20. The legal process of taking out a patent was lengthy and expensive, and although Scotland was officially joined to England by the Act of Union of 1707, it still had a separate legal system, which would require Talbot to pay twice for protection. Since Scotland was a smaller and poorer country than England, it was less likely to repay the cost. In practice, Scottish photography benefited from this useful fact, not simply in terms of commercial profit but because the Scots were free to experiment with a number of processes and inventions patented in England, which included the Daguerreotype and Wolcott's mirror camera (see p. 000).
21. Brewster to Talbot, 22 October 1842, NMPFT 1937-4912.
22. The album contains only the small square calotypes (about $4 \times 3\frac{11}{16}$ inches), in the collection of the FTM, so it may be assumed that they bought the two bigger cameras, taking calotypes about $6\frac{1}{4} \times 4\frac{1}{2}$ inches and $8\frac{1}{4} \times 6$ inches, afterwards.
23. The scrapbook is in the collection of the Royal Museum of Scotland, T.192.1.2.
24. Brewster to Talbot, 9 May 1843, FTM, LA43–53.
25. *British Journal of Photography* (22 August 1879), p. 400.
26. The date is on the negative, which is in the SNPC from the collection of the Edinburgh Photographic Society.
27. Hugh Miller, 'The Two Prints', *The Witness* (24 June 1843).
28. The speculation that the Annan and Adamson families knew each other is based on evidence from family correspondence; Thomas Annan's sister was reported to be much distressed by Robert Adamson's death.
29. Album given by D. O. Hill to Lord Cockburn, 1850 or after, in the collection of the London Library, calotype no. 4.
30. Nasmyth to Hill, 27 March 1847, ROE.
31. Carl Gustav Carus, *The King of Saxony's Journey through England and Scotland in the year 1844*, trans. S. C. Davison, London 1846, p. 337.
32. I am indebted to Larry Schaaf for this information.
33. In the late nineteenth century, the enthusiasm for the calotypes was transmitted through the Annan family, who had known Hill personally. The international response between then and the mid-twentieth century tends to reduce and occasionally ignore Robert Adamson's contribution. Later criticism has attempted to redress the balance.
34. John Brown, 'The Disruption – The Signing of the Deed of Demission. A Picture by D. O. Hill', *The Scotsman* (24 May 1846).
35. Quoted in Anon (presumed to be D. O. Hill), *The Disruption of the Church of Scotland: An Historical Picture... Painted by D. O. Hill*, Edinburgh 1866, p. 4.
36. Brewster to Talbot, 3 July 1843, NMPFT 1937-4926.
37. Advertisement in *The Witness*, 8 July 1843.
38. Brewster to Talbot, 3 July 1843, NMPFT 1937-4926.
39. Sir Thomas Dick Lauder to Hill and Adamson 22 December 1843, RSA MS.
40. Advertised in *Edinburgh Evening Courant* (3 August 1844)
41. Hill to Roberts, 14 March 1845, NLS TD 1742
42. Quoted by Heinrich Schwarz, 'The Calotypes of D. O. Hill and Robert Adamson: Some Contemporary Judgements', *Apollo* (February 1972), p. 124.
43. *Edinburgh Evening Courant* (24 October 1844).
44. Noted later in a letter, Roberts to Hill, 9 November 1849, RSA MS.
45. Hill to Roberts, 25 February 1845, NLS TD 1742.
46. Hill to Roberts, 14 March 1845, NLS TD 1742.
47. Hill to David Roberts, 12 March 1845, NLS TD1742.
48. Wilson to Hill, April 1845, RSA MS.
49. Catalogue of the annual exhibition, Royal Scottish Academy, Edinburgh 1846.
50. Comment presumably by Hugh Miller, *The Witness*, 28 May 1843.
51. Monica Thorp, 'Hill and Adamson without Adamson? The Ballochmyle Calotypes', *Scottish Photography Bulletin*, no. 2 (1989), pp. 25–9
52. Hill to Ruthven, December 1847, draft letter, RSA MS.
53. Hill to Paton, 18 January 1848, NLS Acc 11315.
54. Hill to Samuel Carter Hall, 21 August 1848, Edinburgh Central Library MS.
55. See Pat Hudson, 'Financing Firms, 1700–1850', Maurice W. Kirkby and Mary B. Rose (eds), *Business Enterprise in Modern Britain from the Eighteenth to the Twentieth Century*, London and New York 1994, p. 90. 'The principle of limited liability was finally adopted in 1855 only after heated debate.' P. L. Payne, *British Entrepreneurship in the Nineteenth Century*, 2nd ed., London 1988, p. 16.
56. M. J. Daunton, *Progress and Poverty. An Economic and Social History of Britain 1700–1850*, Oxford 1995, p. 246.
57. In the collection of the Museum Ludwig, Agfa Photo-Historama, Cologne.
58. See A. D. Morrison-Low, 'Dr John Adamson and Thomas Rodger: Amateur and Professional Photography in Nineteenth-Century St Andrews' in Julie Lawson, Ray McKenzie and A. D. Morrison-Low (eds), *Photography 1900: The Edinburgh Symposium*, Edinburgh 1992, pp. 19–37.

CHAPTER TWO

1. See A. D. Morrison-Low, 'Brewster, Talbot and the Adamsons: The Arrival of Photography in St Andrews', *History of Photography*, vol. 25, no. 2, 2001, pp. 130–41 and 'Sir David Brewster and Photography', *Review of Scottish Culture*, no. 4, Edinburgh 1988, pp. 63–73, and also, Graham Smith, *Disciples of Light: Photographs in the Brewster Album*, Malibu 1990.
2. Quoted in H. J. P. Arnold, *William Henry Fox Talbot, Pioneer of Photography and Man of Science*, London 1977, p. 80. For the extraordinary range of Brewster's work, see A. D. Morrison-Low and J. R. R. Christie (eds), *'Martyr of Science': Sir David Brewster 1781–1868*, proceedings of a bicentenary symposium, Edinburgh 1984.
3. Mrs Gordon, *The Home Life of Sir David Brewster*, Edinburgh 1869, p. 299.
4. Ibid., p. 302.
5. See A. D. Morrison-Low, 'Photography in Edinburgh in 1839: the Royal Scottish Society of Arts, Andrew Fyfe and Mungo Ponton', *Scottish Photography Bulletin*, no. 2 (1990), pp. 26–35. See Larry J. Schaaf, 'Henry Talbot's First Exhibition in Scotland', *Studies in Photography* (1998), pp. 25–8.
6. The Froment photograph is in a collection assembled by James Nasmyth, which also includes examples of Cundell's work, NLS MS 3241. See Larry J. Schaaf, 'The First Photograph James Nasmyth Ever Saw', *Scottish Photography Bulletin*, no. 2 (1990), pp. 15–22, and George Smith Cundell, 'On the Practice of the Calotype Process of Photography', *London, Edinburgh and Dublin Philosophical Magazine and Journal of Science*, 3rd series, vol. 24 (1844), pp. 160 and 321–32.
7. Hugh Miller, 'The Two Prints', *The Witness* (24 June 1843).
8. Hill to Gordon, June 1843, New College Library, autograph folder 240.
9. Brewster to Talbot, 18 November 1843, NMPFT 1937-4928.
10. Dr C. G. Carus, *The King of Saxony's Journey through England and Scotland in the Year 1844*, trans. S. C. Davidson, London 1846, p. 336.
11. Brewster to Talbot, 28 November 1843, NMPFT 1937-4929.
12. Brewster to Talbot, 18 April 1844, NMPFT 1937-4935.
13. See Katherine Michaelson, 'The First Photographic Record of a

Scientific Conference' in Van Deren Coke (ed.), *One Hundred Years of Photographic History: Essays in Honor of Beaumont Newhall,* Albuquerque 1975, pp. 109–16.
14. Hill to Talbot, 21 September 1844, FTM LA 44-67.
15. Hill to Talbot, 28 September 1844, FTM LA 44-70.
16. Hill to Roberts, 12 March 1845, NLS TD 1742.
17. The account for this is in the FTM, uncatalogued.
18. Hill to Roberts, 14 March 1845, NLS TD 1742.
19. Talbot notebook 1843/4, FTM, LA-49.
20. Hill's name appears in Talbot's list for copies, notebook 1843/4. On the loose page the general list includes 'Mr Hill's / coloured ones' but the numbering in the list for part five makes it clear that Talbot was not thinking of Hill, but of Calvert Jones as painting calotypes. FTM LAA-49.
21. Hill to Roberts, 12 March 1845, NLS TD 1742.
22. Hill to Roberts 14 March 1845, NLS TD 1742.
23. Elizabeth Rigby, review of books on modern German painting, *Quarterly Review*, vol. 78 (March 1846), p. 338.
24. Murray to Talbot, 14 or 19 May 1846, FTM LA 46-65.
25. Brewster to Talbot, 18 November 1843, NMPFT 1937-4928.
26. See Graham Smith, 'William Henry Fox Talbot's Calotype Views of Loch Katrine', *Bulletin of the University of Michigan Museums of Art and Archaeology*, vol. 7 (1987), pp. 49–77.
27. See Francis Haskell, *Rediscoveries in Art: Some Aspects of Taste, Fashion and Collecting in England and France*, London 1976, pp. 78–9. Stirling's collection was described in G. F. Waagen, *Galleries and Cabinets of Art in Great Britain,* London 1857, pp. 448–53.
28. Arnold, *William Henry Fox Talbot, Pioneer of Photography and Man of Science*, pp. 158–9.
29. David Brewster, 'Photography', *North British Review*, vol. 14 (1847), p. 479.
30. David Brewster, review of Goethe's *Theory of Colours*, trans. Charles Lock Eastlake, *Edinburgh Review*, vol. 72 (October 1840), p. 124.
31. John Brown, review of Hill's work in the Scottish Academy exhibition, *The Witness* (22 April 1846).
32. Brewster 'Photography', *North British Review*, vol. 14 (1847), p. 479.
33. Ibid., pp. 487 and 504.
34. Cockburn to William Empson, 22 November 1847, NLS Dep 235.
35. Sir David Brewster, 'Transactions regarding the recent improvements in photography', *Report of the Twentieth Meeting of the British Association for the Advancement of Science*, relating to the meeting in Edinburgh, July and August 1850, London 1851, p. 6.
36. Sir David Brewster, 'President's address', in ibid. p. xxxvi.
37. The terms of praise include the following: For Ross and Thomson: 'In addition to the extreme clearness observable in the details of their landscape scenery, and the great delicacy of their delineation of objects in general, we may take notice of the excessive beauty of the tints which their works exhibit. Not only are the shadows deep and Rembrandt-looking, where suitable to the effect required, but the middle distances display a beauty of colour.' For Henneman and Malone: ' These are all natural and pleasing, and great delicacy is observable in the lights and shades, the tone of which is a fine warm sepia brown ... The coloured portraits in this collection are very good, and no little credit is due to the artistic skill which they display.'
38. *Exhibition of the Works of Industry of All Nations, 1851. Reports of the Juries*, London 1852, p. 278. The entry for Ross and Thomson has 52 lines, that for Hill and Adamson has only 8.
39. See Mark Haworth-Booth, *Photography: An Independent Art. Photographs from the Victoria and Albert Museum 1839–1996*, London 1997, pp. 25–9.
49. Hill to Roberts, 14 January 1852, NLS Acc 7723.
41. Hill to Roberts, 12 March 1845, NLS TD 1742.
42. William Henry Fox Talbot, *The Pencil of Nature*, part 4, 21 June 1845, quoted in Mike Weaver (ed.), *Henry Fox Talbot, Selected Texts and Bibliography*, Oxford 1992, p. 97.
43. Hill to Roberts 12 March 1845, NLS TD 1742.
44. Talbot, *The Pencil of Nature*, Part 3, 14–29 May 1845, quoted in Weaver (ed.), *Henry Fox Talbot, Selected Texts and Bibliography*, p. 95.
45. Identified as Robert Cranston's Hotel in Larry J. Schaaf, *The Photographic Art of William Henry Fox Talbot*, Princeton and Oxford 2000, p. 202.
46. Talbot's mother passed on a critical comment in response to his calotype of Chambord, taken in 1843 in poor weather, 'as if you could not have remained there until the weather was clear, particularly with such an interesting object before you.' Quoted in ibid., p. 166.
47. In 1845, Talbot took calotypes in York with Calvert Jones, who chose the viewpoints. Talbot wrote, 'Crowds of admiring spectators surrounded the camera wherever we planted it.' Talbot to Constance Talbot, 29 July 1845, FTM LA 45-110.
48. The artificiality of this battle may be judged by the experience of George Harvey, a member of the Photographic Society of Scotland, who was attacked as the opponent of art photography on the grounds that he had moved Oscar Reijlander's *Two Ways of Life* to a poor position in the Arts and Manufactures Exhibition in Edinburgh, when in fact he had a high opinion of it and had hung it in a good position. This situation is discussed in Sara Stevenson, 'David Octavius Hill without Robert Adamson', *The Photographic Collector,* vol. 2, no. 3 (1981), pp. 14–24.
49. James Ross, 'A Few Extracts from an Old Photographer's Ledger', *The British Journal of Photography* (14 February 1873), p. 75.
50. 'Paper read by Sir David Brewster, at the first monthly meeting of the Photographic Society of Scotland, held April 8th, 1856', *Photographic Notes*, vol. 1, no. 1 (1856), p. 8.
51. G. S. Kinnear to Hill, 12 April 1856, SRO.
52. Draft letter Hill to Kinnear, 14 December 1856, RSA.
53. Anon (presumed to be John Brown), review of the Photographic Society of Scotland's exhibition, *The Edinburgh News* (26 December 1857). See also David Brewster, *The Stereoscope*, London 1856.
54. The exhibition set of these photographs is in the collection of the Metropolitan Museum of Art, New York.
55. John Brown, 'Mr Hill's Calotypes', *The Scotsman* (10 February 1862). Taylor is quoted in a notice of the International Exhibition, *The British Journal of Photography* (15 May 1862), p. 129. *Horae Subsecivae* (leisure hours) is the title of John Brown's published essays.

CHAPTER THREE

1. Hill to Roberts, 12 March 1845, NLS TD 1742.
2. Quoted in Helmut and Alison Gernsheim, *L. J. M. Daguerre. The History of the Diorama and the Daguerreotype,* New York 1968, p. 85.
3. Talbot to Forbes, 27 February 1839, and Forbes to his sister, 20 May 1839, quoted and discussed by Graham Smith, 'James David Forbes and the Early History of Photography' in Kathleen Collins (ed.), *Shadow and Substance. Essays on the History of Photography in Honor of Heinz K. Henisch*, Michigan 1990, pp. 9–11.
4. Hill to Roberts, 14 March 1845, NLS TD 1742.
5. Hill to Henry Bicknell, 17 January 1849, George Eastman House Collection MS AC H645 acc 830.
6. Mary Warner Marien, *Photography and its Critics: A Cultural History, 1839–1900*, Cambridge 1997, p. 97, and Lady Eastlake, 'Photography' (1857), republished in *Photography: Essays and Images. Illustrated Readings in the History of Photography*, ed. Beaumont Newhall, London 1981, p. 91.

7. Ibid.
8. He recommended 'damning Prick-the-louse [a derogatory term for a tailor] "with a spot" – and putting in his place a stalwart black-browed smith', Hill to Combe, 27 August 1844, NLS MS 7272 fo. 54.
9. Elizabeth Rigby, review of books on modern German painting, *Quarterly Review*, vol. 78 (March 1846), p. 333.
10. Eastlake 'Photography' (1857), republished in *Photography: Essays and Images. Illustrated Readings in the History of Photography*, p. 91.
11. I Corinthians 13: 11.
12. The painting was exhibited in the RSA with a long quotation from the *Quarterly Review* (September 1843) in the catalogue.
13. Edmund Burke, *A Philosophical Inquiry into the Origin of our Ideas of the Sublime and Beautiful, with an Introductory Discourse Concerning Taste*, London 1823, p. 83.
14. 'The Art of Poetry', *The Collected Works of Horace*, trans. Lord Dunsany and Michael Oakley, London 1961, p. 292.
15. Hugh Miller, *My Schools and Schoolmasters*, Edinburgh 1852, pp. 171–2.
16. Kenneth J. Cameron, *The Schoolmaster Engineer*, Dundee 1988, p. 22.
17. Quoted in Beaumont Newhall, *The Daguerreotype in America*, 3rd revised ed., New York 1976, p. 16.
18. John Brown, review of the RSA exhibition, *The Witness* (22 April 1846).
19. Nasmyth to Hill, 30 April 1845, ROE.
20. Sir Joshua Reynolds, *Discourses Delivered to the Students of the Royal Academy*, intro. Roger Fry, London, 1905, p. 308.
21. Ibid., p. 230.
22. Ibid., p. 247.
23. Quoted in John M. Gray, 'The Early History of Photography' in Andrew Elliot, *Calotypes by D. O. Hill and Robert Adamson*, Edinburgh 1928, p. 6.
24. Larry Schaaf proposes that Talbot understood the concept, for the opposite reason, because he was 'not shackled by a past body of artistic endeavors and was able to accept immediately a whole new type of visual representation'. See Larry J. Schaaf, *The Photographic Art of William Henry Fox Talbot*, Princeton 2000, p. 15.
25. Heinrich Schwarz, *David Octavius Hill, Master of Photography*, trans. Helene E. Fraenkel, George G. Harrap & Co., London, 1932, pp. 38–9.
26. At a meeting of the Photographic Society of Scotland in December 1856, reported in *Photographic Notes*, vol. 1 (1857), p. 8.
27. Henry Bankes, *Lithography; or the Art of Making Drawings on Stone*, Bath 1813, facsimile reprint, London 1976, p. 22. This was the first independent work on lithography published in English. It was used in the article on lithography in David Brewster (ed.), *The Edinburgh Encyclopaedia*, vol. 13, 1830, pp. 44–7.
28. Antony Griffiths, *Prints and Printmaking. An Introduction to the History and Techniques*, 2nd ed., London 1996, p. 102.
29. Hugh Miller, 'The Calotype', *The Witness* (12 July 1843).
30. Quoted in Daphne Foskett, *John Harden of Brathay Hall 1772–1847*, Kendal 1974, p. 52.
31. One of Harden's sketches is illustrated in Sara Stevenson, *Hill and Adamson's 'Fishermen and Women of the Firth of Forth'*, Edinburgh 1992, p. 42.
32. Quoted in Pieter van der Merwe, *The Spectacular Career of Clarkson Stanfield 1793–1867*, exhibition catalogue, Tyne and Wear County Museums 1979, p. 101.
33. John Ruskin, *Modern Painters*, vol. 1, in E. T. Cook and Alexander Wedderburn (eds), *The Works of John Ruskin*, vol. 3, London 1903, p. 223.
34. Hill to Roberts, 26 February 1845, NLS TD 1742.
35. Haydon to Hill, 13 April 1846, NLS Acc 11782, and *The Life of Benjamin Robert Haydon, Historical Painter*, ed. and compiled by Tom Taylor, London 1853, p. 85.
36. Elizabeth Rigby, review of books on modern German painting, *Quarterly Review*, vol. 78 (March 1846), p. 333.
37. Miller 'The Calotype', *The Witness* (12 July 1843).
38. Ibid.
39. Ibid.
40. Journal entry, 29 January 1846, quoted in *The Life of Benjamin Robert Haydon, Historical Painter*, ed. and compiled by Tom Taylor, vol. 3, p. 300. Haydon was in Edinburgh from 20 February to 13 March 1846, lecturing on Fuseli and Wilkie. Hill may have given him a group of the calotypes on this occasion.
41. Eric George, *The Life and Death of Benjamin Robert Haydon, Historical Painter, 1786–1846*, Oxford 1967, p. 54.
42. Quoted by Aaron Scharf, *Art and Photography*, London 1968, p. 4.
43. For a positive view, see Heinrich Schwarz, *Art and Photography: Forerunners and Influences*, ed. William E. Parker, Rochester 1985; Peter Galassi, *Before Photography: Painting and the Invention of Photography*, exhibition catalogue, Museum of Modern Art, New York 1981.
44. David Hockney, *Secret Knowledge: Rediscovering the Lost Techniques of the Old Masters*, London 2001, pp. 12–13.
45. Edward MacCurdy, *The Notebooks of Leonardo da Vinci*, vol. 1, London 1938, p. 243.
46. Reynolds, *Discourses Delivered to the Students of the Royal Academy*, p. 360.
47. John H. Hammond, *The Camera Obscura: A Chronicle*, Bristol 1981, p. 47. Reynolds's camera, which is in the Science Museum, London, is illustrated on p. 48.
48. F. M. Redgrave, *Richard Redgrave: A Memoir Compiled from his Diary*, London 1891, pp. 295–6.
49. Richard Wendorf, *Sir Joshua Reynolds, The Painter in Society*, London 1996, p. 236.
50. Quoted in ibid., p. 117.
51. Martin Kemp, *The Science of Art: Optical themes from Brunelleschi to Seurat*, New Haven and London 1990, p. 193.
52. Daniele Barbaro, *La Pratica della Perspettiva*, quoted in ibid., p. 190.
53. Journal entry, 20 July 1818, quoted in K. M. Lyell, *Life, Letters and Journals of Sir Charles Lyell*, vol. 1, London 1881, pp. 78–9. Secondary methods of viewing dramatic reality may also have been designed for people too feeble to cope with the terrors of the Sublime. D. G. Goyder, on viewing the Falls of Clyde in the 1820s, reported: 'They were the first falls I had ever beheld, except as delineated in books, but I was awe-stricken by them, and began to turn dizzy, but my friend suddenly pushed me into a little room, where there were mirrors so arranged as to present all the grandeur of the scene without feeling any danger. I was told this room had been constructed at considerable expense in order to enable the nervous and timid to behold the magnificence of the falls without danger, several tragical occurrences having taken place previously.' *My Battle for Life. The Autobiography of a Phrenologist*, London 1857, p. 189.
54. Count Francesco Algarotti, *Essay on Painting* (1764), quoted in Aaron Scharf, *Art and Photography*, London 1968, p. 4
55. Galassi, *Before Photography: Painting and the Invention of Photography*. For further examples, see Philip Conisbee, Sarah Faunce and Jeremy Strick, *In the Light of Italy: Corot and Early Open-Air Painting*, exhibition catalogue, National Gallery of Art, Washington 1996.
56. Lawrence Gowing, *The Originality of Thomas Jones*, London 1985, p. 52.
57. See A. D. Morrison-Low and A. D. C. Simpson, 'A New Dimension: A Context for Photography before 1860', *Light from the Dark Room*, exhibition catalogue, National Galleries of Scotland, Edinburgh

1994, pp. 15–28. In 1835, Maria Short opened a Popular Observatory on Calton Hill, with equipment including a camera obscura and a camera lucida. The list of patrons includes the painters James Skene and Alexander Nasmyth, as well as the photographic inventor, Mungo Ponton. See Veronica Wallace, 'Maria Obscura', *Edinburgh Review*, vol. 88 (1992), pp. 101–9.

58. His drawing is illustrated in Morrison-Low and Simpson, 'A New Dimension: A Context for Photography before 1860', *Light from the Dark Room*, p. 25.
59. 23 September 1801, *The Diary of Joseph Farington*, ed. Kenneth Garlick and Angus MacIntyre, vol. 5, New Haven and London, 1979, p. 1631.
60. Hill to Roberts, 12 March 1845, NLS TD 1742.
61. Robert Hunt, 'On the Fading of Photographic Pictures', *The Art Journal*, new series, vol. 1 (1855), p. 210.
62. In a collection of manuscript letters relating to the exhibition, Mitchell Library, Glasgow, quoted by A. D. Morrison-Low, 'Dr John Adamson and Thomas Rodger: Amateur and Professional Photography in Nineteenth-century St Andrews' in Julie Lawson, Ray McKenzie and A. D. Morrison-Low (eds), *Photography 1900: The Edinburgh Symposium*, National Museums and National Galleries of Scotland, Edinburgh, 1992, p. 26.
63. There are examples in the University of St Andrews Library, Special Collections Department, album 4.
64. I am indebted to Mike Ware for his comments on this.
65. Peter Bower, *Turner's Papers. A Study of the Manufacture, Selection and Use of his Drawing Papers 1787–1820*, exhibition catalogue, Tate Gallery, London 1990, pp. 43 and 64.
66. Hill may have bought this lens, which was owned by his wife after his death. It passed to J. T. Cochrane and J. Craig Annan and is now in the collection of the Royal Photographic Society, see Katherine Michaelson, *A Centenary Exhibition of the Work of David Octavius Hill 1802–1870 and Robert Adamson 1821–1848*, exhibition catalogue, Scottish Arts Council, Edinburgh 1970, no. 295.
67. On 12 June 1843, Thomas Davidson delivered a talk to the Royal Scottish Society of Arts on a compound achromatic camera. 'A number of very beautiful specimens of Daguerreotype and of Calotype, taken by Major Playfair and by Mr Adamson, by means of this Camera, both portrait and landscape, were exhibited.' Report in the *Edinburgh Evening Courant* (19 June 1843). See also, Thomas Davidson, *The Art of Daguerreotyping, with the Improvements of the Process and Apparatus*, Edinburgh 1841; John Nichol, 'Reminiscences of Thomas Davidson, a Weaver Lad', *British Journal of Photography*, vol. 26 (1879), p. 391 and A. D. Morrison-Low and J. R. R. Christie (eds), *'Martyr of Science', Sir David Brewster 1781–1868*, Edinburgh 1984, pp. 94–5.
68. Jones to Talbot, 29 May 1841, FTM, LA 41–34.
69. Jones to Talbot, 1 October 1845, FTM, LA 45-133. I am indebted to Michael Gray for these references.
70. Letter to the editor, *Photographic Journal*, vol. 6, no. 103 (1859), p. 264. This passage also suggests a connection with the Bryson family of instrument makers. Hill and Adamson calotyped Robert Bryson, a notable watch and clock maker; his son, Alexander, claimed to have taken the first portrait daguerreotype in Scotland, in 1840, and his younger brother, James Mackay Bryson, was involved in photography in the 1850s. See T. N. Clarke, A. D. Morrison-Low and A.D.C. Simpson, *Brass and Glass. Scientific Instrument Making Workshops in Scotland*, Edinbrugh 1989, pp. 112–22.
71. From the way he begins by referring to 'Adamson & Hill', it may be assumed that having known Adamson first he would not, as later writers did, have assigned actions or authority to Hill, which properly belonged to Adamson.
72. Report of a paper by Andrew Fyfe, given on 27 March 1839, *Proceedings of the Royal Scottish Society of Arts*, vol. 1 (1841), appendix, p. 33.
73. Hill to Kinnear, 14 December 1856, RSA MS.
74. See Floyd and Marion Rinhart, 'Wolcott and Johnson; their camera and their photography', *History of Photography*, vol. 1, no. 2, April 1977, pp. 129–34, and NLS Acc 534/107.
75. Joseph Lewis, 'Practical Notes and Suggestions on Various Processes' in W. Gamble (ed.), *The Process Year Book*, vol. 3 (1897), p. 100. His mirror, made by Messrs Chadburn of Liverpool, had a five-inch focus. I am indebted to Michael Gray for this reference.
76. Hill to David Roberts, 29 December 1846, NLS TD 1742.
77. Hill to Scott, 25 October 1848, inserted in the John Scott album of calotypes, NLS.
78. James Pittendrigh Macgillivray, 'The Art of Photography', *The Photographic Journal*, vol. 70 (1930), p. 10.
79. E. W. Dallas, letter to the editor, *The Journal of the Photographic Society* (April 1853), p. 44. According to R. C. Hungerford, this was 'possibly the first proposal to use deliberately, a lens with optical faults.' 'The Soft-focus Lens – its origin and use', *Royal Photographic Society Historical Group Quarterly*, no. 80 (Spring 1988), p. 8.
80. Mrs William Sharp, 'D. O. Hill, R. S. A.' *Camera Work*, no. 28 (October 1909), p. 19.
81. Robert Louis Stevenson, *Edinburgh Picturesque Notes*, London 1954, p. 78.
82. Robert Hunt, 'Photography, with some of its peculiar phenomena' *The Art Journal*, vol. 4 (1852), p. 101.
83. Hill wrote to Constable in 1830 requesting the loan of 'one or more of those triumphs of your pencil which have so often excited the admiration of many members of our Institution on their visit to the Metropolis', RSA letter book, December 1830, p. 23. Hill's familiarity with prints after both Turner and Constable can be assumed from his brother's print selling business. Alexander Hill promoted English as well as Scottish prints, which are mentioned in his obituary: 'many of the works of Lawrence, Wilkie, Landseer, and Leslie; and in landscape, of Turner, Constable, Collins, Stanfield and Roberts.' *Edinburgh Evening Courant* (18 June 1866).
84. John Adamson, 'Photography', in William and Robert Chambers (eds), *Chambers's Information for the People*, vol. 2, Edinburgh and London 1857, p. 779.
85. Ruskin, *Modern Painters*, vol. 1, in E. T. Cook and Alexander Wedderburn (eds), *The Works of John Ruskin*, vol. 3, London 1903, p. 157.
86. Elizabeth Rigby, 'The Art of Dress' (first published in *Quarterly Review*, March 1847), republished as *Music and the Art of Dress*, London 1852, pp. 90–2.
87. Draft letter, Hill to Ruthven, probably 1847, RSA.
88. Hill to Roberts, 14 March 1845, NLS TD 1742.
89. Anon (presumed to be D. O. Hill), *The Disruption of the Church of Scotland: An Historical Picture*, Edinburgh 1866, p. 3.
90. Hill to Roberts, 18 October 1850, NLS TD 1742.
91. John Adamson to the Photographic Society of Scotland, 29 November 1861, SRO GD 356/12/71.
92. See A. D. Morrison-Low, 'Dr John Adamson and Thomas Rodger: Amateur and Professional Photography in Nineteenth-century St Andrews', *Photography 1900: The Edinburgh Symposium*, Edinburgh 1992, pp. 18–37.
93. Quoted in Sara Stevenson, *Thomas Annan 1829–1887*, Edinburgh 1990, p. 8.
94. Quoted in Dorothy Norman, *Alfred Stieglitz, An American Seer*, New York, 1960, p.56.
95. Beaumont Newhall, *Focus: memoirs of a life in photography*, Boston 1993, p. 137.

96. Quoted by Beaumont Newhall in 'The Challenge of Photography to this Art Historian', Peter Walch and Thomas F. Barrow (eds), *Perspectives in Photography: Essays in Honor of Beaumont Newhall*, Albuquerque 1986, p. 3.
97. Alvin Langdon Coburn, 'The Old Masters of Photography', *Century Magazine,* vol. 90 (1915), p. 909.
98. Ansel Adams, *Making a Photograph*, New York 1936, p. 13.

CHAPTER FOUR

1. Tom Taylor (ed.), *Life of Benjamin Robert Haydon, Historical Painter, from his Autobiography and Journals*, vol. 1, London 1853, pp. 381 and 383.
2. Quoted in Rosalind K. Marshall, *Virgins and Viragos. A History of Women in Scotland from 1080 to 1980*, London 1983, p. 178.
3. Henry Cockburn, *Memorials of his Time*, Edinburgh 1856, p. 41. The text was written between 1821 and 1830.
4. Samuel Smiles (ed.), *James Nasmyth, Engineer, An Autobiography*, London 1891, p. 53.
5. Ibid., p. 336.
6. Nasmyth to Hill, 5 August 1845, ROE.
7. See D. F. MacDonald, *Scotland's Shifting Population 1770–1850*, Glasgow 1937.
8. Thomas Frognall Dibdin, *A Bibliographical Tour in the North Counties of England and Scotland*, vol. II, London 1838, p. 578.
9. Anon, biographical note on D. O. Hill, *The Art Journal*, new series, vol. 2 (October 1850), p. 309.
10. Anon, 'Death of Mr D. O. Hill, R. S. A.', *Edinburgh Evening Courant* (18 May 1870).
11. Ibid.
12. Nasmyth to Hill, 30 April 1845, ROE.
13. 'Death of Mr D. O. Hill', *Edinburgh Evening Courant* (18 May 1870).
14. Hill to Paton, 17 January 1853, NLS Acc 11315.
15. Alice Liddell, quoted in Morton N. Cohen, *Lewis Carroll, A Biography*, New York, Toronto and London 1995, p. 86.
16. C. L. Dodgson, 'A Photographer's Day Out', quoted in Helmut Gernsheim, *Lewis Carroll – Photographer*, London 1949, p. 118.
17. Colin Ford and Roy Strong, *An Early Victorian Album. The Photographic Masterpieces (1843–1847) of David Octavius Hill and Robert Adamson*, New York 1976, p. 54.
18. Thomas Rodger, 'The Collodion Process', *Journal of the Photographic Society* (21 May 1857), p. 278.
19. In 1841, he was living with four women and his two-year-old daughter and, in 1851, the household included five women and two teenage girls.
20. Hill refers to the 'Lady Superintendent', as 'Our kind friend Miss Murray of the Institution.' Hill to Paton, 6 January 1852, NLS Acc 11315.
21. Hill to Paton, 11 August 1852, NLS Acc 11315.
22. Thomas to Jane Welsh Carlyle, Charles Richard Sanders (ed.), *The Collected Letters of Thomas and Jane Welsh Carlyle,* vol. 7, Durham, North Carolina 1977, p. 150. Carlyle reversed his opinion and in 1840 spoke of her as 'No bad person at all; a great deal of *heart* in her, a kind of unsubduable courage, which is the ground root of all.' Ibid., vol. 12, p. 79.
23. Hill to Mr and Mrs Nasmyth, 24 November 1852, MS in a private collection.
24. 'Obituary of Lady Ruthven', *The Scotsman* (7 April 1885).
25. Thomas Wemyss Reid, *Memoirs and Correspondence of Lyon Playfair*, Ilkley 1976, p. 196.
26. Hill to Macdonald, July 1853, NLS Acc 11782.
27. Hill to Paton, 25 October 1851, NLS Acc 11315.
28. J. Craig Annan, 'David Octavius Hill, R.S.A. – 1802–1870', *Camera Work*, no. 11 (July 1905), p. 19.
29. William Milligan Sloane (ed.), *The Life of James McCosh*, Edinburgh 1896, pp. 61–2.
30. See Pat Jalland, *Death in the Victorian Family*, Oxford 1996.
31. Hill to John and Jane Macdonald, 29 December 1869, NLS Acc 11782.
32. See Jalland, *Death in the Victorian Family*, p.4.
33. Hill to Roberts, 26 April 1845, NLS TD 1742.
34. Hugh Miller, 'The Two Prints', *The Witness* (24 June 1843).
35. Announcement in *The Scotsman* (November 1862).
36. D. G. Goyder, a phrenologist and Swedenborgian minister, described a visit to J. N. Paton, senior, 'then a member of the Society of Friends', and after a long conversation with him 'felt happy that my entertainer responded to my opinion in almost every particular.' D. G. Goyder, *My Battle for Life. The Autobiography of a Phrenologist*, London 1857, pp. 274–6.
37. Hill to Paton, 19 November 1853, NLS Acc 11315.
38. See Dominique Brachlianoff, *Le Poème de l'âme. The Poem of the Soul. Louis Janmot*, Paris 1995.
39. Hill to Paton, 18 September 1854, NLS Acc 11315.
40. Janmot's work took a new direction in 1854–5. His first works were oil paintings, but at this time he turned to charcoal on paper. He had been and continued to be unsuccessful in his exhibitions of this work and eventually published the whole cycle in a set of carbon prints. Connections between his painting and that of the 'English Pre-Raphaelites' have been proposed, but 'no direct link has been established.' Brachlianoff, *Le Poème de l'âme. The Poem of the Soul. Louis Janmot*, p. 22. There is a possibility that he was influenced by either or both Hill and Paton and that the apparent Pre-Raphaelite connection could have been made in Scotland.
41. Hill to Paton, 11 December 1851, NLS Acc 11315.
42. Katherine Michaelson, *A Centenary Exhibition of the Work of David Octavius Hill 1802–1870 and Robert Adamson 1821–1848*, exhibition catalogue, Scottish Arts Council, Edinburgh 1970, p. 11.
43. Hill to Mrs James Hogg, undated *c.* 1840, NLS MS 2245, fo. 305.
44. Ann Hill to Jane Macdonald, 4 July 1840, NLS Acc 11782. Their second daughter died within hours of the birth about 23 July. The 1841 census records Hill, Ann and Charlotte, with Isabella Nasmyth, described as of 'independent means', and two female servants, Elizabeth Hill and Margaret Donaldson, living at 28 Inverleith Row.
45. Hugh Miller, 'Characteristics of the Crimean War' in Rev. John Davidson (ed.), *Leading Articles on Various Subjects*, Edinburgh 1870, p. 298.
46. Hill to Paton, 11 July 1853, NLS Acc 11315.
47. Hill to Macdonald, July 1853, NLS Acc 11782. This letter quotes Robert Burns, 'Ye Banks and Braes o' Bonnie Doon', Susanna Blamire, 'The Siller Crown', John Keats, 'Endymion', Milton, 'L'Allegro', and apparently parodies Shakespeare, 'Take, O take those lips away,/ That so sweetly were forsworn/And those eyes, the break of day/ Lights that do mislead the morn.' *Measure for Measure,* Act 4, Scene 1, 1.
48. Hill to Ann Hill, 19 October 1840, NLS Acc 11608.
49. Hill to Charlotte, 9 April 1850, negative copy of letter in GUL.
50. The April 1851 census lists D. O. Hill as the head of the Calton Hill household, with his sister, noted as a widow and 'annuitant', with her daughters, Margaret, aged 21, Sarah, aged 19, and Ann, aged 13, the two last described as scholars.
51. Hill to Paton, 19 November 1851, NLS Acc 11315.This is a parody of the Robert Burns's poem, 'Whistle oe'r the lave [shame or pity] o't', James Kinsley (ed.), *The Poems and Songs of Robert Burns*, Oxford 1968, p. 434.
52. Sarah Watson to Paton, 23 December 1851, NLS Acc 11315.

53. Hill to Paton, 5 August 1854, NLS Acc 11315.
54. Hill to Macdonald, 23 September 1862, NLS Acc 11608.
55. Quoted in Sarah A. Tooley, 'A Famous Lady Sculptor. An Interview with Mrs D. O. Hill', *The Young Woman*, no. 35, August 1895, p. 365.
56. Ibid. p. 364.
57. Ibid.
58. Ibid., p. 365.
59. Mrs William Sharp, 'D. O. Hill, R. S. A.', *Camera Work*, no. 28 (October 1909), p. 18
60. See Robin Lee Woodward 'Nineteenth-Century Scottish Sculpture', Ph.D. thesis, Edinburgh University 1977, vol. 1, pp. 75–6.
61. Henrietta Ward, who married another painter when she was seventeen, in 1848, later wrote: 'In my young days most people would have agreed ... that a wife and mother had no right to be a practitioner in paint, and I think in most households it would have been rendered impossible by the husband's and relations' combined antagonism to the idea', quoted in Pamela Gerrish Nunn, *Victorian Women Artists,* London 1987, p. 137.
62. Whitney Chadwick, *Women, Art, and Society*, 2nd ed., London 1996, p. 217.
63. Tooley, 'A Famous Lady Sculptor. An Interview with Mrs D. O. Hill', p. 363.
64. Hill to John and Jane Macdonald, 29 December 1869, NLS Acc 11782. One copy of this bust is in the collection of the SNPG, another stands on his grave in the Dean Cemetery in Edinburgh.
65. NLS MS 2629 f. 248.
66. Quoted in *Autobiography of Thomas Guthrie, D.D. and Memoir by his sons, Rev. David K. Guthrie and Charles J. Guthrie*, 3rd. ed., vol. 2, London 1874, pp. 417–19.
67. *Journal of Henry Cockburn 1831–1854,* vol. 2, Edinburgh 1874, p. 2.
68. The Rev. Thomas Malthus, in his *An Essay on the Principle of Population* (1798).
69. Quoted in Mrs Oliphant, *Thomas Chalmers*, London 1905, p. 102.
70. Ibid. p. 129.
71. 'Distraining', which means seizing goods in payment of debt, is an English legal term, which apparently gives the picture an English rather than Scottish context.
72. Tom Taylor (ed.), *Life of Benjamin Robert Haydon, Historical Painter, from his Autobiography and Journals*, vol. 1, London 1853, p. 284.
73. In *Little Dorrit* (which he thought of calling *Nobody's Fault*, in a letter quoted by Una Pope-Hennessy, *Charles Dickens*, Harmondsworth 1970, p. 487), Dickens addressed this idea that legal and bureaucratic procedure could be wholly opposed to moral right and the working of society.
74. William Hogarth's moral paintings were satirical and directed at the individual. Wilkie was widening the responsibility and looking at his subjects as real, unexaggerated people.
75. John Brown, review of the Scottish Academy exhibition for *The Witness*, republished in a pamphlet for the academy visitors, 1846.
76. Hill to Roberts, 7 February 1846, NLS TD 1742.
77. Ibid.
78. Obituary of Dr George William Bell, *Edinburgh Medical Journal*, vol. 34, no. 2 (1889), pp. 772–3.
79. George Bell, *Day and Night in the Wynds*, Edinburgh 1849, p. 78.
80. James Ballantyne, 'Introductory Scraps', *The Gaberlunzie's Wallet*, Edinburgh 1842.
81. Ibid.
82. Walter Geikie's etchings of street characters in the 1820s and 1830s are lively and convincing likenesses. He was associated with the academy and Hill owned a set of his engravings. See Sir Thomas Dick Lauder (ed.), *Etchings illustrative of Scottish Character and Scenery by the late Walter Geikie*, Edinburgh, 1885 and Duncan Macmillan, *Walter Geikie*, exhibition catalogue, Talbot Rice Arts Centre, Edinburgh 1984.
83. Duncan Macmillan has traced the concern for the relation between actual and moral vision from the model of Allan Ramsay and Gavin Hamilton in the eighteenth century through David Wilkie and Alexander Nasmyth to the calotypes and Hill's Disruption picture in *Scottish Art, 1460–1990*, Edinburgh 1990, pp. 188–96.
84. Ballantyne, 'Introductory Scraps', *The Gaberlunzie's Wallet.*
85. R. S. Rintoul, 'Encouragement of Art in Scotland', extract from the *Spectator*, no. 3 (1846), Hill had an offprint of this article, which is now in the ECL MSS C52527.
86. See Sara Stevenson, *Hill and Adamson's 'Fishermen and Women of the Firth of Forth'*, National Galleries of Scotland, Edinburgh 1991.
87. Edgar March, *Sailing Drifters*, London 1952, p. 226.
88. Captain John Washington, *Report on the loss of life and damage caused to fishing boats on the East coast of Scotland, in the gale of 19 August, 1848. Parliamentary Papers: Accounts and Papers*, vol. 51, 1849, p. 47.
89. James Wilson, *A Voyage Round the Coasts of Scotland and the Isles in 1841*, Edinburgh 1842, p. 160.
90. Frances Ann Kemble, *Record of a Girlhood*, vol. 1, London, 1878, p. 244.
91. Kate Douglas Wiggin, *Penelope's Experiences in Scotland, being extracts from the commonplace book of Penelope Hamilton*, Gay and Bird, London 1901, p. 209.
92. Wilson, *A Voyage Round the Coasts of Scotland and the Isles in 1841*, p. 161.
93. A comparison may be made with George Walker's series *Costume of Yorkshire* (1814), which is a distanced study of working-class life. See Roger Young, 'George Walker's *Costume of Yorkshire* (1814)', *Art History*, vol. 19, no. 3 (1996), pp. 393–417.
94. See Graham Smith, 'John Adamson, Sanitary Reform and the St Andrews Fishing Community', *History of Photography*, vol. 25, no. 2, Summer 2001, pp. 180–9.
95. There were sharply differing opinions of Playfair's reforms, which are quoted by Smith, ibid., pp. 184–7.
96. Thomas Guthrie, *Speaking to the Heart or Sermons for the People*, London 1862, p. 145.
97. 19 February 1843, *Memoirs and Correspondence of Lady Eastlake*, ed. Charles Eastlake Smith, London 1895, pp. 53–4.
98. Ibid., p. 92.
99. Charles Reade, *Christie Johnstone*, London, Paris and New York 1908.
100. For example, the calotypes include an unexplained group of English yachtsmen and Newhaven fishermen; the book's dramatic climax involves the fishermen and Christie Johnstone with the yachtsmen of the English viscount.

CHAPTER FIVE

1. Samuel Smiles (1812–1904) trained in medicine at Edinburgh University at the same time as Dr John Brown. Although he did not publish *Self-Help* until 1859, he first expressed the idea in a lecture in 1845. See Adrian Jarvis, *Samuel Smiles and the Construction of Victorian Values*, Stroud 1997.
2. Ibid., pp. 2–3.
3. The moral and rational difficulties raised by the proposal of predestination were presented in a nightmare fiction by James Hogg in *The Private Memoirs and Confessions of a Justified Sinner* (1824). Hill illustrated a shortened version of this in the selected *Tales and Sketches of the Ettrick Shepherd* (1837).
4. Hill to Paton, 15 March 1853, NLS Acc 11315.
5. See Charles Colbert, *A Measure of Perfection. Phrenology and the Fine*

Arts in America, Chapel Hill and London 1997, and Roger Cooter, *The Cultural Meaning of Popular Science. Phrenology and the Organization of Consent in Nineteenth-century Britain*, Cambridge 1984.
6. Quoted in ibid., p. 106.
7. Dr Wilkinson, quoted in D. G. Goyder, *The Autobiography of a Phrenologist*, London 1857, p. 183.
8. Cooter, *The Cultural Meaning of Popular Science*, pp. 140–2.
9. James Gall's diary, 22 March 1842, NLS Acc 5745.
10. Hugh Miller, 'The Calotype', *The Witness* (12 July 1843).
11. *The Fife Herald* (6 July 1843).
12. Colbert, *A Measure of Perfection*, pp. 52–5.
13. Alexander Hill was involved as a publisher of Audubon's *Birds of America*, see advertisement in D. O. Hill, *Views of the Opening of the Glasgow and Garnkirk Railway*, Edinburgh 1832.
14. Goyder, *The Autobiography of a Phrenologist*, pp. 293–4.
15. George Combe, *Phrenology Applied to Painting and Sculpture* (first published in the *Phrenological Journal* in 1844), London and Edinburgh 1855, pp. 46–7 and 88.
16. John Brown, review of the RSA exhibition, *The Witness* (22 April 1846).
17. Mungo Campbell, *David Scott 1806–49*, Edinburgh 1990, p. 14 and plate 9. Hill's letters on the subject are published in William Bell Scott, *Memoir of David Scott, R.S.A.*, Edinburgh 1850, pp. 334–7.
18. See Tom Taylor (ed.), *Life of Benjamin Robert Haydon, Historical Painter, from his Autobiography and Journals*, London 1853 and Eric George, *The Life and Death of Benjamin Robert Haydon, Historical Painter, 1786–1846*, Oxford 1967.
19. Quoted in *The Fife Herald* (2 July 1846).
20. Haydon to Hill, 13 April 1846, NLS Acc 11608.
21. Hill to Paton, 5 November 1853, NLS Acc 11315.
22. Walter Scott, *The Bride of Lammermoor. Waverley Novels*, vol. 13, Edinburgh and London 1831, p. 263.
23. Ibid., p. 270.
24. Quoted by Carol McGuirk, *Robert Burns and the Sentimental Era*, Phantassie 1997, p. 66.
25. Nasmyth to Hill, 5 August 1835, ROE.
26. James Skene, 'Painting', in David Brewster (ed.), *Edinburgh Encyclopaedia*, Edinburgh 1823.
27. Hugh Miller, *My Schools and Schoolmasters*, Edinburgh 1879, p. 168.
28. Advertisement, *The Scotsman* (13 October 1832).
29. Bell to Hill, 14 August 1836, ECL YTR 140.
30. Anon (D. O. Hill), 'Sir William Allan', *The Art Journal*, vol. 11 (1849), pp. 108–9.
31. Thomas Frognall Dibdin, *A Bibliographical Tour in the North Counties of England and Scotland*, vol. II, London 1838, p. 590.
32. Brown to John Taylor Brown, 10 March 1846, *Letters of Dr John Brown*, ed. his son and D.W. Forrest, London 1907, p. 64.
33. Hill to Paton, 15 January 1855, NLS Acc 11315.
34. Quoted in John Guille Millais, *The Life and Letters of Sir John Everett Millais,* London 1899, p. 161.
35. Ruskin to his parents, 19 August 1853, quoted in Introduction, 'Lectures on Architecture and Painting, Etc.' Cook and Wedderburn (eds), *Library Edition of Ruskin's Works*, vol. 12, p. xxvii.
36. See Tim Hilton, *John Ruskin. The Early Years 1819–1859*, New Haven and London 1985.
37. Quoted in Cook and Wedderburn (eds), *The Letters of John Ruskin 1827–1869, Library Edition of Ruskin's Works*, London 1909, p. 177. Presumably 'unobtrusive' has the meaning of someone who does not push himself forward.
38. Ruskin to Hill, 29 May 1867, NLS Acc 11608.
39. Henry Cockburn, *Memorials of his Time*, Edinburgh 1856, pp. 463–4.
40. For the history of the academy, see also Esmé Gordon, *The Royal Scottish Academy of Painting Sculpture and Architecture 1826–1976*, Edinburgh 1976.
41. *The Exhibition of the Scottish Academy of Painting, Sculpture and Architecture*, Edinburgh 1830, p. 6.
42. See Anon (Alexander Monro), *Scottish Art and National Encouragement*, Edinburgh 1846. Despite the Royal Charter, which the academy secured in 1838, the funding for the arts provided by the government grant remained in the hands of the Board and Institution. By contrast, both the London Royal Academy and the Hibernian Academy were directly funded by the government.
43. Letter published in ibid., pp. 8–9.
44. Hill to Roberts, 8 January 1846, NLS TD 1742.
45. Nasmyth to Hill, 28 April 1845, ROE.
46. Hill to Paton, 22 January 1855, NLS Acc 11315.
47. Hill to Paton, undated, Autumn 1853, NLS Acc 11315.
48. 'Lewis Carroll' (C. L. Dodgson), *The Annotated Alice: Alice's Adventures in Wonderland & Through the Looking Glass,* intro. and notes by Martin Gardiner, London 1960, p. 269. Gardiner points out that for Dodgson, an Oxford academic, Humpty Dumpty's argument was mediaeval nominalism; he may have encompassed senility within that idea.
49. Hugh Miller, 'An Unspoken Speech' in Rev. John Davidson (ed.), *Leading Articles on Various Subjects*, Edinburgh 1870, p. 277.
50. *Circuit Journeys by the late Lord Cockburn*, Edinburgh 1888, p.19.
51. Kinnear to Roberts, 22 January 1848, NLS Acc 7723.
52. Harvey to Roberts, 19 May 1848, NLS Acc 7723.
53. Hill to Roberts, 25 February 1845, NLS TD 1742.
54. Hill to John and Jane Macdonald, 29 December 1869, NLS Acc 11608.
55. George Harvey, *Notes of the Early History of the Royal Scottish Academy*, Edinburgh 1873, p. 86.
56. For a critical account of the political and social background to the setting up of the academy and the Association, see Duncan Forbes, 'Private advantage and public feeling: the struggle for academic legitimacy in Edinburgh in the 1820s', *Art and the Academy in the Nineteenth Century*, Manchester 2000, pp. 86–101.
57. Esmé Gordon, *The Royal Scottish Academy of Painting Sculpture and Architecture 1826–1976*, Edinburgh 1976, p. 58.
58. *The New Statistical Account for Scotland*, Edinburgh and London 1845, vol. 1, p. 706.
59. John Brown, review of *Modern Painters*, *The North British Review*, vol. 6 (1847), pp. 412–13.
60. Hill to Roberts, 3 February 1845, NLS TD 1742.
61. *Annual Report of the Royal Scottish Academy*, Edinburgh 1851.
62. Hill to Paton, 15 February 1853, NLS Acc 11315.
63. Hill to Paton, 7 February 1854, NLS Acc 11315.
64. Anonymous pamphlet for the academy visitors, republishing Dr John Brown's review of the academy exhibition for *The Witness* (1846).
65. Minute Book, 17 April 1846, Royal Scottish Academy.
66. Hill to Roberts, 20 February 1845, NLS TD 1742.
67. See Forbes 'Private advantage and public feeling: the struggle for academic legitimacy in Edinburgh in the 1820s' in *Art and the Academy in the Nineteenth Century*.
68. Hill to Roberts, 8 January 1851, NLS Acc 7723. Hill's interest in gas lighting may have been stimulated by Adam Anderson: 'He invented a method for purifying the gas, equally ingenious and simple. Its brilliancy is yet unrivalled.' *The New Statistical Account of Scotland: Perth*, vol. 10, Edinburgh and London 1845, p. 86.
69. Hill to Paton, 15 February 1853, NLS Acc 11315.
70. Hill to Paton, 2 January 1855, NLS Acc 11315.
71. Ruskin to Hill, 12 December 1853, NLS Acc 11608.

72. First published by his father, Thomas Hill, in George Street, Perth, and sold through William Blackwood in Edinburgh, and Rodwell and Martin and R. Ackermann in London at six and seven shillings. Fifteen of the prints were advertised for sale again in 1832 in his *Views of the Opening of the Glasgow and Garnkirk Railway*, along with *Five Views on the Clyde*, as published by Alexander Hill.
73. 'His [i. e. Hill's] engravers were as skilful as those who worked for Turner, being in some cases the very same men', P. G. Hamerton, *The Life of J. M. W. Turner*, London 1879, p. 229.
74. Anon (probably S. C. Hall), biographical note on Hill, *The Art Journal*, new series, vol. 2 (1850), p. 309.
75. Hill to Paton, 10 April 1851, NLS Acc 11315.
76. 'The Burns Gallery. The Exhibition of the Original Oil Pictures (upwards of Sixty in number) of the Beautiful and Romantic Scenery of The Land of Burns Painted by D. O. Hill R. S. A. Now open in Alex. Hill's Galleries, 67 Prince's Street'. Advertisement in *The Scotsman* (25 February 1852).
77. Hill to Paton, 17 February 1852, NLS Acc 11315.
78. Anon, 'Death of Mr D. O. Hill', *The Scotsman* (17 May 1870).
79. Hill to Constable, 25 November and 31 December 1842, NLS MS 3109 fo. 154 and 163.
80. Anon, 'Death of Mr D. O. Hill', *The Scotsman* (17 May 1870).
81. His son presented to the academy 'a portfolio of artist's proofs of the most important of his later publications.' *Royal Scottish Academy Report*, Edinburgh 1866, p. 16. See also, Anon, 'The Late Mr Alexander Hill', *The Edinburgh Evening Courant* (18 June 1866).
82. Thomas Frognall Dibdin, *A Bibliographical Tour in the North Counties of England and Scotland*, vol. II, London 1838, p. 590.
83. Ibid.
84. Hugh Miller, 'The Calotype', *The Witness* (12 July 1843).
85. See Graham Smith, ' "Calotype Views of St Andrews" by David Octavius Hill and Robert Adamson', *History of Photography*, vol. 7, no. 3 (1983), pp. 207–36.
86. Quoted in Francis Haskell, *Rediscoveries in Art: Some Aspects of Taste, Fashion and Collecting in England and France*, London 1976, p. 104. Haskell outlines the search for experience of paintings and the need for accurate reproductions of art at this time.
87. Thomas Annan obituary, *The British Journal of Photography*, vol. 34 (1887), p. 803. For a discussion of photographic art reproduction, see Anthony J. Hamber, *'A Higher Branch of the Art', Photographing the Fine Arts in England 1839–1880*, Amsterdam 1996.
88. Discussed in Sara Stevenson, *Thomas Annan 1829–1887*, Edinburgh 1990, pp. 6–7.
89. Hill to John and Jane Macdonald, 29 December 1869, NLS Acc 11608.
90. Hill to Roberts, 13 August 1860, NLS MS 14836 fo. 165.
91. Quoted by John Brown, 'The Disruption – The Signing of the Deed of Demission. A Picture by D. O. Hill', *The Scotsman* (24 May 1846).
92. Wilson to Hill, April 1845, RSA.
93. Elizabeth Rigby, review of books on modern German painting, *Quarterly Review*, vol. 78 (March 1846), p. 338.
94. Hill to Paton, 25 November 1853, NLS Acc 11315. This was presumably a reduced version of the picture.
95. The impact of Delaroche's painting on British art is discussed by Haskell, *Rediscoveries in Art*, pp. 9–11. See also Stephen Bann, *Paul Delaroche: history painted*, London 1997.
96. Sidney Gilpin, *Sam Bough, R.S.A., Some account of his life and works*, London 1905, p. 124. Bough had a lengthy quarrel with the academy and was an aggressive opponent both of Hill and Noël Paton.
97. S. C. Hall, review of the RSA exhibition, *The Art Journal*, vol. 13 (1868), p. 65.
98. Heinrich Schwarz, *David Octavius Hill, Master of Photography*, trans. Helene E. Fraenkel, London 1932, p. 25.
99. Helmut Gernsheim, 'The David Octavius Hill Memorial Lecture', *Creative Camera*, (September 1971), p. 301.
100. Colin Ford and Roy Strong, *An Early Victorian Album. The Photographic Masterpieces (1843–1847) of David Octavius Hill and Robert Adamson*, New York, 1976, p. 43.
101. The *Hémicycle* was designed for the amphitheatre, which was used for the École's prize-giving ceremony, and ' a pleasant scene of instruction could take place … when one more expert connoisseur might take the opportunity of instructing his young companions.' See Bann, *Paul Delaroche*, p. 208.
102. Anon (presumed to be D. O. Hill), *The Disruption of the Church of Scotland: An Historical Picture … Painted by D. O. Hill, R. S. A.*, Edinburgh 1866.
103. Hill to John and Jane Macdonald, 29 December 1869, NLS Acc 11608
104. Anon, 'Death of Mr D. O. Hill', *Edinburgh Evening Courant* (18 May 1870).
105. He is buried in the Dean Cemetery, with a bronze cast of Amelia Paton's bust on the gravestone.

CHAPTER SIX

1. John Taylor Brown, *Dr John Brown. A Biography and Criticism*, London 1903, p. 70.
2. John Brown, review of the RSA exhibition, *The Witness* (22 April 1846). The phrase, 'thick-coming fancies', comes from Shakespeare, *Macbeth*, Act 5, Scene 3, 39.
3. Henry Cockburn, *Memorials of his Time*, Edinburgh 1856, pp. 168–9.
4. Quoted in James Holloway and Lindsay Errington, *The Discovery of Scotland*, exhibition catalogue, National Gallery of Scotland, Edinburgh 1978, p. 109.
5. James Reed, *Sir Walter Scott: Landscape and Locality*, London 1980, p. 6.
6. In relation to *My Schools and Schoolmasters.* Thomas Carlyle, quoted in Sidney Lee (ed.), *The Dictionary of National Biography*, vol. 37, London 1894, p. 409.
7. Quoted in George Rosie, *Hugh Miller, Outrage and Order*, Edinburgh 1981, pp. 224–5.
8. J. B. S. Morritt, quoted by J. G. Lockhart, *The Life of Sir Walter Scott, Bart.*, London 1893, p. 226.
9. Discussed by Marinell Ash, *The Strange Death of Scottish History*, Edinburgh 1980.
10. *The Statistical Account of Scotland. Drawn up from the Communications of the Ministers of the Different Parishes by Sir John Sinclair*, Edinburgh 1792. This was not undertaken in England.
11. J. G. Kinnear to Roberts, 3 July 1844, NLS TD 1742.
12. Review by Thomas Cleghorn, quoted by Mark Haworth-Booth, *The Golden Age of British Photography*, exhibition catalogue, Victoria and Albert Museum, London 1984, p. 19. Cleghorn married Lord Cockburn's daughter in 1849.
13. Quoted in John Knox Laughton, *Memoirs of the Life of Henry Reeve*, London 1898, p. 357.
14. David Robinson, 'Introduction: Shows and Slides', *Magic Images. The Art of Hand-painted and Photographic Lantern Slides*, London 1990, p. 7.
15. Advertisement in the *Edinburgh Evening Courant,* 7 October 1843.
16. Dr John Ker, quoted in *Autobiography of Thomas Guthrie, D. D. and Memoir by his Sons, David K. Guthrie and Charles J. Guthrie*, London 1875, vol. 2, p. 359.
17. Ibid., pp. 160–1.

18. 'M. H.', 'Rough Pulpit Sketches by a Wayfarer, No.VIII Thomas Guthrie', *The Fife Herald* (17 September 1846).
19. *Autobiography of Thomas Guthrie, D. D. and Memoir by his Sons, David K. Guthrie and Charles J. Guthrie*, vol. 2, p. 189.
20. Discussed in Rensselaer W. Lee, *Ut Pictura Poesis: The Humanistic Theory of Painting*, New York 1967.
21. Guthrie to Hill, 1 December 1847, whereabouts of MS unknown, from a glass negative in GUL.
22. *Autobiography of Thomas Guthrie, D. D. and Memoir by his Sons, David K. Guthrie and Charles J. Guthrie*, p. 339.
23. In the collection of the SNPG.
24. *Autobiography of Thomas Guthrie, D. D. and Memoir by his Sons, David K. Guthrie and Charles J. Guthrie*, p. 436.
25. Laughton, *Memoirs of the Life of Henry Reeve*.
26. C. J. Guthrie, *Thomas Guthrie, Preacher and Philanthropist*, Edinburgh 1899, p. 15.
27. Thomas Chalmers, in his discourse 'Sympathy felt for man in distant places of Creation', quoted in Mrs Oliphant, *Thomas Chalmers*, London 1905, p. 91.
28. Quoted in Harry A. Cockburn (ed.), *Some Letters of Lord Cockburn with pages omitted from the Memorials of His Time*, Edinburgh 1932, p. 109.
29. Henry Cockburn, *Memorials of his Time*, Edinburgh 1856, pp. 57–8.
30. Quoted by Dr John Brown, 'Mystifications', *Horae Subsecivae*, London 1908, p. 134.
31. Hill to Paton, 23 January 1854, NLS Acc 11315.
32. John Stuart Blackie, *Notes of a Life*, ed. A. Stodart Walker, Edinburgh 1910, p. 109.
33. Brown to John Taylor Brown, 10 February 1846, quoted in ibid. pp. 62–3.
34. Hill to John Wilson, published in D. O. Hill, *The Land of Burns, A Series of Landscapes and Portraits, Illustrative of the Life and Writings of the Scottish Poet*, vol. 1, text by Robert Chambers and John Wilson, Glasgow, Edinburgh and London 1840, p. 105.
35. Mrs Gordon, *The Home Life of Sir David Brewster*, Edinburgh 1869, p. 289.
36. John Stuart Blackie, *Notes of a Life,* ed. A. Stodart Walker, Edinburgh 1910, pp. 101–2.
37. Samuel Smiles (ed.), *James Nasmyth, Engineer, An Autobiography*, London, 1891, p. 336.
38. John Brown, review of the RSA exhibition, *The Witness* (22 April 1846).
39. Stanley Cursiter, 'D. O. Hill. Famous Calotypes', *The Scotsman* (28 November 1928).
40. Quoted in Fiona Robertson, *Legitimate Histories: Scott, Gothic and the Authorities of Fiction*, Oxford 1994. This work has a useful chapter on 'Fictions of Authenticity', pp. 117–60, which includes this reference to Sarah Green.
41. Ibid., p. 126.
42. Hill to Paton, 6 January 1852, NLS Acc 11315, based on James and Horace Smith, 'A Tale of Drury Lane. The Burning', *Rejected Addresses*: 'You, Clutterbuck, come, stir your stumps, / Why are you in such doleful dumps? / A fireman and afraid of bumps! – / What are they feared on? fools! "od rot em!" / Were the last words of Higginbottom.' See Dwight Macdonald, *Parodies. An Anthology from Chaucer to Beerbohm – and After*, London 1964, preface, p. 15.
43. Ibid., pp. 13–14.
44. Professor Ferrier, preface, *Noctes Ambrosianae, The Works of Professor John Wilson*, Edinburgh and London 1855, vol. 1, pp. xvii–xviii.
45. In the collection of the SNPG. It was painted in 1844, for the publisher Blackwood.
46. Peter H. Drummond, *Perthshire in Bygone Days*, London 1879, p. 130.
47. Quoted, as a malicious review, in William Whitley, *Art in England 1800–1820*, Cambridge 1928, p. 284.
48. Hugh Miller, *My Schools and Schoolmasters*, Edinburgh 1879, p. 554.
49. Hugh Miller, *Scenes and Legends of the North of Scotland*, Edinburgh 1994, pp. 412–13.
50. Hugh Miller, 'An Unspoken Speech' in Rev. John Davidson (ed.), *Leading Articles on Various Subjects*, Edinburgh 1870, pp. 276–7. The editor thanks Hill for the frontispiece portrait, which is a lithograph taken from the large calotype of Miller as a mason.
51. Victorian anxiety about theatricality, as opposed to sincerity, is discussed in Nina Auerbach, *Private Theatricals: The Lives of the Victorians*, Cambridge, Massachusetts 1990.
52. Cockburn (ed.), *Some Letters of Lord Cockburn*, p. 33.
53. Thomas Carlyle, 'The hero as Poet [Shakespeare]', *On Heroes and Hero-Worship, The Works of Thomas Carlyle.* Centenary Edition, vol. 5, London 1897, p. 106.
54. Hill to Paton, 10 April 1851, NLS Acc 11315. *The Process of Augmentation* is published in *Lyrics Legal and Miscellaneous by the late George Outram*, ed. and intro. J. H. Stoddart, Edinburgh and London 1888, pp. 77–92.
55. See Ian Anstruther, *The Knight and the Umbrella*, London 1963, Mark Girouard, *The Return to Camelot. Chivalry and the English Gentleman*, New Haven and London 1981, and Sara Stevenson and Helen Bennett, *Van Dyck in Check Trousers*, exhibition catalogue, Scottish National Portrait Gallery, Edinburgh 1978.
56. Nasmyth to Hill, 5 August 1835, ROE. This surprisingly elderly sounding passage was written when Nasmyth was twenty-seven.
57. It passed from Hill to W. B. Johnstone and then to Noël Paton and is now in the Royal Museum of Scotland, NMS. A. 1902.429. See A. V. B. Norman, *Arms and Armour in the Royal Scottish Museum*, Edinburgh 1972, pp. 14–15 and fig. 11.
58. Hill showed 'A collection of calotype views of Scottish topographical antiquities and portraits, chiefly of individuals eminent as authors or artists' to the first of the society's evening 'conversaziones' in February, and showed them the door in April. Minute Book of the Society of Antiquaries, no . 5, p. 205. He later gave the society an album of the calotypes, which is now housed in the NMS. See Marinell Ash, ' "A fine, genial, hearty band": David Laing, Daniel Wilson and Scottish Archaeology' in A. S. Bell (ed.), *The Scottish Antiquarian Tradition*, Oxford 1968, p. 105
59. Thomas Chalmers, *On Political Economy in Connection with the Moral State and Moral Progress of Society* (1832), quoted by Donald C. Smith, *Passive Obedience and Prophetic Protest: Social Criticism in the Scottish Church 1830–1945*, New York 1987, p. 57.
60. Miller to John Johnstone, MS attached to a copy of the large Hill and Adamson calotype of Miller, SNPC, PGPR169-42. Lord Glenlyon's contribution seems to have been largely the spending of a vast sum of money on costumes for himself and his following, see Anstruther, *The Knight and the Umbrella*, p. 210.
61. Rensselaer W. Lee, *Ut Pictura Poesis: The Humanistic Theory of Painting*, New York 1967, p. 24.
62. Walter Scott, *The Antiquary. Waverley Novels*, vol. 5, Edinburgh and London, 1831, p. 166.
63. William Bell Scott, *Autobiographical Notes*, vol. 1, 1892, p. 115.
64. Cockburn bought the land in 1811 and had first considered a neo-Tudor design by William Burn. See John Gifford, Colin McWilliam and David Walker, *Edinburgh (The Buildings of Scotland)*, Harmondsworth 1984, p. 518.
65. Thomas Cleghorn proposed to her in 1848, but he was known to Cockburn and presumably his daughter well beforehand.
66. Cockburn to Hill, NLS Acc 10400.

67. See Stephen Bann, 'The historical composition of place: Byron and Scott', *The Clothing of Clio*, Cambridge 1984, pp. 93–111.
68. Cockburn to Hill, 28 October 1847, NLS Acc 11782.
69. Hill to Mrs Cleghorn, 12 May 1849, present whereabouts unknown.

CHAPTER SEVEN

1. Marinell Ash, *The Strange Death of Scottish History*, Edinburgh 1980, p. 13.
2. See, for example, Frank McLynn, *The Jacobites*, London, Boston and Melbourne 1985.
3. For the context and impact of Ossian, see William Ferguson, *The Identity of the Scottish Nation: An Historic Quest*, Edinburgh 1998, pp. 227–49.
4. Discussed, for example, by Robert C. Gordon, *Under Which King? A Study of the Scottish Waverley Novels*, Edinburgh and London 1969.
5. H. J. C. Grierson (ed.), *The Letters of Sir Walter Scott (1811–1814)*, London 1932–7, p. 302.
6. See Gerald Finley, *Turner and George IV in Edinburgh*, London and Edinburgh 1981.
7. Hill to Roberts, July 1859, NLS Acc 7723.
8. Paton's prospectus for the sculpture is discussed as evidence of unionist nationalism by R. J. Morris, 'Victorian values in Scotland and England' in T. C. Smout (ed.), *Victorian Values*, Oxford 1992, pp. 38–41.
9. Hugh Miller, 'The Scott Monument', in Rev. John Davidson (ed.), *Leading Articles on Various Subjects*, Edinburgh 1870, pp. 115–16.
10. Archibald Stodart Walker (ed.), *The Letters of John Stuart Blackie to his Wife*, Edinburgh 1909, p. 169. This is strongly contrasted with John Brown's disapproval, 'This is the great slaughter, the St Bartholomew of Grouse. Campbell of Monzie, that Freekirkman and purist, has wagered that he slays 230 brace this day, besides wounding and sending miserably into Eternity 3 times as many.' 12 August 1846, *Letters of Dr John Brown*, ed. by his son and D. W. Forrest, London 1909, p. 66.
11. This interior is illustrated in Christian Hesketh, *Tartans*, London 1961, p. 96.
12. George Stronach, Introduction, John Sobieski Stolberg Stuart and Charles Edward Stuart, *The Costume of the Clans*, Edinburgh 1892.
13. Charles Eastlake Smith (ed.), *Journals and Correspondence of Lady Eastlake*, London 1895, p. 55.
14. He was expressing doubt about their manuscript, *Vestiarum Scoticum*. Letter to Thomas Dick Lauder, 5 June 1829, *The Letters of Sir Walter Scott 1828–31*, vol. 11, ed. H. J. C. Grierson, London 1936, p. 201.
15. See Helen Smailes, *Kenneth MacLeay 1802–1878*, National Galleries of Scotland, Edinburgh 1992, p.17.
16. Quoted in ibid., p. 14.
17. MacLeay to Hill, 2 February 1847, RSA.
18. Anon (presumed to be D. O. Hill), *The Disruption of the Church of Scotland: An Historical Picture ... painted by D. O. Hill*, Edinburgh 1866, p. 16.
19. Helmut von Erffa and Allen Staley, *The Paintings of Benjamin West*, New Haven and London 1986, pp. 55–68.
20. Ibid., p. 213.
21. Quoted in ibid., p. 56.
22. See Lilly Koltun, 'Regalia of Conversion', *Studies in Photography*, 1999, pp. 9–11.
23. Walker (ed.), *The Letters of John Stuart Blackie to his Wife*, p. 117.
24. *Autobiography of Thomas Guthrie, D.D. and Memoir by his sons, Rev. David K. Guthrie and Charles J. Guthrie*, London 1875, vol. 2, p. 2.
25. Hill to Ruthven, 1847, RSA.
26. Anon (presumed to be D. O. Hill), *The Disruption of the Church of Scotland*, p. 16. Miller's independence of mind brought him into conflict with some of the Free Churchmen, notably R. S. Candlish, and the official history of the Free Church, written after Miller's suicide, omits his name. I am indebted to Michael Taylor for sharing his knowledge of Hugh Miller with me.
27. Hugh Miller, 'The Two Prints', *The Witness* (24 June 1843).
28. Anon (presumed to be D. O. Hill), *The Disruption of the Church of Scotland*, p. 4.
29. *Autobiography of Thomas Guthrie*, p. 67.
30. Quoted in Christopher Harvie, *Scotland and Nationalism: Scottish Society and Politics*, London 1977, p. 60.
31. Ibid. p. 61.
32. Stewart J. Brown and Michael Fry, *Scotland in the Age of the Disruption*, Edinburgh 1993, p. ix.
33. Dr Thomas Elder gave an account of a meeting at Dumfries, when Thomas Guthrie's superior rhetoric circumvented a Chartist attempt to break up the proceedings. Quoted in *Autobiography of Thomas Guthrie*, pp. 25–6.
34. Hill to Wilkie, 8 February 1832, RSA letter book pp. 73–4.
35. Anon (presumed to be D. O. Hill), *The Disruption of the Church of Scotland*, p. 16.
36. Ibid., p. 17.
37. 'The Posie', *The Poems and Songs of Robert Burns*, ed. James Kinsley, Oxford 1968, vol. 2, pp. 638–9.
38. 'Is the House Warm Yet?' set to the tune, 'When the house is rinnin' round about it's time enough to flit', *Legal and Other Lyrics by the Late George Outram*, new ed., ed. J. H. Stoddart, Edinburgh and London 1888, pp. 156–8.
39. Ibid., pp. 7 and 13–14.
40. Ibid., p. 24.
41. Ferguson, *The Identity of the Scottish Nation*, and Andrew Fletcher, 'An Account of A Conversation Concerning a Right Regulation of Governments for the common Good of Mankind', quoted in Paul H. Scott, *Andrew Fletcher and the Treaty of Union*, Edinburgh 1992, p. 98.
42. James Hogg, 'On the changes in the habits, amusements and conditions of the Scottish peasantry', reprinted in Judy Steel (ed.), *A Shepherd's Delight. A James Hogg Anthology*, Edinburgh 1985, p. 41.
43. See Alexander Whitelaw, *The Book of Scottish Song*, Glasgow 1844, which has Hill's frontispiece illustration, 'The Bower of Bessy Bell and Mary Gray', and T. F. Henderson, *Scots Vernacular Literature*, Edinburgh 1910.
44. Rev. Charles Rogers (ed.), *Life and Songs of Baroness Nairne*, Edinburgh 1896, pp. 164–6.
45. Joseph Ritson, in 1794, quoted in Carol McGuirk, *Robert Burns and the Sentimental Era*, Phantassie 1997, p. 125.
46. Discussed in ibid., pp. 103–48.
47. Quoted in ibid., p. 119.
48. John Brown, review of Hill's work in the RSA exhibition, *The Witness* (22 April 1846).
49. Tom Taylor (ed.), *Life of Benjamin Robert Haydon, Historical Painter, from his Autobiography and Journals*, vol. 1, London 1853, p. 284.
50. Eastlake Smith (ed.), *Journals and Correspondence of Lady Eastlake*, p. 56.
51. Leigh Hunt to John Hunter of Craigcrook, undated 1850s, quoted in *Manuscripts: Letters: Documents: Portraits: Artefacts & Works of Art*, sale catalogue, Roy Davids Ltd, Great Haseley 1999, p. 69.
52. Walter Scott, 'Advertisement', *The Antiquary, Waverley Novels*, vol. 5, Edinburgh and London 1831, pp. i–ii.
53. Wilkie to Miss Wilkie, 30 October 1817, quoted in Allan Cunningham, *The Life of Sir David Wilkie*, London 1843, vol. 1, p. 482.

54. Scott, *The Antiquary*, p. 68.
55. In the collection of the British Library.
56. Scott, *The Antiquary*, p. 249.
57. John Wilson writing as 'The Ettrick Shepherd', *Noctes Ambrosianae, The Works of Professor John Wilson*, Edinburgh and London 1855, vol. 1, p. 250.
58. Charles Reade, *Christie Johnstone*, London, Paris and New York 1908, pp. 234 and 239.
59. Ibid., p. 246.
60. Anon, 'Death of Mr D. O. Hill', *The Scotsman* (17 May 1870).
61. Reade, *Christie Johnstone*, pp. 201–2.
62. Quoted from *The Scotsman* in *The Fife Herald* (24 September 1846).
63. Hill to Paton, 18 September 1854, NLS Acc 11315.
64. Hill to Macdonald, July 1853, NLS Acc 11782.
65. John Milton, *L'Allegro*, 1. 127.
66. Burns to Margaret Chalmers, 16 September 1788 in G. Ross May (ed.), *The Letters of Robert Burns*, 2nd ed., vol. 1, Oxford 1985, p. 318.
67. Nasmyth to Hill, 30 April 1845, ROE.
68. Paul Strand, *Tir A'Mhurain*, commentary by Basil Davidson, London 1962, pp. 46–7.

CHAPTER EIGHT

1. J. G. Tunny, 'Early Reminiscences of Photography', *The British Journal of Photography* (12 November 1869), p. 545. Tunny was one of the photographers Hill knew and to some degree encouraged in the 1850s, when he took a series of portraits of the academicians.
2. Reported by Abraham Follett Osler in the first issue of the *Illustrated London News*. Hall credited William Hyde Wollaston with the original idea. The passage is quoted in Derek Howse, *Greenwich Time and the Discovery of the Longitude*, Oxford 1980, p. 86.
3. The minute calculations of time, enabled by the use of the telegraph and electricity, generally postdate the calotype partnership. In 1858, Charles Piazzi Smyth demonstrated, through simultaneous observations of the stars in Edinburgh and Greenwich, that the difference in longitude between Greenwich and Edinburgh was 12 minutes 56.005 seconds. See H. A. Brück and M. T. Brück, *The Peripatetic Astronomer. The Life of Charles Piazzi Smyth*, Bristol and Philadephia 1988, p. 83.
4. John Burnet, *Practical Hints on Composition in Painting*, London 1822, p. 10.
5. Illustrated in Jennifer Montagu, *The Expression of the Passions. The origin and influence of Charles Le Brun's* Conférence sur l'expression, New Haven and London 1995, fig. 140.
6. James Skene, 'Painting', in David Brewster (ed.), *Edinburgh Encyclopaedia*, Edinburgh 1823, p. 198.
7. *The Rent Day* was performed with scenery painted by Clarkson Stanfield. Act One ended with a tableau from Wilkie's painting of that title and Act Two ended with a tableau of *Distraining for Rent*, see Pieter van der Merwe, *The Spectacular Career of Clarkson Stanfield 1793– 1867*, exhibition catalogue, Tyne and Wear County Museums 1979, p. 63.
8. Copy of a letter from Wilkie to Clarkson Stanfield, January 1832, pasted to the back of *Distraining for Rent*, in the collection of the NGS.
9. George Bell, *Day and Night in the Wynds*, Edinburgh 1849, p. 78.
10. Advertisement in *The Witness* (24 May 1843).
11. Quoted from the *Daily Review* in Anon (presumed to be D. O. Hill), *The Disruption of the Church of Scotland: An Historical Picture ... painted by D. O. Hill*, Edinburgh 1866, p. 22.
12. Sara Stevenson, *Thomas Annan 1829–1887*, Edinburgh 1990, pp. 6–7.
13. *John Knox Delivering the Sacrament at Calder House*, was bought by the RSA. In 1842 Hill sketched it and drew up the key. See Lindsay Errington, *Tribute to Wilkie*, exhibition catalogue, National Gallery of Scotland, Edinburgh 1985, pp. 76–7.
14. 'M. H.', 'Rough Pulpit Sketches by a Wayfarer, No.VIII Thomas Guthrie', *The Fife Herald* (17 September 1846).
15. Anon (presumed to be D. O. Hill), *The Disruption of the Church of Scotland*, p. 17. Hill borrowed these from the antiquarian, David Laing, see Hill to Laing, 1867, University of Edinburgh Library, MSS 4814.
16. See Katherine Michaelson, *A Centenary Exhibition of the Work of David Octavius Hill 1802–1870 and Robert Adamson 1821–1848*, exhibition catalogue, Scottish Arts Council, Edinburgh 1970, p. 32.
17. In the UOSA, Album 8. See Graham Smith, 'A St Andrews Ghost Story', *History of Photography*, vol. 14, no. 1 (1990), p. 76
18. There is an affinity with Lewis Carroll's Cheshire Cat and, indeed, in the relation of perception to reality, with early twentieth-century physics and quantum theory. See John Gribbin, *In Search of Schrödinger's Cat*, London 1985.
19. This partial and transparent photographic presence was revived and exploited in the double exposures (the overlaying of two separate takes of photographic time) of both comic and serious spirit photography, later in the century.
20. John Brown, 'Dr. Chalmers', *Horae Subsecivae*, London 1908, pp. 114–15 and 123–4. See also, Sara Stevenson, 'David Octavius Hill and the Use of Photography as an Aid to Painting', *History of Photography*, vol. 15, no. 1 (1991), pp. 47–59
21. Ibid., p. 128.
22. Ibid., pp. 132–3.
23. *Letters of Dr John Brown*, ed. by his son and D. W. Forrest, London 1909, p. 291.
24. Hill to Henry Bicknell, 17 January 1849, George Eastman House Collection MS AC H645 acc 830.
25. Hill to Paton, 15 March 1853, NLS Acc 11315.
26. Hill to Paton, 11 July 1853, NLS Acc 11315.
27. Isaiah, 40: 8
28. 'To a Mountain-Daisy, On turning one down with the Plough, in April – 1786', in James Kinsley (ed.), *The Poems and Songs of Robert Burns*, Oxford 1968, vol. 1, pp. 228–9. The manuscript title of this was 'The Gowan'.
29. William Shakespeare, *Cymbeline*, Act 4, Scene 2, 210–11. Hill's captions appear in the album he gave to James Wilson, in the British Library. Hill exhibited a painting from the play in the RSA in 1834, no. 222, *Sketch: Forest Scene in 'Cymbeline'*.
30. Ibid., 220–4.
31. The Scottish emphasis in the first two paintings is discussed by Murdo Macdonald, *Scottish Art*, London 2000, pp. 65–6.
32. In a private collection.
33. Anon, 'Photography and the Elder Fine Arts', *Journal of the Photographic Society*, vol. 3 (1856), p. 30.
34. Quoted and discussed by Geoffrey Batchen, *Burning with Desire: The Conception of Photography*, Cambridge 1999, pp. 112–20.
35. 'Cuthbert Bede' (Rev. Edward Bradley), *Photographic Pleasures*, London 1855, p. 45.
36. John Brown, 'Mr Hill's Calotypes', *The Scotsman* (10 February 1862).
37. Isaiah, 64: 6
38. Sir John Robison, 'Notes on Daguerre's photography', *The Edinburgh New Philosophical Journal* (July 1839), pp. 155–7, quoted in Helmut and Alison Gernsheim, *L. J. M. Daguerre, the History of the Diorama and the Daguerreotype*, 2nd ed., New York 1968, p. 88.
39. Brown, 'Mr Hill's Calotypes'.

40. See Duncan Thomson, John Dick, David Mackie and Nicholas Phillipson, *The Art of Sir Henry Raeburn*, exhibition catalogue, Scottish National Portrait Gallery, Edinburgh 1997, p. 99.
41. 24 March 1846, Charles Eastlake Smith (ed.), *Journals and Correspondence of Lady Eastlake*, London 1895, p. 183.
42. Mrs Gordon, *'Christopher North' A Memoir of John Wilson*, Edinburgh 1863, vol. II, pp. 304–5.
43. Roger Fry (ed.), Sir Joshua Reynolds, *Discourses delivered to the students of the Royal Academy*, London 1905, p. 285.
44. See Mike Weaver, *Whisper of the Muse. The Overstone Album & Other Photographs by Julia Margaret Cameron*, Malibu 1986.
45. Cameron to John Herschel, quoted by Colin Ford, *The Cameron Collection. An Album of Photographs by Julia Margaret Cameron*, Wokingham and New York 1975, pp. 140–1.
46. Quoted in ibid., p. 21.
47. Malcolm Rogers, *Camera Portraits. Photographs from the National Portrait Gallery 1839–1989*, London 1989, p. 82.

CHAPTER NINE

1. Hill to the Board of Trustees, November 1820, uncatalogued Board of Trustees papers, SRO.
2. Hill to Sir William Arbuthnott, March 1827, uncatalogued Board of Trustees papers, SRO.
3. The illustrated portrait is probably identifiable as the Rev. William Bevan, secretary of the British Evangelical Alliance of Protestant churches, established, after meetings in Scotland in 1843 and 1845, in London in 1846. See John W. Ewing, *Goodly Fellowship: A Centenary Tribute to the Life and Work of the World's Evangelical Alliance 1846–1946*, 1946. Amongst those present were Adolphe Monod and J. H. Merle d'Aubigné, from Europe and Lyman Beecher and Samuel H. Cox from America, who were calotyped and appear in the Disruption picture. The oil sketches are now in the SNPG. I am indebted to Helen Smailes for the information.
4. Brewster to Talbot, 3 July 1843, NMPFT 1937-4926.
5. Helmut Gernsheim interpreted the phrase, 'general purposes of a very popular kind', to mean the enlargements Hill and Adamson made through a solar microscope. Helmut Gernsheim, 'The David Octavius Hill Memorial Lecture delivered at Edinburgh University on 9 May, 1970', *Creative Camera* (September 1971), p. 302.
6. See Helen E. Smailes, 'A History of the Statue Gallery at the Trustees' Academy in Edinburgh', *Journal of the History of Collections*, vol. 3 no. 2 (1991), pp. 125–43.
7. Thomas Frognall Dibdin, *A Bibliographical Tour in the North Counties of England and in Scotland*, vol. 2, London 1838, p. 556.
8. Hill to Roberts, 25 March 1846, NLS TD 1742.
9. George Paul Chalmers, quoted in Lindsay Errington, *Master Class: Robert Scott Lauder and his pupils*, exhibition catalogue, National Gallery of Scotland, Edinburgh 1983, p. 32.
10. William Henry Fox Talbot, 'Bust of Patroclus', *The Pencil of Nature*, London, 1844–1846, pl. V, reprinted in Mike Weaver (ed.), *Henry Fox Talbot: Selected Texts and Bibliography*, Oxford 1992, p. 89.
11. See Martin Kemp and Marina Wallace, *Spectacular Bodies: The Art and Science of the Human Body from Leonardo to Now*, exhibition catalogue, Hayward Gallery, London 2000, and Deanna Petheridge, *The Quick and the Dead: Artists and Anatomy*, exhibition catalogue, Hayward Gallery, London 1997.
12. J. Smith, *The Origin, Progress, and Present Position of the Royal College of Surgeons of Edinburgh 1505–1905*, Edinburgh 1905, p. 20.
13. Ibid., p. 47.
14. John Bruce, 'The Royal College of Surgeons of Edinburgh', *Scottish Medical Journal*, vol. 6, no. 578 (1961), p. 583.
15. Kemp and Wallace, *Spectacular Bodies*, p. 29.
16. Nasmyth to Hill, 5 August 1835, ROE.
17. Minutes of the Board of Manufactures, 12 December 1838 and 17 March 1840, SRO NG1/1/37. I am indebted to Helen Smailes for this reference.
18. See Jennifer Montagu, *The Expression of the Passions: the origin and influence of Charles Le Brun's* 'Conférence sur l'expression générale et particulière', New Haven and London 1994.
19. Harvey to Combe, NLS MS 7272, fo. 4.
20. Allan Ramsay, *Dialogue on Taste* (1755) quoted in Alastair Smart, *Allan Ramsay: Painter, Essayist and Man of the Enlightenment*, New Haven and London 1992, p. 141.
21. J. J. Winckelmann, *Reflections Concerning the Imitation of the Grecian Artists in Painting and Sculpture*, Glasgow 1766, p. 36.
22. The line of connection, from Ramsay to Hill and Adamson, is made by Duncan Macmillan, *Scottish Art 1460–1990*, Edinburgh 1990, pp. 104 and 154.
23. Charles Bell, *The Anatomy and Philosophy of Expression, as Connected with the Fine Arts*, 7th ed., London 1877, first published as *Essays in the Anatomy of Expression* (1806) and substantially revised and republished in 1842, after Bell had visited Italy and examined both paintings and sculpture for their expressiveness.
24. Ibid. pp. 18–19.
25. I have paraphrased Ernst Gombrich's analysis here, see *Art and Illusion: A Study in the Psychology of Pictorial Representation*, Washington 1960, pp. 155–6.
26. John Brown, review of Hill's pictures in the RSA exhibition, *The Witness* (22 April 1846).
27. Bell, *The Anatomy and Philosophy of Expression*, p. 131. This also connects with eighteenth-century ideas of society, expressed for example by Adam Smith in his *Theory of Moral Sentiment*, discussed by Nicholas Phillipson, 'Manners, Morals and Characters: Henry Raeburn and the Scottish Enlightenment', *The Art of Sir Henry Raeburn 1756–1823*, exhibition catalogue, National Galleries of Scotland, Edinburgh 1997, p. 34.
28. Giorgio Vasari, *The Lives of the Painters, Sculptors and Architects*, trans. A. B. Hinds, London and New York 1927, vol. 2, p. 164.
29. G. F. Waagen, *Works of Art and Artists in England*, vol. 1, London 1836, p. 240.
30. Hill to Roberts, 14 March 1845, NLS TD 1742. See Sara Stevenson, 'Cold Buckets of Ignorant Criticism: Qualified Success in the Partnership of David Octavius Hill and Robert Adamson', *The Photographic Collector*, vol. 4, no. 3 (1983), pp. 337–47.
31. Review in *The People's Journal* (1846), quoted by Helmut and Alison Gernsheim, *L. J. M. Daguerre: The History of the Diorama and the Daguerreotype*, New York 1968, p. 161.
32. John Brown, 'Mr Hill's Calotypes', *The Scotsman* (10 February 1862).
33. G.-B. Duchenne de Boulogne, *Méchanisme de la physionomie humaine*, Paris 1862; Charles Darwin, *On the Expressions of the Emotions in Man and Animals*, London 1872. The subject is discussed in Robert A. Sobieszek, '"Gymnastics of the Soul." The Clinical Aesthetics of Duchenne de Boulogne', *Ghost in the Shell: Photography and the Human Soul 1850–2000*, Los Angeles and Cambridge, Massachusetts 2000, pp. 32–79.
34. Particularly for his history paintings. See Jeremy Howard, *William Allan: Artist Adventurer*, exhibition catalogue, City of Edinburgh Museums and Galleries, Edinburgh 2001.
35. Brewster to Talbot, 28 November 1843, NMPFT 1937-4929.
36. Anon, review of Brewster's paper, *The Art Journal*, vol. 4 (1852), p. 312.
37. Quoted by Mrs Gordon, *The Home Life of Sir David Brewster*, Edinburgh 1869, p. 164.

38. R. Esmé Dell, granddaughter of Thomas Duncan, to James A. Finlayson, 9 February 1937, transcribed into Finlayson's notebook, NLS Acc 9297, vol. II, p. 671.
39. Hugh Miller, 'The Calotype', *The Witness* (12 July 1843).
40. There is a helpful discussion of this problem in relation to painting and photography in Montagu, *The Expression of the Passions*, pp. 2–8.
41. Ernst Gombrich, 'The Mask and the Face', *Art, Perception and Reality*, Baltimore and London 1972, p. 17.
42. John Ruskin, *Modern Painters,* vol. 1, *The Complete Works of John Ruskin,* vol. 3, ed. E. T. Cook and Alexander Wedderburn, London 1903, p. 147.
43. In discussing this question of recognition, Gombrich used the example of Emmanuel Shinwell, whose political success might be partly explained by the remarkable way the structure of his face dominated his appearance in photographs, from infancy to old age. Gombrich, 'The Mask and the Face', *Art, Perception and Reality*, p. 4.
44. Stevenson to his cousin, Bob, October 1885, *The Letters of Robert Louis Stevenson,* ed. Bradford A. Booth and Ernest Mehew, vol. 5, Yale 1994, p. 133. A copy of the photograph by A. G. Dew Smith is in the SNPC.
45. Stevenson to Will H. Low, 1886, in ibid., p. 177.
46. See Sara Stevenson and Helen Bennett, *Van Dyck in Check Trousers,* exhibition catalogue, Scottish National Portrait Gallery, Edinburgh 1978, pp. 45–63.
47. Quoted in Allan Cunningham, *Lives of the Most Eminent British Painters, Sculptors and Architects,* London 1833, vol. II, p. 216.
48. Hill to Paton, undated, around 22 December 1852, NLS Acc 11315. Paton exhibited a painting after Keats, in the RSA in 1852.
49. Hugh Miller, 'The Calotype', *The Witness* (12 July 1843).
50. Stanley Cursiter, 'D. O. Hill. Famous Calotypes', *The Scotsman* (28 November 1928).
51. Nasmyth to Hill, 10 December 1856, ROE.
52. Robert Chambers, *Traditions of Edinburgh*, new edition, Edinburgh and London 1868, p. 184.
53. Ibid., p. 160.
54. 'Willie brew'd a peck o' maut' in James Kinsley (ed.), *The Poems and Songs of Robert Burns*, Oxford 1968, pp. 476–7, quoted and discussed by Graham Smith, '*Edinburgh Ale* by David Hill and Robert Adamson', *Source Notes in the History of Art*, vol. 2, no. 3 (1983), p. 15.
55. John Gibson Lockhart, *Peter's Letters to His Kinsfolk*, Edinburgh, London and Glasgow, 1819, vol. 1, pp. 106–43 and vol. 3, p. 133.
56. Chambers, *Traditions of Edinburgh*.
57. John Stevens may have brought this large sculptural head for his portrait, taken at Rock House on 3 August 1844. There are three versions of this bust of Lucius Verus, the co-emperor of Marcus Aurelius, in the collection of casts purchased by the Royal Institution and now in the NGS. This, from the design of its pedestal, would appear to be a fourth.
58. Hill to Paton, 19 November 1851, NLS Acc 11315.
59. An opposition proposed, for example, in Allan Ramsay's *Dialogue on Taste.*
60. Hill to Ann Hill, 19 October 1840, NLS Acc 11608.
61. 'Here Phaeton lies: his father's car he tried/ Though proved too weak, he greatly daring died.' Ovid, *The Metamorphoses*, trans. and intro. Mary M. Innes, Harmondsworth 1970, p. 58.
62. Hill to Roberts, 12 March 1845, NLS TD 1742.
63. Alexander Pope, *The Dunciad*, 1. 318.
64. Smith, '*Edinburgh Ale* by David Hill and Robert Adamson'.
65. Bell, *The Anatomy and Philosophy of Expression*, pp. 200–1.
66. This may be seen in Paul Martin's street photographs taken in the 1890s with the concealed 'facile hand camera'. See Roy Flukinger, Larry Schaaf and Standish Meacham, *Paul Martin, Victorian Photographer*, London 1978, p. 81.
67. Bell, *The Anatomy and Philosophy of Expression*, p. 19.
68. A calotype of two Newhaven fishwives, attributed to a member of the Edinburgh Calotype Club, demonstrates how natural confidence and beauty were submerged by incompetent direction. This is illustrated in Sara Stevenson, *Hill and Adamson's 'Fishermen and Women of the Firth of Forth'*, Edinburgh 1991, p. 34.
69. 'Cuthbert Bede' (Rev. Edward Bradley), *Photographic Pleasures*, London 1855, p. 61. The difficulty of photographing even one fishwife in a natural setting defeated most photographers for some time thereafter. The *carte de visite* photographers of the 1860s and 1870s invited them to pose in the studio and stood them in front of painted backdrops of the reality outside.

CHAPTER TEN

1. Also in the sale were sixteen landscapes engraved after Turner and seven after Rubens. *Catalogue of the Valuable Collection of Pictures, Engravings, Sketches, Drawings, Calotypes, and other art property of the Late D.O. Hill, Esq., R. S. A.*, auction catalogue, T. Chapman, Edinburgh, 18, 19 and 21 November 1870, lot 386D
2. Murdo Macdonald, 'Wood Notes Wild: A Tale of Claude', in Alec Finlay (ed.), *Essays on the Poetry and Art of Ian Hamilton Finlay*, Edinburgh 1995, pp. 124–30.
3. D. O. Hill, *The Land of Burns, A Series of Landscapes and Portraits, Illustrative of the Life and Writings of the Scottish Poet*, text by Robert Chambers and John Wilson, Glasgow, Edinburgh and London 1840.
4. Discussed in Leslie Parris, *Landscape in Britain c.1750 – 1850*, exhibition catalogue, Tate Gallery, London 1973, p. 53.
5. Rensselaer W. Lee, *Ut Pictura Poesis: The Humanist Theory of Painting*, New York 1967.
6. Joshua Reynolds, *Discourses delivered to the students of the Royal Academy*, intro. Roger Fry, London 1905, pp. 360–1.
7. John Brown, review of the RSA exhibition, *The Witness* (22 August 1846).
8. See James Reed, *Sir Walter Scott: Landscape and Locality*, London 1980. For Scott's influence on Scottish landscape painting, see James Holloway and Lindsay Errington, *The Discovery of Scotland*, exhibition catalogue, National Gallery of Scotland, Edinburgh 1978.
9. Harry A. Cockburn (ed.), *Some Letters of Lord Cockburn with pages omitted from the Memorials of His Time*, Edinburgh 1932, p. 35.
10. Hill to Paton, 11 August 1852, NLS Acc 1135.
11. Samuel Smiles (ed.), *James Nasmyth, Engineer, An Autobiography*, London 1891, p. 335.
12. John Gibson Lockhart, *The Life of Sir Walter Scott, Bart.*, London 1893, p. 22.
13. Ibid., p. 754.
14. D. O. Hill, *The Land of Burns, A Series of Landscapes and Portraits, Illustrative of the Life and Writings of the Scottish Poet*, text by Robert Chambers and John Wilson, vol. 2, p.22.
15. Ibid., vol. 1, pp. 104–5.
16. Ibid.
17. Ibid., p. 105.
18. Sir Walter Scott, *Letters on Demonology and Witchcraft* (first published 1830), London 1884, pp. 101– 2.
19. As opposed to the northern spirits –'spirits of a coarser sort, more laborious vocation, and more malignant temper', ibid., p. 102.
20. Ibid., p. 106.
21. Jeremy Maas, *Victorian Fairy Painting*, exhibition catalogue, Royal Academy, London 1997.
22. Gillian Avery, *Nineteenth-Century Children: Heroes and Heroines in English Children's Stories,* London 1965, pp. 41–2.

23. D. O. Hill, *The Land of Burns, A Series of Landscapes and Portraits, Illustrative of the Life and Writings of the Scottish Poet*, text by Robert Chambers and John Wilson, vol. 1, p. 105.
24. Allan Cunningham, *Remains of Nithsdale and Galloway Song*, quoted in David Hogg, *Life of Allan Cunningham*, Dumfries 1875, p. 135.
25. Hill's *Poet's Dream* may well have been the inspiration for Noël Paton's two large-scale works, *The Quarrel* and *The Reconciliation of Oberon and Titania* (exhibited in 1846 and 1847). Hill's enthusiasm for the paintings was great. It is a mark of their respectability as 'national' subjects that *The Reconciliation* won a prize of £300 in the Westminster Hall Competition in 1847 and both pictures were acquired for the nation, now in the NGS.
26. Ralph Hyde, *Panoramania! The Art and Entertainment of the 'all-embracing' View*, exhibition catalogue, Barbican Art Gallery, London 1989, pp. 13 and 62.
27. John Gibson Lockhart, *Peter's Letters to his Kinsfolk*, Edinburgh, London and Glasgow 1819, pp. 8–9.
28. Turner's previous, large-scale watercolour, worked up from sketches made in 1801, is less overtly romantic; the New Town had not advanced so far and he was not then seeing through Scott's eyes. These works are illustrated in Katrina Thomson, *Turner and Sir Walter Scott. The Provincial Antiquities and Picturesque Scenery of Scotland*, exhibition catalogue, National Gallery of Scotland, Edinburgh 1999, p. 27 and pls 5 and 11.
29. Quoted in Gerald Finley, *Landscapes of Memory: Turner as Illustrator to Scott*, London 1980, p. 61.
30. Charles Eastlake Smith (ed.), *Memoirs and Correspondence of Lady Eastlake*, London 1895, p. 151.
31. Letter written by Hill, signed by George Watson, to Turner, December 1830, RSA letter book, p. 26.
32. In 1846, the RSA exhibited Turner's *Ivy Bridge, Devon* and *Mercury and Argus*; in 1849, *The Wreckers*; in 1850, *The Wreck of a Transport Ship*; in 1851, *The Opening of the Vintage of Mâcon* and *The Wreck of the Minatour*; in 1852, *Admiral Van Tromp Putting about in a Stiff Breeze*. See Graham Smith, 'David Octavius Hill, David Roberts, and J.M.W. Turner's Wreck of a Transport Ship', *The J. Paul Getty Museum Journal*, vol. 14 (1986), pp. 153–6.
33. Hill to Roberts, 25 February 1845, NLS TD 1742.
34. Hill to Roberts, 14 January 1852, NLS Acc 7723.
35. Turner also worked in Scotland from 1818, on Scott's *The Provincial Antiquities of Scotland*; in 1822, for the visit of George IV; and in 1831 and 1834, for the *Life, Prose Works* and *Poetical Works* of Scott, for which he made seventy-seven vignettes and views. While most of his book illustrations, from the mid-1820s, were worked up from designs already in his sketchbook: 'the Scott illustrations were treated as a special case and prompted additional visits.' Martin Butlin, Andrew Wilton, and John Gage, *Turner 1775–1851*, exhibition catalogue, Tate Gallery, London 1974, p. 98. Turner was caught up in the Scottish publishing revolution. Hill would have known these works and he owned a number of Turner's engravings. John Macrone, who commissioned Turner to illustrate the work of Thomas Moore, was a close friend of Hill.
36. Ibid., p. 45, quoting A. J. Finberg, *The Life of J. M. W. Turner, R. A.*, 2nd ed., 1961, p. 74.
37. He apparently found Turner difficult and thought his financial demands excessive, but a more balanced view of his appreciation of Turner's work may be see in the analysis by Finley, *Landscapes of Memory*.
38. Lockhart, *Peter's Letters to his Kinsfolk*, vol. 3, p. 280.
39. James Skene, 'Painting', *The Edinburgh Encyclopaedia*, vol. 16, Edinburgh 1831, pp. 263–4. This is discussed as 'the first considered review of Turner's scientific intentions as a painter of the nature of light', prefiguring John Ruskin by twenty years, by James Hamilton, *Turner, A Life*, London 1997, p. 216.
40. Hill to Roberts, 14 March 1845, NLS TD 1742. See Gillian Forrester, *Turner's 'Drawing Book': The Liber Studiorum*, exhibition catalogue, Tate Gallery, London 1996.
41. Hill to Roberts, 10 January 1850, Getty Museum, Acc no 84.XG.1003. For a discussion of this letter, see Graham Smith, 'David Octavius Hill, David Roberts, and J.M.W. Turner's Wreck of a Transport Ship', *The J. Paul Getty Museum Journal*, vol. 14 (1986), pp. 153–6.
42. John Ruskin, quoted in Forrester, *Turner's 'Drawing Book'*, p.149.
43. Brown to John Taylor Brown, 18 March 1846, *Letters of Dr John Brown*, ed. by his son and D. W. Forrest, London 1909, p. 65. 'Maker' or 'makar' is the old Scots word for poet.
44. John Brown, review of Hill's pictures, *The Witness* (22 April 1846). MacCulloch is now generally agreed to be the better painter.
45. John Brown, review of volumes 1 and 2 of *Modern Painters, The North British Review*, vol. 6 (1847), pp. 418–9.
46. Mrs William Sharp, 'D. O. Hill, R. S. A.', *Camera Work*, no. 28 (October 1909), p. 18.
47. Hill to Roberts, 12 March 1845, NLS TD 1742.
48. Ibid.
49. John Ruskin, *Modern Painters, The Works of John Ruskin*, library edition, vol. 3, ed. E. T. Cook and Alexander Wedderburn, London 1903, pp. 225–6.
50. David Roberts, working in London, asked D. R. Hay to send him prints of buildings and one of Hill and Adamson's calotypes of soldiers. From correspondence kindly communicated by Helen Guiterman, present whereabouts unknown.
51. Discussed in Sara Stevenson, 'David Octavius Hill and the Use of Photography as an Aid to Painting', *History of Photography*, vol. 15, no. 1 (1991), pp. 47–59.
52. Brewster to Talbot, 3 July 1843, NMPFT 1937–4926.
53. This complex subject is discussed by Martin Kemp, *The Science of Art: Optical Themes from Brunelleschi to Seurat*, New Haven and London 1990.
54. The importance of geometry in landscape painting may be illustrated by the fact that the mathematician, Mary Somerville, first heard about Euclid's *Geometry* from Alexander Nasmyth, who recommended it to the young ladies in his painting class. See *Personal Recollections from Early Life to Old Age of Mary Somerville*, London 1873, p. 49. See also A. D. Morrison-Low and A. D. C. Simpson, 'A New Dimension', *Light from the Dark Room*, exhibition catalogue, National Galleries of Scotland, Edinburgh 1994, pp. 23–6.
55. Hugh Miller, 'The Calotype', *The Witness* (12 July 1843).
56. The busyness of Hill's foreground partly disguises the energy of the setting and a possible connection with Turner's experiments in wide-angled landscape, such as *George IV at St Giles* (1822). This is discussed in Maurice Davies, *Turner as Professor. The Artist and Linear Perspective*, exhibition catalogue, Tate Gallery, London 1972, pp. 82–96.
57. Ernst Gombrich, in analysing Constable's *Wivenhoe Park*, makes the point that, in a view through a window, 'the house in the distance makes a startlingly tiny image … We all know that distant objects "look small," but we are rarely prepared for the real relationships of objects projected onto a plane.' *Art and Illusion. A Study in the Psychology of Pictorial Representation*, New York 1960, p. 300.
58. James Ross, 'A Few Extracts from a Photographer's Ledger', *The British Journal of Photography*, 14 February 1873, p. 75.
59. Hill painted another picture of Edinburgh, from what may have been an impossible angle, above the castle to the west and full into the

morning sun, more than ten years later. This is illustrated and discussed by Murdo Macdonald, *Scottish Art*, London 2000, pp. 100–2. He says of the painting 'Here he remakes Nasmyth's urban vision in the light of Turner.'

60. RSA Minute Books, 10 November 1851, p. 62. The official correspondence for the academy is missing for this period.
61. Ibid., 27 November 1851, pp. 73–4.
62. Hill to Paton, 19 November 1851, NLS Acc 11315.
63. The interest of artists in geology in the 1850s is discussed by Marcia Pointon, 'Geology and landscape painting in nineteenth-century England' in L. Jordanova and R. Porter (eds), *Images of the Earth. Essays in the history of the environmental sciences*, Chalfont St Giles 1979, pp. 93–123.
64. Quoted in George Rosie, *Hugh Miller: Outrage and Order. A Biography and Selected Writings*, Edinburgh 1981, p. 219.
65. A. W. Schlegel, quoted in William Vaughan, *Romanticism and Art*, London and New York 1994, p. 11.
66. Exhibited in the RSA in 1834.
67. 'The Solemn League and Covenant' in James Kinsley (ed.), *The Poems and Songs of Robert Burns*, Oxford 1968, vol. 2, p. 803, quoted by Chambers in D. O. Hill, *The Land of Burns, A Series of Landscapes and Portraits, Illustrative of the Life and Writings of the Scottish Poet*, text by Robert Chambers and John Wilson, vol. 2, p. 3.
68. Rev. Thomas Doig to Guthrie, 16 July 1837, quoted in *The Autobiography of Thomas Guthrie, D. D. and Memoir by his sons, Rev. David K. Guthrie and Charles J. Guthrie*, vol. 1, London 1875, p. 358.
69. The Protestant unease about iconography within the church had placed a greater emphasis on the meaning of the funeral monument. See Nigel Llewellyn, *The Art of Death: Visual Culture in the English Death Ritual c. 1500–c. 1800*, London 1991, pp. 121–36.
70. The connection with Poussin's *Et in Arcadia Ego* is made by Roy Strong in Colin Ford and Roy Strong, *An Early Victorian Album. The Photographic Masterpieces (1843–1847) of David Octavius Hill and Robert Adamson*, New York 1976, p. 60. See Erwin Panofsky, *'Et in Arcadia Ego', Meaning in the Visual Arts*, London 1970, pp. 340–67.
71. These inscriptions are visible in the engraving in Samuel Smiles (ed.), *James Nasmyth, Engineer, an Autobiography*, London 1891, pp. 11–12.
72. Robert Monteith, *A Theater of Mortality*, Edinburgh 1707, pp. 9–10.
73. Genesis, 2: 9. The interrelated pagan and Christian symbolism of the tree is discussed in Simon Schama, *Landscape and Memory*, London 1995, pp. 214–226.
74. Thomas Gray, *Elegy Written in a Country Churchyard*, xxiii.
75. Thomas Carlyle, 'The Hero as Divinity. Odin. Paganism: Scandinavian Mythology', *On Heroes and Hero-Worship*, lecture given May 1840, *The Works of Thomas Carlyle. Centenary Edition*, vol. 5, London 1897, p. 20.
76. Samuel Smiles (ed.), *James Nasmyth, Engineer, An Autobiography*, London 1891, pp. 36–8. The model tree is illustrated on p. 37.
77. The same subject was photographed by Thomas Keith in the 1850s, with the carved stone showing the skull of death, lit and visible between the branches. See John Hannavy, *Thomas Keith's Scotland*, Edinburgh 1981, p. 30.
78. The interest in memorial portraits and casts is discussed in Pat Jalland, *Death in the Victorian Family*, Oxford 1996, pp. 284–97. However, this chapter on 'The Consolations of Memory', which explores the way the Victorians preserved memory as part of the mourning process, does not include the idea of landscape painting.
79. *In Memoriam: The Calton* is in the collection of the Edinburgh City Art Centre. The whereabouts of *Newington* is currently unknown.
80. Illustrated and discussed in Leslie Parris, Ian Fleming-Williams and Conal Shields, *Constable: Paintings, Watercolours, and Drawings*, exhibition catalogue, Tate Gallery, London 1976, pp. 186–8 and Butlin, *Turner 1775–1851*, pp. 145–6.
81. 'Euphranor' (J. B. Manson), *Contemporary Scottish Art. A Series of Pen and Ink Sketches Drawn from the Exhibition of 1864*, Edinburgh 1864, p. 38.
82. Lord Cockburn, *Circuit Journeys*, Edinburgh 1888, pp. 310–11.
83. Hill to Roberts, 3 April 1845, NLS TD 1742. This committee expressed concern about Drummond of Hawthornden's determination to shut out the public from the Esk valley and re-published articles from journals on the Glen Tilt closure, as *No Passage This Way. The Opinions of the Press on the Stopping of the Highland Passes*, Edinburgh n.d. (1 July 1847).
84. *Journal of Henry Cockburn 1831–1854*, vol. 2, Edinburgh 1874, pp. 80–1.
85. Hugh Miller, *The Cruise of the Betsey*, Edinburgh 1870.
86. Anon, *Illustrations of the Principles of Toleration in Scotland*, Edinburgh, Glasgow, London, Manchester and Liverpool n. d. (1846). The drawings were by Hill, James Drummond and the lithographer, Andrew Maclure.
87. Royal Institution papers, SRO NG3/5/15 (27).
88. *Views of the Opening of the Glasgow and Garnkirk Railway, by D. O. Hill Esq ... Also, an Account of that and other Railways in Lanarkshire, drawn up by George Buchanan, Esq., Civil Engineer*, Alexander Hill, Edinburgh 1832.
89. Jack Simmons, *The Victorian Railway*, London 1991, p122. This is an interesting echo of the remark of Constable's brother: 'When I look at a mill painted by John, I see that it will *go round*, which is not always the case with other artists.' C. R. Leslie, *Memoirs of the Life of John Constable*, London 1949, p. 24.
90. Exhibited in the RSA, 1842, no. 154. Sir Samuel Brown invented a link enabling the construction of suspension bridges on a newly enlarged scale. His first bridge of this kind was the Union Bridge over the Tweed at Berwick. Alexander Nasmyth painted the scene and bridge, before it was built, to show the effect. Since Nasmyth died in 1840, Hill may have inherited the Irish commission from him. See the entry on Samuel Brown, *Dictionary of National Biography*, ed. Leslie Stephen, vol. 7, London 1886, pp. 27–8.
91. Hill to Ann Hill, 19 October 1840, NLS Acc 11608.
92. He advertised this series in 1842 and a group of drawings for the project appeared in the sale of his pictures (see n. 1).
93. John Gage, *Turner: Rain, Steam and Speed*, London 1972, p. 19.
94. Simmons, *The Victorian Railway*, p. 128.
95. RSA exhibition catalogue, 1850, no. 220.
96. Quoted in the RSA exhibition catalogue, Edinburgh 1850, no. 292.
97. Illustrated and discussed in Conal Shields, *Landscape in Britain*, exhibition catalogue, Tate Gallery, London 1973, pp. 67–8 and 73.
98. Hill to Bennet Woodcroft, 3 May 1858, Science Museum, London, Z27B 137. The painting was unsold at his death and appears in his sale catalogue (see n. 1).
99. Cockburn, *Circuit Journeys*, p. 129.
100. Hill to Roberts, 3 April 1845, NLS TD 1742.
101. See Nicholas M. McQ. Holmes, *Trinity College Church, Hospital and Apse*, Edinburgh 1988 and Graham Smith, 'A Calotype view of Trinity College, Edinburgh', *Burlington Magazine*, vol. 126 (1984), pp. 781–2.
102. For example, Thomas Annan's photographs of *The Old Closes and Streets of Glasgow*, taken between 1859 and 1861.
103. Hill to Cockburn, 28 March 1854, NLS MS 10994 fo. 67.

104. It was resold in 1858. 'Yesterday the property purchased in 1851 by the Town Council for the sum of £1,260, for the purpose of providing a site for Trinity College Church, as proposed to be restored on the old "style and model" was exposed to public roup in the saloons of Messrs Dowells and Lyon, at the upset price of £650 … The property has for the last few years been let to Mr D. O. Hill at the annual rent of £42.' *Edinburgh Courant* (10 June 1858). It fetched £880.

105. David Bryce produced a design for this, which is illustrated in Holmes, *Trinity College Church*, p. 23.

CONCLUSION

1. Sir Joshua Reynolds, *Discourses Delivered to the Students of the Royal Academy*, intro. Roger Fry, London 1905, p. 233.
2. David Brewster, review of Goethe's *Theory of Colours*, trans. Charles Lock Eastlake, *Edinburgh Review*, vol. 72 (October 1840), p. 124.

SELECT BIBLIOGRAPHY

Primary Texts

Adamson, John, 'Photography', in William and Robert Chambers, eds, *Chambers's Information for the People*, vol. 2, Edinburgh and London 1857, pp. 777–85.

Annan, James Craig, 'David Octavius Hill, R. S. A., 1802–1870', *Camera Work*, no. 11 (July 1905), pp. 17–21.

___, *J. Craig Annan. Selected Texts and Bibliography*, William Buchanan, ed., Oxford 1994.

Bell, Charles, *Essays on the Anatomy of Expression in Painting*, London 1806.

___, *The Anatomy and Philosophy of Expression as Connected with the Fine Arts*, seventh edition, London 1877.

Bell, George, *Day and Night in the Wynds of Edinburgh*, second edition, Edinburgh 1849.

Blackie, John Stuart, *Notes of a Life*, Archibald Stodart Walker, ed., Edinburgh 1910.

Brewster, Sir David, 'Photogenic Drawing or Drawing by the Agency of Light', *Edinburgh Review*, vol. 76 (1843), pp. 465–504.

___, 'Photography', *North British Review*, vol. 14 (1847), pp. 465–504.

___, 'President's address' and 'Transactions regarding the recent improvements in photography', *Report of the Twentieth Meeting of the British Association for the Advancement of Science*, London 1851, pp. xxii–xliv and 6.

___, *The Stereoscope*, London 1856.

___, 'Paper read by Sir David Brewster, at the first monthly meeting of the Photographic Society of Scotland, held April 8th, 1856', *Photographic Notes*, vol. 1, no.1 (1856), p. 8.

Brown, John, 'Review of the Royal Scottish Academy exhibition', *The Witness* (22 April 1846).

___, 'Review of the Photographic Society of Scotland's exhibition', *The Edinburgh News* (26 December 1857).

___, 'Mr. Hill's Calotypes', *The Scotsman* (10 February 1862).

Burnet, John, *Practical Hints on Light and Shade in Painting*, London 1826.

Burns, Robert, *The Poems and Songs of Robert Burns*, James Kinsley, ed., four volumes, Oxford 1968.

Carlyle, Thomas, 'On Heroes and Hero-Worship' (first published 1841) in *The Works of Thomas Carlyle*, centenary edition, volume 5, London 1897.

Carus, Carl Gustav, *The King of Saxony's Journey through England and Scotland in the Year 1844*, translated by S. C. Davidson, London 1846.

Chambers, Robert, *Traditions of Edinburgh*, new edition, Edinburgh and London 1868.

Cockburn, Lord, *Memorials of his Time*, Edinburgh 1856.

___, *Journal of Henry Cockburn, being a continuation of the memorials of his time, 1831–1854*, Edinburgh 1874.

___, *Circuit Journeys by the late Lord Cockburn*, Edinburgh 1888.

Combe, George, *Phrenology Applied to Painting and Sculpture*, London and Edinburgh 1855.

Cundell, George Smith, 'On the practice of the Calotype Process of Photography', *London, Edinburgh and Dublin Philosophical Magazine and Journal of Science*,third series, vol. 24 (May 1844), pp. 160 and 321–2.

Cunningham, Allan, *The Life of Sir David Wilkie*, London 1843.

Dafforne, James, 'David Octavius Hill', *The Art Journal*, new series, vol. 8 (1869), pp. 317–18 and vol. 9 (1870), p. 203.

Davidson, Thomas, 'The Solar Camera', letter to the editor, *The Photographic Journal*, vol. 6 (1859), p. 264.

Eastlake, Lady (Elizabeth Rigby), 'Review of books on modern German painting', *Quarterly Review*, vol. 78 (March 1846), pp. 332–48.

___, *Music, and The Art of Dress*, reprinted from *Quarterly Review*, London 1852.

___, *Memoirs and Correspondence of Lady Eastlake*, Charles Eastlake Smith, ed., London 1895.

___, 'Photography', first published in *Quarterly Review* (1857); republished in Beaumont Newhall, ed., *Photography: Essays and Images*, London 1981, pp. 81–95.

Farington, Joseph, *The Diary of Joseph Farington*, Kenneth Garlick, Angus MacIntyre and Kathryn Cave, eds, New Haven and London 1978–84.

Gordon, Mrs (Margaret Maria Brewster), *The Home Life of Sir David Brewster*, Edinburgh 1869.

Gordon, Mrs (Mary Wilson), *Christopher North: A Memoir of John Wilson*, Edinburgh 1862.

Guthrie, Rev. Thomas, *Autobiography of Thomas Guthrie, D. D. and Memoir by his sons, Rev. David Guthrie and Charles J. Guthrie, M. A.*, third edition, London 1874.

Harvey, Sir George, *Notes of the Early History of the Royal Scottish Academy*, Edinburgh 1873.

Hill, David Octavius, *Sketches of Scenery in Perthshire*, Perth 1821.

___, *Views of the Opening of the Glasgow and Garnkirk Railway. Also an account of that and other railways in Lanarkshire, drawn up by George Buchanan*, Edinburgh 1832.

___, *The Land of Burns, A series of landscapes and portraits, illustrative ofthe life and writings of the Scottish poet. The landscapes from paintings made expressly for the work, by D. O. Hill, Esq., R. S. A. The literary department by Professor Wilson … and Robert Chambers Esq.*, two volumes, Glasgow, Edinburgh and London 1840.

___, *Illustrations of the Principles of Toleration in Scotland*, lithographs by D. O. Hill, James Drummond and Andrew MacLure. No place or date, probably 1846.

___, 'Sir William Allan', *The Art Journal*, vol. 11 (1849), pp. 108–9.

___, (presumed to be Hill), *The Disruption of the Church of Scotland: An Historical Picture, (containing four hundred and fifty portraits) representing the Signing of the Deed of Demission of the First General Assembly of the Free Church. Painted by D. O. Hill, R. S. A.*, Edinburgh 1866.

HOGG, James, *The Poetical Works of the Ettrick Shepherd with an autobiography; and illustrative engravings chiefly from original drawings by D. O. Hill*, five volumes, Glasgow, Edinburgh and London 1838.

HUNT, Robert, 'Photography, with some of its peculiar phenomena', *The Art Journal*, vol. 4 (1852), pp. 101–2.

___, 'On the Fading of Photographic Pictures', *The Art Journal*, new series, vol. 1 (1855), pp. 210–11.

LAWSON, John Parker, *Scotland Delineated, A Series of Views*, vol. 2, London 1854.

LOCKHART, John Gibson, *Peter's Letters to his Kinsfolk*, second edition, three volumes, Edinburgh, London and Glasgow 1819.

___, *The Life of Sir Walter Scott, Bart.*, London 1893.

MILLER, Hugh, 'The Two Prints', *The Witness* (24 June 1843).

___, 'The Calotype', *The Witness* (12 July 1843).

___, *My Schools and Schoolmasters*, Edinburgh 1852.

___, *Leading Articles on Various Subjects*, Rev. John Davidson, ed., Edinburgh 1870.

MONRO, Alexander, *Scottish Art and National Encouragement*, Edinburgh 1846.

NASMYTH, James, *James Nasmyth, Engineer, An Autobiography*, Samuel Smiles, ed., London 1891.

OLIPHANT, Mrs. (Margaret), *Thomas Chalmers*, London 1905.

OUTRAM, George, *Legal and other Lyrics*, J. H. Stoddart, ed., Edinburgh and London 1888.

READE, Charles, *Christie Johnstone* (first published 1851), London 1889.

REYNOLDS, Sir Joshua, *Discourses Delivered to the Students of the Royal Academy*, introduced by Roger Fry, London 1905.

RIGBY, Elizabeth, *see* Eastlake, Lady.

RUSKIN, John, *Ruskin's Works*, Cook and Wedderburn, eds, library edition, 39 volumes, London 1903–12.

SCOTT, Sir Walter, *The Antiquary. Waverley Novels*, vols 5 and 6, Edinburgh and London 1831.

___, *Letters on Demonology and Witchcraft*, first published 1830, London 1884.

SHARP, Mrs William, 'D. O. Hill, R. S. A.', in Alfred Stieglitz, ed.,*Camera Work*, no. 28 (October 1909), pp. 17–19.

TALBOT, William Henry Fox, *Henry Fox Talbot, Selected Texts and Bibliography*, Mike Weaver, ed., Oxford 1992.

TOOLEY, Sarah A., 'A Famous Lady Sculptor. An Interview with Mrs D. O. Hill', *The Young Woman*, no. 35 (August 1895), pp. 361–7.

WILSON, John, *Noctes Ambrosianae. The Works of Professor Wilson of the University of Edinburgh*, vols 1–4, Professor Ferrier, ed., Edinburgh and London, 1856.

ANON. (probably Samuel Carter Hall), 'Biographical note on David Octavius Hill', *The Art Journal*, new series, vol. 2 (October 1850), p. 309.

___, 'The Late Mr Alexander Hill', *Edinburgh Evening Courant* (18 June 1866).

___, 'Death of Mr D. O. Hill', *Scotsman* (17 May 1870).

___, 'Death of Mr D. O. Hill, R. S. A.', *Edinburgh Evening Courant* (18 May 1870).

___, *Catalogue of the Valuable Collection of Pictures, Engravings, Sketches, Drawings, Calotypes, and other art property of the Late D. O. Hill, Esq., R. S. A.*, auction catalogue, T. Chapman, Edinburgh, 18, 19 and 21 November 1870.

___, *Disruption Worthies. A Memorial of 1843*, Edinburgh 1876.

VARIOUS AUTHORS, *The New Statistical Account for Scotland*, Edinburgh and London 1845.

___, *Exhibition of the Works of Industry of All Nations, 1851*, Reports of the Juries, London 1852.

___, *Dictionary of National Biography* Leslie Stephen and Sidney Lee, eds, vols 1–43, London 1885–1900.

SECONDARY TEXTS

ARNOLD, H. J. P., *William Henry Fox Talbot, Pioneer of Photography and Man of Science*, London 1977.

ASH, Marinell, *The Strange Death of Scottish History*, Edinburgh 1980.

BANN, Stephen, 'Erased Physiognomy, Theodore Géricault, Paul Strand and Garry Winogrand', *The Portrait in Photography*, London 1992, pp. 39–40.

BARLOW, Paul, 'Fear and loathing of the academic, or just what is it that makes the avant-garde so different, so appealing?' and 'Rewriting the Academic', *Art and the Academy in the Nineteenth Century*, Manchester 2000, pp. 1–32.

BARTHES, Roland, *The Rustle of Language*, Oxford 1986.

___, *Camera Lucida, Reflections on Photography*, translated by Richard Howard, London 1993.

BATCHEN, Geoffrey, *Burning with Desire. The Conception of Photography*, Cambridge, Massachusetts 1999.

BAXANDALL, Michael, *Patterns of Intention. On the Historical Explanation of Pictures*, New Haven and London 1985.

BENJAMIN, Walter, 'A Small History of Photography', in *One Way Street and Other Writings*, London 1979.

BOWER, Peter, *Turner's Papers. A Study of the Manufacture, Selection and Use of his Drawing Papers 1787–1820*, (exhibition catalogue), Tate Gallery, London 1990.

BROWN, Stewart J., 'Thomas Chalmers and the Communal Ideal', *Victorian Values*, Oxford 1992, pp. 61–80.

___ and Michael Fry, eds, *Scotland in the Age of the Disruption*,Edinburgh 1993.

BRUCE, David, *Sun Pictures: The Hill–Adamson Calotypes*, London 1973.

BUTLIN, Martin, Andrew Wilton and John Gage, *Turner 1775–1851* (exhibition catalogue), Tate Gallery, London 1974.

CHEAPE, Hugh, 'The Culture and Material Culture of Jacobitism', *Jacobitism and the '45*, London 1995, pp. 32–48.

CLARKE, T. N., A. D. Morrison-Low and A. D. C. Simpson, *Brass and Glass. Scientific Instrument Making Workshops in Scotland as Illustrated by Instruments from the Arthur Frank Collection at The Royal Museum of Scotland*, Edinburgh 1989.

COOTER, Roger, *The Cultural Meaning of Popular Science. Phrenology and the Organization of Consent in Nineteenth-century Britain*, Cambridge and elsewhere 1984.

DAUNTON, M. J., *Progress and Poverty. An Economic and Social History of Britain 1700–1850*, Oxford 1995.

DAVIES, Maurice, *Turner as Professor. The Artist and Linear Perspective* (exhibition catalogue), Tate Gallery, London 1972.

DEWITZ, Bodo von, Sara Stevenson, Larry Schaaf, Enno Kaufhold, Andreas Kase and Erich vom Endt, *David Octavius Hill und Robert Adamson: Von den Anfängen der künstlerischen Photographie in 19. Jahrhundert* (exhibition catalogue), Museum Ludwig, Agfa Photo-Historama, Cologne 2000.

ERRINGTON, Lindsay, *Tribute to Wilkie* (exhibition catalogue), National Gallery of Scotland, Edinburgh 1985.

___, 'Chiaroscuro in the Calotype', *Scottish Photography Bulletin* (Autumn 1986), pp. 4–7.

___, *David Wilkie 1785–1841*, Edinburgh 1988.

FERGUSON, William, *The Identity of the Scottish Nation: An Historic Quest*, Edinburgh 1998.

FINLEY, Gerald, *Landscapes of Memory: Turner as Illustrator to Scott*, London 1980.

FORBES, Duncan, 'Private advantage and public feeling: the struggle for academic legitimacy in Edinburgh in the 1820s', *Art and the Academy in the Nineteenth Century*, Manchester 2000, pp. 86–101.

FORD, Colin, *The Cameron Collection. An Album of Photographs by Julia Margaret Cameron, Presented to Sir John Herschel*, Wokingham, New York and elsewhere 1975.

___ and Roy Strong, *An Early Victorian Album. The Photographic Masterpieces (1843–1847) of David Octavius Hill and Robert Adamson*, New York 1976.

FORRESTER, Gillian, *Turner's 'Drawing Book', The Liber Studiorum* (exhibition catalogue), Tate Gallery, London 1996.

GALASSI, Peter, *Before Photography: Painting and the Invention of Photography* (exhibition catalogue), Museum of Modern Art, New York 1981.

GASSER, Martin, 'A Masterpiece: Heinrich Schwarz's Book on David Octavius Hill', *Image*, vol. 36, nos 1–2. (1993), pp. 33–53.

GERNSHEIM, Helmut, 'The David Octavius Hill Memorial Lecture, delivered at Edinburgh University on 9 May, 1970', *Creative Camera* (September 1971), pp. 300–5.

GIFFORD, William, 'The Patons of Dunfermline', *Dunfermline Press* (25 July 1903).

GOMBRICH, Ernst, *Art and Illusion: A Study in the Psychology of Pictorial Representation*, Washington 1960.

___, 'The mask and the face', *Art, Perception and Reality*, Baltimore and London 1972.

GORDON, Esmé, *The Royal Scottish Academy of Painting, Sculpture and Architecture 1826–1976*, Edinburgh 1976.

GRAY, John Miller, introduction and articles in *Calotypes by D. O. Hill and Robert Adamson*, Andrew Elliot, ed., Edinburgh 1928.

GUITERMAN, Helen, *David Roberts, R. A. 1796–1864*, London 1978.

HAMILTON, James, *Turner, A Life*, London 1997.

HAMMOND, John H., *The Camera Obscura: A Chronicle*, Bristol 1981.

HARVIE, Christopher, *Scotland and Nationalism: Scottish Society and Politics*, London 1977.

HAWORTH-BOOTH, Mark, *Photography: An Independent Art. Photographs from the Victoria and Albert Museum 1839–1996*, London 1997.

HENDERSON, T. F., *Scots Vernacular Literature*, Edinburgh 1910.

HILLS, Richard L., *Papermaking in Britain 1488–1988*, London 1988.

HOCKNEY, David, *Secret Knowledge. Rediscovering the Lost Techniques of the Old Masters*, London 2001.

HOLLOWAY, James and Lindsay Errington, *The Discovery of Scotland* (exhibition catalogue), National Gallery of Scotland, Edinburgh 1978.

HYDE, Ralph, *Panoramania! The Art and Entertainment of the 'all-embracing' View* (exhibition catalogue), Barbican Art Gallery, London 1989.

IRWIN, David and Francina, *Scottish Painters at Home and Abroad 1700–1900*, London, 1975.

JALLAND, Pat, *Death in the Victorian Family*, Oxford 1996.

JARVIS, Adrian, *Samuel Smiles and the Construction of Victorian Values*, Stroud 1997.

KEMP, Martin, *The Science of Art: Optical Themes in Western Art from Brunelleschi to Seurat*, New Haven and London 1990.

___ and Marina Wallace, *Spectacular Bodies: The Art and Science of the Human Body from Leonardo to Now* (exhibition catalogue), Hayward Gallery, London 2000.

KIRKBY, Maurice W. and Mary B. Rose, eds, *Business Enterprise in Modern Britain from the Eighteenth to the Twentieth Century*, London and New York 1994.

KOLTUN, Lilly, 'Regalia of Conversion: The Hill and Adamson Portraits of the Reverend Peter Jones or Kahkewaquonaby', *Studies in Photography* (1998), pp. 9–11.

LEE, Rensselaer W., *Ut Pictura Poesis: The Humanist Theory of Painting*, New York 1967.

LYDEN, Anne M., *In Focus: Hill and Adamson, Photographs from the J. Paul Getty Museum*; with the text of a colloquium between David Featherstone, Anne M. Lyden, A. D. Morrison-Low, Weston Naef, Jonathan Reff, Sara Stevenson and Michael Wilson, Los Angeles 1999.

MACDONALD, Murdo, 'Wood Notes Wild: A Tale of Claude', *Essays in the Poetry and Art of Ian Hamilton Finlay*, Alec Finlay, ed., Edinburgh 1995, pp. 124–30.

___, *Scottish Art*, London 2000.

MACGILLIVRAY, James Pittendrigh, 'The Art of Photography', *The Photographic Journal*, vol. 70 (1930), pp. 2–10.

MCLYNN, Frank, *The Jacobites*, London, Boston and Melbourne 1985.

MACMILLAN, Duncan, 'D. O. Hill and the Origins of Photography', *British Photography in the Nineteenth Century*, Mike Weaver, ed., Cambridge 1989, pp. 25–36.

___, *Scottish Art 1460–1990*, Edinburgh 1990.

MAYOR, A. Hyatt, 'The First Victorian Photographer', *The Metropolitan Museum of Art Bulletin*, vol. 17, no. 4 (December 1958), pp. 113–19.

MERWE, Pieter van der, *The Spectacular Career of Clarkson Stanfield 1793–1867* (exhibition catalogue), Tyne and Wear County Museums 1979.

MICHAELSON, Katherine, *A Centenary Exhibition of the Work of David Octavius Hill 1802–1870 and Robert Adamson 1821–1848* (exhibition catalogue), Scottish Arts Council, Edinburgh 1970.

___, 'The First Photographic Record of a Scientific Conference', *One Hundred Years of Photographic History: Essays in Honor of Beaumont Newhall*, Van Deren Coke, ed., Albuquerque 1975, pp. 109–16.

MONTAGU, Jennifer, *The Expression of the Passions: The Origin and Influence of Charles Le Brun's* 'Conférence sur l'expression générale et particulière', New Haven and London 1994.

MORRISON-LOW, A. D., 'Dr John Adamson and Robert Adamson: An Early Partnership in Scottish Photography', *The Photographic Collector*, vol. 2 (autumn 1983), pp. 198–214.

___, 'Sir David Brewster and Photography', *Review of Scottish Culture*, vol. 4 (1988), pp. 63–73.

___, 'Photography in Edinburgh in 1839: the Royal Society of Arts, Andrew Fyfe and Mungo Ponton', *Scottish Photography Bulletin*, no. 2 (1990), pp. 26–35.

___, 'Dr John Adamson and Thomas Rodger: Amateur and Professional Photography in Nineteenth-century St Andrews', *Photography 1900: The Edinburgh Symposium*, Edinburgh 1992, pp. 18–37.

___ and J. R. R. Christie, eds, '*Martyr of Science*': *Sir David Brewster 1781–1868*, proceedings of a bicentenary symposium, Edinburgh 1984.

NEWHALL, Beaumont, *Photography: Essays & Images*, New York 1980.

NICHOL, John, 'Reminiscences of Thomas Davidson, a Weaver Lad', *British Journal of Photography*, vol. 26 (1879), p. 391.

PETHERIDGE, Deanna, *The Quick and the Dead: Artists and Anatomy* (exhibition catalogue), Hayward Gallery, London 1997.

REED, James, *Sir Walter Scott: Landscape and Locality*, London 1980.

ROBERTS, Fiona, *Legitimate Histories: Scott, Gothic, and the Authorities of Fiction*, Oxford 1994.

ROSENTHAL, Michael, *Constable: The Painter and his Landscape*, New Haven and London 1983.

ROSIE, George, *Hugh Miller: Outrage and Order. A Biography and Selected Writings*, Edinburgh 1981.

SCHAAF, Larry J., *H. Fox Talbot's The Pencil of Nature, Anniversary facsimile*, introductory volume, New York 1989.

SCHAMA, Simon, *Landscape and Memory*, London 1995.

SCHARF, Aaron, *Art and Photography*, London 1968.

SCHWARZ, Heinrich, *David Octavius Hill, der Meister der Photographie*, Leipzig 1931; translated by Helene Fraenkel, New York 1931 and London 1932.

___, 'The Calotypes of D. O. Hill and Robert Adamson. Some Contemporary Judgements', *Apollo* (February 1972), pp. 123–8.

___, *Art and Photography: Forerunners and Influences*, William E. Parker, ed., New York 1985.

SHIELDS, Conal and Leslie Parris, *Landscape in Britain* (exhibition catalogue), Tate Gallery, London 1973.

SIM, Kathleen, *David Roberts, R. A. 1796–1864*, London, Melbourne and New York 1984.

SIMMONS, Jack, *The Victorian Railway*, London 1991.

SMAILES, Helen E., 'A History of the Statue Gallery at the Trustees' Academy in Edinburgh', *Journal of the History of Collections*, vol. 3, no. 2 (1991), pp. 125– 43.

SMART, Edward, *History of Perth Academy*, Perth 1932.

SMITH, Graham, 'Hill & Adamson at St Andrews: the Fishergate Calotypes', *The Print Collector's Newsletter*, vol. 12 (1981), pp. 33–7.

___, '*Edinburgh Ale* by David Hill and Robert Adamson', *Source Notes in the History of Art*, vol. 2, no. 3 (1983), p. 15.

___, 'A Calotype view of Trinity College Church, Edinburgh', *Burlington Magazine*, vol. 126 (1984), pp. 781–2.

___, 'A Group of Early Scottish Calotypes', *The Princeton University Library Chronicle*, vol. 46 (1984), pp. 81–94.

___, *Sun Pictures in Scotland* (exhibition catalogue), University of Michigan Museum of Art, Ann Arbor 1989.

___, 'James David Forbes and the Early History of Photography', in *Shadow and Substance. Essays on the History of Photography in Honor of Heinz K. Henisch*, Kathleen Collins, ed., Michigan 1990, pp. 9–11.

—, 'John Adamson, Sanitary Reform and the St Andrews Fishing Community', *History of Photography*, vol. 25, no. 2, summer 2001, pp. 180–9

___, *Disciples of Light: Photographs in the Brewster Album*, Malibu 1990.

SOBIESZEK, Robert A., *Ghost in the Shell: Photography and the Human Soul 1850–2000*, Los Angeles and Cambridge, Massachusetts, 2000.

STEINERT, Otto and Marlis, *David Octavius Hill/Robert Adamson: Inkunabeln der Photographie* (exhibition catalogue), Museum Folkwang, Essen 1963.

STEVENSON, Sara, *David Octavius Hill and Robert Adamson. A Catalogue of their Calotypes in the Collection of the Scottish National Portrait Gallery*, Edinburgh 1981.

___, 'David Octavius Hill without Robert Adamson', *The Photographic Collector*, vol. 2, no. 3 (autumn 1981), pp. 14–24.

___, 'Cold Buckets of Ignorant Criticism: Qualified Success in the Partnership of David Octavius Hill and Robert Adamson', *The Photographic Collector*, vol. 4, no. 3 (1983), pp. 336–47.

___, 'David Octavius Hill and Robert Adamson', in *British Photography in the Nineteenth Century. The Fine Art Tradition*, Mike Weaver, ed., Cambridge 1989, pp. 37–53.

___, *Thomas Annan 1829–1887*, Edinburgh 1990.

___, 'David Octavius Hill and the Use of Photography as an Aid to Painting', *History of Photography*, vol. 15 (1991), pp. 47–59.

___, *Hill and Adamson's 'Fishermen and Women of the Firth of Forth'*, Edinburgh 1992.

___, 'Drawing the Crowd: An Approach to Democracy in the Calotypes of D. O. Hill and Robert Adamson', *Scotlands*, vol. 3, no. 2 (1996), pp. 73–85.

___ and John Ward, *Printed Light. The Scientific Art of William Henry Fox Talbot and David Octavius Hill with Robert Adamson*, Edinburgh 1986.

STRAND, Paul, 'A Picture Book for Elders', *The Saturday Review of Literature*, no. 8 (12 December 1931), p. 372.

___, *Tir A'Mhurain: Outer Hebrides*, text by Basil Davidson, London 1962.

THOMSON, Duncan, John Dick, David Mackie and Nicholas Phillipson, *The Art of Sir Henry Raeburn* (exhibition catalogue), Scottish National Portrait Gallery, Edinburgh 1997.

THORP, Monica, 'Hill and Adamson without Adamson? The Ballochmyle Calotypes', *Scottish Photography Bulletin*, no. 2 (1989), pp. 25–9.

VAUGHAN, William, *Romanticism and Art*, London and New York 1994.

WEAVER, Mike, 'The Hard and Soft in British Photography', *The Photographic Collector*, vol. 4, no. 2 (1983), p. 197.

___, *Whisper of the Muse. The Overstone Album & Other Photographs by Julia Margaret Cameron*, Malibu 1986.

WENDORF, Richard, *Sir Joshua Reynolds, The Painter in Society*, London 1996.

WOLF, Sylvia, *Julia Margaret Cameron's Women* (exhibition catalogue), Art Institute of Chicago 1998.

INDEX